World Economic Outlook

April 1986

A Survey by the Staff
of the
International Monetary Fund

International Monetary Fund
Washington, D.C.

© 1986 International Monetary Fund

International Standard Serial Numbers: ISBN 0-939934-66-3
ISSN 0256-6877

Address orders to:
External Relations Department
Attention Publications
International Monetary Fund,
Washington, D.C. 20431
U.S.A.
Tel: (202)–623-7430   Cable: Interfund

Distributed to the college and university textbook adoption market by:
Oxford University Press

Contents

Page

Page

List of Tables in Chapters and Supplementary Notes

Page

Conventions and Symbols

A number of standard conventions have been employed in arriving at the projections in the report. It has been assumed that the average real exchange rates for the major currencies of a recent period (March 3-7, 1986) will prevail throughout the balance of 1986 and 1987; that "present" policies of national authorities will be maintained; and that the average price of oil will be $15 a barrel from the second quarter of 1986 to the end of 1987. These are, of course, working assumptions rather than forecasts, and the uncertainties surrounding them add to the margins of error that would in any event be involved in the report's projections. The estimates and projections themselves are based on statistical information available on or before March 21, 1986.

The following symbols have been used throughout this report:

...   to indicate that data are not available;

—   to indicate that the figure is zero or less than half the final digit shown, or that the item does not exist;

–   between years or months (e.g., 1984–85 or January–June) to indicate the years or months covered, including the beginning and ending years or months;

/   between years (e.g., 1984/85) to indicate a crop or fiscal (financial) year.

"Billion" means a thousand million.

Minor discrepancies between constituent figures and totals are due to rounding.

*   *   *

It should be noted that the term "country" used in this report does not in all cases refer to a territorial entity that is a state as understood by international law and practice. The terms also covers some territorial entities that are not states but for which statistical data are maintained and provided internationally on a separate and independent basis.

Preface

The projections and analysis contained in the *World Economic Outlook* are the product of a comprehensive interdepartmental review of world economic developments by the staff of the International Monetary Fund. This review is carried out annually and draws on the information the Fund staff gathers through its regular and special consultations with member countries as well as through its econometric modeling techniques. The project is coordinated in the Research Department and draws on the specialized contributions of staff members in the Fund's five Area Departments, together with those of staff in the Exchange and Trade Relations and Fiscal Affairs Departments.

An earlier version of the material in this report was the basis for a discussion of the world economic outlook by the Fund's Executive Board on March 21 and March 24, 1986. The present version has benefited from comments made during those discussions by Executive Directors. However, the descriptions of developments and policies that the report contains, as well as the projections for individual countries and the contents of supplementary notes, are those of the Fund staff and should not necessarily be attributed to Executive Directors or their national authorities.

The *World Economic Outlook* has been published annually by the Fund since 1980. Since 1984, a shorter, updated version of the *World Economic Outlook,* containing revised projections, has also been published in the second half of the year.

Chapter I

The World Economy to 1991: Prospects and Issues

The year 1985 was somewhat disappointing from the viewpoint of economic growth. Expansion fell back by more than expected in the industrial world, and world trade increased only modestly. As a result, the real export earnings of developing countries stagnated, and their rate of economic growth slowed. This, in turn, made the debt situation more difficult to manage.

Nevertheless, progress was made toward alleviating some of the financial imbalances that threaten the sustainability of global expansion. The United States took steps toward a major program of fiscal consolidation; the large industrial countries committed themselves to policies that should help avoid serious exchange rate misalignments and combat protectionism; and an important initiative was launched to underpin the management of the debt situation. At the same time, inflation in the major countries receded further and international interest rates declined. While the impact of these various developments cannot be seen clearly at the present time, they should improve the prospects for sustainable, noninflationary growth throughout the world economy.

Looking ahead, the staff sees a consolidation in the pace of economic growth at around 3 percent in the industrial countries. In the developing world, growth would remain at about 3 percent in 1986, then firm gradually to around 4¾ percent per annum in 1988–91. To achieve this result, however (and especially to improve on it), determined pursuit of the required macroeconomic and structural policies will be needed. Monetary, fiscal, and exchange rate policies will have to concentrate on maintaining a stable climate for the growth of private sector activity. Structural policies must be designed to enhance the incentives for the private sector to take advantage of such a climate by increasing investment, savings, output, and employment.

The remainder of this chapter elaborates on these themes. It begins with a discussion of recent economic developments and the short-term outlook for the world economy. The following section deals with medium-term prospects and presents some of the key results of the staff's scenario analysis. Against the background of these two sections, the concluding part of the chapter reviews some of the major policy issues that require attention if global economic performance is to be sustained and improved.

This general survey is based on the more extended analysis contained in the other chapters of the *World Economic Outlook*. These include a background review of recent developments and short-term prospects in the world economy (Chapters II and III); an analysis of policy interactions in the industrial countries (Chapter IV); and a comprehensive assessment of the debt situation and prospects (Chapter V). A series of supplementary notes provide detailed analysis of specific topics, and a Statistical Appendix contains more comprehensive statistical information.

Current Situation and Short-Term Outlook

The Economic Setting

Considerable uncertainties exist concerning the international economic environment that is likely to prevail in 1986 and 1987. Among the more significant uncertainties are those surrounding the scope and impact of efforts to reduce the U.S. budget deficit; the effect of these and other factors on the pattern of international exchange rates; the likely evolution of interest rates; the path of oil and other commodity prices; the willingness of private creditors to increase their lending to heavily indebted countries; the pace of structural reforms in the industrial countries; and the ability of governments to resist protectionist pressures.

The future path of oil prices is particularly difficult to forecast at the present time. As may be seen in Chart 1, oil prices have been on a downward trend,

Chart 1. Oil Prices, 1972–March 1986

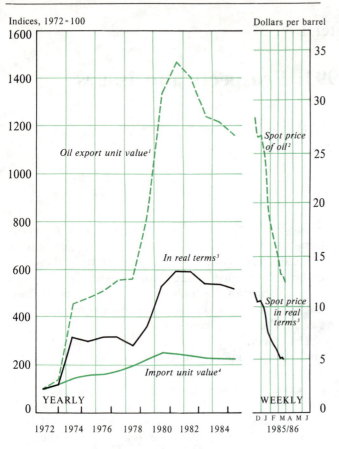

Indices, 1972 = 100

Dollars per barrel

Oil export unit value[1]

Spot price of oil[2]

In real terms[3]

Spot price in real terms[3]

Import unit value[4]

YEARLY

WEEKLY

1972 1974 1976 1978 1980 1982 1984

D J F M A M J
1985/86

[1] In U.S. dollar terms.
[2] Unweighted average of Brent and West Texas Intermediate spot prices in U.S. dollar terms.
[3] Oil price deflated by import unit value of oil exporting countries.
[4] Import unit value of oil exporting countries in U.S. dollar terms.

in U.S. dollar terms, since 1981, and averaged about $26.50 a barrel in 1985. Beginning in January 1986, however, oil prices began to drop more sharply, and by early March, had fallen below $15 per barrel. For purposes of projection, the staff has made the assumption that oil prices will average $15 a barrel from the second quarter of 1986 until the end of 1987. This would represent a drop of 45 percent in nominal terms (or over 50 percent in real terms) from the level that prevailed in 1985. It must be recognized, however, that prices could well be significantly higher or significantly lower than this level, or could fluctuate in a volatile manner. If oil producers continue to compete for market shares, prices could be driven down well below $15 per barrel; on the other hand, an agreement among major producers to reimpose production restraint might be associated with a price closer to $20 a barrel. In any event, compared with 1985, there is likely to be a substantial shift of real incomes from oil exporting to oil importing countries. Such a shift would tend to reduce demand in the former group and to

support demand in the latter group, but it is not easy to determine whether these effects would be symmetrical in their magnitude and timing. Non-oil commodity prices (exclusive of coffee) are expected to rise moderately in U.S. dollar terms during 1986 and 1987, but not by enough to prevent a further erosion in the terms of trade of commodity-producing countries. Coffee prices are a special case, having risen sharply in the closing months of 1985 following the drought in Brazil.

Macroeconomic policies in industrial countries are likely to be directed toward the medium-term objective of maintaining financial stability, while reducing the claims of governments on economic resources. In the United States, although questions have been raised about the constitutionality of certain provisions of the recent legislation to reduce the budget deficit, it nevertheless seems likely that the fiscal deficit will be reduced in 1986, after having grown rapidly in the previous several years. A further substantial decline in the deficit is projected for 1987. The fiscal position of the other industrial countries is expected to continue to be aimed at budgetary consolidation, so that, for the industrial countries as a group, fiscal policy may well exert a contractionary influence. Monetary policy has been implemented fairly flexibly for some time, reflecting two main factors: (1) the increased room for maneuver the authorities have acquired as the credibility of their anti-inflationary commitment has grown; and (2) the need to adapt monetary targets to velocity shifts caused by financial innovation and declining inflation. This flexibility, together with the moderation of growth and improved prospects for reducing the budget deficit in the United States, permitted a substantial decline in interest rates in the latter part of 1985 and early 1986. The staff expects these somewhat easier monetary conditions to persist during the projection period.

Macroeconomic policies in developing countries reflect the considerable diversity of circumstances of the countries included in this group. Virtually all developing countries, however, continue to face external financial constraints, and at the same time are seeking to promote a revival of domestic private investment. In these circumstances, the staff anticipates that there will be considerable pressure to curb fiscal deficits, and that lower borrowing requirements will facilitate the pursuit of credit policies designed to bring down inflation.

Exchange rate developments will be heavily influenced by the actual and expected evolution of macroeconomic policies and performance in the industrial countries. Since March 1985, the U.S. dollar has depreciated significantly against European currencies and the Japanese yen (Chart 2). This decline has been encouraged by the actions of the five largest industrial

Chart 2. Nominal Effective Exchange Rates, 1980–March 1986

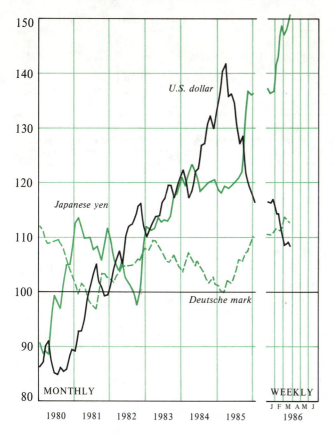

policy reforms in the borrowing countries, as well as of resisting protectionism and ensuring adequate growth in the industrial countries that are the main markets for the indebted countries' exports.

Output and Employment

Real *output* in the industrial countries grew by 2¾ percent in 1985, slightly less than had been expected at the beginning of the year, and considerably below the expansion of 4¾ percent recorded in 1984 (Table 1). The slowdown was largely attributable to developments in the United States, which had grown by 6½ percent in 1984 under the combined influence of a strongly expansionary fiscal policy, favorable investment incentives, declining interest rates, and rising consumer confidence. In 1985, however, the effects of these factors began to taper off, and the negative effects of a sharp deterioration in international competitiveness and a reversal of the inventory cycle began to make themselves felt. As a result, output in the United States expanded by only 2¼ percent. Japan also experienced a modest slowdown in growth in 1985, although much milder than that in the United States. The slowing of growth in Japan was attributable to a smaller positive stimulus from the foreign sector, as Japanese export growth slowed in line with the growth of world trade generally. In the industrial countries of Europe, output growth in 1985 was maintained at the same relatively modest pace (2¼ percent) as in 1984. However, an encouraging sign was the tendency of activity to pick up toward the end of the year, led by a further acceleration of business fixed investment.

The developing world felt the consequences of the slowdown in the industrial countries rather rapidly. World trade growth fell from almost 9 percent in 1984 to 3 percent in 1985. The weakness in the volume of trade was transmitted to prices, which declined slightly in SDR terms. As often happens, the cyclical weakness of trade prices was considerably more pronounced for primary commodities than for manufactured goods; on this occasion, however, commodity prices were also kept down by unusually ample supplies, particularly of agricultural commodities. As a result, the terms of trade of developing countries deteriorated by 2 percent, and the purchasing power of their export earnings declined.

The weakness of exports had both direct and indirect effects on economic activity in developing countries. Directly, it lowered output in sectors producing tradable goods and in ancillary industries; indirectly, it acted as a constraint on imports and thus forced cutbacks in domestic activities dependent on imported

countries, designed to bring about a more sustainable pattern of exchange rates. The projections reported in this *World Economic Outlook* are based on the working assumption that exchange rates will remain unchanged, in real terms, from the pattern prevailing in early March 1986. It has to be recognized, however, that exchange rates can move by substantial amounts in response to market reappraisals; the scope for such reappraisals is greater when, as at present, external imbalances are large, and there are significant uncertainties about the course of policy in major countries.

Lastly, a major element in the economic setting will be the flow of financial resources available to indebted countries, and their access to the markets of the industrial world. Bank lending to 15 heavily indebted countries was virtually zero, on a net basis, in 1985, and the prospect of a continuation of this trend was a major reason for the initiative announced by the Secretary of the U.S. Treasury, James A. Baker III, in October 1985. If the U.S. initiative meets with success, this would obviously brighten the prospects for growth in the countries concerned. It should be noted, however, that taking on additional debt would be prudent only if the means of servicing this debt are enhanced. This underscores the importance of effective

3

Table 1. Changes in World Output, 1968–87[1]

(In percent)

	Average 1968–77[2]	1978	1979	1980	1981	1982	1983	1984	1985	1986	1987
World	4.5	4.5	3.3	2.0	1.6	0.5	2.6	4.4	2.9	3.1	3.3
Industrial countries	3.5	4.2	3.3	1.2	1.4	−0.4	2.6	4.7	2.8	3.0	3.2
Developing countries	6.2	5.1	4.3	3.5	2.2	1.6	1.3	4.1	3.2	3.0	3.4
Fuel exporters	8.4	2.7	3.7	1.1	0.9	−0.1	−1.8	1.2	−0.1	−0.6	0.3
Non-fuel exporters	5.4	6.1	4.6	4.6	2.7	2.5	3.0	5.5	4.8	4.6	4.8
Other countries[3]	6.2	4.8	2.1	3.0	1.9	2.8	4.3	3.4	3.0	3.8	. . .

[1] Real GDP (or GNP) for industrial and developing countries and real net material product (NMP) for other countries. Composites for the country groups are averages of percentage changes for individual countries weighted by the average U.S. dollar value of their respective GDPs (GNPs or NMPs where applicable) over the preceding three years. Because of the uncertainty surrounding the valuation of the composite NMP of the other countries, they have been assigned—somewhat arbitrarily—a weight of 15 percent in the calculation of the growth of world output. Excluding China prior to 1978.

[2] Compound annual rate of change.

[3] The U.S.S.R. and other countries of Eastern Europe that are not members of the Fund.

inputs. Together, these various factors resulted in a decline in economic growth in developing countries from 4 percent in 1984 to a little over 3 percent in 1985 (Table 1). This decline was not evenly distributed, however. The fuel exporters were particularly hard hit, with output stagnating in 1985. The non-fuel exporting countries, on the other hand, continued to grow at 4¾ percent, against 5½ percent the previous year.

Looking ahead to 1986 and 1987, prospects for economic growth in the industrial world have been favorably affected by recent declines in interest rates and oil prices. The oil price assumption employed by the staff implies a reduction in the combined oil import bill of industrial countries of some $60 billion (almost ¾ of 1 percent of their combined gross national product (GNP)) from the 1985 level. This improvement in the terms of trade should provide a significant stimulus to consumption and investment in 1986–87. Moreover, budgetary consolidation efforts have improved confidence in the sustainability of expansion, and have played an important role in bringing down interest rates, particularly in the United States. Partly offsetting these positive influences on demand, the growth of government spending is likely to slow down, and the weaker prospects for developing countries' export earnings will adversely affect their ability to import from the industrial world. On balance, the staff expects economic growth in the United States to firm somewhat in the period ahead, as the positive effects of lower oil prices, lower interest rates, and a lower value for the dollar outweigh the impact of fiscal restraint and the maturing of the investment cycle. Consumer expenditure is likely to be reasonably buoyant, especially given the beneficial effects on real income of the decline in oil prices and the impact of the boom in securities markets on the willingness to spend. How-

ever, the savings ratio in the United States is already very low, and it seems unlikely that it would fall much further.

The prospects for industrial countries outside the United States are significantly affected by recent exchange rate changes and by the efforts of the U.S. authorities to curb the fiscal deficit. These effects will be strongest for Canada and Japan, which have closer trading links to the United States than the principal European countries. Both Canada and Japan are expected to grow at around 3–3½ percent in 1986–87, compared with an average growth rate of 4½–5 percent in 1984–85. In Japan, the slowdown is attributable in substantial part to the swing in the real foreign balance from being a source of considerable stimulus to the domestic economy to becoming a negative influence. This negative impact more than offsets the effect that lower oil prices are expected to have in sustaining domestic demand growth at over 4 percent. In Canada, by contrast, net exports are expected to be a positive factor, but strong fiscal restraint will act to slow the growth of domestic demand.

European industrial countries have less close trading ties with the United States, and are less affected by changes in domestic demand and the strengthening of competitiveness in North America. European countries will benefit from lower interest rates as well as from recent improvements in their terms of trade. However, the persistence of structural rigidities in many countries makes a major acceleration of output growth in Europe unlikely. The staff nevertheless sees a strengthening of output growth to an annual rate of 2¾ percent in 1986 and 1987. Within this figure, investment is expected to be relatively more buoyant than other sources of demand, providing some basis for hope that the pace of output growth could strengthen further later in the decade.

Output growth in the industrial countries could turn out to be higher than estimated, if increases in real income from terms of trade gains are quickly translated into higher demand. Lower oil prices represent a first round addition to domestic incomes in the industrial countries of almost ¾ of 1 percentage point of GNP. The impact of this on economic activity will depend, however, on whether the price decline is accompanied by measures (such as an acceleration of fiscal consolidation or a lowering of monetary growth targets) that have the effect of limiting demand growth. Questions also surround the extent to which real income losses in oil exporting countries would be reflected back in reduced exports, and therefore GNP, of industrial countries.

Output prospects in developing countries are affected both by the international economic environment and by the policies pursued by these countries themselves. The significant deterioration in the terms of trade of developing countries that occurred during the course of 1985 has not yet been fully translated into lower real imports. Thus, there is probably still some negative impact from past price developments to be felt in economic growth. On the other hand, interest rates have come down more quickly than earlier expected, and there are signs that certain developing countries are making progress toward improving the allocation of resources. The balance of these factors varies considerably across groups of countries. The fuel exporting countries, for example, have been hit hardest by recent price movements and probably face a further period of stagnant or slowly growing real output. Among the non-fuel exporters, prospects are considerably brighter, with output expected to increase at an annual rate of 4¾ percent during 1986–87.

In assessing the implications of these projections for economic welfare, account must be taken of a variety of other relevant considerations, including, most importantly, population growth. A new table in the Statistical Appendix (Table A6) provides estimates for increases in output in developing countries, adjusted for the estimated rate of population growth. This table shows that per capita output in the developing world, on the basis of the staff projections, would be virtually unchanged in 1986 from its level at the beginning of the decade. This average, of course, conceals a wide variety of experience across countries; while considerable progress has been made in raising output per head in Asia, per capita output levels in much of Africa and Latin America are expected to remain substantially lower than in 1980. Even deflating by population does not provide a full measure of the divergence in economic welfare among regions. African and Latin American countries have generally suffered substantial deterioration in their terms of trade

or have been obliged to bring about major strengthening of their balance of payments positions. Both of these factors have tended to reduce the share of output available for domestic absorption to a much greater extent than has been the case for Asian or European developing countries.

The continuation of world economic growth at only a moderate pace means that relatively little progress will be made in dealing with the serious *unemployment* problem faced by many countries. Of course, the relationship between unemployment and aggregate demand is neither simple nor clear cut, either in the industrial or in the developing countries. Nevertheless, barring an acceleration of output growth or—particularly in Europe—a deceleration of real wage growth, employment creation will be limited, and unemployment rates are likely to remain high.

In the industrial countries, the implications of the staff's output projections are that total employment would continue to rise at a rate of 1½ percent, slightly more than the growth in the labor force. Nevertheless, the average unemployment rate is unlikely to be reduced more than marginally over the next two years. A positive development in 1985 was the resumption of employment growth in Europe (after four consecutive years of decline, during which the total number in work fell by over 3 percent). The continuation of employment growth in 1986 and 1987 should at last arrest the rise in joblessness that has persisted in most European countries throughout the recovery. Still, recorded unemployment in Europe is expected to remain close to the current level of 11¼ percent—a figure that does not take account of the considerable number of unregistered or discouraged workers, or of younger workers being absorbed temporarily in government-sponsored training schemes or spending additional years in further education.

In the developing world, the concepts of unemployment that are most relevant for the analysis of economic or social conditions are rather different from those in industrial countries. In addition, the dearth of comparable statistics makes it necessary to infer unemployment trends from circumstantial data. For example, the fact that the growth of output per head outside the fuel exporting countries slowed from 3 percent per annum during the period 1968–80 to only 1½ percent per annum since then seems unlikely to be fully accounted for by a decline in the rate of productivity growth, or the completion of a process of absorbing previously unemployed workers. Thus, it is probable that problems of unemployment and underemployment intensified. By the same token, the fact that output growth per head has accelerated from ½ of 1 percent per annum during 1981–83 to almost 3 percent in 1984–85 suggests that the demand for labor may not be quite as weak now as in the early 1980s. To the extent that direct evidence is available, it tends to confirm the above hypothesis. The average unemployment rate in 12 Latin American countries for which data are available (mostly relating to urban unemployment) rose by 3.2 percentage points between 1981 and 1984, but tended to fall in 1985.

Inflation and Interest Rates

In contrast to the experience in most earlier recovery periods, *inflation* in industrial countries has continued its downward trend throughout the current upswing in activity. Having declined from a peak of 9.3 percent in 1980 to 4.3 percent in 1984, the weighted average of inflation rates in industrial countries—as measured by changes in the GNP deflator—fell further to 3.9 percent in 1985. The staff expects an additional decline, to 3.4 percent in 1986 and 3.0 percent in 1987. Lower oil prices are one of the major reasons for expecting continued progress on the price front in 1986 and 1987. By itself, the 45 percent decline in oil prices assumed by the staff is estimated to reduce the average rise in consumer prices in industrial countries by close to 3 percentage points over a two-year period, and the GNP deflator by not quite half that amount. In addition, the factors that were successful in reducing inflation over the past several years are expected to continue to play a role in restraining price pressures. Most important, central banks remain committed to cautious monetary policies, and although such policies may be implemented in a flexible way, the targets that have been announced for monetary aggregates imply that there would be little scope for an acceleration of inflation. Second, wage increases are likely to remain moderate, because of the persistence of high unemployment rates and perhaps also reflecting growing flexibility in the wage determination process. Third, deregulation in goods markets is serving to intensify competition and hold down costs. And fourth, raw material prices have continued to be weak and are not expected to recover more than partially in 1986 and 1987.

Another aspect of inflation performance in industrial countries that is worthy of mention is the narrowing divergence in national inflation rates. The standard deviation of national inflation rates around the industrial country mean had been 5.3 percentage points in 1980, and had fallen to 3.1 percentage points in 1984. It fell further to 2.6 percentage points in 1985, and is expected to remain in that range in 1986 and 1987. The principal reason for this convergence is the improved performance on the part of several previously high-inflation countries. Since 1983, for example, Italy

and France have had considerable success in bringing down above-average rates of inflation. This performance has been all the more gratifying since exchange rate factors had, until 1985, tended to push up costs and prices outside the United States. The partial reversal of the dollar's earlier appreciation is one of the factors contributing to an expected further improvement in price performance in Europe in 1986.

The inflation picture in developing countries is less satisfactory, at least at first glance. The weighted average of rates of consumer price inflation in these countries has accelerated in every recent year, and reached almost 40 percent in 1985. This weighted average gives a somewhat misleading picture, however, since it includes the effects of triple-digit (or even quadruple-digit) rates of inflation in a small number of countries (Argentina, Bolivia, Brazil, Israel, and Peru). Using the median rate of inflation to exclude the influence of these extreme cases suggests that price pressures have been kept under rather better control than in earlier years. The median rate of inflation has been brought down from 14½ percent in 1980 to 9 percent in 1985, and is expected to be held in that range in 1986 before falling further in 1987. One reason to look forward to an abatement of price pressures in 1986–87 is that significant adjustment measures have already been taken in several high-inflation countries (notably Argentina, Bolivia, Brazil, and Israel) resulting in significant, and in some cases dramatic, declines in month-to-month inflation rates. If these efforts persist, the staff expects a sharp fall in inflation rates in the coming period. (As a cautionary note, however, it should be remembered that similar expectations have been reported, and confounded, regularly in the past.)

The continuing decline in overall inflation rates in industrial countries has facilitated a decline in nominal *interest rates*. The decline observed in 1985 was considerably greater than can be attributed to the concurrent decline in inflation, so that estimated real interest rates have fallen as well. Factors contributing to the decline in nominal U.S. dollar interest rates include (besides falling inflation) the weaker evolution of economic activity, increasing confidence that lower inflation would persist, better prospects for a durable improvement in the fiscal position of the U.S. Government, and the growing belief that the Federal Reserve would continue to allow interest rate declines. The easing of interest rates was also a feature of monetary developments in most other industrial countries. The only significant exceptions were the United Kingdom and (on a temporary basis) Japan, where exchange rate considerations have at times weighed heavily in setting the course of monetary policy.

Looking ahead, prospects seem reasonable for maintaining downward pressure on interest rates, even if in most cases they would remain quite high in historical perspective. In particular, a strengthening of the U.S. federal budget position will tend to reduce government demands on credit markets. At the same time, confidence in the continuance of low inflation seems to be fairly well established, and recent developments in oil and commodity markets will, if anything, tend to reduce price pressures further. Of course, the possibility of exchange market disturbances still exists, and these could give rise to a tightening of monetary policy in the United States that would induce a rise in interest rates. On the whole, however, the risks of such a development have probably diminished as a result of the exchange rate movements that have taken place since March 1985, and the actions that are being considered in the United States to bring fiscal policy under better control.

External Adjustment and Debt

The pattern of *payments balances* that had emerged by 1984 continued to prevail in 1985. The United States had a further small rise in its already substantial current account deficit (to reach almost 3 percent of GNP). Japan's large surplus grew by a further sizable amount, and the surplus of the Federal Republic of Germany also increased significantly. The current account deficit of developing countries was roughly stable at about 5 percent of exports of goods and services (less than half the figure of 1982). And the statistical discrepancy, which reflects net underrecording of receipts (or overrecording of payments) remained large.

The similarity of the external payments picture from 1984 to 1985 (and, indeed, the prospect of a similar picture in 1986) does not, of course, connote an absence of strains. The continuation of a current account deficit of well over $100 billion for the United States implies an accumulation of foreign debt that will continue to make heavy demands on global savings and that will make existing exchange rate patterns vulnerable to shifts in investor sentiment. The surpluses of Japan and the Federal Republic of Germany also pose difficulties from a number of standpoints, not least the encouragement they give to protectionist tendencies in other countries. Among developing countries, the deficits that were recorded in 1985, while relatively low in historical perspective, have not resulted in an increased willingness of commercial creditors to roll over existing debt, much less to substantially increase the level of new lending.

The recent depreciation in the dollar (about 25 percent in real effective terms from March 1985 to March 1986), together with the convergence of growth rates among industrial countries, has had a favorable effect on the external prospects of the United States. However, given the fact that imports are already so much larger than exports, a favorable shift in their relative rates of growth may reduce the trade deficit only modestly. At the same time, growing interest payments abroad mean that the invisibles surplus will continue to shrink. Assuming the continuation of the exchange rate pattern prevailing in early March 1986, the U.S. current account deficit is projected to average some $110 billion per annum in 1986–87, still over 2½ percent of GNP. In the short run, both Germany and Japan are projected to have a substantial widening in their surpluses in dollar terms, as a result of the operation of J-curve effects. However, in the medium and longer term, recent exchange rate movements will help reduce their surpluses.

For the developing countries, the balance of payments on current account is largely determined by the available financing, with some flexibility provided through fluctuations in the rate of reserve accumulation and in the level of outstanding arrears. In the non-fuel exporting group, a modest increase in capital inflows in 1986–87 is expected to be more than matched by a faster buildup of external reserves, so that the combined current account deficit of these countries would be held to around 4 percent of exports of goods and services. As a result, the volume of imports into these countries would grow at much the same rate as the volume of their exports—around 5 percent.

The situation in the fuel exporting developing countries is significantly different. Given the price assumption used by the staff, these countries are likely to be faced with a decline in the purchasing power of their exports of 30–40 percent. Despite a sharp cutback in the volume of their imports, fuel exporting countries would nevertheless see a sharp widening of their current account deficit, to perhaps 25–30 percent of exports of goods and services in 1986. To some extent, this increase in the combined deficit can be financed through drawing on reserves and lines of credit; over time, however, it is to be expected that the fuel exporting countries will undertake further adjustment efforts to reduce their current account deficits to a significantly lower level.

It was noted earlier that the process of current account adjustment in developing countries is closely linked to changes in the availability of external sources of finance. In considering *financial flows* to capital importing developing countries (which are all developing countries except the major Middle Eastern oil exporters), it is convenient to distinguish between sources of finance that are relatively "stable" (i.e., that do not vary by very much from year to year according to global economic conditions) and those that are liable to change as a result of reappraisals by creditors or borrowers. The first category includes non-debt-creating flows (official transfers and direct investment) and long-term official lending. These flows averaged about $53 billion per annum from 1981–85 and are expected to increase slightly (to an average of $56 billion per annum) in 1986 and 1987. The second category includes other forms of external borrowing, which have in practice proved highly vulnerable to changes in market assessments. Such borrowing reached a peak of $73 billion in 1981, then fell rapidly to $13 billion in 1984. There was a further fall to about $11 billion in 1985, but the staff projects that such private lending would yield about $14 billion per annum in 1986–87 on the basis of existing policies. At such a level, the increase in private lending to capital importing developing countries is little, if any, more than would be required for the normal financing of increases in import trade.

As may be inferred from these figures, the growth in the *external indebtedness* of developing countries has slowed dramatically in recent years. The gross international indebtedness of capital importing developing countries, which had increased at an average annual rate of almost 20 percent in dollar terms, in 1978–81, grew by only 5½ percent in 1984 and in 1985. The rate of increase in outstanding debt is expected to be slightly faster in 1986, in part because exchange rate changes will cause an upward revaluation of non-dollar liabilities.

Although the rate of debt accumulation has been slowing quite markedly, the ratio of debt to exports has not been reduced, owing to the recent weakness of export markets. For the group of capital importing developing countries, this ratio increased in 1985 to a record level of 163 percent. Increases were quite widely experienced in all categories of countries, and were perhaps particularly disturbing for the small low-income countries, which now face a debt ratio of 383 percent. Debt service ratios have been less severely affected for most countries, since declining interest rates on their variable rate debt have helped cushion the effects of further increases in amortization payments. Countries that have benefited less from falling interest rates (because a relatively high proportion of their debt represents official borrowing at fixed, concessional, interest rates) have continued to have a sharp rise in the share of their export earnings needed to cover interest payments on external debt. Small low-income countries now devote 12½ percent of their export earnings to interest payments, and this proportion is expected to rise to 13 percent by 1987. In contrast, the capital importing countries as a group are expected to have some easing in their interest payments ratios in the coming period, from just over 13 percent in 1985 to 12 percent in 1987. (A further discussion of debt issues is contained in Chapter V.)

Medium-Term Prospects

The analysis of medium-term prospects presented here, and in Chapters IV and V, is based on a "scenario" of economic developments to 1991. It should be recognized that a scenario is in no sense a forecast; it represents an assessment of the consequences of certain assumptions about exogenous economic conditions, given other assumptions about the behavioral relations that link these conditions to actual developments. Only to the extent that the assumptions are considered plausible, and the underlying "model" is reasonable, can the scenario be considered a realistic projection. Even then, it must be recognized that policies and conditions may change—perhaps in recognition of the consequences if they do not—thus invalidating the projections of the scenario.

Assumptions

In present circumstances, a key assumption in the construction of any medium-term scenario concerns the stance of *macroeconomic policies* in industrial countries, particularly the United States. For the purposes of the scenario analysis, a baseline scenario has been constructed on the cautious assumption that, following the budgetary cuts the United States is implementing in 1986, further expenditure cuts (equivalent to $12 billion per annum from "current services" estimates) are instituted in each year of the period 1987–91. (The implications of the full implementation of the automatic expenditure cuts provided for under the Gramm-Rudman-Hollings Act are considered in Chapter IV.) In other industrial countries, fiscal policy is assumed to be moderately restrictive, in line with recent trends, and to involve a slight further withdrawal of stimulus. Monetary policy in all industrial countries is assumed to be such as to prevent any significant acceleration of inflation from the underlying rate expected to prevail in 1987, while accommodating the real growth rate being projected for the medium term. Economic policies in developing countries are those judged "most likely" by the Fund's area department staff. Such policies, on the whole, involve continued restraint on the demand-management side, and an intensification of structural measures leading to some improvement in export performance.

The underlying *rate of inflation*, following the assumptions made about monetary policy, would tend to be stabilized at around 3¾ percent for the industrial countries as a group. (This is marginally higher than the rate projected for 1987, but makes allowance for the fact that the once-for-all benefit of lower oil prices will not persist in the medium term.)

The foregoing assumptions are believed to be consistent with a nominal *interest rate* on short-term U.S. Government securities of just over 7 percent, and a LIBOR (London interbank offered rate) of around 8 percent. The reduction in average fiscal deficits in industrial countries would be a factor tending to lower interest rates, but the weakening of the dollar (see below) and the assumed action of the Federal Reserve to limit inflationary pass-through effects, could work in the opposite direction.

The pattern of *exchange rates* among industrial countries is particularly difficult to project. For reasons given in more detail in Chapter IV, it is assumed that the U.S. and Canadian dollars will depreciate by 10 percent in real terms relative to the other major currencies over the period to 1991, but that real bilateral rates among the other major currencies will remain unchanged.

Oil prices are assumed by the staff to average $15 per barrel from the second quarter of 1986 until the end of 1987, and then to be unchanged in real terms throughout the remainder of the medium-term scenario period. Given current uncertainties in the oil market, this is clearly no more than a working hypothesis.

Non-oil commodity prices (other than coffee) are projected to rise over the medium term, at approximately the same rate as prices of manufactured goods. (Coffee prices, having risen sharply in late 1985 and early 1986, would tend to recede, in real terms, in the medium term.)

Implications for Industrial Countries

The implications of the foregoing assumptions for medium-term economic developments are set out in Table A53 of the Statistical Appendix. They suggest an annual growth rate in the industrial countries of about 3 percent for the four years of the medium-term scenario period, 1988–91. This reflects the fact that the shift in fiscal policies (measured by the reduction in actual fiscal deficits) would be relatively mild and gradual, while monetary policies would be broadly accommodative. Thus the rise in actual output would approximate the estimated growth in potential output, once the initial adjustments to changes in fiscal stance had taken place. In European countries, growth would exceed the increase in estimated productive potential by a small margin to reflect the implementation of structural policies and a marginal reduction in existing very high unemployment levels. By 1991, unemploy-

ment in Europe, under this scenario, would have come down to around 10 percent. At this level it would be 1 percentage point below the current level, but more than 4 percentage points above the level prevailing in 1978–80.

Of just as much interest as the results of the baseline scenario shown in Statistical Appendix Table A53 is the sensitivity of the scenario to alternative developments. In this connection, particular interest attaches to the implications of the application of the full provisions of the Gramm-Rudman-Hollings Act in the United States. The consequences of such a development are explored in more detail in Chapter IV, but the broad conclusions can be stated quite briefly. Empirical evidence suggests further cuts in government expenditure in the United States, sufficient to produce a balanced budget in 1991, could, especially if unaccompanied by any policy changes in other countries, tend to reduce the rate of growth of world output in the short run and increase it thereafter. It is possible, however, that the effects on confidence of firm action to reduce the budget deficit could tend to dampen the initial negative effects, or reduce the lag before positive effects emerged. (The strength of equity and bond markets in late 1985 and early 1986 would be consistent with this interpretation.) The distribution of any change in output would depend very much on what happened to the exchange rate for the U.S. dollar and hence to the pattern of international trade flows. On plausible assumptions, it seems likely that any initial decline in output (as well as the subsequent rise) would be largest in the United States, relatively large also in Japan and Canada, and more modest in the industrial countries of Europe.

It is not necessarily the case, of course, that policies in other countries would remain unchanged in the face of a downturn in activity. (Nor would U.S. monetary policy necessarily be unaffected.) If countries outside the United States were to offset part of the impact of a fiscal contraction through a temporary postponement of fiscal restraint, this would tend to reduce the initial loss of output. However, by the same token, such a temporary relaxation would also postpone the attainment of the longer-term gains from a stronger fiscal position. An easing of monetary conditions would tend to improve the path of real output, but at the cost of risking an acceleration of inflation.

Implications for Developing Countries

The implications of the assumptions of the baseline scenario for economic prospects in developing countries are set out at some length in Chapter V, "The Debt Situation: Prospects and Policy Issues." The main results of the analysis presented there can be briefly summarized, however.

(1) The developments that are expected for the capital importing developing countries with regard to export earnings should permit a growth in these countries' import volumes of just under 5 percent per annum during the period 1988–91. In the *World Economic Outlook, April 1985*, import volume growth of 6¾ percent was considered possible over the medium term; the revision reflects less favorable projections for export volume growth and terms of trade developments.

(2) Taking into account the stance of domestic policies, including the effects of policies on the relationship between the rate of growth of imports and that of real gross domestic product (GDP), the combined output of the capital importing developing countries could grow at about 4¾ percent per annum during the medium-term scenario period. This is the same rate as the projection made in last year's *World Economic Outlook*. Recent evidence has caused the staff to increase its estimate of the output increases that can be achieved from a given growth of imports, and this factor tends to offset the expected lower rate of growth of imports.

(3) Current account deficits are expected to increase only slightly in relation to exports of goods and services (to about 6 percent). This reflects the fact that availability of finance (or in some countries the desire to avoid additional debt) is the main constraint on external positions, and is not likely to ease in the medium term.

(4) While the current account deficits being projected are similar to those in last year's *World Economic Outlook*, they result in a much slower decline in the external debt ratio in the present scenario analysis. The reason for this is to be found in the slower growth of export earnings rather than in a faster accumulation of debt. Export earnings were considerably weaker than expected in 1985, and thus the projected medium-term increase starts from a lower base. At the same time, the rate of increase in world trade prices is now expected to be more modest than was foreseen last year. The net result is that the average debt ratio in capital importing developing countries is now projected to decline from 163 percent at the end of 1985 to 140 percent in 1991. (A decline to 108 percent in 1990 was envisaged in last year's scenario.)

(5) Despite the less satisfactory outlook with regard to debt ratios, the burden of debt service is seen to be only slightly greater than last year. The improved prospects for the continuation of interest rates at their recent lower level broadly offsets the impact of higher debt levels on the ratios of both amortization and interest payments.

(6) Differences among countries remain an important feature of the scenario analysis. Recent developments have had a particularly heavy impact on countries depending on exports of oil and other primary commodities. Declining export earnings in real terms have forced these countries to restrict their imports severely, and this has resulted in a sharp downward revision in prospective growth rates for many of these countries. This downward revision is most marked for the oil producing countries in the short term, but also has effects extending forward. For example, the projected rate of growth for the indebted fuel exporting countries is now expected to average about 3 percent over the entire period 1986–91 (against a corresponding estimate of some 5 percent per annum made in early 1985). For small low-income countries exporting chiefly primary products other than oil, the corresponding downward revision is from 4¼ percent to 4 percent.

The scenario displays considerable sensitivity to alternative assumptions. This sensitivity is reflected more in projected rates of economic growth than in current account positions. Since borrowing possibilities are severely constrained for most developing countries, changes in export earnings (or in import costs) tend to generate adjustments in the volume of imports so as to bring the current account back to its "baseline" level.

Higher oil prices would change the pattern of output growth among developing countries considerably. Naturally, oil importing countries would tend to lose while exporting countries would benefit. On balance, abstracting from secondary effects resulting from higher international interest rates or lower activity in industrial countries, the gains would tend to predominate. This reflects the fact that the developing world, in the aggregate, is a net exporter of oil. A price of oil $5 per barrel higher than assumed in the baseline scenario is estimated to raise the average growth rate in indebted fuel exporting countries by about 2 percentage points, while reducing marginally the average growth rate in other capital importing developing countries.

Lower interest rates would have positive consequences, and would benefit all groups of developing countries. A 1 percentage point decrease in interest rates (holding other assumptions constant) is estimated to increase output growth by about ¼ of 1 percentage point. It would have very little effect on debt ratios over the medium term, since lower borrowing costs would be largely balanced by higher imports, leaving the rate of debt accumulation little changed. A further depreciation of the dollar would tend to push up the price of traded goods, thus tending to lower debt-export ratios, and perhaps facilitating an improvement in creditworthiness.

A different rate of growth in the industrial countries

from the one envisaged in the baseline scenario would have potentially significant effects for developing countries. For example, a 1 percentage point decline in output is estimated to result in a 1½ percentage point drop in the real exports of developing countries. Even if there were no accompanying terms of trade effects, a weakening of industrial country growth to 2½ percent per annum in 1988–91 would cause the annual growth rate in developing countries to fall to 4 percent. Given the likelihood that lower export volumes would be associated with lower prices, the drop in real export earnings would probably be larger, and could cause the growth rate in developing countries to fall even further.

A general conclusion of the foregoing is that while it remains possible to combine an acceleration of per capita income growth in developing countries with declining debt ratios, the scope for achieving such a result has narrowed over the past year. This makes it all the more urgent to pursue policies that will help lead to a more favorable outcome.

Policy Issues in Industrial Countries

For the past several years, economic policy in industrial countries has generally been framed in a medium-term context. This strategy has been based on the objective of restoring financial stability, controlling the growth of government spending, reducing fiscal deficits, and fostering the more efficient working of private markets for goods, services, and factors of production. Short-term policy adaptations, or "fine-tuning," have been seen as inimical to the process of building confidence in the medium-term stability of the policy environment.

This broad strategy has been unevenly implemented. There have been notable successes, but also significant shortfalls. Among the successes, the most striking is the widespread and continued reduction in inflationary pressures. A number of factors have contributed to this improved price performance, but the most important is certainly the commitment of monetary authorities to a policy of continued restraint, expressed in many cases through gradual reductions in target rates of growth of monetary aggregates. Several countries have also enjoyed success in curbing the growth of public expenditure, and encouraging more efficient working of private markets; these successes have contributed to the revival of investment and output in the recent recovery.

Nevertheless, it must be recognized that there have been important weaknesses in the implementation of the industrial countries' overall strategy. The budget deficit in the largest industrial country (the United States), as well as in certain others (Canada and Italy), has not been brought under adequate control. This has contributed to the persistence of real interest rates that remain very high in historical perspective; it has also contributed to a pattern of exchange rates and balance of payments positions that threatened (and still threatens) to generate a potentially destabilizing pattern of indebtedness. Outside the United States, European countries have made only limited progress in tackling structural rigidities in their economies, and have made virtually no progress in bringing down disturbingly high rates of unemployment, while Japan has been unable to prevent its already large current account surplus from growing, and has thus accumulated increasing amounts of foreign assets. In many countries, protectionist pressures have continued to mount, and protectionist actions have been taken in several cases.

Some important initiatives have now been taken to deal with these recognized weaknesses in the implementation of the economic strategy. As discussed above, the United States has adopted the ambitious objective of eliminating the federal deficit by 1991. The five largest industrial countries have committed themselves to pay greater attention to exchange rate developments, and to act in a coordinated fashion to avoid serious exchange rate misalignments. And Japan and the major European countries have pledged themselves to pursue policies that will foster stable noninflationary growth of demand and output in their economies. In addition, all countries have reconfirmed the necessity of resisting protectionist pressures.

In this new environment, the nature of the policy issues facing industrial countries has changed somewhat, but the need for effective solutions has not become any less urgent. A first question concerns the setting of macroeconomic policies. In particular, would the implementation of the Gramm-Rudman-Hollings Act call for policy adaptations, either in the United States through a change in monetary policy, or in the other industrial countries? Second, given the somewhat disappointing experience of recent years, how can structural policies more effectively promote the growth of investment and employment where these have lagged? Third, does the growing awareness of the need to avoid misalignment of exchange rates call for additional efforts at international coordination? This last question embraces both the procedural and substantive aspects of coordination.

Macroeconomic Policies

The increased determination of the U.S. Administration and Congress to deal effectively with the problem of the federal budget deficit is certainly to be welcomed. The growth of this deficit represented a threat to domestic and international financial stability, and its removal or reduction would be a beneficial development of the first importance. Of course, the Gramm-Rudman-Hollings Act, if implemented according to its automatic provisions, would limit the flexibility with which fiscal policy can be implemented. If prior agreement between the Administration and Congress can enable flexibility to be regained, consistent with maintaining the credibility of major cuts in the deficit, this would be all to the good. In any event, a major issue in the formulation of macroeconomic policy in member countries is to gauge the impact of the likely fiscal stance in the United States, and to assess whether adaptations in policies elsewhere are called for.

Substantial budget cuts in the United States would have a positive effect on the sustainability of economic activity in the medium term. There may, however, be an initial dampening effect on domestic demand. The budget cuts would also act to lower domestic interest rates and thus to exert downward pressure on the exchange rate. (To a significant extent this has already happened, perhaps in anticipation of the change in the fiscal stance.) Econometric evidence cannot be regarded as conclusive (particularly given the importance of expectations) but quantitative studies suggest that the negative effects on U.S. output of lower government expenditure would initially outweigh the positive output effects of a more favorable external balance and lower interest rates. In countries outside the United States, negative trade effects (resulting from the loss of competitiveness vis-à-vis the United States) would also be partly offset by favorable effects from lower interest rates. Nevertheless, in countries with close trading links to the United States (for example, Japan and Canada), the net effects are likely to be negative in the short run. In other industrial countries (for example, in Europe), the short-run effects would be less strong but still probably negative. (A more detailed analysis of these effects is provided in Chapter IV.)

Given these results, it is tempting to conclude that countries outside the United States should adjust their fiscal stance so as to mitigate the short-run contractionary effects emanating from the U.S. action. Such a conclusion needs to be qualified, however, in at least three important respects. First, an important purpose of budget cuts is to permit savings that are currently being absorbed by the public sector to be released for private sector use. To compensate for spending cuts in one country by increasing the budget deficit in another would retard this process. Second, all countries have suffered a loss of fiscal flexibility as a result of high ratios of public debt to GNP, and the high and growing share of debt service payments in government expenditure. The reduction of deficits over the medium term continues to be necessary in order to restore this flexibility and to prepare for the expected growth in government transfer payments that most countries face as a result of the working of demographic forces. Third, the imbalance in fiscal policies is much more in the direction of "too high" deficits in the United States and some other countries, than toward "too low" deficits elsewhere.

While there is no disagreement that countries should maintain their medium-term objective of reducing fiscal deficits, it can be argued that a change in the fiscal strategy of the largest country influences the scope for flexibility in other countries in the management of their fiscal policies. If the United States is successful in reducing substantially its deficit, other countries are likely to face a situation of declining worldwide interest rates, lower inflation, and softer demand in which to frame their macroeconomic policies. Germany and Japan, for example, may have somewhat more room for maneuver. In the case of Japan, the prospective weakness of output, combined with the progress already made in reducing the general government deficit and the high savings propensity of the Japanese private sector, argues for a somewhat less restrictive fiscal position in fiscal year 1986/87, particularly, given the high central government deficit, at the non-central government level. There may also be scope to reduce the incentives to save that are inherent in existing tax provisions.

The Federal Republic of Germany, like Japan, has a sizable external surplus and has made good progress in bringing down inflation and the deficit of the public sector. Unlike Japan, however, Germany is expected to have a moderately expansionary fiscal stance in 1986 (the consequence of tax cuts introduced at the beginning of the year) and is expected to grow in 1986 at a rate (3¾ percent) higher than the growth of productive potential. The justification for a change of fiscal plans in Germany would thus seem to be more prospective than immediate. However, if U.S. budget cuts are implemented as planned, if the pace of output growth in Germany tends to slow down during the coming year, and if signs of excess demand pressure remain absent, there could, in the staff's view, be a case for considering action to make the stance of fiscal policy in 1987 more supportive than currently envisaged.

It has been argued above that fiscal policies in countries outside the United States should be assigned a relatively modest role in compensating for any temporary weakness of activity caused by the implementation of U.S. budget cuts. The question remains, however, of whether monetary policies would need to be adapted. In assessing this issue, it is important to draw a distinction between monetary *policies*—the ex ante stance adopted by the monetary authorities—and monetary *conditions*—the terms of borrowing set by the interaction of supply and demand for credit. If government demands for credit are reduced in a situation in which the rate of growth of monetary aggregates remains unchanged, real and nominal interest rates will tend to fall, other things equal. It is important that this decline in interest rates be allowed to occur, since it is the mechanism by which private expenditure is "crowded in" to absorb the resources released by budgetary restraint. Beyond this, there may be scope for some additional relaxation of monetary policy in circumstances where policy had previously been kept very tight because of exchange rate constraints, and where these constraints are seen to have eased. Further scope for a planned easing in monetary conditions may come from the lowering of inflationary pressures as reductions in oil prices work their way through the economic structure. It should be emphasized, however, that the scope for such judgmental flexibility is limited: the credibility of the anti-inflationary commitment of the monetary authorities in industrial countries is a valuable asset that was painstakingly acquired. Preserving this credibility must remain the central objective of monetary policy.

Structural Policies

Structural rigidities are a widespread problem in the industrial world. In varying degrees, they affect all countries and all markets—goods, labor, and capital. There seems to be a consensus, however, that such rigidities are particularly troublesome in labor markets, and that such problems are at their most acute in Europe and to a lesser extent, in Australasia and Canada. Certainly, the high levels of unemployment prevailing in these countries serve to focus attention on their labor markets.

For some time, economic analysts have debated the role of "classical" or "structural" factors relative to "Keynesian" or "demand deficiency" factors in explaining the rise in unemployment. A consensus view on this extremely controversial issue is unlikely to emerge in the foreseeable future, in part because of the difficulties associated with empirical verification of the various hypotheses for any individual country. Nevertheless, a considerable body of evidence points to the conclusion that the differences in labor market performance as between, in particular, Europe and the United States, primarily reflect classical or structural factors. These factors include much stronger trend

growth of real wages in Europe than in the United States, lack of flexibility in European wage behavior in the face of adverse disturbances, substantial tax wedges between wage costs to producers and net earnings of employees, government policies favoring capital deepening over capital widening, and lack of occupational and geographical mobility. These factors may be considered in turn.

Real wages have grown much more rapidly in Europe over the past decade and a half than in the United States, and during certain periods have significantly outstripped accompanying rises in productivity. Recently, the growth of real labor costs has tended to moderate, which should enhance prospects for labor demand. However, this moderation probably owes more to the impact of high unemployment than to any fundamental change in wage behavior. It is sometimes suggested that a further decline in real wage growth should be engineered through the application of incomes policy. According to this proposal, organized labor would be asked to accept lower wage settlements in return for an undertaking by the authorities that fiscal or monetary measures would be used to sustain demand and promote output. An agreement of this general kind could perhaps be attempted in countries where centralized wage bargaining remains the rule and safeguards against slippages exist. In many other countries, however, experience suggests that such "social contracts" are difficult to sustain. The risk is that the authorities' part of the bargain (demand stimulus) is implemented more fully than the wage restraint, so that there may be a short-run, Keynesian spurt of output and employment, but no underlying improvement in structural conditions.

The relatively rapid growth of real wages in Europe seems largely to have reflected *inadequate flexibility* of wages in the face of adverse disturbances, such as higher energy prices and a decline in the growth of overall factor productivity. To the extent that real wages do not respond to such shocks, employers are likely to substitute capital for labor. The Japanese system of providing a substantial share of total compensation in the form of variable annual or semiannual bonuses is often thought to have contributed substantially to wage flexibility (and hence employment) in that country. While the bonus system may not be applicable in Europe in precisely the Japanese form, mechanisms for increasing wage flexibility could nevertheless play an important role in increasing employment levels.

The high *share of payroll taxes* in the total labor bill of producers can be important in reducing the impact of such wage flexibility as exists. A given percentage cut in direct wage receipts by workers translates into a much smaller percentage decline in employers' wage costs if indirect labor costs are substantial and fixed in absolute amounts. There may be scope for reducing the absolute burden of these nonwage costs, and making them more flexible in the face of changes in direct wage costs. Similar considerations apply to both direct and indirect taxes, even though the scope for major tax reductions is limited by budgetary constraints.

Government policy toward investment is a controversial subject. Government policies have traditionally favored higher levels of investment on the grounds that investment has positive "externalities" (through higher real wage and employment levels) not captured in the return to the individual or company undertaking the investment. It has to be recognized, however, that higher investment may also have negative externalities, in particular if it results in the displacement of a factor of production that is taxed (labor) by one that is subsidized (capital). If an appropriate balance is to be restored—whereby efficient and employment-creating capital formation is encouraged, but less efficient investment is not—greater selectivity in the design of investment incentives may well be necessary.

Occupational and geographical immobility can only be tackled by measures addressed to its specific causes. Improved training facilities are part of the answer, and so is action to enhance the transferability of acquired rights (such as pension and medical benefits), and assistance with relocation costs (through, for example, tax deductibility of moving expenses).

Policy Coordination

One aspect of international policy coordination has already been discussed, namely, the advantages and disadvantages of countries outside the United States taking deliberate action in light of the effects stemming from a change in the U.S. fiscal position. The conclusion reached was that while changes in the U.S. fiscal stance could increase the scope for certain other countries to use flexibility in the pursuit of their medium-term economic objectives, they did not fundamentally detract from the desirability of those objectives. In particular, they did not diminish the importance of strengthening the fiscal position in most countries over the medium term.

This lack of direct linkage between policy actions in one country and responses in another should not be construed as denying the importance of coordination. In current circumstances, coordination is being pursued through a convergence of fiscal policies toward a more similar and sustainable position. Beyond the issue of fiscal policy, however, is the question of whether, in the wake of the September 22, 1985 meeting

of the Group of Five finance ministers and central bank governors, a new approach to policies affecting exchange rates is called for. This meeting did not, of course, suggest that exchange rates could be viewed in isolation from their fundamental determining factors. What was suggested in the communiqué was that the participating countries were committed to actions that changed these fundamentals, and that such a commitment had not at that time been reflected in exchange markets.

Exchange markets can be influenced by different types of action, each having a rather different time horizon. In the very short term, exchange market intervention can have a substantial effect on the pattern of market exchange rates. This was clearly illustrated in the immediate aftermath of the Group of Five meeting. To the extent that intervention is sterilized, however, it has only a transitory effect on the fundamental factors determining the balance of supply and demand in the foreign exchange market. Monetary policy shifts can have a more lasting effect, because such action influences interest rates and hence validates the exchange rate that results from intervention. (The employment of monetary policy in this role may be seen in the actions of the Bank of Japan in the last quarter of 1985.) As time passes, however, a sustained shift in the stance of monetary policy is likely to exert an impact on the course of demand and prices, thus tending to erode the earlier change in the real exchange rate. A lasting change in real exchange rates requires a shift in underlying saving/investment balances that, in the absence of a change in the private sector's propensity to save or invest, requires an adjustment to the government's fiscal position.

The implication of the foregoing is that a policy of paying greater attention to exchange rate factors in the implementation of a macroeconomic strategy requires a set of intervention, monetary, and fiscal policies that is internally coherent, and internationally consistent. Specifically, intervention will be of limited value unless supported by monetary policy, and adaptations of monetary policy will be counterproductive unless buttressed by a shift in underlying savings/investment balances. If, for example, the exchange rate between two currencies has become unsustainable through a divergence in their underlying savings/investment balances, using monetary policy to correct this situation will tend to compound the adverse domestic consequences of the underlying divergence.

While monetary policy decisions must be taken with due regard to exchange rate considerations in any individual country, there may be better scope for adjusting monetary policy simultaneously in several countries, without significantly affecting the prevailing pattern of exchange rates. This point may be illustrated by the concerted cut in official discount rates in the three largest countries early in March 1986. However, there again it must be underlined that the recent easing of monetary conditions has been made possible by the improved prospects of fiscal retrenchment in the United States (as well as by the decline in oil prices).

The policy coordination that has occurred as a result of the Group of Five meetings has been aimed at encouraging a desired movement in the pattern of exchange rates. Since the actions that have been taken by the major countries were planned in advance, adequate coordination was assured. A rather different situation could emerge, however, if the need was to respond to an unexpected or potentially disruptive exchange rate change. While there might be agreement that it was desirable to resist such a change, the consequences would be quite different depending on whether the action were taken by the country whose currency was appreciating or the country whose currency was depreciating. If an undue share of the resistance was provided by the authorities of the country with the depreciating currency, this would require a tightening of monetary conditions that would tend to weaken global growth prospects. It is therefore important that actions to resist sudden exchange rate movements be consistent with medium-term economic objectives.

Policy Issues in Developing Countries

For several years, developing countries have been pursuing a strategy aimed at re-establishing international creditworthiness and restoring the momentum of domestic growth. To achieve these goals, they have been seeking to narrow their balance of payments deficits on current account, and to put in place domestic reforms aimed at improving the functioning of their economies. However, while substantial progress has been made in improving current account positions, external creditworthiness remains fragile, and growth has continued to be quite moderate. The reasons for this are twofold: first, the international economic environment has remained inhospitable, with high real interest rates, weak commodity prices and only modest growth of world trade; second, the needed policies have not been fully implemented, so that domestic economic performance has not improved sufficiently, and these countries' vulnerability to adverse developments in the external environment has not been substantially reduced.

For the future, the task facing the developing countries is to strengthen both net exports and domestic sources of growth, against the background of a realistic appraisal of international economic prospects. With respect to the latter, it would not be prudent to count on any substantial further reduction in real interest rates, nor on any greatly increased willingness of foreign creditors to lend without policy improvements. It is also unrealistic to expect a substantial strengthening of export prices or a rapid growth in the volume of trade. The staff's medium-term scenario suggests that developing countries' exports might rise at about 5 percent per annum in volume (about 10 percent per annum in value) over the medium term. With no improvement in the terms of trade, this would permit imports as well to rise at about 5 percent per annum in real terms over the medium term—to be compared with an average growth of 8½ percent in the decade and a half to 1981.

In these circumstances, demand management policies must continue to be directed toward the mobilization of domestic resources for investment and net exports, and toward the creation of a stable financial setting for a revival of private sector activity. In addition, structural reforms are needed that will improve the efficiency of the price mechanism, enabling countries to better exploit their comparative advantage, and thereby reduce the import intensity of increments to output. In what follows, the policy implications of these objectives are considered from the standpoint of macroeconomic policies and structural policies in turn.

Macroeconomic Policies

Over the past two or three years, developing countries have made moderate progress in reducing the share of national savings used to finance government deficits. The weighted average size of central government deficits has fallen from 5 percent of GDP in 1982–83 to 4½ percent in 1984–85. This reduction has freed resources for the needed improvement in the net foreign balance. Despite the progress that has been made, however, the shift in the pattern of absorption of resources remains seriously incomplete, for two main reasons. First, fiscal deficits are still considerably higher than their historical average levels. In 1985, for example, the average size of fiscal deficits in developing countries was still 2 percentage points above the average figure for 1978–80. For the capital importing countries alone, the corresponding figure was 1 percentage point (though from a higher base). Second, the reductions in domestic absorption that have formed the counterpart of balance of payments improvements have fallen disproportionately on investment. As a share of GDP, consumption in developing countries has barely changed; it is investment that has declined—

15

by an estimated 3 percentage points of GDP from 1981 to 1985—as the counterpart of reduced net imports.

The implications of the foregoing for future policy adjustments are several. First, a further reduction in the absorption of national savings by governments is still required. This is particularly important for those countries that encountered slippages in 1985, and for countries where the access of the private sector to credit markets is having to be restricted. Second, in the process of reducing deficits, viable investment projects in the public sector should be protected. In present circumstances, special priority should be given to those public sector investment projects that help increase capacity or improve factor productivity in the private sector. Third, special focus should be given to measures of domestic resource mobilization. Difficult though it is to cut the growth of consumption in already poor countries, additional resources have to be devoted to investment if growth prospects are to be enhanced. Improved revenue collection, undertaken in connection with fiscal consolidation, will play a role in raising national saving, and so too will increasing the attractiveness of private savings outlets. More attractive terms for saving are a crucial factor in containing capital flight, and eventually encouraging the repatriation of assets held abroad.

Exchange rate policy also plays an important role in managing the structure of aggregate demand. An appropriate exchange rate is essential if a country is to achieve the export growth of which it is capable. Just as important, however, the right exchange rate enables scarce foreign exchange to be allocated efficiently among competing domestic uses and provides appropriate incentives for efficient kinds of import substitution. The fact that real export earnings are likely to grow more slowly in the future than they did during the 1960s and 1970s means that growth in developing countries will have to be less import dependent if it is to regain its earlier dynamism. A more competitive exchange rate enhances the profitability of import-competing sectors (for example, the agricultural sector in African countries) and encourages investment in existing and potential industries without the need for costly and artificial subsidy mechanisms. There is already some evidence that increased exchange rate flexibility in developing countries has permitted them to adapt to weakness in international markets at less cost to domestic output growth than might otherwise have been the case.

A willingness to adjust exchange rates downward reinforces the need for monetary policy to be oriented toward containing the secondary inflationary consequences of higher import costs. Of course, monetary policy in developing countries is hard to separate from fiscal policy, because of the linkages between govern-

ment borrowing requirements and the credit expansion of the banking system. Nevertheless, the close association between inflation and monetary growth shows that control over credit expansion has to be an important component of any program of financial stabilization. Closely related to overall monetary policy is the setting of interest rates that bear a realistic relationship to current and prospective inflation rates. As just noted, this is not only a key element in mobilizing domestic savings and allocating scarce investment funds, but also in avoiding capital flight and inducing residents to repatriate foreign assets.

Structural Policies

Structural policies are by their nature specific to the needs and circumstances of individual countries. Nevertheless, it is possible to identify several important problems that appear to be common to a number of countries. One of these that links up with issues of fiscal improvement mentioned above is the excessive dependence of many countries on international trade taxes as a source of budgetary revenues. This has disadvantages from a macroeconomic viewpoint, since the fiscal position tends to weaken in periods when trade growth is relatively subdued. It also has structural disadvantages, since it tends to bias the pattern of output away from the often more dynamic traded-goods sectors. An important priority in many developing countries will be to orient their revenue structure toward other sources, and toward forms (such as taxes on consumption) that also enhance savings incentives.

A second source of widespread problems is rigidity in pricing policies. This extends from macroeconomic prices, such as the exchange rate and interest rates, to microeconomic prices, such as the cost of services provided by government entities and the setting of government-regulated private sector prices, notably agricultural producer prices. Where possible, it is more efficient to allow prices to be set in free and competitive markets. Where this is not possible, governments should administer prices with a full awareness of the opportunity costs of the resources used and the scarcity value of the goods or services provided.

Closely connected with the issue of public sector pricing policy is that of the efficiency of state enterprises. Over the years, inefficiency has flourished in many state enterprises, its overt consequences masked by the ready availability of budgetary support. State enterprises have often been vehicles for the implementation of social policy, for example, by being forced to locate in particular regions, or being required to hire excessive quantities of labor. They have had decisions influenced in other respects too, for example, by being required to purchase inputs from domestic suppliers, or to adopt particular types of technology. While each individual decision affecting the operation of a state enterprise usually has a legitimate motivation, their combined effect has been highly detrimental to economic efficiency. It is important that state enterprises be conducted according to efficient operating principles, and that departures from such principles for reasons of government policy be clearly identified, and preferably provided for through distinct budgetary appropriations.

A further important structural issue concerns the size and distribution of investment expenditure. Ideally, investment would be determined as the outcome of decentralized decisions undertaken at the enterprise level on the basis of adequate information of government policy and the likely evolution of final demand. As a practical matter, however, this does not happen in many developing countries, and the national investment strategy is often planned at the government level. The mistakes that have most often been made in this process include underestimation of the gestation period of major investment projects; excessive concentration on "state-of-the-art" as opposed to "appropriate" technology; the favoring of large or prestige projects; and inadequate flexibility in investment plans, making it difficult to cut back particular projects without adverse effects on the overall efficiency of the investment plan.

A final issue that may be mentioned is the role of import liberalization. A number of countries have felt that trade restrictions are the most effective way of curbing imports without inducing a decline in output and a sharp increase in inflation as a result of exchange depreciation. In anything other than the short run, however, the maintenance of restrictions has consequences that impair the functioning of an economy and reduce its capacity to adapt to external disturbances. Trade restrictions enable the exchange rate to be maintained at a higher level than would otherwise be the case. Thus, while specific industries are protected, others, which could be competitive at a realistic exchange rate, are prevented from becoming established. A structure of production emerges that is based on administrative decision rather than comparative advantage. Inevitably, this process tends to favor existing industries over potential ones. The fact that new traded-goods industries do not come into existence complicates the task of responding to a sudden loss of export earnings in the future, since the domestic productive base that can be used to cushion the economy from a fall in imports is narrower. For these reasons, it remains highly desirable for developing countries, as well as industrial countries, to resist protectionist pressure, and to adopt a medium-term strategy of dismantling trade barriers.

International Cooperation and the Role of the Fund

During the past year there has been a renewed emphasis on the role of international coordination in improving the functioning of the world economy. The largest five industrial countries have committed themselves to the pursuit of policies aimed at promoting convergence, reducing exchange rate misalignment, and combating protectionism; a new initiative has been launched to strengthen growth and buttress the adjustment efforts of developing countries; and the Interim Committee of the Board of Governors (of the Fund) on the International Monetary System (Interim Committee) has taken up the subject of reform of the international monetary system. If these initiatives are to bear fruit, however, important challenges remain for the international community.

Concerning the improvement of economic policy coordination in industrial countries, an important first step was taken with the Group of Five meeting in New York in September, 1985. In a modest way, the present World Economic Outlook exercise attempts to carry this process forward through more explicit consideration of economic policy interactions among the industrial countries. It should be noted that coordination does not connote either fine tuning or joint formulation of policy. It is rather a matter of increasing mutual awareness of policy interactions, designed to arrive at mutually compatible medium-term strategies, and internationally consistent responses to short-term divergences.

A second major development in the field of international collaboration was the debt initiative introduced by the Secretary of the U.S. Treasury in October 1985. This initiative underlined the joint responsibility of three sets of agents in the debt situation: that of the indebted countries, to intensify their efforts to improve the functioning of their economies; that of the multilateral development banks, to increase their disbursements to heavily indebted countries; and that of the commercial banks, to step up their lending to these same countries. There is, in addition, an implied responsibility of the industrial countries, to ensure that markets for developing country exports are kept open and growing and to provide the needed funding to maintain appropriate levels of official development assistance. The Fund will play an important role in this process, not only through the contribution of its own financial resources, but because its function of assisting countries to design, implement, and monitor growth-oriented adjustment programs will act as a catalyst for other financial flows. It will also play a role, through surveillance, in fostering the adoption of policies in industrial countries that take adequate account of the interests of other members.

In this connection, special mention should be made of the need to avoid protectionism. It is heartening that the leaders of the major countries have reaffirmed their joint determination to avoid protectionism. Other countries, both in the developed and developing world, have evinced a similar determination. What is therefore needed is to translate the existing political will into a strategy designed not just to prevent the spread of restrictions, but to roll back those that already exist.

Lastly, the improvement of the functioning of the international monetary system is currently under study by the Fund's Executive Directors and by the Interim Committee. A key element in this is reaching agreement on the kinds of policies and institutional arrangements that will promote greater stability of exchange rates, an orderly basis for providing international liquidity, and a reliable source of resource transfers to developing countries that does not lead to avoidable difficulties of indebtedness. Agreement in these areas would provide a framework within which new procedural arrangements would enable the Fund to carry out its surveillance responsibilities more effectively.

Chapter II

Toward Better Balanced Growth in Industrial Countries

The industrial countries appear now to have entered a period of sustained and better balanced growth. Until recently, the cyclical recovery that began late in 1982 had been characterized by sharp divergences in both policies and economic performance among the major countries. There are now several indications that policies and performance are beginning to converge. In particular, a more sustainable pattern of growth across countries seems to be emerging, while inflation rates continue to decline and inflation differentials are narrowing further. In addition, both the September 1985 exchange rate initiative by the Group of Five and the adoption of a balanced budget act in the United States in December 1985 indicate that the authorities in the largest countries intend to deal with several serious manifestations of imbalances, in particular the high value of the dollar and the large U.S. budget and current account deficits. Although many uncertainties persist, it does appear that some of the downside risks to the outlook for industrial countries have diminished in importance.

The rate of growth in the industrial countries slowed to a moderate 2.8 percent in 1985, which was significantly below the 4.7 percent recorded in 1984. The slowdown was dominated by developments in the United States, where growth fell to 2.2 percent, compared with 6.5 percent in 1984. But the rate of expansion also moderated in Japan. In the industrial countries of Europe, growth averaged only 2.3 percent, which was not sufficient to prevent a further rise in unemployment. Price increases have continued to moderate, particularly in countries with above-average inflation rates. The rate of increase in the composite GNP deflator for industrial countries fell to 3.9 percent in 1985, the lowest inflation rate since 1967.

In 1986 and 1987, the main forces that are expected to influence the industrial economies comprise a tighter fiscal policy stance in North America, somewhat easier fiscal policy in Europe, and a tendency for monetary conditions to ease in most countries. In Japan, the fiscal stance is assumed to remain tight. The significant depreciation of the dollar since March 1985 will also affect the pattern of growth, and will help to reduce inflation further outside the United States. In addition, price performance and real income developments in the industrial countries are expected to be favorably influenced by the recent marked decline in oil prices and, hence, by a significant improvement in the terms of trade vis-à-vis the oil exporting countries. Together with revaluation effects in bond and stock markets, these influences are likely to have a beneficial impact on confidence of consumers and investors. Overall, growth in the industrial countries is projected to average some 3 percent in 1986, rising to 3¼ percent in 1987, with rates of expansion in most countries expected to cluster in the 2½–3½ percent range.

The projections are based on the assumptions that the price of internationally traded oil, which is estimated to have declined to $19 per barrel in the first quarter of 1986, will average $15 per barrel for the remainder of 1986 and in 1987, and that exchange rates will remain unchanged in real effective terms from their level in the first week of March 1986. These assumptions imply that nominal oil prices are assumed to decline by as much as 40 percent in 1986 in dollar terms; in real terms—when deflated by the projected increase in export prices of manufactures—oil prices are assumed to be approximately halved. For the effective exchange rate of the dollar, the estimated depreciation by early March 1986 was about 25 percent from the peak a year earlier. If the dollar were to remain at its early March level through 1986, the effective depreciation would amount to about 15 percent for 1986 on average. With rates of inflation projected to converge across the industrial countries—in part because of the lower value of the dollar—the real depreciation of the dollar would be of the same order of magnitude.

While the dollar depreciation primarily affects the

pattern of growth and inflation across countries, the oil price decline is likely to have a substantial net beneficial impact on the industrial countries in general. Such benefits comprise a real income gain (of almost ¾ of 1 percent of GNP in 1986), lower consumer price inflation (between 1 and 1½ percent lower in 1986 and 1987 than would otherwise have been predicted), and favorable influences on confidence. With lower inflation, monetary conditions would be likely to ease, and lower energy prices would also have beneficial supply-side effects, in particular through their impact on profitability and real labor costs. Overall, these effects are expected to more than offset the impact of reduced exports to the oil exporting developing countries, and the negative implications of an oil price decline for the industrial countries' domestic energy sectors and, perhaps, for some parts of their financial sectors.

Apart from the uncertainty about the extent and timing of budget deficit reductions in the United States, and about the debt situation in the developing countries (analyzed in Chapter V), the principal remaining concerns for the industrial countries are the continuation of large external payments imbalances in the United States, Japan, and the Federal Republic of Germany, and the persistence of high unemployment rates in Europe and Canada. The significant depreciation of the dollar over the past year and the assumed adjustment of fiscal policy in the United States will help prevent larger current account imbalances among the industrial countries but are unlikely to reduce these imbalances much in the short run. Uncertainty will therefore persist both in the area of exchange rates and with respect to protectionist sentiment which continues to constitute an important downside risk. In Europe, growth is not expected to accelerate enough to make major inroads into unemployment, which, it is increasingly recognized, reflects structural factors to a considerable extent. While the possibility of further downward pressure on oil prices cannot be ruled out, it is important to recognize that in the event that some form of restraint on oil production is re-established, a partial reversal of the recent decline in oil prices could take place. (For a detailed discussion of oil market conditions, see Supplementary Note 4.)

This chapter reviews the outlook for the industrial countries in more detail. The first section outlines the setting of economic policy, dealing both with policy objectives and with the difficulties connected with the implementation of policies. The following section discusses the macroeconomic implications of the recent decline in oil prices. This is followed by a review of demand and output developments in 1985, together with a presentation of the staff's projections for 1986 and 1987. The next sections analyze developments in labor markets and in inflation. A main topic dealt with in these sections is the impact of the projected improvement in the industrial countries' terms of trade on employment and inflation. The review of domestic developments is followed by an analysis of developments in exchange rates and balances of payments. The chapter concludes with a discussion of some of the principal uncertainties in the projections.

The Policy Setting

Following the Group of Five initiative in September 1985 and the adoption of a balanced budget act in the United States in December, both the pattern and the mix of economic policies in the industrial countries are expected to change significantly in 1986 and 1987 compared with the past four years. The policy assumptions underlying the projections in this *World Economic Outlook*, which are based on existing or announced policies, suggest that fiscal policy in the major countries as a group will tighten somewhat over the forecast period. The assumptions also point to a tendency for fiscal policy stances across countries to converge. This convergence would be in sharp contrast to the divergent pattern of policies that has prevailed since the beginning of the decade and should contribute to reducing imbalances in foreign trade and in financial markets. As illustrated by the concerted reduction of official discount rates in the three largest countries early in March 1986, the prospect of tighter and more convergent fiscal policies has already contributed to lower interest rates and has facilitated the efforts of the authorities of major countries to bring about a more sustainable pattern of exchange rates. At the same time, it is apparent that the risk of a substantial renewed rise in interest rates has diminished.

Since the beginning of the 1980s, policy objectives in the industrial countries have been formulated in a medium-term framework, with particular emphasis on the need for significant reductions in rates of inflation, in the size of the public sector, and in government budget deficits. These objectives have been viewed as necessary conditions for achieving a sustainable improvement in profitability, investment, and growth over the medium to longer run. At the same time, many governments have striven to improve the functioning of markets, particularly those for labor and financial services. In some countries, privatization of publicly controlled enterprises has also been pursued in an effort to enhance competition and efficiency in markets for both goods and non-financial services.

The strategy adopted has had a number of notable successes. Substantial progress has been achieved both in the area of inflation control and, albeit not in all countries, in budget positions. However, it has to be recognized that there have been several setbacks in implementing the strategy. The rising budget deficit in the United States, in particular, has been a cause of concern, both because of its impact on exchange rates and because of the upward pressure on real interest rates to which it contributes. If, indeed, the United States is now on the path of medium-term deficit reduction, a major element of uncertainty will have been, if not eliminated, at least reduced in importance.

Fiscal Policy

According to fiscal impulse estimates for the broader definition of government (general government), the thrust of fiscal policy in the major industrial countries, taken together, is expected to become somewhat more restrictive over the forecast period than it has been during the last four years (Chart 3). This mainly reflects an expected removal of stimulus in Canada and, particularly in 1987, in the United States. The budgetary policy assumptions adopted suggest that policies will continue to differ across countries, in part reflecting the need for budget consolidation in countries with large remaining budget deficits. Nevertheless, compared with the experience over the past four years, the fiscal outlook for 1986–87 exhibits a clear tendency toward policy convergence. It is, however, more than usually difficult to make projections of fiscal developments, given the uncertainties about the constitutionality of recent budgetary initiatives in the United States as well as about the manner in which such initiatives would be implemented. (For a detailed discussion of fiscal policy developments in industrial countries, see Supplementary Note 1.)

There have been several important developments in the budgetary situation in the United States over the past six months. The compromise budget guidelines established in the Congressional Resolution in August 1985 aimed at reducing the federal budget deficit to $175 billion in fiscal year 1986. This compares with a deficit of $210 billion in fiscal year 1985 and a projected deficit of $230 billion in fiscal year 1986 in the absence of policy changes. Notwithstanding some uncertainty regarding the extent to which these budgetary savings would be achieved (in part because of new appropriations, such as the Farm Bill), the subsequent adoption of the Gramm-Rudman-Hollings balanced budget act in December indicates that a fundamental shift in policy priorities may be taking place. The Administration's budget for fiscal year 1987, released early in February, proposed budgetary changes designed to meet the deficit target stipulated by the balanced budget act which requires a deficit of no more than $144 billion (3.2 percent of GNP) in fiscal year 1987 (and a balanced budget in fiscal year 1991).

Chart 3. Major Industrial Countries: Fiscal Impulses, 1982–85 and 1986–87[1]

(In percent of GDP/GNP at annual rates)

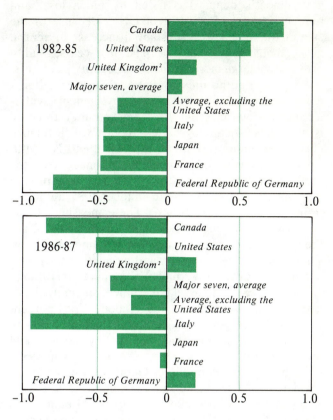

[1] General government, that is, central and local authorities plus social security. Data are on a national accounts basis. A positive fiscal impulse indicates injection of stimulus; a negative impulse indicates withdrawal of stimulus. For the definition of the fiscal impulse, see Supplementary Note 1.
[2] Excluding asset sales.

In light of the uncertainty surrounding the legal status of the Gramm-Rudman-Hollings legislation, the staff has adopted the assumption that the deficit reduction measures actually implemented will not be sufficient to meet the targets fully, in part because of a somewhat lower projection for growth than assumed by the U.S. Administration. According to the staff's projections, the federal deficit would thus decline to around 3½ percent of GNP in fiscal year 1987 (and would remain at about 2½ percent of GNP in fiscal year 1991) compared with a deficit equivalent to 5.4 percent of GNP in fiscal year 1985. Even on this assumption, however, the fiscal stance in the United States would undergo a major change from the sizable injection of stimulus over the four years 1982–85. (The medium-term implications of a more rapid implementation of the balanced budget act are analyzed in Chapter IV, "Policy Interactions in Industrial Countries.")

In Japan, the fiscal balance of the general government sector has strengthened substantially from a peak deficit of 5½ percent of GNP in 1978 to a projected deficit of only 1½ percent of GNP in 1986. The central government's deficit has fallen by much less, and remains close to 5 percent of GNP. Because of the size of the deficit, the substantial increase in central government debt over the past ten years, and a prospective large increase in social security payments, the Japanese authorities continue to emphasize budgetary consolidation at the central government level as a major policy objective. It is their intention to cease issuing deficit-financing bonds—bonds which finance current expenditures—by fiscal year 1990. Notwithstanding this medium-term objective, concern over the outlook for growth led to the adoption of measures to stimulate domestic activity in October 1985 and in the proposed budget for 1986/87. These measures focus on increasing public works expenditure by local authorities, whose budget situation has improved considerably over recent years, and by public enterprises financed by the Government's lending operations. Even with increased local government spending, however, a withdrawal of stimulus of about ½ of 1 percent of GNP at the general government level is likely to occur in 1986. Continuation of this policy stance would imply a further slight withdrawal of stimulus in 1987.

In the Federal Republic of Germany, the stance of fiscal policy is expected to ease somewhat this year as a result of tax cuts amounting to DM 11 billion (0.6 percent of GNP). Nevertheless, it remains an overriding policy objective to reduce the size of the public sector in relation to GNP, and the 1986 budget is characterized by continued restraint on the expenditure side. Because of this restraint, and reflecting also the expected pickup in growth, the general government budget deficit is forecast to decline further, both in 1986 and in 1987. In the latter year, it is projected, on present policies, to be only 0.6 percent of GNP (compared with 1.1 percent in 1985 and 3.7 percent as recently as in 1981). A second stage of tax cuts (amounting to DM 8.5 billion) is scheduled to take effect in 1988.

Fiscal policy in the United Kingdom has been somewhat more expansionary in recent years than intended under the medium-term financial strategy, because of greater difficulties in controlling the growth of public expenditure than had been foreseen. In the light of the recent oil price developments and their adverse impact on North Sea oil revenue, a major improvement in the fiscal position appears unlikely in the period immediately ahead. According to staff projections, which are based on the 1986/87 budget that was made public in March 1986, the public sector borrowing requirement will remain broadly unchanged in 1986 and 1987 from its 1985 level. Substantial increases in sales of public sector assets, together with buoyant non-oil revenues, are expected to offset to a significant degree a projected decline in oil revenues. However, the fiscal impulse measure for the general government sector, which refers to national accounts estimates exclusive of asset sales suggests that the fiscal stance will move marginally in the direction of expansion (by ¼ of 1 percent of GDP) in 1986 and be approximately neutral in 1987.[1]

The budgetary posture in France is expected to remain cautious. Continued curbs on the growth of public expenditure are expected to permit an announced reduction of the tax burden to be financed without any significant increase in the budget deficit, which is projected to remain in the vicinity of 3 percent of GNP at the central government level. Budgetary objectives in Italy are for a small reduction in the central government deficit, which at about 16 percent of GNP in 1985 continues to be clearly the largest among the major industrial countries. In Canada, the budget deficit as a proportion of GNP was little changed in 1985 from a year earlier, notwithstanding a relatively rapid rate of economic growth and the implementation of a number of deficit reduction measures. Staff projections for 1986 and 1987, which are based on the federal budget announced in February of this year, point to a substantial improvement in the budgetary situation, both as a result of tax increases and slower planned growth in public expenditures. The reversal in the budgetary situation is estimated to lead to a large withdrawal of fiscal stimulus at the general government level in 1986 (equivalent to 1¼ percent of GNP), which is in sharp contrast to the injection of stimulus in the 1983–85 period.

Recent budgetary announcements in the smaller industrial countries continue to emphasize the need for deficit reduction. Although the implementation of deficit reductions, as in the major countries, has proven harder to achieve than was envisaged, the impact of budgetary changes in the smaller countries over the forecast period is likely to involve a continued slight withdrawal of stimulus. Nevertheless, with the exception of Denmark and Sweden, budget deficits in the smaller countries are expected to remain substantially higher than they were at the beginning of the decade. Lower oil prices are likely to lead to a sharp reduction of the budget surplus in Norway. With natural gas

---

[1] In the budget, public sector asset sales are treated as negative expenditure. Asset sales therefore reduce the borrowing requirement even though their effects on the economy—abstracting from supply side effects—are likely to be similar to those of bond sales. In the staff's estimates of fiscal balances and of fiscal impulses (see Tables A16 and A17 in the Statistical Appendix), asset sales have been treated as financing items rather than negative expenditure.

prices responding with a lag, the budget deficit in the Netherlands is expected to widen significantly in 1987.

Monetary Policy

Since the beginning of the 1980s, the principal objective of monetary policy in the major industrial countries has been to reduce inflation and inflationary expectations. For most countries, this objective has been achieved by setting progressively lower target growth rates for monetary aggregates. This non-accommodative approach to monetary policy has succeeded in breaking the escalating trend in monetary growth of the 1970s and has established the conditions necessary for a sustained deceleration in inflation (Chart 4). While the pursuit of monetary targets continues to be an important intermediate objective, the implementation of monetary policy has increasingly been adapted to take account of prevailing economic circumstances and of shifts in the underlying velocity of targeted monetary aggregates. As monetary authorities have acquired greater credibility in their commitment to control inflation, they have become more willing to allow shifts in velocity to be reflected in the monetary aggregates rather than in monetary conditions. Nevertheless, the benefits of accommodating such shifts in velocity have continued to be weighed against the risk of unintended easing of monetary conditions which would endanger inflation control.

In 1985, the rate of growth of narrow money in the seven major industrial countries accelerated to 10.1 percent on an end-of-year basis compared with 6.9

Chart 4. Major Industrial Countries: Money Supply, Nominal GNP, and GNP Deflator, 1970–87

(Annual changes, in percent)

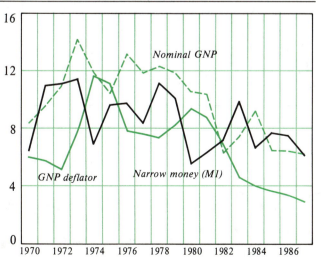

percent during 1984, while the growth rate of broad money rose to 8.9 percent, 1 percentage point above the previous year's rise. However, in several countries the behavior of the velocity of key monetary aggregates was distorted, as it had been in some earlier years, by the effects of financial innovation and by a further reduction in underlying inflation rates. In the United States, the velocity of M1 declined sharply in the first half of the year, although the decline did not extend to the broader monetary aggregates. In part reflecting this development, the authorities de-emphasized the role of M1 as a guide to policy, while giving somewhat greater weight to the broader aggregates and to other economic and financial indicators. In the United Kingdom, the performance of the two targeted aggregates diverged significantly during the year: M0, the wide monetary base, trended along the bottom of its target range while the growth of sterling M3 significantly exceeded the upper end of its range. In view of the recent liberalization of financial markets and the high level of real interest rates, the authorities decided to accept the faster growth of sterling M3 and to assign increased weight to M0 and to the exchange rate, as well as to other financial indicators in the conduct of monetary policy. In the other major industrial countries that announce target (or forecast) growth ranges for monetary aggregates—Japan, France, and the Federal Republic of Germany—the outturns were more consistent with the announced targets (see Chart 32 in Supplementary Note 2).

Short-term interest rates fell significantly in several of the major industrial countries during 1985 (Chart 5). Short-term interest rates in the United States fell by approximately 3½ percentage points from their 1984 peak as the monetary aggregate M1 was permitted to grow more rapidly than targeted in the face of a deceleration of output growth and a continued low rate of inflation. Interest rates also fell quite sharply in France, the Federal Republic of Germany, and Italy. In the United Kingdom, however, the authorities allowed base lending rates to rise by 4½ percentage points early in 1985, on concern about the quickening of the rate of depreciation of sterling and the associated perception that monetary policy had become too loose. Base rates then declined gradually during the year as sterling strengthened on foreign exchange markets. In late 1985 and early 1986, however, sterling again came under pressure, triggering a renewed rise of 1 percentage point in base lending rates in January 1986. In Japan, short-term interest rates were stable at their 1984 level for the first nine months of the year, but rose 1¾ percentage points from September to December, reflecting greater emphasis on exchange market considerations in the conduct of monetary policy.

The first three months of 1986 have witnessed further

Chart 5.   Five Major Industrial Countries: Interest Rates, 1980–86

(In percent)

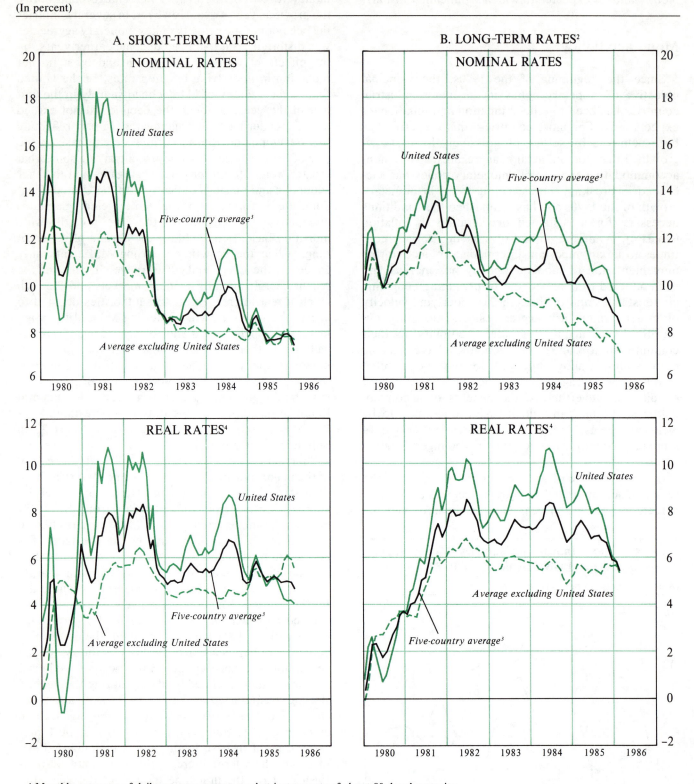

[1] Monthly averages of daily rates on money market instruments of about 90 days' maturity.

[2] Monthly averages of daily or weekly yields on government bonds, with maturities ranging from 7 years for Japan to 20 years for the United States and the United Kingdom.

[3] The United States, Japan, France, the Federal Republic of Germany, and the United Kingdom.

[4] Interest rates deflated by a weighted average of the increase in the private final domestic demand deflator in the current and the following two quarters; for the most recent periods, Fund staff projections of the deflator are used.

significant reductions in short-term interest rates in most of the major countries in response to significant changes in the pattern of exchange rates and to the continued improvement in the outlook for inflation stemming from the sharp drop in oil prices. These developments have permitted a reversal of the firming of interest rates in Japan and the United Kingdom that occurred in late 1985 and early 1986. In early March, the declining trend in interest rates led to a concerted cut in official discount rates by ½ of 1 percentage point in the three largest industrial countries.

Long-term interest rates fell by slightly more than short-term rates in the major industrial countries during 1985 and early 1986, implying that the yield curve tended to flatten in several countries. In the United States, as financial markets reacted to the growing likelihood (and eventual passage) of the balanced budget act, long-term interest rates fell significantly toward the end of the year, thereby narrowing the spread with respect to short-term rates. Long-term interest rates also fell significantly in France, the Federal Republic of Germany, Italy, and Canada during 1985. In Japan, long-term interest rates rose early in 1985 and then declined gradually, falling below short-term rates. In the United Kingdom, the yield curve became inverted in 1985 as long-term interest rates increased by significantly less than short-term rates at the beginning of the year and finished the year below the closing levels of 1984.

Adjusted for changes in the rate of inflation, yield differentials across countries narrowed somewhat last year. In particular, real short-term interest rates fell significantly in North America, whereas they rose somewhat on average in the other major industrial countries.[2] Long-term interest rates also declined significantly in real terms in all the major countries except the United Kingdom, with the most pronounced reduction being in North America. Nevertheless, despite the significant reductions in real interest rates over the past year, both short-term and long-term real interest rates remain high by historical standards.

The target growth ranges for monetary aggregates announced thus far for 1986 reflect the continuing objective of controlling inflation. In the United States, the targets announced in February 1986 call for a continuation of the 3–8 percent growth range for M1 established last July for the remainder of 1985. A 6–9 percent range has been maintained for M2, and a similar range has been established for M3. In France, the authorities have redefined the monetary aggregates as a result of financial innovations and have set an

ambitious target growth range for M3 of 3–5 percent in 1986. The Federal Republic of Germany, which has had one of the best inflation performances among the industrial countries, has raised slightly the target range for the growth of central bank money from 3–5 percent in 1985 to 3½–5½ percent in 1986. This reflects a small increase in the potential rate of output growth (as estimated by the authorities) in 1986 compared with 1985. In the United Kingdom, the authorities have set a 1986–87 target range of 2–6 percent for MO (the wide monetary base). A somewhat higher range of 11–15 percent has been set for sterling M3 to allow for an expected further shift in the allocation of portfolios toward interest-bearing deposits. Overall, in view of the projected developments in real GNP growth and inflation, together with the move toward a more restrictive stance of fiscal policies in the major industrial countries as a group, the announced targets seem to be consistent with some further easing of financial market conditions in most of the major countries during 1986. (Monetary policy developments in the major industrial countries are discussed in more detail in Supplementary Note 2.)

Impact of Lower Oil Prices

The recent decline in oil prices has significantly improved the short-term prospects for domestic demand growth in the fuel importing industrial countries. At the same time, inflation rates are likely to moderate further, which by itself should contribute to prolong the current recovery.

While large fluctuations in oil prices have been observed in the past—in 1973–74 and in 1979–80—the effects of a sharp decline in oil prices are unlikely to be completely symmetrical to those of sharp price increases. In the first place, a key factor behind the recession following each of the two rounds of price increases was a temporary rise in the world's saving ratio, reflecting differences in the short-run spending propensities as between oil exporting and oil importing countries. In the current situation, where many oil exporting countries are already experiencing deficits on their current accounts and severe debt-servicing problems, the decline in oil prices is unlikely to result in a commensurate decline in the world saving ratio. Second, the anti-inflationary tightening of financial policies that followed the oil price increases of the late 1970s also aggravated the subsequent recession. At the current juncture, however, with policies set in a medium-term framework, a corresponding discretionary easing of policies is unlikely. Overall, therefore, it seems unlikely that the effects of the present declines

---

[2] Real interest rates are defined here as nominal interest rates adjusted by the change in the private final domestic demand deflator in the current and the following two quarters.

in oil prices will be as favorable as those of past oil price increases were unfavorable. Nevertheless, the favorable effects for fuel importing countries should be considerably greater than those stemming from the global redistribution of real incomes. On the assumption that monetary targets are not reduced to reflect the decline in inflation, monetary conditions can be expected to ease somewhat. In addition, the reduction in rates of inflation can be expected to result in positive wealth and real balance effects. Both factors should generate a significant net positive impact on output in the oil importing countries.

The direct effect of the assumed decline in oil prices from $26.70 per barrel in 1985 to some $16 per barrel in 1986 (representing an estimated price of $19 in the first quarter and an assumption of $15 thereafter) will be to lower the net oil import bill of the industrial countries by some $60 billion on an annual basis, which corresponds to almost ¾ of 1 percent of the industrial countries' GNP. This real income gain accounts for most of the projected improvement in the industrial countries' terms of trade in 1986. (The continued erosion of real non-oil commodity prices accounts for approximately one fourth of the total terms of trade gain.) For individual countries, the projected terms of trade movements are influenced by changes in the exchange rate as well. As a result, the projected improvement in the United States' terms of trade is somewhat smaller than in the case of Japan and the oil importing countries in Europe (Table 2).

Terms of trade gains in industrial countries will act to raise both profits and the real disposable incomes of consumers more than otherwise would be the case. Exactly how these gains will be distributed between consumers and enterprises is difficult to estimate, but the total impact on real national income is expected to amount to approximately 2½ percent in the case of the oil importing countries in Europe and in Japan. In view of these terms of trade gains, it cannot be excluded that demand and activity in Japan and Europe might in fact turn out somewhat stronger than projected at this juncture. This would partly depend on the impact of the oil price decline on confidence. There are clearly risks to a major decline in oil prices—because of the repercussions on the financial institutions heavily exposed vis-à-vis the oil producing countries, or vis-à-vis the industrial countries' domestic energy sectors. Nevertheless, to judge from the buoyancy of stock markets late in 1985 and early in 1986, the confidence of financial investors has improved dramatically along with the decline in oil prices.

A substantial proportion of the terms-of-trade-induced increase in real incomes stemming from lower oil prices is likely to be offset by reduced exports to the oil exporting countries, even though the adjustment may not be completed until after a few years. The projections assume that import volumes in the fuel exporting developing countries will decline by 15 percent in 1986, and by an additional 8 percent in 1987. This would still leave these countries' current account deficit at $49 billion in 1986, and at some $36 billion in 1987, compared with a deficit of $7 billion in 1985. (The impact on the fuel exporting countries is discussed in more detail in Chapter III.)

The reduction of oil import prices is expected to feed through gradually to consumers, partly through lower prices of other sources of energy. Such sympathetic price responses may not be felt until after a period. (Natural gas prices, for example, are often linked to oil prices with a lag.) Of course, to the extent energy taxes are increased to prevent a reversal of conservation efforts, such effects may not materialize. However, at this stage, most oil importing countries seem prepared to pass on the bulk of the oil price reduction to consumers and enterprises. In addition to the impact on final energy prices, there are likely to be significant effects on inflation in general, including lower nominal wage increases. Indeed, these secondary effects on inflation may turn out to be as important as the direct impact of lower oil prices. Overall, consumer price increases in industrial countries are expected to be reduced by 1–1½ percent in 1986 and 1987 as a result of the decline in oil prices.

Assuming an unchanged growth path for monetary aggregates, the reduction in rates of inflation is expected to have a favorable impact on monetary conditions. As such, the recent decline in interest rates may be interpreted as part of the beneficial effects of lower oil prices. The stance of fiscal policy may also be affected to some extent. In some countries, budgetary expenditures are established in nominal terms, so that as inflation decelerates, the level of real expenditure that is implied by nominal appropriations rises. Offsetting this factor, however, there may be a need for some countries to use the opportunity afforded by lower oil prices to accelerate the process of fiscal consolidation. Governments in oil producing industrial countries may also decide to offset part of the revenue loss from the oil sector by tightening fiscal policy.

Overall, tentative staff estimates suggest that the level of real GNP in the industrial countries at the end of the forecast period could be between ½ and 1 percent higher as a result of the reduction in oil prices. Most of the impact would be attributable to the secondary effects of disinflation and improved business and consumer confidence. Assuming that the price decline is sustained, over the medium-to-longer run there would also be a number of favorable supply-side effects, including in particular lower real labor costs and higher labor intensity of output.

Table 2.   Industrial Countries: Terms of Trade Changes and Real National Income, 1980–87

(In percent)

	1980	1981	1982	1983	1984	1985	1986	1987
Canada								
Changes in terms of trade	−0.8	−3.8	−1.3	2.8	−4.4	−1.6	−3.7	−0.8
Terms of trade impact on real national income (percent of GNP)	−0.2	−1.1	−0.3	0.7	−1.4	−0.5	−1.2	−0.2
Growth of real GNP	1.1	3.3	−4.4	3.3	5.0	4.5	3.3	3.3
United States								
Changes in terms of trade	−7.5	7.9	7.1	6.4	6.8	3.6	2.8	1.1
Terms of trade impact on real national income (percent of GNP)	−1.0	0.9	0.7	0.7	0.8	0.4	0.3	0.1
Growth of real GNP	−0.2	1.9	−2.5	3.5	6.5	2.2	2.9	3.6
Japan								
Changes in terms of trade	−21.1	1.4	0.2	3.3	2.2	3.6	21.6	−0.8
Terms of trade impact on real national income (percent of GNP)	−4.5	0.2	—	0.5	0.4	0.6	2.5	−0.1
Growth of real GNP	4.3	3.7	3.1	3.2	5.1	4.6	3.0	3.2
France								
Changes in terms of trade	−6.3	−4.7	1.8	2.5	0.9	2.5	10.6	0.9
Terms of trade impact on real national income (percent of GDP)	−1.7	−1.3	0.5	0.7	0.2	0.7	2.3	0.2
Growth of real GDP	1.1	0.5	1.8	0.7	1.6	1.1	2.4	2.3
Germany, Fed. Rep. of								
Changes in terms of trade	−6.3	−6.7	3.7	1.6	−2.2	1.4	8.1	0.6
Terms of trade impact on real national income (percent of GNP)	−2.1	−2.2	1.1	0.5	−0.7	0.5	2.4	0.2
Growth of real GNP	1.5	—	−1.0	1.5	3.0	2.4	3.7	2.7
Italy								
Changes in terms of trade	−6.2	−10.5	6.8	4.6	−1.5	0.4	11.1	1.0
Terms of trade impact on real national income (percent of GDP)	−1.8	−3.2	1.7	1.1	−0.4	0.1	2.6	0.3
Growth of real GDP	3.9	0.2	−0.5	−0.4	2.6	2.2	2.3	2.3
United Kingdom								
Changes in terms of trade	3.7	0.5	−1.7	−1.1	−1.0	2.1	−4.1	—
Terms of trade impact on real national income (percent of GDP)	1.1	0.1	−0.5	−0.3	−0.3	0.6	−1.2	—
Growth of real GDP	−2.5	−1.5	1.8	3.3	2.5	3.3	2.8	2.1
Seven major countries								
Changes in terms of trade	−7.2	−1.0	3.1	3.3	1.2	2.3	7.0	0.1
Terms of trade impact on real national income (percent of GNP)	−1.8	−0.3	0.6	0.6	0.2	0.5	0.8	—
Growth of real GNP	1.1	1.6	−0.6	2.8	5.0	2.7	3.0	3.3
All industrial countries								
Changes in terms of trade	−6.4	−1.2	2.7	2.3	1.1	1.8	6.7	0.1
Terms of trade impact on real national income (percent of GNP)	−1.6	−0.4	0.5	0.4	0.2	0.4	0.8	—
Growth of real GNP	1.2	1.4	−0.4	2.6	4.7	2.8	3.0	3.2

Output and Demand

The short-term prospects for the industrial countries suggest that economic expansion is likely to continue in 1986 and 1987 at a slightly faster pace than in 1985, when real GNP rose by 2.8 percent in the industrial countries as a whole. This kind of growth performance would be significantly below the rate of 4.7 percent achieved in 1984, but, given the duration of this recovery, would compare relatively well with the average performance over the two most recent international business cycles. As discussed below, even though the previous upswings were generally more vigorous during the initial two to three years of recovery, they have not typically been as long lived as the current expansion is expected to be.

The projected economic performance of the industrial countries, taken together, is much the same on a year-over-year basis as that presented in the *World Economic Outlook, October 1985*. However, for most countries, growth during 1986 (from the fourth quarter of 1985 to the fourth quarter of 1986) is expected to be significantly more rapid than was expected last October, mainly as a result of the decline in oil prices. In the case of the United States, growth is expected to pick up significantly despite the weaker-than-expected performance in late 1985. The depreciation of the dollar should improve the real foreign balance, and lower energy prices and interest rates will help to support domestic demand. These positive factors should offset the impact of lower growth in public spending as a result of budget cuts. The outlook for Japan has also been affected by exchange rate movements, with the yen having appreciated significantly vis-à-vis both the dollar and some European currencies. In addition, Japan's projected exports to oil exporting developing countries have been revised downward substantially. The contribution of the foreign balance to the growth of output is therefore expected to turn negative in 1986. Even though domestic demand will be stimulated by the substantial improvement in the terms of trade, projected real GNP growth in Japan is now put at only 3 percent in 1986. The projected rate of growth of the European countries for 1986 has been revised upward slightly, reflecting the net effects of a negative contribution from the foreign sector—for much the same reasons as in the case of Japan—and stronger domestic demand growth reflecting both the expected improvement in Europe's terms of trade and, in some countries, an improvement in business and consumer confidence. Overall, real GNP in the industrial countries is expected to grow by 3 percent in 1986, about the same as projected in the October *World Economic Outlook*. More tentatively, a slightly higher growth rate of 3¼ percent is expected for 1987.

As already mentioned, this recovery compares relatively favorably with previous expansion periods in terms of longevity. On average, postwar recoveries have tended to show serious strains by the third or fourth year. The projections suggest that the current recovery will continue through its fourth and fifth years, with growth in each of these years at 3–3¼ percent. While the current expansion so far is not as long as the recovery that began early in 1975, and which to date has been the longest postwar recovery, it is already longer than most earlier expansions and in particular than the recovery that began in 1971 (Chart 6). Growth in the 1971 recovery faltered after about three years, before giving way to the 1973–74 recession, which was partly attributable to the first oil price increase, but also reflected a tightening of financial policies in response to a sharp acceleration of inflation.

The current upswing differs from the two previous expansion periods in three principal respects. First,

the distribution of growth across countries has been more uneven on this occasion. In particular, growth in Europe has been significantly slower during this recovery, while growth in the United States has, on average, been comparable to previous recoveries. Second, the current recovery has so far taken place in a less favorable external environment than earlier recoveries—measured by trade volume developments—with a downward shift in the rest of the world's demand for industrial countries' exports. Finally, the current recovery has been associated with a marked deceleration of rates of inflation, whereas the two previous recoveries were characterized by high or accelerating inflation.

Differences among countries in the growth of output have largely reflected even more pronounced differences in rates of growth of domestic demand (Chart 6a). While domestic demand has grown at least as rapidly in the United States as in earlier upswings, demand has been much weaker this time in Europe and in Japan. If the projections are realized, this pattern will continue during the fourth and fifth years of the current recovery, but with some acceleration likely in the rate of growth of domestic demand in both Europe and Japan.

After growing rapidly in the first two years of this recovery, the U.S. economy slowed abruptly to a more moderate rate over the past year. There were two principal reasons for the marked slowdown in output growth, from 6.5 percent in 1984 to only 2.2 percent in 1985. In the first place, inventory accumulation fell sharply, reflecting a combination of fairly normal cyclical adjustments and prospects of declining commodity prices, which made it advantageous to run down inventories. Second, the trade deficit continued to widen, which meant that a declining share of the growth in demand was being met by domestic producers. In contrast to the weak performance of inventories and net exports, final domestic demand continued to grow at a relatively strong pace, reflecting a significant decline in the household saving ratio and strong growth of defense spending that caused total public expenditure on goods and services to rise by 6 percent in real terms. Business investment also continued to expand, albeit at a slower pace than in 1984.

Because of the decline in inventory investment, total domestic demand in the United States was particularly weak in the first half of 1985 (Table 3). A rebound in final domestic demand in the second half—attributable mainly to defense spending and residential construction—was more than offset by a further sharp deterioration in real net exports. As a result, real GNP growth decelerated to 2.0 percent (annual rate) during the second half of 1985, having grown at a rate of 2.6 percent during the first half.

Chart 6. Major Industrial Countries: Recovery of Real GNP from the 1970–71, 1974–75, and 1980–82 Recessions

(Indices: fourth quarter 1971, first quarter 1975, and fourth quarter 1982 = 100)[1]

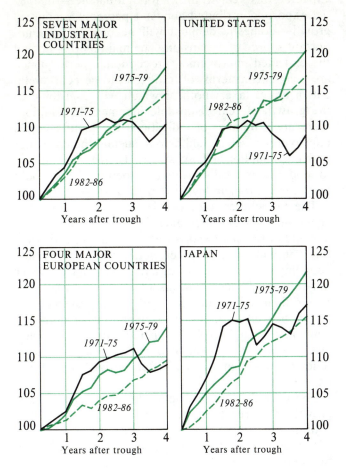

Chart 6a. Major Industrial Countries: Recovery of Real Total Domestic Demand from the 1970–71, 1974–75, and 1980–82 Recessions

(Indices: fourth quarter 1971, first quarter 1975, and fourth quarter 1982 = 100)[1]

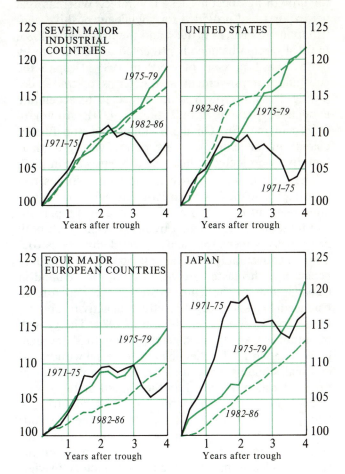

[1] Data for the 1971–75 recovery exclude Italy.

While some of the reasons that led to the pickup in U.S. domestic demand in the second half of 1985 are not expected to persist, other factors are expected to result in a significant strengthening of activity in

Table 3. Stages in U.S. Recovery, 1982–87

(Percent change during period; in real terms at annual rates)

	Q4,1982– Q4,1984	Q4,1984– Q2,1985	Q2,1985– Q4,1985	Q4,1985– Q4,1987
Final domestic demand	5.7	3.6	5.2	2.8
Stockbuilding[1]	1.5	−1.2	−1.2	0.5
Total domestic demand	7.2	2.4	4.0	3.3
Foreign balance[1]	−1.7	—	−2.1	0.3
GNP	5.5	2.4	1.9	3.5

[1] Changes expressed as percentages of GNP at the beginning of the period.

1986–87. The personal saving ratio is unlikely to fall much further from the extremely low level it reached toward the end of 1985; the growth of public expenditure will probably slow significantly; and business surveys suggest that non-residential investment will be less buoyant than over the past two years despite the decline in interest rates. Against this, however, lower oil prices should work to increase real household income, and the effects of the depreciation of the dollar should begin to be felt on the real foreign balance—at least to the extent of halting the earlier deterioration. Following the low level of inventory formation in 1985, this component is also expected to contribute to growth over the forecast period. On balance, real GNP is thus projected to grow at an annual rate of 3¾ percent during 1986 and by 3½ percent during 1987.

Real GNP in Japan rose by 4.6 percent in 1985. A

decline in exports in the second half of the year was largely offset by stronger growth of domestic demand, particularly business fixed investment. In view of the recent appreciation of the yen and the significantly weaker prospects for Japanese exports, the outlook for growth has become less favorable. Whereas real net exports had provided for significant positive contributions to growth in 1984 and the first half of 1985, the real foreign balance is projected to deteriorate by more than 1 percent of GNP in 1986. Despite the substantial improvement in the terms of trade, domestic demand growth is not expected to accelerate enough to prevent a reduction in GNP growth to 3 percent in 1986. On the assumption of no further change in the external value of the yen, growth is tentatively projected to increase to 3¼ percent in 1987.

The slowdown of growth in the United States had little impact on the Canadian economy, which remained quite buoyant in 1985. Real GNP rose by 4.5 percent and total domestic demand by 5.4 percent, with both private investment (particularly residential construction) and consumption sustaining the recovery. Mainly because of the faster growth in domestic demand in Canada than in the United States, the real foreign balance had a small negative effect on activity, following a large positive contribution in 1984. The growth of output in Canada is expected to slow to 3¼ percent in 1986 and in 1987, reflecting a substantial withdrawal of fiscal stimulus as well as the lagged influences of the moderation of growth in the United States.

The rate of growth in the industrial countries in Europe in 1985 was similar to that in the previous year—2.3 percent. In terms of domestic demand, the situation improved somewhat, but the pace of the recovery clearly has remained unsatisfactory in view of the margin of slack in European labor markets. The year-over-year growth rate masks a rather uneven performance during the year. Growth was extremely weak in several countries in the first half of 1985, mainly reflecting an unusually harsh winter. In contrast, during the second half of 1985 there was a marked rebound in demand and activity. In 1986 and 1987, domestic demand in Europe is expected to strengthen markedly, reflecting substantial terms of trade gains as well as easier monetary conditions and a less restrictive fiscal stance. These forces are expected to more than offset the effects of a deterioration in Europe's net exports, attributable mainly to declining imports by the oil exporting countries, and to weaker competitiveness vis-à-vis North American suppliers.

The recent improvement in performance in the Federal Republic of Germany is particularly encouraging. Even though the rebound in the second half of 1985 was not sufficient to prevent a deceleration in

growth, from 3 percent in 1984 to 2.4 percent in 1985 as a whole, the strengthening of demand nevertheless should help to sustain a significantly higher rate of growth in 1986, when real GNP is projected to expand by 3¾ percent. With a small negative contribution expected this year from the foreign balance—in 1985 net exports contributed almost 1 percentage point to growth—domestic demand will become a more important source of expansion. The main factors behind the expected improvement in economic performance are a significant terms of trade gain (8 percent) and a cut in direct taxes, both of which will contribute to the growth of real disposable incomes. In addition, there are a number of indications that confidence is improving, which should help to sustain the growth of both consumption and investment. Growth is projected to moderate in 1987 (to about 2¾ percent), but would nevertheless remain higher than in the rest of Europe.

The French economy experienced sluggish growth again in 1985 (1.1 percent) as the contribution to demand of real net exports turned negative. Prospects for 1986 and 1987, however, suggest that the French economy is now also entering a recovery phase. Lower inflation, a significant terms of trade improvement, easier financial conditions, and an improvement in confidence all point to an acceleration of domestic demand growth, to perhaps 3 percent in both 1986 and 1987. Real GDP is estimated to rise somewhat less, reflecting a slight further deterioration in real net exports.

The United Kingdom had a relatively strong rate of growth of aggregate output (3.3 percent) in 1985, the country's fourth year of recovery. However, because of the influence of the coal miners' strike, which came to an end early in 1985, the recorded growth rate was somewhat higher than the underlying trend. The introduction of less generous depreciation allowances for business investment—which caused investment expenditures to be brought forward into 1985—also seems to have stimulated growth temporarily. As these influences subside, and on the assumption of continued application of restrained monetary policy, the growth of activity is expected to decelerate somewhat over the forecast period, to 2¾ percent in 1986 and to 2 percent in 1987.

The Italian economy is estimated to have grown by only 2.2 percent in 1985, which was slightly less than in 1984 (2.6 percent), mainly because of slower growth of public consumption and a decline in stockbuilding. Growth is expected to remain relatively subdued—at about 2¼ percent—in 1986 and 1987, with the impact of the improvement in the terms of trade being offset by a projected deterioration in real net exports.

In the smaller industrial countries, faster growth of final domestic demand in 1985 was more than offset by a reduction in the contributions to growth from stockbuilding and the foreign balance. These latter factors had been a major source of growth in 1984 but were more nearly neutral in 1985. Real GNP in the smaller countries increased by 2.8 percent in 1985—slightly below the growth rate of the previous year—with individual country outturns ranging from 1 percent in Ireland to 4¾ percent in Australia. In 1986 and 1987, growth in the smaller industrial countries is projected to remain at about 2¾ percent, on average, with domestic demand increasing at a slightly higher rate. Australia is projected to continue to grow faster than the other smaller countries. New Zealand, Belgium, and Sweden are expected to grow by somewhat less than the other countries, reflecting the continuation of efforts to reduce budget deficits.

Labor Market Conditions

Although unemployment rates remain at or near record high levels in many industrial countries, the outlook for employment creation is somewhat more encouraging than in much of the recent past. Employment increased significantly in a large number of countries in 1985, and virtually all countries are expected to experience employment gains over the forecast period. Nevertheless, in many countries, particularly those in Europe, these gains will only keep pace with the number of new entrants into the labor force. The unemployment rate in those countries is therefore unlikely to decline much over the forecast period, if at all.

Total employment in the industrial countries increased by 1.4 percent in 1985, with more evenly balanced gains among countries than in 1984, when a somewhat larger rise in employment was largely attributable to developments in the United States. In the group of countries excluding the United States, employment growth accelerated from 0.3 percent in 1984 to 0.8 percent in 1985. This is the best employment performance in these countries since 1980 and compares favorably with the average employment increase in the 1970s. In the United States, even though employment growth decelerated significantly in 1985, the increase was still more than twice as fast as in the other industrial countries. The number of countries experiencing employment losses was also reduced in 1985. France was the only major country where employment declined, and this decline was much smaller than in the previous year. Among the smaller industrial countries, only Ireland and Spain suffered a loss of employment in 1985, but in these countries as well the declines were appreciably smaller than in 1984.

The principal factors underlying the turnaround in employment in the European countries appear to be the completion of a period of adjustment to earlier disturbances and a trend toward lower real wage increases in recent years. The period from 1980 to 1984 was characterized by severe labor shedding in the European countries, reflecting efforts to bring labor productivity into line with real labor costs in circumstances where the growth of total factor productivity was declining and prices of intermediate inputs were rising. As a result, the growth of labor productivity in that period was surprisingly strong, given the slow growth of output (Chart 7). With output growing at the same pace in 1985 as in 1984, the recovery of employment in the European countries reflected a smaller increase in labor productivity than in 1984. The lower growth in labor productivity seems to suggest that the process of adjustment to the disturbances of the early 1980s may be approaching an end. The moderation of real wage increases since 1982, however, also appears to have played a role by reducing

Chart 7. Industrial Countries: Growth of Output and Employment, 1975–87

(Average and annual changes, in percent)

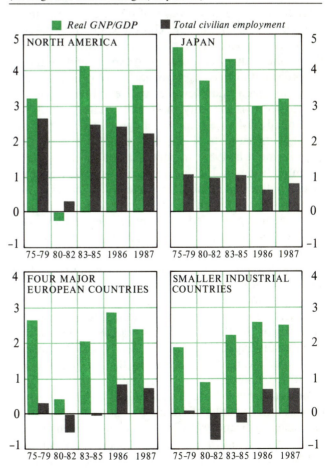

the incentive of firms to substitute capital for labor in the production process. In the United States, the slowdown in employment growth in 1985 broadly matched the deceleration in output growth.

Notwithstanding the gains in employment, the unemployment rate did not decline appreciably in the industrial countries in 1985, because demographic factors and rising participation rates led to an offsetting increase in the labor force. Canada and, to a lesser extent, the United States, were the only major countries in which unemployment fell significantly, whereas France and the United Kingdom recorded further sizable increases. In the group of smaller industrial countries, unemployment rose marginally, despite fairly significant reductions in the Scandinavian countries and in Australia. For the industrial countries of Europe overall, the combined unemployment rate rose to 11.2 percent of the labor force, compared with 10.9 percent in 1984 and 9.4 percent in 1982, when the present phase of expansion began. Since 1982, the U.S. unemployment rate has come down from 9.7 percent to about 7 percent early in 1986.

In most of the industrial countries employment is expected to grow at about the same pace over the forecast period as in 1985. In France, however, job creation is expected to increase slightly in both years after three consecutive years of decline. Employment growth in Canada and the United States is projected to remain considerably stronger than elsewhere. Among the smaller industrial countries, Australia and Denmark are projected to enjoy the strongest employment growth, while in Spain and New Zealand employment is expected to increase only marginally. The outlook for continued moderate employment growth is attributable in large measure to the same forces that led to the improvement in 1985. In particular, labor shedding in manufacturing in Europe is expected to come to a virtual halt, as continued real wage moderation permits a further improvement in profitability. In some countries, including the Federal Republic of Germany and France, faster output growth will also contribute to rising employment.

Although the expected growth in employment in 1986 and 1987 is encouraging, it may not be sufficient to reduce unemployment more than marginally in the industrial countries. North America represents the only region in the industrial world in which unemployment is expected to remain clearly on a downward path over the next two years. In the major countries of Europe, taken as a group, unemployment is expected to be stable, with a moderate decline in joblessness in the Federal Republic of Germany being offset by small increases in France and Italy. Unemployment is expected to decline modestly in the group of smaller industrial countries, mainly because of significant reductions in Australia, Denmark, and Spain. In Japan, where the level of unemployment is much lower than in the other major countries, the proportion of the labor force out of work is expected to rise to 3 percent in 1986 for the first time in recent history, and to continue to increase in 1987.

It should be emphasized that the gains in employment in Europe over the forecast period could be greater than those projected. Whether this potential is realized will depend on the extent to which increases in real labor costs moderate in response to the decline in oil prices and the improvement in Europe's terms of trade. The decline in oil prices, together with the recent appreciation of the European currencies, will result in a substantial, albeit transitory, reduction in the rate of increase of consumer prices in comparison with the prices of domestic products. The increase in real wages measured in terms of consumer prices will therefore translate into a smaller rise in real labor costs relative to output prices—the relevant measure from the employer's point of view. If countries take advantage of this opportunity by containing the rise in real consumption wages—that is, by limiting the extent to which the terms of trade gains are passed on to wage earners—employment can be expected to rise more than would otherwise be the case, even though such gains may show up only after some lag.

Inflation

The continuing deceleration of inflation in industrial countries more than three years into the recovery clearly distinguishes this economic cycle from previous upswings. While the business cycles of the 1960s and 1970s were characterized by a disturbing tendency for inflation rates to ratchet upward to ever higher levels, inflation has continued to moderate in the current recovery (Chart 8). In 1985, the rate of increase of the composite GNP deflator for the industrial countries slowed for the fifth consecutive year, to 3.9 percent, the lowest rate recorded since the late 1960s. Consumer price increases have followed the same overall trend in the past few years, although the deceleration has been from a rather higher level, reflecting the impact of the rise in energy prices in the early 1980s. Differences in inflation performance among countries also continued to narrow in 1985 as countries with higher-than-average inflation rates registered additional significant decelerations in price increases. Over the next two years, inflation is projected to continue to decline, and the dispersion of inflation rates across countries is expected to diminish further.

A number of factors have contributed to the good inflation performance in recent years. First and fore-

Chart 8. Major Industrial Countries: Inflation Paths from the 1970–71, 1974–75, and 1980–82 Recessions

(Change from the corresponding quarter of the previous year, in percent, beginning in trough of each recession: fourth quarter 1971, first quarter 1975, and fourth quarter 1982)

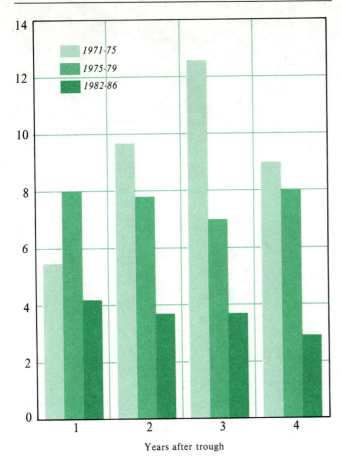

Years after trough

most has been the consistent anti-inflationary stance of government policies in general and monetary policies in particular. The authorities in most countries have made a sustained effort to curtail the growth of monetary aggregates, and to create conditions conducive to continued downward pressure on inflation and inflationary expectations. In addition, public sector wage and pricing policies, together with deregulation and industrial policies, have had a direct impact on the costs of goods and services provided by the public sector and important segments of the private sector.

The consistent commitment of the industrial countries to an anti-inflation policy has made an important contribution to the marked deceleration in nominal wage increases during the 1980s. Subsiding inflationary expectations and high unemployment rates, together with the modification or suspension of indexation clauses, have significantly reduced wage increases in recent years. For the industrial countries as a group, the rate of increase of hourly compensation in manufacturing has fallen from 11.5 percent in 1980 to 5.3

percent in 1985, with the decline being pervasive across countries. At the same time, labor productivity increased, particularly in Europe, resulting in a pronounced deceleration of unit labor cost increases. In 1983–84, for example, reflecting the strong growth of industrial production, unit labor costs in manufacturing were essentially flat in the industrial countries. These costs began to rise again as the growth of output per man-hour moderated in 1985, and their rate of increase is expected to remain at 1½ percent to 2 percent over the next two years (Chart 9). Labor costs, however, are still expected to increase less than GNP deflators, allowing some margin for a further improvement in profitability.

The weakness of import prices has also played an important role in the improved price performance in industrial countries in recent years. For the industrial countries as a group this mainly reflects the weakness in the prices of oil and other primary commodities. Following the sharp rise in 1979–80, average oil prices (measured in U.S. dollar terms) declined by 11.7 percent in 1983, and by 2.1 percent in 1984. Oil prices

Chart 9. Major Industrial Countries: Indicators of Inflation, 1979–87

(Annual changes, in percent)

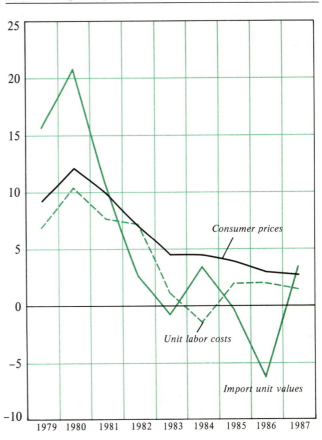

fell an additional 4.4 percent in 1985 and are assumed to fall by 40 percent in 1986. During the first two years of the recovery, prices of non-oil commodities recovered somewhat from a protracted decline during the recession. In 1985, however, there was a broadly based decline in commodity prices of 12.2 percent (in dollar terms) as supplies of many items increased and slower output growth limited the growth of demand.

The substantial decline in the U.S. dollar on foreign exchange markets since March 1985 should, in itself, have been a factor making for higher commodity prices in dollar terms. So far, however, further increases in supply and a considerable inventory overhang in some markets have mitigated these exchange rate influences. Although there was a substantial rise in the price of coffee in the final months of 1985, prices of other primary commodities have remained relatively weak. While non-oil commodity prices are expected to recover somewhat during 1986, their average level in real terms (measured relative to the price index for exports of manufactures) would still be about 2 percent lower than in 1985. (See Supplementary Note 3, "Non-Oil Commodity Price Developments.") Overall, import unit values for the industrial countries as a group, after increasing in local currency terms by only 0.8 percent in 1985, are expected to fall by 7½ percent in 1986 and then to rise by 3¼ percent in 1987.

In 1985, Japan and the Federal Republic of Germany once again recorded the lowest inflation rates among the major industrial countries (Chart 10). The United States and Canada continued to consolidate the substantial reduction in their inflation rates achieved earlier. In the United Kingdom, however, a country which had also significantly lowered its inflation rate, there was some slippage in 1985. Inflation rose noticeably early in the year under the influence of a sharp depreciation of sterling and rising interest rates (which affect the consumer price index directly in the United Kingdom). By the latter half of the year, these temporary influences appeared to have subsided; nevertheless, there has been a noticeable acceleration in the rate of increase of unit labor costs over the past two years (from 1.3 percent in 1983 to 5.2 percent in 1985).

France and Italy made further significant progress in 1985 in reducing their inflation rates. Incomes policies continue to be used as an important adjunct to monetary and fiscal policies in these countries. In France, the rate of increase of the GDP deflator fell by over 1 percentage point and consumer prices decelerated even more, reflecting in part the strengthening of the effective exchange rate in the latter half of the year. Wage increases also have decelerated significantly over the past three years, and France had one of the smallest increases in unit labor costs among the major industrial countries in 1985. The Italian

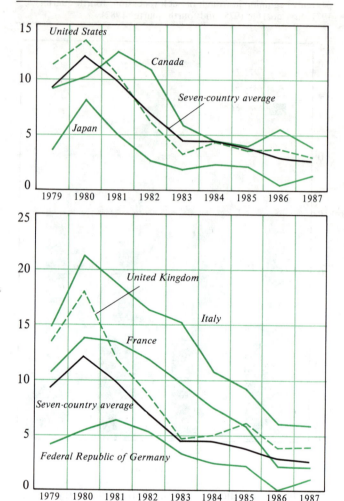

Chart 10. Major Industrial Countries: Consumer Price Inflation, 1979–87

(Annual changes, in percent)

inflation rate slowed by almost 1¾ percentage points on a GDP deflator basis last year, but at 9 percent it was still more than double the average rate in the other major countries. The Italian authorities took further steps in 1985 to delay and reduce the responsiveness of nominal wages to price increases under the national wage indexation scheme.

The smaller industrial countries achieved a further reduction in their inflation rates in 1985, as had been the case in 1983 and 1984. The easing of price pressures was fairly widely spread, with Austria and Spain achieving the largest declines. Nevertheless, for the smaller industrial countries as a group, inflation has remained almost 2 percentage points higher than in the major industrial countries.

The projected further improvement in inflation performance in industrial countries in 1986 is primarily attributable to the lower oil prices that are assumed to prevail. The rate of consumer price inflation is expected to decline by an additional full percentage point, with a somewhat smaller drop in the rate of increase in the combined GNP deflator. As far as the relative inflation performance among industrial countries is concerned, this will be significantly affected by recent movements in exchange rates. While the rate of increase in consumer prices is expected to decline slightly in the United States in 1986, a deceleration of almost 2¾ percentage points is projected for the European countries. As a result, in the European countries as a group, consumer price increases would be slightly lower than in the United States, after having significantly exceeded the U.S. inflation rate in every year since 1980.

The projections for 1987 are somewhat more tenuous; however, no significant changes in inflation trends are anticipated even though the effects of the reduction in oil prices are expected to continue to dampen price pressures. Since exchange rates are assumed constant from early March 1986, changes in consumer prices will not be further influenced by this factor. Overall, the rate of increase of consumer prices is expected to rise slightly in Europe and Japan in 1987, as the immediate benefits from terms of trade gains are absorbed in the price level.

Exchange Market Developments

The U.S. dollar, after four consecutive years of strong appreciation, depreciated significantly beginning in March 1985. For the 12 months through March 1986, the depreciation amounted to almost 25 percent in nominal effective terms (Chart 11). Correspondingly, most of the currencies of the other major industrial countries appreciated against the U.S. dollar in nominal effective terms. Most notably, the effective rate of the Japanese yen rose by 24 percent and that of the deutsche mark by 13 percent. These exchange rate movements brought the real effective exchange rate of the three largest industrial countries closer to their average values for the 1975–84 decade (Chart 12). Based on nominal exchange rate values and on extrapolations of normalized unit labor costs, in the first quarter of 1986, the real exchange rate of the U.S. dollar was 8 percent above its average value for the past decade, that of the deutsche mark 6 percent below its average, and that of the Japanese yen above its average value by 3 percent.

The depreciation of the U.S. dollar followed a steep rise from mid-November 1984 through the latter part of February 1985 that capped the seemingly interminable appreciation that had begun in the third quarter of 1980. The reasons for the turnaround appear to be rooted in several developments that began during the

second half of 1984. First, short-term interest rate differentials had generally moved against dollar-denominated assets from August 1984 through January 1985. Although these movements were partially reversed during the next two months, the net changes remained substantial (Chart 13). Second, growth of the narrow monetary aggregate in the United States (M1) had accelerated considerably beginning in November 1984, and by March 1985 it had moved outside the target range. The continuation of rapid growth after the breaching of the upper limit of the target range may have contributed to a view that monetary policy was in fact being relaxed. Third, there were a number of signs indicating a slowing of real economic growth in the United States, while the rate of expansion was showing little change on average in other large industrial countries. Fourth, there may have been a speculative bubble affecting the value of the dollar during the months leading up to February 1985, which then ran its course, contributing to the subsequent decline; the timing of this effect appears to have been influenced by sizable coordinated intervention at the end of February.

From March through August 1985, the U.S. dollar depreciated by 19 percent against the deutsche mark and by 9 percent against the Japanese yen. Even so, both the deutsche mark and the yen were still well below their average levels of the preceding decade in real terms, and the prospective current account surpluses of the Federal Republic of Germany and Japan remained large.

The exchange rate movements that had taken place from March through August were given a further impetus in the aftermath of the September meeting of Finance Ministers and Central Bank Governors of the Group of Five countries (the United States, Japan, the Federal Republic of Germany, the United Kingdom, and France). It was agreed at that meeting that a further appreciation of the non-dollar currencies against the dollar would be desirable, inasmuch as it was thought that the current levels did not fully reflect changes in policy and in underlying economic conditions that had already taken place or that were in prospect. Consequently, the Group of Five countries—in cooperation with the other countries constituting the Group of Ten (Italy, Canada, the Netherlands, Belgium, Sweden, and Switzerland)—undertook sizable coordinated intervention in foreign exchange markets throughout the remainder of the year.

The September 1985 Group of Five meeting was also followed by a temporary shift toward a somewhat tighter monetary stance in Japan. Domestic short-term interest rates rose from about 6½ percent—a level that had prevailed since the latter part of 1983—to around 8 percent in late October. However, early in 1986,

Chart 11.   Major Industrial Countries: Indices of Monthly Average U.S. Dollar and Effective Exchange Rates, January 1982–February 1986

(Indices: average value for 1975–84 = 100)

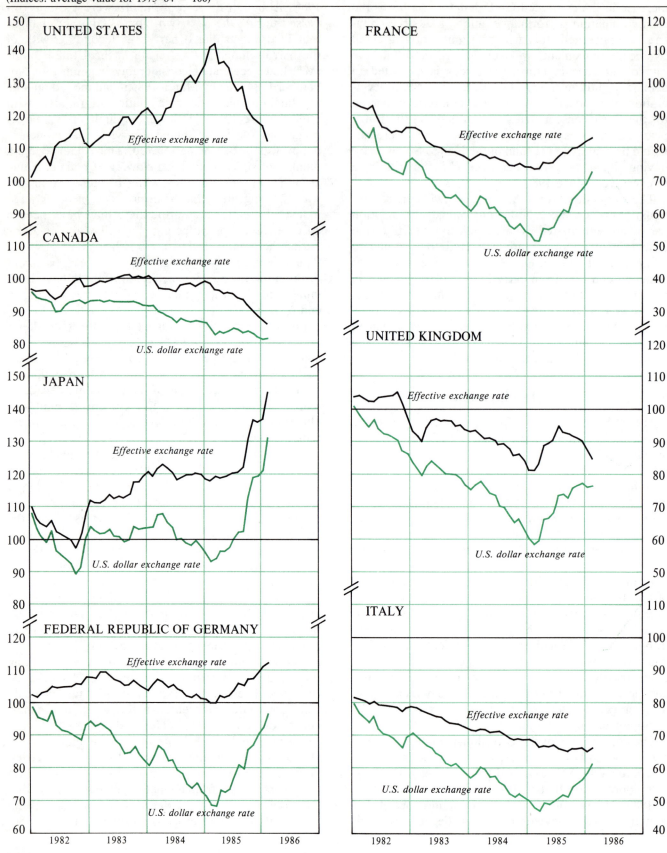

Chart 12.   Major Industrial Countries: Relative Prices of Manufactures Adjusted for Exchange Rate Changes, 1982–86

(Indices: average value for 1975–84 = 100)[1,2]

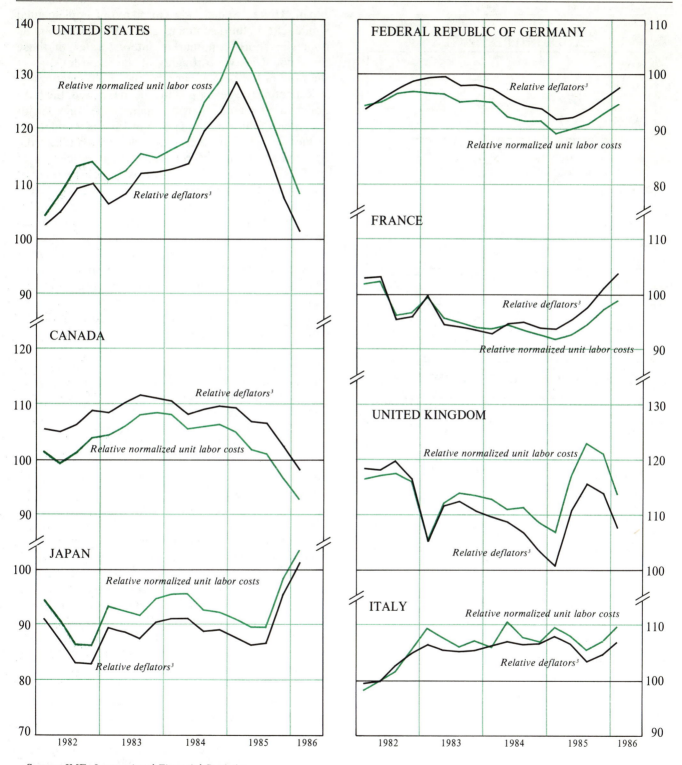

Source: IMF, *International Financial Statistics*.

[1] Indices of the type shown here are frequently referred to as indices of real effective exchange rates.

[2] The data for fourth quarter 1985 and the first quarter 1986 are based on preliminary Fund staff estimates.

[3] Annual deflators for gross domestic product originating in manufacturing with quarterly interpolations and extrapolations (beyond the latest available data) based on wholesale price data for manufactures.

Chart 13.   Major Industrial Countries: Monthly Average Short-Term Interest Rates, January 1982–February 1986[1]

(In percent per annum)

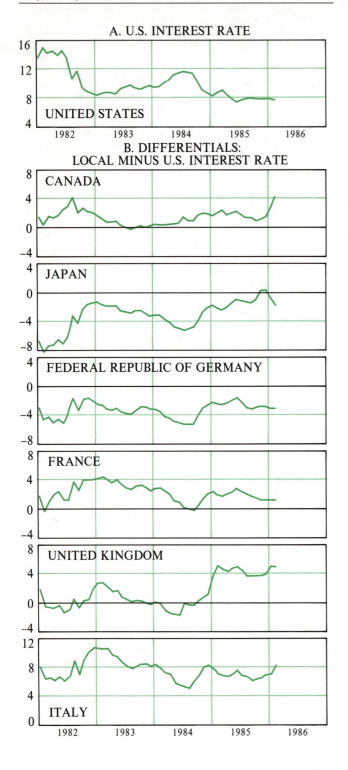

A. U.S. INTEREST RATE

UNITED STATES

B. DIFFERENTIALS: LOCAL MINUS U.S. INTEREST RATE

CANADA

JAPAN

FEDERAL REPUBLIC OF GERMANY

FRANCE

UNITED KINGDOM

ITALY

[1] The rates shown are monthly averages of daily rates on money market instruments of about 90 days' maturity, except for Japan, where the discount rate on 2-month (private) bills is used.

when it became clear that the resultant strengthening of the yen would not be reversed, interest rates were allowed to fall back to and below their September levels. By early March, after the central banks of Japan, United States, and Germany all implemented similar cuts in the discount rate, the differentials among domestic short-term market interest rates in those three countries were roughly at the same level as at the time of the September Group of Five meeting.

Reflecting the developments just described, the U.S. dollar depreciated sharply against all other major currencies following the Group of Five meeting. Subsequently, the markets settled down; overall, from September through March 1986, the depreciation of the U.S. dollar in effective terms was somewhat larger than that which took place between March and September 1985 (Chart 11). However, the pattern of bilateral exchange rate movements changed in the post-meeting period, with the Japanese yen showing a more substantial appreciation against the dollar (over 27 percent from September 20, 1985 to late March 1986, compared with about 21 percent for the deutsche mark).

Another factor that may have helped to push the exchange rates of the larger countries toward more sustainable levels during the latter part of 1985 and the first quarter of 1986 was the improved prospect for fiscal restraint in the United States. Divergences in fiscal policy had been a major factor behind the dollar's appreciation in the early 1980s. Thus the elimination or reversal of this divergence would be expected to work in the opposite direction.

Until the latter part of 1985, the course of U.S. fiscal policy had proved difficult to change. The Congressional Budget Resolution in August provided a first indication that a change in policy was under way. Then, in December, the enactment of the Gramm-Rudman-Hollings balanced budget act mandated gradual reductions in fiscal deficits beginning in the current fiscal year and extending through fiscal year 1991. (The expected economic effects of the legislation on the United States and on other countries are discussed more fully in Chapter IV "Policy Interactions in Industrial Countries.") The decline in long-term interest rates in the United States—from 12 percent in March 1985 to 9 percent in February 1986—may in large measure have been a response to improving prospects for effective action to reduce the deficit, especially toward the end of this period.

The large decline in oil prices during the first quarter of 1986 also reinforced these movements in the exchange rates of the currencies of the major industrial countries. The fall in oil prices appears to have strengthened relatively the external positions of Japan and a number of European countries, and it helped to accelerate the appreciation of the currencies of those countries with respect to the U.S. dollar during February and March 1986. Although the United States is also a large oil importer, it is relatively less dependent on foreign oil supplies, and would benefit less from a drop in oil prices. Over a longer time horizon, however, trade in other commodities will also be affected as lower export earnings from oil exporters are translated into lower imports from industrial countries. This effect could mitigate these exchange market implications somewhat.

The depreciation of the dollar during 1985 does not appear to have resulted in severe pressure on the parities within the European Monetary System (EMS) until around the end of the year (Chart 14). This relative smoothness was perhaps surprising in view of the fact that movements out of the dollar have in the past tended to go predominantly into deutsche mark. It may be that the potential for tensions within the EMS has been reduced in recent years by the convergence of production cost increases among most member countries, although it also appears that substantial intervention was required on a number of occasions.

One EMS realignment was undertaken, in July, when the Italian lira was devalued by 6 percent against the European Currency Unit (ECU) and the other participating currencies were revalued by 2 percent. Among the countries adhering to the narrow EMS band, the Belgian franc was the weakest currency during most of the year (Chart 14). Major pressures, however, were avoided through intervention and through occasional tightening of the stance of monetary policy.

The pound sterling, which had depreciated by over 12 percent in nominal effective terms during 1984, fell by a further 3½ percent in January 1985, until a sharp rise in domestic interest rates halted the decline. Once the dollar began to decline broadly in March, the pound appreciated strongly in effective terms, rising by 16 percent in nominal effective terms from January to July. Thereafter, sterling began to weaken again in effective terms. Downward pressure on the pound became quite strong toward the end of 1985 and early in 1986 in anticipation of (and then in response to) lower oil prices. It is noteworthy, however, that the real value of the pound (measured by reference to normalized unit labor costs) remains high by historical comparison, especially vis-à-vis the EMS currencies. In March 1986, for example, the real bilateral rate with respect to the deutsche mark is estimated to have been almost 15 percent above the 1975–84 average.

The Canadian dollar depreciated by 5½ percent against the U.S. dollar during 1985 and the first quarter of 1986, and by about 13 percent in both nominal and real effective terms. While the Canadian dollar had been depreciating steadily against the U.S. dollar for

Chart 14. European Monetary System: Relative Positions of the Currencies Participating in the Narrow Band, 1985–86[1]

(In percent)

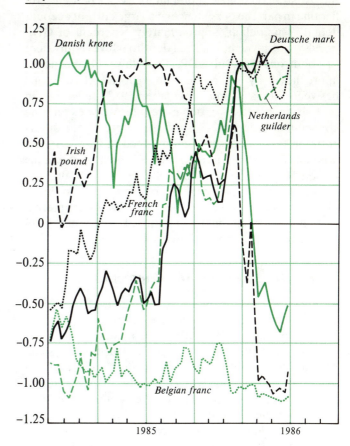

Sources: IMF Data Fund; and Fund staff calculations.
[1] Based on weekly averages, January 6, 1985 to March 21, 1986. The vertical distance between any two currencies is equal to the percentage deviation from their bilateral central parity rate.

a number of years, until early in 1985 it had been appreciating quite strongly against other currencies. The fact that the Canadian dollar did not share, even in some degree, in the general appreciation of currencies against the U.S. dollar appears to have been associated with a decline in interest differentials and also with difficulties experienced by some small banking institutions. Interest differentials favoring investment in Canadian-dollar-denominated assets over those in U.S. dollars fell from 2½ percent in March 1985 to 1 percent in November 1985, reflecting the intention of the Canadian authorities to accommodate domestic economic expansion as long as there were no strong pressures on the exchange rate or on inflation. However, interest differentials widened abruptly early in 1986—reaching 4 percent in February—in response to the downward pressure on the Canadian dollar. This pressure was reinforced by the decline in oil prices.

The largest exchange rate movements among the smaller industrial countries during 1985 involved the Australian and New Zealand dollars. Both of these currencies are independently floating.[3] During 1985, the Australian dollar depreciated by 26 percent, reflecting in part the persistence of a large current account deficit. This deficit, approximately 5 percent of GDP in 1985, has brought external debt to a level equivalent to about one third of GDP. The New Zealand dollar appreciated by 15 percent in real effective terms between January and November 1985, reflecting in part sharp increases in domestic interest rates and the consequent emergence of a large interest rate differential in favor of assets denominated in New Zealand dollars. This appreciation reversed most of the gains in competitiveness that had followed the devaluation of July 1984. A sharp drop of the New Zealand dollar in December, however, associated with lower interest rates and a weaker economic outlook, left it at a level similar to that of the beginning of the year.

Balance of Payments Developments

The combined current account deficit of the industrial countries (including official transfers) narrowed by $10 billion in 1985 to an estimated $54 billion (Statistical Appendix Table A31). During the same period, the combined current account deficit of developing countries narrowed by $2 billion to $33 billion, while the current account of other countries is estimated to have shifted from a surplus of $2.3 billion in 1984 to a deficit of a similar magnitude in 1985 (Statistical Appendix Table A30). Thus, the large statistical discrepancy, which reflects either under-recorded surpluses, or over-recorded deficits, or some combination of the two, decreased by $7 billion to about $90 billion.[4]

These developments in current account positions took place in an environment of sluggish growth of world trade and falling trade prices. While the combined dollar value of overall merchandise trade by the industrial countries grew by about 3 percent from 1984 to 1985, the value of overall trade of the developing countries fell in value by a similar magnitude. In contrast, in 1984 the dollar value of total world trade

expanded by over 6 percent. At least three major factors were responsible for the slowdown in world trade. First, the pace of economic expansion was slower in both the industrial and the developing countries. Among the industrial countries, the slowdown was concentrated in the United States, where the increase in total domestic demand declined from 8.5 percent in 1984 to 2.8 percent in 1985. Second, slower economic expansion and further conservation measures in the industrial countries contributed to a fall in both the volume and price of oil exports from the oil exporting countries. This decline implied a significant drop in the export revenue of these countries and hence their imports as well. Third, mainly reflecting excess supply conditions, primary commodity prices fell by an average of 12.2 percent from 1984 to 1985. Consequently, the terms of trade of most developing countries deteriorated significantly, contributing to the contraction in the value of their total trade.

One of the major factors contributing to the generally improved current account positions of the industrial countries in 1985 was a decline in the value of oil imports. This decline was explained almost equally by the reduction in the price of oil and by the continued reduction in oil consumption by the major importing countries. These developments in turn reflected mainly the slowing of economic growth in the industrial countries, but also the continuing effects of conservation measures and a further substitution of other forms of energy for oil.

The current account positions of the United States and Japan continued to diverge in 1985, albeit at a slower pace than in the past several years (Chart 15). The deficit of the United States widened by about $10 billion, to $118 billion (2.8 percent of GNP), while Japan's surplus increased by $15 billion, to $50 billion (3.7 percent of GNP). The extent of deterioration in the deficit of the United States was much less pronounced than in the previous two years. It is also significant that the current account surplus of the Federal Republic of Germany increased by over $6 billion, to an estimated $13 billion (2.1 percent of GNP). Among other major industrial countries showing an external improvement, the current account surplus of the United Kingdom rose from $1.1 billion in 1984 to $3.8 billion in 1985 (owing in part to the ending of the miners' strike), while the current account position of France shifted from a deficit of $0.8 billion to a small surplus. On the other hand, Italy's current account deficit widened by about $0.7 billion, and the position of Canada turned from a surplus of $2 billion into a deficit of $1.9 billion. The current account positions of the smaller industrial countries either strengthened marginally or were essentially unchanged from 1984 to 1985. The major exceptions were Sweden,

---

[3] The Australian dollar was allowed to float after December 1983. The New Zealand dollar was devalued by 20 percent in July 1984 and then allowed to float from March 1985.

[4] The large discrepancy in the global payments statistics on current account has been analyzed in more detail in earlier *World Economic Outlook* reports, and it is currently the subject of an in-depth study by an international working party commissioned by the Fund and the Organization for Economic Cooperation and Development (OECD). The statistical discrepancy reveals a large margin of error in the levels of reported current account balances, but the staff does not believe that these errors seriously distort an analysis of year-to-year changes in the position of individual countries or groups of countries.

Chart 15.   Major Industrial Countries: Payments Balances on Current Account, Including Official Transfers, 1982–85

(In percent of GNP)

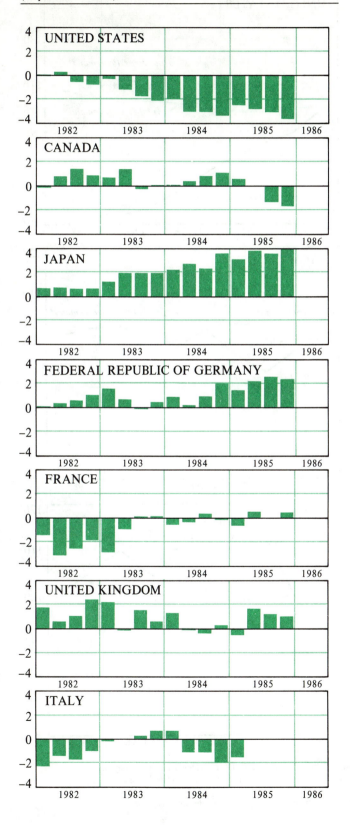

where the current account position deteriorated from a small surplus to a deficit of $1.3 billion, and Denmark, where the deficit widened from $1.7 billion in 1984 to $2.6 billion in 1985.

Cyclical factors and terms of trade changes both played important parts in the current account developments of the United States and Japan during 1985. In the United States, the rate of growth of real domestic demand fell sharply in 1985, as noted above, while the growth of foreign demand was virtually unchanged. Reflecting this, the rate of growth in the volume of U.S. imports dropped from 29 percent to less than 7 percent, with a small decline in the volume of exports. An improvement in the terms of trade of some 4 percent served to limit further the deterioration in the U.S. current account. For Japan, the sharp slowdown in the rate of growth of export markets (amounting to 7 percentage points) was reflected in a decline in export volume growth from 16 percent in 1984 to 5 percent in 1985. However, since imports stagnated and lower oil and commodity prices resulted in a 4 percent improvement in the terms of trade, the Japanese current account surplus widened substantially.

Terms of trade changes played a more limited role in the current account developments of the other industrial countries. For Canada, the terms of trade even deteriorated somewhat, reflecting its position as a net exporter of primary commodities and the continued weakness of the Canadian dollar. Slower demand expansion in the United States and rapid expansion domestically further contributed to the deterioration of Canada's current account. For the remaining industrial countries, changes in current account positions in 1985 seem to have largely reflected the lagged effects of shifts in competitive positions in earlier years. The improvement in the current account positions of the Federal Republic of Germany, France, and the United Kingdom mirrored the cumulative real depreciation of their currencies during 1984 and early 1985; the deutsche mark depreciated by 7 percent, the pound sterling by 5 percent, and the French franc by over 2 percent from the first quarter of 1984 to the first quarter of 1985. Similarly, the deterioration in the current accounts of Italy and Sweden was associated with the real appreciation of their currencies during 1984, amounting to 2 percent and 4 percent, respectively.

Factors underlying developments in non-oil trade positions are illustrated in Chart 16, which shows indices of the real non-oil trade balance (non-oil export volumes relative to non-oil import volumes), the real effective exchange rate, domestic demand, and foreign demand. As the chart indicates, the large shifts in these major industrial countries' competitive positions that took place from 1981 to 1984 began to be reversed

Chart 16.   Major Industrial Countries: Real Non-Oil Trade Balances and Determinants, 1981–85

(Indices: first half of 1981 = 100)

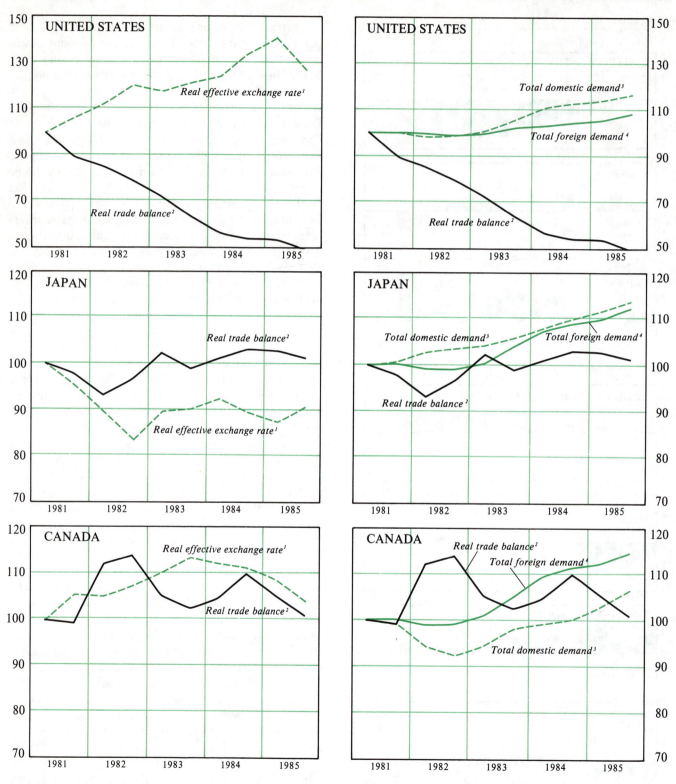

[1] The real effective exchange rate is measured as relative normalized unit labor costs adjusted for exchange rate changes.
[2] The real non-oil trade balance is an index of non-oil export volumes divided by an index of non-oil import volumes.
[3] Real total domestic demand.
[4] Real total domestic demand in foreign markets weighted by the share of each market in the indicated country's exports.

Chart 16 (*concluded*). Major Industrial Countries: Real Non-Oil Trade Balances and Determinants, 1981–85

(Indices: first half of 1981 = 100)

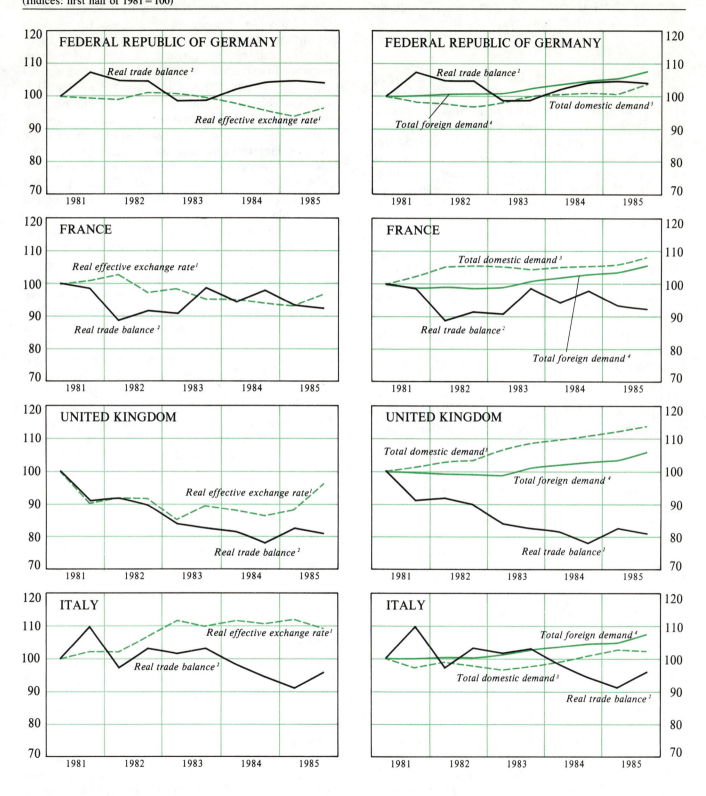

[1] The real effective exchange rate is measured as relative normalized unit labor costs adjusted for exchange rate changes.
[2] The real non-oil trade balance is an index of non-oil export volumes divided by an index of non-oil import volumes.
[3] Real total domestic demand.
[4] Real total domestic demand in foreign markets weighted by the share of each market in the indicated country's exports.

during 1985. These reversals in relative competitive positions did not immediately translate into corresponding shifts in current account positions during 1985. It is expected, however, that the effects will begin to be felt on trade flows during 1986 and, more strongly, in 1987.

Another striking feature of developments underlying non-oil trade balances during 1985 was a narrowing of growth differentials among the major industrial countries, largely reflecting the slowdown in economic activity in the United States. From 1982 to 1984, the growth of foreign demand was greater than that of domestic demand in all countries except the United States and the United Kingdom. For example, the rate of growth of domestic demand in Japan, the country with the fastest GNP growth outside of the United States during 1982–84, averaged just 3 percent in 1982–84, compared with a rate of growth of foreign markets of 4½ percent. Conversely, in the United States the rate of growth of domestic demand during the same period averaged close to 7 percent, compared with foreign market growth of a little over 2 percent. From 1984 to 1985, however, the rate of growth of domestic demand in the United States decreased to 3 percent, while the rate of growth of U.S. export markets increased at about the same pace. In the industrial countries of Europe, reflecting the high share of trade among European countries, domestic and foreign demand moved more closely together. These cyclical changes seem to have already had some impact on current account developments in 1985, and they are expected to continue to influence developments throughout 1986, as a further convergence of domestic and foreign demand growth is expected over the coming months.

The divergence in current account positions of the United States and Japan and, to a lesser extent, the Federal Republic of Germany during 1982–85 have corresponded to large net private capital inflows into the United States and large net outflows from the other two countries. In the United States most increases in net capital inflows took the form of changes in banking flows during the early part of the period and, increasingly, securities in transactions during more recent months. On a gross basis, the increase in U.S. banks' foreign liabilities declined steadily from $66 billion in 1982 to $32 billion in 1984, while net foreign purchases of U.S. securities rose from $13 billion in 1982 to $35 billion in 1984. In 1985, the increase in U.S. banks' foreign liabilities rose somewhat to $41 billion, while net foreign purchases of U.S. securities continued to rise to an estimated $72 billion. In Japan, increases in residents' purchases of foreign securities more than accounted for the increase in net outflows of long-term capital, which rose from $50 billion in 1984 to $64 billion in 1985.

Projections of balance of payments developments in 1986–87 have been made on the basis of the working assumption that real exchange rates among major countries will remain unchanged from the pattern prevailing in early March 1986. Oil prices are assumed to average $16 per barrel in 1986 and $15 per barrel in 1987. On this basis, the combined current account position of industrial countries is projected to improve by some $68 billion to a surplus of $14 billion in 1986, reflecting largely more favorable terms of trade. The U.S. payments position in the coming period will be favorably affected by the lagged effects of recent changes in competitiveness (the consequence of the falling dollar) and by lower oil and commodity prices. The latter development is expected to generate a terms of trade improvement for the United States of 3 percent in 1986. The depreciation of the dollar is expected to contribute to a strengthening of the invisibles balance, as direct investment receipts are projected to rise significantly faster than net interest payments in 1986. Cyclical factors will be broadly neutral, as the rate of growth of domestic demand is expected to be similar in the United States and in its major trading partners. However, since U.S. imports are already so much larger than exports, there is an underlying tendency for the current account deficit to widen, even when imports and exports are growing at the same pace. The net effect of these factors is expected to lead to a U.S. current account deficit in 1986–87 that is somewhat smaller (at 2.5 percent relative to GNP) than that recorded in 1985 (2.9 percent).

In the other industrial countries, competitiveness has deteriorated somewhat as a result of the falling dollar. For the short term, however, "J-curve" effects are likely to cause a continued strengthening in current account positions expressed in U.S. dollars. Lower oil and commodity prices will also tend to increase the aggregate current surplus of industrial countries outside the United States. Looking further ahead, however, recent developments in exchange rates are expected to exert a growing influence on trade flows in volume terms. At the same time, financial constraints facing oil exporting countries will probably lead to significant cutbacks in their imports from the industrial world. The net effect of these factors for European countries is to produce a substantial increase, in dollar terms, in their current account surpluses in 1986, followed by a moderate erosion. A similar pattern is projected for Japan, whose current account surplus is expected to reach 3.9 percent of GNP in 1986, before declining to 3.1 percent of GNP in 1987. For the Federal Republic of Germany, the corresponding figures would be 2.9 percent and 2.2 percent, respectively.

Uncertainties in the Projections

The projections presented in the foregoing sections constitute the staff's view of the most likely outcome for the industrial countries. It is important to recognize, however, that a significant margin of uncertainty attaches to any point estimate of future economic developments: both policies and behavior by individuals and enterprises may turn out to be different from the assumptions adopted in elaborating the projections. At the present time, the most important uncertainties for the industrial countries are those that surround the behavior of the business cycle, the policy stance to be adopted by major countries, the evolution of exchange rates, and developments in oil prices.

The Business Cycle

An important feature of the projections is the relatively smooth continuation of the recovery at a pace that is expected to be broadly similar to the rate of growth of potential output in the industrial countries as a whole. Historically, however, recoveries that have reached the same maturity as the present one—about three years—have typically started showing signs of strain, with output approaching capacity and inflation beginning to pick up. In such circumstances economic policy has often been tightened, which together with declining profits and procyclical movements in saving ratios, inventories, and investment has generated a new cyclical downturn, frequently in the fourth or fifth year after the start of an upswing. A repetition of this type of cyclical pattern cannot be excluded. Nevertheless, there are a number of factors that justify a more optimistic view. First, inflation has continued to decelerate, and the outlook for high-inflation countries in particular continues to point to the likelihood that inflation will moderate further. Second, capacity utilization, though tending to rise, has not yet approached the point where bottlenecks seem likely to impede the growth of demand (Chart 17). Since the outlook for business investment continues to be favorable, there is a reasonable prospect that capacity will grow sufficiently rapidly to prevent the short-term re-emergence of constraints. Third, the terms of trade gains of industrial countries will stimulate real incomes while moderating the growth of producers' costs.

Adaptation of Economic Policies

The assumptions underlying the projections suggest that the setting of policies in the major industrial

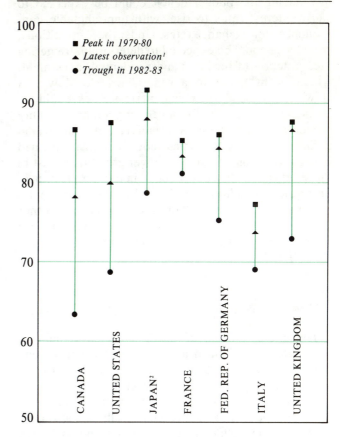

Chart 17. Major Industrial Countries: Rates of Capacity Utilization in Manufacturing

- ■ Peak in 1979-80
- ▲ Latest observation[1]
- ● Trough in 1982-83

Sources: OECD, *Main Economic Indicators*; Ministry of International Trade and Industry, Japan; *Industrial Statistics Monthly*; Commission of the European Communities, *European Economy*, Supplement B.

[1] Canada, United States, Federal Republic of Germany: third quarter 1985; Japan: November 1985; France, United Kingdom: October 1985; Italy: fourth quarter 1985.

[2] Index: historical peak = 100.

countries is undergoing a number of changes which have reduced, if not eliminated, some of the main negative risks in the outlook. In some countries that have already made substantial progress in eliminating imbalances, the stance of fiscal policy in 1986 is expected to be somewhat less restrictive, while countries that have postponed policy adaptations have started implementing the necessary measures. Beneficial effects of these policy adjustments have already materialized in the form of a significant realignment of exchange rates and easier monetary conditions. Despite these developments, a number of uncertainties remain with regard to the continued adaptation of economic policies.

The speed of implementation of the objective of balancing the federal budget in the United States, in particular, could have substantial implications for the performance of the United States and other countries in 1987 and beyond. On the one hand, major slippages in reducing the budget deficit could be expected to cause interest rates to rise, with unpredictable consequences for exchange rates. Under these conditions, confidence could be expected to deteriorate, triggering a contraction of business and residential investment, which might result in a generalized slowdown. A slowdown caused by rising interest rates could be particularly serious for the developing countries' ability to service their debt. Alternatively, a more rapid implementation of the deficit reductions than assumed in the projections might also lower growth, at least in the short run. This would depend in part on the impact on financial conditions, and on the interest elasticity of demand, as well as on the response of other countries. (These issues are discussed in detail in Chapter IV, "Policy Interactions in Industrial Countries.")

Exchange Rates

The exchange rate of the U.S. dollar remains a major element of uncertainty. The agreement among the Group of Five countries last September to encourage exchange rates of key currencies to move more closely into line with underlying "fundamentals" has been successful in achieving a substantial depreciation of the dollar vis-à-vis the yen and the EMS currencies. At the same time, the likelihood of a new sharp appreciation of the dollar has diminished, if not disappeared. However, given the high import propensity of the United States, together with the existing gap between exports and imports and the rise in net investment income to other countries, the maintenance of the real external value of the dollar at its March 1986 level is estimated to be sufficient only to stabilize the current account. The amount of dollars in foreign investors' portfolios would therefore continue to increase at a rate of over $100 billion a year. Since there must be some doubt about the willingness of foreign investors to finance the U.S. current account deficit indefinitely at current exchange rates and interest rates, the dollar may well depreciate further at some stage. This could take the form of a gradual adjustment over time—as assumed in the medium-term baseline scenario discussed in Chapter IV on "Policy Interactions in Industrial Countries." Alternatively, sudden changes in investors' confidence might generate a sharper depreciation; the likelihood of such an eventuality would appear to be higher in the absence of deficit-reducing measures in the United States. (The possible implications of a further depreciation of the dollar are also discussed in Chapter IV.)

Oil Prices

The effects of the substantial declines in oil prices that had occurred by early 1986, and the future development of these prices, are of considerable importance in gauging economic prospects in industrial countries. The projected decline in the fuel exporting countries' export earnings is expected to be partly reflected in lower imports of these countries, which explains the projected sizable deterioration of the industrial countries' real net exports in 1986.

The staff's projections have been developed on the basis of oil prices averaging $16 per barrel in 1986 and $15 per barrel in 1987. This represents a decline of 40 percent in 1986 in U.S. dollar terms from the average 1985 level, and an even greater decline in real terms. As discussed above, this price drop is expected to have a significant favorable effect on real incomes and inflation in the industrial countries—probably cutting an average of 1 to 1½ percent per annum off the combined rate of inflation in the Consumer Price Index in 1986–87 and adding ½ to 1 percent to the level of aggregate output at the end of the forecast period, compared with what otherwise would have been projected.

The projections have been elaborated on the assumption that the oil price change is sustained, or at least perceived to be lasting by market participants. To the extent that the price change was perceived to be transitory, the effects would of course become smaller and, in the limit, would tend to disappear altogether. While the fuel exporting countries would have a strong incentive to finance rather than adjust to the temporary weakening of their external positions, energy users in the fuel importing countries would tend to save a high proportion of the transitory rise in real incomes, thus helping to generate the financing required by the fuel exporting countries. Such financing might, however, not be forthcoming for some of the capital importing fuel exporters, even if it was generally agreed that the price change was temporary. If so, the decline in these countries' imports would probably exceed the expansionary effects in oil importing countries, so that even the latter countries might end up worse off from a temporary fall in the price of oil.

Similarly, adverse effects would follow if oil prices were to become much more variable in the future than they have been in the past. If oil prices were henceforth to fluctuate randomly between, say, $15 and $25 a barrel, this would be equivalent to a succession of shocks to the world economy equivalent to well over ½ of 1 percent of GNP. Shocks of this magnitude could be seriously destabilizing, and it would presumably be a matter of time before countries took action to insulate themselves from them. Fuel importing countries might impose variable levies on oil imports so as to neutralize the effect on domestic energy prices and real incomes. To the extent that domestic prices continued to fluctuate, consumers might be expected to respond with increases in saving rates so as to better cope with the increased variability of their prospective real income streams. Similarly, fuel exporting countries would respond by building up reserves so as to better cope with the increased variability of their prospective export earnings. Aggregated across all countries, the result would be a general rise in world savings as countries sought to cope with the increase in the variability of real incomes. That rise would have a net deflationary effect on the world economy, at least in the short run.

Another set of costs associated with oil price changes is the adjustment costs associated with sustained oil price changes. The oil price increases of the 1970s resulted in large capital losses for oil importing countries as large parts of the capital stock became obsolete given the new and largely unquestioned set of relative prices. More generally, the changes in relative prices induced a large-scale and costly reallocation of re-

sources. Additional costs were incurred by oil importing countries in the form of the output forgone as national authorities in these countries sought to re-establish a non-inflationary environment for sustained growth. By the same token, the price declines since 1980 and especially those of the last year have resulted in a renewed string of capital losses and, potentially, a renewed set of adjustment costs. The most obvious of these are the large energy-related investments made by countries in, for example, oil exploration and extraction, nuclear and hydroelectric energy, strategic petroleum reserves, and new or "alternative" energy sources. Some of these investments were viable only on the assumption that energy prices would remain significantly above present levels.

These adjustment costs tend to get ignored in flow-oriented analyses. Such analyses often conclude that neither the level nor the distribution of world income would be much affected by a sustained change in oil prices that was later reversed. This ignores, however, the fact that because of adjustment costs, global wealth ends up lower under the hypothesized conditions than it would have if actual (or expected) relative prices had not changed.

Chapter III

Adjustment and Growth in Developing Countries

The economic performance of developing countries in 1985 was disappointing, following the encouraging recovery of output that had occurred in 1984. Economic growth decelerated, inflation remained high and external creditworthiness showed few signs of improving. Part of the reason for this weaker performance is traceable to the slowdown in industrial countries, and the associated decline in developing countries' export earnings. In addition, however, adjustment efforts seem to have flagged, particularly in the field of policies aimed at improving domestic economic performance.

Developments in 1986–87 will depend on the extent to which these slippages can be reversed, as well as on the state of the international environment. For most countries the recent sharp fall in oil prices will lead to terms of trade gains or will, in combination with the decline in international interest rates, at least facilitate adjustment to the low prices currently prevailing for most other commodities. Developing countries that are dependent on oil for their export earnings, on the other hand, face a difficult process of adjustment. In this chapter, attention is directed first to the factors determining recent developments and short-term prospects for output and demand in various groups of developing countries. Other domestic issues are then examined, including the outlook for inflation, financial policies, and domestic saving and investment. The concluding sections of the chapter deal with external developments, and focus in turn on trends in the current account position of developing countries and on prospects for external financing and debt.

Demand and Output

The growth of real GDP in the developing world slackened appreciably in 1985, in broad conformity with developments in the industrial countries. For the developing countries as a group, aggregate output

growth, which had accelerated from about 1½ percent per annum in 1982–83 to 4 percent in 1984, fell back to 3¼ percent in 1985. This outturn was about a ¼ of 1 percentage point below the estimate made in mid-1985 and about ¾ of 1 percentage point below that made at the beginning of the year. The downward revisions have been widespread, with output growing by less than projected in all regions except the Western Hemisphere, which was heavily influenced by the strong pace of expansion in Brazil. Overall, therefore, the slowing of growth in the industrial countries appears to have had a fairly immediate and generalized effect on the developing world. This outcome, although perhaps not surprising given the limited room for maneuver in developing countries' external positions, is nevertheless a considerable disappointment, postponing as it does hopes of seeing these countries resume a more satisfactory pace of economic development.

The influence of external developments on developing countries in 1985 can be illustrated by comparing the growth of output relative to that of real export earnings in various groups of countries (Table 4). The

Table 4. Developing Countries: Output and Export Earnings, 1985

(Changes, in percent)

| | Real GDP | Purchasing Power of Exports[1] | | |
		Total	Export volumes	Terms of trade
Developing countries	3.2	−1.8	0.4	−2.2
Fuel exporting countries	−0.1	−8.1	−4.1	−4.2
Non-fuel exporting countries	4.8	2.1	3.4	−1.2
Of which,				
Primary product exporters	3.6	—	3.3	−3.2
Exporters of manufactures	6.6	3.7	3.6	0.1

[1] Export earnings deflated by import prices.

fuel exporting countries confronted the most adverse external conditions in 1985, with the real purchasing power of their exports falling by 8 percent. They also had the weakest output performance, with their combined real GDP actually declining slightly. The non-fuel exporters, by contrast, fared considerably better. Although their terms of trade deteriorated by 1¼ percent, the volume of their exports rose by nearly 3½ percent. As a result, the trade accounts of these countries continued to be a source of support to economic activity and growth remained a quite vigorous 4¾ percent. Within the non-fuel exporting group, the growth of real export earnings was better sustained among the exporters of manufactures than among the exporters of primary products, and this contributed to a more satisfactory rate of output growth in the former group.

The influence of external factors should not, however, be overstressed. Domestic sources of demand are as important to the economies of developing countries as they are in industrial countries. For the past several years, macroeconomic policies have been aimed at limiting domestic absorption to levels that would permit the increases in net exports required to ease external imbalances. However, with the re-establishment of more sustainable external positions in 1984–85, particularly among the larger countries, that context changed. Domestic demand was able to grow more rapidly, and when export growth slowed in 1985, the effects of this slowdown on output were tempered, at least in some groups of developing countries, by the continuation of fairly strong domestic demand growth.

Fuel Exporting Countries

The fuel exporting countries have been the most adversely affected by recent trends in external demand. As oil prices began to recede from earlier peaks, and as export volumes weakened in the face of energy conservation, interfuel substitution, and the development of alternative sources of supply, the purchasing power of fuel exporting countries' exports fell sharply. In 1985, these countries' real export earnings fell 8 percent, and were only 5 percent above the level reached before the second round of oil price increases in 1979–80. Not surprisingly, therefore, the combined output of this group of countries has been hard hit. Their aggregate GDP in 1985 was unchanged from the previous year and was at approximately the level first reached in 1980.

The domestic and external adjustment required of the fuel exporting countries in recent years has been substantial. Initially, the large current account sur-

pluses registered by these countries in 1979–80 had sheltered domestic spending from the effects of falling revenues. By 1982, however, their combined current account was in deficit by some $26 billion, after having been in surplus by $95 billion two years earlier. To cope with this turnaround, firm action was undertaken to curtail domestic expenditure, particularly investment spending. The average ratio of investment to GDP declined from 27¼ percent in 1981 to 23¼ percent in 1985. By 1984–85, despite the continued weakness of oil revenues, the deterioration in these countries' budgetary positions had been arrested, and import cuts had permitted a reduction in the combined current account deficit to less than $10 billion.

These adjustments notwithstanding, it is clear that sizable further adjustments will be required of fuel exporting countries in 1986 and beyond. As described in Supplementary Note 4, oil prices fell sharply in the early part of 1986. In elaborating the projections, the staff has assumed that the oil export price will average $16 a barrel in 1986–87, a decline of some 40 percent from the 1985 level. Since oil accounts for some four fifths of the fuel exporters' exports, a drop in oil prices of this magnitude is expected to imply an overall terms of trade loss of some 37 percent in 1986. Similarly, with oil exports accounting for close to a sixth of output, the immediate loss in real income is also expected to be severe, equivalent to some 6–7 percent of GDP.

A loss of this magnitude will tend to be amplified as domestic economic agents gradually adjust their spending to the reduced level of real income. However, policies in these countries are expected to be oriented toward limiting, at least to some extent, the adverse consequences for the economy as a whole, for example, through sales of foreign assets and, where possible, by allowing increases in public sector deficits. Moreover, governments can be expected to concentrate on adjusting those expenditures, such as technology and import-intensive investment, which result in the greatest import reductions for the lowest adverse consequences for domestic incomes. In the same vein, a number of countries may resort to intensified import restrictions aimed at curbing "non-essential" imports, i.e., those which can be cut without undue adverse consequences for output and employment. Moreover, several of these countries are expected to promote their non-oil exports through exchange rate adjustments and other means. Finally, the task confronting these countries will be eased by the firming of output prospects in oil importing countries and the easing of international interest rates. Nevertheless, even after these mitigating factors are taken into account, the fuel exporters will need to effect large cuts in both real imports and absorption so that, overall, real domestic demand might eventually decline by an amount broadly equivalent to that of the initial terms of trade effect. Real GDP, however, would be somewhat better sustained because of the concurrent improvement in the real foreign balance. In 1986, real GDP for the group of fuel exporters as a whole is expected to decline by 0.6 percent before firming slightly in 1987.

Within the group of fuel exporters, an important distinction may be made between those countries that have typically been capital exporters and those that, despite oil revenues, have tended to remain importers of capital from abroad. The former group is relatively more dependent on oil revenues, with oil exports accounting for the near totality of exports in 1985. Moreover, because of the production cutbacks these countries have had to undertake in recent years, they have experienced a disproportionate share of the loss in oil export earnings recorded by fuel exporting countries since 1980. By 1985, their real export earnings were half their 1980 levels and 16½ percent below those obtaining before the second round of oil price increases. Losses of this magnitude have taken their toll, and governments have responded with wide-ranging expenditure cuts. As a result, domestic demand has slackened appreciably. Imports in particular have been cut sharply in volume terms—by 5 percent in 1983, 9 percent in 1984, and 15½ percent in 1985 (Chart 18).

The decline in oil prices of early 1986 will, if sustained, hit the capital exporting countries hardest because of the overriding importance of oil in most of these economies. The loss in the terms of trade is expected to very nearly equal the drop in oil prices and the immediate loss in real income would reach

some 7 percent of GDP. However, most of these countries were able to accumulate substantial external assets while oil prices were rising. These external assets, as well as the relatively high income levels in their countries, provide something of a cushion against the effects of a loss of export earnings.

As a result, the countries in this group have some latitude as regards the pace of the adjustment. A few of them are expected to remain in current account surplus, and some could at least for a time probably finance the loss in export earnings through running down external financial assets. Nevertheless, these countries as a group are under considerable pressure to adjust, given the 42 percent loss in the real purchasing power of their exports projected for 1986.

The extent by which these countries might curtail imports to compensate for the drop in earnings is difficult to estimate. The data for the years 1982 to 1985 suggest that adjustment has increased over time, with the relationship approaching one-to-one by the end of the period. On the other hand, the compression in imports already undertaken has been so large for some countries that further adjustments will become increasingly difficult. In the projections, the staff has assumed that the adjustment in 1986 would be large, with imports dropping by some 18 percent in volume terms, but nevertheless less than half that which would be required to match the loss in the purchasing power of exports.

The situation of the capital importing fuel exporters (a group that includes Algeria, Indonesia, Mexico, Nigeria, and Venezuela) is rather different. The real export earnings of these countries have been less severely affected than those of the capital exporting group in recent years, partly because oil is a smaller share of their economies, but mainly because terms of trade losses have been largely made up by increases in oil export volumes. Thus, while these countries' earnings were down by some 4 percent in 1985 compared with 1984, they were still above their level in 1982–83. Nevertheless, these countries have been faced with the need for substantial adjustments, as they have not had the same flexibility as most countries in the capital exporting group to draw down external assets. In addition, many of the capital importing fuel exporters were severely affected by the cessation of private bank lending after 1982, which, together with higher debt service payments, prompted sharp cutbacks in absorption, especially investment spending. As a result, imports declined by 28 percent between 1981 and 1983. By the close of 1983, however, most of this initial adjustment had been completed and, under the impetus of the international recovery, output growth resumed in 1984.

After 1984, the momentum of policy adjustment

Chart 18.   Developing Countries: Imports, in Volume, 1972–86

(Indices: 1972 = 100)

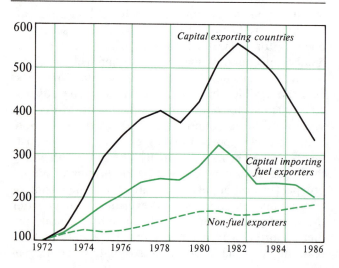

seems to have slackened in this subgroup of the fuel exporting countries. Their combined fiscal deficit rose from 3¾ percent of GDP in 1984 to 5 percent in 1985 and their current account swung back toward deficit. For 1986, however, the substantial weakening of the terms of trade, together with limited opportunities for external borrowing, makes a renewed curtailment of expenditures in these countries unavoidable.

These countries are, by and large, heavily indebted and without ready access to the external financing that would be required to enable them to postpone adjustment to a $30 billion loss in export earnings. Given these financing constraints, governments can be expected to seek pronounced cuts in both fiscal expenditures and imports, as they did in 1982–83. The earlier cuts had been relatively easy, however, coming as they had on the heels of a period of marked buoyancy. Indeed, they did little more than reverse the preceding surge. Further cuts, however, would occur in a context in which there has been no substantive improvement in living standards for close to a decade, and in which per capita GDP and imports are at or below the levels of the mid-1970s. Under these circumstances, the political pressures resisting adjustment could well be considerable and national authorities are expected to seek ways to phase the adjustment over several years.

Some latitude in this respect will be provided by the reserves accumulated by some of these countries in 1983–85, which, at end-1985, amounted to close to 25 percent of imports for the group as a whole. In the main, however, these countries will be able to phase their adjustment only to the extent that they are able to attract additional external financing. For a number of these countries, this financing will in all likelihood not be forthcoming on a voluntary commercial basis. The grounds for such financing will rather reflect various political considerations; concerns for the stability of the financial system; and concerns about maintaining the capital value of existing commercial claims on these countries by, for instance, avoiding arrears on debt service payments. Whatever the reason, such financing is likely to be tied to the implementation of policies that ensure adjustment in these countries' current account balances to the new price of oil within a relatively short time.

Non-Fuel Exporting Countries

Economic activity among the non-fuel exporting countries has been much better sustained than among those countries that are heavily dependent on oil exports. Output growth in non-fuel exporters averaged 2¾ percent in the years 1981–83, and accelerated to 5½ percent in 1984, before falling back to 4¾ percent

in 1985 (Chart 19). A major factor underlying the much stronger performance of these economies has been the relatively stable growth in foreign demand for their exports. This is not to say that these economies did not confront weak international demand or strong adjustment pressures. Indeed, their real export earnings were no better than stagnant during the international recession, at the same time as their interest costs rose sharply, and their access to external private financing virtually dried up. These adverse trends forced a marked squeeze on the growth of domestic absorption during 1981–83. Thereafter, with the onset of recovery in the United States, and aided by the adjustment policies in place, these countries' real export earnings responded strongly to the growth in foreign demand, with real earnings rising by 8½ percent in 1983 and 13½ percent in 1984.

Chart 19. Non-Fuel Exporting Developing Countries: Real GDP, Real Domestic Demand, and Purchasing Power of Exports, 1978–86

(Annual changes, in percent)

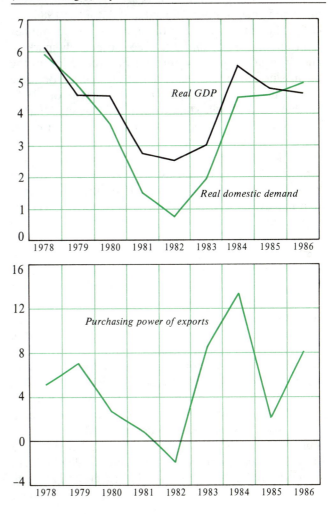

In 1985, however, global conditions once again turned less favorable, with the growth of real export earnings dropping back to only 2 percent. This weakness of external demand would undoubtedly have led to a substantial slowing of GDP growth had it not been for a strengthening of domestic demand growth. This firming of domestic demand seems to have reflected primarily an easing in the stance of demand management policies—not in the sense that policies became actively expansionary but rather that there was an easing in restraint. Fiscal deficits, for example, which had been significantly reduced as a percentage of GDP in 1984, tended to stabilize in 1985. In the same vein, the combined current account deficit—which had fallen steadily in the period 1981–84—ceased to narrow.

For 1986 and 1987, the policy objectives of governments in the non-fuel exporting countries indicate that financial policies will once again become more restrictive, with central government fiscal deficits expected to decline by ½ of 1 percent of GDP in 1986. These adjustment measures, geared as they often are to dramatic cuts in inflation rates in some countries, are expected, in combination with a more favorable set of external developments, to lead to a reasonably well-sustained pace of both demand and output in 1986 and 1987. The improvement in the external circumstances confronting these countries in 1986 is especially marked. The drop in oil prices will result in a reduction in the group's net oil import bill of about $15 billion, or some 4 percent of imports and ¾ of 1 percent of GDP. Further savings will stem from the associated 1 percentage point reduction in international interest rates. Moreover, with the partly oil-induced recovery of domestic demand in industrial countries, the export earnings of these countries are expected to firm in 1986–87. In addition, a number of countries (in particular in Africa and in Central America) will register significant further gains in real incomes because of the large increases in coffee prices.

These gains will be partially offset by losses stemming from the continuing weakness of primary commodity prices other than coffee, by the decline in exports to fuel exporting countries and, for countries in and around the Middle East, by significant reductions in remittance and official transfer receipts from the fuel exporting countries of that region. Nevertheless, the balance of these factors is expected to be distinctly favorable for the group as a whole, with the purchasing power of exports expected to rise by some 8 percent in 1986. While part of this real income gain is expected to be used to buttress adjustment efforts and to replenish reserves, part also is expected to be used for additional imports to sustain domestic demand and output growth. Overall, growth is expected to average 4½ percent in 1986 and to firm to 4¾ percent in 1987.

It needs to be remembered, of course, that the group of non-fuel exporting countries covers a diversity of economies, each facing rather different external and internal circumstances. With respect to 1985, an important distinction can be made between the primary product exporting countries, on the one hand, and the exporters of manufactures, on the other. The importance of this distinction stems from the fact that the primary product exporters incurred terms of trade losses not experienced by the exporters of manufactures. Thus, whereas the terms of trade of the exporters of manufactures were unchanged in 1985, those of the primary product exporters deteriorated by 3¼ percent. This worsening reflected the 13 percent drop in prices of non-oil primary products relative to those for manufactures in 1985. (See Supplementary Note 3 for more details.) The resulting real income losses in primary product exporting countries had depressing effects on domestic demand and output that were largely avoided by the exporters of manufactures.

Within the primary product exporting group, it is important to distinguish developments in Brazil and Argentina from those in most other countries.[1] Brazil, like many other countries, underwent a period of concentrated economic adjustment in the early 1980s, which led to a pronounced decline in output and an even more marked decline in domestic absorption. Partly because of this adjustment and partly because of the resurgence in U.S. demand for its goods, Brazilian exports increased sharply in both 1983 and 1984. As a result, output growth had recovered to 4½ percent by 1984 and balance had been established in the current account, after a $16 billion deficit only two years earlier. After the elections late in 1984, the Brazilian authorities used the scope provided by their stronger external position to support the growth of domestic demand through large increases in real wages. The result was a consumption-led boom in domestic demand and an acceleration in GDP growth to 8 percent in 1985, despite a significant loss in real export earnings. This performance was achieved with only a small deterioration in the current account, owing in large part to the relatively small size of the tradable goods sector in Brazil—imports account for 4 percent of GDP—and to rigid controls over the flow of imports. Internal disequilibria were significantly exacerbated,

---

[1] Brazil is an economy in transition to becoming an exporter of manufactures. It does, however, meet the criterion for a primary product exporter—that at least 50 percent of its exports of goods were primary products in 1980. Moreover, Brazil continues to meet that criterion on the basis of more recent data. This is, however, partly a consequence of the staff's reliance on the Standard International Trade Classification (SITC) for its definition of manufactures. That definition defines processed foods, such as fruit juices and soluble coffee, which are important in Brazil's exports, as non-manufactures.

however, as evidenced by the acceleration of inflation from average twelve-monthly rates of less than 140 percent in 1984 to well over 200 percent in 1985. As a result, the Brazilian authorities announced in early 1986 a major set of policy measures intended to re-establish control over inflation (see below).

Developments in Argentina were also atypical in 1985, but for quite different reasons. Adjustment efforts in Argentina had had a somewhat mixed record until 1984. After 1984, however, policies moved increasingly toward controlling internal and external disequilibria. The fiscal deficit was reduced from 18 percent of GDP in 1983 to 5 percent in 1985; inflation was lowered dramatically after mid-1985; and the current account deficit was roughly halved. Nevertheless, the costs of earlier policy errors have been high. Real output declined by 4½ percent in 1985 and domestic absorption by perhaps twice that amount.

Developments in most other primary product exporting countries in 1985 were less striking than those in Argentina and Brazil. The international recovery had led to a strengthening of their growth rates from an average of ¾ of 1 percent in 1982–83 to 3¼ percent in 1984. Partly because of inadequate policy adaptations, however, substantial fiscal imbalances and exposed external positions remained prevalent in these countries. As a result, when 1985 brought a slowdown of export growth and a sharp deterioration in the terms of trade, these countries had little choice but to continue policies of demand restraint. Fiscal deficits were curtailed further and imports were cut. Rates of output and domestic demand growth thus faltered, with real GDP growth slowing to 2 percent in 1985.

For many of the primary product exporting countries the growth of output is likely to be considerably more buoyant in 1986. The decline in oil prices will cut over $7 billion from their combined import bill, thus freeing, in combination with reduced debt service payments, foreign exchange for other pressing uses. The 50 percent rise in coffee prices occasioned by the drought in Brazil will be even more beneficial for the twenty or so countries in the group that export coffee. Not only will these countries benefit from the rise in price, but they will also benefit from being able to export large amounts of coffee out of existing stocks. Accordingly, except for Brazil where coffee production is expected to be quite weak, these countries' export earnings are projected to rise by some 18½ percent in 1986, fueling an acceleration in output growth from 2½ percent in 1985 to almost 6 percent in 1986. Growth among the other primary product exporters is expected to be more subdued, with the favorable terms of trade effects originating in the decline in oil prices being more than offset by the continuing deterioration in the relative price of non-coffee primary products vis-à-vis

manufactures. For the group of primary product exporters as a whole, the weighted average growth rate is expected to remain around 3¾ percent in 1986. This unchanged overall growth rate is, however, swayed by developments in several of the larger countries. For the typical or median country, a distinct firming of growth is anticipated, from 2¾ percent in 1985 to nearly 4 percent in 1986 and 1987.

The exporters of manufactures have had rather different experiences. As noted earlier, these countries did not experience the terms of trade losses incurred by the primary product exporters in 1985. Nevertheless, they were significantly affected by an unexpected weakness in export demand. Over the five years leading up to 1985, these countries' real exports had increased at an average rate some 7 percentage points faster than that of world trade. The deceleration of these countries' export growth to 3½ percent in 1985—a rate barely in line with world trade, which was itself unexpectedly weak—was therefore a considerable setback. Although this weakness of exports was accompanied by a firming of domestic sources of demand, overall GDP growth among the exporters of manufactures nevertheless slowed from 8¼ percent in 1984 to 6½ percent in 1985.

The strengthening of domestic demand among the exporters of manufactures reflects in part developments in China, which has a large weight in the output of the group. The Chinese economy, propelled by an ambitious program of economic reform, grew at a steadily accelerating rate from 1981 to 1984, when output expanded by some 14 percent. In 1985, the pace of demand expansion, especially that of investment demand, increased further, outstripping the economy's ability to increase production at the same rate. Hence, despite real GDP growth of 12 percent, the current account swung from a surplus of $2½ billion in 1984 to a deficit of almost $11 billion in 1985—a swing equivalent to some 4 percent of GDP. In the face of this shift, the authorities have acted to restrain domestic demand and the flow of imports. These actions are expected to bring about some diminution of the current account deficit and a slowing of growth.

Developments among the other exporters of manufactures were similar to those in China, but of lesser amplitude. Thus, confronted with a marked slowing of export growth in 1985, these countries used the room for maneuver afforded by the current account surplus they had built up in 1984 to cushion contractionary external influences. Domestic demand growth, which had been relatively subdued in 1984, firmed appreciably in 1985. In effect, therefore, these countries compensated for the weakening of world demand by lessening their past strenuous efforts at external adjustment. In terms of policies, this development

53

took the form of increases in fiscal deficits in a number of countries. For the future, given the generally more cautious approach of these countries to economic management, it is to be expected that renewed restraint will be exercised so as to preserve external and internal financial balance. For the group as a whole, growth is expected to stabilize around 6 percent in 1986–87.

The economic prospects of developing countries can be differentiated on other bases besides that of their foreign trade structure. Countries that have succeeded in avoiding external debt-servicing difficulties, for example, have generally fared better in terms of GDP growth in recent years than countries that have encountered such difficulties. This pattern is expected to be repeated in 1986–87, with growth in the former group expected to be close to double the rate in the latter group. These divergent prospects serve to underline the variety of constraints facing different groups of developing countries, and point to the need for adequate differentiation in analysis.

Per Capita Output

Another perspective on the divergence of economic performance among developing countries is provided by the data in Table 5 on the cumulative growth of per capita output during the first half of the 1980s. Two points emerge from this table. First, per capita GDP was unchanged for the developing world as a whole during the period, while in the industrial countries the corresponding measure rose by some 9 percent. Second, there was considerable diversity among the regional groups of developing countries. Output per head has actually grown quite buoyantly in Asia, where real per capita incomes rose by almost a fifth over the period. In Africa, the Middle East, and Latin America, on the other hand, large declines were pervasive. Moreover, these divergences in output per head understate, if anything, developments in living standards. Asian countries tend to be exporters of manufactures and have thus not suffered serious terms of trade losses. In Africa and the Western Hemisphere,

by contrast, an increasing share of real output has had to be channeled to net exports in order to compensate for terms of trade losses and to bring about a reduction in external deficits. For these countries, per capita absorption has fallen by perhaps twice as much as the measured decline in output per head. (The Middle East is a special case, since a sharp decline in output per capita between 1980 and 1985 has been cushioned by a reversal in the balance between exports and imports.)

Price Developments

Inflation remained a serious problem in the developing world in 1985, but an improvement is expected over the forecast period. The weighted average inflation rate in developing countries was 38 percent in 1984–85, reflecting primarily the very high rates of price increase experienced in Argentina, Bolivia, Brazil, Israel, and Peru. However, the median inflation rate, which is perhaps more representative of the "typical" country, has been much lower and has tended to fall in recent years (Chart 20).

The increasing divergence between these two measures of inflation is largely a reflection of the dramatic worsening in inflation rates in the five high-inflation countries noted above. The composite inflation rate for this group accelerated from about 105 percent in 1981–82 to 250 percent in 1984 and close to 300 percent in 1985. Recently, however, most of these countries, as well as others, have introduced measures aimed at strengthening their adjustment efforts and bringing inflationary pressures under better control.

For example, the economic rehabilitation program initiated in Argentina in June 1985 featured a major reduction in the deficit of the public sector and a virtual cessation in the expansion of bank credit. This tightening was accompanied by a wage-price freeze and monetary reform, including the adoption of a new currency. In the same vein, the Brazilian authorities announced and implemented in late February 1986 a major package of economic reforms. The main features of this package were wage and price controls, the de-indexation of financial and other markets, and currency reform. These measures are expected to lead to a drastic cut in the country's triple-digit inflation rate. Assuming these policies and others like them in other high-inflation countries are vigorously and uninterruptedly pursued, significant declines in inflation can be expected in the developing countries in 1986 and beyond.

Inflationary pressures in other developing countries have been less severe. Although inflation remains a serious problem in many of them (such as Chile, Ecuador, Mexico, Nicaragua, Uganda, Uruguay,

---

Table 5. Growth of Per Capita GDP, 1980–85

(In percent)

Industrial countries	9
Developing countries	—
Africa	−11
Of which, sub-Sahara	−7
Asia	19
Europe	7
Middle East	−20
Western Hemisphere	−7

Chart 20.   Developing Countries: Consumer Prices and Broad Money, 1978–86

(Annual changes, in percent)

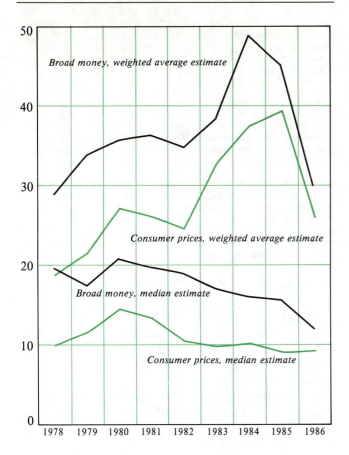

Financial Policies

As was noted above, policy implementation in the developing world in 1985 was somewhat mixed. This is most evident in the field of fiscal policy. In 1984, under the impetus of firm adjustment policies and strong growth in foreign trade, central government fiscal deficits declined by ¾ percent in relation to GDP, to 4½ percent. Although concentrated in those countries and regions where adjustment was most urgent, the declines were fairly widespread. In 1985, on the other hand, fiscal deficits stabilized overall and tended to edge upward among those groups where pressures for external adjustment had become less urgent, for example, in countries without a recent history of debt-servicing difficulties (Table 6).

The stabilization of deficits in 1985 can be traced to developments both on the revenue and the expenditure side of the fiscal accounts. A weakening of revenues seems to be closely linked to the parallel weakening of the foreign trade sector. The downturn in commodity prices of 1985 had a significant impact on fiscal revenues in those countries where commodity export earnings are a major source of government receipts. Similarly, import cuts necessitated by external adjustment had a depressing impact on revenues from customs duties. Overall, foreign trade taxes account for about a third of tax revenues in developing countries. In addition, however, corporate income taxes, collected mostly from firms extracting minerals for exports, account for another sixth. Finally, many "domestic" excise taxes on goods and services are in fact levied on imported goods so that fully half of tax revenues in many developing countries appears to be directly related to trade.

Spurred by the need to improve fiscal positions, many countries have explored means of expanding and diversifying their sources of revenue, turning mostly

Yugoslavia, and Zaïre), most countries experienced a moderation of price increases in 1985. This is reflected in the lower median rates of inflation in 1985 for all regional groupings except the Western Hemisphere, where the consequences of financial imbalances, price distortions, exchange rate depreciations, indexation mechanisms, and inflationary expectations have been particularly pronounced.

Inflationary pressures in developing countries have been exacerbated because of difficulties in supporting price adjustments with effective measures of domestic financial restraint. Since adjustment often requires initial increases in administered prices, the liberalization of controlled market prices, reductions in subsidies, increases in public utility and other tariffs, and sizable exchange rate depreciations, it has often led to upward pressures on costs. In these circumstances, firm fiscal and credit restraint is required to prevent a spiral of further price increases from being set in train. Such restraint has not always been applied with sufficient vigor.

Table 6.   Developing Countries: Central Government Fiscal Balances, 1983–85

(In percent of GDP)

	1983	1984	1985
Developing countries[1]	−5.2	−4.4	−4.4
Africa	−7.3	−5.1	−4.7
Asia	−3.5	−3.2	−4.0
Europe	−2.2	−2.3	−3.2
Middle East	−9.9	−10.3	−9.0
Western Hemisphere	−4.1	−2.3	−2.0
By financial criteria[2]			
Countries with recent debt-servicing problems	−4.6	−2.8	−2.8
Countries without recent debt-servicing problems	−4.6	−4.7	−5.1

[1] Data are weighted averages.
[2] Does not include capital exporting developing countries.

to various types of indirect taxation. In addition, many have taken measures to improve tax collection procedures and the efficiency of public sector enterprises, as well as to rationalize their pricing policies. Public utilities, such as electricity and transport services, have been subject to particular scrutiny. In some cases, these enterprises have been divested to the private sector to improve efficiency.

Although budgetary revenues have fallen considerably among the capital surplus oil exporting countries, revenues were relatively well sustained among the capital importing countries (Table 7). Budgetary difficulties in these countries were instead concentrated on the expenditure side, with the share of expenditures in GDP rising from 1984 to 1985.

One of the main factors putting upward pressure on government deficits in developing countries has been interest payments on outstanding government debt. Available data through 1984 point to a steep rise in the share of interest payments in total expenditure. Starting from some 6½ percent in 1980, this ratio rose progressively to reach 13 percent in 1984. The rise was especially marked among the countries of the Western Hemisphere. Relatively smaller increases were recorded among Asian countries, and the ratios among Middle Eastern countries have been both low and tending to fall (Table 8). A good part of the rise in the share of interest payments in government expenditure reflects the rise in interest payments to foreign creditors. However, these payments, unlike total interest payments, crested in 1982–83 and then receded with the easing of international interest rates. This suggests that the continuing rise of interest payments in government expenditures stems from a rapid rise in payments to domestic holders of government debt. This is in line with the general shift toward more market-determined interest rates in developing countries. It also reflects the large increases in government debt resulting from the unusually large deficits of the past several years.

Given the sharp rise in interest payments and the political sensitivity of expenditures for national defense and public sector employment, fiscal retrenchment has in good part fallen on capital outlays (Table 9). In-

Table 8. Developing Countries: Central Government Interest Payments, 1980–84[1]

(In percent of expenditure and net lending)

	1980	1981	1982	1983	1984
Developing countries	6.5	7.5	9.1	11.4	13.0[2]
Of which,					
Asia	7.2	7.4	8.4	9.8	...
Middle East	1.9	1.1	0.8	—	...
Western Hemisphere	7.7	9.6	12.3	16.0	...
Oil exporting countries	3.9	3.1	3.8	4.9	...
Non-oil developing countries	7.2	8.5	10.4	12.9	...

Sources: IMF, *Government Finance Statistics Yearbook*, 1985; and Inter-American Development Bank, *Economic and Social Progress in Latin America*, 1985.

[1] Estimates shown in this table are less comprehensive in terms of their geographic coverage than those shown in most other tables included in this report. That limitation, together with the restriction of the coverage to the central government as opposed to the entire public sector, is thought to result in a significant understatement of the role of interest payments in public finances, especially for the Western Hemisphere.
[2] Estimated.

vestment expenditures have been severely cut in a wide range of countries, but the cuts have been most severe in the countries undergoing the most pronounced external adjustment, such as those in the Western Hemisphere.

To some extent, this curtailment of investment has been salutary. Part of the difficulties confronting the developing countries has stemmed from over-ambitious and inefficient investment programs. As a result of the financial constraints of the past several years, governments have generally sought to rationalize their investment plans, for example, by giving greater priority to the projects with the greatest rates of return and with the shortest gestation periods. Consequently, and in light of the easing of interest rates and of oil prices, some improvement in the productivity of investment might be forthcoming in the years ahead. Nevertheless, given the implications for the longer-term growth potential of these countries, it is unfortunate that such a major reduction in capital outlays has taken place when current expenditure has been cut by much less.

Monetary policies have generally held to a course of gradual disinflation, except in those countries where inflation accelerated to triple-digit rates or more. Thus, the median rate of expansion of broad money has fallen in each recent year from a high of 21 percent in 1980 to 16 percent in 1984 and to an estimated 15½ percent in 1985. Similarly, domestic credit expansion has slowed from a high of 24½ percent in 1981 to about 14 percent in 1985. Finally, interest rate policies in a number of countries continue to aim at restoring and maintaining positive real rates for both borrowing

Table 7. Capital Importing Developing Countries: Fiscal Indicators, 1983–85

(In percent of GDP)

	1983	1984	1985
Revenues	20.1	20.1	20.0
Expenditures	24.7	23.8	24.1
Balance	−4.6	−3.7	−4.1

Table 9. Developing Countries: Central Government Capital Expenditures, 1979–84

(In percent of total expenditure and net lending)

	1979	1980	1981	1982	1983	1984[1]
Developing countries	19.2	19.0	19.6	19.0	17.3	15.0
Of which,						
Asia	18.8	19.5	21.2	20.9	20.2	. . .
Western Hemisphere	16.6	16.7	16.5	14.6	11.9	. . .
Oil exporting countries	28.9	27.2	30.0	31.4	30.6	. . .
Non-oil developing						
countries	16.7	16.8	16.9	15.9	14.0	. . .

Sources: IMF, *Government Finance Statistics Yearbook*, 1985; and Inter-American Development Bank, *Economic and Social Progress in Latin America*, 1985.

[1] Estimated.

and lending instruments. These trends reflect the important role given to credit policies in adjustment efforts designed to curb inflation, mobilize domestic savings, and reduce distortions in the allocation of resources.

The decline in the rate of domestic credit expansion has often fallen heavily on the private sector. Given the limited availability of foreign financing and, in some cases, the reluctance of countries to increase their foreign indebtedness, there has been increasing recourse to domestic credit to meet public sector financing needs. Recent reductions in fiscal deficits have tended to be associated more with cutbacks in external financing than with reduced claims on domestic saving.

If the analysis is broadened to take full account of developments in the high-inflation countries, a rather less favorable picture of monetary developments emerges. On a weighted average basis, rates of monetary expansion in the developing countries tended to accelerate through 1985 or at least to remain at very high levels. Moreover, these accelerations seemed to be almost wholly tied to the financing of public sector deficits. In 1985, growth in credit to government was a substantially higher proportion of the growth in total domestic credit than in preceding years. Beginning about mid-1985, however, a number of the high-inflation countries began to bring their finances into better order. Although these developments occurred too late in the year to have a visible effect on the aggregates for 1985, they are expected to have a more marked effect in 1986. The main reductions are expected in the rates of broad money expansion of Argentina, Bolivia, and Brazil. Smaller but still significant reductions are also projected for Mexico, Nicaragua, Peru, Uganda, Uruguay, and Yugoslavia—all countries with relatively high rates of inflation. Also noteworthy is the reduction, both actual and projected, in money growth in Israel as part of an adjustment

program that has already resulted in some abatement of inflationary pressures.

Exchange Rates

The year 1985 seems to have been characterized by considerable flexibility in exchange rate policy. Exchange rate adjustments in that year represent the continuation of a process that had begun in the wake of the debt crisis of 1982. Since then, there has been a greater willingness to change exchange rates to correct misalignments in relative prices and to improve competitiveness. These changes have helped achieve adjustment at somewhat higher levels of economic activity than would have been possible through exclusive reliance on policies of demand restraint.

On a weighted average basis, real exchange rates of developing countries declined by some 13 percent during 1985, in good part because of the parallel effective depreciation of the U.S. dollar, which is the key reference currency for many developing countries. This development stands in contrast to events in 1984 when, in part because of the strength of the dollar and the buoyancy of exports, countries had allowed their real exchange rates to stabilize or even appreciate. In 1985, with world trade considerably less buoyant, countries accepted (or sought) real exchange rate depreciations in order to support export competitiveness and to encourage domestic production of tradable goods. This tendency was quite widespread. Real exchange rate indices for the five regional groups of developing countries show declines during the year ranging up to 20 percent.

Needless to say, these averages cover a wide diversity of changes for particular currencies. In some countries, exchange rate policies were aimed at a phased real depreciation, sometimes following an initial step devaluation. Other countries initiated policies to unify their foreign exchange markets. Yet others that have traditionally linked their currencies to the U.S. dollar maintained their existing peg and allowed the decline in the dollar to bring about a real effective depreciation of their own currencies. In countries where earlier exchange rate action had achieved the desired real depreciation, subsequent changes in nominal rates were often necessary to maintain competitiveness.

The increasing resort to exchange rate action during the past several years has been largely a consequence of the need to take prompt and effective measures to strengthen balance of payments positions at a time when the availability of external finance was declining sharply. In these circumstances, a realistic and predictable exchange rate policy has been seen as essential to encourage needed supply responses in agriculture and industry, to promote a more effective allocation of resources, to stimulate investment, and to contain capital flight. Moreover, growing experience with the use of exchange rate policy in adjustment programs may have allayed some earlier misgivings about the use of this instrument.

Savings and Investment

A critical condition for the success of adjustment in developing countries is the achievement of higher rates of domestic savings. Additional domestic savings are needed to compensate for the declining availability of external financing and the increased share of net factor payments abroad. However, the ratio of gross domestic savings to GDP has, if anything, tended to fall since the late 1970s. Taking into account the increase in net factor payments abroad, the proportion of GDP left to finance domestic investment has thus dropped appreciably.

Much of the decline in saving rates took place in the period up to 1983. Since then, saving rates have stabilized or even risen somewhat. This development is closely related to developments in public sector finances. The net dissaving of the public sector reached a peak in 1982–83, after which fiscal deficits have tended to come down. Private savings were also adversely affected in the early 1980s by deteriorating terms of trade, high unemployment, real wage reductions, and low income growth. Moreover, in some countries, the presence of high inflation and economic uncertainty has eroded both the incentive and capacity to save. An extreme case in point is Bolivia, where the gross domestic saving rate fell to 3 percent in 1985 from 18 percent in 1980, in part as a result of hyperinflation. Given the clear need to encourage private saving, many countries have recognized the impor-

tance of a stable, noninflationary environment and of increasing the returns on savings. Thus, with a view to mobilizing domestic resources, curtailing capital flight, and attracting foreign capital inflows, governments have sought to control inflation and to relax restrictions imposed on nominal interest rates. The limited success achieved to date in each of these areas underscores the need for a more determined implementation of policies of structural adjustment.

Because of the steep decline in the availability of foreign and domestic saving, investment spending as a share of GDP has been sharply reduced in recent years. As shown in Chart 21, for the developing countries as a whole, the rate of investment spending has fallen by some 4½–5 percentage points between 1978 and 1985. This decline was, however, rather unevenly distributed. On a regional basis, the declines were concentrated in Africa, Europe, and the Western Hemisphere, which experienced declines equivalent

Chart 21. Developing Countries: Gross Capital Formation, 1978–85

(In percent of nominal GDP)

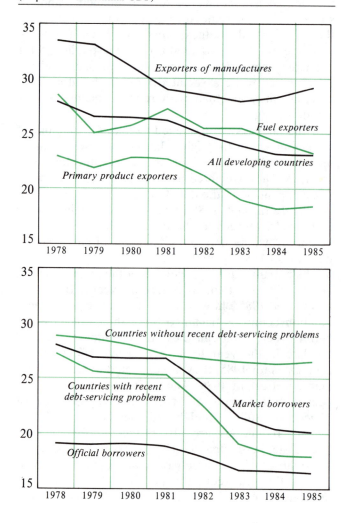

to 7–9 percent of GDP. Reductions in Asia, and especially the Middle East, on the other hand, were of much smaller magnitude.

The influence on investment spending of increased debt service payments and reduced external financing can be illustrated by the divergent trends between countries that borrow primarily from market sources (the "market borrowers") and those that rely on official development assistance (the "official borrowers"). Market borrowers, not surprisingly, have been considerably more sensitive to changes in interest rates and the availability of finance. Accordingly, the decline in the investment ratio among these countries was three times as great as that among official borrowers. The role of external influences is further exemplified by the contrasting development in the investment ratios of countries that did and did not encounter debt-servicing problems. The decline was four to five times as great among the former group.

The widespread reduction in the proportion of developing country output devoted to capital formation was probably an unavoidable initial consequence of the economic retrenchment measures adopted in these countries in the early 1980s. As noted earlier, the process of fiscal consolidation led to a disproportionate share of the cuts falling on capital outlays. Similarly, tight credit and monetary policies adversely affected investment by the private sector. In a somewhat longer time frame, however, it was intended that prudent financial policies, rising private savings, and the resumption of foreign capital inflows would permit expenditures on viable investment projects to grow once again. To the extent that such viable projects have continued to be postponed, the preference thereby given to current expenditures must be regarded as a source of concern.

By the same token, however, it is important that any increases in investment expenditures be such as to enhance rather than impede longer-term growth prospects. In the past, investment programs have too often included projects that require continuing subsidies, either explicitly in the form of government transfers or implicitly in the form of distortions to relative prices. More generally, the rates of return on investment have been disappointing. Decisions have frequently been made on the basis of noneconomic considerations or unrealistic assessments of likely rates of return. Frequently, too, insufficient attention has been given to the long-term viability and robustness of some of the assumptions underlying the cost-benefit analyses attaching to the projects. Finally, and more generally, governments have seriously underestimated the critical role of prudent financial policies in ensuring that scarce resources are directed to the most productive uses.

An important reason why external adjustment has tended to be associated with falling investment is the close association between investment and imports because of the high import content of investment (Chart 22). The initial phases of adjustment often involve some element of import compression—brought about by a combination of exchange rate depreciation, higher tariffs, and import controls—that has a major effect on investment spending. Over time, however, economies should adapt to new patterns of relative scarcity, and while the composition of investment may be changed, the overall level of capital spending should tend to rise again. The continued weakness of investment spending in developing countries is thus disturbing, and suggests that needed domestic adjustments have not taken place nearly as rapidly as the required reduction in balance of payments deficits. Present investment levels, in particular in many heavily indebted developing countries, appear too low to generate rates of growth over the medium term that will permit the servicing of external debt obligations together with an adequate and sustained increase in

Chart 22. Developing Countries with Recent Debt-Servicing Problems: Gross Capital Formation, Imports, and Real GDP, 1973–85

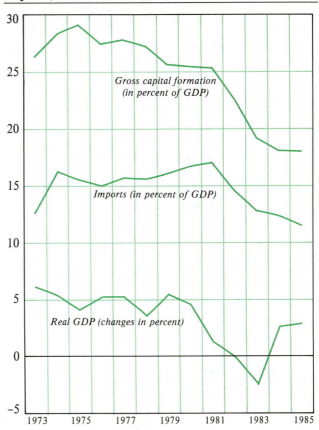

domestic living standards. Fortunately, declines in investment spending appear to be tapering off and, indeed, investment ratios have begun to rise in some countries. For the developing countries as a whole, the rate of investment is estimated to have stabilized in 1985 and, apart from the fuel exporters, is expected to firm gradually in 1986 and 1987, assisted by the favorable effect of lower oil prices and declining interest rates, which should help release resources for financing capital expenditures and buttress the impact of adjustment measures.

Current Account Balances

Tight financing constraints caused the combined current account deficit of developing countries to be held to $34 billion in 1985.[2] This deficit was equivalent to 5 percent of exports, unchanged from the 1984 level but less than half the deficit recorded in 1982 (Chart 23).

The financial constraints that developed after 1981 had uneven effects on developing countries. The most severely affected were the market borrowers. However, the bulk of the current account adjustment of these countries had been achieved by the end of 1984, and the continuation of financing constraints required little further change in their combined external balance in 1985. In fact, the market borrowers had almost eliminated their current account deficit in 1984 and moved into surplus in 1985. The official borrowers, on the other hand, were relatively less affected by cutbacks in external financing after 1982. This group of countries was able to sustain a current account deficit in 1985 that, at 25 percent of exports, was little changed from the average deficit in 1982–84 (Table 10).

The aggregate data for the above-mentioned groups tend to mask developments in individual countries. Many smaller countries did achieve a modest degree of current account adjustment in 1985, but the changes in their current balances were often more than offset by sizable changes in the opposite direction for a few larger countries. Thus the large deterioration in China's current balance conceals the underlying improvement in other countries in the groups to which China belongs (the diversified borrowers and the countries without recent debt-servicing difficulties). Similarly, the large reduction in Mexico's surplus on current account in 1985 in large part offsets an aggregate improvement in

[2] The current account includes unrequited transfers (both private and official). It may be noted that this treatment differs from earlier *World Economic Outlook* reports, in which current account positions of developing countries excluded official transfers. Net receipts of official transfers by developing countries in 1985 were some $14 billion, about 2 percent of exports of goods and services.

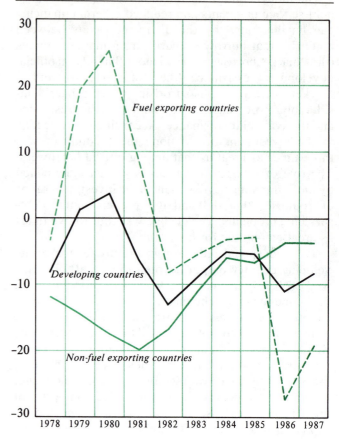

Chart 23.   Developing Countries—By Predominant Export: Current Account Balances, 1978–87

(In percent of exports of goods and services)

the other 14 heavily indebted countries. Conversely, the strong improvement in South Africa's current account exaggerates the degree of strengthening of other countries in the African region.

Because of the decline in oil prices, the staff expects the combined current account deficit of developing countries, relative to exports, to double in 1986 compared to its 1985 level. This increase is, of course, concentrated in the fuel exporting group, whose aggregate current account deficit is expected to increase from 2¾ percent of exports in 1985 to 27¼ percent in 1986, before falling back to around 19 percent in 1987. For the non-fuel exporters, by contrast, the corresponding ratio is projected to decline from 6½ percent in 1985 to about 4 percent in 1986–87.

The deterioration in the fuel exporting countries' current account balance stems from the sharp fall in oil prices in early 1986. The reaction of the fuel exporting countries to this development is expected to depend to a great extent on their financial position. The capital importing fuel exporters, several of which experienced recent debt-servicing problems, remain

Table 10. Developing Countries—By Financial Criteria: Current Account Balances, 1982–87

(In percent of exports of goods and services)

	1982	1983	1984	1985	1986–87
Developing countries	−13.1	−8.9	−5.0	−5.1	−9.4
Capital exporting countries	−0.6	−7.5	−8.6	−5.8	−28.5
Capital importing countries	−17.8	−9.4	−4.1	−4.9	−6.4
Market borrowers	−20.0	−7.5	−0.9	0.4	−2.5
Official borrowers	−29.0	−26.3	−28.1	−25.4	−23.2
Diversified borrowers	−6.6	−10.0	−7.7	−16.4	−13.4
Countries with recent debt-servicing problems	−29.9	−10.2	−3.9	−2.2	−5.7
Countries without recent debt-servicing problems	−9.2	−8.8	−4.3	−6.6	−6.8
Memorandum					
Market borrowers, excluding Mexico and South Africa	−20.5	−10.7	−1.9	−0.6	−3.1
Diversified borrowers, excluding China	−15.5	−18.5	−13.0	−9.7	−8.1
15 heavily indebted countries, excluding Mexico	−35.0	−10.1	−0.6	−0.1	−4.3
	−39.0	−18.2	−4.2	−0.9	−4.7

under severe financial pressures and are expected to take adjustment measures that will restrict the deterioration in their current account balance in 1986 to a level, in relation to exports, which is slightly less than that in 1982. The capital exporting fuel exporters, however, are expected to finance a substantial deterioration in their current account balance, and their deficit in 1986 will be approximately as large relative to exports as was their average surplus in 1979–80. Adjustment measures in both the capital exporting and the capital importing fuel exporting countries are expected to produce a marked reduction in the current account deficit in 1987. Nevertheless, the remaining deficit, at 19 percent of exports, would still be much larger than could be considered sustainable over the longer term.

The expectation that current account deficits, relative to exports of goods and services, will continue to be low by historical standards among the non-fuel exporters reflects the prospect of little or no relaxation of the financing constraints facing many countries. Moreover, it also reflects the apparent reluctance of countries that are not financially constrained to absorb larger capital inflows at prevailing market interest rates. However, attitudes toward borrowing might change if export prospects weakened or if the terms under which funds could be borrowed became more favorable.

The prevalence of external financing constraints and the importance of meeting scheduled interest payments to avoid jeopardizing existing financing arrangements ensure that changes in the purchasing power of developing countries' exports tend to be reflected rather quickly in import volumes. The purchasing power of exports, after rising by 8½ percent in 1984, declined by 1¾ percent in 1985. This represents a substantially less favorable outcome than was envisaged at the beginning of the year (Table 11). The exports of fuel exporting countries were especially weak, and these countries were obliged to cut their imports by 9 percent.

Foreign Trade Prices

The disappointing weakness in the purchasing power of developing countries' exports relative to earlier expectations was caused by a combination of unexpected deterioration in the terms of trade and sharply lower export volume growth. Non-oil commodity prices turned out to be much weaker in 1985 than had been generally expected. These prices declined by some 12 percent in U.S. dollar terms, compared with the projection of a 2¼ percent decline in *World Economic Outlook, April 1985.* (For more details, see Supplementary Note 3.) Part of this weakness may be explained by demand factors. Growth of both total output and industrial production in the industrial countries slowed sharply in 1985, particularly in the early part of the year. Moreover, inflation in these countries continued to recede, which might have further dampened commodity prices. Finally, demand for some commodities appears to have been adversely affected by longer-term substitution possibilities and technological improvements. Nevertheless, even taken together, these factors cannot explain the sharp fall in real commodity prices (relative to manufactures) that occurred in 1985.

It appears, therefore, that much of the fall in real commodity prices can be traced to unusually ample supplies. Available indicators suggest that the increases in supplies of non-oil commodities in 1984 and

Table 11.   Developing Countries: Purchasing Power of Exports, 1983–87[1]

(Changes, in percent)

	1983	1984	1985	1986–87	April 1985 Estimates for 1985	Revision
Developing countries	−1.1	8.4	−1.8	−2.3	4.6	−6.4
Fuel exporting countries	−12.2	1.8	−8.1	−19.8	0.5	−8.6
Non-fuel exporting countries	8.5	13.4	2.1	6.7	7.3	−5.2

[1] Export value deflated by import prices.

1985 were particularly large. The increase was especially pronounced among agricultural crops, which, in many parts of the world, had benefited from good weather (until the impact of the drought on coffee output in Brazil). Prices for food and beverage crops declined by an average of 15 percent in 1985 and those for agricultural raw materials by 12 percent, whereas those for metals fell by less than 3 percent. It should be noted, however, that prices of metals had been quite weak in the preceding year and had not responded to the recovery in industrial output as in the past. It is possible that metal prices have been subject both to secular shifts in production technology, as well as higher production levels in countries seeking to raise export earnings. A particular factor affecting the price of metals was the financial collapse of the International Tin Agreement (ITA) in the latter part of 1985. The exhaustion of the ITA's funds led to concerns for the orderly financing of trade in tin, and of trade in some other metals. As a result, metal prices fell by 6 percent in the fourth quarter of 1985.

Trade barriers and the associated price support policies of industrial countries were another factor that exerted a depressing influence on the international prices of traded commodities. This is a particularly serious problem for agricultural commodity exporters. For example, sugar-producing countries, and especially those for which sugar is a monoculture, have been severely affected by protection of domestic sugar producers in the European Community and the United States.

A development that was widely expected to induce a strengthening in the dollar price of primary commodities, although in fact it did not, was the depreciation of the dollar during 1985. It is generally accepted that real commodity prices (that is, commodity prices relative to the price of manufactures) are largely independent of exchange rates among major currencies. That is, a given depreciation of the dollar should lead eventually to roughly commensurate changes in both non-oil primary commodity prices and in world trade prices for manufactures. There is, however, less agreement as to how rapidly this tendency asserts itself. During 1985, this ambiguity left some scope for interpreting the observed real decline in commodity prices as a temporary and soon-to-be-reversed exchange rate factor. The plausibility of this hypothesis has, however, been undermined by the persistence of lower real commodity prices beyond what might reasonably be regarded as a transitional period. It would seem, therefore, that the supply factors discussed above provide the more satisfactory explanation of recent commodity price trends.

It should be noted that not all relative price changes were adverse to primary product exporting countries in 1985. The cost of borrowing—as measured by the six-month LIBOR—declined substantially, from 11.3 percent in 1984 to 8.6 percent in 1985. This change is particularly important to the market borrowers because interest payments are equivalent, on average, to about one fifth of their payments for merchandise imports.

World oil prices also declined in 1985, although on an annual average basis by considerably less than the average price of non-oil primary commodities. This limited decline, however, masked the increasing tenuousness of the prevailing price as the year wore on, reflecting the growing reliance on a single producer to support the price. As discussed in Supplementary Note 4 on the "World Oil Situation," the conditions in the oil market eventually led to far-reaching changes in the policies of the members of OPEC in the latter part of 1985. The major elements were a shift toward market-related prices and a substantial relaxation (or de facto abandonment) of the previous policy of concerted output restraint. The consequent large increase in oil production and exports of the major oil exporting countries quickly led to a substantial imbalance between demand and supply in early 1986. Prices in the spot markets for both crude oils and refined products began to fall sharply, with a major break occurring in the latter part of January. Although the average price of oil in international trade in the early part of 1986 cannot be estimated with any precision, spot market prices for some crude oils had, by mid-March 1986, fallen well below $15 a barrel. Prices in this period were also highly volatile, being influenced by speculative trading.

The commodity price movements described above led to a 2 percent deterioration in the merchandise terms of trade of developing countries in 1985. The terms of trade of fuel exporting countries, which import relatively few primary commodities, deteriorated by 4 percent, reflecting mainly the change in the price of oil relative to that of manufactures. The non-fuel exporting countries—which export a large amount of manufactures and benefit from the lower oil prices—experienced a much smaller deterioration in their terms of trade of just over 1 percent. Within the group of non-fuel exporting countries, the largest terms of trade deteriorations were, not surprisingly, concentrated in countries that export predominantly primary commodities. The terms of trade of these countries deteriorated by 3¼ percent (and by 5 percent if Brazil is excluded from this group). By contrast, exporters of manufactures, which are significant importers of both oil and other primary products, experienced virtually no change in their terms of trade for the second year in succession.

Prospects for foreign trade prices in 1986–87 are dominated by those for oil. As noted in Supplementary Note 4, the uncertainty attaching to oil prices is considerable and largely contingent on developments on the supply side of the oil market. If production should remain at the levels prevailing in the first quarter of 1985, there would be scope for significant further declines in spot prices from the $12–$14 prevailing in mid-March. If, on the other hand, production is significantly curtailed, oil prices could rise sharply. In the light of this uncertainty, the staff has adopted the working assumption that oil prices will average $15 a barrel over the period from the second quarter of 1986 to the end of 1987. Year on year, this implies a 40 percent drop in oil prices, expressed in terms of U.S. dollars, from 1985 to 1986.

Prospects for non-oil commodity prices in 1986 are heavily influenced by the effects of drought on Brazil's coffee crop. Coffee prices are projected to increase by 50 percent in 1986, and this accounts for virtually all of the expected 12 percent increase in the overall index of non-oil commodities. The price of manufactured goods entering world trade will be strongly affected by recent exchange rate changes and is projected to be some 14 percent above the 1985 level in dollar terms in 1986. Given the above constellation of price developments, and excluding the highly localized effect of the rise in coffee prices, the developing countries' terms of trade would deteriorate by almost 15 percent in 1986. The bulk of this drop would be experienced by the fuel exporters, which would incur a 37½ percent deterioration in their terms of trade. The terms of trade of primary product exporters, other than those that are heavily dependent on coffee, would worsen by 2 percent while those of exporters of manufactures, some of which are significant importers of both oil and other primary commodities, would improve by 2 percent.

Foreign Trade Volumes

A further source of disappointment to developing countries in 1985 was the unexpected weakness of world trade. In volume terms, world trade increased by only 2.9 percent in 1985, barely in step with the rise in world output. This is a significantly smaller rise than was expected a year ago when, on the basis of a projected 3.4 percent rise in world output, trade was expected to increase by 5.4 percent. The unexpected weakness of trade is partly traceable to the sharper-than-expected slowdown in activity in industrial countries, as a result of which the volume of developing countries' exports virtually stagnated in 1985. Imports into fuel exporting countries were also much lower than anticipated earlier in the year.

The commodity composition of developing countries' exports is one of the main factors that influence the degree to which growth in industrial countries is translated into demand for developing countries' exports (Chart 24). In recent years, non-fuel exporting countries have generally been able to sustain the growth of their total exports, in volume terms, at a much faster rate than the growth of industrial countries' output; the opposite has been the case, however, for the fuel exporting countries. Within the non-fuel exporting group, there have also been significant differences: the apparent income elasticity of demand for the exports of the exporters of manufactures has been over twice that of the primary product exporting countries.

Another factor that can have a decisive influence on export performance is price. This is particularly evident for the fuel exporting countries. The oil price increases of 1979–80 led to large declines in these countries' export volumes, both because of conservation by consumers and because of the development of alternative sources of supply. Changes in relative prices have also affected other developing country trade flows. Indeed, the very high apparent income elasticity of demand of industrial countries for manufactured goods from developing countries may in part reflect the growing price competitiveness of developing country producers.

A source of concern in this respect has been the effect of protectionism in industrial countries on developing countries' ability to increase their export earnings. Many of the most dynamic exports of developing countries are increasingly being constrained by restrictions. The problems are most evident for the

Chart 24. Developing Countries: Export Volumes and Industrial Countries' Real GDP, 1972–87[1]

(Indices: 1980 = 100)

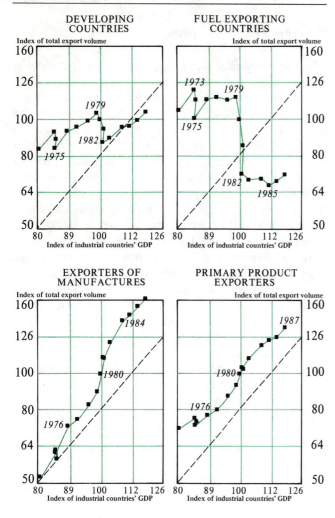

[1] Charts are in ratio scale on both the horizontal and vertical axes. Thus the slope of the line joining any two points indicates the apparent income elasticity of demand. The dashed lines indicate an income elasticity of demand of two and are shown for reference purposes.

simpler types of manufactures, such as shoes and textiles. But the problem is more widespread and covers a large number of the commodities or products which are both exported by developing countries and produced by industrial countries. A particular concern at the current juncture is the extent to which protectionism accounted for the very sharp slowing of developing country exports in 1985. Although the slowdown can be partially explained by cyclical factors, it is noteworthy that the deceleration was especially marked for the exporters of manufactures, the group most likely to be affected by quantitative restrictions.

Especially troublesome in this respect is the decline in the real exports of the heavily indebted countries in 1985 after two years of rapid increases. Although these countries' export performance depends upon many factors, including the quality of their own policies, it is essential to the resolution of these countries' payments difficulties that they not face undue restrictions on their exports.

The geographical distribution of a country's exports is another important influence affecting the link between industrial countries' output growth and developing countries' export volumes. In recent years, countries whose exports have traditionally been directed to the U.S. market have, not surprisingly, enjoyed a more buoyant export performance than developing countries generally.

A last factor which may weaken the direct relationship between the growth of output in industrial countries and developing countries' export volume is the scope that exists for expanding trade among developing countries. For example, intra-regional trade among developing countries in Asia has been growing, both in absolute terms and in relation to the region's exports to the rest of the world (Chart 25). Intra-regional trade in the Western Hemisphere has also been significant, although it has tended to decline in relative importance following the onset of the debt crisis. (This is both because of the weakness of the region's imports and because heavily indebted countries have been compelled to shift their exports away from trading partners in regional payments arrangements toward convertible currency markets, in order to earn the foreign exchange required to service debt.) The critical role of these intra-regional developments to overall performance is illustrated in Table 12. The recent much faster rise of total exports in Asia than in the Western Hemisphere may be seen to be very largely due to intra-regional trade.

The staff expects that export volume growth of developing countries will accelerate modestly in 1986–87, to a rate of about 5 percent per annum in the latter year. But the growth of trade volumes is likely to be distributed rather unevenly (Table 13). The agricultural exporters should achieve only average volume growth, while the mineral exporters would be below the average. The largest increases will probably once again be found among the exporters of manufactures. However, because of the disappointing performance of these countries' exports in 1985 and because of shifts in the geographic distribution of industrial country imports, these countries' exports are expected to increase at only about half their "normal" rate, given the cyclical circumstances expected to prevail over the forecast period. The moderate increase projected for the fuel exporters, following the strong

Chart 25. Developing Countries: Intra-Regional Trade, 1978–84

(In percent of total exports)

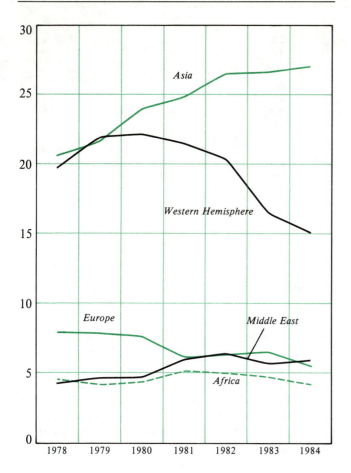

Table 12. Developing Countries: Growth of Exports in Value, 1980–84

(Changes, in percent; in terms of U.S. dollars)

	Asia	Western Hemisphere
Total exports	24	3
To own region	39	− 27
To other countries	19	12

downward trend since 1980, reflects both a significant expansion in non-oil exports of some of these countries and a moderate recovery in the volume of their oil exports as world oil demand begins to rise at a slightly more rapid rate.

Turning to the import side of the trade accounts, there has been a significant shift in recent years in the factors determining the level of real imports. During much of the 1970s and early 1980s, import needs were determined in the context of development plans and were sustained through external borrowing when the growth of export earnings was inadequate to finance them. After 1982, however, the availability of finance became an active constraint, and the level of imports became much more dependent on movements in the purchasing power of exports.

The result of these developments has been that imports have been subdued for the past several years. For developing countries as a group, the volume of imports in 1985 was still 5 percent below the 1981 peak. This behavior contrasts strongly with that in the

preceding decade and a half, when real imports grew at an average rate of over 8 percent per annum. Imports were at their weakest in 1982–83, as countries adjusted to low export receipts, sharply rising debt service burdens, and a marked reduction in the availability of external finance. With the recovery of the world economy, the easing of interest rates, and the stabilization of current account deficits, imports began to recover in 1984. Nevertheless, the overall rise was fairly modest and gave way to renewed stagnation in 1985 as the purchasing power of exports slackened once again.

The weakness of imports is distributed unevenly among developing countries (Table 13). The countries that encountered debt-servicing problems have been those most seriously affected. Not only were they the hardest hit by the rise in interest payments and the sudden unwillingness of private creditors to extend further credit, but they also included some of the economies most exposed to the international recession. As a result, these countries' imports declined by 15 percent both in 1982 and 1983 before stabilizing in 1984. Despite this import compression, their external positions remained precarious and, with a renewed terms of trade loss of 2½ percent in 1985, they were once again forced to curtail imports. Countries that avoided debt service problems, on the other hand, have experienced much more limited import cuts. Indeed, in only one recent year did their average import growth fall below 5 percent. This occurred in 1982 when a number of countries in this group took early action to reduce current account imbalances, and imports declined by a little less than 1 percent. However, the strength of these countries' trade flows also reflects their relatively low levels of external indebtedness and the concentration of their exports in manufacturing.

Imports by capital exporting developing countries, all of which are fuel exporters, followed a rather different trend, at least in terms of timing, from that of the two groups of capital importing countries just described. These countries' imports grew rapidly in the early years of this decade, rising by almost 50 percent from 1979 to 1982. Since then, however, large

Table 13. Developing Countries—By Predominant Export: Growth of Trade Volumes, 1981–87

(In percent)

	1981	1982	1983	1984	1985	1986–87
Growth in export volume						
Developing countries	−5.7	−8.1	2.9	7.1	0.4	4.6
Fuel exporters	−15.1	−16.5	−3.7	0.7	−4.1	3.4
Non-fuel exporters	6.5	0.7	8.3	11.7	3.4	5.0
Of which,						
Agricultural exporters	9.5	2.2	6.7	11.6	1.9	5.0
Mineral exporters	−9.1	−2.0	4.3	0.6	7.4	1.6
Exporters of manufactures	10.3	0.6	10.2	14.5	3.6	5.6
Growth in import volume						
Developing countries	7.1	−4.2	−3.2	2.2	−0.3	0.7
Fuel exporters	20.0	−1.6	−12.0	−4.5	−8.8	−11.6
Non-fuel exporters	1.5	−5.5	1.6	5.2	3.3	5.2
Of which,						
Agricultural exporters	−4.8	−5.7	−1.5	0.3	−2.2	7.9
Mineral exporters	12.7	−16.0	−13.4	4.3	−9.0	6.0
Exporters of manufactures	1.7	−4.9	6.5	8.9	9.3	5.3

declines in export earnings have led to substantial cuts in imports. As noted earlier, the fall in imports has proceeded at an accelerating rate and exceeded 15 percent in 1985.

Turning to prospects, the staff foresees a small decline in developing country imports in 1986 and only modest growth of about 2 percent in 1987. This stagnation in developing country imports is due entirely to the expected declines in the imports of the fuel exporters. Because of the fall in oil prices, the fuel exporting countries are expected to intensify existing adjustment policies. These will result in sharp reductions in import volumes, by 15 percent for the fuel exporting group in 1986, and by 8 percent in 1987. However, there are likely to be significant differences between the two groups of fuel exporters stemming both from the countries' external financial positions and from the intensity of the countries' recent adjustment efforts.

Since 1982 the capital exporting countries have increasingly attempted to protect the strength of their net foreign asset position by compressing imports in line with reductions in export earnings. However, the magnitude of the price shock in 1986, in combination with the increasing difficulty of curbing imports further, suggests that adjustment of imports to the loss of export earnings in 1986–87 will not be as great, in proportionate terms, as it was in 1985. Nevertheless, imports are expected to be cut sharply, by almost 18 percent in volume in 1986 and by a further 13 percent in 1987. As a result, the capital exporting countries' trade balance will begin to improve in 1987, although import volume will then be only half of the 1982 level. The improvement in the current account in that year

will be more marked because of the accompanying efforts in these countries to boost and diversify exports and to curtail service and transfer payments. The latter reductions will have a significant adverse impact on those countries which have been major recipients of these payments.

The capital importing fuel exporting countries were obliged by external financing constraints to adjust more vigorously during 1982–85 than were the capital exporters. Against this background, as well as that of no substantive improvement in living standards during the 1980s, national authorities in the indebted fuel exporting countries are likely therefore to attempt to phase adjustment over several years. In particular, these countries are expected to make major efforts to increase exports other than oil, to increase external borrowing, and, if need be, to draw on official reserves. Notwithstanding these actions, cuts in import volumes will be severe: import volumes are expected to decline by 12¼ percent in 1986, and by a further 3¼ percent in 1987, by which time import volume will be only three fifths of the 1981 level (Chart 18).

For the non-fuel exporting countries, positive import growth is projected for 1986–87 at a rate (5¼ percent annually) which is only marginally lower than the long-run average for the group. Any faster growth of imports by these countries would lead to increases in current account deficits and imply an increased ability or willingness on their part to step up borrowing from commercial sources. The chief exceptions are the coffee exporters (other than Brazil), which, because of the very rapid increase in their export earnings, are expected to increase their imports by nearly 14 percent in 1986.

External Financing

The external financing situation of most capital importing developing countries remained as tight in 1985 as it had been in 1984, and current account deficits were limited accordingly. Nevertheless, there were some encouraging signs that countries may have completed the main part of the adjustment to the reduced levels of borrowing from private creditors. These signs included the leveling out of payments arrears outstanding, the continued, albeit modest, rebuilding of official reserves, the successful conclusion of a number of rescheduling arrangements, and the reduction in the net use of Fund credit. Nevertheless, external financing constraints remain severe and are likely to continue to be so for many countries until such time as their creditworthiness is re-established.

Four developments that characterized the payments position of capital importing developing countries in 1981–84 continued to be important in 1985. First, the deficit on goods, services, and private transfers, which had been reduced by almost two thirds from 1981 to 1984, remained at approximately its new lower level in 1985. It was thus largely covered by two relatively stable sources of finance: non-debt-creating flows and long-term borrowing from official creditors. Much of the reduction in deficits after 1981 was, of course, in response to the loss of access to private sources of credit. Net borrowing from private creditors fell from $73 billion in 1981 to less than $11 billion in 1985.

A second important trend in recent years has been the curbing of capital flight. The outflow of residents' capital from the capital importing countries (defined as net asset transactions plus recorded errors and omissions) declined from $36½ billion in 1982 to $10 billion in 1985. Capital outflows are expected to stabilize in 1986–87. The reduction in capital outflows had a number of causes. Perhaps the most important factor in reducing capital flight has been the reduced level of capital inflows, which, because of the resulting shortages of foreign exchange, has restricted the ability of residents to purchase foreign assets. In addition, some countries have introduced adjustment measures that have increased the attractiveness of domestic financial assets compared with foreign assets—through increases in domestic interest rates, for instance, and devaluation of overvalued currencies—and that ought to have a lasting effect on capital flight. Other countries, however, have delayed the adoption of appropriate adjustment policies or have allowed slippages to occur in the implementation of an orderly adjustment strategy.

A third development is that the rate of growth of external debt has slowed substantially. This deceleration occurred because cuts in deficits on goods, services, and private transfers left deficits at levels that could more nearly be financed with non-debt-creating flows. Furthermore, as just noted, domestic adjustment in many countries, by helping to limit capital flight, reduced the need to borrow to finance outflows of residents' capital. Consequently, the rate of growth of total debt has fallen sharply: from 16½ percent in 1981 to 5½ percent in 1985 in terms of U.S. dollars. (The 1985 figure would have been even lower if the depreciation of the dollar had not caused the value of existing debt in non-dollar currencies to rise.) In 1986–87 the value of outstanding debt is expected to continue to rise at 5½ percent, in part because of valuation effects.

Fourth, progress in strengthening the balance between external assets and liabilities, as well as in improving the maturity structure of external debt, has continued to be made. Reserves have increased in value by almost one third since the end of 1982, and the reserves-to-imports ratio, at 22¾ percent in 1985, is now at its highest level since 1979. The accumulation of arrears, which had been a record $10½ billion in 1982, declined to $1½ billion in 1984. In 1985, there was a small net repayment of arrears (a reduction in the outstanding arrears), for the first time since 1979.

Part of the reduction in arrears was attributable to the successful conclusion of a series of annual and multiyear rescheduling agreements (MYRAs) (Table 14). MYRAs have the merit of stabilizing the debt repayments schedule over the medium term for countries that are seen to be pursuing appropriate medium-term adjustment policies. Consequently, MYRAs are in some respects more closely related to the voluntary arrangements for the early refinancing of debt that were common in the late 1970s than to the

Table 14. Capital Importing Developing Countries: Rescheduled Debt Service, 1980–87

(In billions of U.S. dollars)

	1980	1981	1982	1983	1984	1985	1986	1987
Capital importing developing countries	4.7	2.0	6.8	21.5	36.8	31.6	31.7	32.9
Of which,								
Africa	0.8	1.4	0.4	2.7	4.2	4.5	4.1	2.2
Europe	3.0	0.1	1.8	2.5	1.8	2.0	1.4	1.3
Western Hemisphere	0.9	0.5	4.4	16.3	30.6	23.0	23.0	27.2

"distress" arrangements for annual debt reschedulings that became common in the first half of the 1980s. More generally, rescheduling arrangements have become an increasingly accepted method of refinancing outstanding debt for many countries which have encountered debt-servicing difficulties and are not yet ready to resume borrowing on a spontaneous basis. The sum forecast for debt rescheduling in 1986–87 does not, therefore, necessarily indicate a persistence of debt servicing-problems at the same intensity as in 1983–84.

The problems associated with rebuilding creditor confidence show clearly in the external financing situation of the market borrowers. These countries were the most affected by the increased reluctance of private creditors to lend to developing countries. In response, their deficit on goods, services, and private transfers was cut from $74 billion in 1982 to less than $1 billion in 1985; outflows of their residents' capital fell from $33 billion to $9 billion in the same period; their official reserves were rebuilt by $27 billion in 1984–85; and arrears were reduced by $3 billion in the same two years. Yet net borrowing from private creditors has fallen in every year since 1981, from $76 billion in 1981 to $4½ billion in 1985.

There are three principal reasons why these adjustments have not elicited a greater response from private creditors. First, creditors remain skeptical about the ongoing commitment of national authorities to sound financial and market-oriented structural adjustment policies. Until creditors become persuaded of the underlying creditworthiness of countries—of their ability to service debt—they are unlikely to be forthcoming with new lending. Second, the process of rebuilding creditor confidence in any case takes time. The market borrowers rescheduled more than $80 billion of debt service that was due to be paid during 1982–85, and rescheduling arrangements in place or in immediate prospect will defer a further $52 billion of payments in 1986–87. Creditors are obviously concerned to see how these countries will cope with the new payments schedules. Third, some of the creditworthy debtor countries may now be averse to both the cost and risks associated with market sources of finance. The market borrowers have in fact borrowed as much from official creditors as from private creditors since 1982. These official inflows, in combination with non-debt-creating flows, constitute a much less expensive source of funds than market borrowing. Moreover, some countries appear to have decided that it is not only expensive, but also risky, to depend on the market sources of finance.

The official borrowers, by contrast, have traditionally relied almost exclusively on official transfers and on long-term borrowing from official creditors to finance their deficit on goods, services, and private transfers. The result has been a considerable stability of net resource inflows—a stability that has enabled the official borrowers to avoid the severe current account adjustment problems that confronted the market borrowers. It is only when the official borrowers have lost the confidence of their official creditors, especially that of the export credit guarantee agencies (for example, as a result of the incurrence of arrears to these agencies), that the cost in terms of the loss of access to credit has been considerable.

The weakness of the official borrowers' reserve position is therefore a cause of concern because the availability of reserves can mean the difference between prompt payment of debt service and the emergence of arrears. The stock of official reserves held by the official borrowers was only $9 billion at the end of 1985. At such a level, reserves were equivalent to only eight weeks of imports. (In 1978, by contrast, reserves were almost three months of imports.) Clearly, the official borrowers need to rebuild reserves in order to reduce the risk that unexpected adverse developments might precipitate debt-servicing problems that could subsequently be magnified by the loss of access to new loans from official creditors.

Three other groups of capital importing countries also merit particular attention: the heavily indebted countries—because of their recent history of debt-servicing difficulties and low growth; the indebted fuel exporting countries—because of the prospective weakness in their export earnings; and the small low-income countries—because of the growing size of their debt ratios.

The reluctance of private creditors to resume spontaneous lending to many capital importing countries is causing particular difficulties for the 15 heavily indebted countries mentioned in the U.S. debt initiative. Their import volumes fell by two fifths between 1981 and 1985, in large part because the availability of private credit contracted sharply, and the growth of real GDP has been quite sluggish. The U.S. debt initiative has two main features. First, debtor countries are expected—in collaboration with the Fund and the World Bank—to intensify their pursuit of sound macroeconomic and structural adjustment policies designed to facilitate a reactivation of growth. Second, commercial and multilateral development banks have been asked to increase their lending to these countries during 1986–88, by $20 billion for the commercial banks and $9 billion for the World Bank and the Inter-American Development Bank.

A successful implementation of the plan would clearly ease the financing constraints on the 15 countries. For example, the $29 billion of additional lending, phased evenly over the three years, would enable the countries to increase their imports by about 12½ percent in value compared to the 1985 level. However, because of uncertainties regarding the commitment of authorities in the debtor countries on the requisite policies and regarding the export earnings prospects of these countries, such financing has not yet been incorporated into the staff's projections for a number of these countries. Net borrowing from all private creditors is projected to be negative for these countries taken as a group in 1986–87. It should be noted, however, that this overall development masks opposing tendencies for subgroups of countries. In particular, significant reductions in bank exposure are anticipated for several countries where adjustment efforts are lagging, whereas significant lending is anticipated for countries which are carrying out policies of structural adjustment.

A second category of countries that is a source of concern in the forecast period is the capital importing fuel exporters. These countries are expected to experience a deterioration in their terms of trade of about one third from 1985 to 1987. Moreover, because about half of the group has recently experienced debt-servicing problems, there is a risk that the weakening of their terms of trade might precipitate further debt-servicing difficulties and could result in further large cuts in import volumes. Indeed, external payments arrears are forecast to increase by about $2 billion annually during 1986–87. However, these countries undertook significant adjustment measures in 1982–85, which resulted in a strengthening in their balance of payments position during that period (Table 15). Further adjustment is expected from most countries in this group, which, in combination with some use of

Table 15. Developing Countries—Capital Importing Fuel Exporters: Current Account, Debt, and Debt Service, 1981–87

(In percent of exports of goods and services, or indices)

	1981–82	1984–85	1986–87
Current account balance[1]	−18	2	−18
Debt	148	182	255
Debt service payments	25	35	42
Memorandum			
Terms of trade (index, 1980 = 100)	104	96	63
Import volume (index, 1980 = 100)	112	86	74

[1] Including official transfers.

Fund credit and additional borrowing from official and private creditors, should ensure that cuts in import volumes in 1986–87, though sizable, will not have to match the decline in real export earnings. However, prospects for this group are extremely sensitive to the future path of oil prices and to the attitude of their creditors. The staff expects that these countries will be able to attract the necessary additional financing only if adjustment measures of adequate intensity are adopted urgently. Any delay by these countries, or any attempt to minimize the degree of adjustment, would probably stimulate both a shift away from these countries in the portfolios of foreign private creditors, and a further wave of capital flight by the resident private sector.

A third group that is the focus of concern comprises the group of small low-income countries. In relation to exports, these countries' debt is more than double the average for all capital importing countries (Table 16).

Table 16. Small Low-Income Countries and Capital Importing Countries: Debt and Debt Service, 1981–87

(In percent of exports of goods and services)

	1981	1982	1983	1984	1985	1986–87[1]
Small low-income countries						
Debt	269	321	335	345	383	349
Debt service payments	18	19	20	23	30	29
Of which,						
Interest payments	8	9	9	9	13	13
Memorandum						
Implicit interest rate[2]	3	3	3	3	3	4
Capital importing countries						
Debt	123	149	159	153	163	164
Debt service payments	21	24	22	23	24	23
Of which,						
Interest payments	11	14	13	13	13	12
Memorandum						
Implicit interest rate[2]	9	9	8	9	8	8

[1] Period average.
[2] Interest payments as a share of debt. In percent per annum.

Moreover, these countries have borrowed relatively heavily in recent years, increasing their debt at more than 8 percent per annum during 1983–85. The small low-income countries have been able to service this large volume of debt because much of it has been on concessional, fixed-interest terms. However, the level of concessional debt is such that debt service payments have reached high levels. These countries' debt service ratio was still below that of the countries with recent debt-servicing problems in 1985, but the two groups' ratios are expected to be nearly equal by 1987. There are evident dangers for the small low-income countries in this situation: approximately one third of their export earnings is required to service debt, and their margin for financial maneuver is further limited by the fact that their reserves cover only slightly more than one month's imports.

External Debt

The growth of external debt of all capital importing countries, taken together, has recently proceeded at a modest pace. As noted above, the rate of growth, in dollar terms, decelerated from about 15 percent per annum in 1981–82 to 5½ percent in 1985. The deceleration was the result of the tightening of external financial conditions described above, and of the greater relative importance of non-debt-creating flows in financing current account deficits. The rate of growth of the dollar value of debt is expected to stabilize during 1986–87, when total debt is forecast to rise by an average 5½ percent annually. Part of this sustained growth of debt reflects the increase in the dollar value of existing borrowing in non-dollar currencies—so that the underlying rate of new debt creation is rather less.

Debt ratios are affected both by the growth of debt in absolute terms and by fluctuations in export earnings. Indeed, in the short term, changes in exports often affect the ratio more strongly than changes in the rate of debt accumulation. Overall, the debt-to-export ratio rose steeply through 1983, but receded in 1984 in response to the cyclical rise in export earnings. However, the renewed weakness of export receipts in 1985, combined with the continued growth of debt, caused the debt ratio of the capital importing developing countries to rise to a new peak of 163 percent. The small low-income countries had the highest debt ratio, but the Western Hemisphere, which is mostly middle income, also recorded a high debt ratio, of 295 percent. Both groups have experienced above-average increases in their debt ratios since 1978. Whereas the debt ratio of all capital importing countries increased by about one fifth between 1978 and 1985, the Western Hemisphere countries increased their debt ratio by one third and small low-income countries by two thirds.

Debt service payments have shown considerable volatility in recent years as a result of debt rescheduling agreements. The interest payments ratio of all capital importing countries—a series that has been less distorted by debt reschedulings than the series for total debt service payments—increased from 7 percent in 1978 to 13½ percent in 1982 before declining to 13 percent in 1985 as interest rates eased. LIBOR fell by 3¾ percentage points between the third quarter of 1984 and the fourth quarter of 1985, and the recent downward movement in long-term U.S. interest rates is likely to exert further downward pressures on the interest rates paid by developing countries during the forecast period. The reductions in market interest rates have provided some relief to capital importing countries, particularly to the market borrowers. Interest payments by all capital importing countries are projected to stabilize at about $74 billion annually in 1986–87, some 2½ percent above the level of payments in 1984. But the interest payments ratio is expected to continue to fall, to about 12 percent in 1987.

The interest payments ratio of the market borrowers is expected to decline more rapidly than the average for all capital importing countries. The market borrowers' interest payments ratio peaked at 15¾ percent in 1982, and remained at high levels during 1983–85. However, the ratio is expected to fall by ½ a percentage point in 1986 and by a further 1¼ percentage points in 1987. The official borrowers, however, have been substantially unaffected by the reduction in interest rates. Their interest payments ratio has been pulled up by the growth of their debt, from under 5 percent in 1979 to 11 percent in 1985. A further increase to 11½ percent is expected in 1986–87.

The debt service ratios discussed above do not include the servicing costs associated with some reserve-related liabilities, notably Fund credit. Servicing costs incurred as a result of using Fund credit have increased since 1978, but, at 1¼ percent of export earnings in 1985, are still relatively small for the capital importing countries as a whole. However, for some groups of countries these servicing costs are relatively more important, being equivalent to 6½ percent of the small low-income countries' exports in 1985, for example, and to 4¼ percent of sub-Saharan Africa's exports (see Statistical Appendix Table A52). If debt service were reported inclusive of payments to the Fund, the consolidated debt service ratios would have been 36¼ percent for the small low-income countries in 1985 and 33 percent for sub-Saharan Africa.

Another relatively neglected topic in relation to the capital importing countries' external indebtedness has been the question of the net debt of these countries.

The gross debt of the capital importing developing countries is estimated at $883 billion in 1985, but the net debt—that is, gross debt less total foreign assets—was probably less than half that amount. Rough estimates of the stock of all foreign assets held by the capital importing countries, excluding the offshore banking centers, suggest that these amounted to some $450 billion in 1985, of which official reserves accounted for about $138 billion. The balance consists mainly of trade-related credits, working balances of trading companies held abroad, and the like, but also includes flight capital. The last factor helps to explain why Western Hemisphere countries hold the largest stocks of foreign assets in value terms. However, the non-oil Middle Eastern countries had the largest stock of assets in relation to exports of goods and services (Chart 26). The existence of the large stocks of foreign assets represents an opportunity for the capital importing countries to ease their financial problems through pursuit of policies conducive to the repatriation of some of the capital that flowed out.

Chart 26. Capital Importing Developing Countries—By Region: External Debt, Foreign Assets, and Official Reserves, 1978–87[1]

(In percent of exports of goods and services)

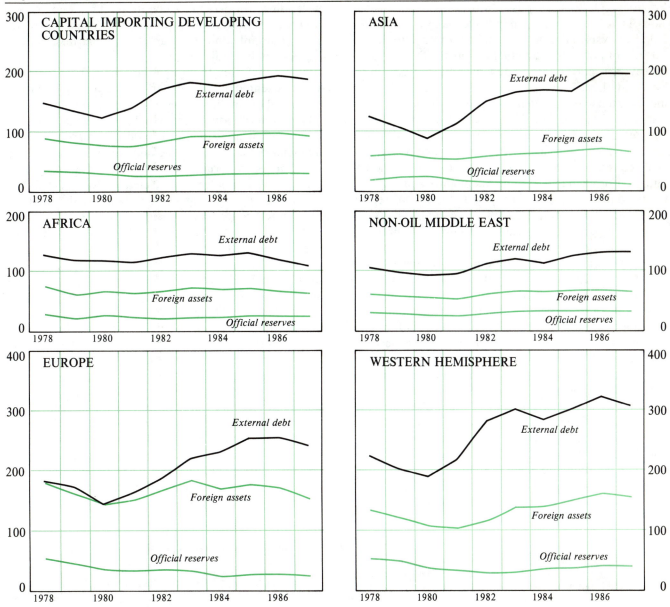

[1] Excluding seven major offshore banking centers.

Chapter IV

Policy Interactions in Industrial Countries

Discussions of policy interactions among countries have always been an important feature of the World Economic Outlook exercise. In the past these discussions have been fairly general and have avoided detailed analysis of the specific implications of alternative settings of policy in individual countries. During 1985, however, reports were issued by both the Group of Ten and the Group of Twenty-Four that called for more extensive and detailed presentations of such issues. The Group of Ten report requested that a chapter of the *World Economic Outlook* be devoted to "analyzing the repercussions of national policies of G-10 countries and of their interaction in the determination of exchange rate developments and international adjustment." The Group of Twenty-Four report states, inter alia, that "The WEO should clearly spell out the repercussions and interactions of national policies of the major industrial countries and contain fairly specific proposals of policies for these countries." This chapter is an initial response to these suggestions. (See also Chapter II for a detailed analysis of recent and prospective balance of payments and exchange rate developments in industrial countries.)

The particular focus of this chapter is on the consequences of the plans to undertake major action to reduce and eventually eliminate the fiscal deficit in the United States over the medium term (defined as the period through 1991). The second section outlines the Fund staff's medium-term "baseline" scenario (in which the U.S. fiscal deficit is substantially reduced) and discusses the potential effects of a variant scenario in which additional expenditure cuts are implemented in the United States.[1] The third section discusses a number of possibly related developments that might alter the outcome of these scenarios, including shifts in monetary policies, changes in non-U.S. fiscal policy, and other possible developments such as an increase in lending to developing countries. The final section reviews the circumstances facing individual countries that would influence their ability to undertake various types of policy adjustments.

One conclusion that might be drawn from the analysis presented in this paper is that a major shift in fiscal policy in the United States would have large enough international effects that a number of countries might find it appropriate to modify temporarily their financial policies during the adjustment period. However, it is important to emphasize that economic forecasting is not an exact science. A major shift in fiscal strategy, such as the one being undertaken by the United States, can change past behavioral relationships. In particular, the speed with which proposed expenditure cuts lead to favorable financial market responses may be positively affected by shifts in expectations. More generally, private market responses to government policy initiatives can differ from those predicted by economic models and can thwart attempts to "fine tune" the international economy in response to disturbances. The first task of policy must be to establish a stable environment for the planning and implementation of private sector decisions. Of course, this prescription need not imply that policy settings should remain unchanged in the face of major external disturbances. Indeed, attempting to hold constant such variables as interest rates, the growth of monetary aggregates, or the level of government borrowing, at times when policy changes in other countries were generating international repercussions, might itself be destabilizing.

The Medium-Term Scenario

The background for any discussion of policy interactions among industrial countries must include a set

---

[1] The expenditure cuts incorporated in the staff's baseline scenario represent a cautious estimate of possible deficit reduction measures; this scenario is not intended to prejudge the extent of the cuts that will eventually be implemented.

of assumptions about the policies to be pursued and the economic outturn that those policies imply. Arriving at realistic policy assumptions is not an easy task, especially under current circumstances, when the United States is in the process of undertaking a major reorientation of fiscal policy over the medium term. Specifically, legislation has been enacted (the so-called Gramm-Rudman-Hollings Act) that is aimed at eliminating the budget deficit of the federal government by 1991. (For more details on this legislation, see Supplementary Note 1.) This legislation designates maximum deficits for each fiscal year through 1991; however, it does not specify how the reductions are to be achieved, and constitutional questions have been raised regarding the mechanism for imposing deficit reductions in the event that the President and the Congress are unable to agree on a budget. A final decision on this matter by the U.S. Supreme Court has not yet been issued.

The most important point to emphasize about the implementation of the Gramm-Rudman-Hollings legislation is that it has reversed the pattern that had prevailed over the past few years, during which time fiscal deficits in the United States had grown to proportions that had threatened the stability of the economy. In the absence of corrective action, these deficits would have been expected to rise still further (Chart 27). As had been argued in several previous *World Economic Outlook* reports, the continued absorption of savings by the U.S. federal government at this pace would eventually have led to one or more serious consequences. By 1983 and 1984, the fiscal deficit, as well as other factors, had contributed to very high real interest rates, a sharp appreciation of the U.S. dollar, and a serious weakening of the current account balance. Over the medium term, real interest rates could have remained very high, crowding out private investment; economic growth might have slowed down more than expected; monetary policy might eventually have been loosened, supporting growth in the short run but leading to an intensification of inflationary pressures in the longer run; and the dollar could have come under severe downward pressure as the size of U.S. deficits and external debt mounted. Although the outcome of the pursuit of unsustainable policies is difficult to foresee, quite possibly some combination of these pressures would have occurred, with adverse effects on growth, both in the United States and abroad.

The shift in policies toward a greater commitment to reducing fiscal deficits in the United States has diminished the likelihood that financial imbalances will pose a major threat to the health of the world economy, and it is expected to lead to a much more favorable outcome both for the United States and for other

Chart 27. United States: Ratios of Federal Government Deficits to GNP, 1970–91[1]

(In percent)

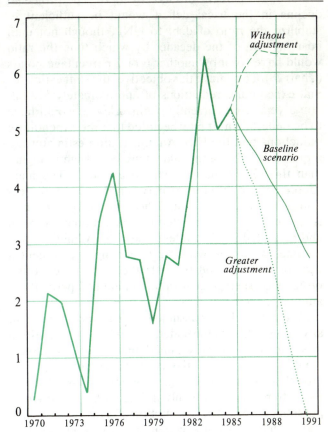

[1] Data are on a fiscal year basis, with actual data through fiscal year 1985. The assumptions for the projections are described in the text. The fiscal year in the United States ends September 30. Prior to fiscal year 1977 the fiscal year ended in June, but the current definition has been applied to the whole period in this chart.

countries than could have been achieved without such an adjustment. It appears already to have had beneficial effects on market expectations and on confidence, as evidenced by a substantial decline in long-term interest rates and a surge in stock prices. Nonetheless, the magnitude of the effort that has now begun is large enough that one cannot ignore the possibility that less-than-full achievement of the fiscal targets may occur. Given the determination of the U.S. Administration to avoid raising taxes, reducing the federal government deficit from 5 percent of GNP in fiscal year 1986 to zero by 1991 will require either very favorable economic growth or large expenditure cuts.

The Baseline Scenario

For expositional purposes, the baseline scenario takes a cautious approach, neither assuming the continuation of large deficits nor assuming their complete elimination. It assumes that the United States will cut spending by enough to reduce the fiscal deficit by half, to about 2½ percent of GNP by 1991. The projected decline in the fiscal deficit would be sufficient to stabilize the ratio of debt to GNP, though not until near the end of the decade, by which time the ratio would have risen by another 6 or 7 percentage points (Chart 28). To achieve this objective, the staff estimates that expenditure reductions of approximately $12 billion a year from currently planned levels would have to be undertaken. It may be noted that the expenditure reductions that the U.S. Administration estimates are required to balance the budget are only slightly higher than this ($15 billion a year on average). The main sources of the differences between the staff's projections of the fiscal deficit and those of the U.S. Administration lie in the projected rate of economic growth and projected interest rates. The U.S. Administration assumes a real growth rate averaging 3¾ percent a year over the period to 1991; the staff, by contrast, projects an average growth rate of about 3 percent per annum.

Monetary policy is assumed to be framed to prevent any acceleration of the underlying inflation rate. Within this constraint, it is assumed that monetary targets would accommodate the continuation of economic growth at the rate that is in prospect for 1986–87, and thereafter at a rate roughly in line with the growth of potential output. The assumption of a monetary policy stance that does not accommodate inflation, together with a declining value of the dollar in exchange markets (see below), are expected to lead to some tightening of domestic monetary conditions (as the real money stock is reduced). Interest rates would therefore be under conflicting pressures in the medium term. The downward movement of the fiscal deficit would be an important factor relieving pressures on real interest rates. On the other hand, the passing of the transitory effects on inflation of oil prices, together with the tightness of monetary conditions just referred to, would tend to work in the other direction. The staff has assumed that the balance of these forces would lead to interest rates remaining lower over the medium term than they were in 1985. However, this interest rate assumption (that short-term rates would average about 4 percent in real terms) is still significantly above the U.S. Administration's assumption of 1¾ percent.

Fiscal policies in other industrial countries are assumed to be broadly consistent (in direction, if not always in degree) with the declared intentions of the authorities concerned. A substantial fiscal consolidation is assumed in Canada, while in European countries and Japan a moderate further withdrawal of fiscal stimulus is assumed. These developments are thought

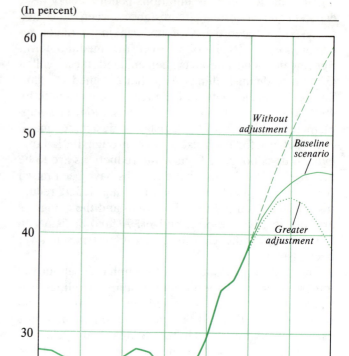

Chart 28. United States: Ratios of Federal Government Debt to GNP, 1970–91[1]

(In percent)

[1] See note 1 to Chart 27.

to be broadly consistent with a reduction in the real exchange rate for the U.S. and Canadian dollars relative to the currencies of other major countries.

The exchange rate assumption underlying the baseline scenario is that the U.S. and Canadian dollars will decline in real terms against the other major currencies by an average of 2½ percent each year from 1988 through 1991.[2] Real bilateral exchange rates among the currencies of European countries and Japan are assumed to remain unchanged.

Against the background of these assumptions, output in the major industrial countries is projected to grow at rates close to the rate of growth of potential output (which is estimated to be about 2¾ to 3 percent per year) throughout the medium-term period (Table 17). Fiscal policy would be exerting a contractionary impact throughout the projection period, but to a relatively

---

[2] In making projections for 1986 and 1987, the conventional working assumption is used that the pattern of real exchange rates among major currencies will be unchanged from that prevailing at a given base period (in this case, early March 1986).

Table 17. Industrial Countries: Outcome of Baseline Scenario, 1984–91

	1984	1985	1986	1987	Average 1988–91
Real GNP			*(Annual change, in percent)*		
Industrial countries	4.8	2.8	3.0	3.2	3.0
Of which:					
United States	6.5	2.2	2.9	3.6	2.9
Europe	2.4	2.3	2.9	2.5	2.7
Japan	5.1	4.6	3.0	3.2	4.1
GNP deflator					
Industrial countries	4.3	3.9	3.4	3.0	3.7
Of which: United States	4.2	3.3	3.3	3.0	3.8
Unemployment			*(Percent of labor force)*		1991
Seven major industrial countries	7.7	7.6	7.6	7.4	6.7
Of which: United States	7.5	7.2	7.0	6.7	6.4
U.S. dollar			*(Annual change, in percent)*		1988–91
Nominal effective exchange rate	8.0	4.5	−11.2	—	−2.1
Interest rates			*(In percent)*		
Six-month LIBOR	11.3	8.6	7.8	7.3	8.0
World trade			*(Annual change, in percent)*		
Volume	8.7	2.9	3.3	3.8	5.0
Unit value (in U.S. dollars)	−2.4	−1.7	6.2	3.6	4.5

mild extent (a withdrawal of stimulus equivalent to somewhat over ¼ of 1 percent of GDP a year for the industrial countries as a group). The dampening effects of such a fiscal stance would tend to be offset in the short run by the favorable effects of lower prices for oil and primary commodities, and in the longer run by the private sector responses to the reduction in government borrowing requirements. Inflation would continue at rates close to those prevailing in 1985 (between 3½ and 4 percent for the average of industrial countries). On the assumption that oil prices average $15 a barrel in 1986–87, there would be downward pressure on inflation during these two years, but as this effect passed, inflation would tend to edge up thereafter. Japan and the Federal Republic of Germany are expected to continue to experience rather lower inflation than the other large countries.

The Effect of Additional Expenditure Cuts

In order to assess how the baseline scenario might be affected by the implementation of a more ambitious deficit-reduction program in the United States, it is necessary to specify assumptions about how the program would be put into effect. In what follows, it is assumed that the reduction would be achieved primarily through further spending reductions across the

whole spectrum of government activities. The staff estimates that the achievement of a balanced budget by 1991 would require additional spending cuts (beyond those assumed in the baseline scenario) averaging $35 billion (about ¾ of 1 percent of GNP) a year.

A further assumption underlying this variant of the medium-term scenario is that monetary policy in the United States (expressed as the target rate of growth of the monetary aggregates) is unchanged, and that fiscal and monetary policies in other countries are also held constant. The assumption of unchanged policies, while analytically convenient, may be regarded as somewhat unrealistic, and the implications of relaxing it are considered further in the third section below.

Empirical estimates of the effects of this more ambitious program, based on past behavioral relationships, suggest that output growth would decline, relative to the baseline projection, by some 1 percent a year for perhaps two or three years, followed by small increases thereafter.[3] Over the longer run, output would be expected to rise above its baseline path, owing to the stimulus to capital formation from the expected decline in interest rates and to the strength-

---
[3] The estimates discussed in this section are based in part on a small model (MINIMOD) developed in the Research Department at the Fund, whose properties are similar to those of a representative group of large-scale internationally linked models.

ening of the current account balance from the expected depreciation of the real exchange rate.

It is possible, of course, that the implementation of additional spending cuts would have only a minor negative effect on economic activity in the short run, if the private sector responded with unusual vigor when faced with the prospect of reduced absorption of savings from the government. In assessing this possibility, however, two considerations should be borne in mind. First, the beneficial effects on market expectations and behavior are already reflected, to some extent, in the baseline scenario, under which output in the United States is projected to grow at rates at or slightly above the rate of growth of potential output in spite of significant cuts in government spending. Second, the spending cuts in this variant scenario are assumed to take place over a number of years; even though the long-run benefits of the first round of cuts might be felt fairly quickly, it could take some time for the net effect of the whole program to be positive. Nonetheless, it must be emphasized that the long-run effects of such a program—which will be positive in any event—could come rather sooner than expected.

Under this variant, the decline in real interest rates relative to the path in the baseline scenario is estimated to amount to around 2 percentage points in the latter years of the program. In spite of the slower growth of nominal incomes, the ratio of government debt to GNP would peak (in 1988) at a level some 3 percentage points below the peak of the baseline scenario. It would then decline steadily, falling to around 38 percent by 1991 (Chart 28).

The effects on exchange rates are even more difficult to assess than those on other major variables, corresponding to the lack of clear empirical evidence on the subject. On the one hand, it seems likely that fiscal expansion played an important role in generating the appreciation of the U.S. dollar during the early part of the present decade, so that a reversal of this expansion might be expected to have the opposite effect. On the other hand, the size (and even the direction) of the effect is open to considerable uncertainty, given the other factors at work and the importance of expectations. Nonetheless, it is reasonable to expect a sizable depreciation. As noted above, interest rates would tend to be lower in the United States, especially in the later years of the program; if monetary and fiscal policies in other countries were unchanged, a depreciation of the dollar against other currencies would be required in order to make people willing to continue to hold the outstanding stock of dollar-denominated assets. For illustrative purposes, it is assumed here that the real value of the U.S. and Canadian dollars would fall by 10 percent against other industrial country currencies relative to their values under the baseline scenario, with half of the depreciation occurring in 1987 and the other half in 1988.[4]

Inflation in the United States (measured by changes in the GNP deflator) is expected to be reduced slightly in the medium term as a consequence of the fiscal retrenchment, even allowing for the effects of the assumed depreciation of the dollar. That is, the deflationary effects on the U.S. GNP deflator of declining domestic demand and of the stimulus to aggregate supply are expected to be somewhat greater than the inflationary effects of the dollar depreciation. However, prices of internationally traded goods would be expected to rise in dollar terms by perhaps 6 percent or 7 percent, relative to the baseline, over about a two-year period. The U.S. current account deficit would be substantially reduced as a result of both the decline in domestic demand and the depreciation of the dollar. Whereas the baseline scenario shows the current account deficit falling from about 2½ percent of GNP in 1986 to about 1¼ percent in 1991, the further fiscal cuts in this variant are estimated to have the effect of producing a small current account surplus by 1991. This would partly reflect lower imports in response to a slowing of economic growth, and partly the effects on competitiveness of the further decline in the dollar.

The impact of additional expenditure cuts in the United States on economic activity in other industrial countries operates through two channels. On the one hand, lower growth of demand in the short term in the United States and the depreciation of the U.S. dollar have negative direct effects on output in other countries, through a weakening in these countries' real foreign balance. On the other hand, the appreciation of other currencies would tend to reduce inflationary pressures in those countries, with favorable effects on real incomes and aggregate supply conditions. Empirical evidence suggests that the balance of these effects would be to cause a temporary decline in output in the other industrial countries, taken together.

Japan and Canada, which have the closest direct trading linkages with the United States, would be most affected by any change in the growth rates in the United States, although the effects would be expected to occur with something of a lag. European countries, which conduct a much smaller portion of their trade with the United States than do either Canada or Japan,

---

[4] In the baseline scenario, real exchange rates are assumed unchanged in 1986–87 from the pattern prevailing in March 1986. Thereafter the U.S. and Canadian dollars are assumed to depreciate in real terms by 2½ percent a year from 1988–91. Thus, under the variant scenario, the real exchange rates of the U.S. and Canadian dollars against other currencies are implicitly assumed to fall by 5 percent in 1987, by 7½ percent in 1988, and by 2½ percent a year thereafter.

should experience somewhat smaller short-term effects. Thus it is unlikely that growth rates in any of the European countries would decline, relative to baseline, by much more than ¼ of 1 percent, given the output effects described above for the United States. Subsequently, as the long-run stimulus to growth begins to accumulate, these initial declines would tend to be reversed.

The developing countries as a group would experience little change in real growth as a result of the U.S. deficit reduction program, owing to the importance of offsetting effects. There would be beneficial effects from the decline in interest rates associated with declining activity in industrial countries. The effects of this benefit on current account balances would, in the aggregate, be offset by the adverse effects of declining demand for developing countries' exports by industrial countries and by the induced worsening of the terms of trade of developing countries. Individual countries might, of course, experience large positive or negative effects, depending on their own circumstances. (These effects are discussed in more detail in Chapter V.)

In assessing the overall impact of expenditure cuts beyond those already included in the baseline scenario, it must be remembered that the reduction in the deficit under the baseline scenario would, in itself, have highly beneficial effects on confidence and thus on the sustainability of expansion. Cuts additional to those in the baseline scenario would, on the basis of empirical evidence, tend to reduce growth in the short run, perhaps for a period of two or three years; thereafter growth would be higher than in the absence of the additional cuts. That the length of the adjustment period is expected to be so long is attributable both to the magnitude of the intended fiscal retrenchment in the United States and to the fact that its implementation is spread out over a period of years. The budget cuts attributable to any given year tend to have positive effects that accrue sooner; but these positive effects are overlaid by the negative short-run effects of subsequent rounds of cuts.

There are, of course, many sources of uncertainty in these projections. Most important, the Gramm-Rudman-Hollings program, if implemented as planned, would mark the first time that the United States had undertaken a major deficit-reduction program over a multiyear horizon. Empirical evidence based on historical data cannot be expected to provide more than a general guide to the evaluation of events that are radically different from the past. To the extent that the deficit reduction program is viewed as appropriate and credible, its beneficial effects on financial markets could well accrue more quickly, so that the short-run consequences for aggregate demand would be diminished. On the other hand, to the extent that people are skeptical about the likelihood of such large spending cuts actually being implemented, it may be more difficult to bring about the desired shifts in conditions in capital and exchange markets. This would make it more difficult to achieve the hoped-for revival in investment and the orderly re-establishment of external competitiveness.

Another uncertainty concerns the nature of the concurrent policy adaptations that will be made, both in the United States and elsewhere. Even though major countries have adopted medium-term economic strategies, it is quite possible that policy settings would be changed in the event that economic developments diverged in a substantial manner from the projected path.

Policy Reactions and Other Possible Disturbances

The foregoing analysis of the implications of eliminating the U.S. budget deficit was predicated on the assumption that U.S. monetary policy, as well as fiscal and monetary policies in other countries, would remain unchanged in the face of a fiscal retrenchment in the United States. It also employed a number of simplifying assumptions about other economic conditions, notably that the U.S. dollar would depreciate by 10 percent over a two-year period (in addition to the depreciation already assumed under the baseline scenario). The purpose of this section is to examine the sensitivity of the analysis to these various assumptions.

The assumed 10 percent depreciation of the U.S. dollar has a major redistributive impact on the estimated effects of the U.S. fiscal program. Specifically, because the dollar's depreciation serves to strengthen the U.S. current account balance, it reduces the short-term output losses in the United States but correspondingly amplifies them for other industrial countries. While the direction of this effect seems plausible, its magnitude and its timing are highly uncertain. The reliance on the simplifying (but perhaps unrealistic) assumption of other policies remaining unchanged adds to these uncertainties. With unchanged monetary policies, the U.S. fiscal cuts are expected, by themselves, to lead to a reduction in interest rates. Nonetheless, faced with temporarily reduced growth of output, the authorities both in the United States and in other countries might decide to seek further reductions in interest rates through an easing of monetary policies. Moreover, in view of the progress achieved in several industrial countries with respect both to inflation control and to budget consolidation, some governments might also decide to ease the stance of fiscal policy.

In most cases, because of the continued consolidation of budgetary positions that is implied by countries' medium-term policy objectives, such a shift in fiscal policy would constitute a postponement of budget consolidation efforts rather than a major injection of stimulus.

A sharp reduction in the U.S. budget deficit, by contributing to a lowering of net capital imports into the United States, would free financial resources that might be used to increase lending to developing countries. This development, which would be consistent with the objectives of the recent initiative by the Secretary of the U.S. Treasury, could lead to an increase in industrial country exports to the developing countries and hence to an increase in the industrial countries' output.

There are thus a number of circumstances in which demand and activity in the industrial countries could be expected to strengthen significantly compared with the results described above. To assess the implications of such developments, the following subsections provide some quantitative evidence of the effects of four possible eventualities: an easing of monetary policies in industrial countries; easier fiscal policy outside the United States; increased lending to developing countries; and a further depreciation of the dollar.[5]

Easier Monetary Policy

As discussed above, a key transmission mechanism in the adjustment of both the United States and other countries to the elimination of the U.S. budget deficit would be a marked reduction in interest rates. An easing of monetary conditions would result automatically from holding the growth of monetary aggregates unchanged as government demands on credit markets were reduced. If the United States or other countries were to decide to ease monetary conditions further, by allowing monetary aggregates to grow somewhat faster for a while, activity could be expected to return to its baseline path rather earlier than would otherwise be the case. For example, if the United States were to expand monetary growth by enough to reduce short-term U.S. interest rates by 1 percentage point more than is allowed for in the baseline scenario, the level of real GNP might increase by approximately ½ of 1

[5] This analysis is based in part on evidence from a number of internationally linked models, including—in addition to the Research Department's MINIMOD model—the Interlink model of the Organization for Economic Cooperation and Development, the Multi-Country Model of the Federal Reserve Board, and Project LINK of the University of Pennsylvania. The Research Department of the Fund wishes to express its gratitude to these institutions for undertaking simulations at short notice, and for generously providing time to discuss the results with Fund staff.

percent more after some two to three years. For Europe and Japan, the corresponding multipliers are estimated to be between ½ and 1½ percent, reflecting the rather different exchange rate effects that are associated with lower interest rates in the various models. Abstracting from exchange rate movements, the evidence for most industrial countries suggests that a reduction of interest rates of 1 percentage point might raise real GNP by about ½ of 1 percent after a period of two to three years.

While easier monetary conditions might help to offset the short-run effects of fiscal contraction in the United States, it is important to recognize that the positive effects of monetary easing on output growth would, for the most part, be temporary, and that an extended acceleration of monetary growth would involve the risk of leading to a rise in inflation.

Postponement of Budget Consolidation in Japan or Europe

In view of the considerable progress that has been achieved in reducing budget deficits in a number of countries outside the United States, questions could arise as to whether some countries might be in a position to ease fiscal policy temporarily to help offset any short-term output losses associated with major reductions in government expenditure in the United States. For illustrative purposes, the staff has examined the possibility of Japan and the European countries acting to shift their fiscal policies in an expansionary direction in 1987 corresponding to 1 percent of GDP, which would be sustained through the medium-term period. It may be recalled that the baseline projections are based on an assumption of the continued removal of fiscal stimulus in several of these countries, in line with their medium-term fiscal objectives. The assumed shift in fiscal policy would therefore involve essentially a postponement of consolidation efforts rather than a major reversal of the fiscal stance. For purposes of simplification no attempt is made in this subsection to differentiate among countries in terms of the appropriateness of these adjustments. However, as discussed below, some countries may be in a better position to ease fiscal policies than others.

An easing of fiscal policy outside the United States would tend to stimulate demand and activity, at least for a period. For the industrial countries as a whole, the short-run adverse effect on output resulting from the additional U.S. fiscal contraction would be reduced by about half as compared with a situation in which policies outside the United States were left unchanged. Assuming a nonaccommodating monetary policy stance, interest rates would fall by less in Europe and Japan

Table 18. Industrial Countries: Effects of a Sustained Change in Government Expenditure Equal to 1 Percent of GNP[1]

(Percentage deviation from baseline levels)

Country Changing Fiscal Policy		United States			Europe			Japan		
		Real GNP	GNP deflator	Budget deficit[2]	Real GNP	GNP deflator	Budget deficit[2]	Real GNP	GNP deflator	Budget deficit[2]
Year	1	1.5	0.2	0.8	1.2	0.1	0.9	1.2	0.1	0.9
	2	1.0	0.5	0.7	1.1	0.5	0.7	1.4	0.4	0.8
	4	0.2	1.2	1.0	0.5	1.2	0.9	0.8	1.0	1.0
		Impact on Europe			Impact on the United States			Impact on the United States		
Year	1	0.2	0.1	−0.1	0.1	—	—	0.1	—	—
	2	0.3	0.2	−0.1	0.1	—	—	0.1	—	—
	4	0.3	0.4	−0.1	—	—	—	—	—	—
		Impact on Japan			Impact on Japan			Impact on Europe		
Year	1	0.4	—	−0.1	0.1	—	—	—	—	—
	2	0.5	0.1	−0.2	0.1	—	—	0.1	—	—
	4	0.3	0.3	−0.1	0.1	—	—	0.1	—	—

[1] Based on an approximate average of the properties of the OECD Interlink Model, the Federal Reserve Board's Multi-Country Model, and the Project LINK model, supplemented with staff estimates and simulations on the MINIMOD model of the Fund's Research Department. The real GNP impact for the country that changes its fiscal policy varies across the models by about ¼ of 1 percentage point. These multipliers assume that monetary policy is non-accommodating, implying unchanged growth rates of money supply.

[2] Change in percent of GNP.

than if no fiscal relaxation were undertaken; the dollar would therefore tend to depreciate more rapidly. These forces would begin to reduce the demand-supporting effects of fiscal relaxation after a period of two to three years. By then, the effects of fiscal contraction in the United States would also begin to taper off. The expected magnitudes of these effects, based on a sampling of recent econometric evidence, are summarized in Table 18.

An important implication of fiscal action outside the United States would be to raise U.S. exports, which in turn would increase the level of U.S. real GNP slightly—by perhaps ¼ of 1 percentage point after two or three years—compared with what otherwise would be predicted. The contribution this would make to the reduction of the U.S. budget deficit would be relatively small, however, and would probably not exceed ¹⁄₁₀ of 1 percentage point of GNP.

For the developing countries, an easing of fiscal policy in the industrial countries outside the United States would raise both the demand for their exports and their export prices. Overall, fiscal action of the size assumed might increase the developing countries' export revenue by 1–1½ percent after a period of two to three years compared with the outcome of the scenario in which the U.S. budget was balanced but no other policy changes occurred. Assuming that the increment to export revenues would be used to finance higher imports, staff estimates suggest that the level

of real GDP in developing countries could also be expected to increase by about 1–1½ percent.

Increased Lending to Developing Countries

An important implication of additional action on the U.S. budget deficit would be to raise total domestic saving in the United States. As a result, both domestic interest rates and the current external deficit in the United States would decline. Lower interest rates would result in a fall in debt service ratios in developing countries, which in turn could facilitate a rise in lending to these countries. That increase would enable them to raise imports, investment, and growth above the levels that would otherwise prevail.

On the assumption that the level of lending to developing countries were to increase by $20 billion above the baseline level in 1987 and to remain at the new level thereafter, staff estimates suggest that the level of both imports and real GDP in these countries could be expected to be some 3 percent higher after a two-to-three-year period. Because of multiplier effects stemming from higher exports to the developing countries, the industrial countries' level of activity would also strengthen, increasing GDP by perhaps ¼ to ½ of 1 percent relative to what otherwise would be the case. Real GNP in the United States would probably increase by a smaller percentage than that of Japan

79

and Europe, although this relationship would depend on the geographical distribution of the increase in lending, which would affect the proportion of the rise in developing countries' imports that would represent increased U.S. exports.

Dollar Depreciation

The balanced budget scenario assumed that the dollar would depreciate by some 10 percent relative to the baseline, as a result of the decline in U.S. interest rates following the implementation of deficit-reducing measures. In view of the uncertainties involved, it is worth examining the implications of different assumptions. In particular, the dollar might fall by significantly more than 10 percent in the short run, perhaps appreciating somewhat in the longer run as the deficit on current account narrowed.

A depreciation of the dollar of, for example, 20 percent instead of the 10 percent assumed earlier, would change the results of the balanced-budget scenario quite significantly. With higher import prices, the rate of inflation in the United States would tend to rise temporarily, raising the price level by 1½–2 percent after a period of two to three years. With unchanged monetary growth (and a higher domestic price level) interest rates would therefore be likely to fall by much less than if the exchange rate decline were more moderate.

The impact of dollar depreciation on U.S. output is more difficult to assess than its impact on prices. Improved net exports would tend to raise real GNP whereas higher inflation and interest rates would tend to depress demand and activity. On the basis of empirical evidence, a central estimate of the likely outcome might be a rise in output of ¼–½ of 1 percent over a period of two to three years. The corresponding negative impact on other industrial countries would be similar in absolute terms, although it would not be evenly spread. In the absence of exchange rate changes among the other industrial countries, the fall in external demand and therefore in output in Japan would be expected to be significantly greater than in Europe, owing to Japan's greater reliance on trade with the United States.

Conclusions

There are, as this discussion has illustrated, a number of developments that might modify the implications for other industrial countries of the implementation of budget deficit reductions in the United States. To the extent that these developments involve fiscal or monetary relaxation, they involve temporary departures from the expressed medium-term stance of policies. The risks inherent in such a course of action must, of course, be balanced against the short-run benefit of supporting existing levels of output and employment. Monetary relaxation, for example, brings with it the danger of stimulating a revival of inflation, while an easing of the fiscal stance outside the United States would limit the extent to which U.S. budget cuts resulted in lower worldwide interest rates. However, it must be recognized that the implementation of credible measures to eliminate the U.S. budget deficit would create circumstances in which global inflation and interest rates would be under considerable downward pressure, increasing the freedom of maneuver that authorities have to use policy to support demand. In weighing the advantages and disadvantages of various policy responses, therefore, a balancing of short-run and longer-run consequences must be undertaken, with due recognition of the fact that countries will be affected in different ways and to varying degrees by deficit reduction measures in the United States.

Because of the relatively small share of foreign trade in U.S. aggregate output, most of the external developments just discussed would have only minor direct effects on U.S output and on the magnitude of the fiscal measures necessary to eliminate the U.S. budget deficit. However, to the extent that the dollar were to depreciate substantially following the budget cuts, for example as a result of an easier stance of U.S. monetary policy, both the magnitude of the required discretionary budgetary cuts as well as the impact on output would be somewhat reduced relative to a scenario with little impact on the dollar and with no change in monetary policy.

Circumstances Affecting Individual Countries

Policy changes of the kind discussed above become more likely to the extent that national authorities feel that their freedom of policy maneuver is increased by a stronger budgetary position in the United States. In present circumstances, the revival of confidence and activity outside the United States is vulnerable to setbacks, and the management of the debt situation could be destabilized by a sharp slowing in industrial country growth. These considerations argue for a willingness to adapt policies to support demand. It is equally clear, however, that to modify policies could be risky in situations where countries have themselves embarked on a path of medium-term adjustment and where inflationary expectations are latent. Whatever adjustments are made to policies in order to cope with external developments must be fully consistent with countries' medium-term strategies, and must not risk destabilizing expectations. This section discusses the circumstances and the constraints that currently prevail in particular countries, as they relate to the possibility of easing monetary or fiscal policies in response to a temporary slowdown that might be induced by the fiscal deficit reduction program in the United States.

United States

Significant action to reduce the fiscal deficit would greatly enhance the prospects for improved macroeconomic balance in the United States. Higher domestic savings would make possible a strengthening of the current account position and a growth in investment, through absorbing resources freed from public sector use. The key to achieving such a smooth reallocation of resources lies in the behavior of interest rates and the exchange rates, as well as in the maintenance of financial stability and private sector confidence.

Obtaining the appropriate evolution of interest rates and the exchange rate will not be easy. A temporary relaxation of monetary policy would help limit the initial weakening of activity stemming from fiscal measures. Such a policy stance would also help to maintain downward pressure on the dollar exchange rate, if that were needed. The danger, however, is that if monetary easing is perceived as going too far, it may be counterproductive. Fears of inflation could produce both a movement out of the dollar and upward pressure on interest rates. If such a development gathered momentum, it could have potentially serious consequences. A rapid depreciation of the dollar would further exacerbate inflationary tendencies, while monetary action to halt depreciation might require a substantial upward movement in interest rates, threatening to undermine domestic economic growth. It is obviously important for the U.S. authorities to seek to avoid being placed in such a dilemma, through exercising prudence in any easing of their monetary stance.

Japan

The recovery of the Japanese economy was, in its initial stages, largely led by exports, benefiting from strong growth in the United States during 1983 and the first half of 1984 and from the relatively low value of the yen in exchange markets. However, while the increasing surplus on current account has been a source of stimulus to the domestic economy, its size has placed a strain on Japan's relations with its trading partners and has aggravated protectionist pressures. The slowdown in the U.S. economy after mid-1984 and the sharp appreciation of the yen against the U.S.

dollar following the Group of Five meeting in September 1985 are reflected in the projection of a negative contribution to growth from external demand in 1986 and 1987.

The importance of maintaining strong growth of domestic demand in Japan under these circumstances raises the question of whether adjustments to the current monetary or fiscal stance might be appropriate. In the area of monetary policy, the options open to the Japanese authorities have been constrained by exchange rate considerations. Following the meeting of the Group of Five in September 1985, interest rates were permitted to rise sharply in order to encourage a further strengthening of the yen. However, the substantial appreciation of the yen, especially since late January 1986, appears to have increased the authorities' freedom of maneuver. As a result, not only was the earlier increase in interest rates reversed, the authorities were able to lower the discount rate by 1 percentage point in two steps at the end of January and the beginning of March 1986. The authorities view the success of their current program of fiscal consolidation as critical to restoring fiscal flexibility and placing the Government in a better position to accommodate the prospective sharp rise in social welfare expenditure. The medium-term fiscal objective is to reduce the central government deficit without recourse to tax increases, so as to eliminate bond financing for current expenditure by fiscal year 1990/91. In view of the constraint on the central government budget, the authorities have increased expenditure by local governments and public enterprises to mitigate the withdrawal of fiscal stimulus. Beyond this, the Japanese authorities have emphasized structural policies, including deregulation and privatization of public enterprises, to ensure strong private demand.

In the baseline scenario, the external constraint on monetary policy would basically remain in place, at least for the time being. A substantial easing of monetary policy would run the risk of a reversal of the appreciation of the yen and a slower current account adjustment. From a cyclical perspective, it would not be desirable for the public sector to withdraw stimulus from domestic demand in 1986 or 1987. However, these short-term considerations need to be weighed against the medium-term fiscal objectives, and it remains important that the medium-term course of fiscal policy not be fundamentally changed. In view of the constraint on the central government budget, there is merit in making use of the scope to support demand through actions at other levels of government to the fullest extent possible. Some short-run flexibility at the central government level might also deserve consideration, if it could be done within the framework of the medium-term objectives of fiscal consolidation.

In the scenario in which the U.S. budget is brought

into balance or a steeper fall of the dollar occurs, the constraint on monetary policy would be greatly eased or removed altogether. Monetary policy could and should then be directed firmly toward supporting demand. If there were to be a large and sustained real appreciation of the yen and a weak U.S. economy, the Japanese economy would experience a severe cutback in net foreign demand, and would therefore need strong growth of domestic demand to avoid the emergence of substantial slack. It would be all the more important in this case that the vitality of the private sector be fully utilized through deregulation and other measures. While both monetary and fiscal policy would also have a role to play, the scope for an easing of monetary policy would be somewhat greater than under the baseline scenario. Such an easing would facilitate a trend toward lower interest rates in other countries.

The possibility of lower oil prices would modify the conclusions just sketched, but it would not change their basic thrust. Lower oil prices should improve real domestic incomes and thus help support demand. However, even at $15 per barrel, the addition to real incomes would not appear to be sufficient to prevent the emergence of some slack in the Japanese economy. At the same time, lower oil prices would be apt to be associated with a stronger yen, thus resulting in a withdrawal of external stimulus.

Federal Republic of Germany

The German economy, which experienced very little growth from 1980 to 1983, has recovered somewhat during the past two years, with real growth averaging about 2½ percent. As in Japan, the recovery has been led by export demand, largely reflecting the strong growth of markets in the United States in 1983 and the first half of 1984. The deceleration in the U.S. growth rate and the recent substantial real appreciation of the deutsche mark against the U.S. dollar thus create a situation for Germany that is similar in many respects to the one described above for Japan. The effects of these international developments, however, are somewhat smaller for the German economy, reflecting the smaller trade linkages with the United States. Moreover, the implementation of tax cuts, an easing of interest rates, and terms of trade improvements are expected to result in a rise in domestic demand in the short term.

Monetary policy in the Federal Republic of Germany remains geared toward maintaining a steady growth in potential output through reducing inflationary pressures. Fiscal policy is also formulated within a medium-term framework and is oriented toward reducing the share of government in the economy and lowering the budget deficit. The authorities believe that the policy of fiscal consolidation that is under way is fundamental to a durable recovery in the private sector and hence to expansion in employment. Considerable progress has already been achieved in fiscal consolidation, with a lowering of the general government deficit from 3½ percent of GNP in 1981 to a projected level of less than 1 percent in 1986. The progressive reduction in the share of general government spending in GNP, from 50 percent in 1982 to an estimated 48 percent in 1985, provided scope for the income tax reductions to be implemented at the start of 1986, which are expected to stimulate private sector activity.

A matter for discussion is whether the German authorities could respond to a program of U.S. fiscal restraint through a relaxation of their fiscal stance. If at the same time monetary policy was left unchanged, the resulting upward pressure on short-term real interest rates in the Federal Republic of Germany and the real appreciation of the deutsche mark against the U.S. dollar would, it might be argued, reinforce the effects of the U.S. fiscal program in reducing current account imbalances. However, the scope in Germany for a further short-term increase in domestic demand growth may not be as great as the relatively high unemployment level implies. Domestic demand picked up significantly in the last three quarters of 1985, and the rate of capacity utilization rose. In addition, the fiscal stance in 1986 is expected to be mildly expansionary, under the influence of the tax cuts introduced in January 1986, and lower oil prices will provide a stimulus to demand as they work their way through the economy.

Much will therefore depend on developments during the course of 1986. The German economy will be less affected than Japan by the possibility of weaker U.S. activity or a lower dollar. Nevertheless, if these developments were to be accompanied by some slackening in the pace of domestic demand, this would strengthen the case for offsetting action. One possibility would be to bring forward the tax cuts projected for 1988. Another would be to ease somewhat the stance of monetary policy. An easing of monetary policy might tend to limit tensions in the EMS, at a time when a weakening of the dollar would probably be tending to exert upward pressure on the deutsche mark.

United Kingdom

The performance of the U.K. economy has strengthened over the past several years, with an average rate of real output growth of about 2½ percent and an inflation rate declining to around 5 percent. However, there continue to be large labor market imbalances, with unemployment at over 13 percent of the labor force. Despite the effects of the recent weakness in oil prices, the pound sterling remains high in real terms in relation to its longer-run historical average level. The real effective exchange rate of the pound in December 1985 (measured by relative normalized unit labor costs adjusted for exchange rate changes) is estimated to have been about 17 percent above its average value for the decade 1975–84, and only 10 percent below the peak level reached in the first quarter of 1981.

The medium-term objective of policy in the United Kingdom is to slow progressively the pace of monetary expansion in order to reduce inflation, supported by a scaling back of the public sector borrowing requirement from about 3¼ percent of GDP in fiscal year 1984/85 to 1¾ percent of GDP by fiscal year 1988/89. Within this broad framework, exchange rate considerations have come to play an increasingly important indicative role in the conduct of monetary policy. The authorities have kept interest rates high relative to those in partner countries, partly in reflection of the judgment that in recent circumstances a narrower differential would be likely to loosen monetary conditions by enough to induce a depreciation of sterling and rekindle inflationary pressure. Of course, the authorities are well aware that downward pressure on the pound stemming from factors having lasting influences on the external position—such as a sustained lower level of oil prices—should be accommodated, though not in a way that would compromise the inflation objective. Thus, in reacting to the downward pressure on sterling that began in December 1985, the U.K. authorities permitted interest rates to rise in a manner that was consistent with a moderate effective depreciation of the pound.

Looking ahead to the possible consequences of major budgetary consolidation in the United States, a temporary weakening in the growth of world activity, coupled with a decline in short-term real interest rates in the United States and other countries, could tend to reduce downward pressure on sterling and permit an easing of interest rates in the United Kingdom. Given the authorities' commitment to a policy of fiscal consolidation, there may be little scope for a temporary easing of fiscal policy, particularly in view of the fact that the curbing of budget deficits has relied increasingly on asset sales. Fiscal policy, as gauged by the fiscal impulse at the general government level, has been broadly expansionary since 1982. In addition, fiscal easing would tend to place upward pressure on interest rates and on the exchange rate, neither of which would be appropriate under circumstances where the maintenance of international competitiveness is an important concern. In the longer run, a permanent improvement in the domestic situation can best be achieved by a reduction in short-term and long-term real interest rates through a continuation of the present policy of fiscal consolidation, along with measures to reduce structural rigidities in the labor market.

France

The moderate recovery of the French economy since 1983 has been accompanied by considerable progress in reducing the inflation rate, by an increase in profitability, and by a strengthening of the current account position. However, the recent decline in the inflation differential between France and the Federal Republic of Germany has not quite been sufficient to prevent a small deterioration in France's external competitiveness relative to Germany's. The rate of growth of real GDP in France fell back from 1½ percent in 1984 to ¾ of 1 percent in 1985, and real growth remains considerably below that of France's main trading partners. In addition to the goal of further reducing the inflation rate, the main domestic concern arises from the continuing deterioration of labor market conditions. This deterioration has become of particular concern in view of the rise in unemployment to close to 11 percent of the labor force by 1985, at a time when rates in many other European countries had stabilized.

While the current account of the balance of payments is now in surplus, the external constraint on policy remains of significance. The French authorities have had to maintain a fairly tight monetary stance in order to preserve an interest differential with deutsche mark-denominated assets that is sufficient to limit exchange market pressures. A further decline in U.S. and German interest rates would give the French authorities an opportunity to allow interest rates to fall without creating additional pressure on the parity of the French franc within the EMS. However, as noted earlier, a shift toward a more expansionary monetary policy by Germany (or Japan) would serve to limit any incipient real depreciation of the U.S. dollar and the corresponding reduction in current account imbalances. An additional argument against monetary easing in the French case is that inflation has only recently declined. Any re-awakening of inflationary expectations in France could induce a speculative movement out of French francs, thereby endangering the stability of the French franc within the EMS.

Canada

A slowdown in U.S. economic activity would have a greater effect on Canadian economic growth than on European growth because of the close trading links between Canada and the United States. At the same time, Canadian authorities would face significant constraints on their ability to pursue policies that would counter the effect of a U.S. slowdown. The size of the Canadian budget deficit and the continued buildup in government debt limits the room for maneuver of fiscal policy. Moreover, the need to preserve the progress made in bringing down inflation restricts the ability of the Canadian authorities to pursue a significantly easier monetary policy.

Over the past year and a half, the Canadian Government has taken measures to correct the central government fiscal imbalance and arrest the growth of the ratio of debt to GNP. Yet the deficit remains large and the debt ratio continues to increase. In 1985, the fiscal deficit was almost 7 percent of GNP on a national accounts basis, and central government debt amounted to 42½ percent of GNP. The authorities have therefore indicated that a strengthening of the budgetary position will be a key priority.

Significant fiscal retrenchment in the United States would have some adverse short-run effects on economic activity in Canada that would make it more difficult for the Canadian authorities to achieve a sizable reduction in the Canadian deficit. However, failure to undertake additional deficit reduction measures in Canada in the face of such action in the United States could well generate a loss of confidence and exert downward pressure on the value of the Canadian dollar vis-à-vis the U.S. dollar, thereby limiting the extent to which Canada might benefit from a reduction in U.S. interest rates. There is, therefore, little room for expansionary fiscal policy action in Canada to counteract any adverse real activity effects stemming from a fiscal correction in the United States. The ability of the Canadian authorities to lower interest rates to take advantage of any reduction in U.S. rates is also constrained by the need to resist sharp downward movements in the exchange rate. The most that might be possible would be for a reduction in Canadian interest rates to follow a corresponding decline in the United States, provided that it could be achieved without provoking an adverse reaction in exchange markets.

Italy

The impact of international economic developments on the policy options facing the Italian authorities has to be seen against the background of the fact that the constraints on Italy's financial policies are essentially domestically generated, with favorable developments abroad consequently providing only marginal and short-term relief. Until a substantial improvement in the public sector financial position is achieved, an easing of financial policies in the main partner countries can provide only a limited scope for relaxation of the stance of policies in Italy.

Consistent with Italy's participation in the EMS, the authorities are committed to the pursuit of a steady disinflationary policy, and counteracting domestic sources of inflationary pressures has consequently been a central element of their medium-term strategy. The authorities recognize that a sustained adjustment effort in public finances is an essential condition for a lasting improvement in economic performance, and they have put forward a medium-term budget consolidation plan. The plan targets the elimination of the non-interest deficit of the state sector, an objective that would require substantial expenditure restraint even under the most favorable international circumstances. There would thus be no room to ease fiscal policy even if international economic conditions were to change. Much the same applies to monetary policy. A generalized decline in interest rates abroad may provide some scope for a modest decline in nominal interest rates in Italy as well, particularly as inflation decelerates in the course of 1986. Over the longer term, however, the level of real interest rates in Italy is largely determined by the need to generate the necessary domestic savings in the face of substantial fiscal deficits, and to secure a steady deceleration in the rate of growth of the monetary aggregates. The level of real interest rates that is appropriate from this domestic perspective may well be higher than in most of Italy's EMS partners.

Other Industrial Countries

Among the smaller EMS countries, the scope for changes in monetary policy is quite limited. Movements in short-term interest rates have had to follow closely those in the Federal Republic of Germany in order to maintain parities within the EMS. In some countries, downward pressure on the exchange rate has led to a tightening of monetary policy, with the recent increases in the Belgian discount rate in August and in December 1985 being notable examples.

The maintenance of interest rates in line with those in the Federal Republic of Germany has posed policy dilemmas for the authorities in these countries in view of their large domestic labor market imbalances. At the same time, the need to reduce large fiscal deficits over the medium term leaves little room for any fiscal stimulus. A fall in U.S. interest rates and a depreciation of the U.S. dollar might reduce somewhat the pressures currently faced by the monetary authorities in these countries. At the same time, the large fiscal imbalances would make it inappropriate to respond to a weakening in the international climate through a loosening of fiscal policy. Fiscal easing would mean that monetary conditions would have to be allowed to tighten in order to protect the exchange rate. In the case of the Netherlands, the relatively strong position of the guilder within the EMS, together with the continuation of a large domestic fiscal imbalance, means that scope for combatting incipient weakness in the economy lies more on the monetary side than on the fiscal side. Monetary easing, however, would have the consequences of limiting the appreciation of the guilder and thus postponing the adjustment of the large external surplus.

Spain faces a situation in which its current account surplus is relatively large, but domestic economic performance is weak, with very high unemployment (over 20 percent) and inflation well above the average of other industrial countries. In addition, Spain may well face problems of structural adaptation following membership in the European Communities. The relatively high level of the public sector borrowing requirement makes it inappropriate to respond to a weakening in the international economic environment by significant budgetary easing. Monetary policy also needs to be cautious, in light of the need to improve inflation performance; it may, however, be possible to respond to a decline in international interest rates with an easing of monetary conditions in Spain also.

Smaller industrial countries that have recently experienced large depreciations of their currencies might also benefit from a sustained depreciation of the U.S. dollar. Since the shift to floating exchange rates in Australia in December 1983, and in New Zealand in March 1985, the effective values of the Australian and New Zealand dollars have undergone sharp fluctuations. The depreciation of the Australian dollar during 1985 of about 25 percent and the sharp drop in the New Zealand dollar in December 1985 have raised concerns about the possibility of a revival in inflation. On the other hand, since both countries have strong trading links with the United States and Japan, any weakening in activity in those countries would be expected to exacerbate the existing domestic unemployment problem, especially in Australia. In view of the large fiscal imbalances and strong domestic inflationary impulses already present in both economies, the scope for any relaxation of the present restrictive stance of financial policy is somewhat limited. A decline in U.S. interest rates might allow some fall in domestic interest rates and stimulus to domestic demand without preventing an appreciation of the currency against the U.S. dollar. In the longer term, the restoration of confidence in the exchange rate and accompanying reduction in current account deficits will necessitate a continuation of the present programs of fiscal retrenchment.

Chapter V

The Debt Situation: Prospects and Policy Issues

The heavy burden of external debt remains the dominant factor in assessing medium-term prospects for a large number of developing countries. For these countries, the medium-term outlook remains considerably less favorable than for countries that avoided large increases in debt and debt-service ratios during the period 1973–82. The following section focuses on the evolution of the debt situation over that period. The next section sets out a medium-term scenario for developing countries, together with an analysis of the scenario's sensitivity to certain alternative developments; this analysis gives some indication of the likely future vulnerability of the system to the kinds of global economic disturbances that occurred in 1979–82, and is intended to place in perspective the proposals reviewed in the following section. The final section then sets out some tentative conclusions on the nature of the systemic weaknesses that may impede resolution of existing debt-servicing problems and could lead to a recurrence of similar problems in the future. The section is concluded by a review of relevant policy issues, distinguishing the contributions to be made by governments of debtor and creditor countries, by private creditors, and by the Fund, the World Bank, and other international institutions.

The Debt Situation Since 1973

Sources and Symptoms of the Crisis

In varying degrees, all developing countries were affected by the various shocks to the global economy that occurred in the late 1970s and early 1980s. These shocks complicated domestic economic management and contributed to the loss of creditors' confidence in many developing countries. The resulting curtailment in the growth of private bank exposure to these countries after 1982 left many debtor countries unable to roll over maturing debts and finance current account deficits. While many countries rapidly adjusted their domestic policies, and some were able to avoid serious liquidity problems, for a large number of others adjustment efforts were not sufficiently timely to prevent the emergence of debt-servicing problems. The entire episode was characterized by the apparently rapid emergence of problems of unexpected severity. Optimistic expectations proved unfounded in several respects, namely with regard to the duration of the recession and of high real interest rates, the financial strength of the commercial banks, and the strength of economic policies and prospects in the debtor countries. In retrospect, it is easier now than it was at the onset of the payments difficulties in 1982 to identify the sources of weakness in the system.

There is, of course, long historical precedent for countries in the early stages of their development engaging in net international borrowing in order to raise their rates of investment and economic growth. However, failure to control adequately the growth, structure, and terms of external borrowing can lead to balance of payments difficulties and ultimately a protracted setback to economic development. For example, while external indebtedness may at times grow more rapidly than output, the ratio of debt to GDP cannot increase indefinitely without threatening the solvency of the debtor, namely, its ability to service debt out of current national income. Analogously, a continued tendency for the ratio of debt to exports to grow is a sign that the economy will eventually experience liquidity problems—that it will not be able to generate sufficient foreign exchange to meet both debt service requirements and at the same time pay for essential imports. Furthermore, a persistently negative difference between the rate of growth of exports and the average interest rate on debt suggests a tendency for additional net borrowing to add to long-run debt-servicing difficulties.

In addition to these considerations, there are those relating to the structure and terms of debt. Important indications of these include: the proportion of total debt at commercial terms; the share of total debt at variable interest rates; the average maturity of debt; and the share of short-term debt in the total. The terms and maturity of debt are reflected to some extent in the frequently cited ratio of debt service payments (total interest payments plus amortization on medium- and long-term debt) to exports of goods and services. While rising debt service ratios can be quite compatible with successful economic policies (for instance, if foreign borrowing is used to finance efficient export-promoting or import-substituting investment), a country with a rising debt service ratio is, other things being equal, becoming more vulnerable to adverse external developments (such as higher interest rates, a decline in the terms of trade, or a reduction in new capital inflows). In gauging the extent of such vulnerability, it is sometimes useful to take into account also the ratio of short-term debt to exports of goods and services. While short-term debt (much of which consists of trade financing) is normally rolled over, during a crisis of creditor confidence there may be reluctance to continue lines of credit and other short-term financing facilities.

The total external debt of capital importing developing countries grew rapidly throughout the period 1973–82 and, except during 1979–80, outpaced the growth of exports or GDP; during the ten-year period 1973–82, external debt grew at a compound annual rate of 20½ percent, while the value of exports grew by 16 percent and nominal GDP by 12½ percent.[1] During 1973–78, however, average nominal interest rates on external debt averaged only 5¾ percent—much lower than the rate of growth of exports or GDP in nominal terms—so that debt service ratios, although rising, were still relatively moderate (Table 19). The average interest rate on debt rose substantially during 1979–80. Although the impact of this increase on debt-servicing positions was temporarily masked by a sharp rise in export prices, there were signs of a growing vulnerability to developments in external financial markets. The proportion of total debt subject to variable interest rates continued to rise as a result of the increased reliance on bank lending, and the share of short-term debt in total debt also increased significantly during the second half of the 1970s (Table 19).

[1] In the remainder of this section, references to GDP are to GDP measured in terms of U.S. dollars at current prices. While this measure makes it easier to compare movements in external debt and GDP, it is subject to some distortion for individual countries, since a large shift in a country's real exchange rate—for example, when the exchange rate is adjusted after many years of overvaluation—can result in a substantial change in the dollar value of its GDP.

Chart 29. Capital Importing Developing Countries: Exports, Total Debt, and Interest Rates, 1971–85[1]

(In percent)

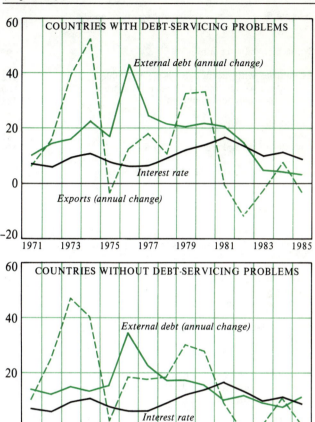

[1] U.S. dollar values of exports of goods and services and of total short- and long-term external debt, and London interbank offered rate on 6-month U.S. dollar deposits.

The consequences of these shifts in the structure of external debt became apparent in the early 1980s. The total external debt of the capital importing countries continued to grow rapidly during 1981–82, at an annual average rate of around 15 percent (Chart 29). High interest rates on world financial markets, together with the increased share of debt subject to variable rates, contributed to a further increase in the average interest rate on external debt, which reached almost 10 percent. At the same time, the value of exports and GDP of the capital importing countries stagnated under the impact of the world recession. As a result, debt and debt service ratios rose substantially, while the large volume of short-term debt relative to export earnings contributed to an increasing incidence of liquidity

Table 19. Capital Importing Developing Countries: Selected Indicators of External Debt Developments, 1973–85

(Period averages; in percent)

	1973–74	1975–78	1979–80	1981–82	1983–85
External debt (as a percentage of exports of goods and services)					
Capital importing countries	95.8	120.1	115.4	135.7	158.2
Countries with recent debt-servicing problems	112.1	154.4	155.9	207.4	252.4
Countries without recent debt-servicing problems	80.8	90.9	81.5	83.3	97.0
15 heavily indebted countries	123.9	169.2	173.7	231.3	280.1
Sub-Saharan Africa[1]	78.2	118.0	140.8	185.3	224.1
Asia	81.1	85.6	72.1	77.8	89.0
Western Hemisphere	139.8	187.6	190.3	238.0	285.3
Debt service payments (as a percentage of exports of goods and services)					
Capital importing countries	12.7	16.7	18.1	22.1	23.0
Countries with recent debt-servicing problems	16.7	24.5	26.5	34.8	35.5
Countries without recent debt-servicing problems	9.0	10.1	11.0	12.7	14.9
15 heavily indebted countries	18.2	28.6	32.0	43.2	42.6
Sub-Saharan Africa[1]	10.0	12.8	15.1	19.0	24.4
Asia	7.4	8.7	8.6	10.4	11.7
Western Hemisphere	21.5	33.3	36.3	45.4	43.2
Share of total debt at floating interest rates					
Capital importing countries	21.1	34.7	44.6	51.1	53.6
Countries with recent debt-servicing problems	29.6	42.4	53.5	59.8	62.8
Countries without recent debt-servicing problems	10.2	23.7	30.4	35.3	37.9
15 heavily indebted countries	31.9	48.7	63.8	70.8	73.5
Sub-Saharan Africa[1]	9.4	15.4	17.8	20.6	19.1
Asia	8.1	21.9	31.3	38.1	45.2
Western Hemisphere	34.1	51.3	66.4	71.7	72.4
Share of short-term debt in total debt					
Capital importing countries	7.3	14.3	18.6	20.8	15.3
Countries with recent debt-servicing problems	10.0	15.1	20.2	23.5	15.8
Countries without recent debt-servicing problems	3.8	13.3	16.0	15.8	14.4
15 heavily indebted countries	7.1	13.8	21.7	25.3	15.7
Sub-Saharan Africa[1]	0.2	4.8	5.7	6.2	4.9
Asia	2.9	10.8	18.4	19.5	15.4
Western Hemisphere	6.3	13.1	21.3	24.4	15.3

[1] Excluding Nigeria and South Africa.

problems, as creditors became reluctant to roll over their short-term commitments to a number of countries. The movements in these indicators differed substantially, however, between the groups of those countries that did, and those that did not, encounter debt-servicing difficulties.[2] The debt-to-exports ratio of

the first-mentioned group almost doubled between 1975 and 1982, rising from 121 percent to 235 percent, while over the same period the ratio for the second group rose only moderately, from 81 percent to 89 percent.

The group of countries with debt-servicing problems also paid higher average interest rates on their external debt than other countries, largely because of the former group's greater reliance on borrowing from private sources, including banks; at the end of 1982, over 70 percent of their total long-term debt was owed to

[2] Countries experiencing debt-servicing difficulties are defined as those that incurred external payments arrears during 1982–84 or rescheduled their debt between the end of 1982 and mid-1985. See the introduction to the Statistical Appendix.

private creditors, compared with less than 50 percent for the non-problem countries. The combination of higher debt-to-export ratios, higher average interest rates, and somewhat shorter maturities contributed to much higher debt service ratios for the countries with debt-servicing difficulties—averaging 35 percent during 1981–82, compared with under 13 percent for the non-problem countries. In addition, the share of short-term debt in total debt was almost 50 percent higher in the debt-problem countries.

The most frequently cited cause of the deteriorating external debt situation of the capital importing countries was the series of external shocks of 1979–83 that to some extent affected all developing countries. But domestic developments prior to that time, as well as earlier external debt management policies, greatly influenced the vulnerability of capital importing countries to these external shocks. Certain key domestic developments are briefly reviewed here, followed by a discussion of the policy background.

The principal rationale of external borrowing is to raise investment, and thereby growth of output, above levels that would otherwise have been attained. There is no direct way of measuring the extent to which the increased external borrowing in the 1970s and early 1980s was used for investment purposes and to what extent it was used to offset a reduction in domestic saving. Indirect evidence is provided, however, by the behavior of saving and investment ratios in the period leading up to, and immediately after, the onset of the debt crisis. For the countries with debt-servicing problems, the domestic saving rate tended to decline after the mid-1970s to the period 1978–82 (Chart 30). Growing inflows of foreign savings were thus used largely to maintain the existing investment ratio, rather than to increase it. In effect foreign saving was, at the margin, financing a reduction in domestic saving. When inflows of foreign savings dried up after 1982, the domestic investment ratio plummeted. Countries that did not encounter debt-servicing difficulties had a rather different history. Although saving in these countries generally represented a smaller share of national income, saving ratios tended to rise after 1977.[3] Hence foreign borrowing seems to have been used largely to support additional investment.

There is also the question of the efficiency of investment, which may be roughly measured by the frequently used incremental output-capital ratio. The wide fluctuations in this ratio across countries and between years are influenced, however, not only by the efficiency of investment but also by annual fluctuations in output, such as the recent declines in GDP

Chart 30.   Capital Importing Developing Countries: Gross Savings and Capital Formation, 1977–85[1]

(Percent of GDP)

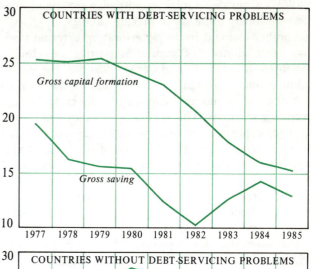

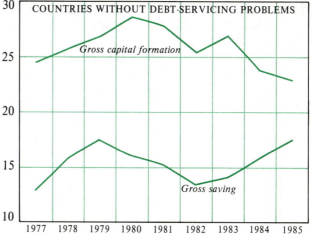

[1] Median values of gross saving and gross capital formation, as a percentage of GDP, in each group of countries.

---

growth in developing countries. Nonetheless, it is worth noting that the countries without debt-servicing problems tended to show significantly higher incremental output-capital ratios than those with debt-servicing problems (see Statistical Appendix Tables A5 and A7).

The external financing requirements of capital importing countries were greatly increased by outflows of resident capital. Such outflows were particularly large in relation to GDP during 1977–80. For capital-importing countries as a whole, capital outflows increased the external financing requirement by about two thirds compared to the needs of current account financing alone; for countries in the Western Hemisphere, the external financing requirement was almost doubled in this manner. While for some countries,

---

[3] The ratios cited here are medians, because of statistical problems with these data.

especially in Asia and the Middle East, capital outflows represented in large part the prudential accumulation of official reserves and, to a lesser extent, trade credits used to promote exports, in other regions the capital outflows from developing countries were mainly accounted for by outflows of private savings.

Another element in the deteriorating external position of a number of capital importing developing countries in the 1970s and early 1980s was the inadequate extent to which borrowed funds were used to increase the economy's capacity to generate foreign exchange earnings. This tendency is suggested by the stronger export performance of countries that avoided debt-servicing problems. These countries' export volumes grew between 1973 and 1982 at a compound average rate of 4¾ percent, as against less than ¾ of 1 percent for debt-problem countries, reflecting in part different export compositions but also a more favorable policy stance.

The domestic developments that have just been briefly outlined had their roots to a considerable extent in the policies pursued in these countries. For a large number of countries, the mid-1970s initiated a long period of expansionary fiscal and monetary policies, accompanied by a set of pricing, interest rate and exchange rate policies, as well as trade and exchange restrictions, that tended to reduce domestic savings, harm the efficiency of investment, encourage capital flight, and discourage the growth of exports (particularly the growth of manufactured exports). In varying degrees, policies of this sort contributed to the rapid accumulation of external indebtedness in countries that eventually developed debt-servicing problems. By contrast, countries that were able to avoid such problems often had domestic policies that to some degree were more successful at encouraging the domestic mobilization of savings, the efficient use of investable resources, and export growth and diversification. This is not, of course, to say that domestic policies were the only cause of the deteriorating external position of the countries with debt-servicing problems, nor that policies in countries without such problems were beyond criticism, but merely to indicate that there is evidence of a tendency to greater policy weakness in the former group compared with the latter. Current and prospective ways in which policies in these countries might be strengthened are reviewed later in this chapter.

Weaknesses in demand management and supply-side policies in the debt-problem countries were often closely associated with the manner in which the external debt was managed. Several aspects of debt management may be noted briefly here. First, there was the rate at which the external indebtedness of the public sector was expanded, which in turn was closely

related to the evolution of the fiscal deficit. Another factor was the effectiveness with which the authorities recorded and monitored both public and privately contracted debt; this influenced the speed of shifting domestic policies in reaction to external difficulties. Vulnerability to such difficulties was influenced by the extent of the shift to borrowing from commercial sources at market-related terms, rather than from official sources at concessional terms, and to short-term rather than medium-term and long-term borrowing. These factors were interrelated: the more rapidly countries increased the relative amount of their external borrowing, the less adequate was available official financing and the heavier was the reliance on commercial sources, while lack of control over external borrowing by the private sector enhanced the danger that short-term debt and overall debt service would grow to unsustainable magnitudes.

Superimposed upon the domestic developments and policy stances just discussed were a series of external shocks beginning in 1979. These shocks not only led initially to higher current account deficits and a larger accumulation of external debt, but eventually also weakened the confidence of creditors and thereby reduced the inflow of new financing.

The first of these external shocks was the series of oil price increases that occurred in 1979 and 1980. Perhaps surprisingly, the countries with the greatest payments difficulties in the early 1980s had benefited as a group from the oil price increases, but oil exporters such as Mexico, Nigeria, and Venezuela soon experienced serious debt-servicing problems from expansionary government expenditure programs, large increases in foreign borrowing, and domestic investments whose prospective yields were mismatched with amortization payments on this borrowing. By 1982, when oil prices began to weaken, some of these governments were heavily overcommitted to debt-servicing payments that were posited on continued high oil prices. At the same time, of course, the price increases of 1979–80 posed serious adjustment difficulties to oil-importing countries, especially countries exporting chiefly non-oil primary commodities, whose terms of trade fell sharply over the period 1979–82.

The recession in the industrial countries in 1980–82 not only contributed to the weakening of non-oil primary commodity prices, as well as to the decline in oil prices from 1982 onwards, but it also led to a cut in the growth, and in some cases even an absolute decline, of export volumes. The resulting fall in the purchasing power of developing countries' exports was concentrated especially heavily in the traditional oil exporters in the Middle East, which are not net capital importers, while Africa was also quite severely affected. For other groups, the purchasing power of exports continued to grow, albeit at a much slower rate than during the 1970s.

The sharp increase in nominal interest rates in industrial countries in 1979–80 quickly fed through to the interest rates that had to be paid on external debt, because a large proportion of the debt was at variable interest rates—especially in the Western Hemisphere and the countries with recent debt-servicing problems. Moreover, since the increase in nominal interest rates occurred shortly before the dollar price of internationally traded goods began to fall (owing to the recession and the appreciation of the dollar), real interest rates rose sharply in 1980. For similar reasons, there was also a sharp increase in the ratio of interest payments to exports: for example, this ratio more than doubled between 1978 and 1984 for debt-problem countries.

The payments problems resulting from the increase in real interest rates did not initially lead creditors to doubt the continued debt-servicing capacity of most indebted countries. Indeed, it is clear in retrospect that there were shortcomings in the risk assessments made by private creditors and bank supervisors. At the same time, while Fund surveillance resulted in the transmission of warning signals to certain debtor countries in the context of Article IV consultations, it did not produce the perception of a global debt problem until a relatively late stage. By 1981, however, doubts as to the solvency of some debtors began to arise as the financial community focused on the debt-servicing problems of Poland. This was followed by concerns about Western Hemisphere and African borrowers in 1982–83. Net lending by private creditors to the debt-problem countries fell from $57 billion in 1981 to virtually zero in 1983 (excluding arrears accumulation to private creditors—see Statistical Appendix Table A42). This development was paralleled by, and to some extent related to, the large shift in current account positions of major creditor countries, in particular, the rapid increase in the current account deficit of the United States.[4]

A final external development of significance to developing countries was the strong appreciation of the U.S. dollar over the period 1981–84. This development was, of course, closely related to the sharp rise in interest rates, but had an analytically distinct impact on the capital importing developing countries by depressing the U.S. dollar prices of internationally traded goods without a corresponding effect on the U.S. dollar magnitude of external debt, about 80 percent of which is estimated to have been denominated in U.S. dollars. For these countries, about two fifths of the rise in debt ratios between 1979 and 1983 is estimated to have been brought about by the real appreciation of the U.S. dollar.

In considering the impact of the external shocks mentioned above, it may be asked why they resulted in serious debt-servicing problems for some countries and not for others. The answer lies in part with the levels and structures of debt that different countries had at the onset of the adverse global developments, but also with the policies pursued in reaction to those changes and in the underlying orientation of trade and development policies. It is perhaps significant that countries with debt-servicing problems allowed their average current account deficit to widen considerably between 1979 and 1982, from 17¾ percent of exports of goods and services to 30 percent, while that of the non-problem countries rose only slightly, from 8 percent to 9¼ percent (see Statistical Appendix Table A35). These current account developments to a substantial extent reflected fiscal developments, as the average central government fiscal deficit of the debt-problem countries grew, as a percentage of GDP, from 2¼ percent to 4¾ percent between 1979 and 1982, while that of the non-problem countries grew by only 1 percentage point during the same period (see Statistical Appendix Table A19).[5] Finally, as noted earlier, the group of countries without debt-servicing problems had considerably larger and more buoyant export sectors: their exports amounted to an average of over 25 percent of GDP during 1979–82, compared with only 20 percent for the debt-problem countries, and grew (in value terms) at an average rate of over 11 percent, more than twice as fast as the exports of the debt-problem countries.

Management of the Debt Crisis, 1982–85

The emergence of widespread payments difficulties after mid-1982 faced the international financial community with the need to take coordinated action in order to avert a breakdown of the international trade and payments mechanism. The strategy that evolved consisted of an appropriate blending of adjustment and finance. Effective adjustment was seen as essential to help restore the confidence of creditors and to lay the basis for a return to sustainable growth in the future. Coordinated financing packages were required to maintain the flow of essential imports, to preserve debtor-creditor relations, and to retain the participation of a

---

[4] For a discussion of the relationship between threse current account developments and available financing to developing countries, see *World Economic Outlook, April 1985,* Supplementary Note 9.

[5] Central government fiscal deficits, however, are only a partial indicator of overall public sector deficits, for which consistent series for cross-country comparisons are not available.

wide range of creditor institutions.[6] These measures have had beneficial results, in terms of both strengthening the balance of payments and the debt structure of capital importing countries, and limiting the extent of the setback to domestic growth. In all these aspects of the international strategy, the Fund has played a leading role: by promoting appropriate adjustment policies, by providing large amounts of financial assistance (purchases of SDR 31 billion during 1982–85), and by coordinating and catalyzing financing from other sources.

The external adjustment achieved by the debtor countries is best measured by changes in the ratio of the current account deficit to exports. For the 15 heavily indebted countries,[7] this ratio fell from 35 percent in 1982 to under 1 percent in 1984. One significant indicator of these adjustments is that many indebted countries now have large surpluses in their merchandise trade accounts, arising from the need to meet large debt-servicing obligations without recourse to heavy additional borrowing. The adjustments producing these results, however, were not easy to carry out. Once payments difficulties arose, the financial imbalances and price distortions already in place increased the difficulty of carrying out speedy and effective adjustment policies. The longer price-distortionary measures had been in force, the more difficult it was, politically and administratively, to carry out corrective policies. Similarly, the longer the period over which an unsustainable level of government expenditure had been in effect, the more difficult it was to bring fiscal deficits down when external sources of credit dried up. Strong initial emphasis on demand management measures, without accompanying supply-side measures of equal effectiveness, led to a disappointing growth performance in a number of countries, despite the recovery of growth in world trade and output in 1984.

A major feature of the debt strategy since 1982 has been an unprecedented number and scale of debt restructurings and financing packages, both by banks and by the official creditors operating through the Paris Club. Beginning in mid-1982, a large number of countries approached banks for new financial arrangements; over the period 1983–85, 31 countries reached agreements with the banks affecting some $140 billion of debt, not counting the amounts involved in further restructuring agreements currently in the process of negotiation. During the same period, the Paris Club

came to agreements with 31 countries to restructure official and officially guaranteed debt.[8] As a result of the restructurings, it was possible to stretch out maturities of large debt repayments already coming due during this period. The financial packages made it possible in a number of cases for debtor countries to reduce substantially their overhang of short-term debt, in effect exchanging it for debt of longer maturities. As a result of these developments, the most heavily indebted countries have been able to reduce both their debt service ratios and the absolute amounts of short-term debt, even though the overall debt ratios have remained relatively stable. For example, the ratio of short-term debt to exports of the 15 heavily indebted countries was reduced from 68 percent in 1982 to 38 percent in 1985, even though their ratio of total debt to exports rose gradually from 263 percent to 286 percent. As a result of the new financing arrangements, together with the accompanying adjustment efforts, the cumulative fall in output for the 15 heavily indebted countries was limited to 4 percent of GDP in 1982 and 1983, before recoveries of 2¼ percent and 3 percent of GDP in 1984 and 1985, respectively. This can, of course, certainly not be considered a satisfactory growth performance over the long term—particularly not for many countries in sub-Saharan Africa where per capita incomes have been falling since the 1970s. As discussed later, bolstering the growth performance of debt-problem countries has become a major objective in the future management of the debt situation.

Medium-Term Scenarios

The efforts made thus far to improve the external position of those capital importing developing countries with recent debt-servicing problems have resulted in a dramatic strengthening of their current accounts. There has, however, been little decline in their total external debt relative to exports, although a substantial improvement in the structure of that debt has occurred. The growth of output and exports of the capital importing countries revived with the economic recovery of 1984–85, although performance in these regards was still unsatisfactory in many countries. This section addresses two key questions for the remainder of the 1980s: (1) the nature of the efforts that will be required on the part of both debtors and creditors to consolidate the progress made in dealing with debt difficulties; and (2) the implication of these efforts for the medium-

---

[6] These arrangements are described in *Recent Developments in External Debt Restructuring*, Occasional Paper No. 40 (Washington: International Monetary Fund, October 1985).

[7] The 15 heavily indebted countries are Argentina, Bolivia, Brazil, Chile, Colombia, Côte d'Ivoire, Ecuador, Mexico, Morocco, Nigeria, Peru, Philippines, Uruguay, Venezuela, and Yugoslavia.

[8] The 31 countries are not the identical set of countries as that involved in bank restructurings. Only partial data is available on the amounts of debt involved in the Paris Club agreements.

term evolution of variables such as GDP growth and the ratio of debt to exports.

As in the *World Economic Outlook* reports of 1984 and 1985, the starting point of the Fund staff's medium-term scenarios is a "baseline" case representing the implications of certain broadly plausible assumptions for certain major variables in the world economy. After exploring the outcomes of this scenario, this section reviews alternative outcomes based on sensitivity analyses of the effects of changes in the following variables: the availability of additional external financing, the growth rate of output in industrial countries, the level of interest rates, the price of petroleum, the effective exchange rate for the U.S. dollar, and the prices of non-oil primary commodities.

Baseline Scenario

The baseline case is built on a set of assumptions that relate in large part to certain key developments in the industrial countries (see Chapter IV for the policy background to these assumptions). Perhaps the most important of these developments is the gradual reduction of the U.S. Federal Government deficit from about 5½ percent of GNP in 1985 to about 2½ percent of GNP in 1991, as a result of expenditure-reducing measures. Because of these measures, real interest rates are assumed to remain fairly close to the lower levels reached at the end of 1985, with the 6–month Eurodollar LIBOR at 7½ percent during 1986/87 and 8 percent for the period 1988–91 (Table 20). (In the absence of measures to reduce the fiscal deficit, the staff would have expected upward pressure on real interest rates to re-emerge in the medium term.)

For reasons explained in Chapter IV, the real value of the U.S. dollar and the Canadian dollar is assumed to decline by 2½ percent a year against all other currencies during 1988–91. No changes in real exchange rates among major floating currencies are assumed to occur in 1986–87, and real exchange rates among non-dollar currencies are assumed to remain unchanged during 1988–91.

The reduction of the U.S. fiscal deficit and the continuation of nominal interest rates near current levels are assumed to result in sustained but moderate growth rates of output among the industrial countries (Table 20). GNP deflators would be close to 4 percent in the United States throughout the period, while for industrial countries as a whole they would remain at 3½–3¾ percent. Prices in world trade would reflect mainly the price and exchange rate assumptions already described, in addition to special developments in specific commodity markets. The world price of manufactures in U.S. dollar terms is projected to rise

by 14 percent in 1986, following a series of annual declines in 1981–84 and a small upturn in 1985. This largely reflects exchange rate developments that had already occurred by early 1986. After 1986 prices of manufactures are assumed to move broadly in line with U.S. price level developments, rising by about 4½ percent in 1987 and (reflecting the influence of the effective depreciation of the U.S. dollar) at the same annual rate in 1988–91. The U.S. dollar price of non-oil primary commodities, having fallen sharply in 1985, is projected to rise by about 12 percent in 1986 (reflecting chiefly a rise in coffee prices), by 1 percent in 1987, and by about 4¼ percent for each year during 1988–91. Oil prices are assumed to average $16 per barrel in 1986 and $15 per barrel in 1987, and then to remain constant in real terms during 1988–91. Because of current uncertainties in the oil market, this should be regarded solely as a working hypothesis, and in light of recent developments in that market a sensitivity analysis described later in this section considers the implications of a rise in oil prices after 1986.

A further important set of assumptions concerns the availability of external financing for developing countries. For the group of capital importing developing countries as a whole, it is assumed that flows of official development assistance will remain approximately constant in real terms and foreign direct investment will rise roughly in step with real GDP in host countries, while trade credits increase in line with imports. The attitude of commercial banks with regard to non-trade-related financing would remain cautious, although showing some continued response to the recent U.S. initiative. Reflecting these assumptions, private lending to the capital importing developing countries is projected to rise at an annual average rate of about 3 percent over the period 1988–91.

A final important set of assumptions underlying the baseline scenario concerns the policies being pursued by the capital importing developing countries themselves. In constructing the scenario, Fund desk economists for the countries surveyed were asked to describe the policies most likely to be pursued by each country's authorities over the forecast period. The resulting policy projections reflect the fact that external circumstances are continuing to compel the authorities in many countries to follow policies directed toward reducing internal and external financial imbalances. This is particularly true of countries with recent debt-servicing difficulties and sub-Saharan African countries, which are projected to reduce fiscal deficits, raise investment-GDP ratios, and moderate inflation, all to a significant degree. Such developments result in the continuation of low ratios of current account deficits to exports—still only 6 percent in 1991 for the capital importing developing countries as a group

Table 20. Summary Results of Baseline Medium-Term Scenario, 1977–91

(In percent)

	Average 1977–81[1]	1982	1983	1984	1985	1986	1987	Average 1988–91[1]
Industrial countries								
Growth of real GNP	2.7	−0.4	2.6	4.7	2.8	3.0	3.2	3.0
Real six-month LIBOR[2]	3.4	7.1	6.2	7.1	5.3	4.2	4.5	4.2
Increase in GNP deflator	8.4	7.3	4.9	4.3	3.9	3.4	3.0	3.7
World economy								
Change in world price of manufactures[3]	8.7	−2.5	−3.3	−3.7	1.0	14.0	4.5	4.5
Change in world price of oil[3]	23.6	−4.2	−11.7	−2.1	−4.4	−40.0	−6.3	4.5
Change in world price of non-oil primary commodities[3]	4.6	−10.1	7.1	3.7	−12.2	12.0	1.0	4.2
Growth of total external credit to capital importing countries[3] [4]	19.7	13.5	6.2	5.3	5.7	6.2	5.0	5.3
Private	21.4	14.4	3.7	3.6	4.1	4.3	3.3	3.1
Official	16.2	11.6	12.3	9.0	9.1	9.9	8.4	9.0
Capital importing developing countries								
Growth of real GDP	4.9	2.1	1.6	4.7	4.2	3.5	4.2	4.7
Growth of import volume	7.1	−6.5	−2.7	4.6	2.6	2.3	4.2	4.9
Growth of export volume	5.1	−1.5	7.5	10.7	2.5	4.1	5.6	4.8
Countries with recent debt-servicing problems								
Growth of real GDP	4.0	−0.1	−2.5	2.6	2.8	1.9	3.3	4.1
Growth of import volume	5.1	−14.6	−15.0	1.8	−2.7	2.3	2.8	4.8
Growth of export volume	3.3	−4.2	5.4	7.0	1.4	0.6	4.5	4.2

	Average 1977–81	1982	1983	1984	1985	1986	1987	1989	1991
Capital importing developing countries	(As a ratio of exports of goods and services)								
Current account balance	−14.1	−17.8	−9.4	−4.1	−4.9	−6.8	−6.0	−5.8	−5.9
Total external debt	122.6	148.6	158.8	152.8	163.0	166.6	160.7	150.0	140.2
Debt service payments	18.4	23.6	22.0	22.9	24.1	24.2	22.6	23.7	21.7
Interest payments	8.1	13.6	13.0	13.1	13.2	13.0	12.1	11.3	10.3
Amortization payments	10.3	10.1	9.1	9.8	10.9	11.3	10.5	12.5	11.4
Countries with recent debt-servicing problems									
Current account balance	−20.6	−29.9	−10.2	−3.9	−2.2	−6.8	−4.6	−3.6	−2.4
Total external debt	166.8	234.5	252.3	244.2	260.6	275.4	261.0	232.7	206.4
Debt service payments	27.4	38.2	34.4	35.1	36.9	37.7	34.8	38.1	31.9
Interest payments	11.9	23.3	22.4	22.6	23.0	23.0	21.0	19.3	16.9
Amortization payments	15.5	14.9	12.0	12.5	13.8	14.7	13.8	18.8	15.0

[1] Compound annual rates of change.
[2] London interbank offered rate on six-month U.S. dollar deposits, deflated by the U.S. GNP deflator.
[3] In U.S. dollars.
[4] Includes trade financing.

(Table 20). A steady decline in the ratio after 1986 is foreseen for countries with recent debt-servicing problems—especially fuel exporters, where these ratios are projected to rise sharply in 1986—but a slight rise for countries that have managed to avoid debt-servicing problems (Statistical Appendix Table A54).

The continuation of policies such as those described above, together with relatively weak export prospects and still fairly high real interest rates, produces an outcome of steady but rather modest rates of growth of output for the capital importing developing countries. GNP is projected to rise at an average annual rate of about 4¾ percent during 1988–91, virtually in line with the projected rates of export growth. Imports, after relatively slow growth in 1986–87, are projected to grow at a slightly higher rate than output in 1988–91, representing a partial recovery from the severe cutbacks in imports in 1982–83. These growth projections are similar to those of the baseline scenario in the *World Economic Outlook, April 1985* as the effects of slightly lower economic growth in the industrial countries are offset by those of slightly lower interest rates.

There are large differences in projected growth performance among groups of countries: for example, the average annual growth rate of output during 1988–91 in sub-Saharan Africa is some 2½ percentage points lower than that of Asia (Statistical Appendix Table A56). Another quite striking contrast is between countries with and without recent debt-servicing problems. For countries that are still recovering from debt service problems, the average annual growth of GDP in 1988–91 is projected at just over 4 percent, while countries that have avoided such problems are projected to grow at an annual rate of nearly 5½ percent. These differences in growth prospects are closely related to parallel differences in export performance, which influences the growth of GNP directly, through the contribution of the export sector to output, and indirectly, through the effects of foreign exchange earnings on import capacity. These results suggest that countries in the slower-growing groups still face serious structural problems, including the limited degree of outward-orientation of their growth process, while the countries without such problems have a stronger underlying basis for sustained growth. Nevertheless, these projections imply for certain groups—in particular, the small low-income countries—improvements in export performance that would require major policy shifts. The results also show the impact of the lower oil prices that are already included in the baseline scenario. Lower oil prices have a net negative effect on the group of countries with recent debt-servicing problems. Capital importing fuel exporters are projected to have lower rates of growth of output and imports than nonfuel exporters (Statistical Appendix Table A56).

Compared with the outcome of the baseline scenario in the *World Economic Outlook, April 1985*, the 1986 scenario shows somewhat smaller current account deficits relative to exports during the projection period.[9] Nevertheless, the debt-to-export ratios in 1990 are considerably higher than for the same year in last year's scenario. This reflects disappointing export levels for the developing countries in 1985 and lower expected export growth rates in 1986 and 1987 rather than any major change in growth rates expected over the medium term. Another important factor is the net negative effect of the fall in oil prices on capital importing developing countries as a whole. The ratio of debt service to exports, however, is only a little higher than in last year's projection, as the effect of

higher debt-export ratios is offset by lower nominal interest rates, an assumption justified by the recent fall in interest rates and the improved outlook for fiscal action in the United States.

For the capital importing developing countries as a group, the debt-export ratio is projected to decline from 163 percent in 1985 to 140 percent in 1991, while the ratio of debt service to exports falls from some 24 percent to 21¾ percent (Table 20). The fall in the debt service ratio is entirely on account of a reduction in the ratio of interest payments to exports, occurring because of both lower interest rates and the fact that exports are growing more rapidly than debt over this period. Despite the latter fact, the amortization ratio rises slightly, because of the rescheduling of payments originally due before the scenario period. There are considerable differences, however, between the groups of countries with and without recent debt-servicing problems. For the debt-problem countries, the debt-export ratio declines from 261 percent in 1985 to 206 percent in 1991. The debt-service ratio of these countries falls from 37 percent to some 32 percent, despite a slight rise in the amortization ratio. For the non-debt-problem countries, by contrast, the debt-export ratio increases slightly (remaining a little above 100 percent), reflecting the fact that the initial ratio was more nearly viable. The debt service ratio of this group of countries remains at close to 16 percent throughout the scenario period (Statistical Appendix Table A55).

The results of the baseline scenario may be briefly summarized as follows. If the capital importing developing countries continue strong adjustment efforts, in the face of moderate rates of economic growth in the industrial countries, they may expect a gradual strengthening of their external position together with moderate rates of output growth. Among particular groups of countries, however, outcomes will differ significantly. For both the highly indebted countries and the sub-Saharan African countries, the prospective growth performance will remain barely adequate and, in the case of the African countries, will not be accompanied by a marked lightening of the external debt burden. For the capital importing fuel exporters, maintaining a moderate rate of growth over the medium term would be consistent with only a slow improvement in their external debt position, which is likely to receive a severe setback in 1986. By contrast, however, groups of countries without debt-servicing problems, especially the Asian countries, enjoy far more buoyant growth prospects, and are able to countenance the continuation of debt and debt-service ratios at close to their current levels. In comparing the groups with better and worse growth prospects, there is a close association between the growth of exports and of GDP.

---

[9] In the present document, current account deficits include official transfers, whereas in earlier *World Economic Outlook* reports, current transfers were excluded. Adjusting for this factor, projected deficits are similar to those foreseen last year.

Alternative Projections

Six alternative projections were carried out to test the sensitivity of the baseline results to changes in six key variables in the global environment: the amount of external financing, growth of output in the industrial countries, interest rates in international financial markets, the price of petroleum, the real effective exchange rate of the U.S. dollar, and the prices of non-oil primary commodities. Policies in the capital importing developing countries are assumed to be unchanged, with targeted reserve-import ratios assumed to be the same as in the baseline scenario. Unless otherwise indicated, it is assumed such policies are constrained by the availability of external financing. The alternative projections are described briefly below and shown in detail in Statistical Appendix Tables A57–A62; key results are shown in Table 21.

Each of the sensitivity analyses focuses on the effect of altering a single variable. Of course, it is also of interest to consider alternative scenarios, in which several variables change together. For example, a

strategy in which additional lending was accompanied by improved policies (and perhaps also by higher market growth in the industrial countries) would have different consequences from simply a change in lending flows. Some of these considerations are explored at the end of this section.

The first of the sensitivity analyses examines the consequences of additional lending, from both commercial and official sources, to countries with debt-servicing problems; there is assumed to be no change in lending to the non-debt-problem countries. The total amount of increased lending was assumed to lead to an additional annual growth of private exposure to the debt-problem countries of 1¾–2 percentage points for the period 1987–91 (with an increase of perhaps half this amount in 1986) and an additional annual increase in official exposure of about 3 percent. The only change in GDP in this alternative projection results from changes in import volumes, as no change occurs in the growth of export markets. This approach was taken in order to isolate the effects of the lending per se. The possible orders of magnitude of additional in-

Table 21. Capital Importing Developing Countries: Alternative Medium-Term Projections

(In percent)

	Base-Line	Additional Lending	Lower Growth in Industrial Countries	Lower Interest Rates	Higher Oil Prices	U.S. Dollar Depreciation	Lower Prices of Non-oil Commodities
Capital importing developing countries				(Average 1987–91)[1]			
Growth rate of real GDP	4.6	4.7	3.3	4.8	4.9	4.6	4.2
Growth rate of import volume	4.8	5.0	3.4	5.1	5.2	4.9	4.4
Growth rate of export volume	4.9	4.9	3.3	4.9	4.9	4.9	4.7
Countries with recent debt-servicing problems							
Growth rate of real GDP	4.0	4.1	2.7	4.2	4.4	4.0	3.5
Growth rate of import volume	4.4	4.7	2.8	4.7	5.0	4.4	3.7
Growth rate of export volume	4.2	4.2	2.8	4.2	4.2	4.2	4.0
Capital importing developing countries				(As a ratio of 1991 exports of goods and services)			
Current account balance	−5.9	−8.0	−6.6	−5.9	−5.7	−5.8	−6.1
Total external debt	140.2	150.2	149.1	140.5	136.3	138.5	142.9
Debt service payments	21.7	23.0	23.1	20.9	21.1	21.4	22.1
Interest payments	10.3	10.9	11.0	9.5	10.0	10.2	10.5
Amortization payments	11.4	12.1	12.1	11.4	11.1	11.2	11.6
Countries with recent debt-servicing problems							
Current account balance	−2.4	−8.1	−2.8	−2.4	−2.3	−2.3	−2.6
Total external debt	206.4	234.2	217.7	206.8	198.9	203.7	211.8
Debt service payments	31.9	35.4	33.6	30.7	30.7	31.5	32.7
Interest payments	16.9	18.7	17.8	15.7	16.3	16.7	17.3
Amortization payments	15.0	16.6	15.8	15.0	14.4	14.8	15.4

[1] Compound annual rates of change.

creases in GDP growth resulting from improved domestic policies in developing countries, and of additional export growth resulting both from such policies and higher industrial country imports, are examined at the end of this section.

The outcome of the projection for additional lending is a combination of somewhat higher growth of both imports and output in 1986–88, and a much more moderate decline in the ratio of debt to exports. By the last three years of the scenario period, however, the additional financing would be insufficient to finance the continued acceleration of import growth, in part owing to the accumulated addition to debt service payments. For the debt-problem countries as a whole, the average growth of real GDP during 1986–88 is 1½ percentage points higher than under the baseline assumptions, but by 1988 the debt-export ratio is 14 percentage points higher; the debt service ratio, 1 percentage point higher; and current account deficits as a ratio of exports have steadily increased (from 2¼ percent in 1985 to 9¾ percent in 1988) instead of declining slightly as in the baseline case. Although growth of GDP in 1989–91 is ½ of 1 percentage point below that in the baseline outcome, the level of real GDP exceeds that in the baseline throughout the period. On the other hand, the final debt-export ratio is some 28 percentage points higher than in the baseline scenario, with little improvement in the debt service ratio between 1986 and 1991 (Table 21 and Statistical Appendix Table A57).

A second sensitivity analysis focuses on the impact of slower growth in the industrial countries, other things held equal. Specifically, growth of GNP in the industrial countries was assumed to be 1 percentage point lower throughout the period 1987–91. (It may be noted that the resulting magnitudes, with signs reversed, give indications both of the possible gains from an increase in industrial country growth and of the impact of a series of trade liberalizing measures by these countries taken over the scenario period.) The results of this sensitivity analysis are relatively straightforward (and dramatic) for the capital importing developing countries: a sharp fall in the rate of growth of exports, and, on the assumption of no additional external borrowing to meet the shortfall in foreign exchange earnings, a concomitant fall in the rate of growth of imports and consequently in that of output (Table 21). While overall levels of external debt are thus the same as in the baseline scenario for all country groups, debt-export and debt service ratios are somewhat higher, owing to the lower level of exports. For the capital importing developing countries as a whole, the average rate of growth of exports during 1987–91 (the years for which the lower growth in industrial countries is assumed) is just over 3 percent, or about

1½ percentage points lower than in the baseline scenario. This leads to a fall of about 1¼ percentage points in the average annual growth rate of GDP. The outcomes of this alternative projection for all of the various sub-groups follow this pattern closely, with somewhat greater sensitivity to the changed assumption shown by countries with relatively greater dependence on exports of manufactures. Although for this reason the growth rates of output for sub-Saharan African countries fall less sharply than do those of most of the other groups, the resulting economic growth implies zero or negative growth of per capita income for many of the countries in this region.

Another element of the global economic environment to which great interest attaches is the level of interest rates in financial markets in the industrial countries. Strictly speaking, the interest rate on loans to the developing countries also contains a variable element of spreads and charges, which reflect the creditworthiness of the borrower. Although variations in the size of these spreads and other charges are of significant importance to the cost of the loan to the borrower, movements in the base interest rate have nevertheless tended to be more volatile. To examine the effects of these movements, an alternative projection was prepared on the assumption that the level of interest rates (LIBOR) was 1 percentage point lower than in the baseline scenario throughout the period 1987–1991. The impact of this change is felt chiefly in 1987, the year in which lower rates are assumed to take effect, with all variables after that year growing at the same rates assumed in the baseline projection. The chief impact is on the rate of growth in output, as the lessened burden of interest payments, in the face of little change in exports and unchanged amounts of external financing, result in a rise of over 1 percentage point in the growth of imports in 1987 and a consequent increase of over 1 percentage point in the growth rate of GDP. While there is a subsequent reversal in the rate of growth of output, the level of output is permanently slightly higher (four tenths of 1 percent) than in the baseline case, and there is also a permanent reduction of about a percentage point in the debt service ratio. For countries with debt-servicing problems, however, these outcomes tend to be more marked (Table 21).

Because of the possibility that oil prices might differ from those assumed in the baseline scenario, an alternative projection was calculated in order to isolate the impact of this variable on the medium-term outcome. It was assumed that the price of oil would increase[10] by $5 a barrel compared with the baseline assumption

---

[10] For computational convenience, the increase was assumed to occur at the end of 1986.

(that the price of oil will average $15 a barrel in 1985 and remain unchanged in real terms thereafter).[11] The chief impact of this scenario is a sharp rise in output in capital importing fuel exporters, and a fall in output (though of smaller magnitude) of non-fuel exporters, which are assumed to offset the cost of additional import payments by reducing their overall import volumes (Statistical Appendix Table A60). While the change in oil prices has a continuing effect on the level of output in the two groups, growth rates return virtually to normal by 1988. Debt and debt service ratios become lower for the fuel exporters, because of higher export receipts. For capital importing countries as a whole, the net effect is positive: perhaps this is best explained by the fact that the value of net exports by developing to industrial countries increases. To assess the full implications of higher oil prices, it would of course be necessary to take account of induced changes in other variables, such as the level of international interest rates and the growth of demand in industrial countries.

Because of the importance of the U.S. dollar exchange rate, an alternative projection was prepared based on the assumption of an additional 5 percent real depreciation of the U.S. and Canadian dollars occurring at the end of 1986 (and taking effect in 1987). It was assumed that the prices of manufactures and non-oil primary commodities in world trade were held the same in SDR terms as under the baseline scenario. These prices would thus rise by an additional approximately 3 percent in U.S. dollar terms. The nominal price of oil in U.S. dollars was, however, assumed to be unaffected by the additional depreciation. As in the case of the sensitivity analysis for a lower interest rate and higher oil prices, the impact of the additional dollar depreciation influences several variables in 1987, but has little or no subsequent effect on their rates of change. For countries with a net surplus on non-oil merchandise trade, the more rapid growth of prices of manufactures and non-oil primary commodities yields an increase in export revenues greater than additional import payments, hence an increased capacity for real imports, supporting a higher rate of growth. The opposite is the case for those with a deficit on non-oil trade, typical both of most oil exporting countries but also for some oil importers with very large overall trade deficits. For the capital importing countries as a whole, the net growth effect over the medium term is negligible (Statistical Appendix Table A61). For countries with debt-servicing problems, the overall once-for-all rise in foreign trade prices as a whole, combined with the dominance of U.S. dollar-denominated ex-

ternal debt in the total, results in a decline of about 3 percentage points in the debt-export ratio.

For a large number of countries, especially low-income countries, a crucial factor in the global economic environment has been the movement of prices of non-oil primary commodities, relative to those of petroleum and manufactures. An alternative projection was carried out based on the assumption that the U.S. dollar prices of these commodities increase by 3 percent per annum over 1988–91, instead of the 4.2 percent assumed in the baseline scenario, and compared to the 4.5 percent per annum increase in the dollar prices of manufactured traded goods. Not surprisingly, the impact of the relative decline in non-oil primary product prices depends mainly on the structure of foreign trade of the countries involved. For the capital importing developing countries as a whole, annual growth rates of output are lowered by ½ of 1 percentage point over 1987–91, but for sub-Saharan Africa, the difference is closer to 1 percentage point. For all groups, however, there is a significant change in the ratios of debt and debt service to exports, since the U.S. dollar value of exports changes by more than that of the debt variables. For the entire group of capital importing countries, the debt-export ratio is almost 3 percentage points higher by 1991, and the debt service ratio ½ of 1 percentage point higher, than the baseline outcome; this impact is more pronounced for the groups with especially heavy debt burdens.

Future Prospects

The prospects of the capital importing countries, especially of the most highly indebted groups, are vulnerable to external factors, especially to a slowdown of growth in the industrial countries. For the highly indebted groups and for sub-Saharan African countries, there is little or no margin for downside developments: any substantial external setback will result either in a decline in the already very moderate growth projected under baseline assumptions, or in a reversal of improvements in the external debt situation, or in some combination of the two. Whatever the precise outcome, it would have serious implications both for the state of creditor confidence and for the internal political support for needed policy reforms.

Two recent developments provide examples of possible changes in the external environment that would affect the prospects of developing countries in more complex ways than those described in the foregoing sensitivity analysis. In the U.S. debt initiative, for example, additional external financing is intended to be combined with growth-oriented adjustment policies to boost borrowing countries' growth rates. It will be

---

[11] It should be emphasized that this scenario is purely illustrative: the impact of a decline in oil prices might also have been projected, with results of similar magnitude.

recalled that the impact of additional financing on commercial terms, taken by itself, is to raise the rate of growth for the next few years, but at the cost of retarding the decline in debt and debt service ratios. One way such an outcome could be avoided would be through improved domestic policies that, inter alia, helped raise not only the growth of output but also the growth rates of exports. For example, improved domestic policies that raised a country's saving and investment ratios by 10 percent (say, from 20 percent to 22 percent of GDP) and that lowered the incremental capital-output ratio by 10 percent (say, from 4 percent to 3.6 percent) would raise the output growth rate by about 1 percentage point. If, in addition, pricing and exchange rate changes were such as to encourage exports to expand in line with output, there need be no significant deterioration of the current account: of course, exports might expand even more rapidly, and the same policies are also likely to encourage some degree of efficient import substitution. It should also be noted that a sound domestic policy framework— particularly as regards demand management, interest rate, and exchange rate policies—is the best instrument available to reduce, or even reverse capital outflows, which is a necessary component of policies to raise saving and investment ratios without undue reliance on additional lending.

If such policies were to be pursued by a large group of heavily indebted developing countries, exploiting the full potential for a debt strategy based on these policies would need to be accompanied by a stronger expansion in industrial country markets for the exports of indebted countries. This in turn would require some combination of faster growth of GNP and more liberal import policies in the industrial countries. If, for example, the additional lending foreseen in the sensitivity analysis was accompanied by policies, both of industrial and developing countries, that enabled the latter to increase their export earnings growth by 1 percentage point, growth rates of GDP in borrowing countries could be raised by nearly an additional percentage point, and debt and debt ratios would be somewhat reduced compared with the outcome of the sensitivity analysis. This increase is thus largely complementary to the one cited in the previous paragraph, but additional to the increases in output resulting alone from additional lending. The overall result would be growth rates in excess of 1 percentage point higher than those in the baseline scenario.

Another alternative external environment, in which changes in several variables occur, is the possibility of a more rapid pace of reduction of the U.S. fiscal deficit (see Chapter IV). In such circumstances, industrial countries' output and world interest rates might be lower in the short run than in the baseline scenario,

and the U.S. dollar might depreciate more rapidly in real terms. If there were no additional external financing available to the capital importing countries, the short-term impact on these countries would be to lower the growth of output (because of the initially adverse impact on the global economy of the sharp reductions in the U.S. fiscal deficit) but also to reduce debt and debt service ratios, because of greater real depreciation of the U.S. dollar and lower interest rates, respectively. If more external financing became available—for instance, because of the easing of pressures on capital markets in the industrial countries—many developing countries might be able to increase their borrowing and thereby support a faster growth of output in the medium term. In the longer run, with a recovery in industrial country growth, the recovery of exports in capital importing developing countries would permit a reduction of such a dependence on external borrowing.

Policy Issues

Recent experience with the external debt situation has brought general recognition of a number of weaknesses in the policies of creditors and debtors, in the practices of private creditors, and in international financial arrangements generally, all of which contributed to the widespread payments difficulties arising in the early 1980s. Recognition of these weaknesses implies various steps that might be taken to avoid a recurrence of such difficulties in the future. At the same time, the precarious medium-term prospects for the more highly indebted capital importing countries underline the need to further develop the efforts that have been underway since 1982 to strengthen the position of these countries. In this section, after a review of the systemic weaknesses revealed by emergence of the debt problem and the short-term requirements for dealing with it, the relevant policy issues are discussed. For convenience these issues can be grouped under four main headings: the challenges facing governments of creditor countries, governments of debtor countries, private creditor institutions, and the Fund and other multilateral institutions.

Policy and Systemic Weaknesses Revealed by the Debt Crisis

Earlier in this chapter, the payments difficulties encountered by a large number of borrowing countries in the early 1980s were reviewed. For many of these countries, the foundations of debt-servicing problems were laid with the heavy borrowing of the 1970s; these problems then came to a head through the conjunction of an unusually unfavorable set of global economic conditions (reflecting to a considerable extent developments in major industrial countries), inadequate demand management and supply-side policies in many debtor countries, and inappropriate levels and modalities of external financing (for which both creditors and debtors share the responsibility). Any one of these factors would have sufficed to create serious payments difficulties for a number of borrowing countries; the combination of all three explains the depth and breadth of the problems that in fact emerged.

The medium-term scenario described in the previous section illustrates the continued vulnerability of developing countries to changes in the global environment. The fact that the domestic policies of the larger industrial countries have powerful effects beyond their own borders suggests the desirability of expanding the use of procedures, such as Fund surveillance, for ensuring that the interests of the international community are fully taken into account by the authorities in those countries in framing their policies.

With regard to the organization and modalities of international finance, the systemic weakness displayed various aspects. These have to some extent been discussed in the first section of this chapter, as well as other places,[12] and will be only briefly summarized below.

(1) The vulnerability of market-borrowing countries to external disturbances has been greatly increased by the growth in the relative importance of private sources of financing, and by the sharp increase in the percentage of external debt on which interest is paid at market or market-related interest rates, and at floating (rather than fixed) interest rates. In addition, the increasing relative dependence on debt rather than equity financing meant that borrowers' debt service obligations were independent of fluctuations in export receipts—caused, for example, by variations in world prices of primary commodities—and ran the risk of increasing if interest rates moved perversely with levels of economic activity (as occurred in 1980–83). For private creditors, in this instance, the advantage of a floating-rate debt—namely, reducing the interest rate risk—was offset by the disadvantage of increasing the risk of arrears and default on both interest and amortization.

(2) The shift of commercial bank lending from trade-related or project-related loans extended to specific enterprises or individuals, to general balance of payments support extended to sovereign borrowers, meant that banks' judgments of creditworthiness were based solely on the borrowing country's overall prospects

and policies, which were more uncertain and difficult to evaluate than specific purposes for borrowing. It was not until a "debt crisis" had clearly emerged that regulatory agencies pressed banks to improve their capital ratios and to dilute the concentrations of exposure in their balance sheets in response to the overall economic situation in debtor countries.

(3) On the debtor country side, however, there was also in many instances insufficient attention given to both the monitoring and management of external debt. Even in certain major borrowing countries, where public and publicly guaranteed external debt was reasonably well accounted for, there was lack of information on the magnitude, terms, and amortization profile of external debt contracted by the private sector. In some smaller countries, accounting for the external debt of even the public sector was in disarray, so that debt-servicing problems came with little warning and therefore without enough time to adopt the measures needed to avoid accumulation of arrears.

(4) The increased dependence on borrowing from commercial banks at shorter average maturities increased the vulnerability of borrowers because the amortization of loans was scheduled before the average gestation period of investments (especially public sector, infrastructural investment) was over. This problem was exacerbated when borrowing was undertaken, as occurred in some instances during the 1980–82 period, not to finance additional investment, but to avoid painful adjustment measures in response to the balance of payments strains created by weakened trade balances and higher interest rates.

(5) A decade or so of rapidly increased dependence on commercial sources of financing also served to diminish pressure for more rapid expansion of official bilateral and multilateral sources of finance, that is, officially guaranteed loans of export credit agencies, assistance from multilateral development institutions, and bilateral governmental grants and loans. Hence, when commercial bank financing suddenly dried up after 1982, there was little existing impetus for a stronger growth of financing from other sources.

Immediate Adjustment and Financing Needs

The debt-servicing difficulties that came to a head in 1982 were handled with a considerable degree of success by strong measures and cooperative efforts of debtor country governments, creditor institutions (and their respective monetary authorities), and the Fund. Nevertheless, as indicated earlier, the countries that encountered debt-servicing problems remain, on the whole, highly vulnerable to unfavorable global eco-

---

[12] For instance, in the *World Development Report, 1985* of the World Bank.

nomic developments. Despite strong adjustment efforts in these countries and despite a recovery of growth in world trade and output, for many of these countries debt and debt service ratios have been brought down only slightly, if at all. Preventing further increases in the debt service ratio, in the face of high interest rates, a large overhang of short-term debt, and heavy amortization payments initially scheduled for each of the years since 1982, was in itself a major accomplishment. For many heavily indebted countries, however, especially in Africa and Latin America, the adjustment that has occurred has yet to yield a favorable growth performance.

It is this weak growth performance that has led to a set of proposals put forward by the United States Secretary of the Treasury at the Annual Meeting of the World Bank and the Fund at Seoul, Korea, in October 1985. These proposals (referred to as the U.S. initiative) included the pursuit of effective growth-oriented adjustment programs by the debtor countries; net increases in exposure by private creditor institutions; increased lending by the World Bank and other multilateral development banks; and a continued central role for the Fund, in collaboration with the Bank, with regard to financial assistance, policy advice and surveillance, and the catalyzing of financing from private creditors. As illustrative figures for a key group of 15 heavily indebted countries (referred to earlier in this chapter), additional new commercial bank lending of $20 billion and $9 billion in additional new official financing over 1986–88 were mentioned, but the same framework could apply to other countries with debt problems and should be accompanied by continued lending to countries that have avoided debt problems.

The disappointing growth performance of a number of countries has been due both to the relative weakness of the recovery in the industrial world, and to the fact that many indebted countries have given insufficient emphasis to the adjustments needed to stimulate the growth of domestic productive capacity. This has been reflected in a tendency to cut investment rather than current outlays when reducing government expenditure, to delay price adjustments for key commodities or factors of production, and to favor administrative control over imports rather than more efficient means of rationing scarce foreign exchange. While the measures that have been taken to improve macroeconomic balance should have positive long-term effects on output growth, there is still a clear need for a greater emphasis on supply-side measures (discussed below). Furthermore, despite the general objective of reducing the ratio of debt to exports, additional external financing may be necessary in some instances to stimulate investment in new export-oriented capacity, and the magnitude of the financing gaps in some cases

requires that some financing take the form of general balance of payments lending by commercial banks.

From the side of creditor institutions, however, it has often proved difficult to mobilize funds for new financing, as smaller commercial banks have at times expressed reluctance to continue their participation in financing packages, and both large and small banks in some countries have also had to adjust to stricter bank regulations and supervision. In this latter regard, the governments of creditor countries are faced with the need to balance their efforts to strengthen bank regulations and supervision with a recognition that continued lending to countries undertaking economic adjustments would also serve to improve the quality of commercial bank balance sheets.

Another crucial element in the role played by the banks is the effective continuation of the Fund's advice, support, and surveillance of members' adjustment programs. In some cases, this may take the form of further use of Fund resources; in others, the technique of enhanced surveillance may facilitate the negotiation of a MYRA with commercial and official creditors. At the same time, the greater emphasis on growth-oriented adjustment programs, urged in the U.S. initiative, strengthens the efforts of the Fund in promoting policies conducive to economic growth and implies the enhanced importance of close collaboration between the Fund and the World Bank.

The terms and modalities of debt restructurings or financial packages remains an urgent issue in some cases. For certain countries, a combination of especially unfavorable external circumstances and inadequate economic management has resulted in situations in which debt service payments are far in arrears and normal restructuring arrangements would not suffice to keep future payments schedules within the country's capacity to pay. Some arguments have been put forward for financial arrangements that would ease both current and future burdens for debtor countries. Whatever the benefits and drawbacks of such an approach, a strong case can be made for the appropriateness of private creditors responding to the financing needs of adjustment programs that, if successful, would result in more adequate debt-servicing capacity in the future.

Finally, the success of adjustment programs and the effectiveness of new financing continue to depend crucially upon a favorable global economic environment. What combination of domestic policies in the major industrial countries will produce such an environment, and whether it is desirable or possible to coordinate policies among these countries, remain questions of pressing urgency. Real interest rates are still high by long-run historical standards; much excess capacity and unemployment remain in a large part of

101

the industrial world, discouraging new investment and productivity growth; protectionism, far from being rolled back as would be desirable, threatens to make new advances. For indebted countries, these developments retard progress in reducing debt-servicing burdens and increasing export earnings, and thereby tend to depress their own growth of output.

The Policy Challenge: Governments of Debtor Countries

At the outset, it should be noted that a large number of developing countries have continued to service their debt without interruption and without especially critical payments difficulties even throughout the late 1970s and early 1980s. Some of these countries were oil exporters or countries benefiting from workers' remittances or other service receipts from petroleum-producing neighbors. Others had pursued over a period of years prudent debt management policies, strictly limiting either the amount of nonconcessional borrowing or the overall use of external financing. In addition, some of these countries had undertaken either long-run policy reforms or timely adjustment measures that made it possible for them to adapt themselves rapidly to the changed external environment after 1979.

For the countries that faced less favorable conditions or whose policies had proved less timely and effective, the emergency measures adopted to deal with severe payments difficulties tended, as mentioned above, to be focused primarily on demand restraint, import controls, and exchange rate adjustments. To varying degrees, these were accompanied also by supply-side measures, but in a number of cases much remains to be done to accompany the necessary initial reductions in expenditure with private sector incentives and public sector initiatives that will stimulate savings, investment, and growth. Among such measures are: (1) improved mobilization of domestic savings, through more attractive interest rates on deposits and fostering the development of financial institutions and instruments; (2) policies to discourage capital flight and encourage repatriation of private foreign assets, through maintaining appropriate exchange rates, interest rates, and investment incentives, as well as a generally sound demand-management framework; (3) careful choice and monitoring of public sector investment projects, and, in general, more efficient allocation of public sector expenditures; (4) reform of public sector enterprises, putting their activities on a cost-efficient basis with realistic pricing of their goods and services, thereby reducing the fiscal burden of subsidization, and, where appropriate, privatizing the enterprises; (5) reduction and eventual elimination of price subsi-

dies to consumers and producers; (6) establishing agricultural producer prices in line with prices in world markets and realistic exchange rates; (7) elimination of trade and exchange controls, and reduction of excessively high tariffs, which serve to distort the domestic structure of production; and (8) realistic exchange rate policies, to maintain the desired degree of international competitiveness of domestic producers.

In addition to these measures, an important aspect of a debtor country's overall economic strategy is the management of its external debt. Where public and publicly guaranteed debt is not already being registered and monitored by a centralized agency—often, for example, the debt of public enterprises is incompletely recorded—such a procedure should be initiated. Next, procedures need to be established to report and monitor foreign borrowing and lending by private institutions and individuals; in a number of countries, significant progress has recently been made in this area with the support of technical assistance from the Fund. Once a proper reporting and monitoring mechanism is in place, the authorities should carefully examine the choices available to them: the amount and terms of borrowing (between fixed and floating interest rates, for example); the currencies in which debt is denominated; the possibilities for attracting equity investment instead of debt-creating borrowing; and the level and composition of international reserves. Finally, and most broadly, the borrowing strategy pursued is inseparable from the overall objectives and implementation of domestic policies: the amounts by which debt and debt service are planned to grow are closely related to the size and financing possibilities of fiscal deficits, but in strategic terms need to be geared to projected rates of domestic growth of output and to prospects for the absorption of exports by world markets. These prospects, in turn, depend partly on projections of global economic variables, and partly on a realistic appraisal of the results of economic policies. In both respects, recent experience has proved the wisdom of choosing projections that are based on realistic assumptions and that make prudent allowances for downside risks.

The Policy Challenge: Private Creditors

The policy issues faced by private creditors fall in several categories. First, there is the organization of continued concerted lending for countries where new debt restructurings and financial packages still need to be carried out and spontaneous lending has not resumed. Second, there are a number of complex questions regarding the terms and modalities of such restructurings or packages, as well as longer-term questions with respect to the modes of future financial instruments that would be best designed to meet the needs of both creditors and debtors. Third, there are issues concerning the policy conditions that should accompany both restructurings and new financing, and the future role of the Fund and Bank with regard to such conditionality. Finally, there are various continuing issues regarding the supervision and regulation of banking practices by governments in creditor countries.

The expressions of support for the U.S. initiative by the commercial banks of major creditor countries in December 1985 encourage hope that these issues will ultimately be resolved. A major problem is how to ensure the continued participation of smaller banks in financing packages. Another is how to gain support of the banking community for financial packages in cases where the record of debt service payments and adjustment programs has thus far not been such as to encourage confidence. The mechanisms for cooperation among banks in the areas of joint negotiation and monitoring of financial packages also have scope for further evolution; these mechanisms are themselves related to further issues, such as the roles of the Fund and the World Bank in the formulation and monitoring of adjustment programs in borrowing countries, and the possible development of new financial mechanisms (such as marketable bank claims) that could, over time, supersede the familiar approach of syndicated loans; these issues are taken up below.

In making decisions on appropriate financial packages, the views of private creditors, individually or collectively, necessarily differ widely depending on the individual borrowing country concerned. For a number of countries that were able to avoid serious payments difficulties during the past five years, spontaneous capital flows have never been suspended. For others, temporary payments difficulties have been successfully dealt with through a combination of effective adjustment policies and financing packages, and as a result the resumption of spontaneous flows is at least foreseeable. For a third group, adjustment policies, while producing some positive results, have not yet met major objectives of the initial program, and the resumption of spontaneous flows seems more remote. Nevertheless, in these cases, it may still be possible to organize needed financial packages on the basis of concerted lending. A last group of countries is at a yet earlier stage of dealing with payments difficulties. The wide variety of these cases underlines the necessity of maintaining a case-by-case approach both to determining financing arrangements and to evaluating the effectiveness of policies in the borrowing country.

Viewing the longer-run future evolution of the debt situation, it is apparent that developing countries should attempt to return eventually to a structure of new financing more like that of the 1960s and early 1970s, namely one that is less dependent on bank lending at commercial terms and variable interest rates. There may also be ways in which commercial bank lending could be packaged and organized that would make it less vulnerable to downswings in the economic situations of borrowing countries and less likely, under such circumstances, to engender threatened pull-outs by participating banks.

An eventual change in the structure of new financing would depend on increases in two forms of capital assistance. One would be an increase in official development assistance, from both multilateral institutions and bilateral sources, the latter including official export credits; these are discussed briefly below. Another would be an increase in various forms of bond and equity financing. For one important type of equity financing, foreign direct investment, the issues are clear enough. Much depends on the policy environment—as well as the political and social climate—within the host country, its willingness to accept higher levels of such investment, the opportunities made available for acquiring assets in the host country, and the regulatory and tax environment offered the foreign investor. Tax and foreign trade policies in the home countries of investors also play an important role: for instance, an easing of protectionist import restrictions tends to encourage investment in export industries in developing countries.

The volume of bonds issued by developing countries on international capital markets declined in the late 1970s, as use of bank credit increased, but a recovery is now possible with the widespread use of floating rate notes and other innovations in this market.[13] Most developing countries, however, are not yet sufficiently creditworthy to enter the bond market. One proposal aimed at encouraging the provision of new commercial bank finance is for the official guaranteeing of commercial bank loans. Certain types of guarantees already exist—for example, the partial guarantees offered by the World Bank on certain of its cofinancing arrangements, and guarantees by official export credit agencies of export credits from banks. There are strong reasons to oppose the generalization of official guarantees, which would tend to weaken the responsibility of private creditors for their lending decisions. Never-

---

[13] A discussion of these instruments may be found in *International Capital Markets: Developments and Prospects*, by Maxwell Watson, Donald Mathieson, Russell Kincaid, and Eliot Kalter, Occasional Paper No. 43 (Washington: International Monetary Fund, February 1986).

theless, in view of the likely preference of banks for trade rather than general purpose financing, an expansion of export credit guarantee facilities by the official agencies in favor of countries with effective adjustment programs could be an important move toward resuming normal financing flows to these countries, without altering established practices.

The Policy Challenge: Governments of Creditor Countries

As suggested earlier, the governments of creditor countries face a wide range of direct and indirect responsibilities in connection with successful management of external debt problems. An immediate issue is the compatibility of regulations and guidelines imposed by bank supervisors with the kinds of financing arrangements that seem called for from the viewpoint of stabilizing the external position of debtors (and in the long run, protecting the assets of creditors). The supervisors are understandably concerned with the deterioration in the financial soundness of some banks, which in a number of cases has arisen from poor performance of domestic as well as foreign loans. In some cases, however, the need to restore ratios of capital to certain types of assets (including outstanding loans to certain countries or groups of countries) has affected the willingness or ability of banks to participate in restructurings or packages that involve refinancing or new financing. In such circumstances, regulatory authorities have to take fully into account the contribution that maintaining flows of credit to heavily indebted countries can make toward improving the medium-term prospects of these countries and thus strengthening the soundness of existing loans.

Another crucial set of issues revolves around the creditor countries' direct and indirect contributions to official development assistance. Through contributions to and participation in major policy decisions of the multilateral institutions, especially the Fund and the Bank, the industrial countries, particularly the largest ones, can set the pace and direction in which a joint debt strategy can develop. The magnitude and direction of bilateral assistance, and policies guiding the nature and scope of guarantees offered by official export credit agencies, also raise a number of issues.

Perhaps the most important potential contribution of the creditor countries to the amelioration of the debt situation lies in their predominant influence over developments in the world economy. The sources of this influence are well-known and documented extensively, for instance in past and current *World Economic Outlook* reports. They require, therefore, only brief summary here. Sustainable, stable growth rates in the major industrial countries form the basis of adequate growth rates of trade volumes and output throughout the world, as well as the stability and buoyancy of prices of primary commodities. From the standpoint of the developing countries, access to industrial country markets is crucially linked to the growth of those markets, for on those two variables depends in large part the growth of exports, imports, and output in the developing countries. It is in this respect that easing trade restrictions is such an important element in improving the latter countries' economic prospects. For heavily indebted countries, another crucial economic variable in industrial countries is the level of interest rates, which in turn depends on the fiscal-monetary mix in the largest of these countries.

The Role of the Fund and Other Multilateral Institutions

To a considerable degree, the role of the Fund in dealing with problems of heavily indebted members may be expected to remain very similar to its role in the past, especially the functions it has performed since 1982. Many countries will continue to carry out Fund-supported programs, receiving both policy advice and financial support from the Fund and also the benefit of the Fund's catalytic role with regard to mobilizing support from both the commercial banks and official bilateral lenders. In some instances, as is already true for Venezuela, member countries may carry out adjustment programs without use of Fund of resources but under the regime of "enhanced surveillance," under which the Fund periodically reports on the progress of adjustment policies and such reports are made available to the pertinent bank advisory groups.

Another issue that arises is the relationship between Fund conditionality and the conditionality of the World Bank's structural adjustment programs. The two institutions share the aim of fostering a set of policies leading to financial stability, higher rates of investment and growth, and improved rates of growth of exports. Means will need to be found to build on existing Bank-Fund collaboration with regard to the advice given to members on the formulation of policy objectives and instruments. Such collaboration will involve in a number of cases the joint examination of a country's economic situation and prospects and the arrival at concerted views on policy measures to be taken, while taking care to avoid cross-conditionality.

Since the onset of widespread payments difficulties in 1982, there have been a number of suggestions revolving around the notion that the Fund or the Bank would provide guarantees of private debt or even more direct intermediary functions between private creditors and debtor governments. The objections to the widespread use of official guarantees have been stated earlier. Cofinancing arrangements between the Bank and private banks have occasionally included a partial guarantee by the Bank. With regard to the Fund, no direct participation in commercial financing operations is possible under the Articles of Agreement, except for the possibility of market borrowing to replenish the Fund's ordinary resources.

The Fund and Bank, as well as other multilateral financial institutions, have been mentioned as sources of expanded multilateral development assistance. There has been discussion of increasing Bank disbursements, or of increasing the permissible ratio of commitments to capital, as well as of future increases in capital subscriptions and in International Development Association (IDA) funds. The use of Fund resources does not, of course, fall under the heading of development assistance, but the new terms of the Structural Adjustment Facility, based on repayments of the original Trust Fund loans, do fall under the category of medium-term assistance to low-income countries on concessional terms. As for expansion of the activities of multilateral development institutions other than the Bank, these depend principally on expanded resources drawn either from donor country contributions or market offerings.

The discussion earlier in this section emphasized the importance of global economic developments for the efforts of indebted countries to improve their external positions. In this connection, a principal task of the Fund is to exercise multilateral surveillance over these developments, especially with respect to those policies in major industrial countries that have a significant influence. While most other multilateral institutions do not have analogous functions, mention might be made of the potential importance of the activities of the General Agreement on Tariffs and Trade in both opening further export markets for developing countries and in inducing them, through the process of trade negotiations, to gear their own economies more closely to world prices and export opportunities.

Supplementary Notes

Fiscal Developments in Major Industrial Countries Since 1980

In the 1980s, fiscal policies in the industrial countries have been generally more restrictive (or less expansionary) than they were during the middle and latter 1970s. Since about 1979, the governments of all the major industrial countries have been committed—at least in principle—to reducing both their fiscal deficits and the relative size of government transactions in their economies. In practice, however, these goals have proved elusive in most countries. Because of such factors as miscalculation of economic prospects, unforeseen external developments, and persistent political pressures, effective implementation of measures required to reduce deficits and to reverse the relative growth of government transactions has been widely frustrated or postponed. In some cases, and particularly in the United States, the effects on the fiscal deficit of the programs actually implemented have diverged markedly from the declared intentions of the authorities. Among the seven major industrial countries, indeed, only two have succeeded in preventing outright increases in the deficits of their general government sectors since 1979, and none of them has yet achieved a major reduction in the ratio of government expenditures to GNP.

This supplementary note reviews the principal factors contributing to the partial frustration of fiscal plans during the first half of the 1980s, describing the changes in fiscal balances and in the overall size of government transactions during 1980–85, the factors affecting government revenues, and summarizing expenditure trends and policies. Against this background, the note then deals with the current and immediately prospective impact of fiscal developments on the economies of the major industrial countries. It includes a special note on an important new law adopted by the United States in December 1985 (the Balanced Budget and Emergency Deficit Control Act of 1985—popularly known as the "Gramm-Rudman-Hollings" legislation), and a technical note on the concepts and statistical techniques underlying the "fiscal impulse" estimates used in assessing the thrust of fiscal policy.

Changes in Fiscal Balances

Judged in terms of prima facie changes in general government fiscal balances, the deviations of actual from planned fiscal outcomes appear to have been most pronounced in Italy, the United States, and Canada (Table 22).[1] The deficits of these countries, expressed as percentages of GNP/GDP, rose from 1979 to 1985 by some 4–4½ percentage points. The apparent slippage was somewhat more moderate in France, amounting to about 1¾ percent of GNP. Contrasting with these results were the changes that occurred in the Federal Republic of Germany, Japan, and the United Kingdom. Over the same six years, Japan's general government deficit was reduced by about 3 percentage points in relation to GNP and Germany's by 1½ percentage points. The ratio of the deficit to GDP in the United Kingdom showed virtually no cumulative change over this period.

Both among the countries with rising deficits and among those whose deficits were reduced, the prima facie comparisons of actual outcomes just summarized convey some misleading impressions of policy-directed shifts in fiscal positions. From 1979 to 1985, the change in general economic conditions was much more adverse in the four European countries than in the two North American countries or in Japan. The degree of deterioration of fiscal positions in this period attributable to purely cyclical factors is estimated (in row 4 of

---

[1] See Statistical Appendix Table A17, for the annual balances underlying this table, and Statistical Appendix Table A16 for separate data on central governments.

Table 22. Major Industrial Countries: Summary of General Government Fiscal Developments, 1980–85

(Percent of GNP/GDP)

	Canada	United States	Japan	France	Germany, Fed. Rep. of	Italy	United Kingdom
Cumulative change in deficit	4.3	4.0	−3.1	1.8	−1.5	4.5	0.1
Cumulative change in revenue[1]	4.2	0.5	4.2	4.7	1.2	9.2	3.3
Total cumulative change in expenditures (actual):	8.5	4.5	1.1	6.6	−0.3	13.7	3.3
Cyclically neutral	*1.5*	*1.7*	*0.5*	*5.1*	*2.9*	*5.3*	*3.8*
Structural	*7.1*	*2.8*	*0.7*	*1.5*	*−3.2*	*8.4*	*−0.5*
Cumulative structural change in deficit[2]	2.9	2.3	−3.5	−3.2	−4.4	−0.8	−3.8

[1] According to the criteria described at the end of Supplementary Note 1, a constant ratio of revenue to GNP is considered cyclically neutral. Any change in that ratio may thus be considered structural, and the figures shown in row 2 may be viewed (with reversal of algebraic signs) as cumulated contributions from the revenue side of the government accounts to the fiscal impulses shown in Statistical Appendix Table A17.

[2] Row 5 minus row 2—the difference being equivalent to a cumulation of the annual "fiscal impulses" shown in Statistical Appendix Table A17.

Table 22)[2] to have been equivalent to more than 5 percent of GNP for Italy and France to more than 3½ percent for the United Kingdom and just below 3 percent in the Federal Republic of Germany. For the United States and Canada, on the other hand, the cumulative deterioration ascribable to cyclical influences over the same period is calculated to have been equivalent to only about 1½ percent of GNP, and for Japan, it was even lower—roughly ½ of 1 percent.

Adjusting for these rather sharp contrasts in the fiscal effects of cyclical developments, one can focus on budgetary shifts of an essentially structural character (summarized in the last row of Table 22). This perspective throws a different light on some of the cumulative changes in actual deficits as listed in the first row of the same table. The contractionary impact of changes in the German budget during the 1980s, for example, is much larger (roughly 4½ percent of GNP) than that implied by the actual change in the fiscal balance, and substantial structural reductions (3–3¾ percent of GNP) in fiscal deficits are also shown for the United Kingdom and France. Even in Italy the net impact of structural changes appears to have been restrictive.

Since most of the changes in Japan's fiscal balance during the 1980s were structural, a cyclical adjustment of the Japanese figures does not greatly alter the degree of contractionary influence implied by the cumulative

reduction in that country's general government deficit. As estimated in the last row of Table 22, this restrictive influence was broadly similar to that exerted by structural shifts in the fiscal positions of most of the large European countries. (It should be noted, however, that the Japanese deficit at the beginning of the period was considerably larger than that of any of the major European countries except Italy, and that similar changes over the period under review do not necessarily imply similar current levels of structural deficits in any absolute sense.)

On a cyclically adjusted (or structural) basis, the cumulative changes in fiscal balances of the United States and Canada stand in striking contrast to those of all the other major industrial countries. During a period in which the structural changes in the other five countries were all in the direction of lower deficits, and in most cases quite substantially so, the corresponding changes in the U.S. and Canadian deficits were strongly upward. Cumulatively over the period 1980–85, these increments amounted to about 2¼–3 percent of GNP.

Generally speaking, the major industrial countries have made less progress in reducing the overall scale of their government transactions than in the companion goal of shrinking fiscal imbalances.[3] For 1980–85 as a whole, the most that can be said is that earlier upward trends in ratios of government revenues and expend-

[2] Since the cyclically neutral change in the revenue/GNP ratio is zero by definition, according to the concepts utilized here, the row showing the cyclically neutral change in expenditures also measures the cyclically neutral change in the deficit. (This measure is identical to the difference between row 1 and row 6 of Table 22.)

[3] In some countries with federal systems (such as the United States and Canada), the objective of reducing the scale of government transactions was pursued, strictly speaking, only at the central government level—sometimes with expansionary implications for regional and local government transactions.

Chart 31.   Major Industrial Countries: General Government Fiscal Aggregates and Balances, 1979–86

(Percent of GNP)

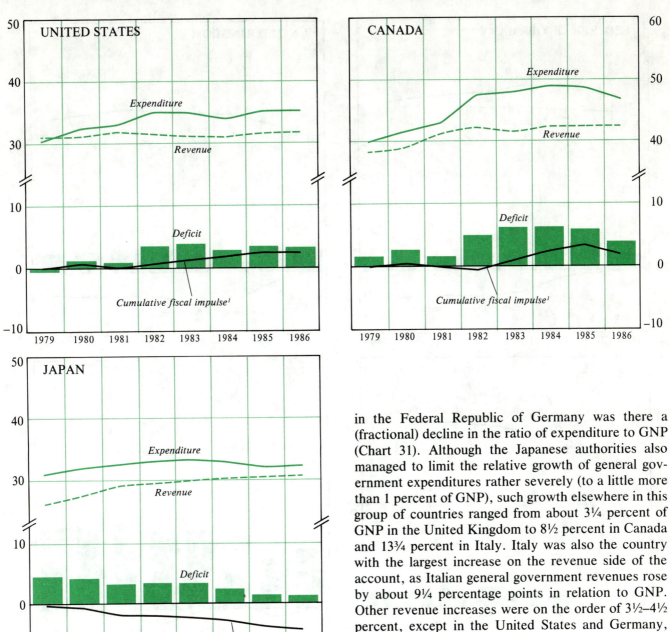

[1] Fiscal impulse as defined in text, cumulated from 1979.

in the Federal Republic of Germany was there a (fractional) decline in the ratio of expenditure to GNP (Chart 31). Although the Japanese authorities also managed to limit the relative growth of general government expenditures rather severely (to a little more than 1 percent of GNP), such growth elsewhere in this group of countries ranged from about 3¼ percent of GNP in the United Kingdom to 8½ percent in Canada and 13¾ percent in Italy. Italy was also the country with the largest increase on the revenue side of the account, as Italian general government revenues rose by about 9¼ percentage points in relation to GNP. Other revenue increases were on the order of 3½–4½ percent, except in the United States and Germany, where they were held to about ½ of 1 percentage point and 1¼ percentage point, respectively.

Factors Affecting Revenues

Revenue growth can be analyzed in terms of the relative contributions of "fiscal drag" and policy-determined changes in tax rates or in the tax base. The exceptionally slow growth of U.S. general government revenue from 1979 to 1985 was essentially a

itures to GNP were flattened in most cases, and that in some cases trends were tilted downward during the last two or three years of the period.

In no major industrial country was the ratio of revenue to GNP lower in 1985 than in 1979, and only

Chart 31 (*concluded*). **Major Industrial Countries: General Government Fiscal Aggregates and Balances, 1979–86**
(Percent of GNP)

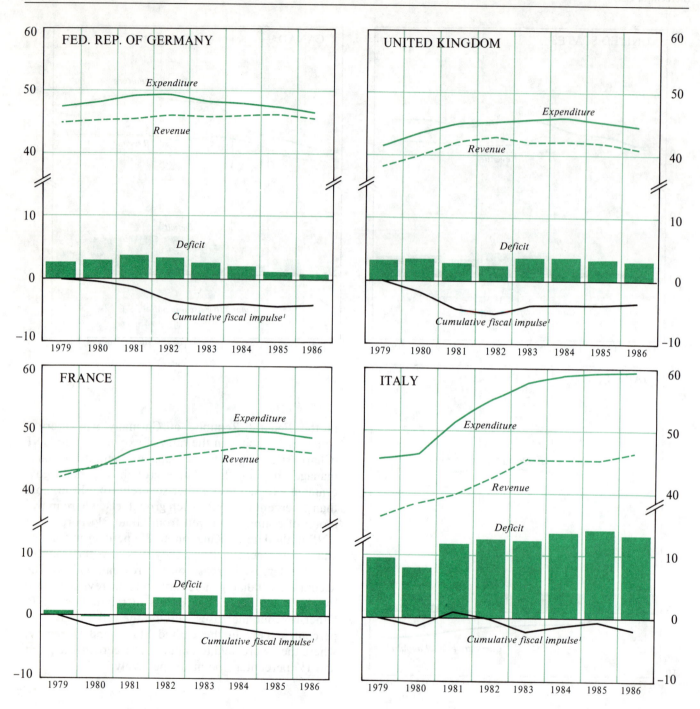

[1] Fiscal impulse as defined in text, cumulated from 1979.

function of the large federal income tax reductions introduced in 1981 and implemented over a three-year period. Despite a subsequent partial reversal of some elements of the original tax-reduction legislation, the cuts were almost sufficient over the period as a whole

(and more than sufficient during 1982 and 1983) to offset two major influences working to raise the ratio of revenue to GNP. One of these was the continued operation of a "fiscal drag," reflecting the elasticity of the revenue system in response to inflation and the trend growth of real income.[4] Another major factor tending to raise the U.S. revenue ratio during the 1980s has been a series of progressive increases in both the tax base and the applicable rates for social security contributions. Although the tax changes implemented under the 1981 legislation (which included provisions for indexing of personal exemptions and of the tax brackets through which progressive marginal rates are imposed) have probably reduced the longer-term income elasticity of the U.S. revenue system, a considerable element of fiscal drag is likely to remain a feature of U.S. fiscal developments. It may soon become more evident again in the absence of further reductions in U.S. income tax rates, since 1985 was the last year in which settlements of personal tax liabilities were significantly affected by the phased reductions enacted in 1981.

In relation to GNP, the rise in general government revenue in the Federal Republic of Germany during the first half of the 1980s was only slightly larger than that in the United States. With both real growth and inflation lower in Germany than in the United States, the impact of fiscal drag and cyclical influences tended to be smaller. In addition, income tax adjustments to "correct" for fiscal drag were introduced by the German authorities early in the period, and significant cuts in taxes on business incomes were provided, chiefly through credits designed to encourage investment and structural shifts in the composition of output.

Reflecting the opposing influences of the fiscal drag and the above-mentioned tax changes, direct taxes as a share of GNP remained virtually unchanged over the period. However, social security contributions as a proportion of GNP increased by 1 percentage point as a result of gradually increasing contribution rates. On the other hand, because of a fall in tax rates for specific indirect taxes in real terms, the share of indirect taxes in GNP declined by ½ percentage point, despite increases in selected consumer taxes and in the value-added tax. Thus, within a relatively stable overall tax

burden, there was a shift away from indirect taxation toward a higher degree of reliance on direct taxes and social security contributions.

Japan's major fiscal policy objective during the 1980s has been to reduce the deficit through curbing growth on the expenditure side of the budget. Revenues have risen substantially in relation to GNP because of the considerable elasticity of the tax system, increases in social security contribution rates, and some increases in corporate and indirect taxes in the early 1980s. The relative rise in taxes and social security contributions was facilitated by the fact that Japan's general government revenues at the beginning of the period were still by far the lowest, in relation to GNP, of any major industrial country. They remain the lowest, although the spread has narrowed considerably in comparison with some of the other countries (notably, the United States and the Federal Republic of Germany).

The fiscal restraint sought by the U.K. authorities during the early 1980s was achieved chiefly by revenue increases, although strenuous efforts were also made to contain the growth of expenditures. The rise in world oil prices played a significant role in bolstering revenues. A feature of the fiscal strategy adopted by the U.K. Government in 1979 was a major shift in the tax structure from income taxation to taxes on expenditures. This shift continued in the budgets of 1982/83, 1983/84, and 1984/85, which resulted in very little cumulative change in the ratio of general government revenues to GNP. During those years, further cuts in taxes on both personal and company incomes were substantially offset by upward adjustments of excise taxes (mainly to take account of inflation), by increases in national insurance contributions, and by a significant rise in oil-related revenues. Partly because of the substantial shift in the tax structure, as well as widespread use of indexation, fiscal drag appears to have been a less important factor in revenue growth in the United Kingdom than elsewhere.

In France, where reliance on income and profits taxes is lower (about 18 percent of total revenue) than in any other major industrial country, a very substantial portion of the rather steady annual increments in the ratio of revenue to GDP ratio during the 1980s has come from successive increases in social security contributions. Measures initiated in 1979 to restore the integrity of the social security system were instrumental in launching this upward trend early in the current decade, and further increases in social security contributions were necessitated in subsequent years by the expansionary trend in social expenditures. In 1983, when a significant reorientation of fiscal policy occurred in response to pressures on the French franc, an income tax surcharge—introduced for the benefit of the family allowance fund—resulted in a relatively

---

[4] The effects of pure "fiscal drag" are very difficult to distinguish statistically from those of cyclical and other short-term influences on revenue yields. In this context, however, some impressions of the potential magnitudes involved may be inferred from certain estimates relating to the U.S tax legislation of 1981. The cumulative reduction of individual income tax liabilities under that legislation amounted to 30 percent. By 1984, the ratio of personal taxes to personal income was calculated to remain at about 10¾ percent, compared with 11½ percent in 1980. However, it was also calculated that the interplay of inflation and real growth with progressivity of the rate structure would have led to a ratio of about 14¾ percent by 1984 under the previous tax arrangements. The combined effects of both cyclical improvement and longer-term fiscal drag (coupled with some predetermined changes in social security contributions) would thus have been more than 3 percentage points. With the U.S. unemployment rate no lower in 1984 than in 1980, the greater part of this hypothetical increase can probably be interpreted as a reflection of fiscal drag, as it operated before the 1981 tax cuts, rather than of purely cyclical influences.

comfortable surplus in the social security accounts, but contributed to a further increase in the revenue to GDP ratio. This trend was finally arrested in 1985, when reductions in the personal income and business tax were introduced with a revenue impact equal to about 0.7 percent of GDP, which offset the impact of some further increases in the social security payroll tax rates, an increase in the domestic tax on petroleum products, and certain other measures.

Cumulatively, the growth of general government revenue relative to GNP in Canada during the 1980s has been similar to the average of the other major industrial countries, although somewhat more irregular. Revenue growth was very strong early in the decade, as a result of large increases in energy taxation. In 1983, however, fiscal policy was directed toward promoting recovery from the 1981–82 recession, while energy tax receipts declined somewhat as a result of both the domestic recession and the weakness in world oil prices. During 1983 and 1984, there was also a slowdown in the growth of revenue from personal income taxes. This slowdown apparently stemmed in part from a shift in the relationship between assessed income for tax purposes and total personal income, reflecting such factors as greater than expected use of exemptions, deductions, and tax credits. In addition, however, there was a decline in the ratio of tax collections to tax liabilities.

Toward the end of 1984 and in early 1985, Canadian fiscal policy was redirected onto a path of restraint by a new government. Although this was done predominantly through measures to curb spending, tax increases were also instituted. Sales tax rates were raised by 1 percentage point, and the base of the tax was broadened; tax brackets and exemptions were partially deindexed; and a temporary surcharge was levied on both individual and corporate incomes. The result was a reversal of the 1983 drop in the ratio of Canadian general government revenues to GNP, partly through restoration of an element of fiscal drag that had been suppressed by indexation.

In Italy, the persistently high rate of inflation and the steep progressivity of personal income tax rates combined to produce an unusually large degree of fiscal drag during the early 1980s, despite periodic steps to reduce its effects. In addition, upward adjustment of various tax rates, particularly for indirect taxes, plus fiscal amnesties and a shortening of lags in revenue collections contributed to a series of marked annual increases in the ratio of revenue to GNP ratio from 1980 through 1983. The fact that the growth of government spending during that period was even more rapid prevented major steps to reduce the rapid rise in the tax burden. Revenue increases were especially large in 1982 and 1983, reflecting various tem-

porary measures to boost receipts. Subsequently, the expiration of those temporary measures, coupled with a reduction of fiscal drag (undertaken in conjunction with an agreed reduction of wage indexation), led to an abrupt leveling off of the ratio of revenue to GNP ratio in 1984 and 1985. The current medium-term strategy of the Italian authorities appears to be geared broadly toward maintenance of the tax burden at its recent level. Within this overall objective, some redistribution of incidence from wage to non-wage income is being sought, along with an increase in the share of indirect taxes. Improved enforcement and measures to reduce the erosion of the tax base (especially for the value-added tax and for income from unincorporated businesses) are prominent among the means through which these aims are being pursued.

Expenditure Trends and Policies

Government expenditure trends in all of the major industrial countries have been strongly affected during the 1980s by two pervasive influences: the difficulty in arresting the rapid growth of spending under various social welfare programs; and the dramatic increase in interest payments generated by large increments in government debt and high interest rates. Both demographic changes and the impact of the prolonged international recession tended to generate automatic or quasi-automatic increases in payments to beneficiaries whose "entitlements" had been established under earlier policy decisions. Although many of the relevant entitlement programs had been introduced at times when prevailing conditions were quite different from those characterizing the 1980s, social and political pressures against curtailment of benefits were almost universal.

Debt service payments were, of course, even more intractable. With the scale of such payments sharply higher in relation to GNP during the early 1980s, containment of the overall ratio of government expenditures to GNP could not be accomplished by any of the major industrial countries except through outright reduction in the relative magnitude of noninterest outlays. The degree to which the national authorities of the seven nations have succeeded in reaching or approaching that target has varied even more widely from country to country than their respective results on the revenue side of the fiscal accounts.

At one extreme is the record of the Federal Republic of Germany, where the rise in total general government expenditures, expressed as a percentage of GNP, was limited to about ½ of 1 percentage point per annum from 1979 through 1982 and then rolled back to a level

Table 23. Major Industrial Countries: General Government Expenditures and Selected Components, 1979–86[1]

(Percent of nominal GDP/GNP)

	1979	1983	1984	1985 (Estimated)	1986 (Projected)
Canada—total	40.2	47.9	48.9	48.5	46.6
Interest payments, gross	*5.2*	*7.2*	*7.9*	*8.4*	*8.2*
Transfers and subsidies	*12.4*	*16.4*	*16.6*	*16.2*	*15.3*
Other (mainly purchases of goods and services)	*22.6*	*24.3*	*24.4*	*23.9*	*23.1*
United States—total	30.6	35.0	33.9	37.1	37.1
Interest payments, gross	*2.7*	*4.3*	*4.6*	*4.8*	*5.0*
Transfers and subsidies	*10.8*	*13.2*	*12.1*	*12.2*	*12.0*
Other (mainly purchases of goods and services)	*17.1*	*17.5*	*17.2*	*20.1*	*20.1*
Japan—total	31.0	33.3	32.8	32.2	32.6
Interest payments, gross	*2.6*	*4.2*	*4.4*	*4.6*	*4.7*
Transfers and subsidies	*11.6*	*13.3*	*13.0*	*12.7*	*12.9*
Other (mainly purchases of goods and services)	*16.8*	*15.8*	*15.5*	*14.9*	*15.0*
France—total	42.9	49.2	49.8	49.4	48.7
Interest payments, gross	*1.5*	*2.6*	*2.8*	*2.7*	*2.7*
Transfers and subsidies	*26.3*	*30.2*	*30.7*	*30.7*	*30.2*
Other (mainly purchases of goods and services)	*15.1*	*16.4*	*16.3*	*16.0*	*15.8*
Germany, Fed. Rep. of—total	48.0	48.7	48.4	47.9	46.9
Interest payments, gross	*1.7*	*3.0*	*3.0*	*3.0*	*2.9*
Transfers and subsidies	*23.3*	*23.2*	*23.1*	*22.5*	*21.9*
Other (mainly purchases of goods and services)	*23.0*	*22.5*	*22.3*	*22.3*	*22.1*
Italy—total	45.6	57.8	58.9	59.4	59.8
Interest payments, gross	*5.8*	*9.1*	*9.5*	*9.2*	*9.4*
Transfers and subsidies	*17.4*	*21.4*	*21.1*	*23.0*	*23.1*
Other (mainly purchases of goods and services)	*22.4*	*27.3*	*28.3*	*27.2*	*27.3*
United Kingdom—total	41.7	45.7	46.0	45.3	44.5
Interest payments, gross	*4.6*	*4.9*	*4.9*	*5.1*	*4.8*
Transfers and subsidies	*14.9*	*17.1*	*17.6*	*17.2*	*. . .*
Other (mainly purchases of goods and services)	*22.2*	*23.7*	*23.5*	*23.0*	*. . .*

[1] The fiscal data used in computing the ratios shown in this table are on a national accounts basis.

in 1985 fractionally below that of 1979. Since interest payments increased over those six years by the equivalent of 1¼ percent of GNP (Table 23), the decline in the relative magnitude of other outlays was appreciable. Moreover, inasmuch as those other outlays in 1985 included much larger unemployment insurance benefits, as well as other components pushed upward by cyclical influences, the compression of cyclically adjusted expenditures was substantial. As measured according to the concepts of the cyclically neutral budget analysis, it amounted to about 3¼ percentage points in relation to GNP over the period 1980–85 (Table 22). The restraint was distributed fairly evenly between government purchases of goods and services and transfer payments. It was also applied gradually, through a succession of relatively small steps in the annual budgets of recent years, rather than through any major fiscal reform. Contributory steps have included, for example, reductions of unemployment benefits, a temporary (nine-month) freeze on civil service wages, changes in the calculation of pension payments, and measures to limit the cost of health insurance.

Japan's fiscal restraint program, although applied under somewhat different economic circumstances, has also been characterized by gradualism and effectiveness. Given the revenue increases produced by the greater buoyancy of the Japanese economy in recent years and the relatively high elasticity of the Japanese tax system, the Japanese authorities have been able to lower the general government deficit substantially without a major cutback in the overall ratio of government expenditure to GNP, which rose moderately from 1979 to 1983, then fell back slightly during the past two calendar years. However, a considerable restructuring of expenditures was carried out.

The authorities' main objective has been to reduce the deficit in the general account of the central government so as to eliminate by fiscal year 1990/91 the issuance of bonds to cover current spending. A reduction in the deficit is believed to be needed both to prevent the further erosion of fiscal flexibility and to place the government in a better position to accommodate the increased social welfare expenditure that will inevitably accompany the rapid aging of the population in the next two decades.

Given the heavy upward pressure on expenditure arising from social security outlays caused by the aging of Japan's population and the maturing of its social security schemes, as well as the rise in interest payments on government debt, the burden of expenditure restraint has fallen heavily on other categories of expenditure. Whereas the ratios of transfer payments and of interest payments to GNP rose by 1.1 percentage points and 2.0 percentage points, respectively, between 1979 and 1985, the ratio of other expenditures was reduced by nearly 2 percentage points. Initially, the expenditure restraint was achieved mainly by across-the-board cuts of nonpriority, discretionary expenditures. However, room for reductions in these areas has become smaller and, in recent years, the authorities have undertaken an important reform of social security programs.

In both the United Kingdom and the United States, the growth of general government expenditures in relation to GNP during the period 1980–85 was close to the average for all seven major industrial countries. However, a considerably larger share of the rise in the expenditure ratio can be attributed to cyclical factors in the United Kingdom than is the case in the United States. Indeed, the "cyclically neutral budget" analysis would impute the entire rise since 1979 in U.K. general government expenditure (as a percentage of GDP) to such factors, whereas the corresponding share in the United States was only about one third (Table 22).

The composition of the respective increases in these two countries also differed. Interest payments and expenditures for national defense were the predominant expansionary elements in the United States, while a rise (relative to GNP) in transfers and subsidies accounted for more than half of the cumulative growth in total expenditures of the general government sector in the United Kingdom. Government interest payments in the United Kingdom, which were already relatively high in 1979, rose less (as a percentage of GDP) over the following six years than in any other major industrial country. In both the United Kingdom and the United States, transfers and subsidies rose more sharply in relative importance during the first several years of the period, but have fallen back somewhat (relative to GNP) since 1983, especially in the United States.

Another change of considerable significance in the United States was an appreciable reduction in the relative importance of transfers to state and local governments. Partly because of this development, which did not affect spending programs of the state and local governments commensurately, the latter units have been much more disposed toward revenue increases than the federal government. Accordingly, their share of U.S. general government receipts has

risen, in relation to GNP, by about ½ of 1 percentage point during the first half of the current decade.

In France, the cumulative rise in general government expenditure during 1980–85 was appreciably larger than the average for all major industrial countries, and was more heavily concentrated on social welfare transfers and subsidies. This increase, together with a virtual doubling of the ratio of government interest payments to GNP, accounted for more than 85 percent of the cumulative growth of total French government spending. Most of the increment occurred during 1981 and 1982, as a consequence of the highly stimulative (but short-lived) fiscal policy introduced to cushion the 1980–81 recession and hasten recovery. However, a major reorientation of French fiscal policy occurred in early 1983, when measures of restraint adopted to help defend the franc included steps to reduce public sector spending. Since then, the French authorities have arrested the increase in the ratio of expenditure to GDP and, despite the continued relatively slow growth of GDP, managed to reduce it slightly in 1985.

The course of general government spending during the 1980s in Canada has been broadly similar to that of France, except that the main surge occurred a year later (1982) and the cumulative rise in relation to GNP was moderately larger (8½ percentage points). Half of the cumulative increase occurred in 1982, reflecting countercyclical efforts of that year, including a large increase in the relative magnitude of unemployment insurance benefits. However, the ratio of government expenditures to GNP did not recede during 1983 and 1984, as might have been expected on cyclical grounds. On the contrary, the ratio rose in each of those years, and did not begin to recede until 1985.

One reason for difficulty in slowing the increase in the expenditure ratio in Canada has been an exceptionally persistent escalation of interest payments. Although the Canadian central government's debt ratio is not particularly high (relative to other countries), Canadian provinces and municipalities have quite large amounts of debt outstanding. With the relatively high level of Canadian interest rates, increases in general government interest payments outpaced the growth of nominal GNP in 1984–85 by a wider margin than in any of the other major industrial countries except Italy.

Throughout much of the period since 1980, the Italian authorities have been unable to obtain the expenditure cuts or revenue increases (beyond those resulting from fiscal drag) that would have been required to meet their established goal of containing the government deficit. General government expenditures rose faster than nominal GDP in every year—and by a strikingly wide margin from 1981 through 1983. Cyclical conditions explain part of the expansion during those years, but the rise in government spending also reflects improvements in social welfare benefits, sizable wage increases in the public sector, larger transfers to troubled enterprises, and rapid growth of debt service costs. Government interest payments in Italy, expressed as a percentage of GDP, increased from less than 6 percent in 1979 to a little over 9 percent in 1983—easily the highest such ratio among the major industrial countries (Table 23). Further increases since 1983 have been considerably slower, in broad conformity with the general trend in most of the other major industrial countries toward a leveling off of this relationship. Further deceleration sufficient to permit the growth of revenues to be applied to reduction of the deficits may depend crucially on the future evolution of real interest rates.

Recent and Prospective Fiscal Influences on Economic Activity

This section, after recapitulating the most recent changes in fiscal balances reviews the prospects for 1986 and 1987, focusing on the restrictive or stimulative effects likely to be imparted to economic activity in the major industrial countries, using an analytical approach that measures the direction and strength of policy-induced changes in underlying fiscal positions. The particular concept utilized here is that of the "fiscal impulse" (expansionary or contractionary) calculated in terms of the "cyclically neutral budget" technique described below. The main provisions are summarized of what might prove to be the most important single fiscal measure of recent years—the "Balanced Budget and Emergency Deficit Control Act of 1985" enacted by the U.S. Congress and approved by the President toward the end of 1985. Although the results likely to flow eventually from this legislation are highly uncertain at the present time, some of the potential consequences are of far-reaching importance, not only for the United States, but for the world economy generally.

Fiscal Developments in 1985

The combined fiscal deficit of the major industrial countries increased marginally in relation to GNP in 1985 at the central government level and was stable at the level of general government (Statistical Appendix Tables A16 and A17). The virtual stability of the combined fiscal balance, however, resulted from contrasting movements in the balances of individual countries. The deterioration in the budgetary position of the United States in 1985 was more than large enough to offset a small decline in the composite fiscal deficit of the other six countries. For the entire group, with account taken of cyclical changes in the respective economies, the underlying fiscal impulse was expansionary at the central government level, but broadly neutral at the general government level.

The difference between the expansionary thrust of U.S. fiscal policy and the generally restrictive impulse in the other major industrial countries, taken together, was somewhat greater in 1985 than in 1984. At the general government level, the U.S. fiscal impulse was again equal to about ½ of 1 percent of GNP, while the composite for the other countries shifted appreciably toward restraint. In the United States, the expansionary impulse stemmed from the expenditure side of the fiscal account, being fueled primarily by the defense buildup and secondarily by expansion of state and local government spending. Part of the expenditure impulse, however, was offset by revenue growth associated with the built-in elasticity of the tax system.

Outside the United States, the moderate composite swing toward restraint in 1985 was largely due to developments in Japan and the Federal Republic of Germany. In each of these countries, the general government deficit was reduced by approximately 1 percentage point in relation to GNP. Occurring in a context of little or no change in cyclical influences, these reductions imparted restrictive impulses of broadly similar size. In Japan, the degree of restraint was smaller at the central government level than for the general government sector, while in Germany it was about that same at either level. Moreover, the sources of the restrictive impulses differed in other ways. In Japan, the negative impulse came to a considerable extent from the revenue side of the account, reflecting mainly the built-in elasticity of the tax system, whereas in the Federal Republic of Germany the decline in the fiscal deficit was due mainly to a fall in public investment outlays and restrained growth of social transfers. Although these categories of expenditure were also strongly restrained in Japan, the total withdrawal of stimulus from the expenditure side of the Japanese account was limited by built-in increases in social security outlays and the rise in interest payments.

In France, the thrust of fiscal policy was contractionary in 1985, particularly at the general government level, where the unadjusted deficit is estimated to have declined from 2.8 percent of GDP in 1984 to 2.5 percent in 1985. The central government deficit is estimated to have been marginally reduced from 3.4 percent to 3.3 percent of GDP, and thus to have slightly overshot the target of 3.0 percent of GDP. This withdrawal of stimulus was attributable to a slowing of expenditure growth. The decline in government expenditures as a percentage of GDP was attributable to restraints on increases in both employment and real wages in the government sector, and to deceleration in the growth of social security transfers and subsidies.

In the United Kingdom, government revenue declined in relation to GDP in 1985, reflecting the impact of lower oil prices and certain tax changes introduced in the March 1985 budget. Notwithstanding this relative decline in revenues, the government deficit also decreased moderately as a result of a sharper deceleration in the growth of government spending. In a year of relatively strong expansion of economic activity, however, much of the decline in the ratio of expenditure to GDP was due to cyclical developments. With allowance for those, the moderate change in the actual deficit must be interpreted as essentially neutral in terms of the implied fiscal impulse.

Italy was the only major European country in which the fiscal deficit widened substantially in 1985. The increase amounted to about ½ of 1 percentage point in relation to GDP, whether measured at the general government level or for the central government alone. In either case, about one third of the change could be attributed to cyclical influences in a year of rather weak GDP growth, but the greater part represented growth in the structural deficit. Slower growth of non-tax revenue, increased outlays associated with social security benefit payments and other transfers to households, and termination of discretionary measures of restraint in effect during the previous year were the principal factors underlying Italy's reversion to a more stimulative fiscal stance in 1985.

In Canada, a relatively high rate of economic growth and the implementation of a number of deficit-reducing measures adopted in the context of the May 1985 budget resulted in little change in the fiscal deficit, after three consecutive years of large and growing imbalances. The revenue measures in the budget included an increase in the sales tax, a partial de-indexation of personal income tax brackets, and temporary corporate and personal income tax surcharges. Partly because of lags in collection of the newly increased taxes and partly because government spending declined less in relation to GNP than might ordinarily have been expected in a year of rather buoyant economic activity, the thrust of central government fiscal policy in 1985 was moderately expansionary. In the broader general government accounts, because of the weight of provincial and municipal government transactions not directly affected by the shift in federal government policy, the fiscal impulse calculated for 1985 was also somewhat expansionary, although less than in the preceding two years.

The Outlook for 1986 and 1987

The projections for 1986 presented in Tables A16 and A17 of the Statistical Appendix are generally based on proposed and, in some cases, adopted budgets and medium-term fiscal plans. For the seven countries as a group they indicate a moderately contractionary thrust at the general government level and a somewhat more contractionary thrust at the central government level. On the basis of staff estimates consistent with the general assumption of "present policies," a further contractionary impulse is indicated for 1987 at both the central and general government levels.

For the United States, the projections are based on the authorities' "current services" estimates.[5] Their estimates of the deficit on this basis have been revised downward substantially from those presented in the fiscal 1986 budget. Current services estimates for expenditures have been lowered, reflecting sizable reductions in estimates of defense spending and the first-year spending reductions required under the Gramm-Rudman-Hollings Act (described below). In deriving the projections for 1986, the staff has adjusted the U.S. authorities' current services estimate for differing assumptions regarding economic growth, employment, inflation, and interest rate developments. According to the staff projections, the federal government deficit (on a "unified budget" basis) would decline by about 1 percentage point to 4¾ percent of GNP in 1986. With little change in the U.S. cyclical position, the thrust of fiscal policy would thus turn contractionary for the first time since 1979. This prospective shift is mostly attributable to cuts in spending and to a reduction in interest rates. Revenue is also projected to increase at a marginally faster rate than GNP, and thus, to impart some contractionary impulse. This essentially reflects the elasticity of the tax system, rather than new discretionary measures.

The overall fiscal deficit at the general government level is expected to remain unchanged in 1986 at about 3½ percent of GNP. An expansionary impulse emanating from the state and local government sector would offset the withdrawal of stimulus by the central government. (Part of the difference between the two "impulse" estimates is also due to differences in coverage between the "unified budget" and the national income accounts, as well as to timing differences between cash transactions and accruals in the federal government account.)

For the other six countries as a group, the 1986 projections indicate little change in the composite fiscal stance. In Japan, the projections for 1986, which are based on the authorities' budget proposals (with some adjustment) and estimates made by the staff, reflect the expectation of continued efforts to reduce the budget deficit and a further withdrawal of stimulus

---

[5] The current service deficit is the deficit projected under the present tax system and existing spending programs.

equivalent to ½ of 1 percent of GNP at either level of government. The Japanese authorities continue to stress the containment of expenditures in a situation featuring strong growth of "entitlement" spending. Social security transfers, in particular, are growing rapidly in response to demographic factors and increasingly wide eligibility of the elderly for pensions. Against this background, containing total expenditures implies that growth in discretionary outlays will have to be especially firmly restrained. Implementation of such an expenditure policy would mean that the steady rise in revenue, which is expected to add about ¼ of 1 percentage point to the revenue-GNP ratio, would produce an equivalent withdrawal of stimulus. For the most part, this prospect reflects the elasticity of the tax system, rather than any significant new discretionary measures.

In the Federal Republic of Germany, the 1986 budget has been formulated in line with the authorities' commitment to medium-term fiscal consolidation. The overall budget deficit is projected to decline by about ¼ of 1 percent of GNP at both levels of government, notwithstanding a larger relative decline in revenue (½ of 1 percent in relation to GNP) due to implementation of previously announced measures of personal income tax relief. The strengthening of the financial position is to be effected by restricting the growth in general government expenditure so as to lower the total by about 1 percent in relation to GNP. This result would reflect above-trend growth in GNP, as well as some futher decline in the underlying share of government expenditure in total output. After allowance for cyclical factors, the withdrawal of stimulus from the expenditure side does not appear to be quite enough to offset the expansionary thrust originating from the revenue side. Accordingly, the overall fiscal impulse is expected to be slightly expansionary, both at the central government level and for the entire general government sector.

In France, the principal objective of the central government's financial policy in 1986 will again be to limit the budget deficit to 3 percent of GDP. This objective is to be achieved through absolute reductions in some types of outlays and by reducing the real growth rates of other categories of discretionary expenditure. This expenditure restraint would more than offset the effects of a decline in the ratio of revenue to GDP, reflecting, inter alia, an income tax reduction. The net effect at the central government level is expected to be marginally contractionary after cyclical adjustment. At the general government level, the appreciably lower rate of inflation now in prospect will help to lower the rate of increase in social security transfers. The contractionary impulse from the expenditure side will be offset by a fall in the ratio of revenue to GDP stemming from income tax reduction and less rapid growth of social security revenues, and both the stance of fiscal policy and the deficit will be unchanged.

The projections for the United Kingdom are based on the 1986/87 budget made public on March 18, 1986. In 1986, the budget deficit (national income accounts basis) at the central government level is projected to decline slightly as a percentage of GDP. Central government receipts are forecast to fall by almost 1½ percentage points of GDP, with oil revenues dropping sharply and non-oil revenues rising by slightly less than the forecast growth in GDP. Overall, central government outlays are projected to decline by a somewhat greater amount, with the growth in real expenditure held to about 1½ percent. On balance, the contractionary effect of the expenditure restraint would not be large enough to offset the stimulus from slower revenue growth, and the overall thrust of fiscal policy at the central government level would be slightly expansionary in 1986 (equivalent to about ¼ of 1 percent of GDP). In the 1985/86 budget, the authorities had penciled in a "fiscal adjustment" for 1986/87, amounting to about 1 percent of GDP in terms of possible reductions in personal income taxes. In the event, the steep drop in oil prices absorbed most of the scope for such reductions, and the actual budgeted cut—a 1 percentage point drop in the basic rate of income taxation—is less than one third of the originally envisaged amount. The staff forecast for 1987 assumes further steps along these lines. A broadly similar picture to that sketched above emerges by focusing on the transactions of the general government.

For Italy, the projections are based on the authorities' "current trends" estimates, with adjustments for the deficit-reducing measures included in the proposed budget, for the effects of income tax reform, and for expected delays in budget implementation. The central government deficit in 1986 is expected to decline to about 15 percent of GDP, from 16 percent of GDP in the preceding year, which would be about 1 percentage point above the authorities' target. The ratio of revenue to GDP is expected to grow by ½ of 1 percentage point, more than offsetting the structural growth of expenditure. A relatively contractionary impulse is thus implied, and is expected to be reflected also at the general government level. The projected increase in the relative magnitude of government revenue is partly attributable to tax measures proposed in the budget, including those to increase social security contributions and local taxes.

The 1986 projections for Canada are based on the authorities' latest estimates as announced in the federal budget of February 1986, with adjustments for differing staff assumptions with respect to growth, inflation, and interest rates. The fiscal deficit is expected to decline by about 1½ percentage points in relation to GNP at the central government level and by almost 2 percent at the general government level. The declines reflect a modest increase in taxes, as announced in the budget of February 1986, and the full-year effects of expenditure restraints and revenue measures contained in the May 1985 budget that will greatly exceed the part-year effects reflected in the 1985 outturn. Deceleration of expenditure growth will result mainly from cuts in federal government employment. In relation to GNP, however, part of the decline in expenditure is expected to stem from a sizable drop in unemployment insurance benefits and other cyclical influences. With allowance for these factors, the overall contractionary impulse imparted to the Canadian economy is projected to be about 1¼ percent of GNP at both the central and general government levels.

For 1987, highly tentative staff projections of the central government fiscal balances of major industrial countries indicate a contractionary composite fiscal thrust equivalent to about ¾ of 1 percent of GNP. This would include significant moves toward restraint in the United States, Japan, Italy, and Canada, while fiscal impulses in the Federal Republic of Germany, France, and the United Kingdom are projected to be moderately contractionary or expansionary. The projections for the United States are based on the working assumption that significant cuts in expenditure would be made in relation to the staff's estimate of the current services deficit for 1987; however, the projections assume that less than half of the potentially very large spending cuts implied by the recently adopted "Gramm-Rudman-Hollings" legislation, described in the following subsection, will be implemented. The full implementation of the cuts provided for under this legislation would imply a further significant reduction of the federal budget deficit in 1987. The contractionary impulse in the United States would be 0.6 percentage points greater than indicated in Statistical Appendix Table A16, and the combined contractionary impulse for all seven major industrial countries would be greater by about ¼ of 1 percentage point. The 1987 projections at the general government level (Statistical Appendix Table A17) broadly parallel those for the central government in all countries.

The "Gramm-Rudman-Hollings" Legislation in the United States

On December 12, 1985, the President signed legislation—the Balanced Budget and Emergency Deficit Control Act of 1985 (widely known as the "Gramm-Rudman-Hollings" Legislation)—stipulating that the

federal budget deficit, which reached $210 billion in fiscal year 1985, must be reduced in each fiscal year from fiscal year 1986 to fiscal year 1991 to attain a balanced budget in the latter year. The maximum deficit amounts specified in the Act are shown in the following tabulation:

Fiscal Year	Maximum Deficit (*In billions of dollars*)
1986	171.9
1987	144.0
1988	108.0
1989	72.0
1990	36.0
1991	—

The Act provides that automatic spending cuts would be triggered if the Administration and Congress are unable to reach agreement on measures that would achieve these targets. With the exceptions of fiscal years 1986 and 1991, the deficit may exceed the target by up to $10 billion without triggering the mandatory spending cuts; once triggered, however, those cuts must be sufficient to bring the deficit down to the target for that year. For fiscal year 1986, the reduction in outlays is limited by the Legislation to a maximum of $11.7 billion regardless of the amount by which the projected deficit for that year exceeds the maximum; no leeway is allowed for fiscal year 1991.

The first step in the process of expenditure reduction will involve the presentation of a joint report, on August 20 of each year, by the Office of Management and Budget and the Congressional Budget Office to the Comptroller General, who is head of the General Accounting Office. The reports are required to provide:

(1) estimates of the amount by which the projected deficit exceeds the maximum deficit for the fiscal year covered by the report;
(2) a set of economic assumptions, including the estimated rate of real economic growth in the fiscal year covered by the report; and
(3) calculations of the percentages and amounts by which various budget categories must be reduced to eliminate any difference between the projected deficit and the maximum deficit.

The Comptroller General will then review the joint report and issue his own report on August 25 to the President and to the Congress; this report should either confirm or modify the estimates provided by the Office of Management and Budget and the Congressional Budget Office. An order by the President implementing the spending cuts specified by the Comptroller General must be issued on September 1, 1986. Unless Congress acts—and the President agrees—to modify the spending reductions in the Comptroller General's report by adopting an alternative deficit reduction plan (which could include tax increases as well as alternative spending cuts), the expenditure reductions will take effect on October 1. Any Congressional action taken during September to reduce the gap between the estimates and the maximum allowable deficit will be reflected in a final Presidential order to be issued on October 15, 1986.

Special procedures are to be followed in the event of a recession. Specifically, the Director of the Congressional Budget Office must notify Congress at any time:

(1) if during the current and preceding quarter, and with respect also to the four quarters following the notification, the Congressional Budget Office or the Office of Management and Budget has projected real economic growth to be less than zero in two consecutive quarters within this six-quarter period; or (2) if the Department of Commerce reports that actual real economic growth for the most recent and immediately preceding quarter is less than 1 percent.

Upon receiving such notification, both Houses of Congress will suspend the obligation to achieve the maximum deficit target for the current fiscal year and the next fiscal year, as it applied to Congressional budget resolutions and the President's budget submissions.

Certain federal programs and activities are exempt from mandatory cuts under the Act. These include social security benefits, veterans' compensation and pensions, regular state unemployment insurance benefits, medicaid, aid to families with dependent children, food stamps, supplemental security income, and interest on the federal debt. Certain other programs, while not exempt, are subject to special rules limiting the extent of the cuts. For example, programs such as medicare and veterans' medical care cannot be cut by more than 1 percent in fiscal year 1986 and 2 percent in subsequent fiscal years. Programs with provisions for annual cost of living adjustments, such as pensions, can be cut by no more than the total cost of living adjustment in any one year.

The Act requires that 50 percent of the mandatory cuts come from domestic programs and 50 percent from the defense budget. For fiscal year 1986 only, the Act gives the President authority to exempt all or part of military personnel from cuts; he has chosen to use this authority, and has exempted 93 percent of the fiscal year 1986 appropriations in this area from cuts. The Act also permits the President (for fiscal year 1986 only) to adjust to a limited extent the percentage reductions for particular programs within a given category of defense spending. Except for these special provisions applying to fiscal year 1986, and subject to the exemptions and limitations described above, all programs must be cut on a uniform percentage basis, computed separately for defense and nondefense programs.

For fiscal year 1986, the average of the deficits recently estimated by the Office of Management and Budget and the Congressional Budget Office is $220.5 billion. As indicated above, the Act limits spending reductions to $11.7 billion for the current fiscal year. This figure reflects the fact that the Act restricts deficit reduction measures to a maximum of $20 billion at an annual rate for fiscal year 1986; as the reductions will not take effect until March 1, 1986, the maximum deficit reduction is seven twelfths of $20 billion. The President's order specifying these cuts was issued February 1, 1986.

On February 7, 1986, a federal court ruled that a crucial provision of the Balanced Budget and Emergency Deficit Control Act of 1985 (the "Gramm-Rudman-Hollings" law) was unconstitutional because it violated the separation of powers among the three branches of government. The court stated that powers conferred by the law on the Comptroller General as part of the provision for the automatic spending reductions were executive powers that could not be exercised by an official who is removable by Congress. The court stayed the effect of its order pending the outcome of an appeal to the Supreme Court.

Calculation of Fiscal Impulse and Fiscal Data Base

This section provides a brief description of how the "fiscal impulse" measure is derived from the "cyclically neutral budget" model, and of the fiscal data used in the analysis undertaken earlier in this Note. The "cyclically neutral budget" technique involves a distinction with respect to government revenues and expenditures between changes considered to be associated with cyclical fluctuations in the output of an economy and other changes, which may be viewed as imparting expansionary or contractionary impulses to the economy independently of the more or less automatic responsiveness of government transactions to cyclical developments. Revenue is regarded as cyclically neutral when it grows in proportion to actual GNP at current prices, and is contractionary (expansionary) when it increases faster (more slowly) than actual GNP. Expenditure other than unemployment insurance benefits is regarded as cyclically neutral if it parallels the movement of potential GNP at current prices, and is expansionary (contractionary) when it increases faster (more slowly) than potential GNP. Year-to-year variations in unemployment insurance benefits are viewed as cyclically neutral—that is, merely reflecting cyclical developments in the economy.[6] The net "impulse" from changes in revenue and expenditure (that part of any net change in the fiscal balance that cannot be attributed to "cyclically neutral" changes in revenue or expenditure) may be interpreted as a cyclically adjusted indicator (according to the criteria just specified) of stimulative or restrictive shifts in government fiscal operations.[7] Such changes may be viewed as policy determined either (1) by the introduction of new measures or (2) by the operation of previously existing measures that automatically result in revenue (expenditure) changing disproportionately to the change in GNP (potential GNP) by which "neutrality" is judged.

The fiscal impulse measure, as defined above, differs from the measure of "discretionary changes" in budget items employed by the Organization for Economic Cooperation and Development in its *Economic Outlook* reports. The latter measure is calculated by deducting from the change in the fiscal balance the estimated effect on the budget of the operation of automatic stabilizers. The deduction is based on structural estimates of the automatic responsiveness of revenue and expenditure to cyclical fluctuations in real output, rather than on equiproportionate revenue and expenditure rules.

The fiscal impulse measure also has not taken account of the potentially different aggregate demand effects associated with increases in noninterest expenditure or decreases in revenue as opposed to increases in expenditure due to the effects of inflation on interest payments. In a situation of increasing inflation, nominal interest rates may rise sharply, leading to a significant increase in interest payments and a deterioration in the fiscal position. It has been argued that the implicit amortization component of these interest payments (reflecting the erosion of outstanding debt, in real terms, through inflation) has a much weaker impact on aggregate demand than other types of expenditure or revenue measures. The appropriate adjustment of the fiscal balance for the effects of inflation is itself a matter of controversy, but the effects of such adjustments on the measure of fiscal impulse are likely to be important only in periods when the inflation rate accelerates or decelerates rather sharply. If movements in the expected inflation rate could be assumed to closely parallel movements in the actual inflation rate, then adjustment of the fiscal impulse measure for the effects of inflation would impute a more expansionary (contractionary) character to fiscal policy in a period of declining (increasing) inflation than would be implied by the unadjusted fiscal impulse measure.

The data on central government fiscal balances shown in Statistical Appendix Table A16 generally conform to the standards used in the Fund's *Government Finance Statistics Yearbook*, which call for the recording of government transactions on a cash basis and the classification of net government lending (loan disbursements less repayments) with expenditures rather than with financing. For the United Kingdom and Canada, however, and for Japan (in large part), the data are on a national income accounts basis; for the Federal Republic of Germany and France, the data are on an administrative basis and do not incorporate social security transactions in the latter case; and for Italy, the data cover the transactions of the state budget as well as those of several government-owned enterprises but, instead of including the gross revenue and expenditure transactions of social security institutions, include only net transfers from the central government to these institutions. The data on general government fiscal balances, in Statistical Appendix Table A17, cover the consolidated balances of central, regional, and local government units engaged in performing governmental functions but exclude government-owned industrial and commercial enterprises. These data are on a national income accounts basis, and thus exclude net government lending from expenditure. The data in Statistical Appendix Tables A16 and A17 are derived from national sources and Fund staff estimates. The base year for the calculation of the fiscal impulse is 1978. In general, definitions and statistical sources used are the same as in the April 1985 World Economic Outlook exercise except for the Federal Republic of Germany and the United Kingdom. The central government data on Germany have been shifted from a cash to an "administrative" basis in order to remain in agreement with government practice, which first introduced the shift. In addition, the data on growth of potential output in Germany have been revised to take account of new estimates reported by the Bundesbank. The figures related to the Central Government of the United Kingdom have been changed

---

[6] This view, although somewhat simplistic in that it ignores changes in the scale of benefits or in eligibility requirements, is adopted on grounds of expediency. Alternative methodologies with conceptually improved treatment of the unemployment insurance benefits have been attempted by the staff, but the empirical results were found to be barely different from the current estimates. Moreover, data for a more refined treatment of unemployment insurance benefits are not readily available for all of the major industrial countries.

[7] The net fiscal impulse (FI) may be expressed in terms of the change in revenue (T), expenditure other than unemployment insurance benefits (G), actual GNP (Y), and potential GNP (YP), as follows:

$$FI = -(\Delta T - t_0 \Delta Y) + (\Delta G - g_0 \Delta YP)$$

where t_0 and g_0 are the base year ratios of revenue to actual GNP and of expenditure other than unemployment insurance benefits to potential GNP, respectively.

from a cash to a national accounts basis; this shift has been introduced to facilitate the interpretation and forecasting of central government finances in view of recently observed wide and erratic fluctuations in central government net lending to other entities within the public sector. In addition, several other fiscal data series for both central and general government and some of the GNP series have been revised since the publication of the *World Economic Outlook, April 1985*.

Supplementary Note 2

Monetary Developments in Major Industrial Countries

During the past decade, a number of major industrial countries specified target ranges for the growth of key monetary aggregates as part of a medium-term policy framework that gave special emphasis to controlling inflation. These monetary targets have played an important role in establishing the credibility of the authorities' commitment to anti-inflation policy and have thereby increased the policy's effectiveness. Partly as a result of this policy, the average rate of inflation (as measured by the GNP deflators) in the major industrial countries has declined from over 9 percent in 1980 to 3.6 percent in 1985. This represents the lowest average rate of inflation in these industrial countries since 1967.

While the period since 1980 has witnessed a decline in inflation in all major countries, the implementation of policies involving monetary aggregates targeting has faced a number of difficulties. The substantial changes in exchange rates, nominal and real interest rates, and financial market structures that occurred in the early 1980s made it difficult for the authorities in some countries to control and to interpret movements in monetary aggregates. These developments also complicated the operational problems associated with the conduct of monetary policy by introducing increased variability into the relationships between the growth rates of monetary aggregates and the expansion of nominal income. The extent and nature of this variability has differed across countries. The velocities of some key monetary aggregates (such as M2 in the United States) have oscillated over a wider range than previously experienced while showing no clear trend, whereas the velocities of certain other key aggregates (such as sterling M3 (£M3) in the United Kingdom) have shifted trend in a reversal of previous behavior.

In some cases, central banks have specified their targets without being able to predict the sharp movements in velocity that would occur during the target year, especially when market innovations or changes in regulations led to the creation of new types of financial instruments. Changes in financial market regulations generally tended to increase the velocity of narrow monetary aggregates, which usually include a relatively high proportion of assets with controlled interest rates; whereas the velocity of more broadly defined aggregates did not change as substantially.[1] To a considerable extent, the pressures that gave rise to financial deregulation resulted from the rapid growth of new forms of financial instruments with market-related yields, which in turn reflected the strong incentives for the public to reduce its holdings of instruments with fixed or controlled yields in a period of high market interest rates.

The uncertainties surrounding the nature and stability of the linkages between the monetary authorities' policy instruments, their intermediate monetary targets, and their overall macroeconomic objectives have affected both the priority given to achieving monetary targets and the range of economic and financial variables used by the authorities in evaluating monetary conditions. As a result of these uncertainties, the growth rates of monetary aggregates have in a number of cases been allowed to move outside their target ranges. In some cases, target ranges have been modified prior to the end of the original target period and, in certain countries, the new bases that have been set for the monetary targets have incorporated the overshooting of the target ranges in the previous period. Several countries have established target ranges for more than one aggregate simultaneously, and in some cases the targeting of particular monetary aggregates has been de-emphasized or abandoned.

Of course, the monetary authorities in the major industrial countries have for some time examined a broad range of indicators of economic activity and financial market developments in evaluating monetary conditions. Nevertheless, the general decline in infla-

---

[1] Where the narrow aggregates also include new financial instruments, however, velocity has tended to decline to the extent that these new instruments have been attractive substitutes for deposits not included in the narrow aggregates.

tion and the instability of the linkages between money and income in some countries have led some authorities to give relatively more weight than previously to movements in such variables as the exchange rate, interest rates, and nominal or real income. The behavior of monetary aggregates relative to their targets nonetheless remains an important consideration in the formulation of policy in most major countries. However, the renewed focus on short-term movements in exchange rates, interest rates, output, and employment raises issues concerning the extent to which the authorities can pursue these objectives through monetary policy without jeopardizing the credibility of their long-term commitment to an anti-inflation policy.

Recent monetary policy in the major industrial countries is examined in the next section. The first part of that section considers developments in these countries as a group while the second contains notes on individual countries' experiences. The final part of that section of the note examines prospects for 1986.

Recent Monetary Policy Developments

While the average rate of growth of both narrow and broad money in the group of major industrial countries was lower in 1984 than in 1983, the average rate of monetary growth accelerated during 1985 (Tables 24 and 25). The slower monetary growth in 1984 reflected both reductions in the target growth rate ranges for key monetary aggregates and greater success in keeping actual rates of monetary growth within the target ranges (Chart 32). As a result, the average rate of growth of narrow money in the major countries declined from 8.6 percent in 1983 to 6.9 percent in 1984, while the average growth rate of broad money fell from 10.1 percent to 7.9 percent. In 1985, by contrast, the rate of growth of broad money rose to 8.9 percent, while narrow money growth accelerated to 10.1 percent—the highest rate of expansion for this aggregate since the late 1970s. The acceleration of monetary growth reflected both overshooting of target

Table 24. Major Industrial Countries: Selected Composite Data on Monetary Aggregates and Other Variables, 1978–85[1]

(Annual percentage changes, except as noted)

	1978	1979	1980	1981	1982	1983	1984	1985
Real GNP	4.6	3.4	1.1	1.6	−0.6	2.7	5.0	2.8
GNP deflator	7.3	8.2	9.3	8.7	6.9	4.6	3.9	3.6
Nominal GNP	12.2	11.7	10.5	10.3	6.2	7.4	9.1	6.4
Nominal monetary aggregates								
Narrow money (M1)[2]	11.3	7.9	5.5	6.6	8.7	8.6	6.9	10.1
Broad money (M2 or M3)[2]	11.1	9.9	9.5	9.6	9.3	10.1	7.9	8.9
Real monetary aggregates[3]								
Narrow money (M1)[2]	3.5	−0.6	−3.8	−1.4	3.1	4.1	3.1	6.3
Broad money (M2 or M3)[2]	3.3	1.4	−0.2	1.5	3.7	5.6	4.1	5.2
Income velocity of money[4]								
GNP/M1	1.1	1.5	4.5	3.6	−0.8	−2.4	2.6	−1.8
GNP/M2 or M3	1.0	1.1	0.9	0.4	−3.0	−2.8	1.3	−2.3
Nominal interest rates[5] (in percent per annum)								
Short term	7.3	9.8	12.6	14.1	11.8	9.2	9.7	8.4
Long term	8.4	9.3	11.2	13.1	12.4	10.9	11.1	9.9
Real interest rates[6] (in percent per annum)								
Short term	−0.3	—	3.3	6.4	6.9	5.3	6.1	5.3
Long term	0.8	−0.5	1.9	5.4	7.6	7.0	7.5	6.7

[1] All of the data shown are weighted averages for the seven major industrial countries (with weights for each year's calculation proportionate to U.S. dollar values of the respective GNPs in the preceding three years).
[2] Changes from year-end to year-end.
[3] Constructed by dividing nominal monetary aggregates by GNP deflators.
[4] Based on average stock of money during the year.
[5] Annual average.
[6] Average of quarterly data calculated by adjusting the nominal rates by the effect of expected changes in prices. The expected change in prices is calculated from a weighted average of the rate of inflation in the current quarter and the next two quarters, with the deflator of private final domestic demand being used as the price variable.

Table 25. Major Industrial Countries: Changes in Stocks of Narrow Money and Broad Money, 1978–85

(Percentage changes from year-end to year-end)

	1978	1979	1980	1981	1982	1983	1984	1985
Narrow money (M1)								
Canada	8.1	3.5	10.4	1.1	3.3	8.6	0.3	9.4
United States	8.2	7.5	7.5	5.1	8.7	10.4	5.3	11.9
Japan	13.4	3.0	−2.0	10.0	5.7	−0.1	6.9	4.5
France	11.1	12.0	6.8	14.5	10.5	11.7	9.5	10.0
Germany, Fed. Rep. of	14.2	3.7	4.2	−0.8	6.6	8.1	5.9	5.3
Italy	25.8	24.4	13.5	10.2	16.7	12.9	12.2	12.9
United Kingdom	14.6	15.2	4.2	10.3	12.3	11.4	15.6	17.5
Average, above countries[1]	11.3	7.9	5.5	6.6	8.7	8.6	6.9	10.1
Average, four major European countries[1]	15.2	11.4	6.4	7.5	10.6	10.7	10.3	10.5
Broad money[2]								
Canada	12.5	17.7	18.1	11.7	8.1	3.5	7.2	10.7
United States	8.0	8.1	9.0	9.3	9.1	12.2	7.9	8.6
Japan	13.1	9.1	7.2	11.0	7.9	7.3	7.8	9.0
France	12.2	14.0	8.4	10.4	10.8	11.2	8.3	8.0
Germany, Fed. Rep. of	11.1	5.8	6.2	5.1	7.2	5.6	4.7	5.1
Italy	22.6	20.8	12.7	10.0	18.0	12.3	12.1	11.2
United Kingdom	17.5	13.4	18.5	13.9	9.1	11.2	9.7	14.5
Average, above countries[1]	11.1	9.9	9.5	9.6	9.3	10.1	7.9	8.9
Average, four major European countries[1]	14.5	11.9	10.2	9.2	10.3	9.5	8.1	9.1

[1] These composites are averages of individual country rates, weighted for each year in proportion to the U.S. dollar values of the respective GNPs in the preceding three years.

[2] M2 for Canada, the United States, and Italy; M2 + CDs for Japan; M2R for France; M3 for Germany; and £M3 for the United Kingdom.

growth rate ranges and modifications of the target ranges during the original target period. Even in those countries where the rates of monetary expansion fell within the target ranges, they were generally near the upper bounds of those ranges.

Despite this more rapid monetary expansion, the weighted average growth of nominal GNP of the major industrial countries slowed sharply from 9.1 percent in 1984 to 6.4 percent in 1985 as the income velocities of both narrow and broad money declined. While the slower expansion of nominal GNP was accompanied by a slight reduction in inflation (the GNP deflator slowed from 3.9 percent in 1984 to 3.6 percent in 1985), real output growth also declined from 5.0 percent in 1984 to 2.8 percent in 1985.

During 1985 and the first few months of 1986, there was a widespread decline in interest rates, whether measured on a nominal or a real basis, for both short-term and longer-term maturities (Chart 33). The average of short-term nominal interest rates fell from 9.7 percent in 1984 to 8.4 percent in 1985; long-term nominal rates declined from 11.1 percent to 9.9 percent. With inflation stable, or declining only slightly, real interest rates are estimated to have fallen in both short-term and long-term markets. However, the declines in interest rates were not uniform across the major industrial countries. In the United States, downward pressures on interest rates were particularly pronounced in the 18 months prior to the end of 1985. Although interest rates also fell in most other countries, the extent of these declines often differed from that in the United States. As a result, there were sizable changes in the pattern of interest rate differentials. In addition, with the exception of the Federal Republic of Germany and Japan, the long-term interest rate differentials in the past two years have been considerably smaller than the short-term yield differentials. In part, this could reflect the fact that short-term rates have been more strongly affected by the operations of the monetary authorities.

Chart 32. Six Major Industrial Countries: Target Ranges and Growth of Targeted Aggregates, 1981–86[1]

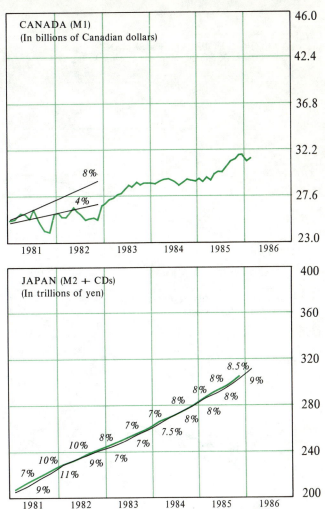

[1] As reported at end of policy period. Target ranges project from base at beginning of policy period, and as bands for the United Kingdom beginning in 1985.

While nominal interest rate differentials have shown a somewhat diverse pattern, real interest rate differentials have shown greater convergence, especially in the period since mid-1984. For each of the major industrial countries except Canada, the real long-term interest rate differential with the United States has declined from the 4 to 5 percent range to less than 2.5 percent.

On average, the income velocities of both narrow and broad money declined in 1985, in contrast to the previous year (Table 24 and Chart 34). These swings in velocity continued a pattern of variability that has been apparent since the late 1970s. Over this period, the behavior of inflation rates and nominal and real interest rates has combined to produce substantial movements in the velocities of the key monetary aggregates. The reduction in the level and variability of inflation and the emergence and persistence of high real interest rates have tended to increase the general attractiveness of financial assets relative to that of real

Chart 32 (*concluded*).   **Six Major Industrial Countries: Target Ranges and Growth of Targeted Aggregates, 1981–86[1]**

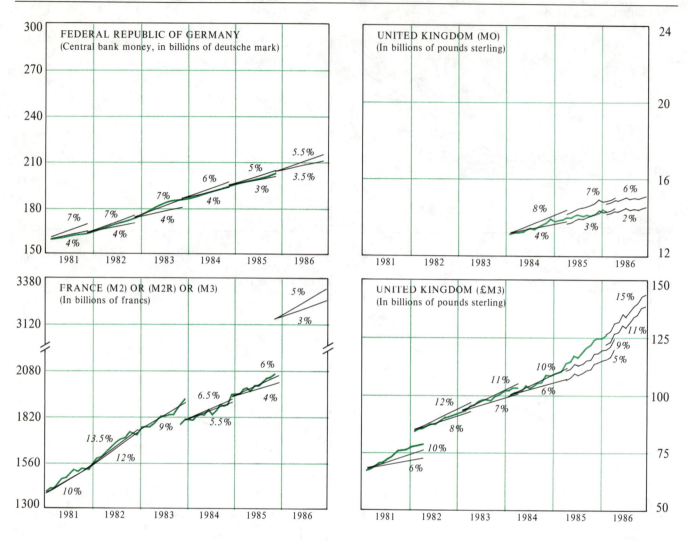

[1] As reported at end of policy period. Target ranges project from base at beginning of policy period, and as bands for the United Kingdom begining in 1985.

assets. During 1982 and 1983, the average velocity of both narrow and broad money declined sharply as inflation slowed and nominal interest rates fell from the peak levels seen in 1981. After mid-1983, however, the decline in inflation slowed and nominal interest rates either stabilized or edged up; reflecting this, in 1984, the velocities of broad and narrow money both changed at rates roughly comparable to the trend rates of increase evident in the period prior to the high inflation era of the late 1970s. In 1985, stable inflation and a renewed decline in interest rates were accompanied by declines in the velocities of both broad and narrow money.

Despite the pronounced variability of velocity for the major industrial countries as a group, certain industrial countries have had relatively stable velocities for their key monetary aggregates. Since the mid-1970s, in particular, the income velocities of central bank money in the Federal Republic of Germany and M2 + CDs in Japan have shown relatively modest variability around a downward trend (Chart 34). In contrast, the velocities for the key monetary aggregates in other major industrial countries have at times shown reversals of trend (such as £M3 in the United Kingdom) or increased variability around an unchanged trend (such as M2 in the United States). While the lower

Chart 33.   Seven Major Industrial Countries: Short-Term and Long-Term Interest Rates and Underlying Inflation, 1981–86[1]

(In percent)

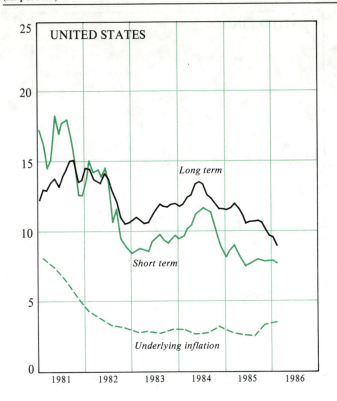

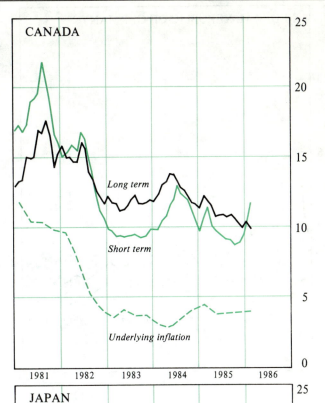

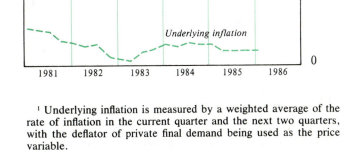

variability of velocity in Germany and Japan has reflected the more stable evolution of inflation and interest rates in those countries, it may also be due in part to the fact that financial markets in the Federal Republic of Germany and Japan have until recently not experienced as extensive a series of institutional changes as financial markets in some other countries.

Country Notes

United States—The monetary growth ranges set at the beginning of 1985 were kept substantially the same as in 1984, and were judged to be consistent with "further sustainable economic growth and progress toward reasonable price stability over time."[2] At the time it was formulating its 1985 objectives, the Federal Open Market Committee projected that both real GNP and the GNP deflator would increase by 3½ percent to 4 percent during 1985, and it was also assumed that the monetary aggregates would not be appreciably influenced by any new statutory or regulatory devel-

---

[2] *Federal Reserve Bulletin*, April 1985, p. 189.

[1] Underlying inflation is measured by a weighted average of the rate of inflation in the current quarter and the next two quarters, with the deflator of private final demand being used as the price variable.

Chart 33 (*concluded*).   Seven Major Industrial Countries: Short-Term and Long-Term Interest Rates and Underlying Inflation, 1981–86[1]

(In percent)

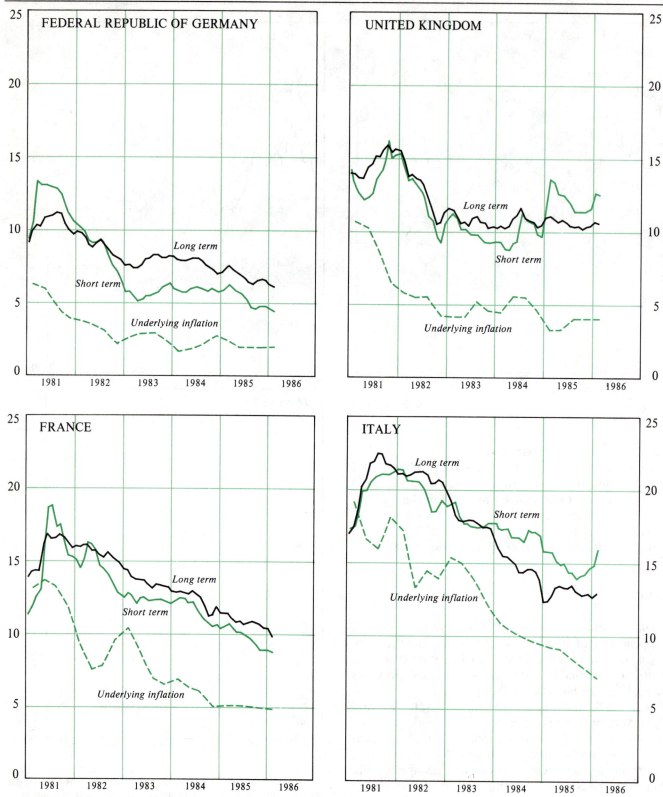

[1] Underlying inflation is measured by a weighted average of the rate of inflation in the current quarter and the next two quarters, with the deflator of private final demand being used as the price variable.

Chart 34. Seven Major Industrial Countries: Velocities of Broad and Narrow Money, 1970–85

(Quarterly GNP at annual rates/average stock of money during quarter)

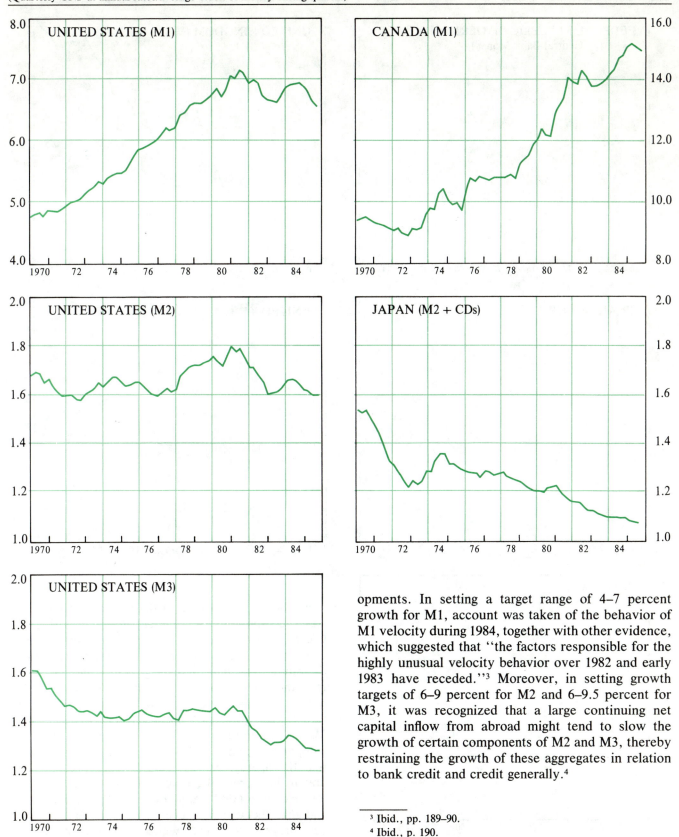

opments. In setting a target range of 4–7 percent growth for M1, account was taken of the behavior of M1 velocity during 1984, together with other evidence, which suggested that "the factors responsible for the highly unusual velocity behavior over 1982 and early 1983 have receded."[3] Moreover, in setting growth targets of 6–9 percent for M2 and 6–9.5 percent for M3, it was recognized that a large continuing net capital inflow from abroad might tend to slow the growth of certain components of M2 and M3, thereby restraining the growth of these aggregates in relation to bank credit and credit generally.[4]

[3] Ibid., pp. 189–90.
[4] Ibid., p. 190.

131

Chart 34 (*concluded*).   **Seven Major Industrial Countries: Velocities of Broad and Narrow Money, 1970–85**
(Quarterly GNP at annual rates/average stock of money during quarter)

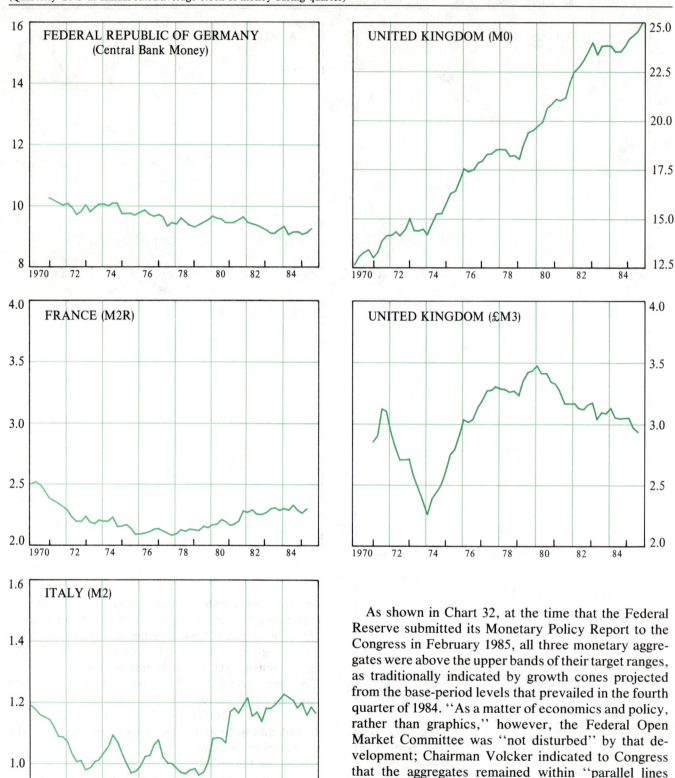

As shown in Chart 32, at the time that the Federal Reserve submitted its Monetary Policy Report to the Congress in February 1985, all three monetary aggregates were above the upper bands of their target ranges, as traditionally indicated by growth cones projected from the base-period levels that prevailed in the fourth quarter of 1984. "As a matter of economics and policy, rather than graphics," however, the Federal Open Market Committee was "not disturbed" by that development; Chairman Volcker indicated to Congress that the aggregates remained within "parallel lines drawn back from the outer bounds of the specified fourth quarter (1985) target ranges to the base period," and that the Committee contemplated that "as the year progresses, growth will slow consistent with the target ranges.''[5] At mid-year, however, only M2 and M3 had been brought back within their cones. By that time, interest rates had drifted lower as industrial output remained little stronger than a year earlier, and the Federal Open Market Committee had lowered by roughly 1 percentage point its projections for both real and nominal GNP growth during 1985. In re-examining its targets in July, the Committee expected that the sharp decline in M1 velocity during the first half of the year would be neither extended nor substantially reversed in the second half; however, the high degree of uncertainty surrounding the behavior of M1 velocity was explicitly recognized. Reflecting these various considerations, the base for the target range for M1 was shifted forward to the second quarter of 1985, and the range itself was widened to 3–8 percent for the second half of the year.

Over the next several months, however, M1 continued to grow rapidly. At the October meeting of the Federal Open Market Committee it was suggested that ''the recent strength in M1 could not be explained fully by such factors as institutional changes and financial innovations'' but should be judged ''in the context of the performance of the economy and the relatively moderate growth in the broader aggregates.''[6] Accordingly, it was decided not to react aggressively to M1 growth above the upper bound of the rebased target range.

For 1985 as a whole, M1 in the United States expanded by nearly 12 percent (fourth quarter 1984 to fourth quarter 1985), while the growth rates of M2 and M3 were held within their target ranges. Nominal interest rates continued to decline in 1985 and early 1986, most markedly for long-term maturities, and the Federal Reserve lowered its discount rate by ½ of 1 percentage point in May 1985 and by another ½ point in early March 1986. The monetary targets for 1986, as adopted in February, have retained the 6–9 percent range for M2 growth while narrowing the M3 range slightly, also to 6–9 percent. The range for M1 was set at 3–8 percent, the same as the revised range that the Federal Open Market Committee adopted last July for the second half of 1985.

Federal Republic of Germany—In 1985, monetary developments in the Federal Republic of Germany were consistent with the plans established by the authorities at the end of 1984. For the period from the fourth quarter of 1984 to the fourth quarter of 1985, the Central Bank Council had indicated a target range of 3–5 percent for the growth of central bank money. This range was based on projections that both potential output and prices would increase about 2 percent. No

allowance for a change in the velocity of circulation was included. During the target period, central bank money expanded at a seasonally adjusted annual rate of about 4½ percent, toward the top end of the target corridor (Chart 32) and much the same as the rate experienced in 1984.

Both short-term and long-term interest rates declined steadily from March until August–September 1985 (Chart 33). These declines reflected a number of factors, including the continued slowing of domestic inflation and strong foreign demand for deutsche-mark-denominated financial assets. Although German interest rates declined by somewhat less than comparable U.S. dollar interest rates during this period, the reduction in market interest rates had created a situation by mid-August in which the Bundesbank was able to lower both its discount and Lombard interest rates by ½ of 1 percentage point to 4 percent and 5.5 percent, respectively. German interest rates increased somewhat in the fourth quarter of 1985, but began to decline again in 1986. In early March 1986, the Bundesbank reduced its discount rate by another ½ of 1 percentage point to 3.5 percent.

In December 1985, the Deutsche Bundesbank set a new target range of 3.5–5.5 percent for the growth of central bank money for the period from the fourth quarter of 1985 to the fourth quarter of 1986. This target range is based on an estimated potential real output growth of 2.5 percent in 1986 and a projection of around 2 percent for underlying price inflation. The target range does not make any allowance for changes in the income velocity of central bank money.

During 1985, the monetary authorities also took measures to increase the competitiveness of the German financial markets. In May, for example, the range of assets available on German markets was expanded with the admission of various new financial instruments (such as floating rate notes, zero-coupon bonds, dual-currency bonds, and bonds linked to currency and interest rate swaps), which had previously been excluded. Moreover, in December, the Central Bank Council recommended a reduction and restructuring of reserve ratios, having the effect of reducing the reserves credit institutions are required to hold by about DM 8 billion. As part of these changes, liabilities in foreign currencies to non-residents will largely be freed from the minimum reserve requirement, but certain newly issued bank bonds with an original maturity of less than two years will be subjected to minimum reserve requirements. In addition, the Bundesbank indicated that it would not object if credit institutions domiciled in the Federal Republic of Germany issued deutsche-mark-denominated paper having the character of certificates of deposit.

Japan—In recent years, monetary policy in Japan

---

[5] Ibid., p. 216.
[6] *Federal Reserve Bulletin*, January 1986, p. 23.

has attempted to influence interest rates and the growth of money and credit through intervention in the money markets and through variations in the discount rate. While credit ceilings are still a potential instrument of monetary control, they have not been used for several years. The change in the implementation of monetary policy reflects the evolution of the Japanese financial market that has occurred in response to a gradual process of financial deregulation. In the past two years, this has included the liberalization of the foreign exchange market (for example, by increasing the scope of transactions that could be undertaken by foreign exchange banks and currency brokers), the introduction of new financial instruments (such as bankers' acceptances, bond futures, and money market certificates), expansion of the Euroyen bond market, and allowing foreign financial institutions improved access to Japanese markets. As a result, market forces have played an increasingly important role in the determination of domestic interest rates, and the linkages between Japanese and international financial markets have been strengthened.

The Japanese authorities have regarded movements in the broad money stock (M2+CDs) and interest rates as the primary indicators of monetary conditions. The demand for M2+CDs is regarded as more stable than that for narrower aggregates, while data for even broader aggregates are available only with longer reporting lags.[7] Although there is no formal targeting of monetary aggregates, the Bank of Japan announces in the first month of each quarter a projection, with a loosely specified range, for the year-on-year growth of M2+CDs measured from the same quarter of the previous year. The Bank of Japan's projection for the first quarter of 1986 was 9.0 percent. In general, actual growth rates have been in line with official forecasts (Chart 32).

M2+CDs expanded by 9 percent during 1985 in contrast to an average of approximately 7½ percent during the previous three years (Table 25). During much of last year, however, the primary focus of monetary policy was on exchange rate objectives. The sharpest change in monetary conditions during the year occurred following the September 22 Group of Five meeting, at which the five largest countries expressed themselves in favor of an orderly appreciation of non-dollar currencies (including the Japanese yen). The Bank of Japan decided not to sterilize the shortage of funds in the interbank market that resulted from its intervention in foreign exchange markets, and also decided not to accommodate the seasonal increase

in the demands for funds in the domestic money market. As a result, short-term interest rates increased by 1–1½ percentage points by the end of October, effectively eliminating the short-term differential between nominal interest rates on Japanese and U.S. assets. This rise in short-term interest rates, however, was more than reversed by early 1986 as the yen strengthened further and the Bank of Japan reduced its discount rate by ½ percentage point in order to support domestic demand. The discount rate was reduced ½ of 1 percentage point further in early March.

United Kingdom—Since fiscal year 1980/81, monetary policy in the United Kingdom has been formulated in the context of a medium-term financial strategy designed to achieve lower rates of inflation through a progressive lowering in the growth rates of the targeted monetary aggregates. The specific set of targeted aggregates has varied with changes in their perceived usefulness as indicators of monetary conditions during a period of extensive financial liberalization. In addition, various supplementary indicators, including the exchange rate, have been taken into account in interpreting financial conditions and in determining interest rate policy. The budgets for fiscal years 1985/86 and 1986/87 reaffirmed the Government's commitment to the medium-term financial strategy and to maintaining monetary conditions consistent with declining growth of nominal GDP and inflation, with short-term interest rates to be set at levels needed to achieve this objective.[7]

For fiscal year 1984/85, the authorities had adopted £M3 as the sole broad money target, while the wide monetary base M0 was introduced as the target for narrow money.[8] In accordance with the medium-term financial strategy, the target ranges for 1984/85 were set at 4–8 percent annual growth for M0 and 6–10 percent for £M3, and it was projected that by fiscal year 1988/89 these target ranges would decline to 0–4 percent annual growth for M0 and to 2–6 percent annual growth for £M3. In the 14 months to April 1985, M0 grew within its target range at an annual rate of 5.7 percent, while £M3 grew somewhat above its target range at an annual rate of 11.9 percent (Chart 32).[9] In the new budget year, the growth rates of the two aggregates began to diverge more strikingly: M0 grew at an annual rate of 3.5 percent in the 12 months to February 1986 (compared with its 1985/86 target range of 3–7 percent), while £M3 grew by 14.8 percent (compared with its target range of 5–9 percent).

---

[7] In 1985, the income velocity of M2+CDs declined by 1.9 percent (Chart 34), which was relatively close to the historical downward trend of 2.3 percent (Table 26).

[8] M0 consists of currency in circulation with the public plus banks' till money and their operational balances with the Bank of England. £M3 consists of currency in circulation plus private sector sterling bank deposits.

[9] Since April 1985, the performance of the targeted aggregates has been evaluated by the authorities in terms of rolling 12-month growth rates rather than annualized rates of growth from the start of the target period.

The authorities attributed the strong growth of £M3 to a permanent shift in the demand for broad money, reflecting developments in financial markets arising from decontrol of the banking system and the restoration of positive real interest rates during the early 1980s. The associated downturn in velocity had not been sufficiently factored into the fiscal year 1985/86 target range for £M3, and with financial liberalization having altered the usefulness of the broad aggregates as indicators of financial conditions, the authorities downgraded the role of £M3 and upgraded that of the exchange rate. This development was foreshadowed in January 1985 by the abandonment of the "decoupling policy," which had focused interest rate policy almost exclusively on domestic indicators and objectives. At that time, the authorities allowed short-term interest rates to rise by 4½ percentage points to 14 percent in order to halt the depreciation of the pound relative to the U.S. dollar. Subsequently, as the pound strengthened, interest rates were allowed to decline by 2½ percentage points, despite the overshooting of the £M3 target.

In January 1986, amid falling oil prices, renewed downward pressure on the pound and the continued buoyancy of bank lending prompted the authorities to let base interest rates rise by 1 percentage point. Despite further easing of the exchange rate and upward pressure on interest rates, a further increase was resisted. While the authorities are paying close attention to the exchange rate as an indicator of monetary conditions, they do not have an exchange rate target. Indeed, they appear willing to countenance declines in the effective value of sterling associated with falling oil prices to the extent that the effects of the two factors on the inflation rate are broadly offsetting.

In mid-March 1986 the authorities released their budget for 1986/87, including new monetary target ranges. The target ranges for fiscal year 1986/87 were set as annualized growth rates of 2–6 percent for M0 and 11–15 percent for £M3. The day after the budget was released, base interest rates were reduced by 1 percentage point.

France—In 1985, inflation and interest rates in France continued the declines that began several years earlier. Measured by the consumer price index, inflation has fallen continuously from over 13 percent in 1981 to less than 5 percent from fourth-quarter 1984 through fourth-quarter 1985. Since 1981, both short-term and long-term nominal interest rates have been reduced by more than 5 percentage points. Because inflation and nominal interest rates have moved together in the period since mid-1983, however, real interest rates have generally remained within the range of 4–6 percent.

In 1984, the French authorities began to formulate their monetary target in terms of M2R (M2 held by residents), rather than total M2.[10] In that year, M2R growth somewhat exceeded the upper bound of the target range of 5.5 to 6.5 percent (Chart 32). For 1985, monetary policy was again formulated in terms of M2R and the target growth rate range was set at 4–6 percent. During the first half of 1985, the expansion of M2R generally exceeded the upper bound, and this led the authorities to take measures in June designed to restrict the extension of credit by banks and to restrain capital inflows through the balance of payments. These measures included a lowering of the limits on bank lending not subject to penalty rates, holding down new foreign borrowing, and encouraging the private sector to repay foreign debt in advance of maturity.

In order to reflect recent financial innovations and institutional changes in the banking system, such as the introduction of instruments similar to claims on money markets funds, the authorities have chosen to change their definitions of the monetary aggregates from a classification based on institutional criteria to a new system based on the nature and the substitutability of the financial assets involved. The authorities have adopted the redefined concept of M3 as the target aggregate for 1986.[11] The 1986 target range has been set at 3–5 percent, 1 percentage point lower than the 1985 target range for M2R, to indicate the continuing commitment of the authorities to reduce inflation.[12] The authorities have also reiterated their intention to move away from the present system of credit controls toward a system based on the control of interest rates, in order to give market forces more influence on the allocation of credit.

Canada—From 1975 until late 1982, the Canadian monetary authorities set a specific target range for the growth of M1 as a policy guide in their attempts to achieve sustained economic expansion and long-term price stability. In November 1982, however, the Bank of Canada abandoned the practice of monetary targeting. It was felt that the relationship between the monetary aggregates (particularly M1), nominal income, and interest rates had become unstable as a result of financial innovations (such as the introduction of interest-bearing checkable accounts and the wide-

---

[10] Under the definitions prevailing during 1984 and 1985, M2R consisted of demand, time and savings deposits in banks held by resident nonfinancial agents, plus currency in circulation. Total M2 comprised M2R plus nonresidents' bank deposits.

[11] Under the new definitions, the aggregates continue to represent the money holdings of residents but no longer include an R in their labels. M3 consists of currency, deposits at financial institutions (including term deposits, certificates of deposit, and foreign-currency deposits), repurchase agreements, and short-term bonds (bons).

[12] The base for the 1986 target rate is the average stock of M3 in the fourth quarter of 1985, whereas the base for the previous M2R target was the three-month average centered on December.

spread availability of cash management facilities for businesses). These innovations in the financial sector led to a shift of funds from accounts classified as part of M1 (currency and non-interest-bearing demand deposits) into deposits bearing market-related interest rates.[13] As a result of the inflows into these types of deposits, there was a sharp divergence between the rates of growth of M1 and M1A (which includes interest bearing checking accounts). While M1 increased at an annual average rate of 3.3 percent during 1981–84 (Table 25), the average rate of growth for M1A was 12.0 percent. Consequently, after mid-1981 the income velocity of M1 increased, while that of M1A declined. Since its decision to abandon monetary targeting, the Bank of Canada has implemented its monetary policy with reference to a variety of economic and financial indicators, including in particular the exchange rate between the Canadian dollar and the U.S. dollar.

During 1985, the sharp divergence between the growth rates of M1 and M1A continued, but the growth of both aggregates accelerated substantially relative to their earlier pace. M1 and M1A expanded by 9.4 percent and 38.3 percent, respectively, in 1985, having grown by 0.3 and 21.7 percent, respectively, in 1984. The authorities attributed the acceleration of the growth of M1A to an ongoing substitution of interest bearing checking accounts for other types of deposits. In addition, the more rapid growth of M1 since mid-1985 has been associated in part with changes in the amount of bank float (that is, changes in the amount of checks and other items that have been deposited or cashed but not yet debited from the accounts on which they were drawn).

Under current conditions, one aim of monetary policy has been to try to reduce interest rates so as to promote economic expansion, provided these interest rate movements do not conflict with the objectives of maintaining a reasonably stable exchange rate and low inflation. Thus, when confronted with the downward pressure on the Canadian dollar that resulted from an increase in U.S. interest rates in the first half of 1984, the Canadian authorities allowed domestic interest rates to increase. Similarly, in early 1985, Canadian interest rates, especially short-term rates, were allowed to rise as U.S. interest rates firmed and the U.S. dollar strengthened relative to the Canadian dollar. However, the subsequent decline in U.S. interest rates permitted reductions to take place in Canadian rates also. As a result, average interest rates (both nominal and real) in Canada were about 2 percentage points lower in 1985 than in 1984.

In September 1985, two bank failures occurred (the first in Canada in more than sixty years). One of the banks involved had received considerable support in the form of an infusion of funds from federal and provincial governments and other Canadian banks. These failures led to liquidity problems in certain small Canadian banks as a result of large deposit withdrawals. However, the authorities felt that this episode did not threaten the financial position of the banking system as a whole and did not raise major problems for the implementation of monetary policy.

Italy—Although the Italian authorities do not announce targets for monetary aggregates in their management of monetary affairs, overall economic policy is based on plans that include projections for a broad range of monetary and credit aggregates, including total domestic credit and its components and the financial assets held by the private sector. Since the beginning of 1984, the authorities have sought to influence financial conditions through their policies regarding the monetary base and interest rates, rather than through direct controls over the availability of domestic credit.[14] For 1985, the authorities' plans included a continued deceleration in rates of monetary and credit growth. This was viewed as consistent with both a further reduction in inflation and some expansion of real output. However, the planned deceleration was achieved only for credit to the private sector, which is estimated to have grown by 12.6 percent in 1985 (15.6 percent in 1984).[15] Credit to the state sector expanded by an estimated 21.7 percent in 1985 (22.8 percent in 1984), which was more than 2.5 percentage points above the projected increase of 19.0 percent. M2 is estimated to have increased by about 11.2 percent (the central projection was 10 percent), as the sharp loss in foreign reserves registered in the fourth quarter led to a marked slowdown of the monetary aggregates. The monetary base adjusted for the automatic increase in reserve requirements is projected to have grown by 14.6 percent, 4.6 percentage points above the initial target.

The major source of liquidity growth was the public sector deficit. As in several recent years, it was originally planned to keep the fiscal deficit unchanged in nominal terms. However, the state sector borrowing

---

[13] The interest rates on these deposits are administered rates that are adjusted from time to time to reflect changes in market rates.

[14] In June 1984, however, the authorities supplemented those instruments with limits on additional net foreign borrowings by banks in an effort to limit what was regarded as excessive growth in credit to the private sector. These limits were abolished in December 1985 since they had proved difficult to enforce and were no longer needed, as commercial banks' borrowing abroad fell sharply in the fourth quarter. In January 1986 credit ceilings were reintroduced for a period of six months and short-term interest rates were increased, in an attempt to contain heavy official reserve losses linked to widespread expectations of a depreciation of the lira.

[15] Approximately one fifth of the expansion of credit to the private sector in 1985 reflects the permission that banks were granted late in the year to exceed their credit margins temporarily.

requirement is estimated to have been approximately 13 percent higher in 1985 than originally planned, and the deficit therefore rose to 16.0 percent of GNP instead of the originally projected 14.4 percent. Similar difficulties in controlling the size of the public sector deficit have been experienced during most of the 1980s.

Although the central bank no longer has a legal obligation to underwrite the public sector deficit, it was felt that financing the larger than anticipated deficit through the issuance of nonmonetary obligations would require increases in interest rates that were not warranted in the face of an already weak demand for credit by the private sector. In 1985, 26 percent of the public sector deficit was financed by credit extended by the Bank of Italy, against 11 percent in 1984. As a result, in 1985 central bank credit to the Treasury accounted for approximately 145 percent of the increase in the monetary base, against about 72 percent in 1984.

On average, both short-term and long-term interest rates in Italy were lower during 1985 than during 1984 (Chart 33). Short-term rates fell from slightly more than 17 percent in 1984 to about 15 percent in 1985, and long-term rates fell from 15 percent to around 13 percent during the same period. Given the concomitant reduction in inflation, however, real interest rates showed a much smaller decline, and began to rise again after the middle of 1985.

The authorities' plans for 1986 envisage a 9.5 percent increase in credit to the private sector,[16] along with a 9 percent increase in the stock of M2. Partly because of the recent decline in the cost of oil imports, it is envisaged that these growth rates for money and credit would support a 10.5 percent rise in nominal GNP. The deficit of the state sector is projected to increase somewhat in nominal terms but to decline to about 14½ percent as a share of GNP.

Review of 1985 and Outlook for 1986

Table 26 summarizes the sharp contrasts in the "velocity puzzles" that different central banks encountered in pursuing their 1985 monetary growth targets. In the Federal Republic of Germany and Japan, the changes in velocity during 1985 were similar to the 1984 experiences. In France, the apparent decline in M2R velocity during 1985 (based on incomplete data) more closely resembled the average 1970–85 experience than the experiences of 1983 and 1984, and it appears that the 1985 monetary growth target was exceeded (Chart 32). For each of the targeted aggre-

gates in the United States, and for sterling M3 in the United Kingdom, the sharp declines in velocity contrasted strongly with both the 1984 experiences and the average annual changes over the period since 1970. To some extent, the velocity declines in the United States may have reflected the lower level of interest rates. In any case, however, the rapid growth of money demand relative to nominal GNP led the authorities during the course of the year to stop aiming at the M1 target in the United States and the sterling M3 target in the United Kingdom.

Columns (5) and (6) of Table 26 provide an alternative perspective of the contrasting velocity puzzles and macroeconomic conditions that different central banks encountered in 1985. These columns indicate the ranges for velocity that were implied a year ago by the monetary growth targets that had then been announced, in combination with the nominal GNP forecasts adopted in the World Economic Outlook, April 1985. The sharp declines in velocity that occurred during 1985 in the United States and for sterling M3 in the United Kingdom were substantially outside the ranges implicitly expected a year ago, as was the decline in M2R velocity in France. By contrast, the velocity change for M0 in the United Kingdom exceeded the range of expectations held a year ago, while the velocity changes for central bank money in Germany and M2+CDs in Japan were close to last year's expectations.

Columns (7) and (8) of Table 26 project the velocity changes implied by combining the monetary target ranges that have been announced for 1986 with the staff's nominal GNP forecasts. It should be emphasized that the projections for GNP growth that are used in the construction of these columns are not those of the authorities, and that the year-over-year changes do not correspond to policy periods in any country. It is noteworthy, however, that the 1986 target ranges for the United States suggest that the velocities of all three targeted aggregates most likely will continue to decline, although at more gradual rates than during 1985, while the monetary targets for the United Kingdom imply a continuing sharp divergence of M0 and £M3 velocities. It may also be noted that for Japan, growth of M2+CDs at the recent projection of 9.0 percent would (under WEO output projections) imply an unusually sharp decline in velocity, which has had a remarkably stable downward trend since the mid-1970s.

The variability of velocity in recent years, particularly in the United States, the United Kingdom, and Canada, and the decisions to de-emphasize or abandon certain monetary targets in those countries, has rekindled the debate over the appropriate conduct of monetary policy. The average inflation rate in the major industrial countries has now been reduced to little

---

[16] The planned increase in credit to the private sector amounts to an expansion of 7 percent from the base that includes the excess growth of bank credit in 1985.

Table 26. Five Major Industrial Countries: Recent and Implied Changes in Annual Velocities of Targeted Aggregates, 1970–85[1]

(In percent per annum)

| | Average Annual Change (1) | Yearly Changes | | | Implied Velocity Change Assuming Monetary Growth Target:[2] | | | | Target Ranges 1986 (9) |
| | | | | | Upper bound (5) | Lower bound (6) | Upper bound (7) | Lower bound (8) | |
		1983 (2)	1984 (3)	1985 (4)	1985		1986		
United States	(1970–85)								
M1	2.3	−3.4	3.8	−3.0	1.3	3.1	−2.9	0.1	3–8
M2	−0.3	−4.5	2.8	−3.0	−1.3	0.5	−1.9	−0.1	6–9
M3	−1.4	−2.4	0.9	−3.2	−2.4	−0.4	−1.4	0.3	6–9
United Kingdom	(1970–85)								
M0	4.4	3.0	0.4	4.7	2.2	3.8	0.7	4.3	2–6
£M3	0.2[3]	−1.8	−0.1	−2.7	−1.1	0.4	−7.3	−4.2	11–15
Germany, Fed. Rep. of	(1971–85)								
Central bank money	−0.7	−2.5	0.4	—	0.1	1.3	0.9	2.1	3.5–5.5
Japan	(1970–85)								
M2+CDs	−2.3	−3.1	−1.3	−1.9	−1.8	−1.8	[−4.5][4]	[−4.5][4]	9.0[4]
France	(1970–85)								
M2R	−0.6	1.0	0.5	−0.8	1.6	2.6	...	...	...
M3	...	...	...	...	...	...	1.6[5]	3.6[5]	3–5

[1] The definitions of monetary aggregates used in this table are those employed by the monetary authorities of the individual countries. Velocity changes represent changes from year to year in the ratios of average annual money stocks to annual GNP levels; such changes do not correspond to velocity changes during policy periods.

[2] Percentage changes between implied velocity levels for the indicated year and actual velocity levels for the previous year. Implied velocity levels are based on the nominal GNP projections adopted in the *World Economic Outlook* and the average money stocks that would prevail during the year if money growth coincided with the upper or lower bounds of the target ranges. The actual changes in velocity may fall outside these bounds if the monetary aggregates do not grow in their target ranges or if the GNP projections are incorrect.

[3] 1976–85.

[4] There is no formal targeting of monetary aggregates by the Bank of Japan. This calculation assumes that the projected rate of growth of M2+CDs for the first quarter of 1986 is maintained throughout 1986.

[5] Based on incomplete data for 1985.

more than half of its level in the decade through 1976. With unemployment high and the global economy strained by a widespread need to grow out of severe debt burdens, it has been argued that the formulation of monetary policy in some countries should devote relatively higher priority to sustaining output and employment than could be done when inflation was the major short-run danger. Regardless of the extent of agreement on the desirability of promoting growth, however, there is disagreement both about the inherent ability of monetary policy to achieve this objective, and about the possible long-run inflationary consequences of attempting to do so.

Supplementary Note 3

Non-Fuel Primary Commodity Prices: Developments and Prospects

This note reviews developments in prices of the major non-fuel primary commodities (hereafter generally referred to as "commodity prices") entering international trade. The first section describes recent price movements and examines the main determinants of those movements. The second section assesses the short- and medium-term outlook for commodity prices. The final section contains brief discussions of the implications of changes in commodity prices for the terms of trade of the non-fuel exporting developing countries and of the use of the Fund's special facilities.

Recent Developments

The weakness in world commodity markets that has been in evidence in recent years continued and became more pronounced in 1985. Following a moderate improvement in 1983–84, the overall index of commodity prices, measured in current U.S. dollar terms, fell in 1985 to its lowest average level since 1976, 12½ percent below the average in 1984 (Table 27).[1] The downturn began in the third quarter of 1984 and proceeded through five consecutive quarters during which the dollar price index dropped by more than 20 percent. The final quarter of 1985, however, witnessed a slight recovery in the index primarily because of the special circumstances affecting coffee prices (discussed below). In real terms (deflated by the export price index for manufactures),[2] the overall index dropped by nearly

13 percent in 1985, erasing most of the improvement that had occurred in the two preceding years.

The recent decline in commodity prices was both steep and broad-based, encompassing all the major commodity groups included in the index (Table 27 and Chart 35). The most pronounced declines since mid-1984 were recorded for food items and agricultural raw materials. The index for beverages also declined sharply through the third quarter of 1985 before recovering markedly in the final quarter of the year, when the prolonged drought in key coffee growing areas of Brazil began to exert a strong influence on coffee prices. The average price of metals exhibited the smallest decline of the major commodity groups after mid-1984, but this decline occurred from an already relatively low level, as metal prices largely had failed to share in the general upturn in commodity prices that occurred during the 18 months following the 1981–82 recession. In contrast to the other major commodity groups, prices of metals weakened further in the last quarter of 1985, largely as a result of the sharp downward adjustment of the price of tin, following the suspension in October of buffer stock operations under the Sixth International Tin Agreement. Over the five-year period from 1980 to 1985, prices of metals fell more (by 30 percent) than the overall index of commodity prices (24 percent). The index for beverages, on the other hand, recorded the smallest decline (12 percent) in the period, due in part to the recovery in the fourth quarter of 1985. The five-year movements in the indices for food items and agricultural raw materials were broadly similar to those of the overall index. The separate indices of prices for primary commodities exported by developing countries and by industrial countries closely paralleled each other in the past two years (Chart 35). In some earlier years (such as 1977 and 1981–83), however, those indices had moved apart, reflecting divergent movements of the

---

[1] The commodity price indices in this report are constructed using weights based on 1979–81 average world export earnings. The indices in earlier *World Economic Outlook* reports were constructed using weights based on 1968–70 average export earnings of primary producing countries. Commodity prices in this note refer to the world index in current U.S. dollars (column 1 of Table 27) unless otherwise specified.

[2] The United Nations index for the unit values of manufactured goods exported by industrial countries.

Table 27. Indices of Non-Fuel Primary Commodity Prices, 1970–85[1]

(1980 = 100)

| | In U.S. Dollars | | | | | | | In SDRs | Deflated by Price of Manufactures[2] | | |
| | | | | | | | | | | | |
Year	All	Food	Beverages	Agricultural raw materials[3]	Metals	Commodity exports of developing countries	Commodity exports of industrial countries	All	All	Commodity exports of developing countries	Commodity exports of industrial countries
Weights	100.0	42.9	11.8	23.3	22.0	45.4	54.6	100.0	100.0	45.4	54.6
1970	37.1	38.4	31.8	29.8	45.4	36.8	37.4	48.4	108.9	107.9	109.8
1971	36.2	39.6	28.8	29.5	40.5	34.4	37.7	46.9	100.9	95.8	105.2
1972	38.9	42.8	31.6	33.6	40.7	36.1	41.1	46.6	99.8	92.7	105.7
1973	63.1	77.2	40.1	53.7	58.1	55.4	69.8	68.8	137.9	121.0	152.4
1974	76.4	95.4	48.6	55.9	75.8	71.4	80.4	82.6	140.4	131.3	148.0
1975	64.0	76.5	45.7	47.7	66.6	59.2	67.8	68.6	102.7	95.1	108.9
1976	69.4	71.7	84.6	61.1	65.5	68.9	69.9	78.3	110.8	109.7	111.6
1977	76.7	69.7	147.0	61.7	68.3	84.8	69.8	85.5	112.2	124.2	102.2
1978	77.6	78.9	109.9	65.6	70.3	80.2	75.4	80.6	98.2	101.5	95.4
1979	94.1	92.1	114.4	90.3	91.3	94.4	93.9	94.8	104.1	104.4	103.9
1980	100.0	100.0	100.0	100.0	100.0	100.0	100.0	100.0	100.0	100.0	100.0
1981	89.4	96.8	79.3	85.3	84.8	86.1	92.2	98.6	94.0	90.4	96.9
1982	80.0	82.1	79.6	81.1	74.8	77.4	82.1	94.2	86.2	83.4	88.5
1983	85.2	89.3	86.1	83.6	78.5	82.9	87.2	103.9	95.1	92.5	97.3
1984	86.6	88.6	100.0	87.8	74.2	86.0	87.1	109.9	100.1	99.4	100.8
1985	75.9	74.9	88.3	77.3	69.6	75.4	76.2	97.5	87.4	86.8	87.8
1984											
Q1	89.8	92.4	103.8	88.7	78.3	89.6	90.0	111.4	101.4	101.2	101.7
Q2	91.6	95.2	103.5	93.0	77.0	90.7	92.5	114.0	103.2	102.1	104.2
Q3	84.2	86.2	96.8	86.2	71.2	83.3	84.9	108.2	98.9	97.8	99.8
Q4	80.8	80.8	96.0	83.2	70.2	80.5	81.1	105.8	97.1	96.6	97.4
1985											
Q1	79.0	80.3	92.6	77.4	71.0	78.5	79.4	106.4	97.9	97.1	98.4
Q2	77.6	77.4	85.7	78.3	72.8	77.1	77.9	101.7	91.5	91.0	92.0
Q3	72.8	70.8	81.0	75.9	69.2	72.2	73.3	92.3	81.8	81.1	82.4
Q4	74.1	71.2	94.0	77.8	65.2	73.9	74.2	89.4	78.3	78.1	78.4

[1] Weights are based on 1979–81 average world export earnings from commodities.
[2] Based on the United Nations index of the unit values of manufactures exported by industrial countries.
[3] Including forestry products.

particular primary commodities exported by the two groups of countries.

Because of the large changes in the exchange rates of major currencies in recent years, movements in commodity prices denominated in currencies other than the U.S. dollar have, of course, diverged markedly from the changes in the dollar price indices shown in Table 27 (Chart 36). With the large appreciation of the U.S. dollar from 1980 through the first quarter of 1985, commodity prices denominated in terms of the French franc and the pound sterling stood in the latter period some 86 percent and 65 percent, respectively, above their levels in 1980, while the overall U.S. dollar index declined by 21 percent; the index measured in terms of the Japanese yen was in the first quarter of 1985 some 10 percent below the 1980 level. Mainly as a result of the depreciation of the U.S. dollar in the last three quarters of 1985, the differences between the commodity price indices denominated in various cur-

rencies have narrowed substantially or have been reversed. Thus, while the overall dollar price index fell by 6 percent between the first and the fourth quarters of 1985, the reductions in terms of other major currencies ranged from 26 percent to 29 percent. Whereas the indices for the French franc, the pound sterling, and the deutsche mark were still considerably above the U.S. dollar price index in late 1985 (on a base of 1980 = 100), the index of commodity prices denominated in the Japanese yen was, in fact, about 9 percent below the dollar price index. The index of commodity prices, measured in terms of the SDR, was in the final quarter of 1985 some 20 percent above the dollar price index.

Changes in real commodity prices have been more important—at least from the perspective of the commodity exporting countries—than the changes in nominal prices discussed above. Real changes are measured here by changes in nominal commodity prices relative

Chart 35. Dollar Commodity Price Indices, 1980–85

(1980 = 100)

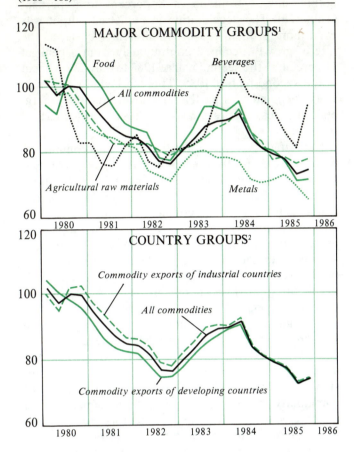

¹ Weights are based on 1979–81 average world export earnings.
² Weights are based on 1979–81 average export earnings of the respective country groups.

Chart 36. Commodity Price Indices in Terms of SDRs and Five Major Currencies, 1980–85

(1980 = 100)¹

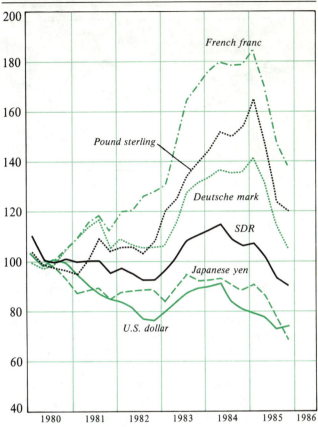

¹ Weights are based on 1979–81 average world export earnings.

to changes in the unit values of manufactured exports from the industrial countries. With the general slowdown of world inflation during the past few years, and reflecting the impact of the appreciation of the U.S. dollar over the 1980–85 period, real commodity prices declined less from 1980 through 1984 than the index measured in nominal U.S. dollar terms would indicate (Table 27 and Chart 37). However, given the dollar's depreciation during 1985, by the end of the year the level of the real and nominal indices was nearly equivalent.

Commodity prices in real terms were quite weak throughout this five-year period, particularly when viewed against a longer time perspective. After declining considerably during the 1981–82 recession, and then recovering in 1983 and 1984 to a point slightly above the 1980 level, real commodity prices fell by about 13 percent in 1985. Despite the small rise in nominal dollar commodity prices in the final quarter of 1985, the average real price in the second half of

1985 was about 20 percent below the level of 1980. Moreover, real commodity prices so far in the 1980s have averaged about 16 percent below the average for the 1970s and in 1985 were some 20 percent below the average for 1960–80.

While annual fluctuations in commodity prices have resulted mainly from various specific influences operating on the demand and the supply sides of the various markets (discussed later in this section), the general weakness of commodity prices during the past five years can be attributed in large measure to the slower economic growth experienced in the industrial world—the major market for primary commodities—than during the 1970s. The sluggishness of economic activity in Western Europe since 1980 is of particular significance as this region accounts for half of total world imports of primary commodities. However, the prolonged weakness of the markets for primary commodities may also, to some extent, have been the result of more deep-seated and fundamental changes in the world economy. One of these factors may well be the structural changes that are taking the economies of the industrial countries away from basic and heavy

141

Chart 37. Real and Nominal Commodity Price Indices, and Unit Value of Manufactures, 1980–85

(1980 = 100)[1]

[1] Weights are based on 1979–81 average export earnings of developing countries.

[2] Dollar commodity price index deflated by unit value of manufactures' exports.

industries toward lighter manufacturing (particularly in electronics) and services industries. While such changes were already under way in the 1970s, they were given additional impetus by the sharp rise in energy prices during 1979–81. Structural changes, reflected in lower intensity of commodity use, may have been a particularly important influence on prices of metals, which, as noted earlier, have shown the most pronounced decline since 1980. These changes may also have contributed to the weak state of the market for agricultural raw materials. At the same time, technological progress and the spread of new technology to developing countries may have contributed to an outward shift in the supply curve for some commodities. As a result of the increased use of higher-yielding varieties of foodgrains, for example, several developing countries have managed to achieve self-sufficiency in food production and, in some cases, to develop export surpluses. As drought-related declines in food production generally have affected regions with relatively small populations and markets, such as sub-Saharan Africa, the net increase in supply may be one factor underlying the persistent weakness of food prices during the past five years.

The sharp declines in commodity prices that were recorded in 1985, following the recovery in the two preceding years, must, of course, be attributed primarily to short-term influences, in particular changes in economic activity in the industrial countries and to specific factors operating on the supply side. That such factors have recently played an important role is indicated by the fact that over the last thirty years, a decline in commodity prices of the magnitude experienced in 1985 occurred only in the 1975 and 1981–82 recessions.

On a year-to-year basis, the rate of growth in real GNP in the industrial world fell from 4¾ percent in 1984 to 2¾ percent in 1985, while growth in industrial output slowed from about 8 percent to 3 percent (Table 28). The deceleration in industrial output was even more pronounced on a half-yearly basis, as the rate of growth declined continuously from a peak of 11 percent in the second half of 1983 to only 2½ percent in the second half of 1985. This marked slowdown in world demand was partly responsible for the emergence of excess supply of commodities on world markets in 1985.

Nevertheless, while the severity of the commodity price decline in 1985 resembled those of the major postwar recession periods in the sense that it was both large and shared by virtually all commodities, the major factor depressing commodity prices appears to have been the large worldwide buildup in supplies of primary commodities that occurred during 1984–85. This buildup had the effect of depressing commodity prices even further during a period of continuing, albeit decelerating, world economic growth. The total supply of primary commodities, defined as current production plus beginning stocks, increased by a cumulative 7½ percent during 1984–85 (Table 29), the largest two-year increase since 1960, the first year for which the supply index was calculated. The effect of this expansion in supply availability on the overall level of commodity prices was reinforced by its concentration in commodities for which supply factors are relatively more important in the determination of prices.

The largest cumulative increases in commodity output during 1984–85 were recorded for food and beverages, which together expanded by about 11 percent in the two-year period. With allowance for the impact of stock changes, the total supply of food items increased by about 9 percent and that of beverages by about 8 percent in the period. In addition to relatively favorable weather conditions, these increases appear to have resulted mainly from an expansion in productive capacity (including technological improvements), which in turn reflected mainly the lagged response to earlier changes in real prices. As the gestation lags are estimated to be relatively long (an average of about four years for food items and about seven years for beverages),[3] the 1984–85 production increases can be traced in part to the high levels of food prices in 1980–81 and to the high prices of beverages in 1977–79. As, in addition, the utilization of productive capacity in food and beverage production is responsive to the

---

[3] See K. Chu and T. Morrison: "World Non-Oil Primary Commodity Markets: A Medium-Term Framework of Analysis," *Staff Papers,* International Monetary Fund (Washington), Vol. 33 (March 1986).

Table 28. Non-Fuel Commodity Prices and Major Underlying Factors, 1981–85

(Annual percentage changes)

	1981	1982	1983	1984	1985
Commodity prices (in U.S. dollar terms)					
All commodities	−10.6	−10.6	6.5	1.6	−12.5
Food	−3.2	−15.2	8.7	−0.7	−15.5
Beverages	−20.7	0.4	8.2	16.1	−11.7
Agricultural raw materials	−14.7	−4.9	3.1	5.0	−12.4
Metals	−15.2	−11.8	4.9	−5.5	−6.2
Underlying factors					
Real GNP[1]	1.4	−0.4	2.6	4.7	2.7
Industrial production[2]	0.3	−3.6	3.4	8.2	3.1
Inflation[3]	9.9	6.9	4.4	4.4	3.8
U.S. dollar exchange rate[4]	12.7	11.7	5.8	7.9	4.5
World production of commodities[5]	3.1	−0.8	−0.6	7.2	1.6
Food and beverages	5.3	1.1	−1.7	7.5	3.1
Agricultural raw materials and metals	0.4	−3.0	1.4	6.5	−0.3

[1] Real average GNP for all industrial countries.
[2] Index for seven major industrial countries.
[3] Index of consumer prices in seven major industrial countries.
[4] Positive figures indicate appreciation of the effective exchange rate of the U.S. dollar.
[5] Using same weights as in commodity price index, adjusted to exclude commodities for which no production data are available. Data for 1985 are estimates.

previous year's real prices, the increased output of these commodities in 1984–85 may also have been attributable partly to the rise in prices of these items from late 1982 through mid-1984.

Other factors that may have contributed to the increase in agricultural production in 1984–85 may be related to price support policies pursued by major producing countries and pressures on debtor countries to maximize their foreign exchange earnings. Agricultural price support policies are widely applied in the major industrial countries. Although it is not clear that these policies intensified during 1984–85, the maintenance of support policies by these countries at a time when world production was increasing had the effect of inhibiting adjustment in output, thereby exacerbating pressures on prices of the commodities concerned. The lack of response to price signals was particularly evident in 1985 when production of most agricultural commodities continued to rise despite substantial declines in market prices beginning in the middle of 1984.

Total supplies of agricultural raw materials and metals also increased during 1984–85, but these increases were much less pronounced than in the case of the two commodity groups discussed above. While production of agricultural raw materials and metals increased in 1984 by about 7½ percent and 5 percent, respectively, small contractions of output were recorded for both these groups of commodities in 1985. For agricultural raw materials, these developments were accompanied by lower-than-expected increases in consumption and a consequent sharp rise in stocks, which tended to depress price expectations. Supply

factors had a particularly depressing influence on prices of cotton and, to a lesser extent, rubber and wool. In the case of metals, an important factor was the existence of large unutilized production capacity that continued to depress prices despite the fact that consumption growth outpaced production growth in 1984–85. This is particularly noteworthy as metal stocks declined significantly in the period. In addition, some of the major metal producers achieved substantial reductions in costs of production.

The differential rates of growth in supplies of the various commodity groups, discussed above, had a significant impact on the overall movement of commodity prices in 1985, since changes in production of food commodities and beverages are much more important determinants of short-term price developments than is the case for agricultural raw materials and metals; for the two latter groups changes in economic activity have been shown to be the more important factor.[4] Demand for food and beverages is more stable than demand for industrial raw materials. In addition, the production of food crops and beverages cannot easily respond to short-term demand changes (such as

[4] The elasticities of prices with respect to changes in production are estimated at −2.5 for food commodities and −1.3 for beverages, while for the other two commodity groups the elasticities are not statistically significant. On the other hand, the elasticities of prices with respect to changes in the economic activity of industrial countries are estimated to be 3.4 for agricultural raw materials and 2.6 for metals, while in the case of food and beverages these elasticities are not statistically significant. These estimates were calculated from equations that are part of a model of commodity price determination; see Chu and Morrison (1986) cited in footnote 3.

Table 29. World Supply of Commodities, 1980–85

(Annual percentage changes)

	1980	1981	1982	1983	1984	1985
All commodities						
Production	0.2	3.1	−0.8	−0.6	7.2	1.6
Beginning stocks	−4.9	6.2	14.6	10.8	−10.3	10.4
Total supply	−0.3	3.2	1.5	1.5	4.5	2.9
Food						
Production	−0.9	4.2	4.9	−3.9	7.5	2.7
Beginning stocks	1.2	2.4	9.8	15.1	−18.6	20.1
Total supply	−0.8	4.0	5.4	−1.3	4.2	4.5
Beverages						
Production	4.0	9.2	−12.5	6.0	7.3	4.7
Beginning stocks	10.1	21.6	27.5	−5.4	−5.6	4.0
Total supply	5.5	12.0	−1.8	2.0	3.2	4.5
Agricultural raw materials						
Production	−0.7	1.6	0.3	2.0	7.9	−0.4
Beginning stocks	−5.8	2.6	11.2	6.7	−0.5	30.4
Total supply	−1.0	0.5	0.5	3.9	5.8	3.0
Metals						
Production	1.5	−0.9	−6.5	0.8	5.1	−0.1
Beginning stocks	−23.3	5.1	16.3	20.0	−1.7	−11.5
Total supply	−1.6	−0.2	−3.5	4.8	4.4	−1.7

those during a crop year), whereas output of most industrial raw materials, particularly metals, can usually adjust somewhat more quickly.[5]

The relatively large increases in output of food items and beverages in 1984–85, therefore, had a strong depressing impact on prices of these commodities as well as on the overall level of commodity prices. With the large supply increases in 1984, prices began to fall sharply in the second half of the year in response to the actual supplies themselves and to lower price expectations, and these price reductions continued in 1985 when output increased further. The impact on prices of the large rise in output of these commodities in 1984–85 can be illustrated by examining a hypothetical scenario of alternative output developments. It is estimated that if food production had recovered in 1984 only to the 1982 level and then remained unchanged in 1985, and if output of beverages had remained at the 1983 level, the prices of these commodities in 1985 would have been some 15 percent higher than the levels actually attained. This would have resulted in the overall index of commodity prices being 8 percent higher than the level actually experienced. While the rise in output of food items and beverages had a particularly important impact on prices, specific supply factors also tended to depress prices of certain agricultural raw materials and metals, as noted earlier.

Market intervention operations through supply control measures, such as export quotas and buffer stocks, under international commodity agreements were in effect in respect of three commodities in 1985: coffee, natural rubber, and tin.[6] Reductions in December 1984 and July 1985 in the export quotas for coffee exporting countries established under the International Coffee Agreement served to contain the downward tendency in coffee prices in the first three quarters of 1985.

---

[5] Food production is, therefore, more influenced by the previous year's prices, whereas production of industrial raw materials is more influenced by the current year's prices. In addition, supply shocks (such as those caused by weather) are generally a much more dominant factor affecting production of food crops and beverages than they are in the case of other commodities. These different characteristics of the various commodity groups result in a significant inverse correlation between production and prices of food items, and a significant positive correlation between production and prices of industrial raw materials.

[6] The 1977 International Sugar Agreement expired at the end of 1984 and sugar-exporting members were then free to release the special stocks of sugar accumulated under that Agreement. While the 1980 International Cocoa Agreement remained in force in 1985, no purchases for, or sales from, the buffer stock established under that Agreement (apart from rotation of the stock of 100,000 tons accumulated earlier) have been made since March 1982 when purchase operations were suspended because of the depletion of funds.

However, increases in quotas in the final quarter failed to contain the sharp upward movement in coffee prices beginning in October 1985 as a result of adverse weather in Brazil. Large-scale intervention by the buffer stock manager of the International Rubber Agreement during 1985 was required to keep prices from falling below the agreed floor level. The semi-automatic downward revision of the price range of 3 percent was triggered in August 1985 after buffer stock purchases reached 300,000 tons. In contrast to the relative success during the year of operations under the Rubber Agreement, it was necessary to end market intervention operations under the International Tin Agreement on October 24, 1985, as a result of the exhaustion of financial resources in the face of continued downward price pressures in an already depressed tin market. Until that date, the price of tin had been kept within the agreed range only through large-scale intervention by the buffer stock manager of the Tin Agreement. Trading in tin on the London Metal Exchange was suspended and the market remained closed through March of 1986. It is unlikely that price stabilization operations will resume in the period immediately ahead.

In addition to the supply and demand influences discussed above, changes in worldwide inflation and in the exchange rate for the U.S. dollar have, of course, continued to have a significant impact on commodity prices in 1985. The further moderate deceleration of inflation in the industrial countries continued to constrain current commodity prices through its influence on the prices of substitutes, through pressures to reduce costs in commodity-using industries, and by reducing speculative demand for stocks. Moreover, the decline in the price of petroleum, which, apart from its widespread effects on production costs, is a raw material for many synthetic substitutes for primary commodities, also acted to depress commodity prices.

The impact of the changes in the U.S. dollar on commodity prices in 1985 is more difficult to ascertain. Although the U.S. dollar depreciated significantly after the first quarter of 1985, its average value in 1985 was about 4.5 percent above the 1984 level, a factor that probably contributed to the lower average level of commodity prices in U.S. dollar terms in 1985. The significant fall in the value of the U.S. dollar during the last three quarters of the year would, by itself, have tended to push up commodity prices in dollar terms during the year. However, it provided only a partial offset to the depressive impact of other factors, and dollar-denominated commodity prices continued to fall until the final quarter of the year. At that time, the dollar index, as noted earlier, recovered slightly under the influence of the sharp rise in coffee prices.

In summary, the major factor affecting the markets for primary commodities in 1985 was the large expansion in supplies, particularly of food items and beverages, that took place during 1984–85 and which was the largest two-year increase recorded since 1960. When combined with the worldwide deceleration of economic activity, and in an environment of continued low inflation in the industrial countries, the rise in output resulted in a broad decline in commodity prices in both nominal and real terms.

Outlook for Commodity Prices

Movements in the overall index of commodity prices in the near future will be affected in an important way by changes in coffee prices, which are discussed separately below. The markets for most other primary commodities are expected to remain weak in 1986 and 1987, reflecting the large overhang of supplies in combination with only a moderate increase in demand. The marked expansion of agricultural output in the past two years is expected to continue to depress prices of most food items, at least until the next harvest season begins to influence prices around the middle of 1986. Some response of agricultural production to the low prices prevailing in 1985 may lead to reduced output and a strengthening of prices in the latter part of 1986. This lower output is projected to result in price increases in 1987 broadly in line with the rate of inflation. Metal prices are also projected to remain weak in 1986 and to recover only moderately in 1987 because of a combination of rather slow growth in demand and ample supplies.

While supply-side factors are generally expected to continue to be the more important short-term determinants of commodity prices, prospective macroeconomic developments in the major markets for primary commodities also suggest that 1986 and 1987 will witness continued depressed prices for most commodities. Real economic growth in the industrial countries is projected to increase slightly from the subdued pace (2¾ percent) recorded in 1985.

In conjunction with a further moderate fall in the rate of inflation in the industrial countries, as well as the large drop in petroleum prices, and on the assumption that the pattern of exchange rates prevailing in early March 1986 will remain unchanged—implying a 15 percent year-on-year depreciation of the U.S. dollar from 1985 to 1986—these prospective developments on the supply and demand sides are expected to result in an increase of about 4 percent in the nominal dollar price index for all primary commodities excluding coffee in 1986. In real terms, the average price of these commodities is expected to decline further, by about 10 percent, to a level significantly below the long-term trend. In 1987, non-coffee commodity prices are expected to rise by about 7 percent in nominal U.S. dollar terms and by about 3 percent in real terms.

Changes in the overall index of commodity prices in 1986 and 1987 will, as noted earlier, differ markedly from those discussed above because of the special situation affecting the price of coffee, which has a relatively large weight in the index. As a result of the anticipated effects of adverse weather conditions on Brazil's current coffee crop (to be harvested in 1986), coffee prices rose by more than 70 percent during the final quarter of 1985 to their highest levels since before quotas under the International Coffee Agreement were re-introduced in October 1980. While coffee prices were still lower on average in 1985 than in the previous year, prices in 1986 are projected to average about 50 percent above the level in 1985. On the assumptions that Brazil's coffee crop will recover partially in 1987 and that other countries will draw down their stocks, coffee prices are projected to decline by 15 percent in 1987.[7] Because of these developments affecting coffee prices, the overall index of commodity prices in nominal U.S. dollars is projected to increase by about 9 percent in 1986 and by about 4 percent in 1987. In real terms, overall commodity prices would therefore decline by about 5 percent in 1986 and by about 1 percent in 1987. As coffee is exported only by developing countries, the prospective changes in coffee prices discussed above will have a considerably larger impact on the overall index of primary commodities exported by these countries. The latter index is projected to rise by 12 percent in nominal U.S. dollars in 1986 and by 1 percent in 1987. In real terms, the average price of all primary commodities exported by developing countries would decline by 2 percent in 1986 and by about 4 percent in 1987.

Some of the longer-term factors that have tended to depress commodity prices in recent years are expected to continue to influence prices over the medium term. In particular, further structural changes in the economies of the industrial countries are likely to continue to adversely affect the demand for primary commodities, while technological progress may contribute to further expansion of supplies. Nevertheless, on the assumptions that these factors will exert a diminishing influence on commodity prices over time and that aggregate output in the industrial countries will increase at a moderately higher average rate in the 1988–91 period (3 percent per annum)[8] than during the first half of the 1980s, real commodity prices are projected to remain virtually unchanged during the four years after 1987. Under the influence of continued low inflation (assumed to average 3.3 percent a year for the industrial countries), and with the assumed depreciation of the U.S. dollar at an average annual rate of 2.3 percent, commodity prices in nominal U.S. dollar terms are projected to rise at an average annual rate of 4.2 percent in the 1988–91 period, slightly below the 4.5 percent rate of increase assumed for prices of manufactured exports and for petroleum.

Terms of Trade and Use of Special Facilities of the Fund

The weakness in world commodity markets in recent years has been reflected in a significant deterioration in the terms of trade of the non-fuel exporting developing countries. During the six-year period from 1979 to 1985 the terms of trade of these countries declined cumulatively by almost 13 percent. Following a temporary small improvement during the recovery of commodity prices in 1983–84, the terms of trade of these countries declined again in 1985, virtually erasing the small gains recorded in the two preceding years. The fact that the terms of trade of the non-fuel exporting developing countries did not improve over the past three years is particularly significant in view of the decline in the price of petroleum, which accounts for a relatively large portion of the total import bill of these countries. The overall terms of trade of the countries under review are expected to increase by almost 4 percent in 1986, with the coffee-exporting countries benefiting relatively more than most other developing countries.

Total purchases under the Fund's compensatory financing facility in 1985 amounted to SDR 929 million, compared with SDR 816 million purchased in 1984. Purchases during 1984 and 1985 represented a substantial decline from the SDR 2.7 billion in average purchases made in 1982–83. Of the 13 compensatory financing purchases made during 1985, four were at least partly with respect to excesses in the cost of cereal imports, and financing of these excesses accounted for 20 percent (SDR 189 million) of total compensatory financing purchases made in 1985. Repurchases during the year, in respect of previous purchases, were larger than current purchases, so that total outstanding purchases under the facility declined from SDR 7.5 billion at the beginning of 1985 to SDR

---

[7] It should be recognized that these projections are subject to a high margin of error as they are dependent upon uncertain assumptions regarding the disposal of large coffee stocks held by many countries and the extent of the longer-term damage to Brazil's coffee trees.

[8] As assumed in the medium-term baseline scenario discussed elsewhere in this report.

7.0 billion at the end of the year. Use of the facility may increase in 1986 as a result of the marked decline in commodity prices and the related fall in export earnings of many developing countries in 1985. Net use of the facility, however, is likely again to be negative as repurchases of SDR 2.3 billion, partly with respect to the large purchases made in 1982, become due.

No purchases were made in 1985 under the Fund's buffer stock financing facility. Outstanding purchases with respect to previous purchases made in connection with members' contributions to the operations of the buffer stocks of the natural rubber and tin agreements amounted to SDR 179 million at the beginning of 1986. Repurchases of SDR 153 million were made in 1985, of which SDR 95 million was made in connection with operations under the International Sugar Agreement, which expired at the end of 1984.

Supplementary Note 4

World Oil Situation

Developments in the world oil market in early 1986, when the price of both crude oil and refined products fell precipitously, were conditioned by two main factors. In essence, they reflected the culmination of the tendency of the past few years for the price of oil to become more closely related to short-term market forces and the simultaneous substantial relaxation, or de facto abandonment, of the policy of concerted output restraint that had been followed by the members of OPEC since early 1983.[1] While the timing of the price drop was also influenced by other factors, it was the latter development that paved the way for the steep price decline.

Although the international oil market has clearly moved into a new phase, it is uncertain how long lasting the recent changes will prove to be. While the shift from the previous system of fixed official selling prices to market-oriented pricing may be a permanent feature of the oil market, output restraint could be restored at any time. As world demand for oil is expected to rise only moderately in the next few years, the level of oil prices will be determined primarily by factors operating on the supply side of the market. For the immediate future, the interplay of political and economic factors suggests that the oil market may remain weak, and the possibility of continued downward pressure on prices cannot be ruled out. However, in the event that some form of concerted output restraint is re-established, a partial reversal of the sharp fall in oil prices could take place.

The following section of this note reviews recent developments in the world oil market, with particular emphasis on prices. The subsequent section describes recent developments in consumption, production, and world trade in oil. The final section assesses the prospects for the oil market, focusing both on the short-term outlook and medium-term prospects.

Recent Developments in the Oil Market and Prices

In order to provide a fuller background to the present oil market situation, it may be useful first to review briefly underlying developments in a longer time perspective. During the 1963–73 decade, total production of the members of OPEC rose sharply from about 12 to 31 million barrels a day because of a combination of rapid growth in world demand and limited additions to productive capacity in other countries. These developments, which reflected mainly the low price of oil prevailing during the period and the comparatively high rate of growth in the world economy, set the stage for the first round of major oil price increases in 1973–74 when the price approximately quadrupled (in current U.S. dollars) to more than $10 a barrel. Important new oil discoveries were made in the early 1970s (in the North Sea, Mexico, and Alaska) and, with the enhanced price incentives, exploration for oil and additions to productive capacity began to rise substantially in these and other non-OPEC areas. However, because of the long lead times, the new capacity had only begun to come on stream in the latter part of the 1970s. As world oil consumption had also continued to rise, although at a much reduced rate, OPEC production in 1979 was about the same as in 1973 (Table 30). In the meantime, the members of OPEC had gained virtually full control over the determination of both prices and production from the leading international oil companies.

In this situation, the second round of large oil price increases in 1979–81 was triggered by a temporary

---

[1] The membership of OPEC corresponds, except for the inclusion of Ecuador and Gabon and the exclusion of Oman, to the former analytical group of 12 major "oil exporting countries." The aggregate oil balance data for the latter countries (presented in Table 30 together with data for other major groups of countries) are virtually identical with those of OPEC.

Table 30.   World Oil Balances, 1973–86[1]

(In millions of barrels a day)

	1973	1978	1979	1980	1981	1982	1983	1984	1985	1986
Industrial countries										
Production[2]	13.8	14.1	14.7	14.8	14.8	15.2	15.7	16.4	16.8	16.8
Consumption[3]	39.7	40.6	40.8	37.8	35.5	33.6	33.0	33.8	33.2	33.7
Adjustments[4]	−0.3	−0.8	−0.1	−0.4	−1.1	−1.3	−1.2	−0.9	−1.0	−1.0
Net imports	25.6	25.7	26.0	22.6	19.6	17.1	16.1	16.5	15.4	15.9
Net oil importers	*23.2*	*25.0*	*25.9*	*22.9*	*20.3*	*18.1*	*17.5*	*17.9*	*17.1*	*17.6*
Net oil exporters[5]	*2.4*	*0.7*	*0.1*	*−0.3*	*−0.7*	*−1.0*	*−1.4*	*−1.4*	*−1.7*	*−1.7*
Developing countries										
Major oil exporters[6]										
Production[2]	31.1	30.6	31.5	27.8	23.8	19.9	18.3	18.2	17.1	17.9
Consumption[3]	1.0	2.0	2.2	2.4	2.7	2.9	3.1	3.2	3.3	3.4
Adjustments[4]	0.5	0.3	0.8	0.7	0.6	0.6	0.3	0.2	0.2	0.1
Net exports	29.6	28.3	28.5	24.7	20.5	16.4	14.9	14.8	13.6	14.4
Other net oil exporters[7]										
Production[2]	2.8	5.3	5.8	6.4	6.7	7.3	7.5	7.9	8.2	8.2
Consumption[3]	2.2	3.4	3.6	3.8	4.0	4.1	4.1	4.2	4.3	4.4
Adjustments[4]	0.1	0.1	0.1	0.1	—	—	—	—	—	—
Net exports	0.5	1.8	2.1	2.4	2.7	3.2	3.4	3.7	3.9	3.8
Net oil importers										
Production[2]	1.5	1.5	1.5	1.5	1.7	1.9	2.1	2.3	2.5	2.7
Consumption[3]	5.6	7.0	7.4	7.4	7.2	7.2	7.2	7.2	7.2	7.4
Adjustments[4]	—	0.1	0.1	0.1	—	—	—	—	—	—
Net imports	4.1	5.6	6.0	6.0	5.5	5.3	5.1	4.9	4.7	4.7
Other countries[8]										
Production[2]	9.0	11.9	12.2	12.5	12.6	12.7	12.8	12.7	12.5	12.4
Consumption[3]	7.8	10.0	10.4	10.7	10.8	10.8	10.7	10.6	10.5	10.4
Adjustments[4]	—	—	—	—	—	—	—	−0.1	—	—
Net exports	1.2	1.9	1.8	1.8	1.8	1.9	2.1	2.2	2.0	2.0
Net oil exporters	*2.5*	*3.5*	*3.5*	*3.5*	*3.5*	*3.5*	*3.7*	*3.8*	*3.6*	*3.6*
Net oil importers	*−1.3*	*−1.6*	*−1.7*	*−1.7*	*−1.7*	*−1.6*	*−1.6*	*−1.6*	*−1.6*	*−1.6*
Memorandum										
Total consumption	56.3	63.0	64.4	62.1	60.2	58.6	58.1	59.0	58.5	59.3
(Change in percent)		*3.3*	*2.2*	*−3.6*	*−3.1*	*−2.7*	*−0.9*	*1.5*	*−0.8*	*1.4*
Total production	58.2	63.4	65.7	63.0	59.6	57.0	56.4	57.5	57.1	58.0
(Change in percent)		*3.6*	*−4.1*	*−5.4*	*−4.4*	*−1.1*	*1.9*	*−0.7*	*1.5*	
Aggregate oil trade balance	1.6	0.7	0.4	0.3	−0.1	−0.9	−0.8	−0.7	−0.6	−0.4
Asymmetry attributable to:										
Estimated transit lag	*. . .*	*−0.1*	*—*	*−0.6*	*−0.5*	*−0.3*	*−0.1*	*−0.2*	*0.1*	*. . .*
Other[9]	*. . .*	*0.8*	*0.4*	*0.9*	*0.4*	*−0.6*	*−0.7*	*−0.5*	*−0.7*	*. . .*

[1] For the classification of countries in groups shown here, see the Introduction to the Statistical Appendix and footnotes 5–8 below.

[2] Includes crude oil production and output of condensates and natural gas liquids (wherever data are available).

[3] Data for industrial countries include use of oil in refineries and bunker fuel. Data for several other countries are derived from statistics on production and trade in oil and group totals should be regarded as orders of magnitude only.

[4] Includes changes in inventories, processing gains (in industrial countries), bunker sales (in some cases), and statistical discrepancies.

[5] Norway and the United Kingdom.

[6] The 12 countries classified as oil exporting countries according to former analytical criteria—Algeria, Indonesia, Islamic Republic of Iran, Iraq, Kuwait, Libyan Arab Jamahiriya, Nigeria, Oman, Qatar, Saudi Arabia, United Arab Emirates, and Venezuela. The aggregate data for these countries shown here are virtually identical with those of the members of OPEC.

[7] Bahrain, Bolivia, Cameroon, China, Congo, Ecuador, Egypt, Gabon, Malaysia, Mexico, Peru, Syria, Trinidad and Tobago, and Tunisia.

[8] Includes the U.S.S.R., non-member countries in Eastern Europe, Democratic People's Republic of Korea, Cuba, Angola, and Brunei.

[9] In addition to statistical discrepancies, reflects changes in stocks afloat (not included in normal transit lag), inclusion of bunkers in export data for some countries, and transit losses.

supply interruption and was sustained for more than two years—bringing the average price of oil from about $13 a barrel in late 1978 to more than $34 a barrel in the first quarter of 1981—in part because of the bidding up of prices by buyers lacking secure long-term supplies and a consequent large buildup of world oil inventories. The escalation of oil prices took place during a period when oil consumption had already started to decline and was made possible because supply could easily adjust to the lower level of demand in view of the sharply higher export earnings of the oil exporting countries. In these circumstances, there was no need for production-sharing agreements and the fall in export volume was brought about by voluntary adjustments in output by individual countries, which were relatively easy to administer as oil operations are directly controlled by the national authorities of the major oil exporting countries.

The sharp rise in oil prices, combined with the comparatively low rates of growth experienced by both industrial and developing countries, led to a considerable decline in world oil consumption during the first half of the 1980s. With a large expansion in non-OPEC production and a reversal (from mid-1981) of the previous buildup of inventories, total oil production of the members of OPEC fell from 31½ million barrels a day in 1979 to about 17 million barrels a day in 1985, while the volume of exports from these countries dropped by more than 50 percent.[2] When the almost continuous fall in export earnings began to be reflected in mounting balance of payments difficulties for several oil exporting countries, voluntary output limitations by individual countries became increasingly difficult to maintain. In March 1983, therefore, the members of OPEC found it necessary to introduce a policy of concerted output restraint through the establishment of export quotas on individual member countries within an overall ceiling on total OPEC crude oil production of 17½ million barrels a day.[3][4] Saudi Arabia was designated as the swing producer "to supply the balancing quantities to meet market requirements." At the same time, the official price of the benchmark or "marker" crude (Arab Light 34 API) was reduced by about 15 percent from $34 a barrel to $29 a barrel. With the gradual erosion of prices that had occurred over the previous two years, this brought the weighted average export price of the major oil exporting countries to just over $28 a barrel,

representing a decline of about 18 percent from the peak reached in the first quarter of 1981 (about $34.40 a barrel).[5]

During the period from the March 1983 OPEC meeting to late 1985, the world oil market was in a state of fragile balance and the average level of oil prices eased only moderately. The price of the marker crude was reduced on one occasion when, in January 1985, the members of OPEC decided to adjust that price to $28 a barrel. The issue of price differentials between various crude oils, which had become a source of instability in the oil market in 1984, was reduced in relative importance as the members of OPEC at the same time decided to narrow the differential between light and heavy (mainstream) crude oils from $4.50 a barrel to $2.40 a barrel, thereby bringing the relative prices more in line with market price differentials.[6] In July 1985, the price differential was widened slightly as the official export prices of medium and heavier crude oils were reduced by $0.20–$0.50 a barrel, while the official prices of lighter crude oils remained unchanged. The effective average price level was also reduced during the 1983–85 period through increased reliance of several oil exporting countries on the offering of discounts below the official export prices in various direct and indirect ways, for example, through processing arrangements with foreign refineries, extended credit terms, barter-trade arrangements, or sales at spot market related prices.

Nevertheless, the weighted average export price of the major oil exporting countries declined only moderately (by about 5½ percent) in current dollar terms from April 1983 to the fourth quarter of 1985, when that price is estimated to have reached about $26.50 a barrel. Mainly reflecting the large changes in the value of the U.S. dollar in the period, the real price of oil actually increased (by about 4–5 percent) through the first quarter of 1985 before falling by about 12 percent from the first to the fourth quarter of 1985.[7] The annual average oil export price of the major oil exporters declined, in current U.S. dollar terms, by about 2 percent in 1984 and by about 4½ percent in 1985 to a level of about $26.70 a barrel in the latter year. In real terms, the average price remained virtually stable in 1984 and fell by 4½ percent in 1985. Thus, during the

---

[2] Data on production include the output of crude oil, condensates, and natural gas liquids.

[3] An earlier attempt (in March 1982) to establish export quotas lasted only a short period.

[4] The production ceilings excluded output of condensates and natural gas liquids (currently about 1.1–1.3 million barrels a day for OPEC as a whole). Such output is included in production in Table 30.

[5] The weighted average export price of crude oil, condensates, natural gas liquids, and refined oil products.

[6] See *World Economic Outlook, April 1985*, p. 150.

[7] The real price of oil is defined as the average oil export price of the major oil exporting countries in current U.S. dollars deflated by the estimated import prices of these countries (also in U.S. dollar terms). While this definition provides an approximate measure of the real price (or purchasing power) of oil in international trade, it does not provide a measure of the real domestic price of oil in importing countries. Such changes in the industrial countries are discussed in the following section.

Table 31. Changes in the Price of Oil, 1979–85[1]

(In percent)

	1979–81	1982–85	1983	1984	1985
In current U.S. dollars	162	−21	−11½	−2	−4½
In real terms[2]	111	−13	−8½	—	−4½

[1] Annual average oil export price of the major oil exporting countries.

[2] Nominal price deflated by estimated import prices of the major oil exporting countries.

whole period from 1981 to 1985, the annual average price declined by about 21 percent in current U.S. dollars and by about 13 percent in real terms, thereby erasing only a relatively small portion of the price increases in 1979–81 (Table 31).

Prices in the spot market for crude oils, after having strengthened for some months following the March 1983 OPEC agreement, fluctuated during the following two years with an underlying moderate downward trend. From June through November 1985, the spot market firmed considerably, with prices of some crude oils rising by about $4 a barrel to more than $30 a barrel (Chart 38).[8] Prices in this period were influenced by a number of partly transitory factors, for example, reduced supplies from the U.S.S.R., intermittent interruptions of oil shipments from the Islamic Republic of Iran, and relatively low worldwide inventories.

The relative stability of the oil market during most of the 1983–85 period, at least on the surface, resulted in part from a stabilization of world oil demand in the past two years after the continuous and large decline from 1979 to 1983. With the recovery in economic activity in major industrial countries since the latter part of 1983, world oil consumption actually increased (by about 1½ percent) in 1984. Although consumption declined again in 1985, as economic growth moderated significantly in both industrial and developing countries, the annual level of world oil consumption was still higher in that year than in 1983 (Table 30).[9] Nevertheless, as total oil production in areas outside the major oil exporting countries (or the members of OPEC) continued to rise, the annual volume of net oil exports from the latter countries remained virtually stable in 1984 and then declined further by about 8 percent in 1985. In response to the weakening of oil market conditions in the latter part of 1984, the

members of OPEC agreed, with effect from November 1, 1984, to lower the individual production quotas within a reduced overall OPEC ceiling of 16 million barrels a day.

The apparent market stability during most of 1985, as attested by the resilience of the price of oil, masked the precarious state of the oil market that developed during the course of the year and that reflected primarily the increasing reliance on a single producer to support the price. As world demand for oil from the members of OPEC declined significantly during the first nine months of 1985—in the third quarter reflecting in part a drawdown of commercial inventories contrary to the normal seasonal pattern—total crude oil production of these countries had, by the summer of 1985, fallen to about 14–15 million barrels a day, or more than 1 million barrels a day below the reduced production ceiling. Virtually all of the decline was absorbed by Saudi Arabia (the swing producer), whereas several other OPEC members maintained their output, in some cases at levels above the production quotas, through increased reliance on price discounting (from the official export prices) or sales at market-related prices. By August 1985, Saudi Arabia's production had fallen to only about 2–2½ million barrels a day, or less than one fourth of its average output in 1980–81. As at that point there was virtually no room for further reduction, the swing producer had lost the incentive and ability to perform its function in an almost continuously declining market.[10]

It was against this background that a major shift in Saudi Arabia's oil policies took place in the third quarter of 1985. Its major elements were the abandonment of Saudi Arabia's role as a swing producer, a change in the previous practice of selling crude oil only at the official export prices, and the restoration of Saudi Arabia's oil production and market share. The latter objective was achieved mainly by the entering into of a number of crude oil sales agreements under which the price of crude oil was directly linked to the spot market prices of the refined products extracted by the particular crude oil (so-called refinery netback prices).[11]

---

[8] The spot prices depicted in Chart 38 are those of the most widely traded crude oils (Brent and Ekofisk in the North Sea and West Texas Intermediate (WTI) in the United States) as well as the OPEC marker crude (Arab Light, produced by Saudi Arabia).

[9] Recent developments in oil consumption are discussed in more detail in the following section.

[10] The sharp fall in Saudi Arabia's crude oil production had, in addition to bringing about a steep decline in foreign exchange earnings and budgetary revenue, begun to impinge on domestic requirements of associated gas (produced in conjunction with crude oil).

[11] Although the exact formulas differ, a typical netback price is determined by calculating the weighted average spot market price (generally at the time of arrival of the crude oil at the refinery gate) of the refined products extracted by a particular crude oil and subtracting from that price total refining costs (often including an agreed profit margin) and the cost of transporting the crude oil. Such netback prices can differ significantly because of the varying product yield patterns of individual crude oils, regional differences in product prices, and different characteristics of oil refineries.

Chart 38.   Spot Market Prices for Selected Crude Oils, 1982–March 1986

(In U.S. dollars per barrel)

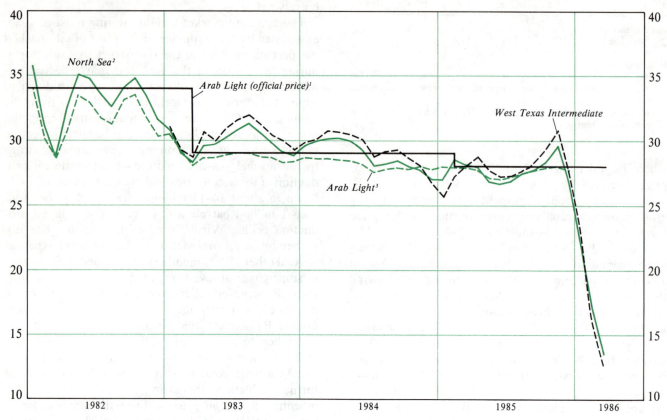

[1] OPEC's marker crude oil.
[2] Average of Brent and Ekofisk.
[3] Representative quotations are not available after 1985.

A further development in late 1985 with major implications for the oil market was the decision reached by the members of OPEC at their meeting on December 7–9, 1985 to ". . . secure and defend for OPEC a fair share in the world oil market. . .''; a ministerial committee was appointed to study the question of how this objective was to be achieved. Although previous decisions on prices and production quotas were not changed, the December OPEC decision was generally interpreted by market participants as a de facto abandonment of the policy of attempting to administer international crude oil prices through the maintenance of agreed official export prices and concerted output restraint.

Largely as a consequence of these developments, total OPEC production increased considerably (by almost 3 million barrels a day) from the third to the fourth quarters of 1985 and remained at a high level in early 1986. Although most of the increase was accounted for by Saudi Arabia, several other oil exporters also raised their output, in part through increased reliance on sales arrangements at netback prices. While the rise in OPEC production since September 1985, coupled with a shift toward market-related pricing, did not have an immediate impact on the oil market, as it occurred during a period of seasonal upturn in oil consumption, it had a powerful effect in early 1986.

Following an initial sharp drop after the announcement of the OPEC communiqué on December 9, spot market prices recovered partially in the latter part of December 1985 to approximately their levels in mid-year. In January 1986, however, the large buildup in OPEC production in combination with lower-than-expected demand for heating fuel—reflecting the unusually mild weather since mid-December in both Western Europe and the northeastern part of the United States—led to the emergence of a major short-term imbalance between supply and demand. Spot market prices for both crude oils and refined products began to fall sharply with a major price break occurring in the latter part of January 1986. Prices continued to fall in the following weeks and by March 1986 spot prices for heavily traded crude oils were in the range of $12–$15 a barrel. Prices in the first quarter of 1986 were also volatile, being influenced by speculative trading in both the spot and forward markets.[12] While the average price of oil in international trade in this period cannot be assessed with any degree of certainty, the fall in product prices had driven down the calculated crude oil netback values to below $15 a barrel in some markets in March 1986.

Although recent developments in the oil market were conditioned by the large reduction in world demand for oil from (and the loss in market share of) the members of OPEC over the past several years, it is important to note that the precipitous drop in oil prices in early 1986 did not take place because of any major or sudden drop in demand for oil at that time. Instead, it occurred because of a major relaxation—if not formal abandonment—of the policy of concerted output restraint by the major oil exporting countries and the simultaneous shift to market-related pricing. In essence, the price of oil had been left free, at least temporarily, to find its own level for the first time in a long period.[13] Because of the low short-term price elasticity of demand for oil and the continued existence of considerable unused production capacity in countries where production costs are very low (often less than $2 a barrel), and which have the ability to reintroduce considerable production restraint at any time, this has created an unstable situation in which the price of oil can swing widely (in either direction) within a relatively short period.

In view of the adverse effects of such swings for producers of oil (and the world economy at large), it is probable that some form of structured oil market system will eventually re-emerge from the present situation. As the maintenance of adequate and flexible output restraint will for some time be a prerequisite for any stability in the general level of oil prices, and as it also appears that such restraint cannot, in current circumstances, be implemented for long by individual producers acting alone, it is likely that any such system will necessitate some form of collective responsibility for managing supplies.[14] Its nature and the configura-

tion of its participants may, however, differ from the system existing in the past few years.

The change in the method of crude oil pricing, from a system of fixed official prices based on the price of a benchmark crude oil—changed from time to time by joint decisions by the members of OPEC—to one of market-related pricing, will probably be more difficult to reverse. The price of oil had already become more directly responsive to short-term market forces because of several related developments over the past few years. These include the growing importance of the spot market for crude oils (at the expense of the term-contract market), the emergence of futures markets for both crude oil and refined products, the increasing fragmentation of the oil market and rise in the number of market participants, the tendency toward disintegration and restructuring of the oil industry following the loss of ownership or control of oil reserves by the major oil companies, the greater flexibility of oil refineries to use different crude oils (which has led to enhanced transmission of price influences between the markets for crude oil and refined products), and a recent shift in world oil trade from crude oils to refined products associated in part with the construction of new export refineries in oil exporting countries. Of major importance, of course, were the practices of several oil exporting countries (inside and outside OPEC) to formally or de facto abandon the official selling prices or to provide varying discounts from these prices.[15] Despite these developments, however, the official selling prices were still important in 1985, at least by providing benchmarks for a significant portion of oil moving in international trade.

With the turn of events in the oil market in the latter part of 1985, the transformation of the pricing system from fixed official selling prices to market-related prices was virtually completed in a short period of time. An important factor was the increasing reliance on netback pricing, as this method of pricing provides a direct link between the price of crude oil and the prices at which petroleum products are traded internationally. At the same time, it provides for a sharing of the risk of short-term changes in oil prices between refineries and crude oil producers.

Although it is not easy to predict the future evolution of the international oil market in the present situation, it is possible that a flexible pricing system—under which crude oil sales will be based on spot prices, netback values, or some other market indicators—will be a permanent feature. The main rationale for such an expectation is not so much the recent events as the

---

[12] Trading activity was concentrated in the Brent and WTI crude oils, the two crudes preferred by speculators, and representative quotations for some other crude oils (including Arab Light) are not available for January–March 1986.

[13] Prior to the assumption of control over the determination of oil prices by members of OPEC in the early 1970s, the major international oil companies exercised a stabilizing influence on the oil market and the level of prices.

[14] In a situation with no restraint on output by any producer, the price of oil would fall to a very low level. Such a development would probably be associated with large shifts in the distribution of world oil production and the price of oil would remain unstable, at least potentially, as output restraint could be reintroduced at any time.

[15] An important development was the shift to market-related prices by the North Sea producers in the latter part of 1984.

likelihood that the structural changes in the oil market over the past several years, noted above, will prove irreversible. As the breakdown of the previous oil market system resulted, to at least some extent, from the difficulties encountered by the major oil exporting countries in attempting to control production through concerted action and simultaneously adhering to agreed and fixed official export prices, a market-oriented pricing system might, in fact, provide for greater longer-term stability in the oil market. At the same time, however, it will pose a challenge in managing supplies in a flexible manner as oil prices will remain volatile in the short run, in part because of the seasonal variations in oil consumption and shifts in demand between various oil products and geographical areas.

Recent Developments in Consumption, Production, and Trade in Oil

The first half of the 1980s witnessed a remarkable shift in the direction and pattern of world energy use. The most important changes occurred in the industrial countries, which currently account for about one half of world energy consumption and more than two thirds of total energy use in the member countries of the Fund. In the developing countries, trends in oil and energy consumption have also departed significantly from previous longer-term trends, but for the developing world as a whole, the more important changes have occurred on the supply side.

While the earlier close link between changes in total output and energy consumption had already begun to weaken in the industrial countries in the second half of the 1970s, the trend toward increased efficiency of energy use gathered strong momentum only after 1979. With the continuing impact of the 1973–74 oil price increases sharply reinforced by the effects of the more important escalation of prices from early 1979, the overall use of energy per unit of output in the industrial world declined by more than 3½ percent a year in the 1980–83 period with only a moderate tendency toward deceleration (Table 32). As the international oil price increases were almost universally passed through to consumers in importing countries and contributed to a considerable rise in prices of other energy products, particularly natural gas, the average real price of energy paid by end-users in the industrial countries rose by almost 40 percent from 1978 to 1982.

Although real domestic prices of oil and total energy products in the industrial world as a whole had already started to fall in 1982 and 1983, respectively, the gains in the overall efficiency of energy use were sustained in 1984 and 1985, albeit at a reduced pace. The rate of decline in energy use per unit of output is estimated

to have been somewhat larger in 1985 (about 1½ percent) than in the preceding year (½ of 1 percent), a development that may be explained in part by the impact on energy consumption of the unusually cold winter in 1983–84 and by the more pronounced shift in industrial activity than in growth of total GNP, as the strong recovery in industrial output in 1984 was followed by a marked deceleration in 1985.[16]

In addition to the sustained trend toward increased efficiency of overall energy use, the period since 1979 also witnessed a marked replacement of oil by other forms of primary energy. Whereas the use of total energy per unit of output in the industrial countries declined cumulatively by about 15 percent from 1979 to 1985, consumption of oil per unit of output fell by almost 30 percent. As a result, the share of oil in total energy consumption of these countries, which had already been reduced from 54 percent in 1973 to 51 percent in 1979, fell to an estimated 43½ percent in 1985. Non-oil energy consumption increased significantly in both 1984 and 1985 with the increase shared by all major energy sources. The growth in production and use of nuclear energy was particularly rapid (about 17 percent a year) because of increased utilization of existing capacity and the commissioning of several new nuclear plants. Coal consumption also rose considerably in the United States, while in Western Europe natural gas had the greatest penetration.

Oil consumption (as well as total energy use) in the industrial countries in the early 1980s was also affected by the prolonged recession and the particular weakness in energy-intensive industrial production, which reflected in part the structural changes in the economies of these countries. As a result of all these factors, total oil consumption in the industrial world fell by nearly 20 percent from 1979 to 1983, although at a gradually declining rate (Table 32). Mainly because of the strong recovery in economic activity in some major countries since the latter part of 1983, oil consumption increased by about 2½ percent in 1984. With the renewed slowing of growth, however, consumption declined again (by an estimated 1½ percent) in 1985. In addition to the changes in economic activity, the levels of total oil consumption in the industrial countries in the past two years were significantly affected by the coal miners' strike in the United Kingdom, which led to a large-scale shift from the use of coal to heavy fuel oil for power generation in that country in 1984 and a subsequent switching back to the use of coal when the strike ended in early 1985. Moreover, because of the cold winter of 1983–84, oil consumption

---

[16] The industrial sector is a relatively large user of energy, and a cyclical upturn in industrial production is often associated with increased utilization of older (and less fuel-efficient) equipment.

Table 32. Industrial Countries: Changes in Oil and Energy Consumption, 1974–85

(Changes in percent, except as noted)

	Average 1974–79	1980	1981	1982	1983	1984	1985
Oil consumption	½	−7½	−6½	−5	−2	2½	−1½
Non-oil energy consumption	2	1½	1½	−1½	1	5	3
Energy consumption	1	−3	−2½	−3	−½	4	1
Consumption per unit of output							
Oil consumption	−2	−8½	−8	−5	−4½	−2	−4
Energy consumption	−1½	−4½	−4	−3	−3	−½	−1½
Ratio of oil consumption to total energy consumption (in percent)	54–51[1]	49	46½	45½	45	44½	43½

[1] For 1973 and 1979 respectively.

in the industrial countries was considerably higher in the first quarter of 1984 than in the corresponding period of 1985. The relatively mild weather in some major consuming areas in December 1985 and January 1986, noted earlier, appears to have led to a temporary weakening of oil consumption in this period.

When allowance is made for the impact of weather conditions as well as the coal miners' strike in the United Kingdom, demand for oil in the industrial countries was relatively stable in the second half of 1985 and has recently tended to firm slightly. It appears, therefore, that the period of falling oil consumption may have come to an end. This development reflects, to some extent, a further lessening of the effects of the oil price increases in 1979–81 and the growing influence of the subsequent fall in prices. Changes in domestic oil prices among the industrial countries have, however, differed markedly in recent years. During the 1982–85 period, the real price of oil for end-users is estimated to have declined by about 23 percent in the United States, by about 10 percent in Japan, and to have remained virtually unchanged in Western Europe.[17]

The different behavior of domestic oil prices in the United States and Western Europe, which to a large extent reflected the impact of exchange rate developments on the landed cost of oil imports in local currency terms (Chart 39), probably served to accentuate the impact on oil demand of the differential rates of economic growth in these regions over the past two years.[18] Whereas all of the increase in total oil consumption in the industrial world from 1983 to 1985

was accounted for by the United States, in Western Europe consumption declined moderately. While oil consumption also declined in Japan, which maintained a high rate of economic growth over the two-year period, this can be explained in part by an unusually large replacement of oil by other forms of energy in that country in 1985.

The lack of comprehensive and up-to-date statistics precludes an adequate analysis of recent developments in total energy demand of the developing countries. Available information indicates that total oil consumption in these countries, after having expanded at a rapid rate (about 7 percent a year) from 1973 to 1979, continued to rise through 1985, in contrast to the

Chart 39. Average Export Price of Petroleum in Terms of Major Currencies, 1978–85[1]

(1978 = 100)

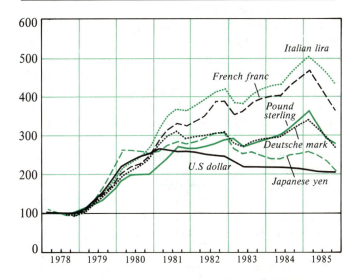

---

[17] According to data prepared by the International Energy Agency.

[18] The different movements in domestic oil prices resulted primarily from the appreciation of the U.S. dollar through the first quarter of 1985. While the subsequent depreciation of the U.S. dollar resulted in a substantial fall in the international price of oil in terms of currencies other than the U.S. dollar in the last three quarters of 1985, the impact on oil demand in 1985 was probably relatively small because of the lags involved.

[1] Average export price of 12 major oil exporting countries in national currency units per barrel. Indices are based on quarterly average prices and exchange rates.

experience of the industrial countries.[19] Nevertheless, the growth in total oil use of the developing world slowed markedly to less than 2 percent a year in the 1980–85 period. Of more significance than changes in the aggregate oil demand of these countries, however, was the experience of different groups of countries. Whereas oil consumption in the 26 net oil exporting developing countries (including the 13 members of OPEC) continued to rise, although at a much reduced rate, total consumption in the much larger group of net oil importing developing countries declined moderately in 1981 and remained virtually unchanged in the following four years at a level of about 7.2 million barrels a day (Table 30).

Although the stability in oil consumption of the net oil importing developing countries in recent years contrasts with the marked decline in oil use by the industrial countries since 1979, it has entailed a considerable effort on the part of many countries to curtail the demand for oil. Apart from their already low level of per capita oil consumption, some of the main obstacles to oil conservation in developing countries include the scarcity of investment capital for the development of oil substitutes, increasing urbanization, and relatively large concentration of oil use in industry and agriculture. Nevertheless, because of the persistent foreign exchange constraints facing the net oil importing developing countries, virtually all of them have taken a number of measures aimed at limiting oil consumption and imports, of which the most important have been increases in domestic petroleum prices.[20] In addition to the direct impact of such measures, the stagnation in total oil consumption of these countries during the past five years has, of course, also reflected the much slower growth experienced by them in this period than during the 1970s.

The stability in total oil consumption of the net oil importing developing countries in recent years conceals important differences between individual countries and regions. Whereas consumption has declined markedly in the Western Hemisphere, with the large drop in Brazil since 1979 being of particular importance, it has continued to rise in several other countries, particularly in the Asian region. In 1985, India appears to have overtaken Brazil as the largest oil consumer among the developing countries.

The trends in consumption of the industrial and developing countries, discussed above, have led to a marked shift in the composition of world oil consumption (excluding the U.S.S.R. and certain other countries that are not members of the Fund) over the last number of years (Table 33).[21] The share of developing countries increased from 18 percent in 1973 to 25 percent in 1979 and rose further to about 31 percent in 1985 due mainly to the continuing rise in consumption of the net oil exporting developing countries. Although the 1985 distribution of world oil consumption is not expected to change markedly in the near future—with all major groups of countries expected to experience a moderate growth in consumption—the trend since 1973 toward relatively greater oil use in developing countries is likely to continue in the medium to longer term.

Changes in aggregate world oil production in recent years have, of course, mirrored the developments in total consumption discussed above, although there have been significant differences in some years, which have resulted mainly from changes in the level of world inventories. While world oil production declined overall by about 13 percent from 1979 to 1985, of greater significance was the marked shift in its distribution that took place in the period. The share of the major oil exporting countries (or the members of OPEC) fell from almost one half in 1979 to only 30 percent in 1985, a marked acceleration of the loss in market share observed in the preceding six-year period (Table 34). While the relative shares of all other major groups of countries increased in the first half of the 1980s, even in absolute terms total production outside the members of OPEC rose considerably in the period, despite the reduction in world oil demand.

The continuing rise in total oil production in areas outside the major oil exporting countries reflected, to a large extent, the development of oil reserves that had been discovered in the early 1970s, particularly in the North Sea, Mexico, and Alaska, but more recently also the impact of the increased incentives for oil exploration resulting from the 1979–81 oil price increases. In part because the new production that was brought on stream entailed a relatively high investment cost—the total cost of production is generally much higher than in OPEC countries—producers have tended to maximize the use of installed capacity by pursuing more flexible pricing policies than OPEC member countries.[22] Although most of the rise in total non-OPEC production was accounted for by countries that have been, or have recently become, net oil exporters,

---

[19] Consumption data for several countries are derived from data on production and trade in oil.

[20] In the past few years, most oil exporting developing countries have also raised domestic oil prices substantially, often with a view to strengthening budgetary positions.

[21] Although available information on developments in these countries (listed in footnote 8 of Table 30) is fragmentary, it appears that their total consumption has tended to decline moderately in the past few years due mainly to significant substitution of natural gas for oil in the U.S.S.R. that was made possible by the continuing large rise in natural gas production in that country. The U.S.S.R. accounts for some 85 percent of total oil consumption in these countries.

[22] In some cases, a substantial part of any reduction in prices is being absorbed by the taxes paid by oil companies.

Table 33. Distribution of World Oil Consumption, 1973–85[1]

(In percent, except as noted)

	1973	1979	1984	1985
Industrial countries	82	75	70	69
Developing countries	18	25	30	31
Net oil exporters[2]	7	11	15	16
Net oil importers	11	14	15	15
Total	100	100	100	100
Total (in millions of barrels a day)	48.5	54.0	48.4	48.0

[1] Excluding consumption in the nonmember countries of the Fund which are included in the group of "other countries" in Table 30.
[2] Includes the 26 net oil exporting countries listed in footnotes 6 and 7 in Table 30.

oil production also increased significantly in a number of net oil importing countries where the producers—in developing countries mostly governments or national oil companies—are often not faced with external competition in their domestic markets. Consequently, almost all producers outside the members of OPEC, with the exception of Mexico, have been producing at close to capacity levels in recent years despite the weakening of demand and prices.[23]

As the residual suppliers of oil to importing countries, the members of OPEC experienced a fall in their total output from 1979 to 1985 that was approximately two and one half times as large as the decline in world oil consumption in the period, and their total export volume dropped by more than one half.[24] Nevertheless, as a significant portion of the rise in output in other countries was absorbed in their domestic markets, the members of OPEC still accounted for almost two thirds of world oil exports in 1985 (Table 34).[25] However, it should be noted that world oil trade has fallen to a considerably greater extent, in both absolute and relative terms, than the decline in world oil consumption since 1979, a circumstance that has tended to narrow the scope for output restrictions.

After having increased, on average, by about 2½ percent a year from 1979 to 1983, total non-OPEC production rose at a somewhat more rapid rate in 1984, mainly because of an upturn in crude oil production in the United States and an acceleration in the growth of oil output of the developing countries, combined with further expansion in North Sea production. In 1985, however, the further rise in total production of

these areas slowed significantly as output in the United States started to level off, while production in the U.K. sector of the North Sea began to near its peak. Elsewhere in the industrial world, Norway's output continued to rise, particularly in the latter part of 1985, and significant production increases were also recorded in Canada and Australia. In the non-OPEC developing countries, output rose at almost the same pace as in 1984, led by sizable increases in China and, to a lesser extent, in Egypt. Approximately four fifths of the further steady rise in oil production in the net oil importing developing countries in the past two years is accounted for by Brazil and India.

An important reason for the slowdown in total non-OPEC production in 1985 was the fall in oil output of the U.S.S.R., the world's largest producer. This decline, which started in 1984 following a continuous upward trend in production for several years, appears to have resulted partly from the gradual loss of productive capacity in some major oil fields (reportedly caused in part by oil field management problems) and the lack of large discoveries in recent years. Although efforts are now being made to improve field operations and recovery methods, it is uncertain whether a further decline in output of the U.S.S.R. can be avoided in the near future.

The changes in world oil consumption and production discussed above, coupled with the large movements in the price of oil, have led to major shifts in world oil trade balances (in U.S. dollar value terms) in recent years. The combined oil export value of the major oil exporting countries, after having more than doubled from 1978 to 1980 (to about $280 billion), fell in each of the following five years and had by 1985 reached approximately the level of 1978 ($134 billion). The main counterpart to this change, of course, was the fall in the net oil import value of the industrial countries from about $260 billion in 1980 to about $150 billion in 1985. Although changes in oil trade balances of the developing countries (outside the major oil

[23] Mexican production has been held virtually stable at a level of about 3 million barrels a day since 1982 and crude oil exports have been limited to an annual ceiling of 1.5 million barrels a day.

[24] As noted in the preceding section, the composition of output among the members of OPEC has also changed significantly, particularly in 1985.

[25] The aggregate of world oil trade balances of countries that are net oil exporters. Excludes exports of the U.S.S.R. to other member countries of the Council for Mutual Economic Assistance (CMEA).

Table 34. Distribution of World Oil Production and Net Oil Exports, 1973–85[1]

(In percent, except as noted)

	1973	1979	1985
World oil production			
Major oil exporters[2]	53	48	30
Other developing countries	7	11	19
Net oil exporters	5	9	14
Net oil importers	2	2	4
Industrial countries	24	22	29
Net oil exporters	—	3	6
Net oil importers	24	19	23
Other countries	16	19	22
Total	100	100	100
Total (in millions of barrels a day)	58.2	65.7	57.1
World net oil exports[3] [4]			
Major oil exporters[2]	95	88	64
Other developing countries	2	6	18
Industrial countries	—	—	8
Other countries[4]	3	6	10
Total	100	100	100
Total (in millions of barrels a day)	31.2	32.4	21.2

[1] For classification of countries, see Table 30.

[2] Members of OPEC, except for the exclusion of Ecuador and Gabon and the inclusion of Oman, three relatively small net oil exporters. The data for this group are virtually identical with those of the members of OPEC.

[3] The aggregate oil trade balances of countries that have been net oil exporters since 1980.

[4] Excluding exports from the U.S.S.R. to other member countries of the Council for Mutual Economic Assistance (CMEA).

exporting group) have been much smaller in absolute terms, the fall in the net oil import bill of the oil importing developing countries of about one third from a peak of $71 billion in 1981 to about $48 billion in 1985 has been of particular importance for these countries. The decline reflected not only the fall in the oil import price but also the growing oil self-sufficiency of these countries, particularly of the two largest consumers (Brazil and India). For the 14 net oil exporters that are not included in the group of major oil exporters, the net oil export value continued to increase through 1984—as the rise in volume more than offset the fall in the average price—but then declined slightly (by about 2 percent) in 1985.

Outlook for the Oil Market and Prices

Given the current situation in the world oil market, it is not possible to predict the average oil price level in 1986 and 1987 with any degree of confidence. Although prices will continue to be affected by developments in oil and energy demand, there can be little

doubt that supply-side factors will be the dominant influence on the evolution of oil prices in this period. As both the distribution and total volume of world oil production may be subject to significant shifts, and with the change to market-related pricing, it also seems likely that oil prices will be quite volatile in the near future.

World oil consumption will be influenced primarily by the level of economic activity in the industrial countries, by further shifts in the composition of total energy consumption, and by the demand response to the recent fall in international oil prices. The latter response will depend importantly on the price level that will eventually emerge, on the expectations for future price changes, as well as on the extent to which the fall in oil prices will be passed through to consumers in oil importing countries. The uncertainties attached to each of these factors obviously makes any projection subject to a significant margin of error. While the impact on world oil consumption of the oil price decline could be significant over time, the initial effect may not be very large if the prime were to settle at $15 or above. In view of the availability of considerable spare capacity in production of other forms of energy and the likely sympathetic responses of prices of such fuels to the oil price decline, the switching from oil to coal, natural gas, and nuclear energy is likely to be retarded only moderately during the next year or two. Prospective changes in world economic activity—with growth in real GNP expected to rise only moderately in 1986 and 1987—also do not point to any major upturn in world oil and energy consumption in the immediate future. Taking all these factors into account, it is expected that world oil consumption will rise at an annual rate of about 1½–2 percent in 1986–87 with some tendency toward acceleration during the period.

The key issue in the determination of oil prices in 1986 and 1987, as discussed earlier, is the extent to which production restraint will be exercised by the major oil exporting countries (inside and outside OPEC). In the circumstances prevailing in mid-March 1986, such restraint would seem to require some form of agreement on concerted action. Without an effective agreement—which may be difficult to achieve because of the different perceptions of the optimal price and appropriate strategies among the oil exporting countries—it is possible that competition for market shares could intensify and drive the price of oil down to very low levels.[26] Although the floor for crude oil prices would, in such a situation, probably be in the $5–$10 range, it would appear unlikely that the price would remain at such a low level, or even significantly below $15 a barrel, for an extended period of time. At a price level in the range of $8–$12 a barrel, some oil production (particularly from high cost stripper wells) will probably be shut in.[27] Moreover, the demand response could be quite significant, as some energy conservation programs would no longer be economical and as considerable switching back to oil from other forms of energy may begin to occur.[28] Such effects would, of course, depend to an important extent on price expectations of market participants and may not be very large if the lower level of prices is expected to be temporary. Of more importance than the demand response to a very low level of oil prices, however, is the probability that it will eventually lead to an agreement to restore considerable production restraint because of the severe financial implications for oil exporting countries. Depending upon the degree of restraint exercised, such an agreement could quickly lead to a significant recovery of oil prices. Short-term changes

in the price of oil could, of course, also be influenced by changes in inventory behavior. However, this factor will probably not be of importance over the 1986–87 period as a whole as the present inventory position is broadly in line with prospective demand.[29]

Given all the uncertainties inherent in the current situation, and in the absence of any obviously plausible alternative assumption, the staff has adopted as a working assumption for this report that the average export price of the major oil exporting countries will be $15 a barrel from the second quarter of 1986 through the end of 1987; the annual average price in 1986 would be about $16 a barrel. This would represent a decline of about 40 percent from the estimated annual average price in 1985 (about $26.70 a barrel) and a further decline of about 6 percent in 1987. In real terms, the price would decline by about 46 percent in 1986 and by about 11 percent in 1987.

World energy developments in the medium term will be conditioned by the as yet uncertain outcome of the events in the world oil market in early 1986. Although the near term impact of lower oil prices may not be very large, as discussed above, the cumulative effects could be significant over time. While the fall in oil prices will affect both the demand for and the supply of oil, the supply-side effects are likely to be the more important, particularly as they will be superimposed upon longer-term tendencies pointing toward slower growth in productive capacity outside the major oil exporting countries in the Middle East.

Although developments since the first round of oil price increases in 1973–74 have shown that the demand for oil is responsive to price changes over a longer period of time, several factors suggest that the response to lower oil prices will be smaller than the response to the earlier rapid escalation of prices. The sustained tendency toward reduced use of energy per unit of output resulted primarily from behavioral changes by end-users of energy that are not easily reversible and from conservation measures mandated by the authorities in consuming countries that are likely to remain in place. Given the considerable time lags in the replacement of the total capital stock (particularly in the housing industry), further gains in the overall efficiency of energy use can, therefore, be expected for some time. Moreover, the substitution of non-oil forms of energy for oil is also likely to be sustained— barring the possibility that oil prices will remain at a low level for an extended period—in view of the

---

[26] This possibility is particularly significant during the forthcoming period of seasonal decline in oil demand.

[27] The overall effect on world oil supply may, however, not be very large since virtually no major oil fields (even in high cost areas such as the North Sea) have operating costs above $10 a barrel.

[28] Such reverse fuel switching would initially affect mainly the use of heavy fuel oil, particularly in electricity generation and industrial plants with dual- or multi-fuel burning capability.

[29] Although the level of commercial stocks has been reduced considerably in the past few years (both in absolute volume and in terms of days of forward consumption), the minimum level of stocks needed for operational purposes has also been reduced because of a more efficient management of stocks and refinery operations by the oil companies.

prospective ample supplies of coal and natural gas and the projected further rise in installed nuclear energy capacity (where the lead times are particularly long).[30] Nevertheless, as the price of oil is becoming more competitive vis-à-vis other fuels and as falling end-user prices will begin to stimulate demand (e.g., in the transportation sector), world oil consumption is expected to expand at a moderately accelerating pace in the medium term. The growth in consumption is likely to be somewhat more rapid in the developing countries than in the industrial countries because of the expected higher rate of growth and closer link between oil use and economic activity in the developing world. Continued financial constraints to interfuels substitution and a rise in energy-intensive industrial production are also expected to stimulate oil consumption in the developing countries.

As discussed in the *World Economic Outlook, April 1985* report, the longer-term prospects for sizable new additions to world oil reserves and productive capacity were already not very promising prior to the recent fall in oil prices, as the returns on world oil exploration have been diminishing with the search for oil increasingly gravitating toward marginal, higher-cost, and less accessible areas. Although recent developments have tended to make the outlook somewhat more favorable in light of significant new finds or improved prospects in some developing countries with active exploration (such as China, Colombia, Oman, the Syrian Arab Republic, and the Yemen Arab Republic), on the whole the longer-term picture has not changed significantly. Of added importance in assessing the prospects beyond 1987 is the likelihood that the recent sharp fall in oil prices will result in a considerable further decline in worldwide drilling activity and overall spending on oil

exploration in the near future, notwithstanding a fall in drilling costs. The decline in capital expenditures by the oil companies, which is already in evidence, is being enhanced by the financial constraints facing some segments of the oil industry, in part because of debts incurred in stock buy-back operations and recent merger activities. As the financial incentives for investments in enhanced recovery techniques are also being reduced, and with oil fields in a number of countries reaching maturity, total productive capacity (outside the major oil exporting countries) is likely to rise at a slow pace.

The trends in world oil demand and supply, discussed above, are likely to result in a gradual firming of the oil market. However, as the changes in both demand and supply conditions will be slow to materialize, they may not have a major impact in the medium-term period considered in this report, that is, through 1991. Moreover, they are subject to uncertainties in at least two important respects: (1) the extent to which governments of consuming countries will allow the fall in oil prices to be passed through to consumers; and (2) the influence of price expectations in a market where the prospective price is likely to remain highly uncertain. As the world will be faced with considerable unused production capacity for several years, the price of oil could fluctuate within a very wide range. Of major importance for the determination of the price, also in the medium term, therefore, is the extent to which the major oil exporting countries will maintain adequate production restraint. Although it would appear that the difficulties currently encountered by these countries will diminish over time as the remaining world oil reserves become increasingly concentrated in a few countries in the Middle East, the medium-term prospects for maintaining sufficient production restraint will depend on factors (partly political in nature) that are difficult to evaluate at the present time.

---

[30] New investments in productive capacity of such energy sources are, however, likely to slow down.

Economic Developments in Eastern Europe and the Union of Soviet Socialist Republics

The year 1985 marked the end of a five-year plan period for Eastern Europe and the Soviet Union in which real net material product (NMP) increased by around 3 percent a year, falling short both of plan objectives and of the rate of economic growth during the preceding five-year-plan period (1976–80). During 1981–85, Eastern European countries confronted a serious external debt problem, which required formal debt reschedulings for Poland and Romania. By 1985, the external position of most Eastern European countries had strengthened considerably. The U.S.S.R. did not experience the same external problems as Eastern Europe in the early 1980s, but now faces a deterioration in its external current account position, related largely to lower receipts from energy exports.

All inferences drawn in this note are subject to statistical uncertainties and gaps of information not experienced to the same extent in the cases of most Western industrial countries and should therefore be treated with caution.

Developments in 1985

Eastern Europe

After a marked upturn in economic activity in 1983 and a further strong expansion in 1984, the six Eastern European members of the Council for Mutual Economic Assistance (CMEA), taken together, experienced a slowdown of economic growth in 1985 under the influence of an exceptionally hard winter generally and the subsequent impact of drought in some countries on agricultural output.[1] The NMP of the region, after

increasing by 4–4½ percent per year in the two preceding years, is estimated to have expanded by about 2½ percent, more than 2 percentage points less than plan targets had called for (Table 35). The shortfall reflected both a deceleration in the growth of industrial production to 3½ percent and a decline in total gross agricultural output of about 1½ percent. Under these conditions, and despite a reduction in net exports of goods and services, real private consumption and real gross fixed investment both grew less rapidly than in 1984. While the deceleration in the growth of private consumption was shared by most countries of the region, the reduction in the rate of growth in investment primarily reflected developments in Poland and Romania. Hungary again recorded a reduction in gross fixed capital formation, although the decline was somewhat slower than in the two preceding years. With few new initiatives of significance, the process of economic reform in Eastern Europe appears to have slowed in 1985.

The slower growth in domestic production in 1985 was accompanied by a significantly smaller increase in the volume of imports than in 1984 (Table 36). The deceleration appears to have been particularly marked in imports from the Eastern European countries themselves and from the U.S.S.R.[2] As a result, the rise in the share of intra-CMEA trade relative to that of East-West trade, which had been observed since about 1980, and which had stemmed largely from the sharp

---

[1] The CMEA comprises six Eastern European countries (Bulgaria, Czechoslovakia, the German Democratic Republic, Hungary, Poland, and Romania), the U.S.S.R., Cuba, Mongolia, and Viet Nam.

[2] The estimation of changes in the value and volume of trade flows for Eastern Europe and the U.S.S.R. is necessarily imprecise. The total value of trade is estimated by converting ruble trade (mostly trade among member countries of the CMEA) into U.S. dollar terms and adding to it trade with the convertible currency area computed in U.S. dollars. However, as similar commodity exports and imports are often priced differently in the two markets, the resulting total trade value, and the decomposition of its changes into price and quantity components, are necessarily rough estimates.

Table 35. Eastern Europe and the U.S.S.R.: Economic Activity and Prices, 1976–86

	Annual Average 1976–80	Annual Average 1981–85	1981	1982	1983	1984	Estimate 1985	Projection 1986[1]
	(Percent change in constant prices)							
Net material product								
Eastern Europe	3½	2	−1½	—	4	4½	2½	3
Eastern Europe excluding Poland	4½	3	3	2	3	4½	2	3½
U.S.S.R.	4½	3½	3½	4	4	3	3	4
Eastern Europe and U.S.S.R.	4	3	2	3	4	3½	3	3½
Gross fixed investment								
Eastern Europe	3	−1	−6½	−6	3	4	2	5
Eastern Europe excluding Poland	5	—	−1½	−3	—	1½	½	5
U.S.S.R.	4	3½	4	3½	5½	2	3	7½
Eastern Europe and U.S.S.R.	3½	2½	1	1	5	2½	2½	7
Gross industrial production								
Eastern Europe	5	2½	−1	1	4	4½	3½	4
Eastern Europe excluding Poland	5½	3½	3	2½	3	4½	3½	4
U.S.S.R.	4½	3½	3½	3	4	4	4	4½
Eastern Europe and U.S.S.R.	4½	3½	2	2½	4	4½	4	4
Gross agricultural production								
Eastern Europe	1	1½	1½	1½	1½	6½	−1½	2½
Eastern Europe excluding Poland	2½	1½	½	3	1	7	−2½	3
U.S.S.R.	1½	2	−1	5½	6	—	—	4½
Eastern Europe and U.S.S.R.	1½	2	−½	4½	5	2	−½	4
	(Percent change)							
Consumer prices								
Eastern Europe	3½	11	7	34	8½	6	5½	5½
Eastern Europe excluding Poland	2	2½	1½	6	3	2	1½	1½
U.S.S.R.	1	½	1	4	—	−3	1	1
Eastern Europe and U.S.S.R.	1½	3½	3	12½	2½	−½	2	2

Sources: Fund staff estimates and projections drawing on national authorities (Hungary, Poland, and Romania) and United Nations publications.

[1] For the U.S.S.R., projections correspond largely to official plan targets.

financially induced contraction of imports in convertible currencies, may have been arrested in 1985. The total volume of Eastern European exports, meanwhile, probably stagnated in 1985, following two years of relatively rapid growth. Adverse climatic conditions contributed to this outcome, but growing difficulties in maintaining market shares in Western industrial countries and in the developing countries also played a role. After having worsened for four consecutive years, Eastern Europe's terms of trade are thought to have remained broadly unchanged in 1985.

With regard to transactions settled in convertible currencies, the region's trade surplus is estimated to have declined by about $2 billion, to a total of around $5 billion in 1985 (Table 37). The decline largely reflected weaker trade performance in Hungary, Romania, and Bulgaria. With the invisibles deficit also narrowing under the influence of lower international interest rates, however, the region's current account surplus declined by somewhat less—probably to about $2 billion. Current account surpluses continued to be recorded by Czechoslovakia, the German Democratic Republic, and Romania in 1985, while Bulgaria and Hungary moved into current account deficit—a position which continued to obtain in Poland.

In addition to the influences noted above on its external transactions in convertible currencies, Eastern Europe began to feel the impact of efforts by the U.S.S.R. to reduce its current account surplus with CMEA partners and to stem a decline in its terms of trade. Some countries experienced a decline in energy imports from the U.S.S.R. other than against convertible currencies, while all countries were required to improve the quality of their exports for nonconvertible currency to the U.S.S.R. In some instances, the latter development was reflected in a reduced readiness on the part of the U.S.S.R. to pay for certain food exports from Eastern Europe in convertible currencies.

Table 36.   Eastern Europe and the U.S.S.R.: Merchandise Trade, 1981–86[1]

(Percent changes based on values and prices expressed in U.S. dollar terms)[2]

	1981	1982	1983	1984	Estimate 1985	Projection 1986
Exports						
Eastern Europe						
Value	1	3	5	4	−3	9
Volume	—	5	9	8	—	4
Prices	1	−2	−3	−4	−3	5
U.S.S.R.						
Value	4	10	5	—	−8	−10
Volume	2	5	3	3	−6	2
Prices	2	5	2	−3	−2	−12
Imports						
Eastern Europe						
Value	−3	−4	3	3	−2	9
Volume	−5	−6	5	5	2	3
Prices	2	2	−2	−2	−3	6
U.S.S.R.						
Value	7	6	3	1	2	5
Volume	8	7	4	5	3	−1
Prices	−1	−1	−1	−4	−1	6
Terms of trade						
Eastern Europe	−2	−3	−2	−2	—	−1
U.S.S.R.	3	6	3	1	−1	−17

Sources: Fund staff estimates and projections drawing on United Nations publications and national trade data.

[1] Trade data are expressed on an f.o.b. basis. Includes trade of the German Democratic Republic with the Federal Republic of Germany.
[2] Figures for value of exports and imports and for terms of trade may not correspond exactly to components because of rounding.

Table 37.   Eastern Europe and the U.S.S.R.: Current Account Balance in Convertible Currencies, 1981–86

(In billions of U.S. dollars)[1]

	1981	1982	1983	1984	Estimate 1985	Projection 1986
Eastern Europe						
Current account balance	−5.5	−0.5	1.5	3.0	2.0	3.0
Trade balance	—	4.5	5.5	7.0	5.0	5.5
Net invisibles	−5.5	−5.0	−4.0	−4.5	−3.0	−2.5
U.S.S.R.						
Current account balance	—	3.0	3.5	4.0	−1.5	−8.0
Trade balance	−2.0	2.0	3.0	3.0	−2.0	−9.0
Net invisibles[2]	2.0	1.0	0.5	1.0	0.5	1.0
Eastern Europe and U.S.S.R.						
Current account balance	−5.5	2.5	5.0	7.0	0.5	−5.0
Trade balance	−2.0	6.5	8.5	10.0	3.0	−3.5
Net invisibles[2]	−3.5	−4.0	−3.5	−3.5	−2.5	−1.5

Sources: Fund staff estimates and projections, drawing on information from national authorities (Hungary, Poland, and Romania), national trade data sources, and United Nations publications.
[1] Components may not add to totals because of rounding.
[2] Including sales of nonmonetary gold.

Table 38. Eastern Europe and the U.S.S.R.: External Debt in Convertible Currencies, 1981–85

(In billions of U.S. dollars)

	1981	1982	1983	1984	Estimate 1985
Gross debt outstanding					
Eastern Europe	67.0	63.5	61.5	59.5	66.0
Poland	25.5	26.5	26.5	27.0	29.5
U.S.S.R.	25.0	25.0	22.5	20.5	26.0
Total	92.0	88.5	84.0	79.5	92.0
Net debt outstanding[1]					
Eastern Europe	61.0	58.0	53.0	48.5	53.5
Poland	24.5	25.5	25.0	25.5	28.0
U.S.S.R.	16.5	15.0	11.5	9.0	14.5
Subtotal	77.5	72.5	64.5	58.0	68.0
CMEA banks	4.0	3.5	3.5	3.5	4.0
Total	81.5	76.0	68.0	61.5	72.0
Memorandum					
Ratio of net debt to convertible currency exports					
Eastern Europe	2.00	1.95	1.75	1.55	1.75
Eastern Europe excluding Poland	1.50	1.30	1.10	0.90	1.00
U.S.S.R.	0.55	0.45	0.35	0.25	0.55
Eastern Europe and U.S.S.R.	1.30	1.15	1.00	0.90	1.20
Ratio of deposits to liabilities in foreign banks[2]					
Eastern Europe	0.14	0.15	0.24	0.34	0.34
Eastern Europe excluding Poland	0.19	0.20	0.31	0.41	0.42
U.S.S.R.	0.53	0.71	0.67	0.68	0.50
Eastern Europe and U.S.S.R.	0.25	0.31	0.38	0.46	0.40
Ratio of short-term debt to banks[2] to total gross debt					
Eastern Europe	0.19	0.17	0.20	0.18	0.17
Eastern Europe excluding Poland	0.28	0.25	0.26	0.27	0.28
U.S.S.R.	0.20	0.27	0.31	0.32	0.34
Eastern Europe and U.S.S.R.	0.19	0.20	0.23	0.22	0.22

Sources: United Nations; Organization for Economic Cooperation and Development; Bank for International Settlements; national authorities (Hungary, Poland, and Romania); and Fund staff estimates.

[1] Gross debt less deposits in banks reporting to the Bank for International Settlements.

[2] Banks reporting to the Bank for International Settlements.

For the Eastern European countries, these changes combined to reduce their ability to achieve continued large current account surpluses in convertible currencies with existing production structures.

Reversing its falling tendency of the three preceding years, the region's external debt in convertible currencies increased in 1985. Taking into account a small increase in deposits with Western banks, net debt increased somewhat less than gross debt, which is estimated to have risen by some $6 billion to a level of about $66 billion at the end of 1985 (Table 38). [3] Although foreign borrowing was stepped up by several countries, much of the increase in debt was accounted

for by valuation effects which, for the first time since 1980, resulted in an increase in the U.S. dollar value of debt denominated in other currencies. The level of net external debt relative to annual exports in convertible currencies increased significantly in 1985, but remained below the level reached in the period 1979–82.

The increase in Eastern European borrowing on Western capital markets in 1985 was facilitated by a more favorable attitude of creditors to most countries in the region following significant improvements in their current account and debt positions. After a period of little or no recourse to the financial markets, Bulgaria, Czechoslovakia, and Romania returned to the syndicated loan market in 1985, and the German Democratic Republic and Hungary continued to be active. In addition, Hungary began to tap other segments of the international capital market (such as note issuance facilities), which have recently been favored

[3] The measure of net debt employed here and in Table 38 does not take into account the rising volume of trade-related credits extended by Eastern European countries to support their convertible currency exports.

by many market participants.[4] There has also been a tendency by the German Democratic Republic and by Hungary to diversify their borrowing in terms of currency of denomination. Poland's access to new borrowing from banks, meanwhile, remained extremely limited.

The terms of bank credits available to Eastern Europe improved further in 1985. Average spreads fell below ¾ of 1 percentage point and were in some cases below ½ of 1 percentage point, while average maturities lengthened. Under these conditions, some countries of the region sought to repay early some older loans carrying significantly higher margins.

U.S.S.R.

After a deceleration in the rate of economic growth in 1984, preliminary indications suggest that in 1985 real NMP in the U.S.S.R. again increased by about 3 percent, somewhat below the officially planned rate of 3½ percent. This brought the average growth rate of real NMP over the plan period 1981–85 to about 3½ percent, which compares with a plan target of 4 percent and growth of almost 4½ percent a year over the previous plan period 1976–80. Gross industrial production appears to have been broadly in line with plan targets in 1985—increasing by 4 percent for the third consecutive year—even though crude oil output is estimated to have fallen by 3 percent. While a higher-than-planned increase in natural gas production partly offset the shortfall in crude oil output, a sizable increase in domestic energy consumption is estimated to have substantially curtailed the availability of energy products for export. Gross agricultural output, meanwhile, is thought to have remained substantially unchanged, as compared with a planned increase of 6 percent. Over the plan period 1981–85 as a whole, agricultural production is estimated to have risen at an average annual rate of only 2 percent, or approximately half the originally targeted rate of increase. Grain output was particularly disappointing with substantial shortfalls from plan occurring in most years during the 1980s. The slowdown in overall growth in 1984–85 was reflected mainly in lower rates of capital formation. Consumption, by contrast, appears to have increased slightly faster than total NMP.

The U.S.S.R. does not publish data on its balance of payments. Rough estimates by the staff suggest that after being in moderate surplus over the three preceding years, in 1985 the trade account in convertible currencies weakened sharply and may have recorded a deficit of some $2 billion.[5] A sharp fall—of perhaps 20 percent—in the value of energy exports, which in 1984 accounted for nearly 80 percent of exports to the developed market economies, was mainly responsible for this outturn. The underlying decline in the volume of energy exports had its origin both in an increase in domestic energy consumption and in lower domestic production, especially of crude oil. Other exports to developed market economies, which have tended to stagnate or fall in recent years, are estimated to have shown a small decline in 1985 as a result mainly of falls in U.S. dollar prices for raw materials.

There is some evidence that the U.S.S.R. reacted to the sharp fall in convertible currency earnings in 1985 by curtailing somewhat the volume of its imports from the West. In addition, and perhaps more importantly, it appears to have benefited from sharply lower prices for grain imports, which have increased in volume following a series of relatively poor harvests. As a result, imports settled in convertible currencies are estimated to have fallen slightly in 1985. By contrast, there are no obvious indications that the U.S.S.R. has sold significantly more gold on international markets to cover its widening trade gap. Rather, this was covered by a considerable rise in net external debt. Correspondingly, an increase in net interest payments is likely to have ensued which, together with the sharp deterioration in the trade account, is estimated to have resulted in a swing in the current account in convertible currencies from a position of surplus of perhaps $4 billion in 1984 to a deficit of $1 billion to $2 billion in 1985.

The substantial current account deficit gave rise to a perceptible increase in borrowing from international financial markets as well as to some reduction by the U.S.S.R. in its deposits with Western banks. In 1985, the lending terms available to the U.S.S.R. were exceptionally favorable, and in general syndicated bank loans were oversubscribed, with margins over LIBOR falling to ¼ of 1 percentage point.

---

[4] Note issuance facilities (or NIFs) involve commitments by an underwriting syndicate to purchase a borrower's short-term notes for several years at a "cap rate"—a fixed spread above a benchmark interest rate.

[5] In estimating the U.S.S.R.'s current account balance in convertible currencies, it is generally assumed that all current account transactions with developed Western countries are settled in convertible currencies, with the exception of those with Finland, which enters into annual bilateral payments agreements with the U.S.S.R. However, major problems arise in trying to estimate which transactions with developing countries and socialist countries take place in convertible currencies. Evidence from partner countries suggests that sizable amounts of the U.S.S.R.'s exports to developing countries are in direct exchange for goods, and that a considerable amount of transactions with developing countries takes place within the framework of bilateral clearing arrangements.

Outlook

For the 1986–90 five-year plan period, Eastern Europe and the U.S.S.R. have set output targets that are generally more ambitious than those in the preceding five-year plan which, as noted above, remained in part unfulfilled. The authorities look for the growth objectives to be reached mainly through economies in labor and material inputs—in particular of energy—with only a modest expansion of productive capital. In order to realize the implied increase in the productivity of capital and labor, emphasis is to be given to accelerating technical progress and to strengthening incentives to managers and workers, in part by improving the supply of consumer goods. The promotion of technological cooperation has been a major theme in the coordination of the new five-year plans within the CMEA. However, there may well be an inconsistency between the likely small increases in gross fixed investment and the generally slow progress of economic reforms, on the one hand, and the expectation of rapidly rising technological standards and improved economic efficiency, on the other. The current account position in convertible currencies could remain weaker for the region as a whole than in 1983–84—perhaps substantially so in the case of the U.S.S.R.

Eastern Europe

Based on the assumption of a recovery in agricultural output, staff estimates for 1986 foresee a modest acceleration in the average rate of growth of real NMP to 3 percent. Gross industrial production is expected to increase by about 4 percent, assuming that bottlenecks in the availability of energy and raw materials (either domestically or under nonconvertible currency clearing arrangements) do not intensify. To the extent that supplies of such intermediate products are obtained from the U.S.S.R. under ruble settlement, Eastern Europe will probably have to offer manufactured products and foodstuffs to the U.S.S.R. that are superior in quality to those supplied in the past. For most countries, this may imply diverting some convertible currency exportables to the nonconvertible currency area and possibly importing more inputs from the convertible currency area in order to raise the quality of their production. Consequently, and despite the posited recovery in agricultural output and stronger expansion of industrial production, the scope for increasing the region's trade surplus in convertible currencies is likely to be limited in 1986, especially as plans call for a somewhat faster increase in domestic absorption, particularly in investment outlays.

After declining in U.S. dollar terms in 1985, total exports and total imports (in convertible and in non-convertible currencies) are both forecast by the staff to increase by nearly 10 percent in 1986. While this is expected principally to reflect a major turnaround in prices in U.S. dollar terms, a stronger volume performance is also foreseen for both exports and imports (Table 36). As regards transactions in convertible currencies, a small increase is expected in the trade surplus in 1986. The deficit on services, meanwhile, is forecast to remain broadly unchanged, with net interest payments subject to the opposing influences of higher net debt and lower interest rates. All told, the current account surplus is projected to rise to around $3 billion from an estimated $2 billion in 1985. Despite the expected rebound of exports in 1986, Eastern European countries continue to face the longer-term challenge of raising the quality and technological standard of their manufactured exports to a level which would make them more easily marketable in Western industrial countries. Recent export achievements have relied to some extent on sales to developing countries which are supported by the extension of trade credits and to that extent do not contribute immediately to cash flow in convertible currencies.

The further evolution of the external debt position in 1986 is likely to differ widely from one country to another. While the German Democratic Republic and Romania remain firmly committed to a further reduction in their net external debt and are again expected to achieve sizable current account surpluses in 1986, Bulgaria, Czechoslovakia, and Hungary are each expected to show approximate balance in their current accounts. In Poland, little change is foreseen in the current account deficit, and the debt situation—complicated by the fact that obligations under earlier reschedulings begin to fall due from 1986 onwards—will be marked by a need for further debt reschedulings.

U.S.S.R.

The economic plan of the U.S.S.R. for 1986–90 calls for the annual rate of growth of real NMP to accelerate to 4 percent. This is to be accomplished mainly by modernizing industry, enhancing labor discipline, and strengthening managerial performance. Fixed investment, which is currently expanding at a rate of 2–3 percent per annum, is planned to rise by 4 percent a year over the five-year period. With the production of raw materials, fuels, and energy targeted to rise by only 2–2½ percent annually, attainment of the output and export targets will be critically dependent on the economy's abililty to realize a substantial decrease in the material- and energy-intensity of production. Agricultural output is planned to increase at an annual rate of 2.7–3.0 percent, which, if achieved, would permit a considerable reduction in grain imports.

For 1986, real NMP is targeted to grow by close to 4 percent, with a surge in the growth rate of fixed investment to 7½ percent. Gross agricultural and gross industrial production are both planned to increase by almost 4½ percent. Achievement of these targets, and of those for the five-year period 1986–90, is to be facilitated by certain reforms within the existing economic system. In addition to steps aimed at improving labor discipline and the performance of management, greater efficiency is to be sought by streamlining the planning and administrative system and enlarging the scope for decentralized decision making. In early 1984, a reform experiment was launched giving more autonomy to enterprises in selected industrial branches and regions, at the expense of centralized administrative powers. This experiment is estimated to have covered about 10 percent of national production in 1985 and is to be extended in 1986 and later years.

Little is known about the U.S.S.R.'s external objectives for 1986 or the 1986–90 plan period. However, in 1986 a further sizable deterioration in the current account in convertible currencies seems to be in prospect, as a result of substantially lower estimated prices for energy exports and considerably higher prices (expressed in U.S. dollar terms) for industrial imports. To a limited extent, the adverse impact of these factors may be offset by an increased volume of energy exports. In addition, an improved agricultural performance would reduce the need for grain imports, while the five-year plan appears to place greater reliance on CMEA-produced capital goods than on imports of Western machinery and technology to modernize and re-equip Soviet industry. Even so, the trade deficit in convertible currencies could widen by as much as $7 billion in 1986, assuming no substantial reduction in the volume of nonagricultural imports.[6] If the surplus on invisibles account were to remain broadly unchanged, this would carry the current account deficit to some $8 billion, necessitating in turn further sizable recourse to international capital markets.

---

[6] The estimate of the trade deficit is based, inter alia, on an assumed decline in the price of oil exports of about 40 percent (to $16 per barrel, on average, in 1986) and an assumed increase in the price of imports of manufactured goods of about 14 percent, expressed in U.S. dollar terms. In addition, a small decline is assumed in the volume of imports.

Statistical Appendix

Statistical Appendix

Assumptions and Conventions

The statistical tables in this appendix have been compiled on the basis of information available on or before March 1986. The recording of the figures for 1985 and beyond with the same degree of precision as the historical figures is solely a matter of convenience. It is not intended to convey any connotation regarding the degree of accuracy attaching to these estimates and projections.

The estimates and projections for 1986 and 1987 are predicated on a number of *assumptions and working hypotheses*:

(1) for the major currencies, the average exchange rates of March 3–7, 1986 will remain unchanged in real terms throughout the balance of 1986 and 1987.

(2) "present" policies of national authorities will be maintained; and

(3) the price of oil will average $15 per barrel from the second quarter of 1986 to the end of 1987.

A few of the tables include series expressed in SDRs (or based on SDR values). The U.S. dollar/SDR conversion rates used in this report are, for the historical period, the geometric averages of daily rates given in the Fund's *International Financial Statistics* (*IFS*). For the years prior to 1970, these data impute to the SDR a value of $1.00. For 1986 and 1987, the exchange rate assumptions specified above imply average U.S. dollar/SDR conversion rates of 1.144 and 1.158, respectively.

Classification of Countries

The basic distinction, adopted by the Fund in December 1979, is between industrial countries and developing countries. *Industrial countries* comprise:

Australia	Iceland	Norway
Austria	Ireland	Spain
Belgium	Italy	Sweden
Canada	Japan	Switzerland
Denmark	Luxembourg	United Kingdom
Finland	Netherlands	United States
France	New Zealand	
Germany, Fed. Rep. of		

The seven largest countries in this group in terms of GNP (Canada, the United States, Japan, France, the Federal Republic of Germany, Italy, and the United Kingdom) are collectively referred to as the *major industrial countries*.

The *developing countries* include all other Fund members (as of January 1, 1986) together with certain essentially autonomous dependent territories for which adequate statistics are available.[1] The regional breakdowns of data for developing countries conform to the regional classification used in *IFS*. It should be noted that, in this classification, Egypt, and Libyan Arab Jamahiriya are part of the Middle East, not Africa.

The analytical groupings currently used by the staff to distinguish among developing countries are (1) countries grouped by predominant export; (2) countries grouped by financial criteria; (3) countries grouped by other criteria; and (4) countries grouped by the former classification criteria. At present, the financial criteria first distinguish among capital exporting and capital importing countries. Countries in the latter, much larger, group are then distinguished on the basis of two additional financial criteria: by predominant type of creditor and by the degree of debt-servicing difficulties faced by countries. The country groups shown under the heading of "by miscellaneous criteria" include capital importing fuel exporters; 15 heavily indebted countries; small low-income countries; and sub-Saharan Africa (excluding Nigeria and South Africa). Table A presents the standard set of headings used in many of the tables for developing countries as well as the proportion of developing country GDP, exports of goods and services, and indebtedness accounted for by the groups in question. Further details on the classification scheme are given below.

The first analytical criterion used to group developing countries is by predominant export category. Four categories are distinguished: fuel (SITC 3); other pri-

---

[1] It should be noted that the term "country" used in this report does not in all cases refer to a territorial entity that is a state as understood by international law and practice. The term also covers some territorial entities that are not states but for which data are maintained and provided internationally on a separate and independent basis.

mary commodities (SITC 0,1,2,4, and diamonds and gemstones); manufactures (SITC 5 to 8, less diamonds and gemstones); and "services and remittances." On the basis of data for 1980, countries are assigned to that commodity grouping which accounts for 50 percent or more of their exports. Specifically, countries are assigned to the "services and remittances" category if their receipts on these transactions account for at least half of their exports of goods and services. If countries do not meet this criterion, they are assigned to that trade category (of the three listed above) which accounts for at least half of their total merchandise exports.[2]

Given these definitions, the *fuel exporters* comprise the following countries:

Algeria	Iraq	Saudi Arabia
Bahrain	Kuwait	Syrian Arab Rep.
Congo	Libyan Arab	Trinidad and
Ecuador	Jamahiriya	Tobago
Gabon	Mexico	Tunisia
Indonesia	Nigeria	United Arab
Iran, Islamic	Oman	Emirates
Rep. of	Qatar	Venezuela

The *primary product exporters*, that is, countries whose exports of agricultural and mineral primary products other than fuel accounted for over 50 percent of their total exports in 1980, comprise:

Afghanistan	Gambia, The	Peru
Argentina	Ghana	Philippines
Bangladesh	Guatemala	Rwanda
Belize	Guinea	São Tomé and
Benin	Guinea-Bissau	Principe
Bhutan	Guyana	Senegal
Bolivia	Haiti	Sierra Leone
Botswana	Honduras	Solomon Islands
Brazil	Jamaica	Somalia
Burma	Kenya	South Africa
Burundi	Lao People's	Sri Lanka
Cameroon	Dem. Rep.	St. Christopher and
Central African	Liberia	Nevis
Rep.	Madagascar	Sudan
Chad	Malawi	Suriname
Chile	Malaysia	Swaziland
Colombia	Mali	Tanzania
Comoros	Mauritania	Thailand
Costa Rica	Mauritius	Togo
Côte d'Ivoire	Morocco	Turkey
Djibouti	Mozambique	Uganda
Dominican Rep.	Nicaragua	Uruguay
El Salvador	Niger	Viet Nam
Equatorial Guinea	Papua New	Zaïre
Ethiopia	Guinea	Zambia
Fiji	Paraguay	Zimbabwe

A further distinction is made among the *primary product exporters* on the basis of whether countries' exports of primary commodities (other than fuel) consisted primarily of agricultural (SITC 0 and 1) or mineral (SITC 2 and 4 and diamonds and gemstones) commodities. The *mineral exporters* comprise:

Bolivia	Liberia	South Africa
Botswana	Mauritania	Suriname
Chile	Morocco	Togo
Guinea	Niger	Zaïre
Guyana	Peru	Zambia
Jamaica	Sierra Leone	Zimbabwe

The *agricultural exporters* are those non-fuel primary product exporters that are not also mineral exporters.

The *exporters of manufactures* (that is, those countries or areas whose exports of manufactures accounted in 1980 for over 50 percent of total exports) include:

China	India	Romania
Hong Kong	Israel	Singapore
Hungary	Korea	Yugoslavia

The *service and remittance countries,* that is, those countries whose receipts from services (such as tourism) and private transfers (such as workers' remittances) amount to at least 50 percent of their exports of goods and services, comprise:

Antigua and	Kampuchea, Dem.	St. Lucia
Barbuda	Lebanon	St. Vincent
Bahamas	Lesotho	Tonga
Barbados	Maldives	Vanuatu
Burkina Faso	Malta	Western Samoa
Cape Verde	Nepal	Yemen Arab
Cyprus	Netherlands	Rep.
Dominica	Antilles	Yemen,
Egypt	Pakistan	People's
Greece	Panama	Dem. Rep.
Grenada	Portugal	of
Jordan	Seychelles	

The primary product exporters, exporters of manufactures, and service and remittance countries taken together are referred to as the "non-fuel exporters."

A second set of analytical groupings of developing countries is based on financial criteria. A first distinction is made between those developing countries that have traditionally been capital exporters and those that have traditionally been capital importers. At present, capital exporters are defined as those developing countries that, on average, recorded a current account surplus during the period 1979–81 and were aid donors over the same period. The *capital exporting countries* comprise:

Iran, Islamic	Libyan Arab	Saudi Arabia
Rep. of	Jamahiriya	United Arab
Iraq	Oman	Emirates
Kuwait	Qatar	

---

[2] Two countries which did not meet any of the above criteria were assigned to that trade category which accounted for the largest share of their exports.

Table A. Developing Countries: Shares of Various Subgroups in Aggregate GDP, Exports of Goods and Services, and Debt Outstanding, 1980

(In percent)

	GDP	Exports of Goods and Services	Debt[1]	Memorandum: Number of Countries in each Subgroup
Developing countries	100.0	100.0	...	132
By region				
Africa	13.7	14.2	16.6	48
Asia	31.2	25.1	23.5	27
Europe	10.2	7.6	12.0	8
Middle East	17.7	36.6	...	16
Western Hemisphere	27.2	16.6	40.6	33
By predominant export				
Fuel exporters	33.4	49.6	...	20
Non-fuel exporters	66.6	50.4	74.9	112
Primary product exporters	33.0	21.6	45.6	73
Agricultural exporters	26.2	14.3	34.5	55
Mineral exporters	6.8	7.3	11.2	18
Exporters of manufactures	28.2	22.8	20.1	10
Service and remittance countries	5.4	5.9	9.1	29
By financial criteria				
Capital exporting countries	15.0	32.4	...	8
Capital importing countries	85.0	67.6	100.0	124
Market borrowers	50.8	49.2	67.8	34
Official borrowers	7.1	5.1	10.7	60
Diversified borrowers	27.1	13.3	21.5	30
Countries with recent debt-servicing problems	43.3	31.2	62.2	61
Countries without recent debt-servicing problems	41.7	36.4	37.8	63
By miscellaneous criteria				
Capital importing fuel exporters	18.4	17.3	25.1	12
Fifteen heavily indebted countries	33.3	21.2	47.1	15
Small low-income countries	5.6	2.8	8.4	41
Sub-Saharan Africa[2]	4.6	4.0	7.3	43
By alternative analytical categories				
Oil exporting countries	25.0	43.7	...	12
Non-oil developing countries	75.0	56.3	86.4	120
Net oil exporters	10.8	10.0	17.9	12
Net oil importers	64.1	46.3	68.5	108

[1] In percent of outstanding debt of capital importing developing countries.
[2] Excluding Nigeria and South Africa.

The *capital importing countries* comprise all other developing countries.

Within the group of capital importing developing countries and areas, two types of financial distinctions are made. The first distinguishes among countries and areas on the basis of their *predominant type of creditor*. *Market borrowers* are defined as those countries which obtained at least two thirds of their external borrowings from 1978 to 1982 from commercial creditors. The group includes:

Algeria	Congo	Korea	Philippines
Antigua and Barbuda	Côte d'Ivoire	Malaysia	Portugal
Argentina	Cyprus	Mexico	Singapore
Bahamas	Ecuador	Nigeria	South Africa
Bolivia	Gabon	Panama	Trinidad and Tobago
Brazil	Greece	Papua New Guinea	Uruguay
Chile	Hong Kong	Paraguay	Venezuela
Columbia	Hungary	Peru	Yugoslavia
	Indonesia		

Official borrowers comprise those countries, except China and India, which obtained two thirds or more of their external borrowings from 1978 to 1982 from official creditors. The countries are:

Afghanistan	Fiji	Malta	Swaziland
Bahrain	Gambia, The	Mauritania	Syrian Arab
Bangladesh	Ghana	Nepal	Rep.
Bhutan	Grenada	Netherlands	Tanzania
Burkina Faso	Guatemala	Antilles	Togo
Burma	Guinea	Nicaragua	Tonga
Burundi	Guinea-	Pakistan	Uganda
Cape Verde	Bissau	Rwanda	Viet Nam
Central	Guyana	São Tomé	Western
African	Honduras	and	Samoa
Rep.	Jamaica	Principe	Yemen Arab
Chad	Jordan	Senegal	Rep.
Comoros	Lao People's	Seychelles	Yemen,
Djibouti	Dem. Rep.	Sierra	People's
Dominica	Liberia	Leone	Dem.
Dominican	Madagascar	Somalia	Rep. of
Rep.	Malawi	St. Lucia	Zaïre
El Salvador	Maldives	St. Vincent	Zambia
Equatorial	Mali	Sudan	
Guinea			

Diversified borrowers comprise those capital importing developing countries that are not market or official borrowers. These countries' external borrowings in 1978–82 were more or less evenly divided between official and commercial creditors. China and India are included in this group.

A second financial distinction among capital importing developing countries is based on whether countries have or have not experienced debt-servicing difficulties in the recent past. Countries that have experienced debt-servicing problems are defined as those countries which incurred external payments arrears during 1983 to 1984 or rescheduled their debt during the period from end-1982 to mid-1985 as reported in the relevant issues of the Fund's *Annual Report on Exchange Arrangements and Exchange Restrictions.* Countries classified as not having experienced debt-servicing problems are defined as all other capital importing developing countries.

Several other analytical groups are also used in the report. One of these is the group of *capital importing fuel exporters*. This group, which is also referred to as the "indebted fuel exporters," comprises those 12 fuel exporters that are not capital exporters. A second is the group of *15 heavily indebted countries*. This group comprises:

Argentina	Côte d'Ivoire	Peru
Bolivia	Ecuador	Philippines
Brazil	Mexico	Uruguay
Chile	Morocco	Venezuela
Colombia	Nigeria	Yugoslavia

A third is the group of *low-income countries*, which comprises 43 countries whose per capita GDP, as estimated by the World Bank, did not exceed the equivalent of $410 in 1980. The countries in this group are:

Afghanistan	Comoros	Kenya	São Tomé
Bangladesh	Equatorial	Lao People's	and
Benin	Guinea	Dem. Rep.	Principe
Bhutan	Ethiopia	Madagascar	Sierra Leone
Burkina Faso	Gambia, The	Malawi	Somalia
Burma	Ghana	Maldives	Sri Lanka
Burundi	Guinea	Mali	Sudan
Cape Verde	Guinea-	Mauritania	Tanzania
Central	Bissau	Mozambique	Togo
African	Haiti	Nepal	Uganda
Rep.	India	Niger	Viet Nam
Chad	Kampuchea,	Pakistan	Zaïre
China	Dem.	Rwanda	

References to the *small or smaller low-income countries* refer to the above group, less China and India. Reference is also made to *sub-Saharan Africa*, which comprises all African countries (as defined in *IFS*) except Algeria, Morocco, Nigeria, South Africa, and Tunisia.

Finally, many of the tables present data on the developing countries grouped in accordance with the *former classification categories*. In this system, which was the one used from 1980 to 1984, the *developing countries* were divided into two groups—"oil exporting countries" and "non-oil developing countries." The countries included under the heading *oil exporting countries*[3] are:

Algeria	Kuwait	Qatar
Indonesia	Libyan Arab	Saudi Arabia
Iran, Islamic	Jamahiriya	United Arab
Rep. of	Nigeria	Emirates
Iraq	Oman	Venezuela

Among the *non-oil developing countries*, four analytical subgroups of countries were distinguished. These subgroupings were based primarily on the character of the countries' economic activity and on the predominant composition of their exports. Since the large "non-oil" group in the basic classification included some countries that had significant production or exports of oil, one of the analytic subgroups shown separately comprised countries (outside the main oil

---

[3] The countries included here were those whose oil exports (net of any imports of crude oil) both accounted for at least two thirds of total exports and were at least 100 million barrels a year (roughly equivalent to 1 percent of annual world exports). These criteria were applied to 1978–80 averages.

exporting group mentioned above) whose oil exports exceeded their oil imports in most years of the 1970s. The countries classified in the subgroup *net oil exporters* were:

Bahrain	Gabon	Syrian Arab Rep.
Bolivia	Malaysia	Trinidad and
Congo	Mexico	Tobago
Ecuador	Peru	Tunisia
Egypt		

The *net oil importers* subgroup comprises all other non-oil developing countries.

Except where otherwise specifically indicated, the Union of Soviet Socialist Republics and other non-member countries of Eastern Europe, Cuba, and North Korea are excluded from the following tables. Also, it has not been possible to include in the tables a number of small countries or territories for which trade and payments data are not available.

List of Tables

Medium-Term Scenario

Table A1. World Output, 1968–87[1]

(Annual changes, in percent)

	Average 1968–77[2]	1978	1979	1980	1981	1982	1983	1984	1985	1986	1987
World	**4.5**	**4.5**	**3.3**	**2.0**	**1.6**	**0.5**	**2.6**	**4.4**	**2.9**	**3.1**	**3.3**
Industrial countries	**3.5**	**4.2**	**3.3**	**1.2**	**1.4**	**−0.4**	**2.6**	**4.7**	**2.8**	**3.0**	**3.2**
United States	2.7	5.3	2.5	−0.2	1.9	−2.5	3.5	6.5	2.2	2.9	3.6
Other industrial countries	4.3	3.5	3.8	2.1	1.1	0.8	2.0	3.4	3.2	3.0	2.9
Of which,											
Japan	6.5	5.2	5.3	4.3	3.7	3.1	3.2	5.1	4.6	3.0	3.2
Germany, Fed. Rep. of	3.7	3.3	4.0	1.5	—	−1.0	1.5	3.0	2.4	3.7	2.7
Developing countries	**6.2**	**5.1**	**4.3**	**3.5**	**2.2**	**1.6**	**1.3**	**4.1**	**3.2**	**3.0**	**3.4**
Median growth rates	5.2	5.9	4.8	3.7	3.1	1.4	1.5	2.8	2.6	3.4	3.6
By region											
Africa	5.3	1.1	3.2	3.8	1.7	0.8	−1.5	1.6	1.6	2.8	2.8
Asia	5.4	9.1	4.4	5.5	5.5	5.0	7.4	7.9	6.1	5.5	5.5
Europe	6.0	5.4	3.8	1.5	2.3	2.4	1.0	3.5	2.5	3.5	3.8
Middle East	9.2	1.7	2.3	−2.1	−1.8	−0.2	0.1	0.7	−1.6	0.2	−0.3
Western Hemisphere	6.0	4.1	6.0	5.3	0.9	−0.9	−3.1	3.1	3.8	1.6	3.5
By analytical criteria											
Fuel exporters	8.4	2.7	3.7	1.1	0.9	−0.1	−1.8	1.2	−0.1	−0.6	0.3
Non-fuel exporters	5.4	6.1	4.6	4.6	2.7	2.5	3.0	5.5	4.8	4.6	4.8
Market borrowers	6.5	4.6	6.0	4.5	2.1	0.4	−1.1	3.4	2.9	2.2	3.6
Official borrowers	3.9	3.6	2.1	3.2	3.1	2.0	1.9	2.8	2.9	4.1	3.4
Other countries[3]	**6.2**	**4.8**	**2.1**	**3.0**	**1.9**	**2.8**	**4.3**	**3.4**	**3.0**	**3.8**	**...**

[1] Real GDP (or GNP) for industrial and developing countries and real net material product (NMP) for other countries. Composites for the country groups are averages of percentage changes for individual countries weighted by the average U.S. dollar value of their respective GDPs (GNPs or NMPs where applicable) over the preceding three years. Because of the uncertainty surrounding the valuation of the composite NMP of the other countries, they have been assigned—somewhat arbitrarily—a weight of 15 percent in the calculation of the growth of world output. Excluding China prior to 1978.

[2] Compound annual rates of change.

[3] The U.S.S.R. and other countries of Eastern Europe that are not members of the Fund.

Table A2. Industrial Countries: Real GNP and Total Domestic Demand, 1968–87[1]
(Annual changes, in percent)

	Average 1968–77[2]	1978	1979	1980	1981	1982	1983	1984	1985	1986	1987	Fourth Quarter[3] 1985	1986	1987
Real GNP														
Canada	4.7	3.6	3.2	1.1	3.3	−4.4	3.3	5.0	4.5	3.3	3.3	4.9	2.6	3.0
United States	2.7	5.3	2.5	−0.2	1.9	−2.5	3.5	6.5	2.2	2.9	3.6	2.1	3.8	3.4
Japan	6.5	5.2	5.3	4.3	3.7	3.1	3.2	5.1	4.6	3.0	3.2	4.4	2.0	3.8
France[4]	4.5	3.8	3.3	1.1	0.5	1.8	0.7	1.6	1.1	2.4	2.3	2.1	2.5	2.0
Germany, Fed. Rep. of	3.7	3.3	4.0	1.5	—	−1.0	1.5	3.0	2.4	3.7	2.7	2.8	3.7	2.3
Italy[4]	3.8	2.7	4.9	3.9	0.2	−0.5	−0.4	2.6	2.2	2.3	2.3	2.5	2.2	2.5
United Kingdom[5]	2.3	3.7	2.6	−2.5	−1.5	1.8	3.3	2.5	3.3	2.8	2.1	2.8	2.0	2.3
Other industrial countries	4.0	2.1	3.0	2.2	0.5	0.5	1.6	3.1	2.8	2.8	2.7	2.5	3.1	2.6
All industrial countries	**3.5**	**4.2**	**3.3**	**1.2**	**1.4**	**−0.4**	**2.6**	**4.7**	**2.8**	**3.0**	**3.2**	**2.6**	**3.2**	**3.1**
Of which, Seven major countries above	3.4	4.6	3.4	1.1	1.6	−0.6	2.8	5.0	2.7	3.0	3.3	2.7	3.3	3.2
European countries	3.7	3.0	3.4	1.4	−0.1	0.5	1.5	2.4	2.3	2.9	2.5	2.4	2.7	2.3
Real total domestic demand														
Canada	5.0	1.7	4.0	−0.2	3.9	−6.5	3.4	3.5	5.4	3.0	2.7	7.4	1.4	3.0
United States	2.8	4.9	1.5	−1.8	2.2	−1.9	5.0	8.5	2.8	3.6	3.3	3.2	3.5	3.1
Japan	6.1	5.9	6.5	0.8	2.1	2.8	1.8	3.8	3.7	4.2	4.4	4.3	3.8	4.7
France	4.4	3.8	4.1	2.1	−0.5	4.1	−0.4	0.6	1.6	3.0	2.9	2.9	2.8	2.5
Germany, Fed. Rep. of	3.9	3.6	5.6	1.0	−2.7	−2.0	2.0	2.0	1.4	4.1	3.6	3.6	3.8	3.2
Italy	3.4	2.0	5.7	7.0	−2.2	−0.3	−1.2	2.9	2.3	3.5	3.4	1.4	4.1	3.5
United Kingdom	1.7	4.2	3.8	−3.3	−1.8	2.4	4.3	2.3	2.7	3.3	2.4	3.3	2.3	2.6
Other industrial countries	3.9	1.0	3.4	2.1	−1.3	0.4	0.3	2.7	2.7	3.5	2.9	3.5	3.2	2.6
All industrial countries	**3.5**	**4.0**	**3.6**	**0.1**	**0.5**	**−0.2**	**2.8**	**5.1**	**2.8**	**3.6**	**3.4**	**3.4**	**3.5**	**3.2**
Of which, Seven major countries above	3.4	4.5	3.6	−0.2	0.8	−0.3	3.2	5.5	2.8	3.6	3.4	3.4	3.5	3.2
European countries	3.5	2.7	4.5	1.6	−2.0	0.8	1.1	1.9	2.1	3.6	3.0	2.9	3.4	2.8

[1] Composites for the country groups are averages of percentage changes for individual countries weighted by the average U.S. dollar value of their respective GNPs over the preceding three years.
[2] Compound annual rates of change.
[3] From fourth quarter of preceding year.
[4] GDP at market prices.
[5] Average of expenditure, income, and output estimates of GDP at market prices.

Table A3. Industrial Countries: Components of Real GNP, 1968–87[1]
(Annual changes, in percent)

	Average 1968–77[2]	1978	1979	1980	1981	1982	1983	1984	1985	1986	1987
Consumer expenditure											
Canada	5.3	2.6	2.0	1.0	1.7	−2.0	3.1	3.7	5.2	3.2	2.3
United States	3.5	4.1	2.2	−0.2	1.2	1.3	4.6	4.4	3.3	2.8	3.5
Japan	6.1	5.4	6.5	1.4	1.3	4.1	3.2	2.8	2.7	3.5	4.0
France	4.8	4.7	3.4	1.5	2.0	3.4	1.0	0.7	2.1	2.8	2.6
Germany, Fed. Rep. of	4.4	3.8	3.6	1.3	−0.5	−1.3	1.2	0.8	1.7	4.4	3.7
Italy	3.8	3.0	5.3	4.3	0.5	0.5	−0.3	1.8	2.0	3.2	3.4
United Kingdom	1.8	5.6	4.5	−0.4	−0.4	0.8	3.8	1.6	3.2	3.9	3.7
Other industrial countries	4.2	1.8	2.7	1.2	−0.1	0.9	0.8	0.9	2.2	4.1	2.8
All industrial countries	**4.0**	**3.9**	**3.4**	**0.8**	**0.8**	**1.4**	**2.9**	**2.8**	**2.9**	**3.3**	**3.4**
Of which, Seven major countries above	4.0	4.3	3.5	0.7	0.9	1.5	3.3	3.1	3.0	3.1	3.5
European countries	3.9	3.4	3.6	1.3	0.1	0.7	1.3	0.9	2.1	3.8	3.2
Public consumption											
Canada	4.5	1.7	0.3	0.4	2.5	0.7	0.6	2.6	2.1	2.8	2.4
United States	0.2	2.6	0.8	1.9	1.5	1.9	0.9	4.3	6.0	1.4	1.1
Japan	5.1	5.3	4.4	2.8	4.8	1.9	2.9	2.5	2.6	2.0	2.0
France	3.7	4.3	1.8	1.8	2.4	2.5	1.5	—	−0.6	1.0	1.0
Germany, Fed. Rep. of	3.4	3.8	3.3	2.6	1.9	−0.9	0.4	2.4	2.1	2.3	2.0
Italy	3.5	2.3	1.7	2.1	3.3	2.6	2.4	2.7	2.0	2.0	2.0
United Kingdom	1.8	2.3	2.2	1.3	0.1	0.9	1.8	1.3	0.6	0.8	0.4
Other industrial countries	4.3	4.7	2.9	2.8	2.3	2.1	2.9	1.9	1.9	1.2	1.4
All industrial countries	**2.3**	**3.4**	**2.1**	**2.1**	**2.3**	**1.6**	**1.6**	**2.9**	**3.6**	**1.6**	**1.4**
Of which, Seven major countries above	1.9	3.2	1.9	2.0	2.2	1.5	1.4	3.1	3.8	1.6	1.4
European countries	3.4	3.7	2.8	2.2	2.0	1.4	1.6	1.4	1.2	1.5	1.3
Gross fixed investment											
Canada	4.4	−0.1	6.8	3.4	6.4	−9.7	−5.7	0.7	7.0	4.9	3.1
United States	3.6	9.8	3.7	−7.9	1.1	−9.6	7.8	17.6	7.5	6.2	4.0
Japan	7.7	8.5	5.3	—	3.1	0.8	−0.3	4.6	5.8	6.0	5.5
France	4.0	1.5	3.7	3.2	−1.1	0.7	−2.3	−2.0	−0.5	5.1	5.3
Germany, Fed. Rep. of	2.3	4.7	7.2	2.8	−4.8	−5.3	3.2	0.8	−0.3	4.7	4.8
Italy	1.8	−0.1	5.8	9.4	0.6	−5.2	−3.8	4.1	4.3	4.0	3.0
United Kingdom	1.2	3.1	2.6	−5.2	−9.3	6.4	4.5	8.2	1.3	4.4	0.5
Other industrial countries	3.0	−0.7	0.5	2.2	−1.9	−2.3	−1.1	3.1	4.8	4.9	4.2
All industrial countries	**3.6**	**5.6**	**4.0**	**−1.8**	**−0.4**	**−4.4**	**2.9**	**9.0**	**5.2**	**5.6**	**4.2**
Of which, Seven major countries above	3.7	6.8	4.6	−2.5	−0.1	−4.8	3.6	10.0	5.3	5.7	4.2
European countries	2.6	1.5	3.6	2.2	−3.9	−1.5	0.7	2.4	1.8	4.8	3.8

Table A3 *(concluded).* **Industrial Countries: Components of Real GNP, 1968–87[1]**
(Annual changes, in percent)

	Average 1968–77[2]	1978	1979	1980	1981	1982	1983	1984	1985	1986	1987
Final domestic demand											
Canada	5.0	1.9	2.7	1.5	2.9	−3.3	0.8	2.9	5.0	3.5	2.5
United States	2.8	4.7	2.2	−1.2	1.2	−0.4	4.4	6.4	4.5	3.1	3.2
Japan	6.5	6.3	5.9	1.1	2.2	2.8	2.1	3.3	3.6	4.1	4.3
France	4.4	3.9	3.3	1.9	1.4	2.7	0.3	0.1	1.2	3.0	2.9
Germany, Fed. Rep. of	3.7	4.0	4.4	1.9	−1.0	−2.1	1.5	1.1	1.4	4.0	3.6
Italy	3.3	2.3	4.8	4.9	1.0	−0.3	−0.5	2.3	2.4	3.2	3.1
United Kingdom	1.7	4.4	3.7	−0.9	−1.9	1.8	3.5	2.7	2.3	3.4	2.4
Other industrial countries	3.9	1.7	2.2	1.8	0.1	0.2	0.7	1.5	2.6	3.7	2.8
All industrial countries	**3.5**	**4.1**	**3.3**	**0.6**	**0.8**	**0.3**	**2.5**	**3.8**	**3.5**	**3.4**	**3.3**
Of which, Seven major countries above	3.5	4.5	3.4	0.4	0.9	0.3	2.8	4.2	3.6	3.4	3.3
European countries	3.5	3.1	3.5	1.7	−0.4	0.3	1.2	1.3	1.9	3.6	3.0
Stockbuilding[3]											
Canada	—	−0.2	1.3	−1.8	1.0	−3.3	2.5	0.6	0.4	−0.5	0.3
United States	—	0.3	−0.7	−0.7	1.0	−1.5	0.6	2.1	−1.6	0.5	0.2
Japan	−0.4	−0.4	0.6	−0.4	−0.1	−0.1	−0.4	0.5	0.1	—	0.1
France	−0.1	−0.1	0.8	0.2	−1.8	1.4	−0.8	0.5	0.4	0.1	—
Germany, Fed. Rep. of	0.1	−0.4	1.2	−0.9	−1.7	0.1	0.5	0.8	0.1	0.1	—
Italy	—	−0.3	0.8	2.1	−3.2	—	−0.7	0.6	−0.1	0.3	0.3
United Kingdom	—	−0.2	0.1	−2.3	0.2	0.6	0.8	−0.3	0.4	—	—
Other industrial countries	—	−0.7	1.2	0.3	−1.3	0.1	−0.4	1.2	0.1	−0.2	0.1
All industrial countries	**—**	**−0.1**	**0.3**	**−0.4**	**−0.3**	**−0.5**	**0.2**	**1.3**	**−0.6**	**0.2**	**0.1**
Of which, Seven major countries above	—	—	0.2	−0.6	−0.1	−0.6	0.3	1.3	−0.7	0.3	0.1
European countries	0.1	−0.4	1.0	−0.1	−1.6	0.5	−0.1	0.6	0.2	—	0.1
Foreign balance[3]											
Canada	−0.3	1.3	−1.1	1.3	−0.4	2.8	−0.4	1.3	−0.6	0.3	0.6
United States	−0.1	0.3	1.0	1.7	−0.2	−0.7	−1.4	−2.0	−0.7	−0.8	0.2
Japan	0.4	−0.8	−1.3	3.7	1.6	0.3	1.5	1.3	0.9	−1.2	−1.1
France	0.1	0.1	−0.7	−1.1	0.9	−2.2	1.2	1.1	−0.5	−0.7	−0.6
Germany, Fed. Rep. of	−0.1	−0.4	−1.6	0.4	2.7	1.0	−0.4	1.1	0.9	−0.4	−0.8
Italy	0.4	0.7	−0.6	−3.0	2.3	−0.2	0.8	−0.2	−0.1	−1.1	−1.0
United Kingdom	0.5	−0.4	−1.4	0.9	0.3	−0.9	−0.8	−0.5	0.9	−0.4	−0.3
Other industrial countries	—	1.0	−0.5	0.1	1.8	0.2	1.3	0.5	0.2	−0.6	−0.1
All industrial countries	**—**	**0.2**	**−0.3**	**1.1**	**0.9**	**−0.2**	**−0.1**	**−0.4**	**—**	**−0.7**	**−0.2**
Of which, Seven major countries above	—	—	−0.2	1.3	0.7	−0.3	−0.4	−0.5	−0.1	−0.7	−0.2
European countries	0.1	0.3	−1.0	−0.2	1.9	−0.3	0.5	0.6	0.3	−0.7	−0.5

[1] Composites for country groups are averages of percentage changes in real terms for individual countries weighted by the average U.S. dollar value of their respective GNPs over the preceding three years.

[2] Compound annual rates of change.

[3] Changes expressed as a percentage of GNP in the preceding period.

Table A4. Industrial Countries: Employment and Unemployment, 1968–87[1]
(In percent)

	Average 1968–77	1978	1979	1980	1981	1982	1983	1984	1985	1986	1987
Growth in employment[2]											
Canada	2.6	3.5	4.1	3.0	2.8	−3.2	0.8	2.5	2.8	3.4	2.2
United States	2.2	4.4	2.9	0.5	1.1	−0.9	1.3	4.1	2.0	2.3	2.2
Japan	0.8	1.2	1.3	1.0	0.8	1.0	1.7	0.6	0.8	0.6	0.8
France	1.0	0.4	—	0.1	−0.6	0.1	−0.5	−1.0	−0.3	0.2	0.5
Germany, Fed. Rep. of	0.5	1.1	1.8	1.5	−0.6	−1.9	−1.7	—	0.8	1.3	0.9
Italy	1.3	0.4	1.0	1.4	0.3	−0.2	0.3	0.4	0.5	0.6	0.5
United Kingdom	−0.1	0.9	1.1	−0.3	−3.9	−1.8	−1.2	1.7	1.1	1.0	0.9
Other industrial countries	0.8	—	0.8	0.2	−0.6	−0.9	−0.9	0.3	0.8	1.0	0.9
All industrial countries	**1.4**	**2.3**	**1.9**	**0.7**	**0.2**	**−0.8**	**0.4**	**2.0**	**1.4**	**1.6**	**1.5**
Of which,											
Seven major countries above	1.5	2.7	2.1	0.7	0.3	−0.8	0.7	2.3	1.4	1.7	1.5
European countries	0.6	0.5	0.9	0.4	−1.1	−1.2	−0.8	0.1	0.5	0.8	0.7
Unemployment rates[3]											
Canada	6.0	8.3	7.4	7.5	7.5	11.1	11.9	11.3	10.5	10.0	9.8
United States	5.7	6.1	5.9	7.2	7.6	9.7	9.6	7.5	7.2	7.0	6.7
Japan	1.5	2.2	2.1	2.0	2.2	2.4	2.7	2.7	2.7	3.0	3.1
France	3.3	5.5	6.2	6.6	7.7	8.4	8.6	10.1	10.8	11.0	11.0
Germany, Fed. Rep. of	1.9	3.8	3.3	3.4	4.9	6.8	8.2	8.1	8.2	7.8	7.6
Italy[4]	6.1	7.2	7.7	7.6	8.4	9.1	9.9	10.4	10.6	10.8	10.8
United Kingdom	3.3	5.7	5.4	6.1	9.5	11.0	12.1	12.6	13.1	13.1	13.0
Other industrial countries	2.5	5.5	5.8	6.7	8.1	9.6	11.0	11.6	11.7	11.3	11.0
All industrial countries	**3.7**	**5.2**	**5.1**	**5.8**	**6.7**	**8.2**	**8.7**	**8.3**	**8.2**	**8.1**	**7.9**
Of which,											
Seven major countries above	4.0	5.1	5.0	5.6	6.5	8.0	8.3	7.7	7.6	7.6	7.4
European countries	3.2	5.5	5.6	6.1	7.9	9.4	10.2	10.9	11.2	11.1	11.0

[1] The figures in the table are not comparable among countries since they are based on the differing labor force definitions and concepts used by the respective national statistical agencies.

[2] Composites for the country groups are averages of percentage changes for individual countries weighted by the average U.S. dollar value of their respective GNPs over the preceding three years.

[3] National unemployment rates weighted by labor force in the respective countries.

[4] Figures for 1968 to 1977 have been adjusted by the staff to allow for a discontinuity in Italian labor force statistics.

Table A5. Developing Countries: Real GDP, 1968–87[1]
(Annual changes, in percent)

	Average 1968–77[2]	1978	1979	1980	1981	1982	1983	1984	1985	1986	1987
Developing countries	**6.2**	**5.1**	**4.3**	**3.5**	**2.2**	**1.6**	**1.3**	**4.1**	**3.2**	**3.0**	**3.4**
Median growth rates	5.2	5.9	4.8	3.7	3.1	1.4	1.5	2.8	2.6	3.4	3.6
By region											
Africa	5.3	1.1	3.2	3.8	1.7	0.8	−1.5	1.6	1.6	2.8	2.8
Asia	5.4	9.1	4.4	5.5	5.5	5.0	7.4	7.9	6.1	5.5	5.5
Europe	6.0	5.4	3.8	1.5	2.3	2.4	1.0	3.5	2.5	3.5	3.8
Middle East	9.2	1.7	2.3	−2.1	−1.8	−0.2	0.1	0.7	−1.6	0.2	−0.3
Western Hemisphere	6.0	4.1	6.0	5.3	0.9	−0.9	−3.1	3.1	3.8	1.6	3.5
By predominant export											
Fuel exporters	8.4	2.7	3.7	1.1	0.9	−0.1	−1.8	1.2	−0.1	−0.6	0.3
Non-fuel exporters	5.4	6.1	4.6	4.6	2.7	2.5	3.0	5.5	4.8	4.6	4.8
Primary product exporters	5.4	3.5	4.6	4.3	1.1	0.3	−0.3	3.6	3.6	3.7	4.3
Agricultural exporters	6.0	3.8	4.8	4.2	0.4	0.9	0.2	3.5	4.1	3.9	4.5
Mineral exporters	3.3	2.3	3.8	4.9	3.8	−2.2	−2.5	4.1	0.9	2.9	3.5
Exporters of manufactures	5.7	9.3	4.3	4.6	4.7	5.0	7.2	8.3	6.6	6.1	6.0
Service and remittance countries	4.6	6.0	5.7	5.7	2.5	3.3	2.0	2.9	3.3	2.5	2.3
By financial criteria											
Capital exporting countries	10.2	0.7	1.4	−4.0	−3.2	−1.0	−0.3	0.5	−2.6	−0.4	−1.0
Capital importing countries	5.7	5.7	4.8	4.7	3.0	2.1	1.6	4.7	4.2	3.5	4.2
Market borrowers	6.5	4.6	6.0	4.5	2.1	0.4	−1.1	3.4	2.9	2.2	3.6
Official borrowers	3.9	3.6	2.1	3.2	3.1	2.0	1.9	2.8	2.9	4.1	3.4
Diversified borrowers	4.9	8.2	3.2	5.3	4.6	5.2	7.0	7.7	6.9	5.9	5.5
Countries with recent debt-servicing problems	5.6	3.5	5.4	4.6	1.2	−0.1	−2.5	2.6	2.8	1.9	3.3
Countries without debt-servicing problems	5.8	8.0	4.1	4.8	4.9	4.3	6.0	6.9	5.5	5.1	4.9
By miscellaneous criteria											
Capital importing fuel exporters	7.1	4.2	5.5	5.2	4.2	0.5	−3.0	1.8	1.8	−0.7	1.4
Fifteen heavily indebted countries	6.4	3.4	6.1	4.8	0.7	−0.4	−3.5	2.2	3.1	1.5	3.3
Small low-income countries	3.7	3.6	2.8	3.2	2.5	2.0	2.6	3.6	4.2	5.1	3.9
Sub-Saharan Africa[3]	3.7	1.9	2.1	3.2	1.9	0.5	0.6	1.9	3.1	4.7	3.5
By alternative analytical categories											
Oil exporting countries	9.2	1.3	2.4	−1.0	−1.2	−0.3	−1.0	0.7	−1.1	−0.1	−0.3
Non-oil developing countries	5.5	6.2	4.9	4.8	3.2	2.2	2.1	5.2	4.6	4.0	4.6
Net oil exporters	6.0	6.0	7.6	7.3	6.7	1.2	−3.0	3.7	3.4	−0.4	2.5
Net oil importers	5.4	6.2	4.5	4.5	2.7	2.4	3.1	5.5	4.8	4.7	5.0

[1] Except where otherwise indicated, arithmetic averages of country growth rates weighted by the average U.S. dollar value of GDPs over the preceding three years. Excluding China prior to 1978.

[2] Compound annual rates of change.

[3] Excluding Nigeria and South Africa.

Table A6. Developing Countries: Per Capita Real GDP, 1968–87[1]
(Annual changes, in percent)

	Average 1968–77[2]	1978	1979	1980	1981	1982	1983	1984	1985	1986	1987
Developing countries	**3.4**	**2.0**	**1.6**	**1.0**	**−0.3**	**−1.1**	**−1.2**	**1.4**	**0.9**	**0.4**	**0.9**
By region											
Africa	2.6	−1.5	0.4	0.9	−1.3	−2.4	−4.7	−1.6	−1.3	—	0.1
Asia	2.4	6.0	1.5	3.2	3.4	2.6	4.6	5.0	3.8	2.9	2.7
Europe	4.8	4.2	2.7	0.4	1.3	1.4	0.2	2.7	1.4	2.4	2.7
Middle East	4.6	−2.4	−1.7	−5.8	−5.7	−4.3	−3.1	−2.8	−4.4	−3.0	−3.5
Western Hemisphere	3.6	1.1	3.7	3.0	−1.2	−3.2	−5.3	0.8	1.7	−0.6	1.3
By predominant export											
Fuel exporters	4.6	−1.7	0.3	−2.1	−2.5	−3.6	−4.7	−2.2	−2.9	−3.5	−2.7
Non-fuel exporters	2.9	3.7	2.1	2.4	0.8	0.3	0.6	3.1	2.7	2.3	2.4
Primary product exporters	3.0	1.4	2.3	1.9	−1.2	−2.2	−2.8	1.2	1.3	1.4	2.0
Agricultural exporters	3.5	1.7	2.5	1.8	−1.8	−1.4	−2.1	1.3	1.9	1.5	2.1
Mineral exporters	0.9	−0.1	1.3	2.5	1.3	−5.1	−5.4	0.9	−1.6	0.4	0.9
Exporters of manufactures	2.9	6.4	1.6	2.7	3.0	3.0	4.8	5.6	4.4	3.5	3.2
Service and remittance countries	2.8	4.2	3.8	3.7	1.0	1.9	0.4	1.3	2.4	1.4	1.2
By financial criteria											
Capital exporting countries	5.0	−3.8	−2.9	−7.7	−7.2	−5.4	−3.7	−3.4	−5.3	−3.6	−4.1
Capital importing countries	3.2	3.0	2.2	2.4	0.9	−0.3	−0.7	2.2	2.0	1.1	1.7
Market borrowers	3.9	1.4	3.2	2.1	−0.1	−1.9	−3.6	0.5	0.6	−0.4	1.0
Official borrowers	1.1	1.0	−0.6	0.5	0.3	−1.1	−1.1	−0.1	−0.1	0.9	0.2
Diversified borrowers	2.6	6.2	1.4	3.4	2.8	3.2	5.2	5.9	5.1	3.9	3.5
Countries with recent debt-servicing problems	3.3	0.8	3.1	2.2	−1.0	−2.5	−4.8	0.2	0.6	−0.5	1.1
Countries without debt-servicing problems	3.1	5.2	1.5	2.6	2.8	2.0	3.4	4.2	3.2	2.6	2.3
By miscellaneous criteria											
Capital importing fuel exporters	4.2	—	2.7	2.4	1.4	−2.3	−5.5	−1.2	−0.9	−3.4	−1.4
Fifteen heavily indebted countries	3.9	0.6	3.7	2.6	−1.5	−2.8	−5.6	−0.2	1.0	−0.7	1.1
Small low-income countries	1.0	1.0	—	0.5	−0.4	−1.1	−0.4	0.7	1.8	2.5	1.4
Sub-Saharan Africa[3]	0.8	−0.7	−1.0	0.1	−1.2	−2.8	−2.8	−1.4	0.9	2.4	1.3
By alternative analytical categories											
Oil exporting countries	5.0	−2.5	−1.2	−4.4	−4.8	−4.1	−4.1	−2.8	−3.9	−3.1	−3.4
Non-oil developing countries	3.0	3.4	2.4	2.7	1.2	−0.1	−0.2	2.8	2.5	1.6	2.2
Net oil exporters	3.2	1.1	4.9	4.6	4.0	−1.4	−5.2	1.1	1.1	−2.7	0.1
Net oil importers	3.0	3.8	2.0	2.4	0.7	0.2	0.7	3.0	2.7	2.3	2.5

[1] Excluding China prior to 1978.
[2] Compound annual rates of change.
[3] Excluding Nigeria and South Africa.

Table A7. Developing Countries: Gross Capital Formation, 1978–86[1]
(In percent of GDP)

	1978	1979	1980	1981	1982	1983	1984	1985	1986
Developing countries	**27.9**	**26.5**	**26.5**	**26.2**	**24.9**	**23.9**	**23.2**	**23.1**	**22.5**
By region									
Africa	28.0	25.0	25.8	28.4	24.8	22.4	21.2	19.8	19.8
Asia	29.4	29.6	28.7	27.5	27.1	26.9	27.0	27.3	26.8
Europe	32.3	31.6	30.4	29.1	27.8	25.9	23.5	23.3	22.9
Middle East	27.5	23.9	24.8	25.8	26.0	29.6	27.5	25.9	23.7
Western Hemisphere	24.7	23.0	23.4	22.8	20.9	17.4	17.2	17.9	17.4
By predominant export									
Fuel exporters	28.5	25.0	25.7	27.2	25.5	25.5	24.3	23.3	22.1
Non-fuel exporters	27.7	27.2	26.8	25.8	24.7	23.1	22.6	23.0	22.6
Primary product exporters	22.9	21.9	22.8	22.7	21.2	19.0	18.2	18.5	18.2
Agricultural exporters	23.3	21.8	22.4	21.6	21.0	18.8	17.6	18.2	17.9
Mineral exporters	21.6	22.0	24.5	27.4	22.1	19.8	20.4	19.7	19.8
Exporters of manufactures	33.5	33.1	31.2	29.0	28.5	28.0	28.3	29.2	28.7
Service and remittance countries	27.2	28.4	27.4	26.6	24.9	22.0	19.5	18.2	17.6
By financial criteria									
Capital exporting countries	27.2	22.4	24.4	26.0	26.4	31.2	29.3	28.0	25.5
Capital importing countries	28.0	27.1	26.8	26.2	24.7	22.8	22.2	22.4	22.0
Market borrowers	28.0	26.9	26.8	26.9	24.6	21.5	20.5	20.2	20.0
Official borrowers	19.1	19.0	19.1	18.9	17.9	16.7	16.6	16.5	16.3
Diversified borrowers	29.8	29.1	28.2	26.6	26.4	26.6	26.9	27.9	26.8
Countries with recent debt-servicing problems	27.2	25.6	25.4	25.3	22.6	19.1	18.0	18.0	17.5
Countries without debt-servicing problems	28.8	28.6	28.1	27.1	26.8	26.5	26.4	26.6	26.1
By miscellaneous criteria									
Capital importing fuel exporters	29.4	26.9	26.6	28.0	24.8	21.7	20.8	19.9	19.4
Fifteen heavily indebted countries	27.0	24.9	24.7	24.6	22.3	18.3	17.2	17.2	16.8
Small low-income countries	17.1	16.8	17.2	16.5	16.1	15.0	15.0	14.9	15.0
Sub-Saharan Africa[2]	21.1	19.3	19.9	20.7	19.8	17.7	16.5	17.2	17.9
By alternative analytical categories									
Oil exporting countries	30.0	24.6	24.9	26.6	26.4	27.1	25.3	23.5	22.4
Non-oil developing countries	27.3	27.1	26.9	26.1	24.5	22.9	22.5	23.0	22.5
Net oil exporters	24.1	25.9	27.0	28.2	23.8	21.9	21.3	21.7	20.7
Net oil importers	27.9	27.3	26.9	25.8	24.6	23.1	22.7	23.2	22.8
Memorandum									
Median estimates									
Developing countries	**25.1**	**25.6**	**25.0**	**25.0**	**24.3**	**21.6**	**20.6**	**19.9**	**19.9**
By region									
Africa	25.7	25.5	23.5	25.7	22.9	19.8	19.2	19.7	19.3
Asia	24.2	26.3	27.9	27.5	25.2	24.5	22.2	20.7	21.3
Europe	33.9	32.3	32.6	31.1	31.6	28.3	23.5	22.3	22.9
Middle East	27.2	25.9	23.7	23.0	24.7	24.2	23.8	24.1	24.0
Western Hemisphere	23.6	25.1	24.8	22.8	20.9	19.7	18.3	17.4	16.9

[1] Except where otherwise indicated, arithmetic averages of country ratios weighted by the average U.S. dollar value of GDPs over the preceding three years.

[2] Excluding Nigeria and South Africa.

Table A8. Inflation, 1968–87[1]
(In percent)

	Average 1968–77[2]	1978	1979	1980	1981	1982	1983	1984	1985	1986	1987
Industrial countries[3]	**7.4**	**7.7**	**8.1**	**9.3**	**8.8**	**7.3**	**4.9**	**4.3**	**3.9**	**3.4**	**3.0**
United States	6.5	7.3	8.8	9.1	9.6	6.5	3.8	4.1	3.3	3.3	3.0
Other industrial countries[3]	8.2	7.9	7.6	9.4	8.3	7.8	5.6	4.4	4.3	3.6	3.0
Of which,											
Japan	8.3	4.8	3.0	3.8	3.2	1.9	0.8	1.3	1.7	1.1	1.4
Germany, Fed. Rep. of	5.3	4.3	4.0	4.8	4.0	4.3	3.3	1.9	2.1	2.6	1.3
Developing countries[4]	**15.2**	**18.7**	**21.5**	**27.1**	**26.0**	**24.5**	**32.7**	**37.4**	**39.3**	**25.9**	**13.7**
Median inflation rates	8.5	9.9	11.6	14.5	13.3	10.4	9.7	10.1	9.0	9.2	7.0
By region[4]											
Africa	10.0	16.9	16.7	16.5	21.3	12.7	18.6	19.8	13.6	13.1	10.3
Asia	8.8	4.0	8.0	13.1	10.6	6.2	6.6	7.1	6.7	5.4	4.8
Europe	9.9	19.8	25.9	37.9	24.1	23.7	23.1	27.9	27.9	25.2	17.6
Middle East	9.8	12.6	11.6	16.7	15.3	12.7	12.1	13.9	13.8	11.9	11.4
Western Hemisphere	27.9	41.9	46.5	54.2	59.1	66.3	102.4	122.6	144.0	76.0	27.0
By analytical criteria[4]											
Fuel exporters	10.7	12.4	12.1	15.5	16.2	17.7	24.7	19.3	14.7	16.5	12.6
Non-fuel exporters	17.1	21.4	25.7	32.3	30.7	28.0	37.1	47.6	53.0	30.6	14.3
Market borrowers	20.8	28.2	31.8	36.4	38.8	38.6	55.6	66.4	70.2	42.9	18.6
Official borrowers	10.3	13.7	19.4	22.4	28.3	16.2	21.9	17.6	19.7	17.3	13.0

[1] As measured by changes in GNP deflators for industrial countries and changes in consumer prices for developing countries.

[2] Compound annual rates of change.

[3] Averages of percentage changes in GNP deflators for individual countries weighted by the average U.S. dollar value of their respective GNPs over the preceding three years.

[4] Percentage changes of geometric averages of indices of consumer prices for individual countries weighted by the average U.S. dollar value of their respective GDPs over the preceding three years. Excluding China prior to 1978.

Table A9. Industrial Countries: GNP Deflators and Consumer Prices, 1968–87[1]
(Annual changes, in percent)

	Average 1968–77[2]	1978	1979	1980	1981	1982	1983	1984	1985	1986	1987	Fourth Quarter[3] 1985	1986	1987
GNP deflator														
Canada	7.2	6.7	10.3	11.4	10.6	10.3	5.3	2.8	3.2	3.9	3.6	3.3	4.5	3.3
United States	6.5	7.3	8.8	9.1	9.6	6.5	3.8	4.1	3.3	3.3	3.0	3.1	3.2	2.9
Japan	8.3	4.8	3.0	3.8	3.2	1.9	0.8	1.3	1.7	1.1	1.4	1.7	1.0	1.6
France[4]	7.9	9.5	10.4	12.2	11.9	12.6	9.5	7.1	5.9	4.3	3.0	5.7	3.6	2.8
Germany, Fed. Rep. of	5.3	4.3	4.0	4.8	4.0	4.3	3.3	1.9	2.1	2.6	1.3	2.9	2.0	1.0
Italy[4]	10.9	13.9	15.9	20.7	18.3	17.8	15.0	10.7	9.0	8.6	6.5	8.9	7.3	6.7
United Kingdom[4]	11.0	11.2	14.5	19.9	11.7	7.3	5.1	4.0	6.1	3.7	3.9	7.6	2.9	3.8
Other industrial countries	8.5	9.6	7.7	9.2	9.3	9.7	7.2	6.6	5.7	4.8	4.2	5.4	4.9	3.7
All industrial countries	**7.4**	**7.7**	**8.1**	**9.3**	**8.8**	**7.3**	**4.9**	**4.3**	**3.9**	**3.4**	**3.0**	**3.9**	**3.2**	**2.9**
Of which, Seven major countries above	7.3	7.3	8.2	9.3	8.7	6.9	4.5	4.0	3.6	3.2	2.8	3.6	3.0	2.8
European countries	8.2	8.9	9.0	11.1	9.8	9.4	7.3	5.6	5.3	4.3	3.4	5.5	3.7	3.2
Consumer prices														
Canada	6.4	8.9	9.1	10.2	12.5	10.8	5.8	4.3	4.0	5.5	4.0	4.1	6.0	3.2
United States	6.1	7.6	11.3	13.5	10.4	6.1	3.2	4.3	3.5	3.1	3.1	3.5	3.0	3.0
Japan	9.3	3.8	3.6	8.0	4.9	2.7	1.9	2.2	2.1	0.5	1.3	1.9	−0.2	2.4
France	8.0	9.1	10.8	13.6	13.4	11.8	9.6	7.4	5.8	2.2	2.1	4.8	1.5	2.2
Germany, Fed. Rep. of	4.5	2.7	4.1	5.4	6.3	5.3	3.3	2.4	2.2	—	1.0	1.6	−0.2	1.6
Italy	9.8	12.1	14.8	21.2	18.7	16.3	15.1	10.7	9.2	6.0	5.8	8.9	5.2	6.1
United Kingdom	11.3	8.3	13.4	18.0	11.9	8.6	4.6	5.0	6.1	3.8	3.9	5.5	3.7	3.7
Other industrial countries	8.1	8.5	7.8	10.2	10.4	9.7	7.6	6.3	5.8	3.7	3.9	5.2	3.5	3.7
All industrial countries	**7.2**	**7.2**	**9.0**	**11.8**	**9.9**	**7.3**	**4.9**	**4.7**	**4.1**	**2.8**	**2.9**	**3.8**	**2.5**	**3.0**
Of which, Seven major countries above	7.1	6.9	9.2	12.1	9.9	6.9	4.4	4.4	3.8	2.6	2.7	3.6	2.3	2.9
European countries	7.8	7.5	8.8	11.8	11.1	9.5	7.3	6.1	5.3	2.6	3.0	4.6	2.2	3.1

[1] Composites for the country groups are averages of percentage changes for individual countries weighted by the average U.S. dollar value of their respective GNPs over the preceding three years.

[2] Compound annual rates of change.

[3] From fourth quarter of preceding year.

[4] GDP at market prices.

Table A10.   Industrial Countries: Hourly Earnings, Productivity, and Unit Labor Costs in Manufacturing, 1968–87[1]

(Annual changes, in percent)

	Average 1968–77[2]	1978	1979	1980	1981	1982	1983	1984	1985	1986	1987
Hourly earnings											
Canada	9.8	7.1	8.8	10.1	12.0	11.7	4.3	4.9	3.8	4.7	4.5
United States	7.8	8.2	9.7	11.7	9.6	8.5	3.5	3.7	4.4	3.9	4.2
Japan	17.3	4.6	6.3	6.7	5.8	5.5	3.3	3.6	4.5	3.4	3.5
France	14.2	13.3	14.8	14.1	15.7	18.2	12.2	7.8	5.9	4.9	3.9
Germany, Fed. Rep. of	11.0	6.7	6.8	8.7	6.9	5.8	3.8	3.1	4.0	4.4	3.4
Italy	18.2	15.5	19.1	18.4	28.6	21.4	20.0	11.4	11.0	9.5	8.5
United Kingdom	14.5	14.7	16.8	22.3	14.8	8.8	8.6	7.9	9.1	8.6	7.9
Other industrial countries	13.5	11.7	11.0	10.8	11.6	10.2	8.4	6.6	6.5	5.7	5.3
All industrial countries	**11.2**	**9.2**	**10.2**	**11.5**	**10.8**	**9.7**	**6.0**	**4.9**	**5.3**	**4.7**	**4.6**
Of which,											
Seven major countries above	10.8	8.8	10.1	11.7	10.6	9.6	5.6	4.6	5.1	4.5	4.5
European countries	14.0	11.6	12.3	13.0	13.3	11.3	9.3	6.8	6.7	6.1	5.3
Output per manhour											
Canada	4.4	3.4	2.7	−0.4	0.3	0.1	6.9	11.3	1.4	1.8	0.9
United States	2.9	1.5	−0.1	—	2.2	2.2	6.6	4.9	2.7	2.5	3.4
Japan	7.3	11.3	6.7	3.5	0.2	0.1	2.9	8.5	3.4	1.5	2.3
France	6.1	5.8	5.0	1.6	3.2	6.5	4.3	5.8	4.3	4.3	3.7
Germany, Fed. Rep. of	5.1	2.9	4.7	1.2	2.1	1.7	4.9	3.8	4.6	2.7	2.8
Italy	5.0	4.0	8.4	3.1	7.3	2.5	4.1	5.8	3.0	3.3	3.3
United Kingdom	3.6	1.3	1.4	0.1	5.1	3.7	7.2	4.4	3.8	3.1	3.0
Other industrial countries	5.9	3.6	5.6	2.7	3.5	2.7	6.2	5.2	3.7	2.9	2.4
All industrial countries	**4.3**	**3.5**	**3.5**	**1.4**	**2.9**	**2.3**	**4.7**	**6.1**	**3.2**	**2.5**	**2.9**
Of which,											
Seven major countries above	4.1	3.5	3.1	1.2	2.7	2.2	4.5	6.2	3.1	2.5	3.0
European countries	5.4	4.0	5.0	2.0	3.7	3.3	5.6	5.1	4.1	3.3	3.0
Unit labor costs											
Canada	5.2	3.6	6.0	10.6	11.7	11.7	−2.4	−5.8	2.3	1.9	3.7
United States	4.8	6.6	9.8	11.7	7.2	6.2	−2.8	−1.3	1.7	1.4	0.8
Japan	9.3	−6.0	−0.4	3.2	5.5	5.4	0.4	−4.5	1.1	1.9	1.2
France	7.6	7.2	9.3	12.3	12.0	11.0	7.6	1.9	1.5	0.6	0.2
Germany, Fed. Rep. of	5.6	3.7	2.0	7.4	4.7	4.0	−1.0	−0.8	−0.6	1.7	0.6
Italy	12.6	11.1	9.9	14.8	19.9	18.4	15.2	5.2	7.7	6.0	5.1
United Kingdom	10.5	13.2	15.2	22.2	9.3	4.9	1.3	3.4	5.2	5.3	4.8
Other industrial countries	7.3	7.9	5.0	8.0	7.8	7.3	2.1	1.4	2.7	2.7	2.8
All industrial countries	**6.6**	**5.7**	**6.6**	**10.0**	**7.7**	**7.2**	**1.2**	**−1.1**	**2.0**	**2.1**	**1.6**
Of which,											
Seven major countries above	6.5	5.2	6.9	10.4	7.6	7.2	1.1	−1.5	1.9	2.0	1.4
European countries	8.2	7.3	6.9	10.8	9.2	7.8	3.6	1.6	2.6	2.8	2.3

[1] Composites for the country groups are averages of percentage changes for individual countries weighted by the average U.S. dollar value of their respective GNPs over the preceding three years.

[2] Compound annual rates of change.

189

Table A11. Developing Countries: Consumer Prices—Weighted Averages, 1968–87[1]
(Annual changes, in percent)

	Average 1968–77[2]	1978	1979	1980	1981	1982	1983	1984	1985	1986	1987
Developing countries	**15.2**	**18.7**	**21.5**	**27.1**	**26.0**	**24.5**	**32.7**	**37.4**	**39.3**	**25.9**	**13.7**
By region											
Africa	10.0	16.9	16.7	16.5	21.3	12.7	18.6	19.8	13.6	13.1	10.3
Asia	8.8	4.0	8.0	13.1	10.6	6.2	6.6	7.1	6.7	5.4	4.8
Europe	9.9	19.8	25.9	37.9	24.1	23.7	23.1	27.9	27.9	25.2	17.6
Middle East	9.8	12.6	11.6	16.7	15.3	12.7	12.1	13.9	13.8	11.9	11.4
Western Hemisphere	27.9	41.9	46.5	54.2	59.1	66.3	102.4	122.6	144.0	76.0	27.0
By predominant export											
Fuel exporters	10.7	12.4	12.1	15.5	16.2	17.7	24.7	19.3	14.7	16.5	12.6
Non-fuel exporters	17.1	21.4	25.7	32.3	30.7	28.0	37.1	47.6	53.0	30.6	14.3
Primary product exporters	23.3	37.8	43.6	51.8	51.3	48.4	69.1	93.5	106.8	55.4	20.3
Agricultural exporters	23.2	41.7	48.2	59.0	59.3	56.4	81.5	113.3	124.4	62.8	20.9
Mineral exporters	23.1	22.3	25.4	23.6	21.7	20.6	28.2	29.8	43.2	22.5	17.0
Exporters of manufactures	8.2	5.3	8.6	15.0	12.7	9.9	10.5	12.3	13.6	9.1	7.7
Service and remittance countries	9.4	12.3	15.1	18.3	16.0	14.7	15.1	15.4	13.4	15.1	12.8
By financial criteria											
Capital exporting countries	9.3	10.7	8.6	11.8	11.8	8.6	7.5	4.9	5.5	7.8	7.9
Capital importing countries	16.0	19.9	23.6	29.6	28.4	27.4	37.7	44.0	46.0	29.3	14.8
Market borrowers	20.8	28.2	31.8	36.4	38.8	38.6	55.6	66.4	70.2	42.9	18.6
Official borrowers	10.3	13.7	19.4	22.4	28.3	16.2	21.9	17.6	19.7	17.3	13.0
Diversified borrowers	7.8	8.3	11.3	20.4	11.9	11.2	11.2	14.1	14.5	9.6	8.2
Countries with recent debt-servicing problems	20.5	31.2	34.4	39.6	44.6	46.6	70.3	85.1	93.3	55.1	23.3
Countries without debt-servicing problems	9.9	9.3	13.5	20.4	14.0	10.3	10.4	11.9	11.4	8.9	7.3
By miscellaneous criteria											
Capital importing fuel exporters	11.7	13.7	15.0	18.7	19.9	25.4	39.7	31.8	22.6	24.2	16.7
Fifteen heavily indebted countries	25.7	37.4	40.8	47.0	52.6	56.0	87.5	110.6	122.5	68.1	25.9
Small low-income countries	10.3	15.2	21.4	24.5	33.0	18.6	26.7	20.0	18.9	16.9	12.7
Sub-Saharan Africa[3]	11.4	22.2	26.7	25.9	30.6	17.7	29.5	21.0	19.6	16.5	11.8
By alternative analytical categories											
Oil exporting countries	10.8	11.4	11.1	13.3	13.6	8.6	9.5	10.0	6.6	8.2	7.5
Non-oil developing countries	16.4	20.8	24.7	31.4	30.1	30.1	41.6	48.0	52.1	32.2	15.8
Net oil exporters	10.3	17.7	17.7	24.2	24.4	43.5	70.1	50.0	48.2	39.2	25.5
Net oil importers	17.5	21.3	25.8	32.5	31.0	27.9	36.9	47.7	52.7	31.0	14.1

[1] Geometric averages of country indices weighted by the average U.S. dollar value of GDPs over the preceding three years. Excluding China prior to 1978.

[2] Compound annual rates of change.

[3] Excluding Nigeria and South Africa.

Table A12. Developing Countries: Consumer Prices—Median Estimates, 1968–87
(Annual changes, in percent)

	Average 1968–77	1978	1979	1980	1981	1982	1983	1984	1985	1986	1987
Developing countries	**8.5**	**9.9**	**11.6**	**14.5**	**13.3**	**10.4**	**9.7**	**10.1**	**9.0**	**9.2**	**7.0**
By region											
Africa	8.3	10.3	11.9	12.9	13.4	12.6	11.5	11.8	10.3	10.0	7.5
Asia	6.9	5.9	7.5	13.9	12.5	7.6	8.1	7.2	5.1	5.3	5.0
Europe	7.8	9.9	14.3	16.2	15.7	19.0	13.8	13.4	12.1	10.0	8.5
Middle East	9.1	10.7	10.6	10.5	8.9	9.2	5.6	7.5	5.8	7.8	5.5
Western Hemisphere	9.8	10.2	14.9	18.1	14.7	9.2	8.8	11.9	14.0	15.0	10.0
By predominant export											
Fuel exporters	8.7	10.5	10.3	11.2	13.3	10.7	9.7	9.2	7.3	8.0	6.5
Non-fuel exporters	8.4	9.4	12.2	14.7	13.3	10.4	9.7	10.5	9.4	10.0	7.0
Primary product exporters	8.6	10.1	12.2	16.5	14.0	11.8	11.5	12.4	13.0	10.9	9.5
Agricultural exporters	8.5	10.0	12.1	17.1	12.7	11.8	11.4	11.9	12.6	10.0	8.0
Mineral exporters	8.2	10.2	12.8	13.8	15.7	11.9	13.7	18.1	16.9	18.0	15.3
Exporters of manufactures	6.8	5.3	9.4	13.3	13.6	7.6	6.3	5.6	4.3	4.5	4.2
Service and remittance countries	8.4	8.2	13.1	14.7	11.7	6.7	5.9	5.6	4.9	5.3	5.0
By financial criteria											
Capital exporting countries	9.4	10.6	9.9	10.0	8.3	7.4	3.7	1.2	3.0	4.0	4.0
Capital importing countries	8.5	9.7	12.0	14.7	13.5	10.6	10.0	10.5	9.4	10.0	7.0
Market borrowers	9.6	10.5	15.4	17.7	15.0	10.0	12.1	12.6	11.1	11.0	9.0
Official borrowers	8.6	9.1	12.0	14.7	12.7	10.0	10.6	10.7	9.9	10.0	8.0
Diversified borrowers	7.7	9.2	10.1	13.5	12.8	11.5	7.8	8.4	8.1	7.3	5.9
Countries with recent debt-servicing problems	8.7	10.2	13.1	18.1	15.0	12.3	14.1	13.0	15.0	15.0	10.0
Countries without debt-servicing problems	8.2	8.7	11.0	13.5	12.5	9.6	7.7	7.2	6.0	6.8	5.6
By miscellaneous criteria											
Capital importing fuel exporters	8.2	10.5	10.6	12.5	14.7	12.6	11.1	11.3	9.1	9.5	8.0
Fifteen heavily indebted countries	14.0	17.5	19.8	26.4	26.3	19.0	40.9	50.3	30.7	22.0	15.6
Small low-income countries	8.5	9.9	12.2	13.8	12.7	11.8	12.0	11.1	10.0	10.0	8.0
Sub-Saharan Africa[1]	8.5	10.3	12.5	13.5	13.3	12.7	11.5	12.0	10.5	10.0	8.0
By alternative analytical categories											
Oil exporting countries	9.0	10.6	10.8	10.6	11.7	7.8	5.6	8.3	4.9	5.0	4.7
Non-oil developing countries	8.5	9.7	12.0	14.7	13.3	11.0	10.0	10.5	9.4	10.0	7.0
Net oil exporters	8.6	10.5	9.0	15.1	14.6	16.2	17.4	13.2	10.5	13.0	12.0
Net oil importers	8.4	9.4	12.2	14.7	13.3	10.4	9.7	10.1	9.0	9.9	7.0

[1] Excluding Nigeria and South Africa.

Table A13. Summary Financial Indicators, 1978–87
(In percent)

	1978	1979	1980	1981	1982	1983	1984	1985	1986	1987
Major industrial countries										
Fiscal balances of central governments[1]										
Seven major countries	−3.2	−2.8	−3.3	−3.6	−4.6	−5.4	−5.1	−5.4	−4.7	−3.9
Of which,										
United States	−2.0	−1.1	−2.3	−2.4	−4.1	−5.6	−4.9	−5.9	−4.8	−3.4
Japan	−5.2	−6.1	−6.2	−5.9	−5.9	−5.7	−5.4	−4.9	−4.8	−4.7
Germany, Fed. Rep. of	−2.1	−1.8	−1.6	−2.1	−2.1	−2.0	−1.8	−1.1	−0.7	−0.6
Fiscal impulses of central governments[2]										
Seven major countries	0.5	−0.4	−0.1	−0.2	—	0.8	0.3	0.4	−0.7	−0.8
Of which,										
United States	0.1	−0.8	0.4	—	0.3	1.6	0.4	1.0	−1.0	−1.3
Japan	0.2	1.1	0.1	−0.5	−0.3	−0.4	−0.1	−0.3	−0.4	−0.4
Germany, Fed. Rep. of	0.1	—	−0.7	−0.8	−1.3	−0.1	0.5	−0.5	0.1	0.1
Growth of monetary aggregates[3]										
Narrow money										
Seven major countries	11.0	10.2	5.6	6.5	7.1	10.0	6.4	8.5	7.6	6.3
Of which,										
United States	8.2	7.7	6.3	7.1	6.6	11.2	6.9	8.9	8.0	5.7
Japan	10.1	10.7	2.6	3.3	5.8	3.6	2.8	5.1	3.0	3.5
Germany, Fed. Rep. of	13.4	7.5	2.4	1.1	3.6	10.3	3.3	4.3	6.4	5.0
Broad money										
Seven major countries	11.2	10.6	9.5	10.0	9.4	10.5	7.7	8.9	7.7	7.4
Of which,										
United States	8.5	8.3	8.1	9.5	9.3	12.5	8.0	9.0	7.2	6.9
Japan	11.7	11.9	9.2	8.9	9.2	7.4	7.8	8.3	8.0	8.0
Germany, Fed. Rep. of	10.6	8.9	5.3	6.4	6.5	6.6	3.9	4.9	5.0	5.5
Interest rates[4]										
Six-month Eurodollars	9.1	11.9	14.0	16.7	13.6	9.9	11.3	8.6	7.5	7.5
Developing countries										
Fiscal balances of central governments[1]										
Weighted averages	−3.4	−2.2	−1.5	−3.4	−4.8	−5.2	−4.4	−4.4	−4.8	...
Medians	−3.9	−3.4	−4.6	−5.7	−6.6	−7.1	−5.2	−4.6	−4.5	...
Growth of monetary aggregates[5]										
Weighted averages	28.9	33.9	35.7	36.3	34.8	38.4	48.9	45.0	30.0	...
Medians	19.5	17.5	20.9	19.7	18.9	17.0	16.0	15.6	12.0	...

[1] In percent of GNP/GDP.

[2] For definition of fiscal impulses, see *World Economic Outlook* April 1985, Supplementary Note 1. See also footnotes to Table A16. It should be noted that estimates for the industrial and developing countries are not necessarily comparable, in part because of the exclusion of the so-called monetary correction from the estimates for some of the high-inflation developing countries.

[3] For definitions of monetary aggregates, see footnotes 3 and 4 to Table A14.

[4] London interbank offered rate on six-month U.S. dollar deposits.

[5] Money and quasi-money. For method of calculation, see Table A18.

Table A14. Major Industrial Countries: Monetary Aggregates, 1978–86[1]

(Annual changes, in percent)

	1978	1979	1980	1981	1982	1983	1984	1985	Fourth Quarter[2] 1984	1985	1986
Narrow money (M1)[3]											
Canada	10.1	7.0	6.3	3.8	0.6	10.1	3.3	4.2	0.3	9.4	7.0
United States	8.2	7.7	6.3	7.1	6.6	11.2	6.9	8.9	5.3	11.9	6.0
Japan	10.1	10.7	2.6	3.3	5.8	3.6	2.8	5.1	6.9	4.5	3.0
France	11.3	13.8	6.8	12.2	13.9	9.9	7.0	8.6	9.5	10.0	6.5
Germany, Fed. Rep. of	13.4	7.5	2.4	1.1	3.6	10.3	3.3	4.3	5.9	5.3	5.2
Italy	23.7	24.2	16.1	10.9	11.8	15.1	12.3	13.8	12.4	11.5	10.5
United Kingdom	19.9	17.7	5.0	10.3	10.0	13.0	12.4	18.5	15.6	17.5	17.0
Seven major countries above	**11.0**	**10.2**	**5.6**	**6.5**	**7.1**	**10.0**	**6.4**	**8.5**	**6.9**	**10.1**	**6.4**
Four major European countries above	15.7	13.8	6.3	7.6	9.2	11.6	8.0	10.4	10.3	10.5	9.2
Broad money[4]											
Canada	11.1	15.7	18.9	15.1	9.4	5.7	4.4	9.5	7.2	10.7	4.5
United States	8.5	8.3	8.1	9.5	9.3	12.5	8.0	9.0	7.9	8.6	7.0
Japan	11.7	11.9	9.2	8.9	9.2	7.4	7.8	8.3	7.8	9.0	8.0
France	13.2	13.0	10.8	11.4	11.5	9.1	8.0	7.9	8.3	8.0	6.0
Germany, Fed. Rep. of	10.6	8.9	5.3	6.4	6.5	6.6	3.9	4.9	4.7	5.1	5.5
Italy	23.7	19.6	14.4	10.7	12.3	16.5	12.3	13.9	12.1	11.2	10.5
United Kingdom	18.4	13.3	16.5	16.4	10.5	11.3	9.7	12.4	9.7	14.5	14.0
Seven major countries above	**11.2**	**10.6**	**9.5**	**10.0**	**9.4**	**10.5**	**7.7**	**8.9**	**7.9**	**8.9**	**7.5**
Four major European countries above	14.9	12.6	10.4	10.5	9.7	10.0	7.8	9.0	8.1	9.1	8.5

[1] Composites for the country groups are averages of percentage changes for individual countries weighted by the average U.S. dollar value of their respective GNPs over the preceding three years.

[2] From fourth quarter of preceding year.

[3] M1 is generally currency in circulation plus private demand deposits. In addition, Canada excludes private sector float; the United States includes traveler's checks of nonbank issues and other checkable deposits and excludes private sector float and demand deposits of banks; the Federal Republic of Germany includes demand deposits at fixed interest rates; and Japan includes government demand deposits and excludes float.

[4] M1 plus quasi-money—generally "M2," except for the United Kingdom, Japan, and the Federal Republic of Germany, for which the data are based on sterling M3, M2 + CD, and M3, respectively. Quasi-money is essentially private term deposits and other notice deposits. The United States also includes money market mutual fund balances, money market deposit accounts, overnight repurchase agreements, and overnight Eurodollars issued to U.S. residents by foreign branches of U.S. banks. France also includes government savings bonds. Sterling M3 is M1 plus private sterling time deposits. For Japan, M2 + CD is currency in circulation plus total private and public sector deposits and installments of Sogo Banks plus certificates of deposit. For the Federal Republic of Germany, M3 is M1 plus private time deposits with maturities of less than four years plus savings deposits at statutory notice.

Table A15. Major Industrial Countries: Interest Rates, 1978–January 1986[1]

(In percent per annum)

	1978	1979	1980	1981	1982	1983	1984	1985	January 1986
Short-term interest rates[1]									
Canada	8.5	11.9	13.4	18.3	14.4	9.5	11.3	9.6	10.2
United States	8.2	11.2	13.1	15.9	12.4	9.1	10.4	8.0	7.8
Japan	4.4	5.9	11.0	7.7	7.1	6.7	6.3	6.7	7.0
France	8.1	9.5	12.2	15.4	14.6	12.4	11.7	9.9	9.0
Germany, Fed. Rep. of	3.7	6.6	9.5	12.0	8.8	5.7	6.0	5.4	4.7
Italy	11.4	12.0	17.5	20.0	20.0	18.0	17.1	14.9	14.9
United Kingdom	9.2	13.6	16.6	13.8	12.3	10.1	9.9	12.2	12.8
Seven major countries above[2]	**7.3**	**9.8**	**12.6**	**14.1**	**11.8**	**9.2**	**9.7**	**8.4**	**8.2**
Four major European countries above	7.2	9.6	12.8	14.6	13.0	10.6	10.3	9.8	9.5
Long-term interest rates[3]									
Canada	9.3	10.2	12.5	15.2	14.3	11.8	12.8	11.0	10.5
United States	8.5	9.3	11.4	13.7	12.9	11.3	12.5	11.0	9.6
Japan	6.1	7.7	8.9	8.4	8.3	7.8	7.3	6.5	5.6
France	9.0	9.5	13.0	15.7	15.6	13.6	12.4	10.9	10.4
Germany, Fed. Rep. of	5.7	7.4	8.5	10.4	9.0	7.9	7.8	6.9	6.3
Italy	13.7	14.1	16.1	20.6	20.9	18.0	15.0	13.0	12.7
United Kingdom	12.5	13.0	13.8	14.7	12.9	10.8	10.7	10.6	10.7
Seven major countries above[2]	**8.4**	**9.3**	**11.2**	**13.1**	**12.4**	**10.9**	**11.1**	**9.9**	**8.9**
Four major European countries above	9.2	10.1	12.0	14.3	13.6	11.8	10.9	9.9	9.5

[1] Composites for the country groups are averages of interest rates for individual countries weighted by the average U.S. dollar value of their respective GNPs over the preceding three years.

[2] Interest rate on the following instruments: Canada, three-month Financial paper; United States, 90-day bank certificates of deposit in secondary market; Japan, discount rate on two-month private bills; Franc the Federal Republic of Germany, Italy, and the United Kingdom, three-month interbank loan rate.

[3] Average yield to maturity of central government bonds with terms of 10 years or more for Canada, 20 years for the United States and the United Kingdom, and over the counter sales yields of interest bearing government bonds with maturities of 10 years or more for Japan. Average yield to maturity of National Equipment Bonds of 1965, 1966, and 1967 for France, public authorities bonds with terms of three years or more for the Federal Republic of Germany, and bonds issued by the Consortium of Credit for Public Works with an average maturity of 15 to 20 years for Italy.

Table A16. Major Industrial Countries: Central Government Fiscal Balances and Impulses, 1978–87[1]

(In percent of GNP)

	1978	1979	1980	1981	1982	1983	1984	1985	1986	1987
Fiscal balance										
(+ surplus, − deficit)										
Canada[2]	−4.6	−3.5	−3.5	−2.2	−5.3	−6.2	−7.0	−6.9	−5.3	−3.9
United States	−2.0	−1.1	−2.3	−2.4	−4.1	−5.6	−4.9	−5.9	−4.8	−3.4
Japan[3]	−5.2	−6.1	−6.2	−5.9	−5.9	−5.7	−5.4	−4.9	−4.8	−4.7
France[4]	−1.6	−1.5	−1.1	−2.6	−2.8	−3.3	−3.4	−3.3	−3.1	−3.0
Germany, Fed. Rep. of	−2.1	−1.8	−1.6	−2.1	−2.1	−2.0	−1.8	−1.1	−0.7	−0.6
Italy[5]	−13.1	−10.8	−10.8	−12.8	−15.1	−16.4	−15.4	−16.0	−15.1	−14.7
United Kingdom[2]	−3.3	−2.2	−2.5	−2.9	−2.7	−3.2	−3.2	−2.8	−2.7	−2.9
Seven major countries above	**−3.2**	**−2.8**	**−3.3**	**−3.6**	**−4.6**	**−5.4**	**−5.1**	**−5.4**	**−4.7**	**−3.9**
Seven major countries except the United States	−4.4	−4.1	−4.1	−4.5	−5.0	−5.3	−5.2	−5.0	−4.6	−4.4
Fiscal impulse										
(+ expansionary, − contractionary)										
Canada[2]	1.2	−0.5	−0.2	−1.1	0.8	0.9	1.6	0.4	−1.3	−1.1
United States	0.1	−0.8	0.4	—	0.3	1.6	0.4	1.0	−1.0	−1.3
Japan[3]	0.2	1.1	0.1	−0.5	−0.3	−0.4	−0.1	−0.3	−0.4	−0.4
France[4]	0.9	0.1	−0.8	1.1	—	0.1	−0.1	−0.3	−0.3	−0.1
Germany, Fed. Rep. of	0.1	—	−0.7	−0.8	−1.3	−0.1	0.5	−0.5	0.1	0.1
Italy[5]	3.8	−1.7	0.1	0.7	0.6	−0.1	−1.2	0.4	−1.1	−0.7
United Kingdom[2]	2.1	−0.8	−1.6	−1.5	−0.5	0.6	—	—	0.3	0.2
Seven major countries above	**0.5**	**−0.4**	**−0.1**	**−0.2**	**—**	**0.8**	**0.3**	**0.4**	**−0.7**	**−0.8**
Seven major countries except the United States	1.0	0.1	−0.5	−0.3	−0.3	—	0.1	−0.2	−0.3	−0.3

[1] Composites for the country groups are weighted averages of the individual national ratios for each year, with weights proportionate to the U.S. dollar value of the respective GNPs in the preceding three years.

[2] Data for Canada and the United Kingdom are on a national income accounts basis.

[3] Data for Japan cover the consolidated operations of the general account, certain special accounts, social security transactions, and disbursements of the fiscal investment and loan program (FILP) except those to financial institutions. Japanese data other than FILP transactions are based on national income accounts.

[4] Data for France are on an administrative basis and do not include social security transactions.

[5] Data for Italy refer to the state sector and cover the transactions of the state budget as well as those of several autonomous entities operating at the state level. They also include the deficit, but not the gross transactions, of social security institutions, and part of that of local authorities.

Table A17. Major Industrial Countries: General Government Fiscal Balances and Impulses, 1978–87[1]
(In percent of GNP)

	1978	1979	1980	1981	1982	1983	1984	1985	1986	1987
Fiscal balance										
(+ surplus, − deficit)										
Canada	−3.1	−1.8	−2.7	−1.6	−5.0	−6.2	−6.3	−6.1	−4.3	−3.4
United States	—	0.5	−1.3	−1.0	−3.5	−3.8	−2.9	−3.5	−3.4	−2.1
Japan	−5.5	−4.7	−4.4	−3.5	−3.6	−3.5	−2.6	−1.6	−1.5	−1.5
France	−1.9	−0.7	0.2	−1.8	−2.7	−3.1	−2.8	−2.5	−2.5	−2.5
Germany, Fed. Rep. of	−2.4	−2.6	−2.9	−3.7	−3.3	−2.5	−1.9	−1.1	−0.8	−0.6
Italy	−9.7	−9.5	−8.0	−11.9	−12.6	−12.4	−13.5	−14.0	−13.1	−12.7
United Kingdom	−4.4	−3.3	−3.6	−2.9	−2.4	−3.7	−3.8	−3.4	−3.1	−3.2
Seven major countries above	**−2.2**	**−1.7**	**−2.5**	**−2.6**	**−3.9**	**−4.1**	**−3.5**	**−3.5**	**−3.3**	**−2.5**
Seven major countries except the United States	−4.2	−3.6	−3.4	−3.8	−4.2	−4.4	−4.1	−3.6	−3.2	−3.0
Fiscal impulse										
(+ expansionary, − contractionary)										
Canada	1.1	−0.6	0.5	−0.7	−0.4	1.4	1.5	0.7	−1.2	−0.5
United States	—	−0.5	0.7	−0.5	0.5	0.6	0.6	0.6	—	−1.0
Japan	1.7	−0.5	−0.4	−1.2	−0.1	−0.4	−0.5	−0.8	−0.4	−0.3
France	1.4	−1.0	−1.8	0.6	0.3	−0.5	−0.7	−1.0	—	−0.1
Germany, Fed. Rep. of	0.4	0.6	−0.4	−0.9	−2.1	−0.9	0.4	−0.6	0.4	—
Italy	1.4	0.4	−1.3	2.2	−1.1	−1.9	0.9	0.3	−1.2	−0.7
United Kingdom	1.9	−0.7	−1.8	−2.8	−0.8	1.4	0.1	0.1	0.3	0.1
Seven major countries above	**0.7**	**−0.4**	**−0.2**	**−0.6**	**−0.1**	**0.1**	**0.3**	**0.1**	**−0.2**	**−0.6**
Seven major countries except the United States	1.3	−0.3	−0.8	−0.6	−0.7	−0.3	—	−0.4	−0.3	−0.2

[1] Data are on a national income accounts basis. Composites for the country groups are weighted averages of the individual national ratios for each year, with weights proportionate to the U.S. dollar value of the respective GNPs in the preceding three years.

Table A18. Developing Countries: Broad Money Aggregates, 1978–85[1]
(Annual changes, in percent)

	1978	1979	1980	1981	1982	1983	1984	1985
Developing countries	**28.9**	**33.9**	**35.7**	**36.3**	**34.8**	**38.4**	**48.9**	**45.0**
By region								
Africa	15.1	15.4	26.5	19.4	17.5	17.4	18.4	15.8
Asia	17.7	25.4	27.4	20.5	21.7	19.4	22.9	17.6
Europe	24.5	29.8	35.6	37.8	30.1	19.8	31.3	29.7
Middle East	27.0	27.0	32.6	31.4	22.8	17.3	21.6	17.1
Western Hemisphere	53.3	60.9	53.4	71.3	73.2	104.2	141.5	143.1
By predominant export								
Fuel exporters	21.9	23.0	30.6	28.4	25.8	22.4	22.1	17.5
Non-fuel exporters	32.0	38.8	38.0	40.1	39.5	47.6	64.6	60.4
Primary product exporters	45.4	51.7	48.2	60.2	56.5	79.2	109.7	109.8
Agricultural exporters	49.1	58.3	51.1	69.3	66.3	96.9	130.9	129.8
Mineral exporters	31.1	26.2	36.1	26.9	23.2	23.7	41.1	38.9
Exporters of manufactures	18.5	26.7	28.6	22.1	24.1	21.7	31.3	23.5
Service and remittance countries	23.2	26.7	28.3	27.3	27.1	21.3	19.6	20.5
By financial criteria								
Capital exporting countries	24.5	23.4	27.0	27.9	17.3	10.1	10.6	7.7
Capital importing countries	29.6	35.5	37.1	37.8	38.0	44.1	56.7	52.5
Market borrowers	37.5	41.9	42.8	46.6	46.9	59.6	75.6	74.7
Official borrowers	23.3	15.3	21.3	23.7	24.4	25.0	20.6	21.9
Diversified borrowers	18.5	30.4	32.0	26.8	25.9	21.9	34.0	24.4
Countries with recent debt-servicing problems	38.8	42.1	43.4	51.7	51.9	69.4	92.0	91.5
Countries without debt-servicing problems	20.8	29.2	31.2	25.1	25.1	21.8	27.8	22.5
By miscellaneous criteria								
Capital importing fuel exporters	20.0	22.7	33.6	28.8	32.8	32.9	32.0	26.1
Fifteen heavily indebted countries	45.1	51.8	50.5	60.9	61.6	88.1	117.7	120.6
Small low-income countries	25.5	16.6	23.6	27.1	25.7	27.3	20.9	20.6
Sub-Saharan Africa[2]	22.9	17.7	22.3	23.1	22.2	23.1	21.4	22.4
By alternative analytical categories								
Oil exporting countries	19.4	20.7	30.8	23.9	15.9	13.8	12.1	11.2
Non-oil developing countries	31.8	38.0	37.2	40.4	41.5	47.9	63.7	58.2
Net oil exporters	31.2	32.5	36.5	41.6	55.7	49.2	57.7	46.0
Net oil importers	31.9	38.8	37.3	40.2	39.2	47.6	64.8	60.4

Table A18 *(concluded).* **Developing Countries: Broad Money Aggregates, 1978–85[1]**
(Annual changes, in percent)

	1978	1979	1980	1981	1982	1983	1984	1985
Memorandum								
Median estimates								
Developing countries	**19.5**	**17.5**	**20.9**	**19.7**	**18.9**	**17.0**	**16.0**	**15.6**
By region								
Africa	19.7	14.6	20.4	19.1	16.3	15.2	17.5	15.8
Asia	18.3	21.0	21.4	19.5	20.7	18.9	14.9	14.3
Europe	17.9	18.6	22.0	24.4	22.1	15.6	20.6	15.5
Middle East	23.1	21.3	28.8	31.5	19.9	18.4	18.7	11.2
Western Hemisphere	19.3	16.9	15.4	14.8	15.1	16.0	16.0	20.0

[1] Except where otherwise indicated, geometric averages of country indices, weighted by the average U.S. dollar value of GDPs over the preceding three years.

[2] Excluding Nigeria and South Africa.

Table A19. Developing Countries: Central Government Fiscal Balances, 1978–86[1]

(In percent of GDP)

	1978	1979	1980	1981	1982	1983	1984	1985	1986
Developing countries	**−3.4**	**−2.2**	**−1.5**	**−3.4**	**−4.8**	**−5.2**	**−4.4**	**−4.4**	**−4.8**
By region									
Africa	−5.5	−4.4	−3.9	−5.5	−6.4	−7.3	−5.1	−4.7	−5.4
Asia	−2.0	−3.7	−3.4	−3.2	−4.4	−3.5	−3.2	−4.0	−3.9
Europe	−3.0	−3.0	−3.5	−3.1	−2.5	−2.2	−2.3	−3.2	−2.7
Middle East	−7.3	0.2	4.3	−3.0	−6.9	−9.9	−10.3	−9.0	−11.3
Western Hemisphere	−2.0	−0.7	−0.6	−3.1	−4.2	−4.1	−2.3	−2.0	−2.0
By predominant export									
Fuel exporters	−4.2	1.0	2.8	−2.6	−5.9	−7.4	−5.6	−5.8	−8.0
Non-fuel exporters	−3.0	−3.6	−3.3	−3.8	−4.3	−4.0	−3.7	−3.7	−3.2
Primary product exporters	−2.9	−2.4	−2.4	−3.8	−4.3	−3.9	−3.0	−2.5	−1.8
Agricultural exporters	−2.4	−2.0	−2.2	−3.6	−3.9	−3.3	−2.4	−1.8	−1.1
Mineral exporters	−4.9	−3.9	−3.2	−4.6	−5.7	−6.0	−5.4	−5.4	−5.0
Exporters of manufactures	−1.8	−3.8	−3.4	−2.5	−2.9	−2.8	−3.0	−3.1	−3.1
Service and remittance countries	−9.8	−10.3	−8.3	−11.2	−11.8	−11.4	−11.7	−13.6	−12.3
By financial criteria									
Capital exporting countries	−5.5	3.6	8.0	−0.5	−4.9	−8.3	−8.0	−6.7	−9.5
Capital importing countries	−3.1	−3.1	−2.9	−3.9	−4.8	−4.6	−3.7	−4.0	−4.0
Market borrowers	−2.3	−1.1	−1.1	−3.5	−4.5	−4.3	−2.4	−2.8	−3.0
Official borrowers	−6.2	−6.3	−6.9	−7.0	−8.7	−7.2	−7.6	−7.9	−7.8
Diversified borrowers	−3.7	−5.9	−5.1	−3.8	−4.5	−4.6	−5.2	−5.1	−4.8
Countries with recent debt-servicing problems	−3.2	−2.3	−1.8	−4.1	−4.8	−4.6	−2.8	−2.8	−2.9
Countries without debt-servicing problems	−3.0	−3.9	−4.0	−3.7	−4.9	−4.6	−4.7	−5.1	−4.9
By miscellaneous criteria									
Capital importing fuel exporters	−3.3	−1.0	−1.4	−4.2	−6.6	−6.6	−3.7	−5.0	−6.8
Fifteen heavily indebted countries	−2.1	−0.8	−0.8	−3.6	−4.3	−4.3	−2.3	−2.0	−2.1
Small low-income countries	−6.0	−6.8	−6.4	−6.3	−7.4	−6.0	−5.6	−6.1	−5.2
Sub-Saharan Africa[2]	−5.8	−6.5	−6.5	−6.8	−7.0	−5.6	−4.6	−5.1	−4.8
By alternative analytical categories									
Oil exporting countries	−4.4	2.2	4.6	−1.4	−5.1	−7.3	−5.5	−5.3	−7.8
Non-oil developing countries	−3.1	−3.5	−3.3	−4.1	−4.8	−4.5	−4.0	−4.1	−3.8
Net oil exporters	−5.8	−4.9	−4.1	−7.7	−9.4	−8.7	−7.1	−8.2	−9.6
Net oil importers	−2.7	−3.3	−3.1	−3.5	−3.9	−3.7	−3.4	−3.3	−2.8
Memorandum									
Median estimates									
Developing countries	**−3.9**	**−3.4**	**−4.6**	**−5.7**	**−6.6**	**−7.1**	**−5.2**	**−4.6**	**−4.5**
By region									
Africa	−5.7	−6.2	−6.0	−7.0	−7.5	−8.1	−5.8	−4.7	−4.5
Asia	−2.8	−3.2	−3.4	−4.1	−5.8	−4.1	−3.5	−4.5	−4.3
Europe	−2.3	−2.9	−3.2	−1.3	−1.9	−2.2	−3.2	−1.6	−1.9
Middle East	−8.2	−0.1	−5.6	−11.6	−9.0	−9.1	−13.7	−12.2	−12.5
Western Hemisphere	−2.2	−2.6	−3.1	−5.3	−5.8	−5.2	−5.1	−3.8	−2.9

[1] Arithmetic averages of country balances, in percent of GDP, weighted by the average U.S. dollar value of GDPs over the preceding three years.
[2] Excluding Nigeria and South Africa.

Table A20. Summary of World Trade Volumes and Prices, 1968–87[1]
(Annual changes, in percent)

	Average 1968–77[2]	1978	1979	1980	1981	1982	1983	1984	1985	1986	1987
World trade[3]											
Volume	7.7	5.4	6.5	1.7	0.8	−2.3	2.8	8.7	2.9	3.3	3.8
Unit value (in U.S. dollar terms)	9.6	10.0	18.7	19.6	−1.2	−4.3	−4.7	−2.4	−1.7	6.2	3.6
(in SDR terms)[4]	7.9	2.6	15.0	18.7	9.1	2.2	−1.6	1.8	−0.8	−5.5	2.6
Volume of trade											
Exports											
Industrial countries	8.1	5.5	7.0	4.1	3.6	−2.2	2.5	9.3	3.9	2.7	3.4
Developing countries	5.7	4.0	5.0	−4.0	−5.7	−8.1	2.9	7.1	0.4	3.8	5.5
Fuel exporters	4.7	−1.6	1.7	−13.1	−15.1	−16.5	−3.7	0.7	−4.1	2.6	4.2
Non-fuel exporters	7.1	9.4	8.4	9.1	6.5	0.7	8.3	11.7	3.4	4.3	5.8
Imports											
Industrial countries	7.4	5.6	8.8	−0.7	−1.5	0.1	5.1	13.0	5.2	5.0	4.3
Developing countries	9.2	7.1	4.8	8.5	7.1	−4.2	−3.2	2.2	−0.3	−0.6	2.1
Fuel exporters	16.7	3.9	−4.3	13.3	20.0	−1.6	−12.0	−4.5	−8.8	−15.1	−7.9
Non-fuel exporters	6.6	8.9	9.3	6.5	1.5	−5.5	1.6	5.2	3.3	5.1	5.4
Unit value of trade (in SDR terms)[4]											
Exports											
Industrial countries	6.7	5.8	11.9	12.0	5.9	2.8	−0.4	1.6	0.6	1.1	2.8
Developing countries	12.8	−3.9	25.9	37.1	15.9	1.9	−4.7	4.2	−2.8	−18.0	1.6
Fuel exporters	20.3	−6.1	40.1	61.7	23.3	3.2	−8.6	3.4	−3.6	−39.4	−0.2
Non-fuel exporters	7.4	−1.6	13.6	12.6	7.5	0.5	−1.2	4.8	−2.4	−5.2	2.5
Imports											
Industrial countries	8.1	1.9	15.1	19.6	7.2	0.1	−2.7	0.5	−1.2	−5.2	2.7
Developing countries	7.4	3.2	13.5	17.5	12.5	3.2	−0.9	2.9	−0.7	−7.1	3.1
Fuel exporters	6.3	4.7	10.4	12.4	10.2	3.1	0.2	2.3	0.6	−3.2	3.7
Non-fuel exporters	7.7	2.3	15.1	19.7	13.5	3.3	−1.5	3.3	−1.2	−8.5	2.9
Terms of trade											
Industrial countries	−1.3	3.9	−2.8	−6.4	−1.2	2.7	2.3	1.1	1.8	6.7	0.1
Developing countries	5.0	−6.8	10.9	16.7	3.0	−1.2	−3.9	1.2	−2.2	−11.7	−1.4
Fuel exporters	13.2	−10.3	26.8	43.8	11.8	0.1	−8.8	1.1	−4.2	−37.4	−3.8
Non-fuel exporters	−0.3	−3.9	−1.2	−5.9	−5.3	−2.6	0.2	1.5	−1.2	3.6	−0.4
Memorandum											
World trade prices (in U.S. dollar terms) for major commodity groups[5]											
Manufactures	8.1	15.6	14.2	10.7	−4.9	−2.5	−3.3	−3.7	1.0	14.0	4.5
Oil	22.7	0.4	45.9	63.5	9.9	−4.2	−11.7	−2.1	−4.4	−40.0	−6.3
Non-oil primary commodities	9.9	−5.5	17.8	5.9	−13.9	−10.1	7.1	3.7	−12.2	12.0	1.0

[1] Excluding China prior to 1978.

[2] Compound annual rates of change.

[3] Averages based on data for the two groups of countries shown separately below and on partly estimated data for the U.S.S.R. and other nonmember countries of Eastern Europe and, for years prior to 1978, China.

[4] For years prior to 1970, an imputed value of US$1.00 has been assigned to the SDR.

[5] As represented, respectively, by the export unit value index for the manufactures of the industrial countries; the oil export unit value of the oil exporting countries (according to the former analytical categories); and the index of market quotations for non-oil primary commodities exported by the developing countries.

Table A21. Industrial Countries: Merchandise Trade, 1968–87
(Changes, in percent)

	Average 1968–77[1]	1978	1979	1980	1981	1982	1983	1984	1985	1986	1987
Total merchandise trade											
Value (in U.S. dollar terms)											
Exports	17.2	19.7	23.6	17.5	−0.6	−5.9	−1.2	6.5	3.6	16.8	7.3
Imports	17.9	15.4	29.3	19.6	−4.4	−6.2	−0.9	8.9	3.0	11.9	8.1
Volume											
Exports	8.1	5.5	7.0	4.1	3.6	−2.2	2.5	9.3	3.9	2.7	3.4
Imports	7.4	5.6	8.8	−0.7	−1.5	0.1	5.1	13.0	5.2	5.0	4.3
Unit value (in U.S. dollar terms)											
Exports	8.3	13.5	15.5	12.9	−4.1	−3.8	−3.6	−2.5	−0.3	13.7	3.8
Imports	9.8	9.3	18.8	20.5	−2.9	−6.3	−5.8	−3.6	−2.1	6.6	3.7
Terms of trade	−1.3	3.9	−2.8	−6.4	−1.2	2.7	2.3	1.1	1.8	6.7	0.1
Non-oil trade											
Value (in U.S. dollar terms)											
Exports	17.1	20.0	22.3	16.5	−1.1	−6.4	−1.2	6.7	3.7	19.5	7.7
Imports	16.3	19.4	25.1	14.2	−5.3	−3.6	2.3	11.4	5.2	21.0	9.5
Volume											
Exports	8.9	5.5	6.9	4.7	3.7	−2.9	2.2	9.5	3.9	2.5	3.5
Imports	8.3	9.0	10.7	3.7	1.6	2.4	7.0	15.1	6.9	5.3	4.5
Unit value (in U.S. dollar terms)											
Exports	7.5	13.8	14.4	11.4	−4.6	−3.5	−3.3	−2.5	−0.2	16.5	4.0
Imports	7.3	9.5	13.1	10.0	−6.8	−5.9	−4.5	−3.2	−1.6	15.0	4.7
Terms of trade	0.2	3.9	1.2	1.2	2.3	2.5	1.2	0.7	1.4	1.3	−0.7
Memorandum											
Real GNP[2]	3.8	3.5	3.3	1.4	0.7	−0.2	2.0	3.8	2.7	2.9	2.9
Apparent income elasticity of non-oil imports[3]	2.2	2.6	3.2	2.7	2.1	−11.8	3.5	4.0	2.6	1.9	1.6
Import volume of developing countries	9.2	7.1	4.8	8.5	7.1	−4.2	−3.2	2.2	−0.3	−0.6	2.1
Market prices of non-oil primary commodities (in U.S. dollar terms)[4]	8.9	−2.4	24.0	6.5	−13.8	−8.7	5.9	1.4	−11.0	11.6	3.0
Unit labor costs in manufacturing (in U.S. dollar terms)	7.3	13.3	9.1	10.1	−1.1	−0.8	−3.1	−5.7	—	14.8	2.1

[1] Compound annual rates of change.

[2] Averages of changes for individual countries weighted by the average U.S. dollar value of their respective non-oil imports over the preceding three years.

[3] Ratio of growth in non-oil imports to growth in real GNP.

[4] Average of individual commodity price indices weighted by the U.S. dollar value of industrial countries' imports of the respective commodities in 1979–81.

Table A22. Industrial Countries: Export Volumes, Import Volumes, and Terms of Trade, 1968–87[1]
(Annual changes, in percent)

	Average 1968–77[2]	1978	1979	1980	1981	1982	1983	1984	1985	1986	1987
Export volumes[3]											
Canada	7.1	10.2	1.5	0.5	3.6	−0.7	8.8	22.2	4.2	4.2	3.4
United States	6.6	10.6	13.8	9.9	−2.5	−11.2	−5.2	5.7	−1.2	3.3	9.2
Japan	15.1	−2.9	0.5	18.9	11.0	−2.1	8.2	15.6	4.8	−1.8	−2.5
France	9.8	6.6	9.0	3.5	4.0	−3.8	3.4	5.7	1.9	3.4	3.6
Germany, Fed. Rep. of	7.7	3.6	5.0	1.4	6.5	2.9	−0.2	9.6	6.4	4.0	3.0
Italy	8.8	10.8	7.7	−7.8	5.5	−0.5	3.5	6.5	6.5	3.5	3.0
United Kingdom	6.8	0.6	4.7	2.2	−1.3	1.7	0.8	7.1	5.8	3.0	2.4
Other industrial countries	7.7	6.0	8.3	1.8	2.3	0.9	5.7	8.5	5.3	3.2	3.5
All industrial countries	**8.1**	**5.5**	**7.0**	**4.1**	**3.6**	**−2.2**	**2.5**	**9.3**	**3.9**	**2.7**	**3.4**
Of which,											
Seven major countries above	8.3	5.3	6.6	4.9	4.0	−3.2	1.4	9.5	3.5	2.5	3.3
European countries	8.0	5.4	6.7	1.0	4.2	0.3	3.1	7.6	5.0	3.5	3.2
Import volumes[4]											
Canada	7.3	4.2	9.0	−5.3	2.7	−15.3	14.1	18.4	8.2	2.0	0.8
United States	7.3	11.9	2.5	−1.5	5.7	−0.3	14.6	28.7	6.5	4.1	3.2
Japan	8.4	4.7	12.0	−5.4	−2.0	−1.0	1.2	10.3	−0.4	5.5	5.0
France	9.8	6.1	11.9	6.2	−3.9	3.3	−1.4	2.7	4.3	6.5	5.8
Germany, Fed. Rep. of	8.8	7.1	7.8	−0.2	−5.0	1.0	4.0	5.5	4.6	6.6	5.8
Italy	5.9	7.4	13.2	2.6	−11.1	3.3	2.0	9.2	7.5	8.5	7.0
United Kingdom	4.1	3.6	13.0	−5.1	−4.6	3.0	5.6	10.4	4.6	3.1	3.9
Other industrial countries	7.0	1.3	9.4	0.8	−3.4	1.2	1.2	6.4	5.9	4.9	4.2
All industrial countries	**7.4**	**5.6**	**8.8**	**−0.7**	**−1.5**	**0.1**	**5.1**	**13.0**	**5.2**	**5.0**	**4.3**
Of which,											
Seven major countries above	7.5	7.3	8.6	−1.3	−0.9	−0.3	6.5	15.1	5.0	5.1	4.3
European countries	7.3	3.7	10.6	0.9	−4.9	1.6	2.3	6.2	5.1	5.9	5.1
Terms of trade[3]											
Canada	0.4	−4.0	5.9	−0.8	−3.8	−1.3	2.8	−4.4	−1.6	−3.7	−0.8
United States	−2.9	2.6	−2.8	−7.5	7.9	7.1	6.4	6.8	3.6	2.8	1.1
Japan	−3.6	16.9	−15.6	−21.1	1.4	0.2	3.3	2.2	3.6	21.6	−0.8
France	−0.3	4.1	−0.5	−6.3	−4.7	1.8	2.5	0.9	2.5	10.6	0.9
Germany, Fed. Rep. of	0.4	4.0	−5.5	−6.3	−6.7	3.7	1.6	−2.2	1.4	8.1	0.6
Italy	−2.1	2.1	−1.8	−6.2	−10.5	6.8	4.6	−1.5	0.4	11.1	1.0
United Kingdom	−2.1	5.8	3.9	3.7	0.5	−1.7	−1.1	−1.0	2.1	−4.1	—
Other industrial countries	−0.5	0.9	−1.0	−4.0	−2.0	1.5	−0.7	0.8	0.4	5.6	0.1
All industrial countries	**−1.3**	**3.9**	**−2.8**	**−6.4**	**−1.2**	**2.7**	**2.3**	**1.1**	**1.8**	**6.7**	**0.1**
Of which,											
Seven major countries above	−1.6	5.0	−3.4	−7.2	−1.0	3.1	3.3	1.2	2.3	7.0	0.1
European countries	−0.7	3.0	−1.5	−3.9	−4.4	2.3	1.0	−0.5	1.1	6.4	0.4

[1] Trade in goods only.

[2] Compound annual rates of change.

[3] Composites for country groups are averages of percentage changes for individual countries weighted by the average U.S. dollar value of their respective merchandise exports over the preceding three years.

[4] Composites for country groups are averages of percentage changes for individual countries weighted by the average U.S. dollar value of their respective merchandise imports over the preceding three years.

Table A23. Developing Countries: Merchandise Trade, 1968–87[1]
(Annual changes, in percent)

	Average 1968–77[2]	1978	1979	1980	1981	1982	1983	1984	1985	1986	1987
Developing countries											
Value (in U.S. dollar terms)											
Exports	21.1	7.2	36.3	32.6	−1.0	−12.4	−5.1	7.0	−3.3	−4.3	8.3
Imports	19.1	18.5	22.7	28.3	9.1	−7.5	−7.1	0.8	−1.9	3.8	6.3
Volume											
Exports	5.7	4.0	5.0	−4.0	−5.7	−8.1	2.9	7.1	0.4	3.8	5.5
Imports	9.2	7.1	4.8	8.5	7.1	−4.2	−3.2	2.2	−0.3	−0.6	2.1
Unit value (in U.S. dollar terms)											
Exports	14.6	3.1	29.9	38.1	5.0	−4.6	−7.7	−0.1	−3.8	−7.8	2.6
Imports	9.1	10.6	17.1	18.3	1.9	−3.4	−4.0	−1.3	−1.6	4.4	4.1
Terms of trade	5.0	−6.8	10.9	16.7	3.0	−1.2	−3.9	1.2	−2.2	−11.7	−1.4
Purchasing power of exports[3]	11.1	−3.1	16.4	12.1	−2.9	−9.3	−1.1	8.4	−1.8	−8.3	4.0
Memorandum											
Real GNP growth of trading partners	5.1	4.6	3.9	2.5	2.0	0.6	2.4	4.2	2.7	3.1	3.2
Market prices (in U.S. dollar terms) of primary commodities (excluding petroleum) exported by developing countries	9.9	−5.5	17.8	5.9	−13.9	−10.1	7.1	3.7	−12.2	12.0	1.0
Fuel exporters											
Value (in U.S. dollar terms)											
Exports	27.9	−0.9	47.0	41.5	−5.2	−19.3	−14.8	−0.2	−8.4	−30.1	5.0
Imports	26.0	16.7	9.1	28.3	19.9	−5.0	−14.6	−6.4	−9.1	−7.6	−3.6
Volume											
Exports	4.7	−1.6	1.7	−13.1	−15.1	−16.5	−3.7	0.7	−4.1	2.6	4.2
Imports	16.7	3.9	−4.3	13.3	20.0	−1.6	−12.0	−4.5	−8.8	−15.1	−7.9
Unit value (in U.S. dollar terms)											
Exports	22.2	0.7	44.5	62.9	11.7	−3.4	−11.5	−0.9	−4.5	−31.9	0.7
Imports	7.9	12.3	13.9	13.2	−0.1	−3.5	−2.9	−1.9	−0.3	8.8	4.7
Terms of trade	13.2	−10.3	26.8	43.8	11.8	0.1	−8.8	1.1	−4.2	−37.4	−3.8
Purchasing power of exports[3]	18.5	−11.8	29.1	24.9	−5.1	−16.3	−12.2	1.8	−8.1	−35.8	0.3
Memorandum											
Oil export volume (in billions of barrels)[4]	9.4	10.4	10.5	9.1	7.6	6.1	5.6	5.5	5.0	5.2	5.4
Average oil export price (in U.S. dollars per barrel)[4]	5.9	12.9	18.8	30.7	33.7	32.3	28.5	27.9	26.7	16.0	15.0
Annual percentage change	22.7	0.4	45.9	63.5	9.9	−4.2	−11.7	−2.1	−4.4	−40.0	−6.3
Real GNP growth of trading partners	5.0	4.6	3.9	2.4	1.9	0.5	2.3	4.1	2.7	3.0	3.2
Export unit value (in U.S. dollar terms) of manufactures[5]	8.1	15.6	14.2	10.7	−4.9	−2.5	−3.3	−3.7	1.0	14.0	4.5
Non-fuel exporters											
Value (in U.S. dollar terms)											
Exports	16.8	15.4	27.1	23.8	3.7	−5.2	3.5	12.2	—	11.1	9.5
Imports	16.5	19.5	29.8	28.4	4.4	−8.7	−3.1	4.2	1.1	8.1	9.5
Volume											
Exports	7.1	9.4	8.4	9.1	6.5	0.7	8.3	11.7	3.4	4.3	5.8
Imports	6.6	8.9	9.3	6.5	1.5	−5.5	1.6	5.2	3.3	5.1	5.4
Unit value (in U.S. dollar terms)											
Exports	9.0	5.5	17.3	13.5	−2.6	−5.9	−4.4	0.5	−3.3	6.5	3.5
Imports	9.4	9.8	18.7	20.6	2.8	−3.3	−4.6	−1.0	−2.1	2.8	3.9
Terms of trade	−0.3	−3.9	−1.2	−5.9	−5.3	−2.6	0.2	1.5	−1.2	3.6	−0.4
Purchasing power of exports[3]	6.8	5.1	7.0	2.7	0.9	−1.9	8.5	13.4	2.1	8.1	5.4

Table A23 *(concluded).* **Developing Countries: Merchandise Trade, 1968–87[1]**

(Annual changes, in percent)

	Average 1968–77[2]	1978	1979	1980	1981	1982	1983	1984	1985	1986	1987
Memorandum											
Real GNP growth of trading partners	5.1	4.6	4.0	2.6	2.0	0.8	2.6	4.2	2.7	3.1	3.2
Market price (in U.S. dollar terms) of primary commodities (excluding petroleum) exported by non-fuel exporters	11.4	−5.6	17.2	7.0	−13.8	−11.2	7.0	3.6	−12.3	12.3	1.0
Gross reserves (end of period) as percentage of total imports of goods and services[6]	26.7	26.6	22.8	17.7	16.3	17.1	19.2	21.1	22.1	23.1	23.2

[1] Excluding China prior to 1978.
[2] Compound annual rates of change.
[3] Export earnings deflated by import prices.
[4] Oil exporting countries, according to the former classification categories.
[5] Exported by the industrial countries.
[6] Gold holdings are valued at SDR 35 an ounce.

Table A24. Developing Countries: Export Volumes, 1968–87[1]
(Annual changes, in percent)

	Average 1968–77[2]	1978	1979	1980	1981	1982	1983	1984	1985	1986	1987
Developing countries	**5.7**	**4.0**	**5.0**	**−4.0**	**−5.7**	**−8.1**	**2.9**	**7.1**	**0.4**	**3.8**	**5.5**
By region											
Africa	3.5	3.6	7.7	—	−16.1	−7.0	3.8	4.6	6.1	3.1	6.1
Asia	10.9	10.4	9.5	9.2	9.3	0.5	10.1	14.0	2.5	6.2	5.6
Europe	7.5	6.7	2.7	4.8	11.5	1.3	8.0	14.6	4.6	4.1	6.4
Middle East	7.2	−3.3	0.4	−15.2	−17.9	−19.8	−8.9	−3.2	−5.9	2.9	4.4
Western Hemisphere	1.3	9.6	7.5	1.2	6.1	−2.2	7.1	7.3	−1.2	−0.2	4.8
By predominant export											
Fuel exporters	4.7	−1.6	1.7	−13.1	−15.1	−16.5	−3.7	0.7	−4.1	2.6	4.2
Non-fuel exporters	7.1	9.4	8.4	9.1	6.5	0.7	8.3	11.7	3.4	4.3	5.8
Primary product exporters	4.2	9.0	7.2	7.2	3.0	0.9	6.0	8.6	3.3	1.9	6.4
Agricultural exporters	4.7	8.3	5.4	6.3	9.5	2.2	6.7	11.6	1.9	2.8	7.2
Mineral exporters	3.6	10.5	10.9	9.0	−9.1	−2.0	4.3	0.6	7.4	−0.7	3.9
Exporters of manufactures	12.4	9.8	8.5	11.8	10.3	0.6	10.2	14.5	3.6	5.7	5.6
Service and remittance countries	3.6	8.9	16.4	3.7	2.5	0.9	8.0	9.2	2.0	8.1	4.3
By financial criteria											
Capital exporting countries	7.7	−3.2	0.3	−16.5	−19.0	−21.4	−9.6	−4.6	−7.5	1.6	4.1
Capital importing countries	5.7	7.6	7.5	4.4	2.3	−1.5	7.5	10.7	2.5	4.1	5.6
Market borrowers	6.3	9.3	8.1	3.9	1.0	−2.4	9.3	10.8	1.9	3.0	5.4
Official borrowers	1.5	−0.3	4.3	1.6	−5.6	−4.0	1.8	−1.4	1.9	8.2	4.3
Diversified borrowers	6.1	5.4	6.5	7.5	11.4	3.0	2.8	14.4	5.0	6.7	6.8
Countries with recent debt-servicing problems	3.2	5.5	6.3	3.3	−3.0	−4.2	5.4	7.0	1.4	0.6	4.5
Countries without debt-servicing problems	8.6	9.4	8.5	5.3	6.8	0.6	9.0	13.2	3.2	6.2	6.3
By miscellaneous criteria											
Capital importing fuel exporters	1.2	1.8	4.8	−6.0	−7.4	−7.4	5.0	7.4	−0.3	3.5	4.3
Fifteen heavily indebted countries	2.5	5.8	7.2	0.7	−2.0	−4.9	5.5	8.7	−0.2	0.4	4.9
Small low-income countries	0.3	2.1	3.5	7.8	−2.7	−0.6	4.0	0.2	4.0	11.3	4.0
Sub-Saharan Africa[3]	2.0	0.2	2.8	4.9	−2.6	4.4	0.4	4.9	0.7	9.1	3.2
By alternative analytical categories											
Oil exporting countries	5.1	−2.7	1.7	−14.9	−17.6	−19.6	−5.7	−0.4	−5.0	2.4	4.8
Non-oil developing countries	6.9	9.4	7.8	8.8	6.8	1.5	8.1	11.1	3.0	4.2	5.5
Net oil exporters	3.8	9.8	5.4	3.3	4.6	9.3	7.1	9.3	1.1	6.1	3.3
Net oil importers	7.3	9.4	8.3	10.0	7.3	—	8.3	11.5	3.4	3.9	5.9

[1] Excluding China prior to 1978.
[2] Compound annual rates of change.
[3] Excluding Nigeria and South Africa.

Table A25. Developing Countries: Import Volumes, 1968–87[1]
(Annual changes, in percent)

	Average 1968–77[2]	1978	1979	1980	1981	1982	1983	1984	1985	1986	1987
Developing countries	**9.2**	**7.1**	**4.8**	**8.5**	**7.1**	**−4.2**	**−3.2**	**2.2**	**−0.3**	**−0.6**	**2.1**
By region											
Africa	7.6	3.6	−3.7	9.3	10.3	−9.0	−10.1	−0.3	−5.2	−0.2	−1.5
Asia	7.8	16.4	13.4	10.2	4.1	−0.2	6.4	6.7	6.3	2.8	5.4
Europe	7.6	0.8	5.4	0.5	2.2	−7.7	2.2	6.9	4.1	5.3	8.0
Middle East	17.1	3.4	−3.6	9.4	16.8	5.9	−2.8	−6.3	−11.4	−13.3	−9.6
Western Hemisphere	7.0	5.5	8.0	9.3	2.6	−17.7	−22.2	2.9	−1.3	3.2	5.1
By predominant export											
Fuel exporters	16.7	3.9	−4.3	13.3	20.0	−1.6	−12.0	−4.5	−8.8	−15.1	−7.9
Non-fuel exporters	6.6	8.9	9.3	6.5	1.5	−5.5	1.6	5.2	3.3	5.1	5.4
Primary product exporters	5.0	3.4	6.8	6.7	−0.2	−8.8	−4.8	1.3	−3.8	9.2	6.0
Agricultural exporters	6.0	5.8	8.2	5.4	−4.8	−5.7	−1.5	0.3	−2.2	9.9	6.2
Mineral exporters	2.7	−2.9	3.1	10.2	12.7	−16.0	−13.4	4.3	−9.0	6.8	5.3
Exporters of manufactures	9.1	14.7	11.1	6.2	1.7	−4.9	6.5	8.9	9.3	4.2	6.4
Service and remittance countries	5.5	7.1	10.5	6.7	6.7	2.0	3.0	2.4	−1.4	−0.8	−0.5
By financial criteria											
Capital exporting countries	22.4	4.1	−6.8	13.3	22.3	7.8	−5.1	−8.9	−15.6	−17.8	−12.9
Capital importing countries	7.6	7.8	7.1	7.7	4.5	−6.5	−2.7	4.6	2.6	2.3	4.2
Market borrowers	9.1	8.3	7.4	8.9	6.9	−7.4	−6.5	3.0	−1.2	2.8	5.2
Official borrowers	3.9	5.1	1.5	0.2	−2.5	−1.4	1.0	1.1	−1.2	5.0	2.5
Diversified borrowers	5.9	7.7	9.0	7.9	1.1	−6.3	6.8	10.2	13.5	0.2	2.6
Countries with recent debt-servicing problems	6.8	4.5	4.6	5.4	3.7	−14.6	−15.0	1.8	−2.7	2.3	2.8
Countries without debt-servicing problems	8.4	10.5	9.1	9.4	5.2	−0.7	5.0	6.0	5.2	2.3	4.8
By miscellaneous criteria											
Capital importing fuel exporters	12.9	3.8	−1.6	13.4	18.0	−10.3	−19.7	1.2	−0.7	−12.3	−3.2
Fifteen heavily indebted countries	9.2	4.1	7.1	7.6	3.8	−16.5	−21.5	−2.2	−2.9	2.0	3.7
Small low-income countries	1.3	17.0	−0.6	2.8	−5.8	1.7	−2.3	5.5	−0.1	7.4	2.3
Sub-Saharan Africa[3]	3.8	8.1	−2.8	6.9	−3.6	−3.5	−7.7	−1.4	1.1	11.1	1.0
By alternative analytical categories											
Oil exporting countries	20.3	2.8	−8.5	12.3	22.1	5.1	−10.1	−7.4	−11.8	−16.5	−10.4
Non-oil developing countries	6.5	9.0	10.0	7.3	2.6	−7.5	−0.3	5.7	3.4	4.1	5.2
Net oil exporters	5.8	6.7	16.7	12.4	12.4	−13.8	−10.9	9.4	1.0	−4.2	−1.0
Net oil importers	6.7	9.3	9.0	6.5	0.9	−6.3	1.6	5.1	3.8	5.5	6.1

[1] Excluding China prior to 1978.
[2] Compound annual rates of change.
[3] Excluding Nigeria and South Africa.

Table A26. Developing Countries: Export Unit Values, 1968–87[1]
(Annual changes, in percent, in terms of U.S. dollars)

	Average 1968–77[2]	1978	1979	1980	1981	1982	1983	1984	1985	1986	1987
Developing countries	**14.6**	**3.1**	**29.9**	**38.1**	**5.0**	**−4.6**	**−7.7**	**−0.1**	**−3.8**	**−7.8**	**2.6**
By region											
Africa	13.2	1.9	28.6	37.9	−0.6	−8.3	−6.9	−1.9	−6.6	−11.5	−1.2
Asia	9.4	7.3	20.1	16.2	−0.1	−4.7	−4.6	1.8	−3.0	1.6	3.9
Europe	7.5	7.6	18.0	14.5	−0.7	−2.1	−7.7	−5.0	−2.2	8.9	4.6
Middle East	21.8	2.0	43.9	63.2	13.4	−2.3	−12.0	−1.9	−4.4	−32.5	1.1
Western Hemisphere	14.3	−2.0	24.0	28.6	0.6	−7.5	−5.8	2.7	−3.4	−3.3	2.8
By predominant export											
Fuel exporters	22.2	0.7	44.5	62.9	11.7	−3.4	−11.5	−0.9	−4.5	−31.9	0.7
Non-fuel exporters	9.0	5.5	17.3	13.5	−2.6	−5.9	−4.4	0.5	−3.3	6.5	3.5
Primary product exporters	10.2	2.2	19.1	14.5	−7.1	−9.2	−2.9	1.5	−5.5	8.4	2.6
Agricultural exporters	11.4	0.4	17.0	11.4	−6.0	−9.1	−3.3	3.9	−4.2	9.2	2.5
Mineral exporters	7.6	6.5	23.7	20.7	−9.0	−9.5	−2.2	−4.4	−9.2	6.1	2.9
Exporters of manufactures	7.4	9.0	15.8	11.6	1.4	−3.0	−5.1	—	−1.8	5.7	4.0
Service and remittance countries	8.4	5.6	15.2	19.8	−0.9	−6.3	−7.4	−1.9	−1.7	2.5	4.5
By financial criteria											
Capital exporting countries	23.1	1.0	45.8	66.1	13.8	−2.2	−12.7	−2.1	−4.7	−36.7	0.5
Capital importing countries	11.4	4.2	22.7	24.1	0.3	−5.7	−5.8	0.5	−3.5	−1.1	3.0
Market borrowers	12.2	3.3	24.7	27.4	0.6	−5.6	−6.2	0.7	−3.5	−2.7	2.8
Official borrowers	11.3	2.7	18.0	14.9	1.9	−6.5	−2.4	3.6	−3.3	5.2	2.0
Diversified borrowers	8.7	8.2	17.5	15.4	−1.9	−5.9	−5.1	−1.1	−3.6	3.2	4.0
Countries with recent debt-servicing problems	12.4	1.6	25.6	28.3	−0.2	−7.5	−5.8	0.6	−4.9	−3.6	3.1
Countries without debt-servicing problems	10.4	6.5	20.3	20.7	0.6	−4.4	−5.7	0.4	−2.6	0.5	2.9
By miscellaneous criteria											
Capital importing fuel exporters	20.3	0.1	41.9	56.3	7.6	−5.4	−9.7	0.7	−4.3	−27.0	0.9
Fifteen heavily indebted countries	14.7	−0.2	28.0	34.1	1.4	−7.1	−6.2	1.9	−3.8	−5.6	3.0
Small low-income countries	10.7	4.4	15.6	7.2	−6.3	−8.8	1.8	6.0	−6.3	10.9	2.2
Sub-Saharan Africa[3]	11.1	2.0	18.6	12.7	−9.1	−10.8	−3.2	2.4	−2.6	2.1	0.6
By alternative analytical categories											
Oil exporting countries	23.1	0.4	44.9	64.9	12.4	−2.6	−12.5	−1.2	−4.5	−34.4	−0.4
Non-oil developing countries	9.4	5.4	19.0	16.0	−1.8	−6.2	−4.6	0.5	−3.4	3.7	3.6
Net oil exporters	12.0	4.4	39.5	33.6	0.7	−8.9	−5.1	0.6	−5.6	−15.8	4.4
Net oil importers	8.9	5.6	15.8	12.7	−2.3	−5.6	−4.5	0.4	−3.0	7.6	3.5

[1] Excluding China prior to 1978.
[2] Compound annual rates of change.
[3] Excluding Nigeria and South Africa.

Table A27. Developing Countries: Import Unit Values, 1968–87[1]
(Annual changes, in percent, in terms of U.S. dollars)

	Average 1968–77[2]	1978	1979	1980	1981	1982	1983	1984	1985	1986	1987
Developing countries	**9.1**	**10.6**	**17.1**	**18.3**	**1.9**	**−3.4**	**−4.0**	**−1.3**	**−1.6**	**4.4**	**4.1**
By region											
Africa	9.0	12.8	18.3	19.7	−2.9	−3.6	−3.7	−4.2	−3.7	5.2	4.2
Asia	9.1	10.1	17.2	18.2	4.8	−4.0	−4.1	0.7	−1.8	3.9	3.8
Europe	9.4	7.8	19.7	19.2	−1.0	−1.8	−6.6	−3.4	−1.3	1.3	4.2
Middle East	8.2	13.4	15.3	15.5	−0.5	−4.4	−3.6	−1.9	−0.9	8.7	4.3
Western Hemisphere	9.3	8.2	16.4	20.1	5.2	−1.8	−3.2	−1.3	−0.4	1.9	4.5
By predominant export											
Fuel exporters	7.9	12.3	13.9	13.2	−0.1	−3.5	−2.9	−1.9	−0.3	8.8	4.7
Non-fuel exporters	9.4	9.8	18.7	20.6	2.8	−3.3	−4.6	−1.0	−2.1	2.8	3.9
Primary product exporters	9.6	9.8	18.6	24.2	3.7	−3.2	−3.8	−2.0	−2.4	1.0	4.4
Agricultural exporters	9.7	9.2	17.3	23.8	5.5	−3.7	−4.2	−1.2	−0.9	1.2	4.7
Mineral exporters	9.3	11.4	22.2	25.5	−0.9	−2.0	−2.8	−4.4	−6.8	0.4	3.5
Exporters of manufactures	9.0	10.5	18.5	18.4	3.3	−3.3	−4.3	—	−1.9	3.4	3.6
Service and remittance countries	9.5	7.4	20.1	17.3	−1.5	−3.8	−7.5	−1.6	−2.2	4.9	3.6
By financial criteria											
Capital exporting countries	7.3	13.6	13.4	11.7	−2.3	−4.0	−3.6	−2.1	−0.2	10.6	4.9
Capital importing countries	9.2	10.0	17.9	19.5	2.7	−3.3	−4.1	−1.1	−1.9	3.5	4.0
Market borrowers	9.2	9.6	17.4	18.0	2.9	−2.7	−3.8	−0.9	−2.0	3.5	4.2
Official borrowers	9.6	9.2	17.5	24.1	6.1	−4.4	−4.5	−1.0	−1.4	—	3.3
Diversified borrowers	8.9	11.8	19.3	21.6	0.5	−4.3	−5.0	−1.8	−1.8	4.6	3.9
Countries with recent debt-servicing problems	9.3	9.4	17.9	20.7	2.7	−2.8	−3.1	−2.0	−2.5	2.4	4.1
Countries without debt-servicing problems	9.1	10.6	17.8	18.6	2.6	−3.6	−4.7	−0.7	−1.6	3.9	3.9
By miscellaneous criteria											
Capital importing fuel exporters	8.3	11.1	14.5	14.7	1.9	−3.0	−2.2	−1.8	−0.5	7.1	4.6
Fifteen heavily indebted countries	9.1	8.6	16.6	18.4	4.5	−2.7	−2.8	−0.8	−0.7	3.1	4.5
Small low-income countries	9.5	10.7	17.7	21.2	2.7	−4.6	−4.2	−0.7	−1.8	2.4	3.6
Sub-Saharan Africa[3]	9.4	12.6	17.7	19.2	−2.0	−4.6	−4.3	−2.5	−0.6	4.0	4.3
By alternative analytical categories											
Oil exporting countries	7.2	13.1	13.4	11.6	−2.0	−4.0	−3.4	−2.0	−0.1	10.5	4.9
Non-oil developing countries	9.4	9.6	18.6	20.5	3.2	−3.2	−4.3	−1.0	−2.1	2.7	3.9
Net oil exporters	9.7	8.8	16.2	19.2	5.6	−2.1	−2.2	−2.2	−1.4	6.9	4.2
Net oil importers	9.3	9.8	19.0	20.7	2.8	−3.4	−4.7	−0.8	−2.2	2.1	3.9

[1] Excluding China prior to 1978.
[2] Compound annual rates of change.
[3] Excluding Nigeria and South Africa.

Table A28. Developing Countries: Terms of Trade, 1968–87[1]
(Annual changes, in percent)

	Average 1968–77[2]	1978	1979	1980	1981	1982	1983	1984	1985	1986	1987
Developing countries	**5.0**	**−6.8**	**10.9**	**16.7**	**3.0**	**−1.2**	**−3.9**	**1.2**	**−2.2**	**−11.7**	**−1.4**
By region											
Africa	3.8	−9.7	8.7	15.2	2.3	−4.8	−3.3	2.4	−3.0	−15.8	−5.2
Asia	0.3	−2.5	2.5	−1.8	−4.7	−0.8	−0.6	1.1	−1.2	−2.3	—
Europe	−1.8	−0.2	−1.4	−3.9	0.3	−0.3	−1.2	−1.6	−1.0	7.5	0.4
Middle East	12.5	−10.0	24.8	41.3	14.0	2.2	−8.8	—	−3.5	−37.9	−3.1
Western Hemisphere	4.6	−9.4	6.6	7.0	−4.4	−5.8	−2.8	4.0	−3.0	−5.1	−1.7
By predominant export											
Fuel exporters	13.2	−10.3	26.8	43.8	11.8	0.1	−8.8	1.1	−4.2	−37.4	−3.8
Non-fuel exporters	−0.3	−3.9	−1.2	−5.9	−5.3	−2.6	0.2	1.5	−1.2	3.6	−0.4
Primary product exporters	0.6	−6.9	0.4	−7.9	−10.4	−6.2	0.9	3.5	−3.2	7.3	−1.7
Agricultural exporters	1.6	−8.0	−0.3	−10.0	−10.9	−5.6	1.0	5.2	−3.3	7.9	−2.1
Mineral exporters	−1.5	−4.4	1.3	−3.8	−8.1	−7.7	0.6	—	−2.6	5.7	−0.6
Exporters of manufactures	−1.4	−1.3	−2.3	−5.8	−1.8	0.3	−0.8	—	0.1	2.2	0.4
Service and remittance countries	−0.9	−1.7	−4.1	2.2	0.6	−2.6	0.1	−0.3	0.6	−2.3	0.9
By financial criteria											
Capital exporting countries	14.8	−11.1	28.6	48.7	16.4	1.9	−9.4	—	−4.5	−42.7	−4.1
Capital importing countries	2.0	−5.3	4.1	3.9	−2.3	−2.6	−1.7	1.7	−1.7	−4.4	−1.0
Market borrowers	2.8	−5.7	6.2	8.0	−2.2	−3.0	−2.6	1.6	−1.6	−6.0	−1.3
Official borrowers	1.5	−6.0	0.5	−7.4	−4.0	−2.2	2.2	4.7	−1.9	5.1	−1.3
Diversified borrowers	−0.2	−3.3	−1.5	−5.1	−2.4	−1.7	−0.1	0.7	−1.9	−1.4	0.1
Countries with recent debt-servicing problems	2.8	−7.1	6.5	6.3	−2.8	−4.8	−2.8	2.7	−2.5	−5.8	−1.0
Countries without debt-servicing problems	1.2	−3.7	2.1	1.7	−1.9	−0.8	−1.0	1.1	−1.0	−3.3	−1.0
By miscellaneous criteria											
Capital importing fuel exporters	11.0	−9.8	24.0	36.2	5.6	−2.5	−7.7	2.5	−3.8	−31.8	−3.5
Fifteen heavily indebted countries	5.2	−8.1	9.8	13.3	−2.9	−4.5	−3.6	2.8	−3.1	−8.5	−1.5
Small low-income countries	1.1	−5.7	−1.8	−11.6	−8.7	−4.4	6.3	6.8	−4.5	8.3	−1.4
Sub-Saharan Africa[3]	1.6	−9.3	0.8	−5.4	−7.3	−6.5	1.2	5.0	−2.0	−1.9	−3.5
By alternative analytical categories											
Oil exporting countries	14.8	−11.2	27.8	47.7	14.7	1.4	−9.4	0.8	−4.4	−40.7	−5.0
Non-oil developing countries	—	−3.9	0.4	−3.8	−4.9	−3.1	−0.3	1.5	−1.4	0.9	−0.3
Net oil exporters	2.2	−4.1	20.1	12.1	−4.6	−6.9	−2.9	2.9	−4.3	−21.2	0.2
Net oil importers	−0.4	−3.8	−2.6	−6.6	−5.0	−2.3	0.2	1.3	−0.8	5.4	−0.4

[1] Excluding China prior to 1978.
[2] Compound annual rates of change.
[3] Excluding Nigeria and South Africa.

Table A29. Developing Countries: Non-Oil Commodity Prices, 1968–87[1]
(Annual changes, in percent)

	Average 1968–77[2]	1978	1979	1980	1981	1982	1983	1984	1985	1986	1987
Non-oil primary commodities	**9.9**	**−5.5**	**17.8**	**5.9**	**−13.9**	**−10.1**	**7.1**	**3.7**	**−12.2**	**12.0**	**1.0**
By commodity group[3]											
Food and beverages	12.4	−11.5	8.7	0.3	−12.9	−11.1	9.7	8.7	−15.3	19.9	−2.4
Food	6.8	12.6	13.1	13.2	−6.5	−19.2	11.2	2.9	−18.7	3.4	7.2
Beverages	18.4	−25.9	4.7	−12.4	−21.1	1.1	7.9	15.9	−11.6	36.6	−9.8
Agricultural raw materials	7.9	6.7	32.4	13.6	−15.0	−7.1	5.9	2.4	−12.2	3.7	5.8
Metals	5.2	4.0	30.7	9.7	−16.8	−10.3	4.4	−7.5	−2.8	1.1	5.0
By region[4]											
Africa	11.3	−11.6	15.7	5.0	−16.4	−9.8	6.2	3.4	−8.7	16.7	−0.5
Asia	7.6	6.5	19.3	9.9	−12.4	−16.8	8.6	10.3	−19.6	0.9	5.0
Europe	6.6	11.3	26.2	8.1	−7.5	−4.9	5.6	0.3	−9.4	4.1	6.1
Middle East	9.0	0.7	11.3	17.1	−7.4	−15.8	11.0	0.1	−14.5	1.3	7.6
Western Hemisphere	11.0	−12.0	15.8	5.1	−14.5	−8.2	6.0	−0.5	−8.3	20.1	−1.5
By predominant export[4]											
Fuel exporters	11.8	−6.7	21.4	4.4	−17.8	−9.3	7.7	4.2	−11.6	12.5	0.4
Non-fuel exporters	9.7	−5.6	17.2	7.0	−13.8	−11.2	7.0	3.6	−12.3	12.3	1.0
Primary product exporters	10.1	−6.9	17.7	6.4	−14.9	−11.0	7.1	2.9	−11.5	13.6	0.4
Agricultural exporters	11.5	−8.5	15.1	4.4	−14.9	−10.4	7.6	5.4	−12.9	14.8	−0.7
Mineral exporters	5.6	0.1	28.9	13.7	−15.1	−13.1	5.4	−6.1	−5.7	9.3	4.9
Exporters of manufactures	7.6	1.3	15.9	8.7	−7.8	−10.4	5.3	9.9	−18.1	6.2	4.5
Service and remittance countries	7.2	6.9	9.9	16.1	−4.9	−17.7	8.1	0.2	−12.5	1.9	5.8
By financial criteria[4]											
Capital exporting countries	6.2	9.4	8.3	15.2	−7.2	−22.1	11.1	3.5	−19.8	6.3	6.5
Capital importing countries	10.0	−5.8	17.7	6.6	−14.3	−11.0	7.0	3.7	−12.2	12.3	0.9
Market borrowers	10.2	−5.6	21.0	4.3	−15.4	−9.7	7.2	3.8	−12.3	12.2	0.9
Official borrowers	10.3	−9.5	14.0	8.5	−16.1	−12.3	7.4	1.4	−7.6	15.5	−1.0
Diversified borrowers	8.8	−2.9	10.6	13.2	−8.6	−13.9	6.3	5.2	−16.0	9.9	2.9
Countries with recent debt-servicing problems	10.0	−7.8	17.8	5.3	−14.6	−10.2	7.4	0.9	−10.0	14.1	0.9
Countries without debt-servicing problems	9.8	−2.8	17.6	8.6	−13.8	−12.1	6.4	7.6	−15.2	9.8	1.0
By miscellaneous criteria[4]											
Capital importing fuel exporters	11.9	−7.1	21.8	4.1	−18.1	−8.9	7.6	4.3	−11.3	12.6	0.2
Fifteen heavily indebted countries	10.7	−9.8	17.5	2.9	−14.3	−8.8	6.4	2.2	−10.4	16.1	−0.1
Small low-income countries	10.8	−11.1	9.4	1.7	−14.0	−11.1	9.0	9.8	−13.0	13.4	−1.4
Sub-Saharan Africa	12.0	−13.1	14.4	1.2	−18.2	−8.3	7.8	4.5	−8.3	17.7	−2.0

Table A29 *(concluded).* **Developing Countries: Non-Oil Commodity Prices, 1968–87[1]**
(Annual changes, in percent)

	Average 1968–77[2]	1978	1979	1980	1981	1982	1983	1984	1985	1986	1987
By alternative analytical categories[4]											
Oil exporting countries	11.1	−2.8	24.8	5.7	−19.4	−9.9	7.8	4.9	−13.1	9.8	1.5
Non-oil developing countries	9.9	−6.1	17.2	6.9	−13.8	−11.2	6.9	3.5	−12.1	12.6	0.9
Net oil exporters	9.9	1.9	24.7	6.1	−16.1	−12.8	8.1	4.9	−14.2	4.3	2.8
Net oil importers	9.9	−7.4	15.6	6.9	−13.3	−10.8	6.7	3.3	−11.7	14.2	0.6
Memorandum											
Oil export unit value[5]	22.7	0.4	45.9	63.5	9.9	−4.2	−11.7	−2.1	−4.4	−40.0	−6.3
Export unit value of manufactures[6]	8.1	15.6	14.2	10.7	−4.9	−2.5	−3.3	−3.7	1.0	14.0	4.5

[1] In U.S. dollar terms.

[2] Compound annual rates of change.

[3] Based on averages of component commodity price indices weighted by the U.S. dollar value of exports of each commodity from developing countries in 1979–81.

[4] Based on averages of individual commodity price indices weighted according to the 1979–81 composition of commodity exports of the respective groups of developing countries.

[5] Of the oil exporting countries (according to the former analytical categories).

[6] Exported by the industrial countries.

211

Table A30. Summary of Payments Balances on Current Account, 1978–87[1]

(In billions of U.S. dollars)

	1978	1979	1980	1981	1982	1983	1984	1985	1986	1987
Industrial countries	**14.5**	**−25.5**	**−61.8**	**−18.9**	**−22.2**	**−23.0**	**−64.1**	**−54.2**	**13.5**	**−9.3**
United States	−15.4	−1.0	1.9	6.3	−8.1	−46.0	−107.4	−117.7	−110.5	−108.8
Other industrial countries	30.0	−24.6	−63.7	−25.2	−14.1	23.0	43.2	63.4	124.0	99.5
Of which,										
Japan	16.5	−8.8	−10.7	4.8	6.9	20.8	35.0	49.7	72.0	62.0
Germany, Fed. Rep. of	9.0	−6.1	−15.8	−5.5	3.4	4.1	6.8	13.2	25.4	20.1
Developing countries	**−34.5**	**7.1**	**27.9**	**−49.2**	**−90.9**	**−58.9**	**−35.1**	**−34.1**	**−69.3**	**−57.9**
By region										
Africa	−12.8	−3.4	−1.6	−21.9	−21.3	−11.6	−6.7	−1.4	−11.6	−10.1
Asia	−6.8	−12.6	−19.3	−20.7	−17.3	−14.3	−4.8	−15.4	−15.4	−16.9
Europe	−7.1	−10.0	−12.3	−9.9	−6.1	−4.2	−1.9	−2.3	1.3	0.4
Middle East	11.2	54.2	90.7	45.8	−5.1	−18.5	−18.1	−10.7	−36.7	−24.7
Western Hemisphere	−19.0	−21.1	−29.5	−42.6	−41.1	−10.3	−3.6	−4.3	−6.9	−6.6
By analytical criteria										
Fuel exporters	−6.1	51.4	95.1	31.0	−25.6	−14.8	−8.6	−6.5	−49.0	−35.6
Non-fuel exporters	−28.4	−44.3	−67.1	−80.2	−65.3	−44.1	−26.5	−27.6	−20.3	−22.3
Market borrowers	−31.8	−29.2	−35.3	−71.2	−72.3	−27.2	−3.6	1.7	−10.3	−9.8
Official borrowers	−7.2	−5.9	−9.1	−11.7	−10.3	−9.2	−9.9	−9.0	−9.1	−9.9
Other countries[2]	**−9.5**	**−6.5**	**−4.6**	**−3.3**	**−0.5**	**1.1**	**2.3**	**−2.4**	**−8.5**	**...**
Total[3]	**−29.5**	**−24.9**	**−38.5**	**−71.5**	**−113.5**	**−80.8**	**−96.9**	**−90.8**	**−64.3**	**−75.7**
Memorandum										
Total, by selected categories										
Trade balance	10.9	17.3	27.0	20.4	−3.4	4.7	9.2	1.4	9.5	8.4
Timing asymmetry[4]	10.0	23.0	11.0	−3.0	−10.0	2.0	—	4.0	11.0	9.0
Residual asymmetry	0.9	−5.7	16.0	23.4	6.6	2.7	9.2	−2.6	−1.5	−0.6
Balance on services	−28.3	−31.5	−50.3	−78.7	−95.0	−75.0	−96.9	−80.9	−60.4	−67.2
(in percent of service payments)	−6.1	−5.3	−6.7	−9.2	−11.1	−9.5	−11.7	−9.7	−6.4	−6.7
Private transfers net	1.0	1.4	0.5	0.1	−1.4	0.9	3.1	3.1	−0.4	−0.7
Official transfers net	−13.3	−12.0	−15.7	−13.3	−13.6	−11.4	−12.3	−14.3	−12.9	−16.2

[1] Including official transfers.

[2] Covers estimated balances on current transactions only in convertible currencies of the U.S.S.R. and other nonmember countries of Eastern Europe.

[3] Reflects errors, omissions, and asymmetries in reported balance of payments statistics on current account, plus balance of listed groups with countries not included. In the estimate for 1987, the current balance for the group of "Other countries" has been assumed to remain at the same level as projected for 1986.

[4] Staff estimates of the difference between the beginning-of-year and end-of-year "float," that is, the value of those exports that have not yet been recorded as imports (usually because the goods are in transit or because of delays in the processing of the documentation). The estimates should be viewed only as rough orders of magnitude.

Table A31. Industrial Countries: Balance of Payments on Current Account, 1978–87[1]

(In billions of U.S. dollars)

	1978	1979	1980	1981	1982	1983	1984	1985	1986	1987
Balance on current account										
Canada	−4.3	−4.1	−1.0	−5.1	2.2	1.4	2.0	−1.9	−4.2	−3.3
United States	−15.4	−1.0	1.9	6.3	−8.1	−46.0	−107.4	−117.7	−110.5	−108.8
Japan	16.5	−8.8	−10.7	4.8	6.9	20.8	35.0	49.7	72.0	62.0
France	7.0	5.2	−4.2	−4.8	−12.1	−4.7	−0.8	0.3	9.0	7.9
Germany, Fed. Rep. of	9.0	−6.1	−15.8	−5.5	3.4	4.1	6.8	13.2	25.4	20.1
Italy	6.2	5.5	−9.7	−8.2	−5.5	0.8	−3.0	−3.7	2.1	−1.1
United Kingdom	1.9	−1.6	7.2	13.2	7.1	4.7	1.1	3.8	3.9	−0.7
Other industrial countries	−6.4	−14.7	−29.6	−19.7	−15.9	−4.1	2.0	1.9	15.9	14.5
All industrial countries	**14.5**	**−25.5**	**−61.8**	**−18.9**	**−22.2**	**−23.0**	**−64.1**	**−54.2**	**13.5**	**−9.3**
Of which,										
Seven major countries above	20.9	−10.8	−32.3	0.8	−6.3	−18.9	−66.1	−56.2	−2.4	−23.8
European countries	22.9	−8.2	−47.1	−15.5	−13.5	7.7	16.1	24.8	63.6	48.0
All industrial countries except the United States	30.0	−24.6	−63.7	−25.2	−14.1	23.0	43.2	63.4	124.0	99.5
Memorandum										
Balance on goods and services										
Canada	−4.4	−4.7	−2.0	−6.3	1.1	0.7	1.2	−2.7	−5.1	−4.3
United States	−10.3	4.7	8.9	13.2	0.1	−37.1	−95.9	−102.8	−98.5	−96.4
Japan	17.2	−7.6	−9.2	6.4	8.2	22.4	36.5	51.4	73.7	63.7
France	10.3	9.2	—	−0.5	−7.5	−0.9	2.1	3.7	13.9	13.2
Germany, Fed. Rep. of	17.9	5.5	−2.3	6.3	15.0	14.7	17.4	23.7	40.1	37.0
Italy	6.6	5.0	−10.9	−8.9	−6.4	−0.4	−4.1	−4.8	0.7	−2.4
United Kingdom	5.3	3.3	12.0	17.2	10.6	8.0	4.2	8.6	6.8	4.0
Other industrial countries	−4.6	−12.9	−26.8	−16.1	−12.4	−0.9	4.7	5.4	21.1	19.4
All industrial countries	**38.0**	**2.5**	**−30.2**	**11.2**	**8.6**	**6.5**	**−33.8**	**−17.6**	**52.6**	**34.2**
Of which,										
Seven major countries above	42.6	15.4	−3.4	27.3	21.0	7.4	−38.5	−23.0	31.5	14.8
European countries	40.1	13.1	−23.3	7.0	8.5	27.1	33.9	45.6	89.4	78.1
All industrial countries except the United States	48.4	−2.2	−39.1	−2.0	8.5	43.7	62.1	85.3	151.1	130.6
Official transfers, net										
Canada	−0.3	0.1	0.3	0.3	0.2	—	−0.2	−0.3	−0.1	−0.2
United States	−3.2	−3.6	−4.7	−4.5	−5.5	−6.3	−8.5	−11.2	−8.5	−8.8
Japan	−0.4	−0.9	−1.3	−1.4	−1.3	−1.4	−1.4	−1.5	−1.5	−1.5
France	−1.5	−1.7	−1.7	−2.0	−2.7	−2.1	−1.9	−1.9	−2.8	−3.0
Germany, Fed. Rep. of	−4.4	−6.1	−7.4	−6.6	−6.7	−5.9	−6.4	−6.2	−8.9	−10.0
Italy	−1.5	−1.0	−0.2	−0.7	−0.6	−0.2	−0.2	−0.3	−0.4	−0.4
United Kingdom	−3.2	−4.3	−4.1	−3.3	−3.2	−3.0	−2.9	−4.5	−2.6	−4.3
Other industrial countries	−1.9	−1.9	−2.9	−3.3	−3.4	−2.8	−2.5	−3.0	−4.1	−3.6
All industrial countries	**−16.4**	**−19.4**	**−22.1**	**−21.5**	**−23.1**	**−21.7**	**−24.0**	**−28.8**	**−28.9**	**−31.9**
Of which,										
Seven major countries above	−14.4	−17.4	−19.2	−18.2	−19.7	−18.8	−21.5	−25.9	−24.8	−28.3
European countries	−11.9	−14.4	−15.6	−15.2	−15.7	−13.3	−13.0	−15.2	−18.0	−20.7
All industrial countries except the United States	−13.2	−15.8	−17.3	−17.0	−17.6	−15.4	−15.4	−17.6	−20.4	−23.1

[1] Including official transfers.

Table A32. Industrial Countries: Current Account Transactions, 1978–87
(In billions of U.S. dollars)

	1978	1979	1980	1981	1982	1983	1984	1985	1986	1987
Exports (f.o.b.)	832.9	1,029.4	1,209.3	1,201.7	1,130.8	1,117.1	1,189.5	1,232.6	1,439.2	1,543.9
Imports (f.o.b.)	824.3	1,065.5	1,274.9	1,219.3	1,143.4	1,132.7	1,233.6	1,270.0	1,421.3	1,536.7
Trade balance	**8.6**	**−36.1**	**−65.5**	**−17.6**	**−12.7**	**−15.6**	**−44.0**	**−37.5**	**17.9**	**7.2**
Services receipts	334.6	435.2	534.9	589.5	584.6	540.3	560.8	583.9	706.8	750.8
Services payments	305.2	396.7	499.5	560.7	563.4	518.2	550.6	564.0	672.1	723.7
Balance on services	29.4	38.6	35.4	28.7	21.2	22.1	10.2	19.9	34.7	27.0
Balance on goods and services	**38.1**	**2.5**	**−30.1**	**11.2**	**8.6**	**6.5**	**−33.9**	**−17.6**	**52.6**	**34.2**
Private transfers, net	−7.1	−8.7	−9.6	−8.7	−7.6	−7.8	−6.4	−7.8	−10.1	−11.6
Official transfers, net	−16.4	−19.4	−22.1	−21.5	−23.1	−21.7	−24.0	−28.8	−28.9	−31.9
Balance on current account	**14.6**	**−25.6**	**−61.8**	**−18.9**	**−22.2**	**−23.0**	**−64.2**	**−54.2**	**13.5**	**−9.3**
Memorandum										
Current account balance as percentage of GNP	0.2	−0.4	−0.8	−0.2	−0.3	−0.3	−0.8	−0.6	0.1	−0.1
Current account balance as percentage of exports of goods and services	1.2	−1.7	−3.5	−1.1	−1.3	−1.4	−3.7	−3.0	0.6	−0.4
Exports of goods and services	1,167.5	1,464.6	1,744.3	1,791.2	1,715.4	1,657.4	1,750.3	1,816.5	2,146.0	2,294.6
Oil trade balance[1]	−119.9	−174.5	−247.1	−237.6	−193.4	−163.6	−159.7	−142.2	−91.0	−87.1

[1] Figures shown are on a balance of payments basis with rough adjustments to those countries' oil trade balance data that are only available on a trade returns basis.

214

Table A33. Developing Countries: Summary of Payments Balances on Current Account, 1978–87[1]

(In billions of U.S. dollars)

	1978	1979	1980	1981	1982	1983	1984	1985	1986	1987
Developing countries	**−34.5**	**7.1**	**27.9**	**−49.2**	**−90.9**	**−58.9**	**−35.1**	**−34.1**	**−69.3**	**−57.9**
By region										
Africa	−12.8	−3.4	−1.6	−21.9	−21.3	−11.6	−6.7	−1.4	−11.6	−10.1
Asia	−6.8	−12.6	−19.3	−20.7	−17.3	−14.3	−4.8	−15.4	−15.4	−16.9
Europe	−7.1	−10.0	−12.3	−9.9	−6.1	−4.2	−1.9	−2.3	1.3	0.4
Middle East	11.2	54.2	90.7	45.8	−5.1	−18.5	−18.1	−10.7	−36.7	−24.7
Western Hemisphere	−19.0	−21.1	−29.5	−42.6	−41.1	−10.3	−3.6	−4.3	−6.9	−6.6
By predominant export										
Fuel exporters	−6.1	51.4	95.1	31.0	−25.6	−14.8	−8.6	−6.5	−49.0	−35.6
Non-fuel exporters	−28.4	−44.3	−67.1	−80.2	−65.3	−44.1	−26.5	−27.6	−20.3	−22.3
Primary product exporters	−19.2	−23.8	−40.2	−57.5	−54.8	−38.2	−26.0	−17.7	−15.1	−17.2
Agricultural exporters	−16.8	−24.3	−38.7	−41.2	−42.5	−33.3	−19.8	−16.8	−14.1	−15.3
Mineral exporters	−2.4	0.4	−1.5	−16.3	−12.3	−4.9	−6.2	−0.9	−1.0	−1.9
Exporters of manufactures	−5.1	−14.6	−20.1	−12.5	−1.5	2.2	7.3	−2.0	4.4	2.5
Service and remittance countries	−4.1	−5.8	−6.8	−10.2	−9.0	−8.1	−7.8	−8.0	−9.5	−7.6
By financial criteria										
Capital exporting countries	13.6	56.3	92.5	50.2	−1.1	−11.8	−12.5	−7.4	−31.0	−20.8
Capital importing countries	−48.2	−49.2	−64.6	−99.5	−89.8	−47.1	−22.6	−26.8	−38.3	−37.1
Market borrowers	−31.8	−29.2	−35.3	−71.2	−72.3	−27.2	−3.6	1.7	−10.3	−9.8
Official borrowers	−7.2	−5.9	−9.1	−11.7	−10.3	−9.2	−9.9	−9.0	−9.1	−9.9
Diversified borrowers	−9.2	−14.1	−20.2	−16.6	−7.2	−10.7	−9.1	−19.4	−18.8	−17.4
Countries with recent debt-servicing problems	−31.7	−31.6	−38.5	−67.2	−62.3	−20.6	−8.4	−4.7	−14.0	−10.3
Countries without debt-servicing problems	−16.4	−17.6	−26.1	−32.2	−27.5	−26.5	−14.2	−22.1	−24.3	−26.8
By miscellaneous criteria										
Capital importing fuel exporters	−19.7	−4.9	2.5	−19.2	−24.5	−3.0	3.9	0.9	−18.0	−14.8
Fifteen heavily indebted countries	−24.7	−24.5	−28.7	−50.0	−50.1	−13.8	−0.9	−0.1	−7.3	−5.1
Small low-income countries	−5.9	−6.9	−8.7	−9.0	−8.6	−6.0	−6.9	−6.8	−6.9	−7.5
Sub-Saharan Africa[2]	−5.4	−5.5	−8.1	−9.4	−8.4	−6.1	−3.9	−3.9	−5.4	−6.0
By alternative analytical categories										
Oil exporting countries	−1.3	56.8	102.4	45.8	−17.8	−18.0	−10.0	−5.5	−44.1	−31.1
Non-oil developing countries	−33.2	−49.7	−74.4	−95.0	−73.2	−40.9	−25.0	−28.7	−25.2	−26.7
Net oil exporters	−5.9	−5.5	−8.1	−21.0	−15.4	−2.9	−2.5	−5.3	−14.0	−11.3
Net oil importers	−27.3	−44.2	−66.4	−74.0	−57.8	−38.0	−22.5	−23.3	−11.2	−15.4

[1] Including official transfers.

[2] Excluding Nigeria and South Africa.

Table A34. Developing Countries: Summary of Payments Balances on Goods, Services, and Private Transfers, 1978–87

(In billions of U.S. dollars)

	1978	1979	1980	1981	1982	1983	1984	1985	1986	1987
Developing countries	**−36.6**	**0.8**	**22.6**	**−56.4**	**−99.4**	**−68.2**	**−45.7**	**−47.7**	**−84.3**	**−72.5**
By region										
Africa	−15.5	−6.7	−5.4	−25.6	−24.8	−15.3	−10.3	−5.7	−15.6	−13.9
Asia	−8.7	−15.1	−21.9	−23.7	−20.2	−17.0	−7.6	−18.2	−18.3	−19.9
Europe	−7.2	−10.1	−12.4	−10.2	−6.8	−5.3	−3.0	−3.3	0.3	−0.6
Middle East	14.2	54.4	92.5	46.5	−5.6	−19.1	−20.0	−14.6	−42.1	−30.0
Western Hemisphere	−19.4	−21.8	−30.2	−43.3	−42.0	−11.4	−4.9	−5.9	−8.6	−8.2
By predominant export										
Fuel exporters	−1.0	54.6	100.1	35.0	−22.6	−12.6	−7.3	−5.3	−48.4	−35.5
Non-fuel exporters	−35.6	−53.8	−77.5	−91.4	−76.7	−55.6	−38.5	−42.4	−35.9	−37.0
Primary product exporters	−23.1	−28.6	−45.5	−63.0	−60.4	−44.2	−32.0	−24.8	−22.1	−23.9
Agricultural exporters	−19.4	−27.4	−42.4	−44.8	−46.7	−37.9	−24.5	−22.2	−19.7	−20.8
Mineral exporters	−3.7	−1.1	−3.1	−18.2	−13.8	−6.3	−7.4	−2.5	−2.4	−3.1
Exporters of manufactures	−6.9	−16.9	−22.5	−14.8	−3.4	−0.1	4.3	−6.5	−0.4	−1.5
Service and remittance countries	−5.7	−8.3	−9.5	−13.5	−12.9	−11.3	−10.8	−11.1	−13.4	−11.7
By financial criteria										
Capital exporting countries	19.8	61.6	99.6	56.7	3.7	−7.8	−9.3	−4.7	−29.0	−19.3
Capital importing countries	−56.4	−60.8	−77.0	−113.0	−103.0	−60.4	−36.4	−43.0	−55.3	−53.2
Market borrowers	−32.8	−30.4	−36.7	−73.1	−74.3	−29.6	−5.8	−0.5	−12.5	−11.9
Official borrowers	−11.0	−12.1	−16.0	−19.0	−17.5	−15.7	−16.3	−15.5	−15.8	−16.7
Diversified borrowers	−12.6	−18.3	−24.2	−21.0	−11.2	−15.2	−14.3	−27.0	−27.1	−24.7
Countries with recent debt-servicing problems	−34.8	−35.2	−42.1	−71.3	−66.7	−25.0	−12.8	−10.5	−20.5	−16.7
Countries without debt-servicing problems	−21.6	−25.7	−34.9	−41.7	−36.4	−35.5	−23.6	−32.5	−34.8	−36.6
By miscellaneous criteria										
Capital importing fuel exporters	−20.8	−7.0	0.5	−21.7	−26.3	−4.8	2.0	−0.6	−19.4	−16.2
Fifteen heavily indebted countries	−25.4	−25.4	−29.4	−50.9	−50.8	−14.8	−1.6	−1.4	−8.4	−5.9
Small low-income countries	−8.7	−10.2	−12.5	−12.9	−12.9	−10.1	−11.2	−11.5	−11.6	−12.4
Sub-Saharan Africa[1]	−7.6	−8.1	−11.3	−12.4	−11.5	−9.4	−7.3	−7.6	−9.1	−9.8
By alternative analytical categories										
Oil exporting countries	4.9	62.0	109.4	52.0	−13.1	−14.1	−6.9	−2.9	−42.1	−29.7
Non-oil developing countries	−41.5	−61.3	−86.8	−108.4	−86.3	−54.2	−38.8	−44.8	−42.2	−42.8
Net oil exporters	−7.5	−7.8	−10.3	−23.4	−17.5	−5.1	−4.7	−7.5	−16.8	−14.2
Net oil importers	−34.1	−53.5	−76.6	−84.9	−68.8	−49.1	−34.1	−37.3	−25.4	−28.6

[1] Excluding Nigeria and South Africa.

Table A35. Developing Countries: Current Account Balances as Percentage of Exports of Goods and Services, 1968–87[1]

(In percent)

	Average 1968–77	1978	1979	1980	1981	1982	1983	1984	1985	1986	1987
Developing countries	**−2.9**	**−8.1**	**1.2**	**3.7**	**−6.3**	**−13.1**	**−8.9**	**−5.0**	**−5.1**	**−10.6**	**−8.2**
Memorandum: Median estimate	−11.1	−15.5	−13.5	−17.8	−27.0	−24.6	−22.5	−15.7	−16.8	−16.9	−16.6
By region											
Africa	−11.1	−21.9	−4.4	−1.5	−23.8	−27.0	−15.3	−8.7	−1.9	−16.2	−13.3
Asia	−6.1	−5.9	−8.4	−10.2	−9.7	−8.3	−6.6	−1.9	−6.3	−5.8	−5.8
Europe	−10.3	−18.7	−21.1	−21.4	−15.8	−9.9	−7.1	−3.0	−3.5	1.7	0.5
Middle East	14.1	7.9	27.1	32.6	16.8	−2.3	−9.8	−10.2	−6.7	−30.0	−19.4
Western Hemisphere	−18.0	−26.5	−22.1	−23.4	−31.0	−33.4	−8.7	−2.8	−3.4	−5.6	−5.0
By predominant export											
Fuel exporters	6.7	−3.3	19.2	25.2	8.3	−8.3	−5.6	−3.3	−2.7	−27.3	−19.1
Non-fuel exporters	−11.3	−11.9	−14.5	−17.5	−19.9	−16.8	−11.2	−6.1	−6.4	−4.2	−4.3
Primary product exporters	−17.5	−18.6	−18.0	−24.5	−35.9	−36.8	−25.5	−15.9	−11.0	−8.5	−8.8
Agricultural exporters	−19.1	−23.3	−27.0	−35.7	−36.7	−40.2	−31.2	−16.3	−13.9	−10.4	−10.2
Mineral exporters	−14.6	−7.8	1.0	−2.7	−34.0	−28.5	−11.4	−14.8	−2.3	−2.3	−4.2
Exporters of manufactures	−3.4	−4.7	−10.5	−11.6	−6.4	−0.8	1.1	3.3	−0.9	1.7	0.9
Service and remittance countries	−15.4	−16.1	−17.7	−15.0	−21.8	−19.6	−18.3	−17.2	−18.0	−20.2	−14.7
By financial criteria											
Capital exporting countries	18.1	11.0	31.9	37.6	21.1	−0.6	−7.5	−8.6	−5.8	−34.3	−22.6
Capital importing countries	−11.0	−16.0	−12.5	−12.6	−18.5	−17.8	−9.4	−4.1	−4.9	−6.8	−6.0
Market borrowers	−11.7	−15.0	−10.3	−9.4	−18.2	−20.0	−7.5	−0.9	0.4	−2.6	−2.3
Official borrowers	−17.8	−26.7	−17.9	−23.4	−30.5	−29.0	−26.3	−28.1	−25.4	−23.0	−23.3
Diversified borrowers	−6.1	−14.7	−17.8	−20.0	−15.2	−6.6	−10.0	−7.7	−16.4	−14.6	−12.1
Countries with recent debt-servicing problems	−14.0	−23.6	−17.7	−16.2	−28.4	−29.9	−10.2	−3.9	−2.2	−6.8	−4.6
Countries without debt-servicing problems	−8.3	−9.8	−8.1	−9.4	−10.7	−9.2	−8.8	−4.3	−6.6	−6.7	−6.8
By miscellaneous criteria											
Capital importing fuel exporters	−11.6	−31.5	−5.5	1.9	−14.2	−21.0	−2.7	3.3	0.8	−20.3	−15.8
Fifteen heavily indebted countries	−14.7	−28.2	−20.4	−17.8	−30.4	−35.0	−10.1	−0.6	−0.1	−5.2	−3.3
Small low-income countries	−24.5	−38.8	−37.4	−40.4	−45.3	−46.9	−31.3	−34.4	−34.8	−29.1	−29.4
Sub-Saharan Africa[2]	−12.4	−26.1	−21.7	−26.7	−34.6	−33.3	−25.1	−15.4	−15.6	−19.2	−20.3
By alternative analytical categories											
Oil exporting countries	11.3	−0.8	24.0	30.8	14.2	−6.9	−8.2	−4.7	−2.8	−31.9	−22.0
Non-oil developing countries	−12.2	−12.7	−14.8	−17.4	−20.9	−16.7	−9.3	−5.2	−6.0	−4.9	−4.7
Net oil exporters	−16.6	−15.1	−9.9	−10.6	−25.8	−19.9	−3.7	−2.9	−6.5	−18.7	−13.8
Net oil importers	−11.5	−12.3	−15.8	−18.9	−19.8	−16.1	−10.5	−5.7	−5.9	−2.5	−3.2

[1] Including official transfers.
[2] Excluding Nigeria and South Africa.

Table A36. Developing Countries—by Region: Current Account Transactions, 1978–87
(In billions of U.S. dollars)

	1978	1979	1980	1981	1982	1983	1984	1985	1986	1987
Developing countries										
Exports (f.o.b.)	342.2	466.5	618.6	612.2	536.5	509.2	544.9	526.8	504.3	546.1
Imports (f.o.b.)	332.8	408.3	524.0	571.9	529.3	491.9	496.1	486.6	505.1	537.1
Trade balance	9.3	58.2	94.6	40.3	7.2	17.3	48.9	40.3	−0.8	8.8
Services, net	−53.1	−66.4	−81.0	−104.4	−111.8	−93.3	−103.0	−97.8	−92.3	−91.3
Goods and services balance	−43.8	−8.2	13.5	−64.1	−104.6	−75.9	−54.2	−57.4	−93.1	−82.5
Unrequited transfers	9.3	15.3	14.4	14.9	13.7	17.0	19.1	23.4	23.8	24.6
Current account balance	−34.5	7.1	27.9	−49.2	−90.9	−58.9	−35.1	−34.1	−69.3	−57.9
Memorandum										
Exports of goods and services	425.0	571.7	760.4	776.5	696.2	659.9	694.6	672.7	656.5	708.6
Investment income, net[1]	−5.6	−8.5	−8.9	−15.4	−28.2	−29.6	−39.5	−44.6	−45.8	−47.2
Of which,										
Interest payments[2]	−25.9	−36.9	−55.3	−74.2	−83.7	−77.8	−87.0	−86.1	−84.5	−83.8
Oil trade balance	110.5	160.0	226.7	213.6	168.3	134.8	137.2	120.3	73.9	76.2
Africa										
Exports (f.o.b.)	49.0	67.9	93.6	78.1	66.6	64.4	66.1	65.5	59.8	62.6
Imports (f.o.b.)	51.4	58.5	76.6	82.0	71.9	62.3	59.5	54.3	57.0	58.5
Trade balance	−2.4	9.3	17.0	−4.0	−5.3	2.1	6.6	11.2	2.8	4.2
Services, net	−13.7	−16.6	−22.8	−22.5	−20.6	−18.6	−18.1	−18.3	−19.6	−19.3
Goods and services balance	−16.1	−7.2	−5.7	−26.5	−25.9	−16.5	−11.5	−7.1	−16.8	−15.2
Unrequited transfers	3.3	3.8	4.2	4.6	4.6	4.9	4.8	5.7	5.3	5.1
Current account balance	−12.8	−3.4	−1.6	−21.9	−21.3	−11.6	−6.7	−1.4	−11.6	−10.1
Memorandum										
Exports of goods and services	58.3	79.1	107.7	91.9	78.8	76.1	77.1	76.2	71.4	75.4
Investment income, net[1]	−2.3	−3.8	−5.0	−5.7	−6.7	−7.0	−7.9	−8.6	−9.6	−9.1
Of which,										
Interest payments[2]	−3.4	−5.1	−7.3	−8.0	−8.2	−8.2	−9.1	−9.7	−10.7	−10.2
Oil trade balance	8.5	12.7	19.5	21.0	19.3	16.5	19.0	18.3	11.5	11.7
Asia										
Exports (f.o.b.)	93.5	122.9	155.9	170.2	163.0	171.1	198.6	197.6	213.1	233.7
Imports (f.o.b.)	102.2	135.7	176.9	192.9	184.8	188.6	202.6	211.5	225.8	247.2
Trade balance	−8.7	−12.8	−21.0	−22.7	−21.8	−17.5	−4.0	−13.9	−12.8	−13.5
Services, net	−4.0	−6.6	−7.8	−7.9	−6.3	−8.0	−11.5	−11.8	−11.8	−12.9
Goods and services balance	−12.7	−19.5	−28.8	−30.5	−28.1	−25.5	−15.5	−25.8	−24.5	−26.4
Unrequited transfers	5.9	6.9	9.5	9.9	10.8	11.2	10.7	10.4	9.1	9.4
Current account balance	−6.8	−12.6	−19.3	−20.7	−17.3	−14.3	−4.8	−15.4	−15.4	−16.9
Memorandum										
Exports of goods and services	115.1	150.3	190.4	212.5	208.7	217.0	245.3	245.6	265.2	290.0
Investment income, net[1]	−2.0	−2.4	−4.0	−5.4	−7.2	−7.1	−7.7	−9.1	−10.3	−11.4
Of which,										
Interest payments[2]	−5.2	−7.2	−10.4	−13.8	−15.6	−15.4	−17.9	−18.9	−19.5	−20.1
Oil trade balance	−2.4	−4.2	−8.6	−9.6	−9.5	−7.5	−3.0	−4.1	−2.4	−2.4

Table A36 *(concluded).* **Developing Countries—by Region: Current Account Transactions, 1978–87**
(In billions of U.S. dollars)

	1978	1979	1980	1981	1982	1983	1984	1985	1986	1987
Europe										
Exports (f.o.b.)	28.6	34.7	41.6	46.0	45.6	45.5	49.5	50.6	57.4	63.9
Imports (f.o.b.)	42.0	53.0	63.5	64.3	58.2	55.6	57.4	59.0	62.9	70.8
Trade balance	−13.5	−18.4	−21.9	−18.3	−12.6	−10.1	−7.9	−8.4	−5.5	−6.9
Services, net	0.5	0.8	1.7	−0.3	−1.4	−1.6	−1.9	−1.5	−0.5	0.2
Goods and services balance	−13.0	−17.6	−20.3	−18.5	−14.0	−11.7	−9.8	−9.9	−6.0	−6.7
Unrequited transfers	5.9	7.6	8.0	8.6	7.9	7.5	7.9	7.6	7.3	7.1
Current account balance	−7.1	−10.0	−12.3	−9.9	−6.1	−4.2	−1.9	−2.3	1.3	0.4
Memorandum										
Exports of goods and services	38.0	47.5	57.7	62.9	61.2	59.2	64.0	65.9	74.8	83.3
Investment income, net[1]	−1.5	−2.8	−4.1	−6.5	−6.7	−6.0	−6.5	−6.6	−6.6	−6.6
Of which,										
Interest payments[2]	−2.2	−3.7	−5.4	−7.9	−7.9	−6.9	−7.7	−8.0	−8.1	−8.1
Oil trade balance	−5.5	−8.0	−13.9	−13.8	−12.1	−10.9	−10.8	−10.6	−6.1	−6.3
Middle East										
Exports (f.o.b.)	116.7	168.6	233.2	217.2	170.1	136.3	129.4	116.4	80.8	85.3
Imports (f.o.b.)	78.9	87.7	110.8	128.8	130.3	122.2	112.3	98.6	93.0	87.6
Trade balance	37.8	80.9	122.4	88.4	39.7	14.2	17.1	17.8	−12.1	−2.3
Services, net	−20.1	−22.6	−23.4	−32.9	−34.1	−24.3	−28.6	−25.4	−24.0	−22.7
Goods and services balance	17.7	58.3	99.0	55.5	5.7	−10.1	−11.5	−7.6	−36.1	−25.0
Unrequited transfers	−6.5	−4.1	−8.3	--9.7	−10.8	−8.4	−6.5	−3.1	−0.6	0.3
Current account balance	11.2	54.2	90.7	45.8	−5.1	−18.5	−18.1	−10.7	−36.7	−24.7
Memorandum										
Exports of goods and services	141.9	199.7	278.4	271.8	224.5	189.2	177.9	160.2	122.4	127.6
Investment income, net[1]	8.5	11.6	20.3	26.5	26.0	23.2	18.7	12.9	9.2	6.6
Of which,										
Interest payments[2]	−2.9	−4.1	−5.7	−6.9	−7.3	−7.0	−7.8	−8.2	−9.7	−10.5
Oil trade balance	103.7	151.9	211.3	193.5	147.7	114.3	106.0	92.4	55.6	57.4
Western Hemisphere										
Exports (f.o.b.)	54.4	72.5	94.3	100.7	91.2	91.9	101.3	96.7	93.3	100.5
Imports (f.o.b.)	58.3	73.3	96.3	103.9	84.0	63.3	64.3	63.2	66.4	73.0
Trade balance	−4.0	−0.8	−1.9	−3.2	7.2	28.7	37.0	33.6	26.9	27.4
Services, net	−15.8	−21.5	−28.7	−40.9	−49.4	−40.8	−43.0	−40.7	−36.4	−36.7
Goods and services balance	−19.8	−22.3	−30.7	−44.1	−42.3	−12.1	−5.9	−7.1	−9.6	−9.2
Unrequited transfers	0.8	1.2	1.2	1.5	1.2	1.9	2.3	2.9	2.7	2.6
Current account balance	−19.0	−21.1	−29.5	−42.6	−41.1	−10.3	−3.6	−4.3	−6.9	−6.6
Memorandum										
Exports of goods and services	71.8	95.1	126.2	137.4	123.0	118.5	130.2	124.8	122.7	132.2
Investment income, net[1]	−8.2	−11.1	−16.2	−24.3	−33.6	−32.6	−36.1	−33.2	−28.5	−26.8
Of which,										
Interest payments[2]	−12.3	−16.7	−26.5	−37.7	−44.7	−40.2	−44.5	−41.3	−36.5	−34.9
Oil trade balance	6.2	7.7	18.3	22.5	22.9	22.3	26.1	24.4	15.3	15.8

[1] Comprises all investment income, except payments of income on foreign direct investment; receipts from direct investment abroad by residents are included.

[2] Including dividends and other investment income payments not related to foreign direct investment.

Table A37. Developing Countries—by Predominant Export: Current Account Transactions, 1978–87
(In billions of U.S. dollars)

	1978	1979	1980	1981	1982	1983	1984	1985	1986	1987
Fuel exporters										
Exports (f.o.b.)	158.4	233.0	329.6	312.4	252.2	214.8	214.5	196.5	137.3	144.1
Imports (f.o.b.)	114.3	124.7	160.0	191.9	182.2	155.6	145.7	132.5	122.5	118.1
Trade balance	44.1	108.3	169.5	120.5	70.0	59.2	68.7	64.0	14.8	26.1
Services, net	−38.4	−46.0	−58.6	−72.8	−77.4	−59.1	−64.1	−58.9	−54.2	−53.6
Goods and services balance	5.7	62.2	111.0	47.7	−7.4	0.1	4.7	5.1	−39.4	−27.6
Unrequited transfers	−11.8	−10.9	−15.9	−16.7	−18.2	−14.9	−13.3	−11.6	−9.6	−8.1
Current account balance	−6.1	51.4	95.1	31.0	−25.6	−14.8	−8.6	−6.5	−49.0	−35.6
Memorandum										
Exports of goods and services	186.2	267.2	377.3	373.3	307.1	266.1	262.9	240.8	179.3	186.0
Investment income, net[1]	4.4	5.3	12.1	16.8	11.6	8.6	3.1	0.2	−1.9	−2.5
Of which,										
Interest payments[2]	−8.1	−11.3	−15.7	−20.7	−23.6	−22.3	−25.6	−24.2	−23.7	−22.9
Oil trade balance	134.5	194.7	283.2	272.6	219.5	179.5	175.7	154.9	93.2	95.8
Non-fuel exporters										
Exports (f.o.b.)	183.7	233.5	289.0	299.8	284.3	294.4	330.4	330.3	367.0	401.9
Imports (f.o.b.)	218.5	283.6	364.0	380.0	347.0	336.3	350.3	354.1	382.6	419.0
Trade balance	−34.8	−50.1	−75.0	−80.2	−62.7	−41.9	−19.9	−23.7	−15.6	−17.2
Services, net	−14.7	−20.4	−22.5	−31.6	−34.4	−34.2	−39.0	−38.9	−38.1	−37.7
Goods and services balance	−49.5	−70.5	−97.4	−111.8	−97.1	−76.1	−58.8	−62.5	−53.7	−54.9
Unrequited transfers	21.1	26.2	30.3	31.6	31.8	32.0	32.4	35.0	33.4	32.7
Current account balance	−28.4	−44.3	−67.1	−80.2	−65.3	−44.1	−26.5	−27.6	−20.3	−22.3
Memorandum										
Exports of goods and services	238.8	304.5	383.1	403.2	389.1	393.9	431.7	431.9	477.2	522.6
Investment income, net[1]	−10.0	−13.8	−21.0	−32.2	−39.8	−38.1	−42.6	−44.7	−43.9	−44.7
Of which,										
Interest payments[2]	−17.8	−25.6	−39.6	−53.5	−60.1	−55.4	−61.5	−61.9	−60.7	−60.9
Oil trade balance	−24.0	−34.6	−56.5	−59.0	−51.2	−44.8	−38.6	−34.5	−19.3	−19.6
Primary product exporters										
Exports (f.o.b.)	85.1	108.6	133.3	127.6	116.9	120.3	132.5	129.3	142.9	156.0
Imports (f.o.b.)	88.4	112.0	148.4	153.6	135.5	124.1	123.1	115.6	127.4	141.1
Trade balance	−3.3	−3.4	−15.1	−26.0	−18.6	−3.8	9.4	13.8	15.4	14.8
Services, net	−22.0	−28.5	−35.0	−42.7	−47.4	−45.9	−47.2	−44.7	−42.8	−44.1
Goods and services balance	−25.4	−31.9	−50.1	−68.7	−66.0	−49.7	−37.9	−30.9	−27.4	−29.3
Unrequited transfers	6.1	8.1	9.9	11.2	11.2	11.5	11.9	13.3	12.3	12.2
Current account balance	−19.2	−23.8	−40.2	−57.5	−54.8	−38.2	−26.0	−17.7	−15.1	−17.2
Memorandum										
Exports of goods and services	103.6	132.4	164.2	160.4	148.8	149.9	162.8	161.0	178.2	194.9
Investment income, net[1]	−7.2	−10.7	−15.5	−23.3	−30.8	−30.0	−33.6	−33.4	−31.0	−31.1
Of which,										
Interest payments[2]	−10.3	−15.4	−22.3	−30.6	−36.4	−34.2	−38.2	−38.2	−35.6	−35.7
Oil trade balance	−12.8	−18.2	−28.1	−29.1	−25.1	−21.9	−17.7	−15.5	−8.2	−8.1

Table A37 *(continued)*. **Developing Countries—by Predominant Export: Current Account Transactions, 1978–87**
(In billions of U.S. dollars)

	1978	1979	1980	1981	1982	1983	1984	1985	1986	1987
Agricultural exporters										
Exports (f.o.b.)	58.9	72.6	86.0	88.5	82.2	84.9	98.5	96.2	107.9	118.6
Imports (f.o.b.)	65.2	82.7	108.0	108.4	98.4	92.9	92.0	89.1	99.1	110.1
Trade balance	−6.3	−10.1	−22.0	−20.0	−16.2	−7.9	6.5	7.1	8.8	8.3
Services, net	−14.9	−19.9	−24.1	−29.6	−35.1	−34.4	−36.1	−34.6	−32.9	−33.6
Goods and services balance	−21.2	−30.0	−46.1	−49.5	−51.3	−42.4	−29.5	−27.4	−24.1	−25.3
Unrequited transfers	4.4	5.7	7.4	8.3	8.8	9.1	9.7	10.8	10.0	10.1
Current account balance	−16.8	−24.3	−38.7	−41.2	−42.5	−33.3	−19.8	−16.8	−14.1	−15.3
Memorandum										
Exports of goods and services	72.3	89.9	108.5	112.4	105.8	106.9	121.2	120.8	135.6	149.3
Investment income, net[1]	−4.6	−7.3	−10.7	−17.5	−23.8	−23.7	−26.2	−26.4	−24.1	−24.0
Of which,										
Interest payments[2]	−7.3	−11.2	−16.0	−23.2	−28.5	−27.1	−29.8	−30.4	−28.1	−27.8
Oil trade balance	−10.0	−14.3	−22.9	−23.0	−19.8	−16.5	−12.5	−10.6	−5.6	−5.4
Mineral exporters										
Exports (f.o.b.)	26.2	35.9	47.3	39.1	34.7	35.4	34.0	33.2	34.9	37.4
Imports (f.o.b.)	23.2	29.2	40.4	45.1	37.1	31.2	31.2	26.5	28.4	30.9
Trade balance	3.0	6.7	6.9	−6.0	−2.5	4.1	2.8	6.7	6.6	6.5
Services, net	−7.1	−8.6	−10.9	−13.2	−12.3	−11.4	−11.2	−10.2	−9.9	−10.5
Goods and services balance	−4.2	−1.9	−4.0	−19.2	−14.7	−7.3	−8.3	−3.5	−3.3	−4.0
Unrequited transfers	1.7	2.3	2.5	2.9	2.5	2.4	2.2	2.5	2.3	2.1
Current account balance	−2.4	0.4	−1.5	−16.3	−12.3	−4.9	−6.2	−0.9	−1.0	−1.9
Memorandum										
Exports of goods and services	31.3	42.5	55.7	48.0	43.0	43.0	41.6	40.2	42.5	45.6
Investment income, net[1]	−2.6	−3.4	−4.8	−5.8	−7.0	−6.3	−7.4	−7.1	−6.9	−7.2
Of which,										
Interest payments[2]	−3.1	−4.2	−6.2	−7.5	−7.8	−7.1	−8.4	−7.8	−7.6	−7.8
Oil trade balance	−2.8	−3.8	−5.2	−6.1	−5.3	−5.4	−5.2	−4.9	−2.6	−2.7
Exporters of manufactures										
Exports (f.o.b.)	86.9	109.2	136.1	152.3	148.6	155.3	177.8	180.7	201.8	221.5
Imports (f.o.b.)	101.1	133.2	167.5	175.9	161.8	164.9	179.5	192.5	207.4	228.6
Trade balance	−14.2	−24.0	−31.3	−23.6	−13.2	−9.6	−1.7	−11.8	−5.6	−7.1
Services, net	2.2	1.6	2.6	2.5	4.2	3.5	0.6	−0.5	−0.3	0.3
Goods and services balance	−12.0	−22.4	−28.7	−21.1	−9.1	−6.0	−1.1	−12.2	−5.9	−6.8
Unrequited transfers	6.9	7.7	8.6	8.6	7.5	8.2	8.5	10.2	10.3	9.4
Current account balance	−5.1	−14.6	−20.1	−12.5	−1.5	2.2	7.3	−2.0	4.4	2.5
Memorandum										
Exports of goods and services	110.0	139.1	173.8	196.1	194.3	199.8	223.3	226.6	251.9	275.9
Investment income, net[1]	−1.7	−2.3	−4.8	−7.3	−7.3	−5.7	−5.5	−6.6	−7.3	−7.4
Of which,										
Interest payments[2]	−4.8	−7.0	−11.3	−14.9	−15.3	−13.6	−14.8	−15.4	−15.8	−15.6
Oil trade balance	−9.2	−13.5	−22.7	−23.8	−20.8	−17.8	−15.9	−14.1	−8.8	−9.1

Table A37 *(concluded).* **Developing Countries—by Predominant Export: Current Account Transactions, 1978–87**
(In billions of U.S. dollars)

	1978	1979	1980	1981	1982	1983	1984	1985	1986	1987
Service and remittance countries										
Exports (f.o.b.)	11.8	15.8	19.6	19.9	18.8	18.8	20.1	20.2	22.4	24.4
Imports (f.o.b.)	29.0	38.5	48.1	50.6	49.7	47.3	47.7	46.0	47.8	49.3
Trade balance	−17.2	−22.7	−28.5	−30.7	−30.8	−28.5	−27.5	−25.7	−25.4	−24.9
Services, net	5.1	6.5	9.9	8.6	8.8	8.2	7.7	6.3	5.0	6.2
Goods and services balance	−12.1	−16.2	−18.6	−22.1	−22.1	−20.4	−19.9	−19.4	−20.4	−18.8
Unrequited transfers	8.0	10.4	11.8	11.9	13.1	12.3	12.0	11.4	10.9	11.1
Current account balance	−4.1	−5.8	−6.8	−10.2	−9.0	−8.1	−7.8	−8.0	−9.5	−7.6
Memorandum										
Exports of goods and services	25.2	33.0	45.1	46.8	46.0	44.2	45.6	44.3	47.2	51.8
Investment income, net[1]	−1.1	−0.8	−0.7	−1.6	−1.7	−2.5	−3.5	−4.7	−5.6	−6.2
Of which,										
Interest payments[2]	−2.6	−3.1	−6.1	−8.0	−8.5	−7.7	−8.4	−8.4	−9.3	−9.6
Oil trade balance	−2.0	−2.9	−5.6	−6.1	−5.2	−5.1	−5.1	−4.9	−2.3	−2.4

[1] Comprises all investment income, except payments of income on foreign direct investment; receipts from direct investment abroad by residents are included.

[2] Including dividends and other investment income payments not related to foreign direct investment.

Table A38. Developing Countries—by Financial and Other Criteria: Current Account Transactions, 1978–87
(In billions of U.S. dollars)

	1978	1979	1980	1981	1982	1983	1984	1985	1986	1987
By financial criteria										
Capital exporting countries										
Exports (f.o.b.)	106.5	155.8	216.1	199.2	153.1	120.9	112.9	99.5	64.0	67.0
Imports (f.o.b.)	58.2	61.5	77.9	93.2	96.4	88.2	78.6	66.2	60.2	55.0
Trade balance	48.3	94.2	138.2	106.1	56.7	32.7	34.2	33.3	3.8	12.0
Services, net	−21.6	−24.6	−27.9	−36.9	−38.2	−27.7	−31.6	−27.5	−23.8	−23.3
Goods and services balance	26.6	69.6	110.3	69.2	18.5	5.0	2.7	5.8	−20.0	−11.3
Unrequited transfers	−13.0	−13.3	−17.7	−19.0	−19.7	−16.8	−15.2	−13.2	−11.0	−9.5
Current account balance	13.6	56.3	92.5	50.2	−1.1	−11.8	−12.5	−7.4	−31.0	−20.8
Memorandum										
Exports of goods and services	123.7	176.5	246.1	237.7	190.5	157.2	144.6	127.9	90.3	92.1
Investment income, net[1]	9.3	12.0	20.5	26.6	26.0	24.2	20.1	15.5	12.7	10.6
Of which,										
Interest payments[2]	−1.1	−1.6	−2.0	−2.5	−2.5	−2.4	−2.9	−3.3	−3.8	−4.4
Oil trade balance	103.2	151.2	210.7	193.0	147.0	113.8	105.1	91.5	54.5	56.3
Capital importing countries										
Exports (f.o.b.)	235.7	310.7	402.5	412.9	383.4	388.3	432.1	427.3	440.3	479.1
Imports (f.o.b.)	274.6	346.8	446.2	478.7	432.9	403.8	417.4	420.4	444.9	482.1
Trade balance	−39.0	−36.1	−43.7	−65.8	−49.5	−15.4	14.6	7.0	−4.6	−3.2
Services, net	−31.5	−41.8	−53.1	−67.5	−73.6	−65.5	−71.5	−70.3	−68.5	−68.0
Goods and services balance	−70.4	−77.9	−96.8	−133.3	−123.1	−80.9	−56.9	−63.2	−73.1	−71.1
Unrequited transfers	22.3	28.6	32.2	33.9	33.3	33.8	34.3	36.6	34.8	34.1
Current account balance	−48.2	−49.2	−64.6	−99.5	−89.8	−47.1	−22.6	−26.8	−38.3	−37.1
Memorandum										
Exports of goods and services	301.4	395.2	514.3	538.8	505.7	502.8	550.0	544.9	566.2	616.5
Investment income, net[1]	−14.8	−20.5	−29.4	−42.0	−54.2	−53.8	−59.6	−60.0	−58.5	−57.8
Of which,										
Interest payments[2]	−24.8	−35.3	−53.3	−71.8	−81.2	−75.4	−84.1	−82.8	−80.7	−79.4
Oil trade balance	7.3	8.8	16.0	20.6	21.3	20.9	32.0	28.9	19.4	19.9
Market borrowers										
Exports (f.o.b.)	168.5	227.2	300.7	305.5	281.4	288.3	321.6	316.2	317.0	343.6
Imports (f.o.b.)	180.1	227.2	291.8	321.0	289.3	260.3	265.7	257.3	273.9	300.2
Trade balance	−11.5	—	8.9	−15.5	−7.9	28.0	55.9	58.9	43.1	43.3
Services, net	−25.8	−35.5	−50.5	−62.9	−70.8	−62.5	−66.8	−64.3	−60.4	−59.9
Goods and services balance	−37.4	−35.5	−41.6	−78.5	−78.7	−34.5	−10.9	−5.3	−17.4	−16.6
Unrequited transfers	5.6	6.4	6.3	7.3	6.4	7.3	7.3	7.1	7.0	6.8
Current account balance	−31.8	−29.2	−35.3	−71.2	−72.3	−27.2	−3.6	1.7	−10.3	−9.8
Memorandum										
Exports of goods and services	212.1	282.9	374.2	391.0	361.3	360.7	396.5	390.8	397.1	429.9
Investment income, net[1]	−11.6	−16.4	−24.2	−34.9	−46.4	−45.2	−49.9	−47.8	−44.1	−41.4
Of which,										
Interest payments[2]	−19.0	−26.8	−41.3	−56.9	−65.1	−59.8	−66.9	−64.7	−60.8	−57.9
Oil trade balance	14.1	18.1	33.8	38.5	35.9	33.2	41.8	37.8	24.3	25.1

Table A38 *(continued).* **Developing Countries—by Financial and Other Criteria: Current Account Transactions, 1978–87**

(In billions of U.S. dollars)

	1978	1979	1980	1981	1982	1983	1984	1985	1986	1987
Official borrowers										
Exports (f.o.b.)	20.4	25.1	29.3	28.2	25.3	25.1	25.7	25.3	28.8	30.6
Imports (f.o.b.)	31.4	37.4	46.6	48.2	45.4	43.8	43.9	42.7	44.9	47.5
Trade balance	−11.0	−12.4	−17.3	−20.0	−20.1	−18.7	−18.2	−17.4	−16.1	−16.9
Services, net	−4.1	−4.5	−4.6	−4.9	−4.4	−4.6	−5.5	−5.3	−5.4	−5.6
Goods and services balance	−15.1	−16.9	−21.9	−24.9	−24.5	−23.3	−23.8	−22.7	−21.5	−22.5
Unrequited transfers	7.9	10.9	12.7	13.2	14.2	14.1	13.9	13.7	12.3	12.6
Current account balance	−7.2	−5.9	−9.1	−11.7	−10.3	−9.2	−9.9	−9.0	−9.1	−9.9
Memorandum										
Exports of goods and services	26.8	33.2	39.0	38.4	35.6	34.9	35.3	35.5	39.8	42.5
Investment income, net[1]	−1.0	−1.3	−1.7	−2.0	−2.5	−2.8	−3.2	−3.9	−4.4	−4.6
Of which,										
Interest payments[2]	−1.7	−2.3	−3.3	−3.8	−4.3	−4.2	−4.6	−5.2	−5.6	−5.7
Oil trade balance	−1.7	−3.0	−5.0	−6.3	−5.5	−5.2	−4.9	−5.0	−2.6	−2.4
Diversified borrowers										
Exports (f.o.b.)	46.7	58.5	72.5	79.2	76.7	74.9	84.8	85.8	94.5	104.9
Imports (f.o.b.)	63.2	82.1	107.8	109.5	98.2	99.6	107.9	120.3	126.1	134.4
Trade balance	−16.4	−23.7	−35.3	−30.3	−21.4	−24.7	−23.1	−34.5	−31.6	−29.5
Services, net	−1.6	−1.8	1.9	0.3	1.6	1.5	0.8	−0.8	−2.6	−2.5
Goods and services balance	−18.0	−25.5	−33.3	−29.9	−19.9	−23.2	−22.2	−35.2	−34.2	−32.1
Unrequited transfers	8.8	11.3	13.1	13.4	12.7	12.5	13.1	15.8	15.4	14.6
Current account balance	−9.2	−14.1	−20.2	−16.6	−7.2	−10.7	−9.1	−19.4	−18.8	−17.4
Memorandum										
Exports of goods and services	62.5	79.1	101.1	109.4	108.8	107.1	118.2	118.5	129.3	144.1
Investment income, net[1]	−2.3	−2.8	−3.4	−5.2	−5.4	−5.7	−6.4	−8.3	−10.0	−11.8
Of which,										
Interest payments[2]	−4.1	−6.3	−8.6	−11.1	−11.8	−11.4	−12.6	−12.9	−14.3	−15.8
Oil trade balance	−5.0	−6.3	−12.8	−11.5	−9.1	−7.1	−4.8	−3.9	−2.3	−2.8
Countries with recent debt-servicing problems										
Exports (f.o.b.)	105.3	140.5	186.2	180.3	159.7	158.5	170.8	164.6	159.7	172.0
Imports (f.o.b.)	119.6	147.5	187.6	199.8	165.7	136.5	136.2	129.3	135.5	145.1
Trade balance	−14.3	−7.0	−1.4	−19.4	−6.0	22.0	34.6	35.4	24.2	26.8
Services, net	−24.1	−31.8	−43.9	−55.6	−63.9	−51.3	−52.2	−50.7	−49.1	−47.7
Goods and services balance	−38.4	−38.8	−45.3	−75.0	−69.9	−29.3	−17.6	−15.3	−24.9	−20.8
Unrequited transfers	6.7	7.2	6.9	7.8	7.6	8.7	9.2	10.7	10.9	10.6
Current account balance	−31.7	−31.6	−38.5	−67.2	−62.3	−20.6	−8.4	−4.7	−14.0	−10.3
Memorandum										
Exports of goods and services	134.5	178.2	237.3	236.4	208.0	202.5	217.5	209.3	205.7	222.4
Investment income, net[1]	−10.6	−14.6	−22.0	−31.7	−42.2	−41.3	−45.2	−43.8	−40.6	−37.9
Of which,										
Interest payments[2]	−15.8	−22.2	−35.0	−47.9	−55.3	−50.8	−56.0	−53.5	−50.0	−47.5
Oil trade balance	5.1	6.6	16.6	23.0	24.4	22.5	29.0	27.3	17.1	17.4

Table A38 *(continued).* **Developing Countries—by Financial and Other Criteria: Current Account Transactions, 1978–87**

(In billions of U.S. dollars)

	1978	1979	1980	1981	1982	1983	1984	1985	1986	1987
Countries without debt-servicing problems										
Exports (f.o.b.)	130.4	170.2	216.3	232.6	223.7	229.8	261.3	262.7	280.6	307.0
Imports (f.o.b.)	155.1	199.3	258.5	279.0	267.2	267.2	281.2	291.1	309.4	337.0
Trade balance	−24.6	−29.0	−42.3	−46.4	−43.5	−37.4	−19.9	−28.4	−28.8	−30.0
Services, net	−7.3	−10.1	−9.2	−11.9	−9.8	−14.2	−19.3	−19.6	−19.3	−20.3
Goods and services balance	−32.0	−39.1	−51.5	−58.3	−53.3	−51.7	−39.2	−48.0	−48.2	−50.3
Unrequited transfers	15.6	21.5	25.3	26.1	25.7	25.1	25.1	25.9	23.9	23.5
Current account balance	−16.4	−17.6	−26.1	−32.2	−27.5	−26.5	−14.2	−22.1	−24.3	−26.8
Memorandum										
Exports of goods and services	166.8	217.0	277.0	302.4	297.7	300.3	332.4	335.5	360.6	394.1
Investment income, net[1]	−4.2	−5.9	−7.4	−10.3	−12.1	−12.5	−14.4	−16.3	−17.9	−20.0
Of which,										
Interest payments[2]	−9.0	−13.2	−18.3	−23.9	−25.8	−24.6	−28.1	−29.3	−30.6	−31.9
Oil trade balance	2.2	2.1	−0.6	−2.3	−3.1	−1.6	3.0	1.6	2.3	2.5
By miscellaneous criteria										
Capital importing fuel exporters										
Exports (f.o.b.)	51.9	77.2	113.5	113.1	99.1	94.0	101.6	97.0	73.3	77.1
Imports (f.o.b.)	56.1	63.2	82.2	98.7	85.9	67.5	67.1	66.3	62.3	63.1
Trade balance	−4.2	14.0	31.3	14.4	13.2	26.5	34.5	30.7	11.0	14.1
Services, net	−16.8	−21.4	−30.6	−35.9	−39.2	−31.3	−32.5	−31.4	−30.4	−30.3
Goods and services balance	−20.9	−7.4	0.7	−21.5	−26.0	−4.8	2.0	−0.7	−19.4	−16.3
Unrequited transfers	1.2	2.4	1.8	2.3	1.5	1.9	1.9	1.6	1.4	1.4
Current account balance	−19.7	−4.9	2.5	−19.2	−24.5	−3.0	3.9	0.9	−18.0	−14.8
Memorandum										
Exports of goods and services	62.5	90.7	131.3	135.6	116.7	108.9	118.3	113.0	89.0	93.9
Investment income, net[1]	−4.8	−6.7	−8.4	−9.8	−14.4	−15.6	−17.1	−15.3	−14.6	−13.1
Of which,										
Interest payments[2]	−7.0	−9.7	−13.6	−18.2	−21.1	−20.0	−22.6	−20.9	−19.9	−18.5
Oil trade balance	31.3	43.4	72.5	79.6	72.5	65.7	70.6	63.4	38.7	39.5
Fifteen heavily indebted countries										
Exports (f.o.b.)	69.1	94.8	128.0	127.3	112.5	111.3	123.2	118.3	112.1	121.0
Imports (f.o.b.)	76.9	96.0	122.4	132.7	107.8	82.3	79.8	76.9	80.9	87.7
Trade balance	−7.9	−1.2	5.6	−5.3	4.7	29.0	43.4	41.4	31.1	33.2
Services, net	−19.7	−26.5	−36.7	−47.8	−56.8	−46.2	−48.0	−45.7	−42.2	−41.5
Goods and services balance	−27.6	−27.7	−31.1	−53.1	−52.2	−17.2	−4.6	−4.3	−11.1	−8.4
Unrequited transfers	2.9	3.2	2.3	3.1	2.1	3.3	3.6	4.3	3.8	3.2
Current account balance	−24.7	−24.5	−28.7	−50.0	−50.1	−13.8	−0.9	−0.1	−7.3	−5.1
Memorandum										
Exports of goods and services	87.6	119.7	161.3	164.8	143.1	136.5	150.7	145.6	141.3	153.0
Investment income, net[1]	−8.3	−12.1	−17.3	−26.2	−36.8	−36.0	−39.5	−37.0	−32.9	−30.0
Of which,										
Interest payments[2]	−12.0	−17.4	−25.7	−37.1	−44.4	−41.0	−45.7	−43.4	−39.1	−36.6
Oil trade balance	8.3	9.9	23.0	28.9	29.4	27.4	33.6	32.1	19.9	20.7

Table A38 *(concluded).* **Developing Countries—by Financial and Other Criteria: Current Account Transactions, 1978–87**

(In billions of U.S. dollars)

	1978	1979	1980	1981	1982	1983	1984	1985	1986	1987
Small low-income countries										
Exports (f.o.b.)	12.3	14.7	17.0	15.5	14.1	14.9	15.8	15.4	19.0	20.2
Imports (f.o.b.)	20.1	23.5	29.3	28.3	27.5	25.7	26.9	26.4	29.0	30.8
Trade balance	−7.8	−8.8	−12.3	−12.8	−13.4	−10.8	−11.1	−11.0	−10.0	−10.5
Services, net	−2.9	−3.6	−3.4	−3.7	−3.8	−4.1	−4.7	−5.0	−5.3	−5.5
Goods and services balance	−10.7	−12.4	−15.7	−16.5	−17.2	−14.9	−15.8	−16.0	−15.3	−16.0
Unrequited transfers	4.8	5.5	7.0	7.5	8.6	9.0	8.9	9.2	8.3	8.5
Current account balance	−5.9	−6.9	−8.7	−9.0	−8.6	−6.0	−6.9	−6.8	−6.9	−7.5
Memorandum										
Exports of goods and services	15.3	18.3	21.5	19.9	18.4	19.1	19.9	19.6	23.8	25.4
Investment income, net[1]	−0.7	−0.8	−1.0	−1.5	−2.0	−2.1	−2.3	−2.7	−3.0	−3.2
Of which,										
Interest payments[2]	−1.0	−1.2	−1.6	−2.0	−2.5	−2.6	−2.8	−3.2	−3.5	−3.6
Oil trade balance	−1.8	−2.9	−4.5	−5.3	−5.3	−4.6	−4.3	−4.2	−2.5	−2.5
Sub-Saharan Africa[3]										
Exports (f.o.b.)	16.8	20.5	24.2	21.4	20.0	19.4	20.9	20.4	22.8	23.6
Imports (f.o.b.)	18.8	21.5	27.4	25.9	23.8	21.1	20.2	20.3	23.5	24.7
Trade balance	−2.0	−1.0	−3.2	−4.5	−3.9	−1.6	0.6	0.1	−0.7	−1.1
Services, net	−5.3	−6.3	−7.3	−7.6	−7.4	−7.7	−8.0	−8.0	−8.6	−8.8
Goods and services balance	−7.3	−7.4	−10.5	−12.1	−11.3	−9.3	−7.3	−7.9	−9.3	−9.9
Unrequited transfers	1.9	1.9	2.5	2.7	2.9	3.2	3.4	3.9	3.9	3.9
Current account balance	−5.4	−5.5	−8.1	−9.4	−8.4	−6.1	−3.9	−3.9	−5.4	−6.0
Memorandum										
Exports of goods and services	20.9	25.2	30.1	27.1	25.2	24.5	25.7	25.3	28.2	29.6
Investment income, net[1]	−0.9	−1.4	−2.0	−2.3	−2.7	−2.7	−3.0	−3.4	−3.7	−3.9
Of which,										
Interest payments[2]	−1.2	−1.8	−2.6	−2.9	−3.2	−3.1	−3.4	−3.8	−4.1	−4.2
Oil trade balance	−0.5	−0.9	−1.1	−0.5	0.2	0.8	1.5	1.3	0.4	0.2

[1] Comprises all investment income, except payments of income on foreign direct investment; receipts from direct investment abroad by residents are included.

[2] Including dividends and other investment income payments not related to foreign direct investment.

[3] Excluding Nigeria and South Africa.

Table A39. Developing Countries—by Alternative Analytical Categories: Current Account Transactions, 1978–87

(In billions of U.S. dollars)

	1978	1979	1980	1981	1982	1983	1984	1985	1986	1987
Oil exporting countries										
Exports (f.o.b.)	143.5	211.5	296.8	274.6	215.0	177.6	174.7	158.5	106.4	111.2
Imports (f.o.b.)	96.7	100.4	125.9	150.6	152.1	132.2	119.8	105.5	97.3	91.4
Trade balance	46.7	111.1	170.8	124.0	63.0	45.4	54.8	53.0	9.1	19.8
Services, net	−34.7	−40.6	−49.8	−58.9	−60.5	−46.4	−49.6	−45.2	−42.0	−41.2
Goods and services balance	12.1	70.5	121.0	65.2	2.5	−0.9	5.3	7.9	−32.9	−21.4
Unrequited transfers	−13.4	−13.7	−18.6	−19.4	−20.2	−17.1	−15.3	−13.3	−11.2	−9.7
Current account balance	−1.3	56.8	102.4	45.8	−17.8	−18.0	−10.0	−5.5	−44.1	−31.1
Memorandum										
Exports of goods and services	164.2	236.5	332.6	321.6	259.1	219.1	211.8	192.5	138.2	141.6
Investment income, net[1]	7.8	9.2	17.7	24.3	22.3	18.5	13.8	9.2	6.4	4.9
Of which,										
Interest payments[2]	−4.0	−6.3	−8.2	−10.6	−10.4	−10.5	−12.4	−12.6	−13.3	−12.9
Oil trade balance	128.8	184.9	264.9	250.9	196.1	157.0	152.7	133.7	80.3	82.6
Non-oil developing countries										
Exports (f.o.b.)	198.7	255.0	321.9	337.5	321.5	331.6	370.2	368.3	397.8	434.8
Imports (f.o.b.)	236.1	307.9	398.1	421.3	377.2	359.8	376.2	381.1	407.7	445.6
Trade balance	−37.4	−52.9	−76.2	−83.8	−55.7	−28.1	−6.0	−12.7	−9.9	−10.9
Services, net	−18.5	−25.8	−31.3	−45.5	−51.3	−46.9	−53.5	−52.6	−50.3	−50.1
Goods and services balance	−55.9	−78.7	−107.5	−129.3	−107.1	−75.0	−59.5	−65.3	−60.2	−61.0
Unrequited transfers	22.7	29.0	33.1	34.3	33.9	34.1	34.5	36.8	35.0	34.3
Current account balance	−33.2	−49.7	−74.4	−95.0	−73.2	−40.9	−25.0	−28.7	−25.2	−26.7
Memorandum										
Exports of goods and services	260.8	335.2	427.8	454.9	437.1	440.8	482.7	480.2	518.4	567.0
Investment income, net[1]	−13.4	−17.6	−26.6	−39.7	−50.6	−48.1	−53.3	−53.8	−52.1	−52.1
Of which,										
Interest payments[2]	−21.9	−30.6	−47.1	−63.6	−73.3	−67.3	−74.6	−73.5	−71.1	−70.8
Oil trade balance	−18.3	−24.9	−38.2	−37.3	−27.8	−22.2	−15.5	−13.4	−6.4	−6.4
Net oil exporters										
Exports (f.o.b.)	26.9	39.6	54.6	57.5	57.3	58.3	64.1	61.2	54.7	58.9
Imports (f.o.b.)	31.0	42.1	56.4	66.9	56.5	49.2	52.7	52.5	53.7	55.4
Trade balance	−4.1	−2.5	−1.8	−9.4	0.8	9.1	11.4	8.7	0.9	3.5
Services, net	−3.7	−6.0	−9.2	−14.5	−18.6	−14.6	−16.4	−16.5	−17.9	−18.1
Goods and services balance	−7.9	−8.6	−11.0	−23.9	−17.8	−5.5	−5.0	−7.8	−17.0	−14.5
Unrequited transfers	2.0	3.0	2.9	2.9	2.4	2.6	2.5	2.5	3.0	3.1
Current account balance	−5.9	−5.5	−8.1	−21.0	−15.4	−2.9	−2.5	−5.3	−14.0	−11.3
Memorandum										
Exports of goods and services	39.2	55.8	75.8	81.3	77.5	78.7	87.2	82.3	75.0	81.7
Investment income, net[1]	−4.4	−4.5	−6.1	−8.7	−12.3	−12.4	−13.6	−12.9	−12.7	−12.3
Of which,										
Interest payments[2]	−5.6	−7.1	−10.1	−13.6	−17.0	−16.0	−18.1	−16.7	−16.2	−16.0
Oil trade balance	7.2	13.5	23.8	27.6	30.0	28.6	29.6	27.2	16.9	17.0

Table A39 *(concluded).* **Developing Countries—by Alternative Analytical Categories: Current Account Transactions, 1978–87**
(In billions of U.S. dollars)

	1978	1979	1980	1981	1982	1983	1984	1985	1986	1987
Net oil importers										
Exports (f.o.b.)	171.8	215.4	267.2	280.0	264.1	273.3	306.1	307.0	343.2	375.9
Imports (f.o.b.)	205.0	265.8	341.7	354.4	320.7	310.6	323.5	328.6	354.0	390.2
Trade balance	−33.3	−50.4	−74.5	−74.4	−56.6	−37.2	−17.4	−21.5	−10.8	−14.4
Services, net	−14.7	−19.8	−22.1	−31.0	−32.7	−32.3	−37.1	−36.1	−32.4	−32.1
Goods and services balance	−48.0	−70.2	−96.5	−105.4	−89.3	−69.5	−54.5	−57.5	−43.2	−46.5
Unrequited transfers	20.7	26.0	30.2	31.4	31.5	31.5	32.0	34.3	32.0	31.2
Current account balance	−27.3	−44.2	−66.4	−74.0	−57.8	−38.0	−22.5	−23.3	−11.2	−15.4
Memorandum										
Exports of goods and services	221.7	279.4	351.9	373.6	359.6	362.1	395.5	397.9	443.3	485.3
Investment income, net[1]	−9.0	−13.1	−20.5	−31.0	−38.2	−35.7	−39.7	−40.9	−39.4	−39.9
Of which,										
Interest payments[2]	−16.3	−23.5	−36.9	−50.0	−56.4	−51.2	−56.5	−56.8	−54.9	−54.9
Oil trade balance	−25.6	−38.4	−62.0	−64.9	−57.8	−50.8	−45.1	−40.6	−23.2	−23.4

[1] Comprises all investment income, except payments of income on foreign direct investment; receipts from direct investment abroad by residents are included.

[2] Including dividends and other investment income payments not related to foreign direct investment.

Table A40. Capital Importing Developing Countries—by Class of Creditor: External Financing, 1978–87

(In billions of U.S. dollars)

	1978	1979	1980	1981	1982	1983	1984	1985	1986	1987
Capital importing countries										
Deficit on goods, services, and private transfers[1]	56.4	60.8	77.0	113.0	103.0	60.4	36.4	43.0	55.3	53.2
Non-debt-creating flows	17.8	24.7	23.7	27.8	26.6	23.2	24.1	26.5	29.0	29.1
Official transfers	8.3	11.6	12.4	13.6	13.3	13.3	13.9	16.2	17.0	16.2
Direct investment flows, net	7.8	10.2	8.9	14.0	13.1	9.6	9.9	10.0	11.4	12.3
SDR allocations, valuation adjustments, and gold monetization	1.7	2.9	2.4	0.2	0.2	0.3	0.3	0.2	0.6	0.7
Use of reserves	−13.9	−21.6	−18.6	5.1	17.2	−9.4	−19.7	−2.2	−8.1	−7.1
Asset transactions, net[2]	−3.5	−4.2	−4.1	−12.5	−10.2	−9.6	−11.8	−6.2	−9.3	−11.1
Recorded errors and omissions[3]	−5.7	−3.8	−14.8	−19.6	−26.3	−10.9	−4.1	−3.8	—	—
Net external borrowing	61.7	65.8	90.9	112.3	95.8	67.2	48.0	28.7	43.7	42.4
Reserve-related liabilities	1.4	−0.8	4.4	9.2	18.9	18.1	5.9	—	2.4	1.5
Liabilities constituting foreign authorities' reserves[4]	1.4	−1.3	2.0	0.9	1.6	−2.0	−0.7	−0.1	−0.3	−0.1
Use of Fund credit[5]	−0.6	0.2	1.5	6.3	7.0	11.4	5.1	0.2	−0.6	−2.9
Arrears	0.5	0.4	0.8	1.9	10.4	8.7	1.5	−0.2	3.3	4.4
Long-term borrowing from official creditors, net[6]	16.5	19.3	25.4	30.1	27.6	31.6	28.7	18.0	27.3	26.6
Other net external borrowing[7]	43.9	47.3	61.1	73.1	49.3	17.5	13.4	10.8	14.1	14.4
Long-term	34.1	39.0	34.9	52.7	34.5	42.8	13.3	23.1	16.9	12.2
From banks[8]	29.2	26.0	19.7	28.4	21.4	40.3	13.0	27.0	16.8	9.4
Other	4.9	12.9	15.2	24.3	13.1	2.5	0.3	−3.9	0.1	2.8
Short-term	9.7	8.3	26.3	20.4	14.8	−25.4	—	−11.3	−3.1	1.9
Of which,										
Market borrowers										
Deficit on goods, services, and private transfers[1]	32.8	30.4	36.7	73.1	74.3	29.6	5.8	0.5	12.5	11.9
Non-debt-creating flows, net	8.8	11.4	10.3	13.2	12.9	10.0	9.6	9.6	10.9	11.4
Official transfers	1.0	1.2	1.5	1.9	2.0	2.4	2.2	2.1	2.1	2.1
Direct investment flows, net	6.4	8.0	7.5	11.3	10.7	7.4	7.2	7.3	8.2	8.6
SDR allocations, valuation adjustments and gold monetization	1.4	2.2	1.3	—	0.2	0.1	0.2	0.2	0.6	0.7
Use of reserves	−10.6	−18.2	−17.3	5.0	24.8	−4.2	−19.8	−7.6	−4.5	−5.5
Asset transactions, net[2]	−3.0	−3.2	−2.8	−11.0	−9.8	−6.9	−8.5	−5.2	−9.0	−10.3
Recorded errors and omissions[3]	−4.5	−3.5	−15.9	−21.4	−23.5	−11.7	−2.6	−4.1	—	—
Net external borrowing	42.0	43.9	62.4	87.3	69.8	42.3	27.1	7.8	15.0	16.3
Reserve-related liabilities	−1.0	−1.9	1.0	2.3	13.3	16.0	3.5	−2.6	1.2	3.5
Liabilities constituting foreign authorities' reserves[4]	—	−1.5	0.2	0.5	1.6	−1.2	−0.7	−0.3	−0.3	−0.1
Use of Fund credit[5]	−1.0	−0.4	0.6	1.8	2.9	7.7	4.2	0.7	0.2	−0.8
Arrears	—	—	0.1	—	8.8	9.5	—	−3.0	1.3	4.4
Long-term borrowing from official creditors, net[6]	6.5	5.1	7.7	9.4	7.3	15.6	11.9	5.8	11.3	8.5

Table A40 *(concluded).* **Capital Importing Developing Countries—by Class of Creditor: External Financing, 1978–87**

(In billions of U.S. dollars)

	1978	1979	1980	1981	1982	1983	1984	1985	1986	1987
Other net external borrowing[7]	36.5	40.7	53.7	75.6	49.2	10.7	11.7	4.6	2.5	4.4
Long-term	29.2	32.3	28.2	53.4	34.5	36.9	14.9	19.7	6.4	3.7
From banks[8]	25.1	20.5	15.7	28.3	21.3	36.4	15.5	27.5	7.4	3.5
Other	4.1	11.8	12.4	25.1	13.2	0.4	−0.6	−7.8	−0.9	0.2
Short-term	7.4	8.5	25.5	22.1	14.6	−26.1	−3.2	−14.1	−4.2	0.4
Official borrowers										
Deficit on goods, services, and private transfers[1]	11.0	12.1	16.0	19.0	17.5	15.7	16.3	15.5	15.8	16.7
Non-debt-creating flows, net	4.5	6.9	7.5	8.1	7.7	6.8	7.0	6.9	7.2	7.4
Official transfers	3.9	6.1	6.9	7.3	7.2	6.5	6.4	6.5	6.6	6.8
Direct investment flows, net	0.6	0.5	0.2	0.9	0.6	0.4	0.4	0.4	0.5	0.6
SDR allocations, valuation adjustments, and gold monetization	—	0.2	0.4	−0.1	—	−0.1	0.2	—	—	—
Use of reserves	−0.8	−0.8	−0.3	0.4	1.1	−1.0	1.4	0.6	0.2	1.2
Asset transactions, net[2]	−0.1	−0.4	−0.9	−0.5	—	−0.1	−0.1	−0.2	−0.1	—
Recorded errors and omissions[3]	0.3	−1.1	−1.4	0.2	−1.5	−0.4	−0.3	−0.3	—	—
Net external borrowing	7.1	7.6	11.1	10.8	10.2	10.4	8.2	8.5	8.6	8.2
Reserve-related liabilities	0.8	0.3	2.1	3.1	3.4	1.8	1.3	2.0	−0.3	—
Liabilities constituting foreign authorities' reserves[4]	0.3	—	1.6	0.7	0.2	−0.4	—	0.5	—	−0.1
Use of Fund credit[5]	0.2	0.5	0.1	2.0	1.3	1.6	0.4	—	−0.6	−0.8
Arrears	0.2	−0.2	0.4	0.4	1.9	0.6	0.9	1.5	0.4	0.8
Long-term borrowing from official creditors, net[6]	3.9	6.3	7.8	9.2	8.8	7.2	7.5	5.6	7.8	7.7
Other net external borrowing[7]	2.5	0.9	1.1	−1.5	−2.0	1.4	−0.6	0.9	1.0	0.5
Long-term	1.9	0.7	0.5	−1.4	−1.3	1.8	−0.3	0.1	0.6	0.3
Short-term	0.6	0.3	0.6	−0.1	−0.7	−0.4	−0.3	0.8	0.3	0.2

NOTE: Except where otherwise footnoted, estimates shown here are based on national balance of payments statistics, which are not always easily reconcilable with year-to-year changes in either debtor- or creditor-reported debt statistics, in part because the latter are affected by changes in valuation.

[1] Equivalent to current account deficit less official transfers. For purposes of this table, official transfers are treated as external financing.

[2] Pertains primarily to export credit.

[3] Positioned here on the presumption that estimates reflect primarily unrecorded capital outflows.

[4] Comprises short-term borrowing by monetary authorities from other monetary authorities.

[5] Projected use of Fund credit includes prospective programs.

[6] Estimates, based on debt statistics reported in Tables A47 and A48, of net disbursements by official creditors (other than monetary institutions).

[7] Residually calculated. Except for minor discrepancies in coverage, amounts shown reflect almost exclusively net external borrowing from private creditors.

[8] Refers only to long-term lending by banks guaranteed by government of debtor country. Bank lending also accounts for large fractions of unguaranteed long-term flows (included in "other" long-term flows) and short-term flows.

Table A41. Capital Importing Developing Countries—by Region: Summary of External Financing, 1978–87[1]

(In billions of U.S. dollars)

	1978	1979	1980	1981	1982	1983	1984	1985	1986	1987
Africa										
Deficit on goods, services, and private transfers	15.5	6.7	5.4	25.6	24.8	15.3	10.3	5.7	15.6	13.9
Use of reserves	1.8	−4.4	−6.2	8.6	4.0	0.5	0.3	−0.5	1.3	1.6
Asset transactions, net	−1.0	−1.7	−1.3	−1.7	−0.8	−0.6	−0.4	−0.1	−0.1	—
Errors and omissions	0.1	−1.4	−1.1	−0.7	−2.3	−2.9	−2.2	−1.1	—	—
Non-debt-creating flows, net	3.6	4.9	4.1	3.5	5.5	4.8	4.7	5.2	5.1	5.0
Net external borrowing	10.9	9.3	9.7	15.9	18.4	13.5	7.9	2.3	9.3	7.3
Long-term borrowing from official creditors	3.9	6.0	6.1	7.3	5.2	7.4	5.6	4.9	5.2	5.0
Reserve-related liabilities	0.5	—	1.6	2.9	7.8	5.1	1.0	0.5	3.2	1.9
Other borrowing	6.5	3.3	2.0	5.7	5.4	1.0	1.4	−3.1	0.9	0.5
Asia										
Deficit on goods, services, and private transfers	8.7	15.1	21.9	23.7	20.2	17.0	7.6	18.2	18.3	19.9
Use of reserves	−5.0	−6.0	−6.7	−6.7	−6.0	−8.8	−9.3	0.5	−4.5	−5.2
Asset transactions, net	−0.2	−1.5	0.9	0.1	−1.9	−2.7	−3.9	−3.2	−5.1	−6.3
Errors and omissions	−1.2	−0.2	−1.8	−3.2	−4.7	−2.3	−2.3	−0.7	—	—
Non-debt-creating flows, net	4.9	5.5	6.5	8.7	6.8	6.8	7.3	7.3	7.9	8.4
Net external borrowing	10.3	17.3	22.9	24.8	25.9	24.1	15.8	14.4	19.9	22.9
Long-term borrowing from official creditors	4.4	4.6	6.9	10.2	9.4	9.3	10.7	6.5	10.0	10.1
Reserve-related liabilities	−0.2	−0.1	1.3	3.4	2.6	4.2	1.4	−3.6	0.1	−0.3
Other borrowing	6.1	12.8	14.8	11.2	14.0	10.6	3.7	11.4	9.8	13.1
Europe										
Deficit on goods, services, and private transfers	7.2	10.1	12.4	10.2	6.8	5.3	3.0	3.3	−0.3	0.6
Use of reserves	−1.0	1.1	−0.9	0.6	1.8	−0.1	−1.6	−1.9	−1.5	−1.7
Asset transactions, net	—	0.5	0.3	−0.8	−1.5	−0.4	−0.2	−0.3	−0.6	−0.5
Errors and omissions	−1.1	0.5	0.2	1.6	0.8	−1.4	−0.1	0.3	—	—
Non-debt-creating flows, net	0.8	1.2	1.0	1.1	1.4	1.9	1.8	1.8	2.0	2.1
Net external borrowing	8.4	6.9	11.8	7.7	4.4	5.2	3.1	3.4	−0.2	0.7
Long-term borrowing from official creditors	2.7	1.2	3.6	2.7	2.4	1.0	2.0	0.5	0.6	0.2
Reserve-related liabilities	0.4	−0.5	−0.2	2.3	—	0.8	0.2	−0.6	−0.9	−1.5
Other borrowing	5.2	6.1	8.3	2.7	2.0	3.4	0.8	3.5	0.1	2.0
Non-oil Middle East										
Deficit on goods, services, and private transfers	5.6	7.2	7.1	10.2	9.2	11.3	10.7	9.9	13.1	10.7
Use of reserves	−1.7	−0.9	−1.3	—	−1.8	1.1	2.5	−1.2	0.1	0.5
Asset transactions, net	0.1	0.5	−1.4	−0.3	1.6	−0.8	−0.3	−0.3	0.5	0.1
Errors and omissions	−0.4	−0.8	0.2	1.0	—	1.4	−0.3	0.5	—	—
Non-debt-creating flows, net	3.5	6.0	5.2	6.2	5.6	5.0	5.3	6.7	7.5	6.9
Net external borrowing	4.1	2.3	4.4	3.4	3.8	4.6	3.5	4.2	5.0	3.1
Long-term borrowing from official creditors	3.0	4.7	4.5	4.6	5.1	4.5	3.1	2.8	2.3	4.4
Reserve-related liabilities	0.9	—	−0.2	−0.5	−0.4	−0.2	—	1.8	1.7	−0.7
Other borrowing	0.2	−2.3	0.1	−0.7	−0.9	0.4	0.4	−0.4	1.1	−0.7

Table A41 *(concluded).* **Capital Importing Developing Countries—by Region: Summary of External Financing, 1978–87[1]**

(In billions of U.S. dollars)

	1978	1979	1980	1981	1982	1983	1984	1985	1986	1987
Western Hemisphere										
Deficit on goods, services, and										
private transfers	19.4	21.8	30.2	43.3	42.0	11.4	4.9	5.9	8.6	8.2
Use of reserves	−8.0	−11.3	−3.6	2.6	19.2	−2.1	−11.6	0.9	−3.5	−2.3
Asset transactions, net	−2.5	−2.1	−2.7	−9.8	−7.6	−5.2	−7.1	−2.2	−4.1	−4.5
Errors and omissions	−3.1	−2.0	−12.4	−18.3	−20.2	−5.8	0.9	−2.7	—	—
Non-debt-creating flows, net	4.9	7.1	6.8	8.3	7.3	4.7	5.0	5.5	6.5	6.6
Net external borrowing	28.0	30.1	42.0	60.6	43.3	19.7	17.7	4.5	3.7	8.4
Long-term borrowing from official										
creditors	2.5	2.8	4.2	5.3	5.6	9.5	7.3	3.3	9.1	6.9
Reserve-related liabilities	−0.3	−0.1	1.9	1.2	9.0	8.2	3.4	1.8	−1.8	2.0
Other borrowing	25.8	27.4	35.9	54.1	28.8	2.0	7.0	−0.6	2.3	−0.5

[1] For definition of stub entries, see Table A40.

Table A42. Capital Importing Developing Countries—by Analytical Subgroup: Summary of External Financing, 1978–87[1]

(In billions of U.S. dollars)

	1978	1979	1980	1981	1982	1983	1984	1985	1986	1987
By predominant export										
Non-fuel exporters										
Deficit on goods, services, and private transfers	35.6	53.8	77.5	91.4	76.7	55.6	38.5	42.4	35.9	37.0
Use of reserves	−16.3	−10.5	−4.9	0.5	0.1	−7.7	−14.1	−2.6	−13.2	−10.3
Asset transactions, net	−0.9	−0.8	−0.5	−5.4	−4.0	−4.5	−7.7	−4.8	−6.2	−8.0
Errors and omissions	−5.9	−1.9	−9.3	−9.1	−11.6	−6.8	−5.4	−2.1	—	—
Non-debt-creating flows, net	14.7	19.3	19.3	22.2	21.2	19.5	20.5	23.4	25.6	25.7
Net external borrowing	44.0	47.7	72.8	83.2	71.0	55.2	45.2	28.5	29.7	29.7
Long-term borrowing from official creditors	13.9	17.3	22.0	25.5	25.1	25.2	26.2	15.2	22.7	22.1
Reserve-related liabilities	1.7	−0.3	4.3	9.3	12.5	11.9	5.0	0.8	−1.2	−2.0
Other borrowing	28.4	30.7	46.6	48.3	33.4	18.2	14.0	12.5	8.2	9.7
Primary product exporters										
Deficit on goods, services, and private transfers	23.1	28.6	45.5	63.0	60.4	44.2	32.0	24.8	22.1	23.9
Use of reserves	−9.9	−7.9	0.3	6.7	9.1	1.8	−6.7	−1.4	−5.5	−3.2
Asset transactions, net	−1.1	−1.4	−0.7	−5.3	−2.9	−2.3	−3.2	−1.1	−1.7	−2.1
Errors and omissions	−5.0	−2.7	−9.6	−9.7	−10.3	−3.5	−2.6	−2.2	—	—
Non-debt-creating flows, net	8.6	10.6	10.3	12.2	12.0	10.8	10.9	11.9	12.5	13.0
Net external borrowing	30.6	29.9	45.3	59.2	52.5	37.5	33.6	17.5	16.8	16.3
Long-term borrowing from official creditors	7.7	9.7	12.8	14.6	14.3	15.5	17.7	8.5	15.3	11.8
Reserve-related liabilities	1.0	0.8	4.0	5.8	10.8	9.8	3.9	0.3	−2.6	0.9
Other borrowing	21.9	19.4	28.5	38.8	27.5	12.1	12.0	8.7	4.1	3.5
Agricultural exporters										
Deficit on goods, services, and private transfers	19.4	27.4	42.4	44.8	46.7	37.9	24.5	22.2	19.7	20.8
Use of reserves	−8.6	−5.6	3.4	4.0	7.5	1.9	−6.9	−0.8	−4.0	−2.5
Asset transactions, net	−0.9	−0.4	−0.6	−4.0	−1.8	−1.9	−3.6	−1.4	−1.7	−1.9
Errors and omissions	−4.6	−1.9	−7.6	−9.3	−9.6	−1.5	−0.6	−1.0	—	—
Non-debt-creating flows, net	7.3	8.8	8.6	9.6	9.5	9.2	9.4	10.3	10.9	11.5
Net external borrowing	26.2	26.5	38.6	44.5	41.1	30.2	26.2	15.1	14.5	13.8
Long-term borrowing from official creditors	5.8	7.1	9.3	11.8	11.5	11.7	15.2	6.6	12.4	9.6
Reserve-related liabilities	0.3	1.3	2.6	4.3	7.2	9.0	2.4	−1.5	−3.9	−0.7
Other borrowing	20.1	18.1	26.7	28.4	22.4	9.4	8.6	10.0	5.9	4.9
Mineral exporters										
Deficit on goods, services, and private transfers	3.7	1.1	3.1	18.2	13.8	6.3	7.4	2.5	2.4	3.1
Use of reserves	−1.3	−2.3	−3.1	2.7	1.6	−0.1	0.2	−0.6	−1.5	−0.7
Asset transactions, net	−0.3	−1.0	−0.2	−1.3	−1.1	−0.4	0.4	0.3	−0.1	−0.1
Errors and omissions	−0.3	−0.8	−2.0	−0.5	−0.7	−2.0	−2.1	−1.2	—	—
Non-debt-creating flows, net	1.2	1.8	1.7	2.6	2.5	1.6	1.5	1.6	1.6	1.5
Net external borrowing	4.3	3.5	6.7	14.7	11.4	7.3	7.4	2.4	2.4	2.4
Long-term borrowing from official creditors	1.9	2.6	3.5	2.8	2.8	3.8	2.5	1.9	2.8	2.2
Reserve-related liabilities	0.6	−0.5	1.4	1.5	3.6	0.7	1.5	1.8	1.3	1.6
Other borrowing	1.7	1.3	1.8	10.4	5.1	2.7	3.4	−1.3	−1.8	−1.4

233

Table A42 *(continued).* **Capital Importing Developing Countries—by Analytical Subgroup: Summary of External Financing, 1978–87[1]**

(In billions of U.S. dollars)

	1978	1979	1980	1981	1982	1983	1984	1985	1986	1987
Exporters of manufactures										
Deficit on goods, services, and private transfers	6.9	16.9	22.5	14.8	3.4	0.1	−4.3	6.5	0.4	1.5
Use of reserves	−4.8	−2.3	−3.5	−6.7	−7.4	−9.6	−9.1	−0.7	−7.8	−7.3
Asset transactions, net	−0.2	0.4	1.0	0.1	−1.3	−1.9	−4.7	−3.6	−5.1	−6.4
Errors and omissions	−0.1	−0.4	−0.5	−0.4	−1.6	−4.3	−2.8	−0.4	—	—
Non-debt-creating flows, net	3.6	4.3	4.9	5.4	4.2	4.5	5.7	7.4	8.0	7.5
Net external borrowing	8.4	14.9	20.6	16.4	9.6	11.4	6.5	3.9	5.3	7.7
Long-term borrowing from official creditors	2.7	4.2	4.5	6.3	5.5	5.0	3.9	2.9	4.2	4.9
Reserve-related liabilities	−0.2	0.1	1.2	3.4	1.7	1.7	1.3	−0.7	—	−1.7
Other borrowing	5.9	10.6	14.9	6.7	2.4	4.6	1.4	1.7	1.0	4.6
Service and remittance countries										
Deficit on goods, services, and private transfers	5.7	8.3	9.5	13.5	12.9	11.3	10.8	11.1	13.4	11.7
Use of reserves	−1.6	−0.3	−1.6	0.5	−1.6	0.1	1.7	−0.5	0.1	0.2
Asset transactions, net	0.5	0.2	−0.8	−0.3	0.2	−0.3	0.1	−0.1	0.7	0.5
Errors and omissions	−0.9	1.2	0.9	1.0	0.3	1.0	−0.1	0.5	—	—
Non-debt-creating flows, net	2.5	4.4	4.1	4.7	5.0	4.2	3.9	4.2	5.0	5.3
Net external borrowing	5.1	2.8	6.9	7.5	9.0	6.4	5.1	7.1	7.6	5.7
Long-term borrowing from official creditors	3.6	3.4	4.7	4.6	5.4	4.6	4.6	3.8	3.2	5.4
Reserve-related liabilities	0.9	−1.2	−0.9	0.1	0.1	0.4	−0.2	1.3	1.4	−1.2
Other borrowing	0.6	0.6	3.1	2.8	3.5	1.4	0.7	2.1	3.1	1.6
By financial criteria[2]										
Diversified borrowers										
Deficit on goods, services, and private transfers	12.6	18.3	24.2	21.0	11.2	15.2	14.3	27.0	27.1	24.7
Use of reserves	−2.5	−2.5	−1.0	−0.3	−8.7	−4.2	−1.4	4.9	−3.8	−2.8
Asset transactions, net	−0.4	−0.6	−0.5	−1.1	−0.5	−2.6	−3.2	−0.8	−0.2	−0.8
Errors and omissions	−1.6	0.8	2.5	1.6	−1.4	1.2	−1.2	0.6	—	—
Non-debt-creating flows, net	4.5	6.3	5.8	6.6	5.9	6.4	7.5	9.9	10.9	10.4
Net external borrowing	12.6	14.4	17.4	14.3	15.8	14.4	12.7	12.4	20.1	17.9
Long-term borrowing from official creditors	6.1	7.9	9.8	11.5	11.5	8.8	9.3	6.5	8.1	10.3
Reserve-related liabilities	1.6	0.9	1.2	3.8	2.2	0.3	1.1	0.6	1.4	−2.0
Other borrowing	4.9	5.6	6.3	−1.0	2.1	5.3	2.3	5.3	10.6	9.5
Countries with recent debt-servicing problems										
Deficit on goods, services, and private transfers	34.8	35.2	42.1	71.3	66.7	25.0	12.8	10.5	20.5	16.7
Use of reserves	−6.9	−12.0	−7.9	12.4	22.8	−2.4	−14.8	1.9	−4.3	−2.3
Asset transactions, net	−3.6	−3.0	−4.3	−12.7	−10.0	−6.9	−7.8	−2.7	−4.0	−4.9
Errors and omissions	−4.2	−4.1	−14.9	−18.9	−20.6	−8.6	0.6	−2.2	—	—
Non-debt-creating flows, net	8.0	11.7	9.1	10.9	11.7	8.1	8.4	9.9	11.4	11.9
Net external borrowing	41.6	42.5	60.1	79.7	62.8	34.7	26.4	3.7	17.4	12.0
Long-term borrowing from official creditors	8.1	9.9	13.8	16.7	13.7	19.6	15.5	10.7	14.8	13.9
Reserve-related liabilities	1.3	0.2	3.9	5.8	16.0	15.0	5.3	0.7	2.8	2.7
Other borrowing	32.1	32.4	42.4	57.2	33.1	0.2	5.5	−7.7	−0.2	−4.5

Table A42 *(continued).* **Capital Importing Developing Countries—by Analytical Subgroup: Summary of External Financing, 1978–87[1]**

(In billions of U.S. dollars)

	1978	1979	1980	1981	1982	1983	1984	1985	1986	1987
Countries without debt-servicing problems										
Deficit on goods, services, and private transfers	21.6	25.7	34.9	41.7	36.4	35.5	23.6	32.5	34.8	36.6
Use of reserves	−7.0	−9.6	−10.7	−7.3	−5.5	−7.0	−4.9	−4.1	−3.9	−4.8
Asset transactions, net	0.2	−1.2	0.1	0.2	−0.2	−2.7	−4.1	−3.5	−5.2	−6.2
Errors and omissions	−1.5	0.3	0.2	−0.7	−5.7	−2.3	−4.7	−1.6	—	—
Non-debt-creating flows, net	9.8	13.0	14.5	16.9	14.9	15.0	15.6	16.6	17.7	17.3
Net external borrowing	20.1	23.3	30.8	32.6	33.0	32.4	21.6	25.0	26.3	30.4
Long-term borrowing from official creditors	8.3	9.3	11.5	13.3	13.9	12.0	13.2	7.3	12.5	12.7
Reserve-related liabilities	—	−0.9	0.5	3.4	2.9	3.1	0.6	−0.7	−0.4	−1.2
Other borrowing	11.8	14.8	18.7	15.9	16.2	17.3	7.9	18.5	14.2	18.9
By miscellaneous criteria										
Capital importing fuel exporters										
Deficit on goods, services, and private transfers	20.8	7.0	−0.5	21.7	26.3	4.8	−2.0	0.6	19.4	16.2
Use of reserves	2.4	−11.2	−13.7	4.6	17.1	−1.7	−5.7	0.4	5.1	3.2
Asset transactions, net	−2.6	−3.4	−3.6	−7.1	−6.3	−5.1	−4.1	−1.4	−3.1	−3.1
Errors and omissions	0.1	−1.9	−5.5	−10.6	−14.7	−4.1	1.4	−1.7	—	—
Non-debt-creating flows, net	3.1	5.4	4.4	5.6	5.4	3.7	3.5	3.0	3.4	3.4
Net external borrowing	17.7	18.1	18.0	29.2	24.8	11.9	2.8	0.2	14.0	12.7
Long-term borrowing from official creditors	2.5	1.9	3.4	4.5	2.5	6.4	2.5	2.8	4.6	4.5
Reserve-related liabilities	−0.3	−0.4	0.1	−0.2	6.4	6.2	1.0	−0.8	3.6	3.5
Other borrowing	15.4	16.6	14.6	24.8	15.9	−0.7	−0.7	−1.8	5.8	4.7
Fifteen heavily indebted countries										
Deficit on goods, services, and private transfers	25.4	25.4	29.4	50.9	50.8	14.8	1.6	1.4	8.4	5.9
Use of reserves	−6.7	−13.1	−8.6	9.0	23.0	−0.2	−13.3	1.2	−3.3	−2.2
Asset transactions, net	−3.0	−1.8	−2.6	−11.4	−9.3	−5.1	−6.6	−2.2	−4.3	−4.7
Errors and omissions	−2.8	−2.1	−12.4	−17.9	−20.0	−7.9	1.4	−2.0	—	—
Non-debt-creating flows, net	5.4	8.0	6.0	7.3	7.4	4.6	4.3	5.3	6.0	5.9
Net external borrowing	32.5	34.4	46.9	63.8	49.7	23.4	15.8	−1.0	10.0	6.9
Long-term borrowing from official creditors	3.7	2.6	4.6	6.5	4.0	12.0	8.1	4.9	9.1	6.2
Reserve-related liabilities	−0.5	−0.2	1.7	1.6	12.9	14.2	3.2	−2.0	1.3	3.6
Other borrowing	29.3	32.1	40.7	55.7	32.7	−2.8	4.5	−3.8	−0.3	−2.9
Small low-income countries										
Deficit on goods, services, and private transfers	8.7	10.2	12.5	12.9	12.9	10.1	11.2	11.5	11.6	12.4
Use of reserves	0.2	−0.3	−0.2	0.1	0.2	−1.2	1.0	1.3	−0.4	0.3
Asset transactions, net	−0.2	−0.3	−0.4	—	−0.1	—	−0.2	—	0.1	0.1
Errors and omissions	0.6	—	0.1	—	−0.1	−0.3	0.1	−0.2	—	—
Non-debt-creating flows, net	3.0	3.8	4.2	4.3	4.5	4.3	4.7	4.9	4.9	5.1
Net external borrowing	5.2	6.9	8.7	8.4	8.3	7.3	5.6	5.6	7.0	6.8
Long-term borrowing from official creditors	2.9	5.1	6.0	6.8	6.8	5.0	5.7	4.5	5.9	6.0
Reserve-related liabilities	0.3	0.1	1.5	2.2	2.2	1.0	0.4	0.8	−0.1	—
Other borrowing	2.0	1.7	1.3	−0.6	−0.8	1.3	−0.5	0.2	1.1	0.8

235

Table A42 *(concluded).* **Capital Importing Developing Countries—by Analytical Subgroup: Summary of External Financing, 1978–87**[1]

(In billions of U.S. dollars)

	1978	1979	1980	1981	1982	1983	1984	1985	1986	1987
Sub-Saharan Africa[3]										
Deficit on goods, services, and										
private transfers	7.6	8.1	11.3	12.4	11.5	9.4	7.3	7.6	9.1	9.8
Use of reserves	0.1	−0.2	0.2	0.3	0.5	−0.3	−0.2	−0.1	−0.5	0.5
Asset transactions, net	−0.1	−0.2	−0.7	−0.6	−0.3	−0.2	−0.2	−0.1	0.1	0.1
Errors and omissions	0.5	−0.2	0.3	0.4	−0.8	−0.5	−0.4	−0.3	—	—
Non-debt-creating flows, net	2.7	3.5	4.1	4.0	3.9	4.0	3.9	4.2	4.3	4.4
Net external borrowing	4.5	5.3	7.3	8.4	8.1	6.4	4.2	3.9	5.3	4.8
Long-term borrowing from										
official creditors	2.2	4.6	4.5	4.9	5.5	3.6	4.6	3.6	4.1	3.9
Reserve-related liabilities	0.7	0.3	1.6	2.6	2.2	1.7	0.7	1.0	0.5	0.3
Other borrowing	1.6	0.4	1.2	0.9	0.4	1.0	−1.1	−0.7	0.6	0.7

[1] For definition of stub entries, see Table A40.

[2] For estimates for the market and official borrowers, see Table A40.

[3] Excluding Nigeria and South Africa.

Table A43. Capital Importing Developing Countries—by Alternative Analytical Categories: Summary of External Financing, 1978–87

(In billions of U.S. dollars)

	1978	1979	1980	1981	1982	1983	1984	1985	1986	1987
Non-oil developing countries										
Deficit on goods, services, and private transfers[1]	41.5	61.3	86.8	108.4	86.3	54.2	38.8	44.8	42.2	42.8
Non-debt-creating flows	17.2	23.3	23.5	27.6	25.4	22.6	23.5	25.8	28.4	28.4
Official transfers	8.3	11.6	12.4	13.4	13.1	13.3	13.8	16.2	17.0	16.1
Direct investment flows, net	7.1	9.6	9.1	13.6	12.2	8.9	9.4	9.5	10.8	11.6
SDR allocations, valuation adjustments, and gold monetization	1.7	2.1	2.0	0.7	—	0.4	0.3	0.2	0.6	0.7
Use of reserves	−16.9	−11.8	−6.7	−1.2	4.1	−10.0	−16.5	0.3	−15.0	−10.7
Asset transactions, net[2]	−1.8	−3.0	−2.5	−9.9	−5.1	−8.6	−10.4	−5.7	−9.0	−10.7
Recorded errors and omissions[3]	−6.2	−1.4	−12.1	−16.8	−22.2	−9.6	−5.6	−4.1	—	—
Net external borrowing	49.3	54.1	84.7	108.6	84.1	59.8	47.9	28.4	37.8	35.9
Reserve-related liabilities	1.4	−0.8	4.4	9.2	14.5	12.1	5.8	2.0	0.4	−1.1
Liabilities constituting foreign authorities' reserves[4]	1.4	−1.3	2.0	0.9	1.6	−2.0	−0.7	0.3	−0.3	−0.1
Use of Fund credit[5]	−0.6	0.2	1.5	6.3	7.0	11.0	5.1	0.6	−0.7	−3.7
Arrears	0.5	0.4	0.8	1.9	5.9	3.2	1.4	1.0	1.4	2.7
Long-term borrowing from official creditors, net[6]	14.9	18.1	23.5	28.1	27.3	27.5	27.1	17.0	25.3	24.4
Other net external borrowing[7]	33.0	36.8	56.8	71.3	42.3	20.2	15.0	9.5	12.1	12.5
Long-term	25.5	31.5	33.0	51.0	29.4	38.8	15.9	22.2	11.2	11.5
From banks[8]	22.4	20.0	17.8	27.4	17.1	40.9	16.4	25.3	11.8	9.5
Other	3.1	11.6	15.2	23.6	12.3	−2.1	−0.5	−3.1	−0.7	2.0
Short-term	7.6	5.2	23.8	20.3	12.8	−18.6	−0.9	−11.7	0.6	0.7
Net oil exporters[9]										
Deficit on goods, services, and private transfers	7.5	7.8	10.3	23.4	17.5	5.1	4.7	7.5	16.8	14.2
Use of reserves	−1.4	−3.6	−3.5	−0.7	3.6	−2.4	−3.4	1.4	−0.6	−0.3
Asset transactions, net	−1.3	−3.0	−3.1	−5.3	−1.3	−6.2	−2.6	−1.2	−2.9	−3.2
Errors and omissions	−1.7	−0.2	−4.0	−7.9	−9.6	−3.0	0.4	−2.5	—	—
Non-debt-creating flows	3.8	5.8	5.3	7.2	5.6	4.6	4.1	3.9	5.1	5.2
Net external borrowing	8.0	8.8	15.5	30.1	19.2	12.0	6.2	6.0	15.2	12.5
Long-term borrowing from official creditors	3.0	3.3	5.6	5.9	5.8	7.0	5.2	3.4	4.4	5.9
Reserve-related liabilities	0.9	−0.2	0.1	−0.2	2.3	0.1	1.4	3.8	5.5	2.5
Other borrowing	4.1	5.7	9.8	24.3	11.2	4.9	−0.3	−1.3	5.4	4.1

Table A43 *(concluded).* **Capital Importing Developing Countries—by Alternative Analytical Categories: Summary of External Financing, 1978–87**

(In billions of U.S. dollars)

	1978	1979	1980	1981	1982	1983	1984	1985	1986	1987
Net oil importers[9]										
Deficit on goods, services, and										
private transfers	34.1	53.5	76.6	84.9	68.8	49.1	34.1	37.3	25.4	28.6
Use of reserves	−15.5	−8.2	−3.3	−0.5	0.5	−7.7	−13.1	−1.0	−14.4	−10.4
Asset transactions, net	−0.5	0.1	0.6	−4.6	−3.7	−2.4	−7.8	−4.6	−6.1	−7.5
Errors and omissions	−4.5	−1.2	−8.1	−8.9	−12.6	−6.6	−6.0	−1.5	—	—
Non-debt-creating flows	13.3	17.4	18.2	20.4	19.8	18.0	19.4	22.0	23.3	23.2
Net external borrowing	41.3	45.3	69.1	78.5	64.8	47.8	41.7	22.5	22.6	23.4
Long-term borrowing from										
official creditors	11.9	14.8	17.9	22.2	21.6	20.5	21.9	13.6	20.9	18.5
Reserve-related liabilities	0.5	−0.5	4.3	9.4	12.2	12.0	4.5	−1.9	−5.1	−3.6
Other borrowing	28.9	31.0	47.0	46.9	31.0	15.3	15.3	10.7	6.7	8.4

NOTE: Except where otherwise footnoted, estimates shown here are based on national balance of payments statistics, which are not always easily reconcilable with year-to-year changes in either debtor- or creditor-reported debt statistics, in part because the latter are affected by changes in valuation.

[1] Equivalent to current account deficit less official transfers. For the purposes of this table, official transfers are treated as external financing.

[2] Pertains primarily to export credit.

[3] Positioned here on the presumption that estimates reflect primarily unrecorded capital outflows.

[4] Comprises short-term borrowing by the monetary authorities from other monetary authorities.

[5] Projected use of Fund credit includes prospective programs.

[6] Estimates, based on debt statistics reported in Table A49, of net disbursements by official creditors (other than monetary institutions).

[7] Residually calculated. Except for minor discrepancies in coverage, amounts shown reflect almost exclusively net borrowing from private creditors.

[8] Refers only to long-term lending by banks guaranteed by government of debtor country. Bank lending also accounts for a large fraction of unguaranteed long-term flows (included in "other" long-term flows) and short-term flows.

[9] For definition of stubs, see footnotes on the non-oil developing countries.

Table A44. Capital Importing Developing Countries: Reserves and Ratios of Reserves to Imports of Goods and Services, 1978–87[1]

(Values in billions of U.S. dollars; ratios in percent)

	1978	1979	1980	1981	1982	1983	1984	1985	1986	1987
Official reserve holdings										
Capital importing countries	**95.9**	**113.0**	**121.0**	**116.6**	**104.8**	**114.0**	**132.2**	**138.2**	**146.8**	**155.3**
By region										
Africa	9.7	14.7	20.4	13.2	8.6	7.9	7.2	9.4	8.6	7.8
Asia	31.0	36.2	39.6	44.2	49.0	58.5	67.4	69.6	74.0	79.5
Europe	10.6	9.6	10.1	9.1	7.7	8.5	9.5	11.2	12.8	14.5
Non-oil Middle East	9.0	9.8	10.6	10.5	11.2	9.8	7.3	8.6	8.6	8.3
Western Hemisphere	35.5	42.7	40.3	39.6	28.2	29.3	40.8	39.4	42.9	45.2
By predominant export										
Non-fuel exporters	76.8	85.7	85.1	84.0	83.2	90.0	103.6	109.3	122.6	133.9
Primary product exporters	39.4	46.4	43.4	37.5	28.8	27.2	34.4	36.8	42.6	46.7
Agricultural exporters	35.0	39.5	34.7	30.1	23.1	21.1	28.3	29.9	34.2	37.0
Mineral exporters	4.4	6.8	8.6	7.4	5.7	6.1	6.1	6.9	8.5	9.7
Exporters of manufactures	26.2	28.0	29.8	35.7	43.0	51.3	60.3	62.6	70.3	77.6
Service and remittance countries	11.2	11.3	11.9	10.8	11.4	11.4	8.9	9.9	9.7	9.6
By financial criteria										
Market borrowers	64.8	78.6	86.9	83.3	65.4	70.0	87.4	95.6	100.3	106.1
Official borrowers	9.6	10.5	10.1	9.8	8.9	9.9	8.7	9.4	9.4	9.2
Diversified borrowers	21.5	23.9	24.1	23.5	30.5	34.2	36.0	33.2	37.1	40.0
Countries with recent debt-servicing problems	43.6	51.8	53.2	43.9	28.0	31.7	44.8	43.7	48.4	51.4
Countries without debt-servicing problems	52.3	61.2	67.9	72.7	76.8	82.3	87.4	94.5	98.4	103.9
By miscellaneous criteria										
Capital importing fuel exporters	19.1	27.4	35.9	32.5	21.6	24.0	28.6	29.0	24.2	21.4
Fifteen heavily indebted countries	38.2	47.6	50.0	41.8	26.3	27.5	39.6	38.4	41.9	44.1
Small low-income countries	4.5	5.0	4.4	4.3	3.7	5.1	4.4	4.3	4.8	5.0
Sub-Saharan Africa[2]	3.6	4.1	3.8	3.5	2.7	2.9	3.0	3.8	4.8	5.2
By alternative analytical categories										
Non-oil developing countries	82.6	92.6	94.1	95.0	90.2	99.0	114.9	117.7	133.1	145.2
Net oil exporters	10.4	13.4	16.8	17.3	13.3	15.4	17.8	16.4	17.3	18.0
Net oil importers	72.2	79.2	77.3	77.6	76.9	83.7	97.0	101.3	115.8	127.2

Table A44 *(concluded).* **Capital Importing Developing Countries: Reserves and Ratios of Reserves to Imports of Goods and Services, 1978–87[1]**

(Values in billions of U.S. dollars; ratios in percent)

	1978	1979	1980	1981	1982	1983	1984	1985	1986	1987
Ratios of reserves to imports of goods and services[3]										
Capital importing countries	**25.8**	**23.9**	**19.8**	**17.3**	**16.7**	**19.5**	**21.8**	**22.7**	**23.0**	**22.6**
By region										
Africa	13.1	17.0	18.0	11.1	8.3	8.5	8.1	11.3	9.7	8.6
Asia	24.3	21.3	18.1	18.2	20.7	24.1	25.8	25.7	25.5	25.1
Europe	20.8	14.8	12.9	11.2	10.3	12.0	12.9	14.8	15.8	16.1
Non-oil Middle East	33.2	28.3	24.3	21.9	23.9	20.9	15.4	18.8	17.9	16.9
Western Hemisphere	38.8	36.4	25.7	21.8	17.1	22.4	30.0	29.8	32.4	32.0
By predominant export										
Non-fuel exporters	26.6	22.8	17.7	16.3	17.1	19.2	21.1	22.1	23.1	23.2
Primary product exporters	30.5	28.2	20.2	16.4	13.4	13.6	17.2	19.2	20.8	20.8
Agricultural exporters	37.4	33.0	22.5	18.6	14.7	14.1	18.8	20.1	21.4	21.2
Mineral exporters	12.4	15.4	14.5	11.0	9.9	12.2	12.3	15.9	18.5	19.4
Exporters of manufactures	21.5	17.3	14.7	16.5	21.1	24.9	26.9	26.2	27.3	27.4
Service and remittance countries	30.0	22.9	18.8	15.7	16.7	17.7	13.6	15.5	14.3	13.6
By financial criteria										
Market borrowers	26.0	24.7	20.9	17.7	14.9	17.7	21.5	24.1	24.2	23.8
Official borrowers	22.9	21.0	16.5	15.5	14.8	16.9	14.7	16.2	15.3	14.1
Diversified borrowers	26.7	22.9	17.9	16.8	23.7	26.3	25.6	21.6	22.7	22.7
Countries with recent debt-servicing problems	25.2	23.9	18.8	14.1	10.1	13.7	19.0	19.5	21.0	21.1
Countries without debt-servicing problems	26.3	23.9	20.7	20.1	21.9	23.4	23.5	24.6	24.1	23.4
By miscellaneous criteria										
Capital importing fuel exporters	22.9	27.9	27.5	20.7	15.2	21.1	24.6	25.5	22.3	19.5
Fifteen heavily indebted countries	33.2	32.3	26.0	19.2	13.5	17.9	25.5	25.6	27.5	27.3
Small low-income countries	17.1	16.3	11.9	11.8	10.5	15.0	12.4	12.1	12.3	12.0
Sub-Saharan Africa[2]	12.8	12.6	9.4	8.9	7.5	8.7	9.2	11.4	12.9	13.1
By alternative analytical categories										
Non-oil developing countries	26.1	22.4	17.6	16.3	16.6	19.2	21.2	21.6	23.0	23.1
Net oil exporters	22.0	20.8	19.4	16.4	13.9	18.3	19.4	18.2	18.8	18.7
Net oil importers	26.8	22.7	17.2	16.2	17.1	19.4	21.6	22.2	23.8	23.9

[1] For this table, official holdings of gold are valued at SDR 35 an ounce. This convention results in a significant underestimate of the reserves of those groups of countries that have substantial holdings of gold.

[2] Excluding Nigeria and South Africa.

[3] Ratio of end-year reserves to imports of goods and services during the year indicated.

Table A45. Developing Countries: Use of Fund Credit, 1978–87[1]
(In billions of U.S. dollars)

	1978	1979	1980	1981	1982	1983	1984	1985	1986	1987
Developing countries	**−0.6**	**0.2**	**1.5**	**6.3**	**7.0**	**11.4**	**5.1**	**0.2**	**−0.6**	**−2.9**
By region										
Africa	0.1	0.1	0.3	1.8	2.1	1.4	0.7	0.2	−0.7	−0.6
Asia	−0.2	—	1.0	3.2	2.3	2.5	0.4	−0.8	—	−0.6
Europe	0.1	0.1	0.6	1.1	1.2	1.4	0.7	−0.6	−0.9	−1.5
Middle East	—	−0.1	−0.2	−0.2	−0.1	—	—	—	—	0.1
Western Hemisphere	−0.6	0.1	−0.2	0.4	1.5	6.1	3.4	1.4	1.0	−0.3
By predominant export										
Fuel exporters	−0.2	−0.2	−0.2	—	0.2	1.7	1.3	—	1.3	1.3
Non-fuel exporters	−0.3	0.3	1.6	6.3	6.8	9.7	3.9	0.2	−1.9	−4.2
Primary product exporters	0.1	0.6	0.9	3.8	3.7	6.8	2.3	1.1	−1.7	−2.1
Agricultural exporters	−0.2	0.6	0.8	2.9	1.8	5.5	1.6	0.9	−0.9	−1.2
Mineral exporters	0.3	−0.1	—	0.9	1.9	1.3	0.7	0.2	−0.8	−0.9
Exporters of manufactures	−0.3	—	1.2	2.3	2.8	2.1	1.3	−0.7	—	−1.7
Service and remittance countries	−0.1	−0.2	−0.4	0.3	0.4	0.8	0.3	−0.1	−0.3	−0.4
By financial criteria										
Capital importing countries	−0.6	0.2	1.5	6.3	7.0	11.4	5.1	0.2	−0.6	−2.9
Market borrowers	−1.0	−0.4	0.6	1.8	2.9	7.7	4.2	0.7	0.2	−0.8
Official borrowers	0.2	0.5	0.1	2.0	1.3	1.6	0.4	—	−0.6	−0.8
Diversified borrowers	0.2	0.1	0.7	2.5	2.8	2.1	0.6	−0.4	−0.3	−1.3
Countries with recent debt-servicing problems	−0.5	0.3	0.5	3.0	4.1	7.9	4.0	1.6	−0.2	−1.6
Countries without debt-servicing problems	−0.1	−0.1	1.0	3.4	3.0	3.5	1.1	−1.3	−0.5	−1.3
By miscellaneous criteria										
Capital importing fuel exporters	−0.2	−0.2	−0.2	—	0.2	1.7	1.3	—	1.3	1.3
Fifteen heavily indebted countries	−0.7	0.1	0.5	1.2	2.2	6.3	3.3	1.6	0.7	−0.4
Small low-income countries	—	0.2	0.2	1.4	1.1	1.2	0.2	—	−0.4	−0.6
Sub-Saharan Africa[2]	0.2	0.4	0.3	1.7	0.7	1.3	0.5	0.1	−0.2	−0.5
By alternative analytical categories										
Oil exporting countries	—	—	—	—	—	0.5	—	−0.4	—	0.8
Non-oil developing countries	−0.6	0.2	1.5	6.3	7.0	11.0	5.1	0.6	−0.7	−3.7
Net oil exporters	—	−0.1	−0.3	0.1	0.6	1.4	1.2	0.1	1.1	0.5
Net oil importers	−0.5	0.3	1.7	6.2	6.5	9.5	3.9	0.5	−1.7	−4.2
Memorandum										
Drawings outstanding at end of year										
Developing countries	8.0	8.3	9.5	14.9	21.2	31.3	34.2	38.6	38.0	35.1

[1] Projected use of Fund credit includes prospective programs.
[2] Excluding Nigeria and South Africa.

Table A46. Capital Importing Developing Countries: External Debt and Debt Service, 1978–87[1]
(In percent of exports of goods and services, except where otherwise noted)

	1978	1979	1980	1981	1982	1983	1984	1985	1986	1987
External debt										
Capital importing countries	**132.4**	**120.4**	**110.4**	**122.9**	**148.6**	**158.8**	**152.8**	**163.0**	**166.6**	**160.7**
(in billions of U.S. dollars)	399.1	475.9	567.8	662.0	751.6	798.4	840.7	888.3	943.1	990.5
By region										
Africa	124.2	106.6	87.6	112.3	148.6	164.4	167.7	168.6	196.0	194.7
Asia	81.0	74.1	70.1	71.5	84.0	89.2	84.2	93.5	96.5	96.9
Europe	126.8	118.4	117.9	114.7	122.8	129.5	126.0	133.1	119.3	109.4
Non-oil Middle East	161.5	154.4	127.7	139.9	162.8	195.7	204.8	229.3	237.0	225.9
Western Hemisphere	217.2	197.8	182.8	208.8	267.2	287.5	273.3	295.0	311.1	296.0
By analytical criteria										
Market borrowers	126.1	112.6	102.8	117.7	146.5	154.6	146.5	154.1	158.0	150.2
Official borrowers	162.6	152.6	156.5	179.0	215.4	239.1	258.7	279.6	273.6	276.3
Diversified borrowers	140.8	135.0	120.6	121.7	133.8	146.7	142.7	157.5	159.9	157.8
Countries with recent debt-servicing problems	179.1	162.9	148.9	180.2	234.5	252.3	244.2	260.6	275.4	261.0
Countries without debt-servicing problems	94.8	85.5	77.4	78.0	88.6	95.8	93.1	102.2	104.5	104.1
Debt service payments										
Capital importing countries	**19.0**	**19.1**	**17.1**	**20.5**	**23.6**	**22.0**	**22.9**	**24.1**	**24.2**	**22.6**
(in billions of U.S. dollars)	57.2	75.3	87.9	110.2	119.5	110.7	126.2	131.4	137.1	139.4
By region										
Africa	15.3	14.6	13.6	15.5	19.6	22.8	24.8	27.0	32.3	31.1
Asia	10.3	9.0	8.2	9.5	11.2	10.8	11.8	12.3	13.0	12.7
Europe	15.8	17.9	18.1	20.6	21.9	21.2	23.8	26.0	24.7	22.4
Non-oil Middle East	18.1	18.8	16.3	18.1	18.6	20.1	22.9	25.8	23.7	22.1
Western Hemisphere	37.9	39.2	33.3	41.1	49.6	43.0	42.4	44.1	43.5	39.7
By analytical criteria										
Market borrowers	21.1	21.2	18.4	22.4	26.3	23.9	24.7	25.3	25.7	23.5
Official borrowers	12.6	11.8	12.6	13.9	15.2	17.0	22.4	25.9	26.8	27.3
Diversified borrowers	14.5	14.6	14.0	15.8	17.5	17.4	17.1	19.6	18.8	18.6
Countries with recent debt-servicing problems	28.4	28.4	24.7	31.4	38.2	34.4	35.1	36.9	37.7	34.8
Countries without debt-servicing problems	11.4	11.4	10.6	11.9	13.5	13.7	15.0	16.1	16.5	15.7

[1] Debt export ratios show the ratio of total debt at the end of a year to exports of goods and services in that year.
Debt service payments and ratios refer to all interest payments plus amortization payments on long-term debt.

Table A47. Capital Importing Developing Countries—by Region: External Debt, by Class of Creditor, End of Year, 1978–87[1]

(In billions of U.S. dollars)

	1978	1979	1980	1981	1982	1983	1984	1985	1986	1987
Capital importing countries										
Total debt	399.1	475.9	567.8	662.0	751.6	798.4	840.7	888.3	943.1	990.5
Short-term	71.8	82.4	112.9	135.6	158.0	132.7	132.7	120.4	117.6	120.9
Long-term	327.3	393.5	454.8	526.4	593.6	665.8	707.9	767.9	825.5	869.6
Unguaranteed[2]	58.2	69.7	82.6	101.7	110.3	106.6	104.0	102.8	98.1	98.3
Guaranteed[2]	269.1	323.8	372.3	424.7	483.3	559.2	603.9	665.1	727.4	771.3
To official creditors	130.4	149.8	174.5	197.8	220.7	247.9	270.3	294.8	323.9	351.1
To financial institutions	102.8	135.8	157.7	184.8	214.3	258.6	280.4	314.3	343.9	356.9
To other private creditors	35.9	38.2	40.1	42.1	48.3	52.7	53.2	56.0	59.6	63.2
By region										
Africa										
Total debt	72.4	84.3	94.3	103.1	117.1	125.1	129.3	128.5	139.9	146.9
Short-term	9.4	9.1	11.0	13.9	21.4	18.2	19.1	15.4	18.3	18.4
Long-term	62.9	75.2	83.3	89.2	95.7	106.8	110.2	113.0	121.6	128.5
To official creditors	23.9	30.2	35.7	41.0	44.8	50.5	54.3	60.1	65.7	70.8
To financial institutions[3]	22.7	27.7	29.8	31.1	35.6	38.4	37.1	35.1	36.3	36.9
To other private creditors[4]	16.3	17.3	17.9	17.1	15.3	18.0	18.7	17.8	19.6	20.8
Asia										
Total debt	93.2	111.4	133.4	151.9	175.3	193.5	206.6	229.7	256.1	281.0
Short-term	14.1	19.0	26.3	29.4	34.3	33.0	32.4	30.7	31.4	31.6
Long-term	79.2	92.4	107.1	122.5	141.0	160.5	174.1	199.0	224.7	249.4
To official creditors	51.5	55.8	63.3	70.4	77.6	85.4	93.2	102.9	113.6	123.9
To financial institutions[3]	12.6	18.8	23.9	29.0	35.5	41.8	45.3	55.8	65.4	73.7
To other private creditors[4]	15.1	17.9	20.0	23.1	28.0	33.3	35.6	40.3	45.7	51.8
Europe										
Total debt	48.1	56.2	68.0	72.2	75.2	76.7	80.7	87.8	89.3	91.1
Short-term	15.0	12.7	14.4	14.6	13.7	13.0	13.7	14.5	15.4	16.5
Long-term	33.1	43.5	53.6	57.6	61.5	63.7	66.9	73.3	73.9	74.6
To official creditors	13.3	14.7	18.0	20.1	22.1	22.6	24.1	25.3	26.0	26.1
To financial institutions[3]	9.6	14.6	18.2	20.4	21.3	23.3	26.3	31.6	33.1	34.3
To other private creditors[4]	10.3	14.2	17.4	17.0	18.1	17.9	16.6	16.4	14.8	14.2
Non-oil Middle East										
Total debt	29.5	35.9	41.3	47.7	55.4	62.6	68.2	74.0	76.1	80.1
Short-term	5.0	6.0	6.3	7.3	8.9	10.6	11.4	11.8	11.6	11.4
Long-term	24.4	29.9	35.1	40.4	46.5	52.0	56.7	62.2	64.5	68.7
To official creditors	17.0	21.7	26.0	30.1	34.9	39.0	41.6	45.1	47.5	52.1
To financial institutions[3]	2.5	2.5	2.6	3.3	4.2	5.0	6.4	7.0	7.0	6.8
To other private creditors[4]	5.0	5.7	6.5	7.0	7.4	8.0	8.8	10.1	10.0	9.8
Western Hemisphere										
Total debt	155.9	188.1	230.7	287.0	328.6	340.6	355.9	368.3	381.8	391.5
Short-term	28.2	35.5	55.0	70.4	79.7	57.9	56.0	48.0	40.9	43.0
Long-term	127.7	152.6	175.7	216.6	248.9	282.7	300.0	320.3	340.8	348.4
To official creditors	24.7	27.5	31.5	36.2	41.3	50.4	57.1	61.3	71.1	78.2
To financial institutions[3]	55.6	72.2	83.3	101.0	117.8	150.1	165.3	184.7	202.2	205.2
To other private creditors[4]	47.3	52.9	60.9	79.5	89.8	82.1	77.5	74.3	67.6	65.0

[1] Excludes debt owed to the Fund.

[2] By an official agency of the debtor country.

[3] Covers only public and publicly guaranteed debt.

[4] Includes all unguaranteed debt on the presumption that this is owed mainly to private creditors.

243

Table A48. Capital Importing Developing Countries—by Analytical Criteria: External Debt, by Class of Creditor, End of Year, 1978–87[1]

(In billions of U.S. dollars)

	1978	1979	1980	1981	1982	1983	1984	1985	1986	1987
By predominant export										
Non-fuel exporters										
Total debt	300.0	357.1	425.5	487.9	555.1	594.6	632.4	675.3	715.5	752.6
Short-term	56.0	61.3	81.3	91.8	108.2	103.7	103.2	91.1	90.2	90.4
Long-term	244.1	295.8	344.2	396.1	446.9	491.0	529.2	584.2	625.3	662.1
To official creditors	110.7	128.4	149.8	169.6	190.7	212.2	233.2	254.3	278.5	301.1
To financial institutions[2]	61.5	84.2	99.2	116.7	136.0	161.7	181.3	216.7	232.0	243.1
To other private creditors[3]	71.8	83.2	95.2	109.9	120.2	117.1	114.7	113.2	114.8	117.9
Primary product exporters										
Total debt	186.8	217.9	259.2	305.6	353.7	379.3	406.9	427.5	451.3	469.5
Short-term	37.1	37.5	50.1	59.5	73.6	70.0	70.4	57.0	56.3	56.4
Long-term	149.7	180.4	209.0	246.2	280.1	309.3	336.5	370.5	395.0	413.0
To official creditors	56.0	65.7	78.1	89.7	101.8	115.2	130.2	141.7	158.0	170.2
To financial institutions[2]	42.8	59.1	67.1	79.1	94.5	115.1	128.2	156.1	164.1	169.8
To other private creditors[3]	50.9	55.7	63.8	77.3	83.8	79.0	78.1	72.7	72.9	73.1
Agricultural exporters										
Total debt	135.3	162.1	195.7	232.4	271.3	293.2	316.3	338.5	358.5	373.4
Short-term	27.2	28.3	39.1	43.7	54.5	51.8	53.1	42.0	39.8	38.8
Long-term	108.2	133.8	156.6	188.7	216.8	241.4	263.3	296.5	318.8	334.6
To official creditors	42.3	49.3	58.5	68.2	78.2	88.5	101.7	110.9	124.2	134.1
To financial institutions[2]	30.0	44.0	52.4	63.9	76.7	94.5	103.2	130.4	137.7	142.4
To other private creditors[3]	35.9	40.5	45.7	56.5	61.9	58.4	58.4	55.2	56.8	58.1
Mineral exporters										
Total debt	51.4	55.9	63.4	73.3	82.4	86.2	90.6	89.0	92.8	96.1
Short-term	9.9	9.2	11.0	15.8	19.0	18.2	17.3	14.9	16.5	17.6
Long-term	41.5	46.7	52.4	57.5	63.3	67.9	73.3	74.0	76.3	78.5
To official creditors	13.7	16.4	19.6	21.5	23.6	26.7	28.5	30.8	33.8	36.1
To financial institutions[2]	12.8	15.1	14.7	15.2	17.8	20.6	25.1	25.7	26.4	27.3
To other private creditors[3]	15.0	15.2	18.1	20.8	21.9	20.6	19.7	17.6	16.1	15.0
Exporters of manufactures										
Total debt	76.7	95.8	114.4	121.7	129.9	136.7	139.3	151.0	162.2	174.5
Short-term	12.2	16.2	22.1	21.7	22.0	20.9	18.8	19.8	19.5	19.4
Long-term	64.5	79.7	92.3	100.0	107.9	115.8	120.5	131.2	142.7	155.2
To official creditors	33.6	38.0	42.6	46.9	51.1	55.1	57.3	61.9	66.4	71.4
To financial institutions[2]	13.7	19.5	24.7	27.8	29.2	31.6	36.0	40.8	46.6	51.4
To other private creditors[3]	17.2	22.2	25.0	25.3	27.6	29.1	27.2	28.4	29.6	32.4
Service and remittance countries										
Total debt	36.5	43.3	51.9	60.5	71.5	78.6	86.2	96.8	102.0	108.6
Short-term	6.7	7.6	9.1	10.6	12.6	12.8	14.0	14.3	14.4	14.6
Long-term	29.8	35.7	42.8	49.9	58.9	65.8	72.2	82.5	87.5	93.9
To official creditors	21.2	24.6	29.1	32.9	37.8	41.9	45.7	50.7	54.0	59.5
To financial institutions[2]	5.0	5.7	7.4	9.8	12.4	14.9	17.1	19.8	21.3	22.0
To other private creditors[3]	3.7	5.3	6.4	7.2	8.7	9.0	9.4	12.0	12.2	12.3

Table A48 *(continued).* **Capital Importing Developing Countries—by Analytical Criteria: External Debt, by Class of Creditor, End of Year, 1978–87[1]**
(In billions of U.S. dollars)

	1978	1979	1980	1981	1982	1983	1984	1985	1986	1987
By financial criteria										
Market borrowers										
Total debt	267.5	318.4	384.8	460.1	529.3	557.7	580.7	602.2	627.5	645.8
Short-term	52.4	62.6	92.0	114.3	135.2	109.0	105.8	90.7	86.8	88.6
Long-term	215.1	255.8	292.9	345.8	394.1	448.7	474.9	511.5	540.7	557.2
To official creditors	49.7	54.3	61.8	69.1	75.0	89.3	99.3	107.8	119.8	128.5
To financial institutions[2]	86.5	110.7	128.2	153.2	181.3	222.9	242.3	272.6	294.9	302.8
To other private creditors[3]	78.8	90.8	102.9	123.5	137.9	136.5	133.3	131.2	126.0	125.9
Official borrowers										
Total debt	43.6	50.7	61.0	68.7	76.8	83.6	91.2	99.3	108.9	117.3
Short-term	2.2	2.6	4.5	4.6	4.9	4.5	5.5	6.0	6.3	6.4
Long-term	41.3	48.1	56.5	64.2	71.9	79.1	85.7	93.4	102.6	110.9
To official creditors	31.5	38.0	45.6	53.2	60.7	66.8	72.7	79.9	88.3	96.2
To financial institutions[2]	5.4	6.2	6.6	7.1	7.4	8.5	9.2	9.6	10.2	10.4
To other private creditors[3]	4.4	3.9	4.2	3.9	3.7	3.7	3.8	3.9	4.2	4.3
Diversified borrowers										
Total debt	88.0	106.8	121.9	133.2	145.6	157.1	168.7	186.7	206.7	227.4
Short-term	17.1	17.2	16.4	16.8	18.0	19.1	21.4	23.7	24.5	26.0
Long-term	70.9	89.6	105.5	116.4	127.6	138.0	147.3	163.0	182.2	201.4
To official creditors	49.2	57.5	67.0	75.5	85.0	91.7	98.3	107.1	115.8	126.4
To financial institutions[2]	10.9	18.9	22.9	24.5	25.6	27.1	28.9	32.1	38.9	43.7
To other private creditors[3]	10.9	13.2	15.5	16.4	17.0	19.1	20.1	23.8	27.5	31.3
Countries with recent debt-servicing problems										
Total debt	240.8	290.2	353.4	426.2	487.8	510.8	531.3	545.5	566.4	580.4
Short-term	42.9	53.4	77.6	98.5	116.1	88.7	88.3	73.4	69.5	70.8
Long-term	197.9	236.8	275.8	327.7	371.7	422.1	443.0	472.1	496.9	509.6
To official creditors	57.1	67.1	80.3	94.7	106.6	124.3	137.5	150.0	165.8	180.0
To financial institutions[2]	72.1	92.5	106.8	127.0	149.7	186.8	201.6	223.7	240.4	242.5
To other private creditors[3]	68.6	77.2	88.6	106.0	115.4	111.0	103.9	98.4	90.7	87.0
Countries without debt-servicing problems										
Total debt	158.2	185.6	214.4	235.8	263.8	287.6	309.4	342.8	376.7	410.1
Short-term	28.8	28.9	35.3	37.2	41.9	43.9	44.4	47.0	48.1	50.1
Long-term	129.4	156.7	179.1	198.7	221.9	243.7	264.9	295.8	328.6	360.0
To official creditors	73.3	82.7	94.1	103.1	114.1	123.6	132.8	144.8	158.1	171.1
To financial institutions[2]	30.7	43.3	50.9	57.8	64.6	71.8	78.8	90.6	103.5	114.4
To other private creditors[3]	25.4	30.7	34.0	37.8	43.2	48.3	53.3	60.4	67.0	74.5

Table A48 *(concluded)*. **Capital Importing Developing Countries—by Analytical Criteria: External Debt, by Class of Creditor, End of Year, 1978–87[1]**
(In billions of U.S. dollars)

	1978	1979	1980	1981	1982	1983	1984	1985	1986	1987
By miscellaneous criteria										
Capital importing fuel exporters										
Total debt	99.0	118.8	142.3	174.1	196.5	203.8	208.2	213.0	227.6	238.0
Short-term	15.8	21.0	31.7	43.9	49.9	29.0	29.5	29.3	27.4	30.5
Long-term	83.2	97.7	110.7	130.3	146.7	174.8	178.8	183.7	200.3	207.5
To official creditors	19.7	21.5	24.7	28.2	30.0	35.7	37.2	40.5	45.4	50.0
To financial institutions[2]	41.3	51.6	58.6	68.1	78.3	96.9	99.1	97.5	111.9	113.8
To other private creditors[3]	22.2	24.7	27.4	34.0	38.4	42.2	42.5	45.7	42.9	43.7
Fifteen heavily indebted countries										
Total debt	178.2	217.4	267.5	328.3	376.8	390.9	403.9	416.2	430.7	436.8
Short-term	32.7	42.0	64.3	81.9	96.8	68.5	66.4	54.9	51.4	53.5
Long-term	145.5	175.4	203.2	246.4	280.1	322.4	337.4	361.3	379.4	383.2
To official creditors	29.9	32.4	36.6	42.0	45.4	56.6	63.7	69.1	78.8	85.2
To financial institutions[2]	59.0	77.8	90.7	109.8	130.2	165.1	179.4	202.8	219.3	220.6
To other private creditors[3]	56.6	65.3	75.9	94.5	104.5	100.8	94.4	89.5	81.3	77.4
Small low-income countries										
Total debt	34.6	40.4	47.9	53.7	59.2	63.9	68.7	75.1	82.4	89.4
Short-term	0.9	1.2	2.2	2.3	2.2	2.2	2.6	2.7	2.8	2.9
Long-term	33.7	39.2	45.7	51.4	56.9	61.7	66.1	72.3	79.6	86.4
To official creditors	27.2	32.4	38.2	43.4	49.0	52.9	57.2	62.9	69.3	75.4
To financial institutions[2]	3.6	4.4	4.9	5.5	5.8	6.4	6.5	6.8	7.5	7.9
To other private creditors[3]	2.8	2.4	2.6	2.5	2.2	2.3	2.4	2.6	2.8	3.0
Sub-Saharan Africa[4]										
Total debt	29.5	36.0	41.7	45.8	50.7	52.8	55.5	60.7	66.5	71.9
Short-term	1.9	2.0	2.5	2.9	3.0	2.8	2.8	2.8	2.8	2.9
Long-term	27.5	34.1	39.2	42.9	47.7	50.1	52.8	57.9	63.6	69.0
To official creditors	16.0	20.8	24.8	28.2	32.7	35.2	38.6	42.9	47.3	51.3
To financial institutions[2]	6.6	8.4	9.1	9.7	10.4	10.3	9.3	9.9	10.8	11.8
To other private creditors[3]	5.0	4.9	5.3	5.0	4.6	4.7	4.8	5.2	5.5	5.9

[1] Excludes debt owed to the Fund.
[2] Covers only public and publicly guaranteed debt.
[3] Includes all unguaranteed debt on the presumption that this is owed mainly to private creditors.
[4] Excluding Nigeria and South Africa.

Table A49. Capital Importing Developing Countries—by Alternative Analytical Categories: External Debt, by Class of Creditor, End of Year, 1978–87[1]

(In billions of U.S. dollars)

	1978	1979	1980	1981	1982	1983	1984	1985	1986	1987
Non-oil developing countries										
Total debt	343.4	409.2	490.5	578.5	662.0	703.5	744.4	789.5	836.3	879.0
Short-term	61.1	68.2	94.3	115.5	135.9	117.3	116.4	103.7	105.5	107.0
Long-term	282.3	340.9	396.3	463.0	526.1	586.2	628.0	685.8	730.8	772.0
To official creditors	118.4	136.9	159.7	181.8	205.0	228.5	250.2	273.1	300.1	325.1
To financial institutions[2]	82.9	109.9	128.6	153.9	178.9	219.6	242.7	276.6	297.0	310.4
To other private creditors[3]	80.9	94.1	107.9	127.3	142.2	138.0	135.2	136.1	133.7	136.5
Net oil exporters										
Total debt	70.7	83.6	101.5	134.2	160.2	172.2	180.7	193.2	205.6	219.1
Short-term	11.0	13.1	19.3	31.1	36.4	24.1	23.5	24.8	30.0	33.8
Long-term	59.7	70.5	82.3	103.1	123.8	148.1	157.2	168.4	175.5	185.3
To official creditors	21.1	24.4	29.9	35.0	40.2	46.6	51.1	55.3	60.0	66.0
To financial institutions[2]	25.4	30.4	33.6	43.5	52.3	70.3	75.0	77.1	83.5	87.7
To other private creditors[3]	13.1	15.7	18.8	24.7	31.2	31.2	31.1	36.0	32.1	31.6
Net oil importers										
Total debt	272.7	325.6	389.0	444.3	501.8	531.3	563.8	596.3	630.7	659.9
Short-term	50.1	55.2	75.0	84.4	99.5	93.2	92.9	78.9	75.4	73.3
Long-term	222.6	270.4	314.0	359.8	402.3	438.1	470.8	517.4	555.3	586.6
To official creditors	97.2	112.5	129.9	146.8	164.7	181.9	199.1	217.8	240.1	259.1
To financial institutions[2]	57.5	79.5	95.0	110.4	126.6	149.4	167.7	199.5	213.5	222.7
To other private creditors[3]	67.8	78.4	89.1	102.6	111.0	106.8	104.0	100.1	101.6	104.8

[1] Excludes debt owed to the Fund.
[2] Covers only public and publicly guaranteed debt.
[3] Includes all unguaranteed debt on the presumption that this is owed mainly to private creditors.

Table A50. Capital Importing Developing Countries: Long-Term and Short-Term External Debt Relative to Exports and to GDP, 1978–87[1]

(In percent)

	1978	1979	1980	1981	1982	1983	1984	1985	1986	1987
Ratio of external debt to exports of goods and services[2]										
Capital importing countries	**132.4**	**120.4**	**110.4**	**122.9**	**148.6**	**158.8**	**152.8**	**163.0**	**166.6**	**160.7**
By region										
Africa	124.2	106.6	87.6	112.3	148.6	164.4	167.7	168.6	196.0	194.7
Asia	81.0	74.1	70.1	71.5	84.0	89.2	84.2	93.5	96.5	96.9
Europe	126.8	118.4	117.9	114.7	122.8	129.5	126.0	133.1	119.3	109.4
Non-oil Middle East	161.5	154.4	127.7	139.9	162.8	195.7	204.8	229.3	237.0	225.9
Western Hemisphere	217.2	197.8	182.8	208.8	267.2	287.5	273.3	295.0	311.1	296.0
By predominant export										
Non-fuel exporters	125.6	117.3	111.1	121.0	142.7	151.0	146.5	156.4	149.9	144.0
Primary product exporters	180.3	164.6	157.8	190.6	237.7	253.0	250.0	265.5	253.3	240.8
Agricultural exporters	187.3	180.3	180.4	206.8	256.4	274.2	260.9	280.1	264.3	250.1
Mineral exporters	164.2	131.4	113.8	152.7	191.7	200.4	217.9	221.4	218.2	210.5
Exporters of manufactures	69.7	68.9	65.8	62.1	66.9	68.4	62.4	66.6	64.4	63.3
Service and remittance countries	144.7	131.2	115.2	129.4	155.4	178.0	189.1	218.6	216.0	209.6
By financial criteria										
Market borrowers	126.1	112.6	102.8	117.7	146.5	154.6	146.5	154.1	158.0	150.2
Official borrowers	162.6	152.6	156.5	179.0	215.4	239.1	258.7	279.6	273.6	276.3
Diversified borrowers	140.8	135.0	120.6	121.7	133.8	146.7	142.7	157.5	159.9	157.8
Countries with recent debt-servicing problems	179.1	162.9	148.9	180.2	234.5	252.3	244.2	260.6	275.4	261.0
Countries without debt-servicing problems	94.8	85.5	77.4	78.0	88.6	95.8	93.1	102.2	104.5	104.1
By miscellaneous criteria										
Capital importing fuel exporters	158.4	131.0	108.4	128.4	168.5	187.2	176.0	188.6	255.7	253.5
Fifteen heavily indebted countries	203.4	181.7	165.8	199.2	263.4	286.3	268.1	285.9	304.8	285.4
Small low-income countries	225.5	220.4	222.6	269.4	320.9	334.6	345.1	382.9	346.9	351.2
Sub-Saharan Africa[3]	141.2	143.3	138.4	169.3	201.3	215.8	216.3	240.3	236.0	242.8
By alternative analytical categories										
Non-oil developing countries	131.6	122.1	114.7	127.2	151.5	159.6	154.2	164.4	161.3	155.0
Net oil exporters	180.6	149.7	133.9	165.0	206.6	218.9	207.1	234.8	274.0	268.3
Net oil importers	123.0	116.6	110.5	118.9	139.6	146.7	142.5	149.9	142.3	136.0

Table A50 *(concluded).* **Capital Importing Developing Countries: Long-Term and Short-Term External Debt Relative to Exports and to GDP, 1978–87[1]**

(In percent)

	1978	1979	1980	1981	1982	1983	1984	1985	1986	1987
Ratio of external debt to GDP[2]										
Capital importing countries	**25.6**	**25.6**	**25.7**	**28.9**	**33.2**	**35.9**	**36.8**	**38.1**	**38.7**	**37.9**
By region										
Africa	32.4	30.3	26.6	30.5	35.9	37.9	39.9	41.5	44.1	42.7
Asia	15.9	16.1	16.5	18.3	20.9	22.0	22.8	25.5	27.6	27.7
Europe	23.7	21.4	25.6	28.9	30.3	35.1	39.4	40.2	36.7	34.9
Non-oil Middle East	52.9	62.9	59.1	62.0	65.7	67.1	69.6	70.5	63.2	78.2
Western Hemisphere	31.8	32.9	32.7	36.2	43.1	48.2	47.3	46.2	46.0	43.8
By predominant export										
Non-fuel exporters	23.7	23.8	24.6	28.0	31.6	33.3	34.9	36.6	36.2	35.3
Primary product exporters	29.7	29.7	30.3	35.0	40.4	43.1	45.0	46.9	45.3	43.3
Agricultural exporters	26.2	27.1	28.8	33.7	38.3	40.8	42.1	43.2	41.4	39.5
Mineral exporters	46.2	41.0	35.9	39.8	49.1	53.0	59.4	69.4	71.6	68.8
Exporters of manufactures	14.5	14.9	15.6	16.8	17.8	18.1	18.5	19.5	20.1	19.7
Service and remittance countries	32.8	35.7	37.1	42.2	48.2	52.6	55.7	60.3	57.7	68.3
By financial criteria										
Market borrowers	29.7	29.5	29.2	32.2	37.9	42.4	42.0	42.6	42.6	40.9
Official borrowers	31.9	32.2	33.1	38.6	42.5	44.3	49.4	56.5	59.0	58.4
Diversified borrowers	16.9	17.2	17.3	19.5	21.3	21.8	23.5	25.2	26.5	27.3
Countries with recent debt-servicing problems	31.3	31.6	31.4	36.2	42.6	47.6	48.0	48.1	48.2	46.8
Countries without debt-servicing problems	20.1	19.8	19.8	21.2	23.6	25.0	26.3	28.6	29.9	29.8
By miscellaneous criteria										
Capital importing fuel exporters	34.2	33.1	29.9	31.8	38.7	46.3	44.2	43.9	49.6	49.1
Fifteen heavily indebted countries	29.9	30.6	31.0	34.9	41.6	47.6	46.4	45.6	45.6	43.0
Small low-income countries	32.3	32.5	33.2	40.6	44.8	46.2	50.6	58.6	62.8	62.1
Sub-Saharan Africa[3]	35.9	36.8	35.3	43.0	48.8	51.4	60.0	62.6	61.7	59.5
By alternative analytical categories										
Non-oil developing countries	24.7	24.7	25.2	28.8	33.4	35.7	36.8	38.2	38.4	37.5
Net oil exporters	40.2	39.3	36.2	39.3	52.7	65.2	60.0	60.9	66.9	72.2
Net oil importers	22.5	22.5	23.4	26.6	29.9	31.2	32.8	34.1	33.7	32.4

[1] Excludes debt owed to the Fund.

[2] Ratio of year-end debt to exports of goods and services or GDP for year indicated.

[3] Excluding Nigeria and South Africa.

Table A51.   Capital Importing Developing Countries: Debt Service Payments on Short-Term and Long-Term External Debt, 1978–87
(Values in billions of U.S. dollars; ratios in percent)

	1978	1979	1980	1981	1982	1983	1984	1985	1986	1987
Capital importing countries										
Value of debt service payments	57.2	75.3	87.9	110.2	119.5	110.7	126.2	131.4	137.1	139.4
Interest payments	21.5	31.5	44.1	60.5	68.6	65.2	72.2	71.8	73.4	74.7
Amortization payments[1]	35.7	43.8	43.8	49.7	50.9	45.6	53.9	59.5	63.8	64.8
Debt service ratio[2]	19.0	19.1	17.1	20.5	23.6	22.0	22.9	24.1	24.2	22.6
Interest payments ratio	7.1	8.0	8.6	11.2	13.6	13.0	13.1	13.2	13.0	12.1
Amortization ratio[1]	11.9	11.1	8.5	9.2	10.1	9.1	9.8	10.9	11.3	10.5
Of which,										
Market borrowers										
Value of debt service payments	44.8	59.9	68.9	87.6	95.1	86.2	98.1	98.9	102.2	101.1
Interest payments	15.9	24.5	35.2	49.3	56.7	53.2	58.5	57.0	56.6	55.3
Amortization payments[1]	28.9	35.4	33.7	38.2	38.4	33.0	39.6	42.0	45.7	45.7
Debt service ratio[2]	21.1	21.2	18.4	22.4	26.3	23.9	24.7	25.3	25.7	23.5
Interest payments ratio	7.5	8.7	9.4	12.6	15.7	14.7	14.7	14.6	14.2	12.9
Amortization ratio[1]	13.6	12.5	9.0	9.8	10.6	9.2	10.0	10.7	11.5	10.6
Official borrowers										
Value of debt service payments	3.4	3.9	4.9	5.4	5.4	5.9	7.9	9.2	10.7	11.6
Interest payments	1.3	1.6	2.0	2.3	2.6	2.7	3.3	4.0	4.6	5.0
Amortization payments[1]	2.0	2.3	2.9	3.1	2.8	3.2	4.6	5.2	6.1	6.6
Debt service ratio[2]	12.6	11.8	12.6	13.9	15.2	17.0	22.4	25.9	26.8	27.3
Interest payments ratio	5.0	4.7	5.1	6.0	7.4	7.7	9.4	11.1	11.5	11.7
Amortization ratio[1]	7.6	7.1	7.5	8.0	7.8	9.3	13.0	14.7	15.3	15.6
By region										
Africa										
Debt service ratio[2]	15.3	14.6	13.6	15.5	19.6	22.8	24.8	27.0	32.3	31.1
Interest payments ratio	5.2	5.7	5.2	6.2	8.4	8.7	9.5	11.1	14.1	13.1
Amortization ratio[1]	10.1	8.9	8.4	9.2	11.2	14.1	15.3	16.0	18.2	18.0
Asia										
Debt service ratio[2]	10.3	9.0	8.2	9.5	11.2	10.8	11.8	12.3	13.0	12.7
Interest payments ratio	3.8	3.8	4.3	5.2	5.8	5.7	5.9	6.0	6.2	6.2
Amortization ratio[1]	6.5	5.2	3.9	4.4	5.4	5.1	5.9	6.3	6.8	6.6
Europe										
Debt service ratio[2]	15.8	17.9	18.1	20.6	21.9	21.2	23.8	26.0	24.7	22.4
Interest payments ratio	5.7	6.4	8.4	11.5	12.1	11.1	11.6	11.8	10.9	10.2
Amortization ratio[1]	10.1	11.6	9.7	9.2	9.9	10.1	12.2	14.2	13.8	12.1
Non-oil Middle East										
Debt service ratio[2]	18.1	18.8	16.3	18.1	18.6	20.1	22.9	25.8	23.7	22.1
Interest payments ratio	9.9	9.4	7.9	8.8	9.4	10.5	12.2	12.5	13.9	13.6
Amortization ratio[1]	8.2	9.3	8.5	9.3	9.1	9.6	10.7	13.4	9.8	8.5
Western Hemisphere										
Debt service ratio[2]	37.9	39.2	33.3	41.1	49.6	43.0	42.4	44.1	43.5	39.7
Interest payments ratio	14.2	16.8	18.2	24.4	31.9	30.7	29.8	29.5	27.8	25.4
Amortization ratio[1]	23.8	22.5	15.1	16.7	17.7	12.3	12.6	14.6	15.7	14.3

Table A51 *(continued)*. **Capital Importing Developing Countries: Debt Service Payments on Short-Term and Long-Term External Debt, 1978–87**

(Values in billions of U.S. dollars; ratios in percent)

	1978	1979	1980	1981	1982	1983	1984	1985	1986	1987
By predominant export										
Non-fuel exporters										
Debt service ratio[2]	17.6	17.0	16.5	19.7	22.3	19.7	20.1	20.6	20.5	19.6
Interest payments ratio	6.5	7.2	8.1	10.6	12.4	11.6	11.6	12.0	11.0	10.6
Amortization ratio[1]	11.1	9.7	8.3	9.1	9.9	8.1	8.4	8.7	9.5	9.0
Primary product exporters										
Debt service ratio[2]	27.2	25.1	24.4	31.6	37.5	32.5	31.8	32.1	33.0	32.0
Interest payments ratio	9.6	10.8	12.0	17.3	21.8	20.6	20.6	21.5	19.1	18.3
Amortization ratio[1]	17.6	14.2	12.4	14.3	15.7	11.9	11.3	10.6	13.8	13.7
Agricultural exporters										
Debt service ratio[2]	27.1	25.7	26.2	34.6	41.0	34.5	32.2	34.5	35.9	34.2
Interest payments ratio	10.0	11.7	13.9	19.6	24.6	23.2	21.7	23.6	20.7	19.3
Amortization ratio[1]	17.0	14.0	12.3	15.0	16.4	11.3	10.5	10.9	15.3	14.9
Mineral exporters										
Debt service ratio[2]	27.5	23.6	21.1	24.5	29.0	27.6	30.7	25.0	23.5	24.5
Interest payments ratio	8.5	8.9	8.3	12.1	15.0	14.1	17.2	15.1	14.2	14.9
Amortization ratio[1]	19.0	14.7	12.7	12.4	14.0	13.5	13.5	9.9	9.3	9.5
Exporters of manufactures										
Debt service ratio[2]	8.5	9.6	9.7	10.4	11.4	9.8	10.7	11.4	11.2	9.6
Interest payments ratio	3.6	4.1	5.0	5.5	5.8	5.1	5.2	5.1	4.9	4.4
Amortization ratio[1]	5.0	5.6	4.7	4.9	5.6	4.7	5.5	6.3	6.3	5.1
Services and remittance countries										
Debt service ratio[2]	17.6	15.3	13.4	17.6	19.1	20.7	24.0	26.2	23.5	26.4
Interest payments ratio	6.9	6.3	6.0	8.9	9.7	10.3	11.3	12.6	13.1	14.1
Amortization ratio[1]	10.7	9.0	7.4	8.7	9.5	10.4	12.7	13.6	10.4	12.3
By financial criteria										
Diversified borrowers										
Debt service ratio[2]	14.5	14.6	14.0	15.8	17.5	17.4	17.1	19.6	18.8	18.6
Interest payments ratio	6.8	6.9	6.9	8.1	8.5	8.7	8.9	9.2	9.5	10.0
Amortization ratio[1]	7.7	7.7	7.1	7.7	8.9	8.7	8.2	10.4	9.3	8.6
Countries with recent debt-servicing problems										
Debt service ratio[2]	28.4	28.4	24.7	31.4	38.2	34.4	35.1	36.9	37.7	34.8
Interest payments ratio	10.1	11.6	12.5	17.8	23.3	22.4	22.6	23.0	23.0	21.0
Amortization ratio[1]	18.3	16.9	12.2	13.6	14.9	12.0	12.5	13.8	14.7	13.8
Countries without debt-servicing problems										
Debt service ratio[2]	11.4	11.4	10.6	11.9	13.5	13.7	15.0	16.1	16.5	15.7
Interest payments ratio	4.7	5.0	5.2	6.1	6.8	6.6	6.9	7.0	7.2	7.1
Amortization ratio[1]	6.7	6.3	5.4	5.8	6.7	7.1	8.0	9.1	9.3	8.7

Table A51 *(concluded).* **Capital Importing Developing Countries: Debt Service Payments on Short-Term and Long-Term External Debt, 1978–87**
(Values in billions of U.S. dollars; ratios in percent)

	1978	1979	1980	1981	1982	1983	1984	1985	1986	1987
By miscellaneous criteria										
Capital importing fuel exporters										
Debt service ratio[2]	24.3	26.1	18.9	22.7	28.2	30.6	33.5	37.4	44.0	39.5
Interest payments ratio	9.4	10.4	9.9	13.0	17.5	18.0	18.7	17.8	23.3	20.7
Amortization ratio[1]	14.9	15.7	9.1	9.7	10.7	12.6	14.8	19.6	20.7	18.7
Fifteen heavily indebted countries										
Debt service ratio[2]	33.4	34.6	29.4	38.5	47.9	42.5	41.6	43.8	45.6	41.1
Interest payments ratio	12.3	14.5	15.8	22.5	30.2	29.5	28.8	28.6	28.2	25.2
Amortization ratio[1]	21.0	20.1	13.6	16.0	17.7	13.0	12.8	15.3	17.4	15.9
Small low-income countries										
Debt service ratio[2]	14.4	12.7	14.5	17.6	19.0	20.4	23.1	29.8	28.4	30.2
Interest payments ratio	6.0	6.0	6.3	7.5	9.1	8.9	9.3	12.5	12.4	13.1
Amortization ratio[1]	8.3	6.8	8.2	10.1	9.9	11.5	13.8	17.2	16.0	17.1
Sub-Saharan Africa[3]										
Debt service ratio[2]	15.1	14.6	15.6	17.9	20.2	21.3	23.3	28.6	29.4	31.0
Interest payments ratio	5.9	6.3	6.7	7.9	10.0	9.8	10.3	12.5	13.3	13.9
Amortization ratio[1]	9.2	8.4	8.9	10.0	10.1	11.5	13.1	16.1	16.2	17.1
By alternative analytical categories										
Non-oil developing countries										
Debt service ratio[2]	19.3	19.6	17.7	21.2	24.1	21.1	22.0	22.7	22.1	20.8
Interest payments ratio	7.1	8.0	8.8	11.6	14.0	13.0	13.1	13.2	12.3	11.6
Amortization ratio[1]	12.2	11.7	8.8	9.6	10.1	8.1	8.9	9.6	9.8	9.2
Net oil exporters										
Debt service ratio[2]	33.7	34.2	24.1	29.9	33.1	29.1	32.5	34.2	31.2	28.6
Interest payments ratio	11.9	12.2	12.1	16.8	21.3	20.2	20.6	19.0	20.3	19.6
Amortization ratio[1]	21.8	22.0	12.0	13.1	11.8	9.0	12.0	15.2	10.9	9.1
Net oil importers										
Debt service ratio[2]	16.8	16.7	16.3	19.3	22.1	19.4	19.6	20.4	20.5	19.5
Interest payments ratio	6.3	7.1	8.1	10.5	12.4	11.4	11.4	12.0	10.9	10.3
Amortization ratio[1]	10.5	9.6	8.2	8.8	9.8	7.9	8.2	8.4	9.6	9.2

[1] On long-term debt only. Estimates for the period up to 1984 reflect actual amortization payments. The estimates for 1985 and 1986 reflect scheduled payments, modified to take account of actual or pending rescheduling agreements.

[2] Payments (interest, amortization, or both) as percentages of exports of goods and services.

[3] Excluding Nigeria and South Africa.

Table A52. Capital Importing Developing Countries: Fund Charges and Repurchases from the Fund, 1978–87[1]

(In percent of exports of goods and services)

	1978	1979	1980	1981	1982	1983	1984	1985	1986	1987
Capital importing countries	**0.5**	**0.7**	**0.5**	**0.4**	**0.5**	**0.7**	**0.9**	**1.2**	**1.5**	**1.5**
By region										
Africa	0.4	0.9	0.5	0.5	0.6	0.9	1.3	1.8	2.8	2.5
Asia	0.4	0.5	0.3	0.4	0.4	0.5	0.8	0.9	0.9	0.9
Europe	0.7	0.6	0.8	0.8	0.9	1.2	1.5	1.5	1.4	1.5
Non-oil Middle East	0.9	0.8	0.6	0.5	0.5	0.2	0.1	0.1	0.2	0.1
Western Hemisphere	0.6	0.9	0.4	0.3	0.3	0.6	0.9	1.2	2.4	2.8
By predominant export										
Non-fuel exporters	0.7	0.8	0.6	0.5	0.6	0.8	1.1	1.4	1.7	1.7
Primary product exporters	0.9	1.3	0.8	0.8	1.0	1.4	1.8	2.4	3.2	3.2
Agricultural exporters	1.0	1.1	0.7	0.7	1.0	1.4	1.8	2.4	2.9	2.9
Mineral exporters	0.8	1.8	1.1	1.0	1.0	1.4	1.9	2.6	4.2	4.1
Exporters of manufactures	0.3	0.3	0.2	0.2	0.3	0.4	0.6	0.7	0.6	0.7
Service and remittance countries	1.2	1.0	1.0	0.9	0.7	0.5	0.7	1.0	1.2	1.5
By financial criteria										
Market borrowers	0.4	0.6	0.3	0.2	0.3	0.4	0.6	0.7	1.1	1.3
Official borrowers	1.3	1.3	1.4	1.7	1.8	2.1	3.1	4.1	4.4	3.8
Diversified borrowers	0.7	0.7	0.7	0.7	0.8	1.0	1.3	1.6	1.8	1.7
Countries with recent debt-servicing problems	0.7	1.0	0.6	0.5	0.6	0.9	1.3	1.7	2.7	2.8
Countries without debt-servicing problems	0.5	0.4	0.4	0.4	0.4	0.5	0.7	0.8	0.8	0.8
By miscellaneous criteria										
Capital importing fuel exporters	0.1	0.3	0.1	0.1	0.1	0.1	0.2	0.3	0.5	0.7
Fifteen heavily indebted countries	0.6	0.9	0.4	0.4	0.5	0.9	1.2	1.5	2.7	2.9
Small low-income countries	2.3	2.4	2.4	2.9	3.1	3.3	4.8	6.4	6.0	5.4
Sub-Saharan Africa[2]	0.7	0.9	0.9	1.2	1.4	2.0	3.1	4.3	4.2	3.8
By alternative analytical categories										
Non-oil developing countries	0.6	0.8	0.5	0.5	0.6	0.7	1.0	1.3	1.6	1.7
Net oil exporters	0.2	0.9	0.5	0.3	0.3	0.4	0.5	0.7	0.9	1.1
Net oil importers	0.7	0.8	0.6	0.5	0.6	0.8	1.1	1.4	1.7	1.8
Memorandum item Capital importing countries : Fund charges and repurchases from the Fund in billions of U.S. dollars										
Total	1.6	2.7	2.3	2.3	2.5	3.3	5.0	6.3	8.4	9.5
Charges	0.4	0.4	0.5	0.7	1.4	2.1	2.9	3.1	3.0	2.5
Repurchases	1.3	2.4	1.9	1.5	1.1	1.2	2.1	3.1	5.4	7.0

[1] Fund charges on and repurchases (or repayments of principal) for use of Fund credit. Projected charges and repurchases do not take into account prospective programs.

[2] Excluding Nigeria and South Africa.

Table A53. Results of Baseline Medium-Term Scenario, 1977-91

	Average 1977–81[1]	1982	1983	1984	1985	1986	1987	Average 1988–91[1]
	(In percent)							
Industrial countries								
Growth of real GNP	2.7	−0.4	2.6	4.7	2.8	3.0	3.2	3.0
Real six-month LIBOR[2]	3.4	7.1	6.2	7.1	5.3	4.2	4.5	4.2
Increase in GNP deflator	8.4	7.3	4.9	4.3	3.9	3.4	3.0	3.7
World economy								
Change in world price of manufactures [3]	8.7	−2.5	−3.3	−3.7	1.0	14.0	4.5	4.5
Change in world price of oil[3]	23.6	−4.2	−11.7	−2.1	−4.4	−40.0	−6.3	4.5
Change in world price of non-oil primary commodities [3]	4.6	−10.1	7.1	3.7	−12.2	12.0	1.0	4.2
Capital importing developing countries								
Growth of total external credit [3,4]								
Private	21.4	14.4	3.7	3.6	4.1	4.3	3.3	3.1
Official	16.2	11.6	12.3	9.0	9.1	9.9	8.4	9.0
Growth of real GDP	4.9	2.1	1.6	4.7	4.2	3.5	4.2	4.7
Growth of import volume	7.1	−6.5	−2.7	4.6	2.6	2.3	4.2	4.9
Growth of export volume	5.1	−1.5	7.5	10.7	2.5	4.1	5.6	4.8

	Average 1977–81	1982	1983	1984	1985	1986	1987	1989	1991
	(In percent of exports of goods and services)								
Current account balance	−14.1	−17.8	−9.4	−4.1	−4.9	−6.8	−6.0	−5.8	−5.9
Total external debt	122.6	148.6	158.8	152.8	163.0	166.6	160.7	150.0	140.2
Debt service payments	18.4	23.6	22.0	22.9	24.1	24.2	22.6	23.7	21.7
Interest payments	8.1	13.6	13.0	13.1	13.2	13.0	12.1	11.3	10.3
Amortization payments	10.3	10.1	9.1	9.8	10.9	11.3	10.5	12.5	11.4

[1] Compound annual rates of change.
[2] London Interbank Offered Rate on six-month U.S. dollar deposits, deflated by U.S. GNP deflator.
[3] In U.S. dollars.
[4] Includes trade financing.

Table A54. Capital Importing Developing Countries: Payments Balances on Current Account—Medium-Term Scenario, 1972-91[1]

	1972	1977	1982	1983	1984	1985	1986	1987	1989	1991
	(In billions of U.S. dollars)									
Capital importing countries	**−6.1**	**−28.7**	**−89.8**	**−47.1**	**−22.6**	**−26.8**	**−38.3**	**−37.1**	**−42.7**	**−51.4**
By region										
Africa	−1.6	−8.0	−21.3	−11.6	−6.7	−1.4	−11.6	−10.1	−6.3	−6.0
Asia	−0.4	0.9	−17.3	−14.3	−4.8	−15.4	−15.4	−16.9	−26.0	−36.4
Europe	0.6	−9.0	−6.1	−4.2	−1.9	−2.3	1.3	0.4	0.7	—
Non-oil Middle East	−0.3	−1.4	−4.0	−6.7	−5.6	−3.3	−5.7	−3.9	−4.0	−3.5
Western Hemisphere	−4.4	−11.3	−41.1	−10.3	−3.6	−4.3	−6.9	−6.6	−7.0	−5.5
By financial criteria										
Market borrowers	−5.2	−18.8	−72.3	−27.2	−3.6	1.7	−10.3	−9.8	−15.0	−20.0
Official borrowers	−1.5	−4.3	−10.3	−9.2	−9.9	−9.0	−9.1	−9.9	−10.0	−10.1
Diversified borrowers	0.6	−5.6	−7.2	−10.7	−9.1	−19.4	−18.8	−17.4	−17.7	−21.2
Countries with recent debt-servicing problems	−5.1	−20.7	−62.3	−20.6	−8.4	−4.7	−14.0	−10.3	−9.3	−7.3
Countries without debt-servicing problems	−1.0	−8.1	−27.5	−26.5	−14.2	−22.1	−24.3	−26.8	−33.4	−44.1
By miscellaneous criteria										
Capital importing fuel exporters	−2.2	−10.5	−24.5	−3.0	3.9	0.9	−18.0	−14.8	−12.5	−12.9
Non-fuel exporters	−3.9	−18.2	−65.3	−44.1	−26.5	−27.6	−20.3	−22.3	−30.2	−38.5
Fifteen heavily indebted countries	−3.6	−16.1	−50.1	−13.8	−0.9	−0.1	−7.3	−5.1	−2.7	0.2
Small low-income countries	−1.2	−3.0	−8.6	−6.0	−6.9	−6.8	−6.9	−7.5	−6.2	−5.6
Sub-Saharan Africa[2]	−1.1	−2.2	−8.4	−6.1	−3.9	−3.9	−5.4	−6.0	−5.4	−4.6
By alternative analytical categories										
Non-oil developing countries	−5.2	−21.3	−73.2	−40.9	−25.0	−28.7	−25.2	−26.7	−37.0	−46.6
Net oil exporters	−1.7	−4.5	−15.4	−2.9	−2.5	−5.3	−14.0	−11.3	−11.3	−12.9
Net oil importers	−3.5	−16.8	−57.8	−38.0	−22.5	−23.3	−11.2	−15.4	−21.7	−29.0
	(In percent of exports of goods and services)									
Capital importing countries	**−6.6**	**−10.9**	**−17.8**	**−9.4**	**−4.1**	**−4.9**	**−6.8**	**−6.0**	**−5.8**	**−5.9**
By region										
Africa	−8.6	−14.7	−27.0	−15.3	−8.7	−1.9	−16.2	−13.3	−7.1	−5.8
Asia	−1.3	1.0	−8.3	−6.6	−1.9	−6.3	−5.8	−5.8	−7.5	−8.8
Europe	3.8	−27.3	−9.9	−7.1	−3.0	−3.5	1.7	0.5	0.7	—
Non-oil Middle East	−5.3	−8.7	−11.8	−20.9	−16.8	−10.3	−17.9	−10.9	−9.8	−7.3
Western Hemisphere	−18.6	−17.5	−33.4	−8.7	−2.8	−3.4	−5.6	−5.0	−4.5	−3.0
By financial criteria										
Market borrowers	−8.7	−10.2	−20.0	−7.5	−0.9	0.4	−2.6	−2.3	−3.0	−3.4
Official borrowers	−13.8	−17.0	−29.0	−26.3	−28.1	−25.4	−23.0	−23.3	−20.2	−17.8
Diversified borrowers	2.6	−10.6	−6.6	−10.0	−7.7	−16.4	−14.6	−12.1	−10.0	−9.8
Countries with recent debt-servicing problems	−11.4	−17.0	−29.9	−10.2	−3.9	−2.2	−6.8	−4.6	−3.6	−2.4
Countries without debt-servicing problems	−2.1	−5.7	−9.2	−8.8	−4.3	−6.6	−6.7	−6.8	−7.1	−7.9

Table A54 *(concluded)*. **Capital Importing Developing Countries: Payments Balances on Current Account—Medium-Term Scenario, 1972-91**[1]

	1972	1977	1982	1983	1984	1985	1986	1987	1989	1991
By miscellaneous criteria										
Capital importing fuel exporters	−14.2	−17.6	−21.0	−2.7	3.3	0.8	−20.3	−15.8	−11.5	−10.3
Non-fuel exporters	−5.1	−9.0	−16.8	−11.2	−6.1	−6.4	−4.2	−4.3	−4.9	−5.2
Fifteen heavily indebted countries	−13.3	−19.9	−35.0	−10.1	−0.6	−0.1	−5.2	−3.3	−1.5	0.1
Small low-income countries	−17.2	−21.7	−46.9	−31.3	−34.4	−34.8	−29.1	−29.4	−20.3	−15.3
Sub-Saharan Africa[2]	−12.8	−11.2	−33.3	−25.1	−15.4	−15.6	−19.2	−20.3	−15.7	−11.6
By alternative analytical categories										
Non-oil developing countries	−6.2	−9.6	−16.7	−9.3	−5.2	−6.0	−4.9	−4.7	−5.5	−5.8
Net oil exporters	−16.1	−13.6	−19.9	−3.7	−2.9	−6.5	−18.7	−13.8	−11.8	−11.4
Net oil importers	−4.8	−8.9	−16.1	−10.5	−5.7	−5.9	−2.5	−3.2	−3.7	−4.2

[1] Current account data include official transfers.
[2] Excluding Nigeria and South Africa.

Table A55. Capital Importing Developing Countries: External Debt and Debt Service—Medium-Term Scenario, 1977-91[1]

(In percent of exports of goods and services)

	1977	1982	1983	1984	1985	1986	1987	1989	1991
Capital importing countries									
Debt ratio	126.9	148.6	158.8	152.8	163.0	166.6	160.7	150.0	140.2
Debt service ratio[2]	16.5	23.6	22.0	22.9	24.1	24.2	22.6	23.7	21.7
Interest payments ratio	5.8	13.6	13.0	13.1	13.2	13.0	12.1	11.3	10.3
Amortization ratio[3]	10.7	10.1	9.1	9.8	10.9	11.3	10.5	12.5	11.4
By region									
Africa									
Debt ratio	112.9	148.6	164.4	167.7	168.6	196.0	194.7	182.6	172.1
Debt service ratio[2]	12.7	19.6	22.8	24.8	27.0	32.3	31.1	32.8	29.1
Interest payments ratio	4.2	8.4	8.7	9.5	11.1	14.1	13.1	11.9	10.7
Amortization ratio[3]	8.5	11.2	14.1	15.3	16.0	18.2	18.0	20.8	18.4
Asia									
Debt ratio	87.7	84.0	89.2	84.2	93.5	96.5	96.9	99.3	102.2
Debt service ratio[2]	8.4	11.2	10.8	11.8	12.3	13.0	12.7	12.9	14.4
Interest payments ratio	3.5	5.8	5.7	5.9	6.0	6.2	6.2	6.0	6.3
Amortization ratio[3]	4.8	5.4	5.1	5.9	6.3	6.8	6.6	6.8	8.1
Europe									
Debt ratio	118.7	122.8	129.5	126.0	133.1	119.3	109.4	92.2	76.2
Debt service ratio[2]	14.2	21.9	21.2	23.8	26.0	24.7	22.4	19.3	16.7
Interest payments ratio	4.5	12.1	11.1	11.6	11.8	10.9	10.2	8.4	7.0
Amortization ratio[3]	9.7	9.9	10.1	12.2	14.2	13.8	12.1	10.9	9.6
Non-oil Middle East									
Debt ratio	163.7	162.8	195.7	204.8	229.3	237.0	225.9	217.7	203.7
Debt service ratio[2]	19.9	18.6	20.1	22.9	25.8	23.7	22.1	23.9	22.2
Interest payments ratio	9.6	9.4	10.5	12.2	12.5	13.9	13.6	13.0	11.9
Amortization ratio[3]	10.3	9.1	9.6	10.7	13.4	9.8	8.5	10.8	10.3
Western Hemisphere									
Debt ratio	191.8	267.2	287.5	273.3	295.0	311.1	296.0	263.5	234.4
Debt service ratio[2]	32.1	49.6	43.0	42.4	44.1	43.5	39.7	45.6	37.4
Interest payments ratio	10.2	31.9	30.7	29.8	29.5	27.8	25.4	23.8	21.0
Amortization ratio[3]	22.0	17.7	12.3	12.6	14.6	15.7	14.3	21.8	16.4
By financial criteria									
Market borrowers									
Debt ratio	119.6	146.5	154.6	146.5	154.1	158.0	150.2	136.4	124.2
Debt service ratio[2]	17.9	26.3	23.9	24.7	25.3	25.7	23.5	24.5	21.8
Interest payments ratio	5.7	15.7	14.7	14.7	14.6	14.2	12.9	11.9	10.7
Amortization ratio[3]	12.2	10.6	9.2	10.0	10.7	11.5	10.6	12.6	11.1
Official borrowers									
Debt ratio	149.6	215.4	239.1	258.7	279.6	273.6	276.3	280.0	280.6
Debt service ratio[2]	12.2	15.2	17.0	22.4	25.9	26.8	27.3	30.6	30.3
Interest payments ratio	5.3	7.4	7.7	9.4	11.1	11.5	11.7	11.0	11.1
Amortization ratio[3]	6.9	7.8	9.3	13.0	14.7	15.3	15.6	19.6	19.2

257

Table A55 *(continued).* **Capital Importing Developing Countries: External Debt and Debt Service—Medium-Term Scenario, 1977-91[1]**

(In percent of exports of goods and services)

	1977	1982	1983	1984	1985	1986	1987	1989	1991
Diversified borrowers									
Debt ratio	141.8	133.8	146.7	142.7	157.5	159.9	157.8	152.4	147.0
Debt service ratio[2]	13.8	17.5	17.4	17.1	19.6	18.8	18.6	19.7	19.2
Interest payments ratio	6.2	8.5	8.7	8.9	9.2	9.5	10.0	9.5	9.0
Amortization ratio[3]	7.6	8.9	8.7	8.2	10.4	9.3	8.6	10.3	10.2
Countries with recent debt-servicing problems									
Debt ratio	162.9	234.5	252.3	244.2	260.6	275.4	261.0	232.7	206.4
Debt service ratio[2]	24.1	38.2	34.4	35.1	36.9	37.7	34.8	38.1	31.9
Interest payments ratio	7.5	23.3	22.4	22.6	23.0	23.0	21.0	19.3	16.9
Amortization ratio[3]	16.6	14.9	12.0	12.5	13.8	14.7	13.8	18.8	15.0
Countries without debt-servicing problems									
Debt ratio	95.9	88.6	95.8	93.1	102.2	104.5	104.1	103.6	103.5
Debt service ratio[2]	10.0	13.5	13.7	15.0	16.1	16.5	15.7	15.7	16.1
Interest payments ratio	4.3	6.8	6.6	6.9	7.0	7.2	7.1	6.7	6.7
Amortization ratio[3]	5.7	6.7	7.1	8.0	9.1	9.3	8.7	8.9	9.4
By miscellaneous criteria									
Capital importing fuel exporters									
Debt ratio	131.2	168.5	187.2	176.0	188.6	255.7	253.5	246.1	241.2
Debt service ratio[2]	20.6	28.2	30.6	33.5	37.4	44.0	39.5	40.1	37.7
Interest payments ratio	6.4	17.5	18.0	18.7	17.8	23.3	20.7	20.1	20.2
Amortization ratio[3]	14.2	10.7	12.6	14.8	19.6	20.7	18.7	20.0	17.5
Non-fuel exporters									
Debt ratio	125.7	142.7	151.0	146.5	156.4	149.9	144.0	133.1	123.1
Debt service ratio[2]	15.3	22.3	19.7	20.1	20.6	20.5	19.6	20.9	19.0
Interest payments ratio	5.6	12.4	11.6	11.6	12.0	11.0	10.6	9.7	8.6
Amortization ratio[3]	9.7	9.9	8.1	8.4	8.7	9.5	9.0	11.2	10.4
Fifteen heavily indebted countries									
Debt ratio	173.9	263.4	286.3	268.1	285.9	304.8	285.4	249.2	216.7
Debt service ratio[2]	27.4	47.9	42.5	41.6	43.8	45.6	41.1	44.5	36.7
Interest payments ratio	8.5	30.2	29.5	28.8	28.6	28.2	25.2	22.9	19.7
Amortization ratio[3]	18.8	17.7	13.0	12.8	15.3	17.4	15.9	21.6	16.9
Small low-income countries									
Debt ratio	210.9	320.9	334.6	345.1	382.9	346.9	351.2	345.2	333.1
Debt service ratio[2]	15.1	19.0	20.4	23.1	29.8	28.4	30.2	32.0	30.3
Interest payments ratio	5.6	9.1	8.9	9.3	12.5	12.4	13.1	11.7	11.6
Amortization ratio[3]	9.5	9.9	11.5	13.8	17.2	16.0	17.1	20.3	18.8
Sub-Saharan Africa[4]									
Debt ratio	122.3	201.3	215.8	216.3	240.3	236.0	242.8	236.5	220.3
Debt service ratio[2]	11.8	20.2	21.3	23.3	28.6	29.4	31.0	31.5	28.8
Interest payments ratio	5.3	10.0	9.8	10.3	12.5	13.3	13.9	12.8	11.4
Amortization ratio[3]	6.5	10.1	11.5	13.1	16.1	16.2	17.1	18.7	17.4

Table A55 *(concluded).* **Capital Importing Developing Countries: External Debt and Debt Service—Medium-Term Scenario, 1977-91[1]**

(In percent of exports of goods and services)

	1977	1982	1983	1984	1985	1986	1987	1989	1991
By alternative analytical categories									
Non-oil developing countries									
Debt ratio	131.9	151.5	159.6	154.2	164.4	161.3	155.0	142.6	131.3
Debt service ratio[2]	17.6	24.1	21.1	22.0	22.7	22.1	20.8	21.3	19.5
Interest payments ratio	6.0	14.0	13.0	13.1	13.2	12.3	11.6	10.5	9.5
Amortization ratio[3]	11.6	10.1	8.1	8.9	9.6	9.8	9.2	10.8	10.1
Net oil exporters									
Debt ratio	190.2	206.6	218.9	207.1	234.8	274.0	268.3	254.2	240.2
Debt service ratio[2]	35.2	33.1	29.1	32.5	34.2	31.2	28.6	29.8	28.7
Interest payments ratio	10.0	21.3	20.2	20.6	19.0	20.3	19.6	18.1	17.4
Amortization ratio[3]	25.2	11.8	9.0	12.0	15.2	10.9	9.1	11.7	11.3
Net oil importers									
Debt ratio	121.6	139.6	146.7	142.5	149.9	142.3	136.0	124.2	113.5
Debt service ratio[2]	14.5	22.1	19.4	19.6	20.4	20.5	19.5	19.9	18.0
Interest payments ratio	5.3	12.4	11.4	11.4	12.0	10.9	10.3	9.3	8.2
Amortization ratio[3]	9.2	9.8	7.9	8.2	8.4	9.6	9.2	10.6	9.9

[1] Covers all short- and long-term debt except debt owed to the Fund.

[2] Amortization payments on long-term debt and total interest payments as a percentage of exports of goods and services.

[3] On long-term debt only. Estimates for the period up to 1985 reflect actual amortization payments. The estimates for the 1986 and 1987 reflect scheduled payments modified to take account of actual or pending restructuring agreements.

[4] Excluding Nigeria and South Africa.

259

Table A56. Capital Importing Developing Countries: Foreign Trade and Output—Medium-Term Scenario, 1968-91
(Annual changes, in percent)

	Averages[1,2]		1982	1983	1984	1985	1986	1987	Average[1]
	1968–72	1973–80							1988–91
Capital importing countries									
Export volume	7.4	5.3	−1.5	7.5	10.7	2.5	4.1	5.6	4.8
Terms of trade	0.5	2.5	−2.6	−1.7	1.7	−1.7	−4.4	−1.0	−0.1
Import volume	7.5	7.5	−6.5	−2.7	4.6	2.6	2.3	4.2	4.9
Real GDP	6.3	5.3	2.1	1.6	4.7	4.2	3.5	4.2	4.7
By region									
Africa									
Export volume	7.1	1.8	−7.0	3.8	4.6	6.1	3.1	6.1	3.1
Terms of trade	−0.3	6.3	−4.8	−3.3	2.4	−3.0	−15.8	−5.2	0.1
Import volume	6.2	6.7	−9.0	−10.1	−0.3	−5.2	−0.2	−1.5	2.9
Real GDP	7.3	3.1	0.8	−1.5	1.6	1.6	2.8	2.8	3.7
Asia									
Export volume	10.4	11.6	0.5	10.1	14.0	2.5	6.2	5.6	5.1
Terms of trade	0.6	0.6	−0.8	−0.6	1.1	−1.2	−2.3	—	0.1
Import volume	6.8	10.1	−0.2	6.4	6.7	6.3	2.8	5.4	6.0
Real GDP	5.9	6.1	5.0	7.4	7.9	6.1	5.5	5.5	5.8
Europe									
Export volume	9.4	5.9	1.3	8.0	14.6	4.6	4.1	6.4	5.8
Terms of trade	−1.1	−2.2	−0.3	−1.2	−1.6	−1.0	7.5	0.4	0.2
Import volume	9.0	4.6	−7.7	2.2	6.9	4.1	5.3	8.0	5.8
Real GDP	6.5	4.8	2.4	1.0	3.5	2.5	3.5	3.8	4.1
Non-oil Middle East									
Export volume	8.7	2.1	−1.8	−2.9	7.5	5.4	8.1	5.1	5.9
Terms of trade	0.3	2.6	1.8	−2.8	0.9	0.1	−12.5	0.3	—
Import volume	8.9	6.5	0.8	3.8	0.4	−1.2	−3.7	−3.6	1.4
Real GDP	6.9	5.2	4.0	2.2	1.8	2.3	2.6	2.4	3.3
Western Hemisphere									
Export volume	3.6	1.4	−2.2	7.1	7.3	−1.2	−0.2	4.8	4.2
Terms of trade	1.9	4.5	−5.8	−2.8	4.0	−3.0	−5.1	−1.7	−0.8
Import volume	8.1	6.5	−17.7	−22.2	2.9	−1.3	3.2	5.1	4.8
Real GDP	6.3	5.5	−0.9	−3.1	3.1	3.8	1.6	3.5	4.3
By financial criteria									
Market borrowers									
Export volume	7.9	5.9	−2.4	9.3	10.8	1.9	3.0	5.4	4.3
Terms of trade	1.1	3.6	−3.0	−2.6	1.6	−1.6	−6.0	−1.3	−0.2
Import of volume	9.3	8.7	−7.4	−6.5	3.0	−1.2	2.8	5.2	5.4
Real GDP	7.2	5.5	0.4	−1.1	3.4	2.9	2.2	3.6	4.4
Official borrowers									
Export volume	4.4	0.6	−4.0	1.8	−1.4	1.9	8.2	4.3	4.2
Terms of trade	−0.8	−0.6	−2.2	2.2	4.7	−1.9	5.1	−1.3	−0.2
Import volume	3.1	3.3	−1.4	1.0	1.1	−1.2	5.0	2.5	2.6
Real GDP	3.6	3.7	2.0	1.9	2.8	2.9	4.1	3.4	3.6

Table A56 *(continued).* **Capital Importing Developing Countries: Foreign Trade and Output—Medium-Term Scenario, 1968-91**

(Annual changes, in percent)

	Averages[1,2]		1982	1983	1984	1985	1986	1987	Average[1]
	1968–72	1973–80							1988–91
Diversified borrowers									
Export volume	7.4	2.9	3.0	2.8	14.4	5.0	6.7	6.8	6.5
Terms of trade	−0.4	0.6	−1.7	−0.1	0.7	−1.9	−1.4	0.1	0.2
Import volume	5.0	6.5	−6.3	6.8	10.2	13.5	0.2	2.6	4.7
Real GDP	6.0	5.4	5.2	7.0	7.7	6.9	5.9	5.5	5.7
Countries with recent debt-servicing problems									
Export volume	5.6	2.3	−4.2	5.4	7.0	1.4	0.6	4.5	4.2
Terms of trade	0.3	3.8	−4.8	−2.8	2.7	−2.5	−5.8	−1.0	−0.2
Import volume	6.4	6.3	−14.6	−15.0	1.8	−2.7	2.3	2.8	4.8
Real GDP	6.1	4.9	−0.1	−2.5	2.6	2.8	1.9	3.3	4.1
Countries without debt-servicing problems									
Export volume	9.6	8.4	0.6	9.0	13.2	3.2	6.2	6.3	5.2
Terms of trade	0.7	1.4	−0.8	−1.0	1.1	−1.0	−3.3	−1.0	0.1
Import volume	8.6	8.4	−0.7	5.0	6.0	5.2	2.3	4.8	5.3
Real GDP	6.5	5.7	4.3	6.0	6.9	5.5	5.1	4.9	5.4
By miscellaneous criteria									
Capital importing fuel exporters									
Export volume	2.4	—	−7.4	5.0	7.4	−0.3	3.5	4.3	3.0
Terms of trade	4.6	17.8	−2.5	−7.7	2.5	−3.8	−31.8	−3.5	0.1
Import volume	7.4	13.2	−10.3	−19.7	1.2	−0.7	−12.3	−3.2	2.7
Real GDP	8.4	5.5	0.5	−3.0	1.8	1.8	−0.7	1.4	4.1
Non-fuel exporters									
Export volume	8.3	6.5	0.7	8.3	11.7	3.4	4.3	5.8	5.2
Terms of trade	−0.3	−1.6	−2.6	0.2	1.5	−1.2	3.6	−0.4	−0.1
Import volume	7.2	6.5	−5.5	1.6	5.2	3.3	5.1	5.4	5.4
Real GDP	5.9	5.3	2.5	3.0	5.5	4.8	4.6	4.8	4.9
Fifteen heavily indebted countries									
Export volume	5.2	1.7	−4.9	5.5	8.7	−0.2	0.4	4.9	4.1
Terms of trade	1.6	7.1	−4.5	−3.6	2.8	−3.1	−8.5	−1.5	−0.3
Import volume	8.2	8.3	−16.5	−21.5	−2.2	−2.9	2.0	3.7	4.7
Real GDP	7.0	5.3	−0.4	−3.5	2.2	3.1	1.5	3.3	4.2
Small low-income countries									
Export volume	3.0	1.1	−0.6	4.0	0.2	4.0	11.3	4.0	5.3
Terms of trade	−1.2	−2.1	−4.4	6.3	6.8	−4.5	8.3	−1.4	0.5
Import volume	1.6	2.3	1.7	−2.3	5.5	−0.1	7.4	2.3	2.5
Real GDP	3.6	3.6	2.0	2.6	3.6	4.2	5.1	3.9	3.7
Sub-Saharan Africa[3]									
Export volume	5.7	1.3	4.4	0.4	4.9	0.7	9.1	3.2	3.5
Terms of trade	−1.4	−0.5	−6.5	1.2	5.0	−2.0	−1.9	−3.5	−0.3
Import volume	5.5	2.6	−3.5	−7.7	−1.4	1.1	11.1	1.0	1.9
Real GDP	4.9	2.4	0.5	0.6	1.9	3.1	4.7	3.5	3.3

Table A56 *(concluded)*. **Capital Importing Developing Countries: Foreign Trade and Output—Medium-Term Scenario, 1968-91**

(Annual changes, in percent)

	Averages[1,2]		1982	1983	1984	1985	1986	1987	Average[1]
	1968–72	1973–80							1988–91
By alternative analytical categories									
Non-oil developing countries									
Export volume	8.1	7.1	1.5	8.1	11.1	3.0	4.2	5.5	5.1
Terms of trade	−0.3	−0.8	−3.1	−0.3	1.5	−1.4	0.9	−0.3	−0.1
Import volume	7.3	6.8	−7.5	−0.3	5.7	3.4	4.1	5.2	5.3
Real GDP	6.0	5.4	2.2	2.1	5.2	4.6	4.0	4.6	4.8
Net oil exporters									
Export volume	3.6	4.5	9.3	7.1	9.3	1.1	6.1	3.3	4.2
Terms of trade	−0.9	6.1	−6.9	−2.9	2.9	−4.3	−21.2	0.2	−0.1
Import volume	2.4	10.2	−13.8	−10.9	9.4	1.0	−4.2	−1.0	3.9
Real GDP	6.1	6.3	1.2	−3.0	3.7	3.4	−0.4	2.5	4.2
Net oil importers									
Export volume	8.9	7.6	—	8.3	11.5	3.4	3.9	5.9	5.2
Terms of trade	−0.2	−1.9	−2.3	0.2	1.3	−0.8	5.4	−0.4	−0.1
Import volume	8.0	6.3	−6.3	1.6	5.1	3.8	5.5	6.1	5.6
Real GDP	6.0	5.2	2.4	3.1	5.5	4.8	4.7	5.0	5.0

[1] Compound annual rates of change.
[2] Excluding China.
[3] Excluding Nigeria and South Africa.

Table A57. Capital Importing Developing Countries: Medium-Term Impact of Additional Private and Official Lending, 1986-91

(Difference from the baseline in percentage points)

| | Ratios to Exports of Goods and Services, in Percent | | | | | | Average Rates of Growth[4] 1986-91 | | |
| | Current account balance[1] | | External debt[2] | | Debt service[3] | | Real GDP | Export volume | Import volume |
	1989	1991	1989	1991	1989	1991			
Capital importing countries	**−2.2**	**−2.1**	**7.0**	**10.0**	**0.8**	**1.3**	**0.3**	**—**	**0.4**
By region									
Africa	−4.1	−4.3	12.5	19.1	1.6	2.6	0.4	—	0.7
Asia	−0.3	−0.3	1.0	1.4	0.1	0.2	—	—	—
Europe	−0.5	−0.5	1.9	2.5	0.3	0.5	—	—	0.1
Non-oil Middle East	−3.9	−3.7	12.2	17.6	1.0	1.6	0.3	—	0.6
Western Hemisphere	−5.8	−5.5	18.8	27.0	2.3	3.5	0.7	—	1.1
By financial criteria									
Market borrowers	−2.0	−1.8	6.6	9.1	0.8	1.3	0.2	—	0.3
Official borrowers	−5.7	−6.2	17.2	26.8	1.4	2.4	0.5	—	0.8
Diversified borrowers	−1.8	−1.8	5.3	7.9	0.6	0.9	0.4	—	0.8
Countries with recent debt-servicing problems	−6.0	−5.8	19.3	27.8	2.2	3.5	0.6	—	1.0
Countries without debt-servicing problems	—	—	—	—	—	—	—	—	—
By miscellaneous criteria									
Capital importing fuel exporters	−3.6	−3.5	11.4	16.8	1.3	2.1	0.3	—	0.6
Non-fuel exporters	−1.9	−1.8	6.2	8.8	0.7	1.1	0.1	—	0.3
Fifteen heavily indebted countries	−5.9	−5.5	19.2	27.2	2.4	3.7	0.6	—	1.0
Small low-income countries	−6.0	−6.3	18.1	27.6	1.2	2.0	0.5	—	0.9
Sub-Saharan Africa[5]	−6.1	−6.2	18.2	27.6	1.7	2.9	0.7	—	1.1
By alternative analytical categories									
Non-oil developing countries	−2.0	−1.9	6.7	9.3	0.7	1.2	0.2	—	0.4
Net oil exporters	−4.6	−4.2	15.2	21.2	1.3	2.1	0.4	—	0.7
Net oil importers	−1.6	−1.5	5.3	7.4	0.6	1.0	0.2	—	0.2

[1] Including official transfers.
[2] Covers all short-and long-term debt except debt owed to the Fund.
[3] Amortization payments on long-term debt and total interest payments.
[4] Compound annual rates of change.
[5] Excluding Nigeria and South Africa.

Table A58. Capital Importing Developing Countries: Medium-Term Impact of Lower Growth in Industrial Countries, 1987-91

(Difference from the baseline in percentage points)

| | Ratios to Exports of Goods and Services, in Percent | | | | | | Average Rates of Growth[4] 1987-91 | | |
| | Current account balance[1] | | External debt[2] | | Debt service[3] | | Real GDP | Export volume | Import volume |
	1989	1991	1989	1991	1989	1991			
Capital importing countries	−0.5	−0.7	5.6	8.9	0.9	1.4	−1.3	−1.6	−1.4
By region									
Africa	−0.3	−0.3	4.7	7.4	0.8	1.3	−0.9	−1.1	−1.1
Asia	−0.7	−1.0	4.3	7.6	0.6	1.1	−1.4	−1.8	−1.6
Europe	−0.2	−0.2	3.6	5.1	0.8	1.1	−1.3	−1.2	−1.6
Non-oil Middle East	−0.3	−0.3	3.6	5.9	0.4	0.6	−0.6	−1.0	−0.6
Western Hemisphere	−0.5	−0.6	8.9	13.4	1.5	2.1	−1.5	−1.5	−1.9
By financial criteria									
Market borrowers	−0.5	−0.6	6.2	9.6	1.1	1.7	−1.6	−1.9	−2.0
Official borrowers	−0.4	−0.6	4.8	8.1	0.5	0.9	−0.5	−1.8	−0.5
Diversified borrowers	−0.4	−0.6	3.0	5.3	0.4	0.7	−0.4	−1.0	−0.2
Countries with recent debt-servicing problems	−0.4	−0.4	7.5	11.3	1.2	1.8	−1.3	−1.4	−1.6
Countries without debt-servicing problems	−0.6	−0.9	4.1	7.0	0.6	1.1	−1.4	−1.8	−1.6
By miscellaneous criteria									
Capital importing fuel exporters	−0.4	−0.5	4.8	7.9	0.8	1.2	−0.8	−0.8	−0.9
Non-fuel exporters	−0.5	−0.7	5.3	8.4	0.8	1.3	−1.4	−1.8	−1.6
Fifteen heavily indebted countries	−0.5	−0.5	10.1	14.8	1.8	2.5	−1.7	−1.7	−2.2
Small low-income countries	−0.4	−0.5	4.8	7.8	0.4	0.7	−0.4	−0.6	−0.4
Sub-Saharan Africa[5]	−0.3	−0.4	4.7	7.4	0.6	1.0	−0.7	−0.9	−0.8
By alternative analytical categories									
Non-oil developing countries	−0.6	−0.7	5.9	9.1	0.9	1.4	−1.2	−1.7	−1.6
Net oil exporters	−0.3	−0.5	4.3	6.9	0.5	0.8	−0.7	−0.8	−0.8
Net oil importers	−0.6	−0.7	5.6	8.7	0.9	1.4	−1.3	−1.9	−1.8

[1] Including official transfers.
[2] Covers all short-and long-term debt except debt owed to the Fund.
[3] Amortization payments on long-term debt and total interest payments.
[4] Compound annual rates of change.
[5] Excluding Nigeria and South Africa.

Table A59. Capital Importing Developing Countries: Medium-Term Impact of Lower Interest Rates, 1987-91
(Difference from the baseline in percentage points)

| | Ratios to Exports of Goods and Services, in Percent | | | | | | Average Rates of Growth[4] 1987-91 | | |
| | Current account balance[1] | | External debt[2] | | Debt service[3] | | Real GDP | Export volume | Import volume |
	1989	1991	1989	1991	1989	1991			
Capital importing countries	—	—	**0.4**	**0.3**	**−0.8**	**−0.8**	**0.2**	**—**	**0.3**
By region									
Africa	—	—	0.2	0.1	−0.8	−0.7	0.1	—	0.2
Asia	—	—	0.3	0.2	−0.5	−0.5	—	—	0.1
Europe	—	—	0.1	0.1	−0.6	−0.6	0.1	—	0.1
Non-oil Middle East	—	—	0.5	0.4	−0.6	−0.6	0.1	—	0.1
Western Hemisphere	—	—	0.8	0.7	−1.9	−1.6	0.3	—	0.5
By financial criteria									
Market borrowers	—	—	0.3	0.3	−1.0	−0.9	0.1	—	0.2
Official borrowers	—	—	0.6	0.5	−0.4	−0.3	—	—	—
Diversified borrowers	—	—	0.4	0.4	−0.5	−0.5	0.2	—	0.3
Countries with recent debt-servicing problems	—	—	0.5	0.4	−1.4	−1.2	0.2	—	0.3
Countries without debt-servicing problems	—	—	0.3	0.2	−0.5	−0.5	—	—	—
By miscellaneous criteria									
Capital importing fuel exporters	—	—	0.5	0.5	−1.6	−1.5	0.2	—	0.4
Non-fuel exporters	—	—	0.3	0.3	−0.7	−0.6	0.1	—	0.1
Fifteen heavily indebted countries	—	—	0.7	0.6	−1.8	−1.5	0.3	—	0.5
Small low-income countries	—	—	0.7	0.7	−0.4	−0.3	—	—	—
Sub-Saharan Africa[5]	—	—	0.3	0.2	−0.6	−0.5	0.1	—	0.1
By alternative analytical categories									
Non-oil developing countries	—	—	0.3	0.3	−0.8	−0.7	0.1	—	0.2
Net oil exporters	—	—	0.5	0.5	−1.6	−1.6	0.2	—	0.4
Net oil importers	—	—	0.3	0.3	−0.7	−0.6	0.1	—	0.1

[1] Including official transfers.
[2] Covers all short-and long-term debt except debt owed to the Fund.
[3] Amortization payments on long-term debt and total interest payments.
[4] Compound annual rates of change.
[5] Excluding Nigeria and South Africa.

265

Table A60. Capital Importing Developing Countries: Medium-Term Impact of Higher Oil Prices, 1987-91

(Difference from the baseline in percentage points)

| | Ratios to Exports of Goods and Services, in Percent | | | | | | Average Rates of Growth[4] 1987-91 | | |
| | Current account balance[1] | | External debt[2] | | Debt service[3] | | Real GDP | Export volume | Import volume |
	1989	1991	1989	1991	1989	1991			
Capital importing countries	**0.2**	**0.2**	**−4.4**	**−3.9**	**−0.7**	**−0.6**	**0.3**	**—**	**0.4**
By region									
Africa	0.4	0.3	−10.7	−9.8	−1.9	−1.7	0.6	—	1.1
Asia	0.2	0.1	−1.7	−1.6	−0.2	−0.2	—	—	—
Europe	—	—	−0.9	−0.7	−0.2	−0.2	−0.3	—	−0.5
Non-oil Middle East	0.6	0.5	−12.1	−11.6	−1.3	−1.3	0.4	—	0.7
Western Hemisphere	0.3	0.2	−11.7	−9.9	−2.0	−1.6	0.7	—	1.1
By financial criteria									
Market borrowers	0.1	0.1	−4.3	−3.7	−0.8	−0.7	0.2	—	0.4
Official borrowers	0.9	0.7	−11.4	−11.4	−1.2	−1.2	—	—	−0.1
Diversified borrowers	0.2	0.2	−3.0	−2.7	−0.4	−0.4	0.3	—	0.5
Countries with recent debt-servicing problems	0.2	0.1	−8.9	−7.5	−1.5	−1.2	0.4	—	0.6
Countries without debt-servicing problems	0.2	0.2	−2.5	−2.4	−0.4	−0.4	—	—	—
By miscellaneous criteria									
Capital importing fuel exporters	1.5	1.4	−28.1	−26.9	−4.6	−4.2	2.0	—	3.3
Non-fuel exporters	0.1	—	−1.7	−1.5	−0.3	−0.2	−0.1	—	−0.2
Fifteen heavily indebted countries	0.2	0.1	−11.6	−9.5	−2.1	−1.6	0.7	—	1.1
Small low-income countries	0.2	0.1	−2.2	−2.4	−0.2	−0.2	−0.3	—	−0.5
Sub-Saharan Africa[5]	0.4	0.3	−6.5	−5.6	−0.9	−0.7	—	—	—
By alternative analytical categories									
Non-oil developing countries	0.1	0.1	−2.7	−2.3	−0.4	−0.3	—	—	—
Net oil exporters	0.9	0.8	−17.7	−15.9	−2.1	−1.9	1.0	—	1.8
Net oil importers	—	—	−1.3	−1.1	−0.2	−0.2	−0.1	—	−0.3

[1] Including official transfers.

[2] Covers all short-and long-term debt except debt owed to the Fund.

[3] Amortization payments on long-term debt and total interest payments.

[4] Compound annual rates of change.

[5] Excluding Nigeria and South Africa.

Table A61. Capital Importing Developing Countries: Medium-Term Impact of Greater Effective Depreciation of the U. S. Dollar, 1987-91
(Difference from the baseline in percentage points)

| | Ratios to Exports of Goods and Services, in Percent | | | | | | Average Rates of Growth[4] 1987-91 | | |
| | Current account balance[1] | | External debt[2] | | Debt service[3] | | Real GDP | Export volume | Import volume |
	1989	1991	1989	1991	1989	1991			
Capital importing countries	**0.1**	**0.1**	**−1.7**	**−1.7**	**−0.3**	**−0.3**	**—**	**—**	**0.1**
By region									
Africa	0.1	0.1	−1.1	−1.2	−0.2	−0.2	—	—	—
Asia	0.2	0.2	−0.9	−1.2	−0.1	−0.2	—	—	−0.1
Europe	—	—	−1.0	−0.9	−0.2	−0.2	—	—	—
Non-oil Middle East	0.1	0.1	−1.5	−1.6	−0.2	−0.2	−0.1	—	−0.2
Western Hemisphere	0.1	0.1	−3.5	−3.2	−0.6	−0.5	—	—	0.1
By financial criteria									
Market borrowers	0.1	0.1	−1.7	−1.6	−0.3	−0.3	—	—	—
Official borrowers	0.3	0.3	−2.5	−2.9	−0.3	−0.3	−0.1	—	−0.2
Diversified borrowers	0.2	0.2	−1.3	−1.5	−0.1	−0.2	—	—	0.1
Countries with recent debt-servicing problems	0.1	0.1	−2.9	−2.7	−0.5	−0.4	—	—	—
Countries without debt-servicing problems	0.2	0.2	−0.9	−1.1	−0.1	−0.2	−0.1	—	−0.2
By miscellaneous criteria									
Capital importing fuel exporters	0.1	0.2	0.1	−0.3	—	—	−0.1	—	−0.2
Non-fuel exporters	0.1	0.1	−1.8	−1.8	−0.3	−0.3	—	—	—
Fifteen heavily indebted countries	0.1	0.1	−3.1	−2.8	−0.6	−0.5	—	—	0.1
Small low-income countries	0.5	0.4	−4.0	−4.4	−0.4	−0.4	−0.1	—	−0.1
Sub-Saharan Africa[5]	0.3	0.2	−2.1	−2.2	−0.3	−0.3	—	—	—
By alternative analytical categories									
Non-oil developing countries	0.1	0.1	−1.8	−1.8	−0.3	−0.3	—	—	—
Net oil exporters	0.2	0.2	−2.5	−2.5	−0.3	−0.3	−0.1	—	−0.1
Net oil importers	0.1	0.1	−1.6	−1.6	−0.3	−0.2	—	—	—

[1] Including official transfers.
[2] Covers all short-and long-term debt except debt owed to the Fund.
[3] Amortization payments on long-term debt and total interest payments.
[4] Compound annual rates of change.
[5] Excluding Nigeria and South Africa.

Table A62. Capital Importing Developing Countries: Medium-Term Impact of Lower Non-Oil Commodity Prices, 1987-91

(Difference from the baseline in percentage points)

| | Ratios to Exports of Goods and Services, in Percent | | | | | | Average Rates of Growth[4] 1987-91 | | |
| | Current account balance[1] | | External debt[2] | | Debt service[3] | | Real GDP | Export volume | Import volume |
	1989	1991	1989	1991	1989	1991			
Capital importing countries	−0.2	−0.2	1.7	2.7	0.3	0.4	−0.4	−0.2	−0.4
By region									
Africa	−0.2	−0.2	3.2	5.1	0.6	0.9	−0.5	−0.3	−0.8
Asia	−0.2	−0.2	1.0	1.8	0.1	0.3	−0.3	−0.2	−0.4
Europe	—	—	0.6	0.8	0.1	0.2	−0.2	−0.1	−0.2
Non-oil Middle East	−0.1	−0.1	0.9	1.5	0.1	0.2	−0.1	—	−0.2
Western Hemisphere	−0.3	−0.3	4.1	6.2	0.7	1.0	−0.6	−0.2	−0.9
By financial criteria									
Market borrowers	−0.1	−0.2	1.6	2.5	0.3	0.4	−0.4	−0.2	−0.5
Official borrowers	−0.5	−0.6	5.0	8.5	0.6	0.9	−0.4	−0.2	−0.6
Diversified borrowers	−0.2	−0.3	1.3	2.2	0.2	0.3	—	−0.1	—
Countries with recent debt-servicing problems	−0.2	−0.2	3.6	5.4	0.6	0.8	−0.5	−0.2	−0.7
Countries without debt-servicing problems	−0.1	−0.2	1.0	1.6	0.1	0.2	−0.3	−0.2	−0.4
By miscellaneous criteria									
Capital importing fuel exporters	−0.2	−0.2	2.0	3.3	0.3	0.5	−0.3	−0.1	−0.4
Non-fuel exporters	−0.2	−0.2	1.6	2.5	0.2	0.4	−0.3	−0.2	−0.5
Fifteen heavily indebted countries	−0.2	−0.2	3.9	5.7	0.7	1.0	−0.6	−0.2	−0.8
Small low-income countries	−0.6	−0.8	7.9	12.8	0.7	1.2	−0.5	−0.4	−0.7
Sub-Saharan Africa[5]	−0.5	−0.5	6.4	10.0	0.8	1.3	−0.8	−0.4	−1.1
By alternative analytical categories									
Non-oil developing countries	−0.2	−0.2	1.7	2.7	0.3	0.4	−0.3	−0.2	−0.5
Net oil exporters	−0.3	−0.4	3.3	5.4	0.4	0.6	−0.4	−0.2	−0.6
Net oil importers	−0.1	−0.2	1.5	2.3	0.2	0.4	−0.3	−0.2	−0.5

[1] Including official transfers.
[2] Covers all short-and long-term debt except debt owed to the Fund.
[3] Amortization payments on long-term debt and total interest payments.
[4] Compound annual rates of change.
[5] Excluding Nigeria and South Africa.